Walleye-Sauger Bibliography

Mark Ebbers, Peter Colby, Cheryl Lewis

The BiblioGov Project is an effort to expand awareness of the public documents and records of the U.S. Government via print publications. In broadening the public understanding of government and its work, an enlightened democracy can grow and prosper. Ranging from historic Congressional Bills to the most recent Budget of the United States Government, the BiblioGov Project spans a wealth of government information. These works are now made available through an environmentally friendly, print-on-demand basis, using only what is necessary to meet the required demands of an interested public. We invite you to learn of the records of the U.S. Government, heightening the knowledge and debate that can lead from such publications.

Included are the following Collections:

Budget of The United States Government
Presidential Documents
United States Code
Education Reports from ERIC
GAO Reports
History of Bills
House Rules and Manual
Public and Private Laws

Code of Federal Regulations
Congressional Documents
Economic Indicators
Federal Register
Government Manuals
House Journal
Privacy act Issuances
Statutes at Large

WALLEYE — SAUGER

BIBLIOGRAPHY

by

Mark A. Ebbers
Minnesota Department of Natural Resources
500 Lafayette Road
St. Paul, Minnesota 55155, USA

and

Peter J. Colby
Ontario Ministry of Natural Resources
Thunder Bay, Ont. P7C 5G6

and

Cheryl A. Lewis
Ontario Ministry of Natural Resources
R.R. 4
Picton, Ont. K0K 2T0

Minnesota Department of
Natural Resources
Investigational Report
No. 396
500 Lafayette Road
St. Paul, Minnesota 55155-4012

Contribution No. 88-02
of the Ontario Ministry
of Natural Resources,
Fisheries Branch,
Fisheries Research Section
Box 50, Maple, Ont. L0J 1E0

July 1988

INTRODUCTION

This bibliography on sauger *(Stizostedion canadense)* and walleye *(Stizostedion vitreum vitreum)* is the result of a joint effort between the Minnesota Department of Natural Resources and Ontario Ministry of Natural Resources. Our goal is to update the work by Addison and Ryder (1970) and to facilitate the revision of the synopsis of biological data on walleye (Colby et al. 1979).

This bibliography was developed on Wordstar[1] with dms4Cite[2] being used to format the references. References were obtained from electronic data base searches, reference documents, lists submitted by various State, Federal and Provincial Governments, and from personal libraries. Only technical and scientific publications were used. We did not include titles from popular magazines. Progress reports are listed only if a completion report was unavailable. Unpublished reports by State or Provincial Governments were included because of their usefulness at a local or regional level. The last date for adding new references was January 1988, however, we continued to add references into 1988 if they were available prior to going to the printers.

References are listed alphabetically by author. Keywords are listed after each reference. A listing of each reference number for each species are also listed by keyword.

We request feedback from the readers as to any correction or omissions. We would also appreciate copies of future publications so that they can be included in revisions of this bibliography. It is currently planned to revise the paper copy of this document every five years. By correcting errors and omissions in this document and adding new publications to the data base, future revisions will increase in accuracy.

KEYWORDS

AGE AND GROWTH: age, growth, size (length and weight), techniques and structures used to obtain ages.

BEHAVIOR: ethology, qualitative behavior, techniques and equipment for observations (including taxis, homing, telemetry).

COMMERCIAL FISHERIES: catch statistics, regulations.

COMMUNITY DYNAMICS: inter- and intra-specific competition, predation, community management (including coarse fish removal), trophodynamics.

CREEL CENSUS: angling catch statistics, techniques, gear.

ECOLOGY: used in its broadest sense — i.e., the relation of the organism to its environment.

EMBRYOLOGY: descriptive, ecological, and physiological embryology.

FISHING GEAR: materials and construction, selectivity.

FISHWAYS: design, operation, and effectiveness of man-made structures which assist migrating fish past obstacles.

FOOD STUDIES: descriptions of food ingested, selective feeding, and feeding behavior and related methodology.

GENETICS: descriptive genetics, hybridization, introgression, and strains.

GEOGRAPHIC DISTRIBUTION: studies of the geographic distributions patterns of the species.

HABITAT DEGRADATION: identification and measurement of pollution and its sublethal and lethal effects, including eutrophication, acidification, dredging, channelization, erosion, sedimentation.

HABITAT IMPROVEMENT: man's alteration of the habitat to increase yield, including such techniques as fertilization, construction of shelters, and artificial spawning grounds, etc.

IMPOUNDMENTS: studies of fish in bodies of water created or altered by a dam or barrier.

INTRODUCTIONS: the stocking of non-indigenous species.

LIFE HISTORY: confined to papers dealing generally with several stages of life history.

MARKING: all means of marking fish for later identification, including tags, chemicals,

---

Wordstar[1] is a trademark of MicroPro Corp.
dms4Cite[2] is the trademark of Sidereal Technologies, Inc.

brands, fin clips, and their associated side-effects.

MORPHOLOGY: all aspects of morphology, especially morphometry.

MORTALITY: its causes, measurement, and effects on populations.

MOVEMENT AND MIGRATIONS: vertical and horizontal fish movements, and distribution within a water body.

PATHOLOGY: all aspects of fish disease, including parasitology.

PHYSIOLOGY: includes metabolic and other functional processes and behavior resulting from same.

POPULATION STUDIES: measurement of population parameters, including mortality, population estimates and exploitation, ages composition, maturity schedules, recruitment, proportional stock density.

PRODUCTIVITY: the measurement or estimation of fish yield (actual or potential), standing crops and their relation to environmental factors.

PROPAGATION: the techniques, equipment and food for artificially rearing fish at all stages.

REGULATIONS: size limits, seasons, sanctuaries, catch limits, gear restrictions.

SAMPLING METHODS: includes the techniques (physical and biometric) and equipment for sampling fish populations.

SOCIO-ECONOMICS OF FISHERIES: description of social and economic factors influencing and/or resulting from fisheries, both sport and commercial.

SPAWNING STUDIES: description of spawning areas, spawning, fecundity, and age at maturity.

STOCKING: locale, techniques and equipment for stocking fish, as well as the assessment of stocking as a management tool.

TAXONOMY: the history and techniques of systematic studies of the North American *Stizostedion* species.

TOXICANTS: the description of chemical agents and their effects on fish, including selective anesthetics and piscidies. Bioassays.

WATER LEVELS: water level fluctuations as stresses on fisheries or as a management tool.

ACKNOWLEDGMENTS

The completion of a project of this magnitude would be impossible without the dedicated assistance of many people. We would like to express our thanks to Daniel O'Shea, MN DNR, Dominic Baccante, Kevin Roberts, Kevin Trimble and Letizia Tamasi of the Walleye Research Unit, OMNR for entering and compiling references and assigning key words. We are also grateful to Char Feist and Colleen Mlecoch, MN DNR Library for their assistance in doing literature searches and requesting copies of publications. We also appreciate the assistance of the Fish and Wildlife Reference Service, Rockville, Maryland. We would also like to thank Daniel O'Shea, Kevin Trimble, and Barry Johnson who assisted in proof reading this document and Jack Wingate who helped to prepare it for publication.

REFERENCES

1. Aadland, L. P. E. 1982. Artificial reefs as a management tool to improve sport fishing in North Dakota reservoirs. M.S. Thesis, N. D. State Univ., Grand Forks, N. D. 75 pp. (WALLEYE; CREEL CENSUS; FOOD STUDIES; HABITAT IMPROVEMENT; IMPOUNDMENTS; SAMPLING METHODS;).

2. Adair, T. 1971. Rice River creel census 1971. Ont. Min. Nat. Res. Rep. 3 pp. (WALLEYE; CREEL CENSUS;).

3. Adams, C. C., and T. L. Hankinson. 1916. Notes on Oneida Lake fish and fisheries. Trans. Am. Fish. Soc. 45:154-169. (WALLEYE; COMMERCIAL FISHERIES; SOCIO-ECONOMICS OF FISHERIES;).

4. Adams, C. C., and T. L. Hankinson. 1928. The ecology and economics of Oneida Lake fish. Roosevelt Wildl. Ann. 1:235-548. (SAUGER; WALLEYE; COMMERCIAL FISHERIES; ECOLOGY; FOOD STUDIES; PATHOLOGY; PROPAGATION; SO-

CIO-ECONOMICS OF FISHERIES; SPAWNING STUDIES;).

5. Adams, G. F. 1978. An historical review of the commercial fisheries of the Boreal Lakes of central Canada: their development, management, and potential. Pages 347-360 *in* R.L. Kendall, ed. Selected coolwater fishes of North America. Am. Fish. Soc. Spec. Publ. No. 11, Washington, D.C. (WALLEYE; COMMERCIAL FISHERIES; SOCIO-ECONOMICS OF FISHERIES;).

6. Adams, G. F., and C. H. Olver. 1977. Yield properties and structure of boreal percid communities in Ontario. J. Fish. Research Board Can. 34:1613-1625. (WALLEYE; COMMERCIAL FISHERIES; COMMUNITY DYNAMICS; PRODUCTIVITY;).

7. Adamstone, F. B. 1922. Rates of growth of the blue and yellow pike perch in the Lake Erie. Univ. Toronto Stud. Biol. Ser. No. 20. Pub. Ont. Fish. Research Lab. No. 5:77-86. (WALLEYE; AGE AND GROWTH;).

8. Addis, J. T. 1966. Annual measurement of fish population levels in selected lakes. Ohio Dept. Nat. Res., Fed. Aid Fish Wildl. Restor. Proj. F-29-R-5, Job No. 2: 13 pp. (WALLEYE; INTRODUCTIONS; POPULATION STUDIES; SAMPLING METHODS;).

9. Addison, W. D., and R. A. Ryder. 1970. An indexed bibliography of North American *Stizostedion* (Pisces, Percidae) species. Ont. Dept. Lands Forest Res., Inf. Pap. (Fish) 38: 318 pp. (SAUGER; WALLEYE; ECOLOGY;).

10. Agassiz, L. 1850. Lake Superior: its physical character, vegetation and animals, compared with those of other and similar regions, with a narrative of the tour by J.E. Cabot. Gould, Kendall and Lincoln, Boston, Mass., 425 pp., 8 plates. (SAUGER; WALLEYE; MORTALITY; TAXONOMY;).

11. Ager, L. M. 1976. A biotelemetry study of the movements of the walleye in Center Hill Reservoir, Tennessee. M.S. Theses, Tenn. Tech. Univ., Cookeville. TWRA Technical Report No. 51: 97 pp. (WALLEYE; BEHAVIOR; IMPOUNDMENTS; MOVEMENT AND MIGRATIONS;).

12. Aggus, L. R., and W. M. Bivin. 1982. Habitat stability index models: regression models based on harvest of coolwater and coldwater fishes in reservoirs. U.S. Fish Wildl. Serv., FWS/OBS-82/10.25: 39 pp. (WALLEYE; HABITAT IMPROVEMENT;).

13. Aitken, W. W. 1940. A preliminary report on a checklist of Iowa teleosts. Proc. Iowa Acad. Sci. 47:387-392. (SAUGER; WALLEYE; GEOGRAPHICAL DISTRIBUTION;).

14. Albright, G. H., and K. J. Wright. 1973. Mississippi River special tailwater sport fishing creel census in Pool 7, March 1 — April 30, 1973. Wis. Dept. Nat. Res., Fish. Manage. Bur., Manage. Rep. No. 64: 27 pp. (SAUGER; WALLEYE; AGE AND GROWTH; CREEL CENSUS;).

15. Alder, J. 1979. Creel census Lake of the Woods 1977. Ont. Min. Nat. Res., Lake of the Woods Fish. Assess. Unit Rep. 1979-1. 28 pp. (SAUGER; WALLEYE; CREEL CENSUS;).

16. Aldridge, E. C., III, and H. A. Loyacano, Jr. 1973. Parasites from fish collected in proximity to catfish cages. Proc. 27th Annu. Conf. Southeast Assoc. Fish Wildl. Agencies 27:630-640. (WALLEYE; PATHOLOGY;).

17. Alexander, A. B. 1905. Statistics of the fisheries of the Great Lakes in 1903. U. S. Bur. Fish., Annu. Rep. (1904): 643-731. (SAUGER; WALLEYE; COMMERCIAL FISHERIES; FISHING GEAR;).

18. Alexander, H. C., P. B. Latvaitis, and D. L. Hopkins. 1986. Site-specific toxicity of unionized ammonia in the Tittabewassee River at Midland, Michigan: Overview. Environ. Toxicol. Chem. 5:427-435. (WALLEYE; TOXICANTS;).

19. Ali, M. A., and M. Anctil. 1968. Relationship between the retinal structure and habitat of *Stizostedion vitreum vitreum* and *S. canadense*. J. Fish. Research Board Can. 25:2001-2003. (SAUGER; WALLEYE; ECOLOGY; PHYSIOLOGY;).

20. Ali, M. A., and M. Anctil. 1977. Retinal structure and function in the walleye *(Stizostedion vitreum vitreum)* and sauger *(S. canadense)*. J. Fish. Research Board Can. 34:1467-1474. (SAUGER; WALLEYE; BEHAVIOR; PHYSIOLOGY;).

21. Ali, M. A., R. A. Ryder, and M. Anctil. 1977. Photoreceptors and visual pigments as related to behavioral responses and preferred habitats of perches (*Perca* spp.) and pike-perches (*Stizostedion* spp.). J. Fish. Research Board Can. 34:1475-1480. (SAUGER; WALLEYE; BEHAVIOR; PHYSIOLOGY;).

22. Allard, L. 1963. Fish spawning in the Kelsey area of Saskatchewan River, 1962. Man. Dept. Mines Nat. Res., Fish. Branch Manuscript Rep. 9 pp. (SAUGER; WALLEYE; SPAWNING STUDIES;).

23. Allbaugh, C. A. 1963. Reducing the oxygen content of lake water used at the Put-in-Bay hatchery. Prog. Fish-Cult. 25:108-109. (WALLEYE; PROPAGATION;).

24. Allbaugh, C. A., and J. V. Manz. 1964. Preliminary study of the effects of temperature fluctuations on developing eggs and fry. Prog. Fish-Cult. 26:175-180. (WALLEYE; EMBRYOLOGY; PHYSIOLOGY;).

25. Allen, J. L., C. W. Luhning, and P. D. Harman. 1972. Residues of MS-222 in northern pike, muskellunge, and walleye. U.S. Fish Wildl. Serv., Invest. Fish Control No. 45: 3-8. (WALLEYE; PHYSIOLOGY;).

26. Allin, A. E. 1940. The vertebrate fauna of Darlington Township, Durham County, Ontario. Trans. Roy. Can. Inst. 23(49), Part 1:83-118. (SAUGER; WALLEYE; GEOGRAPHICAL DISTRIBUTION;).

27. Allison, L. N. 1950. Common diseases of fish in Michigan. Mich. Dept. Conserv., Inst. Fish. Research Misc. Pub. 5: 27 pp. (WALLEYE; PATHOLOGY;).

28. Alvord, W. 1957. Northeast Montana fisheries study, Tongue River. Mont. Fish Game Dept., Fed. Aid Fish Wildl. Restor. Proj. F-11-R-4, Job No. 1-F: 1 p. (WALLEYE; ECOLOGY; STOCKING;).

29. Amin, O. M. 1979. Lymphocystis disease in Wisconsin fishes. J. Fish. Dis. 2:207-218. (SAUGER; WALLEYE; PATHOLOGY;).

30. Anderson, D. 1966. Lake Erie fish population trawling survey. Ohio Dept. Nat. Res., Fed. Aid Fish Wildl. Restor. Proj. F-35-R-4, Job No. 3: 31 pp. (WALLEYE; AGE AND GROWTH; ECOLOGY; POPULATION STUDIES; SAMPLING METHODS;).

31. Anderson, D. W. 1987. Bluegill and associated fish community response to yellow perch and walleye population manipulation. Minn. Dept. Nat. Res., Fed. Aid Fish Wildl. Restor. Proj. F-26-R-18, Study No. 125: 10 pp. (WALLEYE; AGE AND GROWTH; COMMUNITY DYNAMICS; POPULATION STUDIES;).

32. Anderson, D. W., J. J. Hickey, R. W. Risebrough, D. F. Hughes, and R. E. Christensen. 1969. Significance of chlorinated hydrocarbon residues to breeding pelicans and cormorants. Can. Field-Natur. 83:91-112. (SAUGER; WALLEYE; HABITAT DEGRADATION;).

33. Anderson, D. W., and D. H. Schupp. 1986. Fish community responses to northern pike stocking in Horseshoe Lake, Minnesota. Minn. Dept. Nat. Res., Invest. Rep. No. 387: 38 pp. (WALLEYE; AGE AND GROWTH; COMMUNITY DYNAMICS; FOOD STUDIES; MORTALITY; POPULATION STUDIES; PRODUCTIVITY; STOCKING;).

34. Anderson, J. K. 1969. A study of the Lake Champlain walleye. Vt. Fish Game Serv., Fed. Aid Fish Wildl. Restor. Proj. F-12-R, Job No. 2-A: 12 pp. (WALLEYE; MARKING; PATHOLOGY; SAMPLING METHODS; SPAWNING STUDIES;).

35. Anderson, J. K. 1971. Lake Champlain fishery investigations. Vt. Fish Game Dept. 74 pp. (SAUGER; WALLEYE; CREEL CENSUS; MOVEMENTS AND MIGRATIONS;).

36. Anderson, R. O., and A. S. Weithman. 1978. The concept of balance for coolwater fish populations. Pages 371-381 *in* R.L. Kendall, ed. Selected coolwater fishes of North America. Am. Fish. Soc. Spec. Publ. No. 11, Washington, D.C. (WALLEYE; PRODUCTIVITY;).

37. Anjard, C. A., E. Kothas, D. Mathur, and T. W. Robbins. 1974. Meter net catches-results. Pages 3-92-3-102 *in* T.W. Robbins and D. Mathur, eds. Preoperational report on the ecology of Conowingo Pond-Peach Bottom Atomic Station units No. 2 and 3. Ichthyological Assoc., Inc. 357 pp. (WALLEYE; POPULATION STUDIES;).

38. Anjard, C. A., E. Kothas, D. Mathur, and T. W. Robbins. 1974. Meter net catches-results. Pages 3-31-3-36 *in* T.W. Robbins and D. Mathur, ed. Peach Bottom Atomic Power Sta-

tion postoperational report no. 1 on the ecology of Conowingo Pond for units No. 2 and 3. Ichthyological Assoc., Inc. 154 pp. (WALLEYE; POPULATION STUDIES;).

39. Annett, C. S., F. M. D'itri, J. R. Ford, and H. H. Prince. 1975. Mercury in fish and waterfowl from Ball Lake, Ontario. J. Envir. Quality 4:219-222. (SAUGER; WALLEYE; HABITAT DEGRADATION; TOXICANTS;).

40. Annin, J., Jr. 1896. Report of the superintendent of hatcheries. N.Y. Comm. Fish. Game Forest., 1st Annu. Rep. (1895):62-75. (WALLEYE; PROPAGATION; STOCKING;).

41. Annin, J., Jr. 1897. Report of the superintendent of hatcheries. N.Y. Comm. Fish. Game Forest., 2nd Annu. Rep. (1896):112-169. (WALLEYE; PROPAGATION; STOCKING;).

42. Annin, J., Jr. 1898. Report of the superintendent of hatcheries. N.Y. Comm. Fish. Game Forest., 3rd Annu. Rep. (1897):126-190. (WALLEYE; PROPAGATION; STOCKING;).

43. Annin, J., Jr. 1899. Report of the superintendent of the state hatcheries. N.Y. Comm. Fish. Game Forest., 4th Annu Rep. (1898):113-165. (WALLEYE; PROPAGATION; STOCKING;).

44. Annin, J., Jr. 1900. Report of superintendent of hatcheries. N.Y. Comm. Fish. Game Forest., 5th Annu. Rep. (1899):73-186. (WALLEYE; PROPAGATION; STOCKING;).

45. Anonymous. 1887. The fisheries of Canada in 1884. (Extracts from the annual report of the Department of Fisheries, Dominion of Canada, for the year 1884.). U.S. Fish Comm., Bull. 6 (1886):51-56. (WALLEYE; COMMERCIAL FISHERIES; PROPAGATION;).

46. Anonymous. 1889. Jack salmon and black bass in the Ohio at Wheeling. in Notes upon fish and fisheries. U.S. Fish Comm., Bull. 7(1887): 36 pp. (SAUGER; WALLEYE; GEOGRAPHICAL DISTRIBUTION;).

47. Anonymous. 1893. Report of the United States Commissioner of Fish and Fisheries for the fiscal years 1889-90 and 1890-91. U.S. Fish Comm., Rep. (1889 to 1891):1-96. (WALL-EYE; PROPAGATION; STOCKING;).

48. Anonymous. 1903. The fish hatcheries. N.Y. Forest, Fish Game Comm., 9th Annu. Rep. p. 148-152. (WALLEYE; PROPAGATION;).

49. Anonymous. 1911. Fisheries of Manitoba. Comm. Conserv. Can., Fish. Game, Annu. Rep. p. 164-175. (WALLEYE; COMMERCIAL FISHERIES;).

50. Anonymous. 1912. Distribution of fish, fingerlings and fry. Conn. Comm. Fish. Game, 9th Bien. Rep. (1911-1912):69, 84. (WALLEYE; INTRODUCTIONS; STOCKING;).

51. Anonymous. 1922. Effect of drought and extreme heat of summer on fish life. Trans. Am. Fish. Soc. 51:133-135. (WALLEYE; ECOLOGY; MORTALITY;).

52. Anonymous. 1924. Distribution of fish. Conn. Comm. Fish. Game, 15th Bien. Rep. (1923-1924):10, 50. (WALLEYE; INTRODUCTIONS; STOCKING;).

53. Anonymous. 1928. Summary, by species and streams, of distribution of fishes and eggs to applicants of the State of Connecticut by the U.S. Bureau of Fisheries. Conn. State Board Fish Game, 17th Bien. Rep. (1927-1928):128-130. (WALLEYE; PROPAGATION;).

54. Anonymous. 1928. The game fishes of Canada. Can. Pacific Railway Co., Montreal, Que. 45 pp. (WALLEYE; GEOGRAPHICAL DISTRIBUTION; TAXONOMY;).

55. Anonymous. 1932. Division of fish restoration. Conn. State Board. Fish. Game, 19th Bien. Rep. (1931-1932):14,18. (WALLEYE; INTRODUCTIONS; PROPAGATION;).

56. Anonymous. 1940. Potential egg production of walleye pike and black bass. Prog. Fish-Cult. 50:46-47. (WALLEYE; SPAWNING STUDIES;).

57. Anonymous. 1941. Protozoan causes loss of walleyed pike eggs. Prog. Fish-Cult. 56:30. (WALLEYE; MORTALITY; PROPAGATION;).

58. Anonymous. 1945. Fresh water fishery resources — Great Lakes. Pages 111-116 in Fishery resources of the United States. U.S.

Government Printing Office, Washington D.C. (SAUGER; WALLEYE; AGE AND GROWTH; COMMERCIAL FISHERIES;).

59. Anonymous. 1946. Fisheries of the Great Lakes and border lakes 1915 to 1946. U. S. Fish Wildl. Serv., No. 413: 7 pp. (SAUGER; WALLEYE; COMMERCIAL FISHERIES;).

60. Anonymous. 1947. An experiment to check standing crop in two backwater ponds by the use of rotenone. Upper Miss. River Conserv. Comm., Tech. Comm. Fish., 3rd Prog. Rep., Append. 2:24-27. (WALLEYE; PRODUCTIVITY; TOXICANTS;).

61. Anonymous. 1947. Effects of midwinter drawdowns on the upper Mississippi River aquatic wildlife. Upper Miss. River Conserv. Comm., Tech. Comm. Fish., 3rd Prog. Rep., Append. 1:16-23. (SAUGER; WALLEYE; ECOLOGY; IMPOUNDMENTS; MORTALITY; WATER LEVELS;).

62. Anonymous. 1948. Natural history and status of game and pan fishes. Fisheries report for lakes of central Massachusetts 1944-1945. Mass. Dept. Conserv. pp. 91-118. (WALLEYE; STOCKING;).

63. Anonymous. 1948. Fisheries report for lakes of central Massachusetts 1944-1945. Mass. Dept. Conserv. pp. 9-104. (WALLEYE; CREEL CENSUS;).

64. Anonymous. 1949. Richelieu River. Que. Game Fish. Dept., 6th Rep. Biol. Bur. (1948):59-75. (WALLEYE; COMMERCIAL FISHERIES; CREEL CENSUS;).

65. Anonymous. 1955. Fish Conservation highlights of 1955. Sport Fish. Inst., Bull. 60: 72 pp. (WALLEYE; CREEL CENSUS;).

66. Anonymous. 1955. Test of planting walleye fry by plane. Prog. Fish-Cult. 17:128. (WALLEYE; STOCKING;).

67. Anonymous. 1955. The Canadian commercial fisheries of the Great Lakes. Can. Dept. Fish., Markets Econ. Serv., Basebook Fish Stat. 2: 180 pp. (SAUGER; WALLEYE; COMMERCIAL FISHERIES;).

68. Anonymous. 1956. The commercial fisheries of Canada. in W.L. Gordon (Chairman), Royal Commission on Canada's Economic Prospects, Queen's Printer, Ottawa, Ont. 192 pp. (SAUGER; WALLEYE; COMMERCIAL FISHERIES;).

69. Anonymous. 1956. Names of Michigan fishes. Mich. Dept. Conserv., Fish Div. Pamphlet No. 22: 5 pp. (SAUGER; WALLEYE; TAXONOMY;).

70. Anonymous. 1957. Progress report — five lakes project. Wis. Conserv. Dept. 11 pp. (WALLEYE; AGE AND GROWTH; CREEL CENSUS; MARKING; SPAWNING STUDIES; STOCKING;).

71. Anonymous. 1958. Fish planting — 1958. Alta. Dept. Lands Forest. Wildl. 1(3):16-17. (WALLEYE; STOCKING;).

72. Anonymous. 1958. Summary of laws relating to commercial fishing on the Great Lakes. Compiled by U.S. Fish. Wildl. Serv., Bur. Com. Fish., Ann Arbor, Mich. 42 pp. (SAUGER; WALLEYE; COMMERCIAL FISHERIES; REGULATIONS;).

73. Anonymous. 1959. A list of Ontario fishes. Roy. Ont. Mus., Dept. Fish. 8 pp. (SAUGER; WALLEYE; GEOGRAPHICAL DISTRIBUTION;).

74. Anonymous. 1961. Ecological investigations — Canton Reservoir. Okla. Dept. Wildl. Conserv., Fed. Aid Fish Wildl. Restor. Proj. F-7-R-1, Job No. 2-B: 4 pp. (WALLEYE; ECOLOGY; IMPOUNDMENTS; STOCKING;).

75. Anonymous. 1962. Summary of laws relating to commercial fishing on the Great Lakes. Great Lakes Fish. Comm. 42 pp. (SAUGER; WALLEYE; COMMERCIAL FISHERIES; FISHING GEAR; REGULATIONS;).

76. Anonymous. 1962. Some North Carolina freshwater fishes. N.C. Wildl. Res. Comm. 46 pp. (WALLEYE; INTRODUCTIONS; MORPHOLOGY;).

77. Anonymous. 1963. Summary of state and provincial regulations relating to sport fishing on the Great Lakes. Great Lakes Fish. Comm. 15 pp. (SAUGER; WALLEYE; REGULATIONS;).

78. Anonymous. 1965. Warmwater game fishes of California. Calif. Dept. Fish Game, Species Booklet 12: 39 pp. (WALLEYE; INTRODUCTIONS;).

79. Anonymous. 1966. Report on commercial fisheries resources of the Lake Erie basin. U.S. Fish Wildl. Serv., Bur. Com. Fish. 113 pp. Append. 14 pp. (SAUGER; WALLEYE; COMMERCIAL FISHERIES; HABITAT DEGRADATION;).

80. Anonymous. 1967. Commercial fish landings for Lake Erie, Ohio, 1966. Ohio Dept. Nat. Res. No. 200: 9 pp. (SAUGER; WALLEYE; COMMERCIAL FISHERIES;).

81. Anonymous. 1967. Temperatures for hatching walleye eggs. Prog. Fish-Cult. 29:20. (WALLEYE; EMBRYOLOGY; PROPAGATION;).

82. Anonymous. 1968. Report on commercial fisheries resources of the Lake Huron basin. U.S. Fish Wildl. Serv., Bur. Com. Fish. 91 pp. (WALLEYE; COMMERCIAL FISHERIES; ECOLOGY;).

83. Anonymous. 1969. Walleye fry — zooplankton relationship in southeastern Wisconsin lakes. Wis. Dept. Nat. Res., Fed. Aid Fish Wildl. Restor. Proj. F-83-R-5, Wk. Pl. 21, Job No. 1: 26 pp. (WALLEYE; ECOLOGY; FOOD STUDIES; MORTALITY; SPAWNING STUDIES; STOCKING;).

84. Anonymous. 1969. Report on commercial fisheries resources of the Lake Ontario basin. U.S. Fish Wildl. Serv., Bur. Com. Fish. 81 pp. (WALLEYE; COMMERCIAL FISHERIES; ECOLOGY; HABITAT DEGRADATION;).

85. Anonymous. 1969. Report on commercial fisheries resource of the Lake Superior basin. U.S. Fish Wildl. Serv., Bur. Com. Fish. 117 pp. (WALLEYE; COMMERCIAL FISHERIES; HABITAT DEGRADATION;).

86. Anonymous. 1982. Report to the Lake Huron Lake Committee. Mich. Dept. Nat. Res. 10 pp. (WALLEYE; AGE AND GROWTH; SPAWNING STUDIES; STOCKING;).

87. Anonymous. 1984. A fishery management plan for the walleye resource in Franklin Delano Roosevelt (FDR) Reservoir. Wash. Dept. Game 24 pp. (WALLEYE; CREEL CENSUS; IMPOUNDMENTS; POPULATION STUDIES; REGULATIONS;).

88. Anonymous. 1984. Walleye rehabilitation and enhancement newsletter. Can. Dept. Fish. Oceans, Freshwater Inst., Winnipeg, Man. No. 1, Fall 1984: 18 pp. (WALLEYE; ECOLOGY;).

89. Anonymous. 1984. Recommended fish protection procedures for stream crossings in Manitoba. Man. Dept. Nat. Res. 46 pp. (SAUGER; WALLEYE; FISHWAYS; HABITAT IMPROVEMENT;).

90. Anonymous. 1985. Symposium on the role of the fish culture in fishery management. Miss. Dept. of Conserv. 29 pp. (SAUGER; WALLEYE; PROPAGATION;).

91. Anonymous. 1985. Coolwater diet trials — walleye fingerlings. Penn. Fish. Comm. 13 pp. (WALLEYE; PROPAGATION;).

92. Anonymous. 1985. Walleye rehabilitation and enhancement newsletter. Can. Dept. Fish. Oceans, Freshwater Inst., Winnipeg, Man. No. 2, Spring 1985: 18 pp. (WALLEYE; ECOLOGY;).

93. Anonymous. 1985. A fishery management plan for the walleye resource in Washington State. Wash. Dept. Game. 12 pp. (WALLEYE; CREEL CENSUS; IMPOUNDMENTS; POPULATION STUDIES; REGULATIONS;).

94. Anonymous. 1985. Walleye rehabilitation and enhancement newsletter. Can. Dept. Fish. Oceans, Freshwater Inst., Winnipeg, Man. No. 3, Fall 1985: 21 pp. (WALLEYE; ECOLOGY;).

95. Anonymous. 1986. Walleye rehabilitation and enhancement newsletter. Can. Dept. Fish. Oceans, Freshwater Inst., Winnipeg, Man. No. 4, Spring 1986: 26 pp. (WALLEYE; ECOLOGY;).

96. Anonymous. 1986. Walleye rehabilitation and enhancement newsletter. Can. Dept. Fish. Oceans, Freshwater Inst., Winnipeg, Man. No. 5, Fall 1986: 23 pp. (WALLEYE; ECOLOGY;).

97. Anthony, D. D., and C. R. Jorgensen. 1977. Factors in the declining contributions of walleye *(Stizostedion vitreum vitreum)* to the fishery of Lake Nipissing, Ontario, 1960-76. J. Fish. Research Board Can. 34:1703-1709. (WALLEYE; AGE AND GROWTH; COMMUNITY DYNAMICS; CREEL CENSUS;).

98. Anthony, J. D. 1963. Parasites of eastern Wisconsin fishes. Trans. Wis. Acad. Sci., Arts Letters 52:83-95. (WALLEYE; PATHOLOGY;).

99. Anthony, L., and I. W. Dickson. 1965. A biological survey of Garner Lake, Manitoba. August, 1964. Man. Dept. Mines Nat. Res., Fish. Branch, Manuscript Rep. 8: 12 pp. (WALLEYE; AGE AND GROWTH; SAMPLING METHODS;).

100. Appelget, J. G. 1951. A report on the year classes of walleyes taken by anglers from Winnibigoshish Lake and connecting waters during the 1950 angling season. Minn. Dept. Conserv., Invest. Rep. No. 108: 11 pp. (WALLEYE; AGE AND GROWTH; CREEL CENSUS; MORTALITY;).

101. Applegate, R. L. 1983. *Bidens* Achenes cause mortality in young muskellunge and walleyes. Prog. Fish-Cult. 45:107. (WALLEYE; MORTALITY;).

102. Applegate, V. C. 1950. Natural history of the sea lamprey, *(Petromyzon marinus),* in Michigan. U.S. Fish Wildl. Serv., Spec. Sci. Rep. Fish. 55: 237 pp. (WALLEYE; COMMUNITY DYNAMICS; FOOD STUDIES;).

103. Applegate, V. C. 1961. Downstream movement of lampreys and fishes in the Carp Lake River, Michigan. U.S. Fish Wildl. Serv., Spec. Sci. Rep. Fish. 387: 71 pp. (WALLEYE; MOVEMENT AND MIGRATIONS;).

104. Applegate, V. C., J. H. Howell, J. W. Moffett, B. G. H. Johnson, and M. A. Smith. 1961. Use of 3-trifluormethyl-4-nitrophenol as a selective sea lamprey larvicide. Great Lakes Fish. Comm., Tech. Rep. 1: 35 pp. (WALLEYE; TOXICANTS;).

105. Applegate, V. C., and E. L. King, Jr. 1962. Comparative toxicity of 3-trifluormethyl-4-nitrophenol (TFM) to larval lampreys and eleven species of fishes. Trans. Am. Fish. Soc. 91:342-345. (WALLEYE; TOXICANTS;).

106. Applegate, V. C., A. L. Mc Lain, and M. Pattersom. 1952. Sea lamprey spawning runs in the Great Lakes, 1951. U.S. Fish Wildl. Serv., Spec. Sci. Rep. Fish. 68: 37 pp. (WALLEYE; PHYSIOLOGY;).

107. Applegate, V. C., and B. R. Smith. 1950. Sea lamprey spawning runs in the Great Lakes in 1950. U.S. Fish Wildl. Serv., Spec. Sci. Rep. Fish. 61: 49 pp. (WALLEYE; MOVEMENT AND MIGRATIONS;).

108. Applegate, V. C., and H. D. Van Meter. 1970. A brief history of commercial fishing in Lake Erie. U.S. Fish Wildl. Serv., Fish. Leaflet 630: 28 pp. (WALLEYE; COMMERCIAL FISHERIES;).

109. Armbruster, D. C. 1962. Observations on the loss of walleyes over and through Berlin Dam. Ohio Dept. Nat. Res. (W-64): 7 pp. (WALLEYE; CREEL CENSUS; MARKING; MORTALITY; MOVEMENT AND MIGRATIONS; WATER LEVELS;).

110. Armstrong, A. E. 1961. Preliminary report of fisheries inventory work in the Patricias, 1959-1960. Age and growth studies on five northern Ontario lakes. Ont. Dept. Lands Forest., Manuscript Rep. (1961): 19 pp. (WALLEYE; AGE AND GROWTH;).

111. Armstrong, E. R. 1983. Windfall Lake creel census 1983. Ont. Min. Nat. Res. Rep. 13 pp. (WALLEYE; CREEL CENSUS;).

112. Armstrong, E. R. 1983. Summer-Fall creel census on Mindemoya Lake. Ont. Min. Nat. Res. Rep. 41 pp. (WALLEYE; CREEL CENSUS;).

113. Armstrong, E. R. 1984. Kesagami Lake fisheries studies 1984. Ont. Min. Nat. Res. Rep. 30 pp. (WALLEYE; CREEL CENSUS;).

114. Armstrong, E. R., and D. B. Elliott. 1983. The impact of the northeastern Ontario access road (Detour Lake Road) on northern fly-in lakes. I. Baseline Studies — 1981. Ont. Min. Nat. Res. Rep. 76 pp. (WALLEYE; CREEL CENSUS; REGULATIONS; SOCIO-ECONOMICS OF FISHERIES;).

115. Armstrong, E. R., and G. Brown. 1983. The impact of the northeastern Ontario access road (Detour Lake Road) on northern fly-in lakes. II. Little Abitibi Lake creel census. Ont. Min. Nat. Res. Rep. 32 pp. (WALLEYE; CREEL CENSUS;).

116. Armstrong, E. R., and B. Jolkowski. 1984. Detour Lake road fisheries studies V. Fall fecundity studies 1983. Ont. Min. Nat. Res., Cochrane District. 51 pp. (WALLEYE; POPULATION STUDIES; SPAWNING

STUDIES;).

117. Armstrong, F. A. J., and D. P. Scott. 1979. Decrease in mercury content of fishes in Ball Lake, Ontario, since imposition of controls on mercury discharges. J. Fish. Research Board Can. 36:670-672. (WALLEYE; HABITAT DEGRADATION;).

118. Armstrong, J. J. 1965. Report on the use of four inch mesh in harvesting the walleye *(Stizostedion vitreum vitreum)* of Makoop Lake with recommendations of the use of this mesh size in the Patricias. Ont. Dept. Lands Forest., Res. Manage. Rep. (81):46-62. (WALLEYE; AGE AND GROWTH; COMMERCIAL FISHERIES; POPULATION STUDIES; SAMPLING METHODS;).

119. Armstrong, J. J. 1967. A creel census study of Sturgeon Lake, summer — 1965. Ont. Dept. Lands Forest., Res. Manage. Rep. (86):9-30. (WALLEYE; CREEL CENSUS;).

120. Armstrong, J. J., and R. D. Dyke. 1967. Walleye egg deposition on artificial spawning beds constructed in the Otonabee River at Bobcaygeon. Ont. Min. Nat. Res., Manuscript Rep. 14 pp. (WALLEYE; HABITAT IMPROVEMENT; SPAWNING STUDIES;).

121. Arnold, B. B. 1960. Life history notes on the walleye, *Stizostedion vitreum vitreum* (Mitchill), in a turbid water, Utah Lake, Utah. M.S. Thesis, Utah State Univ., Logan, Utah 114 pp. (WALLEYE; AGE AND GROWTH; COMMUNITY DYNAMICS; ECOLOGY; FOOD STUDIES; MARKING; MOVEMENT AND MIGRATIONS; POPULATION STUDIES; SPAWNING STUDIES; STOCKING;).

122. Arnold, B. B. 1961. Spawning habitat and success of the walleye in Utah Lake, Utah. *in* Proc. 41st Annu. Conf. Western Assoc. Game Fish Comm. 41:208-211. (WALLEYE; SPAWNING STUDIES;).

123. Arnold, D. E. 1969. The ecological decline of Lake Erie. N.Y. Fish Game J. 16:27-45. (SAUGER; WALLEYE; COMMERCIAL FISHERIES; ECOLOGY; POPULATION STUDIES;).

124. Arthur, J. W., C. W. West, and K. N. Allen. 1987. Seasonal toxicity of ammonia of five fish and nine invertebrates species. Bull. Environ. Contam. Toxicol. 38:324-331. (WALLEYE; TAXONOMY;).

125. Atton, F. M. 1951. Lac la Ronge creel census, 1950. Sask. Fish. Lab., Tech. Rep. 1951-5: 18 pp. (WALLEYE; CREEL CENSUS;).

126. Atton, F. M. 1952. Lac la Ronge creel census, 1951. Sask. Fish. Lab., Tech. Rep. 1952-4: 10 pp. (WALLEYE; AGE AND GROWTH; CREEL CENSUS;).

127. Atton, F. M. 1955. The relative effectiveness of nylon and cotton gill nets. Can. Fish Cult. 17:18-26. (WALLEYE; COMMERCIAL FISHERIES; FISHING GEAR;).

128. Atton, F. M. 1959. Lac la Ronge creel census, 1958. Sask. Fish. Lab., Tech. Rep. 1959-9: 5 pp. (WALLEYE; CREEL CENSUS;).

129. Atton, F. M. 1963. Lac la Ronge creel census, 1962. Sask. Fish. Lab., Tech. Rep. 1963-4: 3 pp. (WALLEYE; CREEL CENSUS;).

130. Atton, F. M. 1964. Lac la Ronge creel census, 1963. Sask. Fish. Lab., Tech. Rep. 1964-7: 6 pp. (WALLEYE; CREEL CENSUS;).

131. Atton, F. M. 1971. South shore walleye population, Lake Athabasca. Sask. Fish. Lab., Tech. Rep. 1971-4: 6 pp. (WALLEYE; SAMPLING METHODS;).

132. Atton, F. M., and N. S. Novakowski. 1954. Analysis of sampling the commercial fishery of Lake Athabaska, 1951, 1952, 1953. Sask. Fish. Lab., Tech. Rep. 1954-4: 33 pp. (WALLEYE; AGE AND GROWTH; COMMERCIAL FISHERIES;).

133. Atton, F. M., and N. S. Novakowski. 1955. Analysis of sampling the commercial fishery of Lake Athabaska, 1954. Sask. Fish. Lab., Tech. Rep. 1955-3: 8 pp. (WALLEYE; AGE AND GROWTH; COMMERCIAL FISHERIES;).

134. Auer, N. A., and M. T. Auer. 1984. Walleye *(Stizostedion vitreum)* egg hatching success in the lower Fox River (Wisconsin). U.S. Environ. Prot. Agency, Duluth, MN, Grant No. R810076-01-0 27:26-40. (WALLEYE; HABITAT DEGRADATION; MORTALITY; SPAWNING STUDIES;).

135. Avery, C. 1918. Minnesota's experiment in state fishing. Trans. Am. Fish. Soc. 48:57-

64. (WALLEYE; COMMERCIAL FISH-ERIES;).

136. Axon, J. R. 1979. Walleye stocking evaluation at Rough River Lake. Ky. Dept. Fish Wildl. Res., Fed. Aid Fish Wildl. Restor. Proj. F-39-R: 24 pp. (WALLEYE; AGE AND GROWTH; CREEL CENSUS; IMPOUND-MENTS; POPULATION STUDIES; SPAWNING STUDIES;).

137. Axon, J. R., R. V. Jackson, S. Samples, and M. Stephenson. 1985. Ohio River sport fishery investigations. Subsection III. Ky. Dept. Fish Wildl. Res., Fed. Aid Fish Wildl. Res-tor. Proj. F-40,Segment 7: 38 pp. (SAUGER; WALLEYE; AGE AND GROWTH; CREEL CENSUS; IMPOUNDMENTS; POPULATION STUDIES; PRODUCTIV-ITY; SAMPLING METHODS;).

138. Axon, J. R., B. T. Kinman, and C. Gorham. 1985. Sport fishery investigation: Subsec-tion I. Ky. Dept. Fish Wildl., Fed. Aid Fish Wildl. Restor. Proj. F-40, Segment 7: 73 pp. (WALLEYE; AGE AND GROWTH; CREEL CENSUS; POPULATION STUD-IES; SAMPLING METHODS; STOCK-ING;).

139. Axon, J. R., W. N. McLemore, D. E. Bell, B. D. Laflin, J. P. Henley, L. E. Kornman, A. R. Jones, and K. W. Pratter. 1984. Lakes and tailwaters research and management: Sub-section I. Ky. Dept. Fish Wildl. Res., Fed. Aid Fish Wildl. Restor. Proj. F-50, Segment 6: 239 pp. (SAUGER; WALLEYE; AGE AND GROWTH; IMPOUNDMENTS; POPULATION STUDIES; SAMPLING METHODS;).

140. Babaluk, J. A., B. M. Belcher, and J. S. Camp-bell. 1984. An investigation of the sport fishery on Dauphin Lake, Manitoba. Can. Manuscript Rep. Fish. Aquat. Sci. No. 1777: 23 pp. (WALLEYE; CREEL CEN-SUS;).

141. Babaluk, J. A., and J. S. Campbell. 1987. Pre-liminary results of tetracycline labelling for validating annual growth increments of opercula of walleyes. N. Am. J. Fish. Man-age. 7:138-141. (WALLEYE; AGE AND GROWTH;).

142. Baccante, D., and J. Sandhu. 1983. Annulus formation and growth characteristics of tagged walleye (Stizostedion vitreum) in a

lightly exploited lake. Ont. Fish. Tech. Rep. Ser. 9: 5 pp. (WALLEYE; AGE AND GROWTH;).

143. Backer, J. P. 1985. An examination of methods to eliminate adhesiveness and increase sur-vival of walleye eggs for hatchery produc-tion. Mich. Dept. Nat. Res. Fish. Tech. Rep. No. 85-6: 7 pp. (WALLEYE; PROPAGA-TION;).

144. Bahr, M. D. 1977. Homing, swimming behav-ior, range, activity pattern, and reaction to increasing water level of walleye's as deter-mined by radio-telemetry in navigational pools 7 and 8 of the upper Mississippi River during spring 1976. M.S. Thesis. Univ. Wis., La Crosse, Wis. 67 pp. (WALLEYE; BEHAVIOR; IMPOUNDMENTS; MARK-ING; MOVEMENT AND MIGRATIONS; WATER LEVELS;).

145. Bailey, L. R., and J. A. Oliver. 1938. The fishes of the Connecticut watershed. Pages 150-189 in H. E Warfel, ed. Biological survey of the Connecticut Watershed. N. H. Fish Game Dept. (WALLEYE; STOCKING;).

146. Bailey, R. M. 1938. The fishes of the Merri-mack watershed. Pages 149-185 in E. E. Hoover, ed. Biological survey of the Merri-mack watershed. N.H. Fish Game Dept., Rep. 3:. (WALLEYE; INTRODUCTIONS;).

147. Bailey, R. M. 1951. A check-list of the fishes of Iowa, with keys for identification. Pages 187-238 in J. R. Harlan, and E. B. Speaker, eds. Iowa fish and fishing. Iowa State Con-serv. Comm., Des Moines, Iowa. (SAUGER; WALLEYE; TAXONOMY;).

148. Bailey, R. M. 1952. Annual report of commit-tee on names of fishes. Trans. Am. Fish. Soc. 81: 324-327. (WALLEYE; TAXONOMY;).

149. Bailey, R. M., and M. O. Allum. 1962. Fishes of South Dakota. Univ. Mich. Mus. Zool., Misc. Pub. 119: 131 pp. (SAUGER; WALL-EYE; INTRODUCTIONS;).

150. Bailey, R. M., and W. A. Gosline. 1955. Varia-tion and systematic significance of verte-bral counts in the American fishes of the family Percidae. Univ. Mich. Mus. Zool. Misc. Publ. (93): 44 pp. (SAUGER; WALL-EYE; MORPHOLOGY; TAXONOMY;).

151. Bailey, R. M., and H. M. Harrison, Jr. 1945. The fishes of Clear Lake, Iowa. Iowa State

Coll. J. Sci. 20(1):57-77. (WALLEYE; FOOD STUDIES; STOCKING;).

152. Bajkov, A. 1930. Biological conditions of Manitoban lakes. Can. Biol. Fish. 5(12):383-422. (WALLEYE; ECOLOGY;).

153. Bajkov, A. 1930. A study of the whitefish *(Coregonus clupeaformis)* in Manitoban lakes. Contrib. Can. Biol. Fish. 5(15):443-455. (SAUGER; WALLEYE; COMMUNITY DYNAMICS;).

154. Bajkov, A. 1930. Fishing industry and fisheries investigation in the prairie provinces. Trans. Am. Fish. Soc. 60:215-237. (SAUGER; WALLEYE; AGE AND GROWTH; COMMERCIAL FISHERIES; FOOD STUDIES; SPAWNING STUDIES;).

155. Bajkov, A. 1932. Fish population and productivity of lakes. Trans. Am. Fish. Soc. 62:307-316. (WALLEYE; FOOD STUDIES;).

156. Baker, C. T., and H. L. Bower, Jr. 1965. Lake Erie fish population trawling survey. Ohio Dept. Nat. Res., Fed. Aid Fish Wildl. Restor. Proj. F-35-R-3, Job No. 3: 31 pp. (WALLEYE; ECOLOGY; POPULATION STUDIES; SAMPLING METHODS;).

157. Baker, C. T., and R. L. Scholl. 1971. Lake Erie fisheries investigations. Ohio Dept. Nat. Res., Fed. Aid Fish Wildl. Restor. Proj. F-35-R-10, Job 1: 24 pp. (WALLEYE; POPULATION STUDIES;).

158. Baker, C. T., and R. L. Scholl. 1971. Lake Erie fish research — walleye sampling. Ohio Dept. Nat. Res., Fed. Aid Fish Wildl. Restor. Proj. Final Rep., F-35-R-10, Job 2: 16 pp. (WALLEYE; AGE AND GROWTH; COMMUNITY DYNAMICS; FISHING GEAR; MOVEMENTS AND MIGRATIONS; POPULATION STUDIES;).

159. Baker, F. C. 1916. The relation of mollusks to fish in Oneida Lake. N.Y. State Coll. Forest., Syracuse Univ., Tech. Pub. 4: 365 pp. (SAUGER; WALLEYE; FOOD STUDIES; PATHOLOGY;).

160. Baker, F. C. 1918. The productivity of invertebrate fish food on the bottom of Oneida Lake, with special reference to mollusks. N.Y. State Coll. Forest., Syracuse Univ., Tech. Pub. 9: 264 pp. (WALLEYE; FOOD STUDIES;).

161. Balcer, M., D. McCauley, G. Niemi, and L. Brooke. 1986. Ecological assessment of factors affecting walleye ova survival in the lower Fox River. U.S. Environ. Protection Agency, Environ. Res. Lab.-Duluth, MN. Prog. Rep. in partial fulfillment of cooperative agreement #CR-811723-02-0: 110 pp. (WALLEYE; ECOLOGY; HABITAT DEGRADATION; MORTALITY; SPAWNING STUDIES; TOXICANTS;).

162. Baldwin, N. S., and R. W. Saalfeld. 1962. Commercial fish production in the Great Lakes 1867-1960. Great Lakes Fish. Comm., Tech. Rep. 3: 166 pp. (SAUGER; WALLEYE; COMMERCIAL FISHERIES;).

163. Baldwin, R. E., D. H. Strong, and J. H. Torrie. 1961. Flavor and aroma of fish taken from four freshwater sources. Trans. Am. Fish. Soc. 90:175-180. (WALLEYE; HABITAT DEGRADATION;).

164. Ball, C. T., and R. L. Scholl. 1971. Lake Erie fish population gill netting survey. Ohio Dept. Nat. Res., Fed. Aid Fish Wildl. Restor. Proj., Final Report, F-35-R-9, Job No. 4: 24 pp. (WALLEYE; AGE AND GROWTH; COMMUNITY DYNAMICS; FISHING GEAR; POPULATION STUDIES;).

165. Ball, D. R., and R. W. Stewart. 1979. Assessment of the Pierre-Montreuil Park Reserve yellow pickerel and northern pike sport fishery. Ont. Min. Nat. Res., Rep. 63 pp. (WALLEYE; CREEL CENSUS;).

166. Ball, R. C. 1948. Recovery of marked fish following a second poisoning of the population in Ford Lake, Michigan. Trans. Am. Fish. Soc. 75:36-42. (WALLEYE; COMMUNITY DYNAMICS; POPULATION STUDIES; STOCKING; TOXICANTS;).

167. Ball, R. L. 1982. 1980 and 1981 walleye population dynamics, growth and movements, and muskellunge exploitation in Brookville Reservoir. Ind. Dept. Nat. Res., Fish. Research Rep. 32 pp. (WALLEYE; AGE AND GROWTH; CREEL CENSUS; IMPOUNDMENTS; INTRODUCTIONS; MARKING; MORTALITY; MOVEMENTS AND MIGRATIONS; POPULATION STUDIES;).

168. Balon, E. K., W. T. Momot, and H. A. Reigier. 1977. Reproductive guilds of percids: results of the paleogeographical history and ecological succession. J. Fish. Research

Board Can. 34:1910-1921. (SAUGER; WALLEYE; COMMUNITY DYNAMICS; EMBRYOLOGY; SPAWNING STUDIES;).

169. Bandow, F. 1974. Algae control in fish ponds through chemical control of available nutrients. Minn. Dept. Nat. Res., Invest. Rep. No. 326: 22 pp. (WALLEYE; HABITAT DEGRADATION; PROPAGATION;).

170. Bandow, F. 1975. Methods for increasing the growth of walleye fingerlings in ponds. Minn. Dept. Nat. Res., Fed. Aid Fish Wildl. Restor. Proj. F-26-R-2, Wk. Pl. 2, Job 3: 5 pp. (WALLEYE; AGE AND GROWTH; PROPAGATION;).

171. Bandow, F. 1987. Fluorescent pigment marking of seven Minnesota fish species. Minn. Dept. Nat. Res., Invest. Rep. No. 393: 38 pp. (WALLEYE; MARKING;).

172. Bangham, R. V. 1946. Parasites of northern Wisconsin fish. Trans. Wis. Acad. Sci., Arts and Letters 36:291-325. (WALLEYE; PATHOLOGY;).

173. Bangham, R. V. 1955. Studies of fish parasites of Lake Huron and Manitoulin Island. Am. Midl. Nat. 53:184-194. (SAUGER; WALLEYE; PATHOLOGY;).

174. Bangham, R. V. 1963. Studies on fish parasites of Lake Erie, a resurvey. Ohio Dept. Nat. Res., Fed. Aid Fish Wildl. Restor. Proj. F-34-R-1, Job 3, Part 2: 50 pp. (SAUGER; WALLEYE; PATHOLOGY;).

175. Bangham, R. V., and G. W. Hunter, III. 1939. Studies on fish parasites of Lake Erie. Zoologica 24(27):385-448. (SAUGER; WALLEYE; PATHOLOGY;).

176. Bardach, T. E. 1955. Certain biological effects of thermocline shifts (observations from Lake West Okoboji, Iowa). Hydrobiologia 7:309-324. (WALLEYE; BEHAVIOR; ECOLOGY; MOVEMENTS AND MIGRATIONS; PHYSIOLOGY;).

177. Barnickol, P. G., and W. C. Starrett. 1951. Commercial and sport fishes of the Mississippi River between Caruthersville, Missouri, and Dubuque, Iowa. Ill. Nat. Hist. Surv., Bull. 25(5):267-350. (SAUGER; WALLEYE; AGE AND GROWTH; COMMERCIAL FISHERIES; CREEL CENSUS;).

178. Barr, W. C., and J. A. Holbrook II. 1976. A method for analysis of differences in fish community species occurrences. Proc. 30th Annu. Conf. Southeast Assoc. Fish Wildl. Agencies 30:276-279. (SAUGER; COMMUNITY DYNAMICS; IMPOUNDMENTS;).

179. Barrow, F. T. 1987. Nutrient requirements of walleyes (Stizostedion vitreum vitreum). Ph.D. Dissertation, Iowa State Univ., Ames, Iowa. 143 pp. (WALLEYE; FOOD STUDIES; PROPAGATION;).

180. Bartlett, S. P. 1911. Rescue work-the saving of fish from overflowed lands. Trans. Am. Fish. Soc. 40(1910):153-158. (WALLEYE; ECOLOGY; MORTALITY;).

181. Battle, H. I., and W. M. Sprules. 1960. A description of the semi-buoyant eggs and early development stages of the goldeye, Hiodon alosoides (Rafinesque). J. Fish. Research Board Can. 17:245-266. (WALLEYE; EMBRYOLOGY;).

182. Batty, S. 1985. 1985 winter creel census on Marshall, Meta, Abamasagi and Ara Lakes. Ont. Min. Nat. Res., Rep. 25 pp. (WALLEYE; CREEL CENSUS;).

183. Batty, S. 1985. O'Sullivan Lake 1985 summer creel census. Ont. Min. Nat. Res., Rep. 24 pp. (WALLEYE; CREEL CENSUS;).

184. Batty, S. 1985. Summary of the Kenogamisis Fish and Game Protective Association Fish Derby, June 8 and 9, 1985. Ont. Min. Nat. Res., Rep. 8 pp. (WALLEYE; CREEL CENSUS;).

185. Baur, R. J., and R. A. Rogers. 1985. 1983 Illinois sport fishing survey. Ill. Dept. Conserv., Special Fish. Rep. No. 52: 45 pp. (SAUGER; WALLEYE; CREEL CENSUS;).

186. Beamish, R. J. 1979. Design of a trapnet for sampling shallow-water habitats. Fish. Research Board Can., Tech. Rep. No. 305: 14 pp. (WALLEYE; FISHING GEAR; SAMPLING METHODS;).

187. Beamish, R. L., W. L. Lockhart, J. C. Van Loon, and H. H. Harvey. 1975. Long term acidification of a lake and resulting effects on fishes. Ambio 4:98-102. (WALLEYE; HABITAT DEGRADATION;).

188. Bean, B. A., and A. C. Weed. 1911. Recent ad-

ditions to the fish fauna of the District of Columbia. Proc. Biol. Soc. Washington 24:171-174. (WALLEYE; INTRODUCTIONS;).

189. Bean, T. H. 1892. Observations upon fishes and fish-culture. U.S. Fish Comm., Bull. 10 (1890): 49-61. (WALLEYE; COMMUNITY DYNAMICS; POPULATION STUDIES;).

190. Bean, T. H. 1896. Report on the propagation and distribution of food-fishes. U.S. Comm. Fish., Annu. Rep. (1894): 20-80. (WALLEYE; GENETICS; PROPAGATION; WATER LEVELS;).

191. Bean, T. H. 1897. Notes upon New York fishes received at the New York aquarium, 1895 to 1897. in N.Y. Comm. Fish., Game Forest., 2nd Annu. Rep. (1896): 207-251. (WALLEYE; MORPHOLOGY; STOCKING;).

192. Bean, T. H. 1901. Catalogue of the fishes of Long Island. N.Y. Forest., Fish Game Comm., 6th Annu. Rep. (1900): 373-374. (WALLEYE; INTRODUCTIONS;).

193. Bean, T. H. 1901. The fishes of Long Island, with notes upon their distribution, common names, habits, and rate of growth. N.Y. Forest, Fish Game Comm., 6th Annu. Rep. (1900): 375-478. (WALLEYE; ECOLOGY; INTRODUCTIONS; MORTALITY;).

194. Bean, T. H. 1902. Food and game fishes of New York. N.Y. Forest, Fish Game Comm., 7th Annu. Rep. (1901): 251-460. (SAUGER; WALLEYE; ECOLOGY; FOOD STUDIES; PROPAGATION; SPAWNING STUDIES; TAXONOMY;).

195. Bean, T. H. 1903. Catalogue of the fishes of New York. N.Y. State Mus. Bull. 60: 784 pp. (SAUGER; WALLEYE; ECOLOGY; MORPHOLOGY; SPAWNING STUDIES; TAXONOMY;).

196. Bean, T. H. 1903. The food and game fishes of New York: notes on their common names, distribution, habits and mode of capture. N.Y. Forest, Fish Game Comm. 427 pp. (SAUGER; WALLEYE; ECOLOGY; FOOD STUDIES; SPAWNING STUDIES; TAXONOMY;).

197. Bean, T. H. 1910. Report of the state fish culturist. N.Y. Forest, Fish Game Comm., Annu. Rep. (1907-1908-1909): 308-357. (WALLEYE; PATHOLOGY; PROPAGA-

TION; STOCKING;).

198. Bean, T. H. 1912. Annual report of the fish culturist. N.Y. Conserv. Comm., Ann. Rep. 1:161-225. (WALLEYE; PRODUCTIVITY;).

199. Bean, T. H. 1913. Annual report of the fish culturist. N.Y. Conserv. Comm., Ann. Rep. 2:227-280. (WALLEYE; PRODUCTIVITY;).

200. Bean, T. H. 1916. Fish planting in public waters. N.Y. Conserv. Comm., 24 pp. (WALLEYE; PROPAGATION; STOCKING;).

201. Becker, G. C. 1964. The fishes of Pewaukee Lake. Trans. Wis. Acad. Sci., Arts Letters 53:19-27. (WALLEYE; GEOGRAPHICAL DISTRIBUTION;).

202. Becker, G. C. 1964. The fishes of Lakes Poygan and Winnebago. Trans. Wis. Acad. Sci., Arts Letters 53:29-52. (WALLEYE; ECOLOGY;).

203. Becker, G. C. 1966. Fishes of southwestern Wisconsin. Trans. Wis. Acad. Sci., Arts Letters 55:87-117. (SAUGER; WALLEYE; GEOGRAPHICAL DISTRIBUTION;).

204. Becker, G. C. 1969. Key to the Wisconsin percid fishes. Wis. State Univ., Mus. Natur. Hist. 6 pp. (SAUGER; WALLEYE; TAXONOMY;).

205. Becker, G. C. 1969. Preliminary list of fishes of Portage County, Wisconsin. Wis. State Univ., Mus. Natur. Hist., Rep. Fauna Flora Wis. 1: 11 pp. (WALLEYE; GEOGRAPHICAL DISTRIBUTION; HABITAT DEGRADATION;).

206. Becker, G. C. 1983. Fishes of Wisconsin. Univ. of Wis. Press, Madison. 1052 pp. (SAUGER; WALLEYE; LIFE HISTORY; TAXONOMY;).

207. Beckman, L. G. 1987. Relative abundance and distribution of young-of-the-year fishes and minnows in Lake Sharpe, South Dakota, USA 1967-1975. U.S. Fish Wildl. Serv., Fish Wildl. Tech. Rep. 8:30-45. (WALLEYE; IMPOUNDMENTS; POPULATION STUDIES;).

208. Beckman, L. G., and J. H. Elrod. 1971. Apparent abundance and distribution of young-of-

year fishes in Lake Oahe, 1965-69. Pages 333-347 in G. E. Hall, ed. Reservoir fisheries and limnology. Am. Fish. Soc. Sp. Publ. No. 8. Washington, D. C. (SAUGER; WALLEYE; COMMUNITY DYNAMICS; FISHING GEAR; IMPOUNDMENTS; POPULATION STUDIES; SAMPLING METHODS; SPAWNING STUDIES;).

209. Beckman, W. C. 1943. Annulus formation on the scales of certain Michigan game fishes. Pap. Mich. Acad. Sci. Arts, and Letters 28(1942):281-312. (WALLEYE; MORPHOLOGY;).

210. Beckman, W. C. 1952. Guide to the fishes of Colorado. Univ. Colorado Mus. Leafl. (11): 108 pp. (WALLEYE; MORPHOLOGY; SPAWNING STUDIES; TAXONOMY;).

211. Beeton, A. M. 1961. Environmental changes in Lake Erie. Trans. Am. Fish. Soc. 90:153-159. (SAUGER; WALLEYE; ECOLOGY;).

212. Beeton, A. M. 1963. Limnological survey of Lake Erie 1959 and 1960. Great Lakes Fish. Comm. Tech. Rep. 6: 32 pp. (SAUGER; WALLEYE; ECOLOGY;).

213. Beeton, A. M. 1965. Eutrophication of the St. Lawrence Great Lakes. Limnol. Oceanogr. 10:240-254. (SAUGER; WALLEYE; ECOLOGY; PRODUCTIVITY;).

214. Beeton, A. M. 1966. Indices of Great Lakes eutrophication. Univ. Mich. Great Lakes Research Div. Publ. 15:1-8. (SAUGER; WALLEYE; AGE AND GROWTH; ECOLOGY; HABITAT DEGRADATION;).

215. Beeton, A. M., S. H. Smith, and F. H. Hooper. 1967. Physical limnology of Saginaw Bay, Lake Huron. Great Lakes Fish. Comm. Tech. Rep. No. 12: 56 pp. (WALLEYE; ECOLOGY; HABITAT DEGRADATION;).

216. Behmer, D. J. 1964. Movement and angler harvest of fishes in the Des Moines River, Boone County, Iowa. Proc. Iowa Acad. Sci. 71:259-263. (WALLEYE; MARKING; MOVEMENTS AND MIGRATIONS;).

217. Behnke, R. J., and R. M. Wetzel. 1960. A preliminary list of the fishes found in the fresh waters of Connecticut. Copeia 1960(2):141-143. (WALLEYE; INTRODUCTIONS;).

218. Belanger, S. E., and S. R. Hogler. 1982. Comparison of five aging methodologies applied to walleye (Stizostedion vitreum) in Burt Lake, Michigan. J. Great Lakes Research 8:666-671. (WALLEYE; AGE AND GROWTH;).

219. Bell, D. 1980. Round Lake creel census 1980. Ont. Min. Nat. Res., Rep. 36 pp. (WALLEYE; CREEL CENSUS;).

220. Bell, D. 1980. Belmont Lake creel census 1980. Ont. Min. Nat. Res., Rep. 37 pp. (WALLEYE; CREEL CENSUS;).

221. Bell, D. 1982. Stony Lake and Clear Lake creel census report. Ont. Min. Nat. Res., Rep. 63 pp. (WALLEYE; CREEL CENSUS;).

222. Bell, R. J. 1983. Region 4 lowland lakes investigations. Idaho Dept. Fish Game, Fed. Aid Fish Wildl. Restor. Proj. F-71-R-7, Job IV-b: 3-12. (WALLEYE; AGE AND GROWTH; CREEL CENSUS; FOOD STUDIES; IMPOUNDMENTS; STOCKING;).

223. Bellington, N., and P. D. N. Hebert. 1986. Stock discrimination in walleye based on divergence in the mitochondrial genome. Great Lakes Inst. Proj. GR06385: 58 pp. (WALLEYE; GENETICS;).

224. Bennett, D. H. 1979. Probable walleye (Stizostedion vitreum) habitation in the Snake River and tributaries of Idaho. Idaho Univ., Moscow Water Res. Research Inst. Proj. A-060-IDA: 53 pp. (WALLEYE; AGE AND GROWTH; COMMUNITY DYNAMICS; FOOD STUDIES; GEOGRAPHICAL DISTRIBUTION; LIFE HISTORY; SPAWNING STUDIES; TAXONOMY;).

225. Bennett, G. W. 1962. Management of artificial lakes and ponds. Reinhold Publ. Corp., New York, N.Y. 283 pp. (WALLEYE; AGE AND GROWTH; COMMUNITY DYNAMICS; MORTALITY; MOVEMENTS AND MIGRATIONS; PHYSIOLOGY; PRODUCTIVITY;).

226. Bennett, L. H. 1948. Pike culture at the New London, Minnesota, station. Prog. Fish-Cult. 10:95-97. (WALLEYE; AGE AND GROWTH; MORTALITY; PROPAGATION; SPAWNING STUDIES;).

227. Bensley, B. A. 1915. The fishes of Georgian Bay. Contrib. Can. Biol. 1911-1914 (1):1-51. (WALLEYE; COMMERCIAL FISHERIES; ECOLOGY; FOOD STUDIES; LIFE HISTORY; PROPAGATION;).

228. Benson, N. G. 1959. Fish management on Wood's Reservoir. J. Tenn. Acad. Sci. 34(3):172-189. (WALLEYE; CREEL CENSUS; IMPOUNDMENTS; POPULATION STUDIES;).

229. Benson, N. G. 1968. Review of fishery studies on Missouri River main stem reservoirs. U.S. Fish Wildl. Serv. Research Rep. 71: 61 pp. (SAUGER; WALLEYE; AGE AND GROWTH; COMMUNITY DYNAMICS; ECOLOGY; MOVEMENT AND MIGRATIONS; POPULATION STUDIES; SPAWNING STUDIES;).

230. Benson, N. G. 1973. Evaluating the effects of discharge rates, water levels, and peaking on fish populations in Missouri River main stem impoundments. Pages 683-689 in W.C. Ackermann, G. F. White, and E. B. Worthington, eds. Man-made lakes: Their problems and environmental effects. Geophysical Monograph 17. (SAUGER; IMPOUNDMENTS; WATER LEVELS;).

231. Benson, N. G. 1973. North central reservoir investigations. U.S. Bur. Sport. Fish. Wildl. Res. Publ. 121:125-134. (WALLEYE; COMMUNITY DYNAMICS; ECOLOGY; IMPOUNDMENTS; POPULATION STUDIES; SPAWNING STUDIES; WATER LEVELS;).

232. Benson, N. G. 1980. Effects of post-impoundment shore modifications on fish populations in Missouri River Reservoirs. U. S. Fish Wildl. Serv., Research Rep. 80: 32 pp. (SAUGER; WALLEYE; COMMUNITY DYNAMICS; HABITAT IMPROVEMENT; IMPOUNDMENTS; POPULATION STUDIES; SPAWNING STUDIES; WATER LEVELS;).

233. Berard, E. 1978. Statewide fisheries investigations. Investigate the influence of smelt on the walleye population in Lake Sakakawea. N. D. State Game & Fish Dept., Fed. Aid Fish Wildl. Restor. Proj. F-002-R-25, Wk. Pl. 6, Job A & B: 39 pp. (WALLEYE; AGE AND GROWTH; FOOD STUDIES; POPULATION STUDIES;).

234. Berard, E. 1986. Ecological investigations of the Missouri mainstream reservoirs in North Dakota. N. D. Game Fish Dept., Statewide Fish. Invest., Fed. Aid Fish Wildl. Restor. Proj. F-2-R-32, Rep. No. A-1123: 62 pp. (SAUGER; WALLEYE; COMMERCIAL FISHERIES; COMMUNITY DYNAMICS; IMPOUNDMENTS; INTRODUCTIONS; POPULATION STUDIES; WATER LEVELS;).

235. Berard, E., and G. J. Power. 1985. Ecological investigations of the Missouri mainstream reservoirs in North Dakota. N. D. Game Fish Dept., Statewide Fish. Invest., Fed. Aid Fish Wildl. Restor. Proj. F-2-R-31, Rep. No. A-1110: 55 pp. (SAUGER; WALLEYE; AGE AND GROWTH; IMPOUNDMENTS; POPULATION STUDIES; WATER LEVELS;).

236. Bere, R. 1931. Copepods parasitic on fish of the Trout Lake region, with descriptions of two new species. Trans. Wis. Acad. Sci., Arts Letters 26:427-436. (WALLEYE; PATHOLOGY;).

237. Bere, R. 1935. Further notes on the occurrence of parasitic copepods on fish of the Trout Lake region, with a description of the male of *Argulus biramosus*. Trans. Wis. Acad. Sci., Arts Letters 29:83-88. (WALLEYE; PATHOLOGY;).

238. Berg, G. 1920. Report of the superintendent of state hatcheries. Ind. Dept. Conserv., 1st Annu. Rep. (1919):81-96. (WALLEYE; STOCKING;).

239. Berg, G. 1923. Report of the superintendent of hatcheries. Ind. Dept. Conserv., 4th Annu. Rep. (1922):76-82, 119-140. (WALLEYE; STOCKING;).

240. Berger, B. L., R. E. Lennon, and J. W. Hogan. 1969. Laboratory studies on Antimycin A as a fish toxicant. U.S. Fish Wildl. Serv., Invest. Fish Control 26: 21 pp. (WALLEYE; TOXICANTS;).

241. Berkes, F., and D. Pocock. 1987. Quota management and "people problems: a case history of Canadian Lake Erie fisheries. Trans. Am. Fish. Soc. 116:494-502. (WALLEYE; COMMERCIAL FISHERIES; SOCIO-ECONOMICS OF FISHERIES;).

242. Bever, G. C., and J. M. Lealos. 1974. Walleye fishery in Pike and Round Lakes, Price County. Wis. Dept. Nat. Res., Fish Manage. Rep. No. 73: 16 pp. (WALLEYE; AGE AND GROWTH; COMMUNITY DYNAMICS; CREEL CENSUS; MORTALITY; POPULATION STUDIES;).

243. Bever, G. G., and J. M. Lealos. 1977. The walleye in Butternut Lake, Price County, Wisconsin. Wis. Dept. Nat. Res., Fish Manage. Rep. No. 96: 12 pp. (WALLEYE; AGE AND GROWTH; CREEL CENSUS; POPULATION STUDIES; PRODUCTIVITY; REGULATIONS; SPAWNING STUDIES;).

244. Beverton, R. J. H. 1987. Longevity in fish: some ecological and evolutionary considerations. Pages 161-186 in A.D. Woodhead and K.H. Thompson, eds. Evolution and longevity in animals. Basic Life Sciences. Vol. 42. Plenum Press, New York. (WALLEYE; FOOD STUDIES; GENETICS; POPULATION STUDIES;).

245. Beyerle, G. B. 1975. Propagation of walleyes from egg to fry, and fry to fingerling. Mich. Dept. Nat. Res., Annual Prog. Rep.: 41-46. (WALLEYE; FOOD STUDIES; PROPAGATION; STOCKING;).

246. Beyerle, G. B. 1975. Summary of attempts to raise walleye fry and fingerlings on artificial diets, with suggestions on needed research and procedures to be used in future tests. Prog. Fish-Cult. 37:103-105. (WALLEYE; FOOD STUDIES; PROPAGATION;).

247. Beyerle, G. B. 1976. Survival, growth and vulnerability to angling of walleyes stocked as fingerlings in a small lake with bluegills. Mich. Dept. Nat. Res., Fish. Research Rep. No. 1837: 11 pp. (WALLEYE; AGE AND GROWTH; CREEL CENSUS; FOOD STUDIES; MORTALITY; PRODUCTIVITY; STOCKING;).

248. Beyerle, G. B. 1977. Survival, growth, and vulnerability to angling of walleyes stocked as fingerlings in a small lake with minnows. Mich. Dept. Nat. Res., Fish. Research Rep. No. 1853: 12 pp. (WALLEYE; AGE AND GROWTH; CREEL CENSUS; FOOD STUDIES; MORTALITY; PRODUCTIVITY; STOCKING;).

249. Beyerle, G. B. 1978. Survival, growth, and vulnerability to angling of northern pike and walleyes stocked as fingerlings in small lakes with bluegills or minnows. Pages 135-139 in R.L. Kendall, ed. Selected coolwater fishes of North America. Am. Fish. Soc. Sp. Publ. No. 11, Washington D.C. (WALLEYE; AGE AND GROWTH; COMMUNITY DYNAMICS; FOOD STUDIES; INTRODUCTIONS; MORTALITY; PRODUCTIVITY; STOCKING;).

250. Beyerle, G. B. 1978. Hatchery-reared fingerling walleyes unharmed by diet change from pellets to spiny-rayed prey fish. Prog. Fish-Cult. 40:93. (WALLEYE; FOOD STUDIES; PROPAGATION;).

251. Beyerle, G. B. 1979. Intensive culture of walleye fry and fingerlings in Michigan, 1972-1979. Mich. Dept. Nat. Res., Fish. Research Rep. No. 1873: 32 pp. (WALLEYE; PROPAGATION;).

252. Beyerle, G. B. 1979. Extensive culture of walleye fry in ponds at the Wolf Lake Hatchery, 1975-1978. Mich. Dept. Nat. Res., Fish. Research Rep. No. 1874: 28 pp. (WALLEYE; FOOD STUDIES; PROPAGATION;).

253. Beyerle, G. B. 1983. Survival and growth of 5-, 10-, and 15-cm walleye fingerlings stocked in ponds with bluegills. Mich. Dept. Nat. Res., Fish. Research Rep. No. 1910: 9 pp. (WALLEYE; AGE AND GROWTH; COMMUNITY DYNAMICS; MORTALITY; POPULATION STUDIES; STOCKING;).

254. Beyette, D. J. 1978. A comparison of growth rates of walleye (Stizostedion vitreum) from Lake Winnipeg and other water bodies. Man. Dept. Mines, Nat. Res. Envir., Manuscript Rep. No. 78-84: 37 pp. (WALLEYE; AGE AND GROWTH; COMMERCIAL FISHERIES; MORTALITY; POPULATION STUDIES;).

255. Bidgood, B. F. 1966. Spring movement of walleye into Richardson Lake. Alta. Dept. Lands Forest., Manuscript Report. 32 pp. (WALLEYE; COMMERCIAL FISHERIES; FISHING GEAR; POPULATION STUDIES; SPAWNING STUDIES;).

256. Bidgood, B. F. 1968. Ecology of walleyes in Richardson Lake — Lake Athabasca. Alta. Fish & Wildl. Div., Fish. Sec., Research Rep. No. 1: 20 pp. (WALLEYE; ECOLOGY;).

257. Bidgood, B. F. 1971. Ecology of walleyes, Stizostedion v. vitreum, in the Richardson Lake-Lake Athabasca Complex. Pages 187-

203 *in* Proceedings of Peace-Athabasca Delta Symposium, Edmonton, Alta, 14-15 January 1971. (WALLEYE; ECOLOGY; MOVEMENTS AND MIGRATIONS; POPULATION STUDIES;).

258. Bidgood, B. F. 1980. Procuring and transporting walleye eggs from remote locations to a centralized hatchery. Alta. Dept. Nat. Res., Fish. Research Rep. No. 19: 20 pp. (WALLEYE; PROPAGATION;).

259. Biette, R. M., and R. M. Odell. 1975. An assessment of a fish pass manufactured by Aeroceanics Fishway Corporation. Ont. Min. Nat. Res., Internal Rep. 32 pp. (WALLEYE; FISHWAYS;).

260. Billington, N., T. J. Crease, P. M. Grewe, P. D. N. Hebert, and D. J. Stanton. 1987. Development of a small tissue sample technique for the rapid analysis of mitochondrial DNA in walleye and lake trout. Great Lakes Institute Rep. 32 pp. (WALLEYE; GENETICS; PHYSIOLOGY;).

261. Billington, N., and P. D. N. Hebert. 1986. Stock discrimination in walleye based on divergence in the mitochondrial genome. Great Lakes Institute Rep. 58 pp. (WALLEYE; GENETICS; PHYSIOLOGY;).

262. Binkley, L. E. 1944. An analysis of fishing effort at Indian Lake. Ohio J. Sci. 44(3):145-150. (WALLEYE; CREEL CENSUS;).

263. Birnie, J., J.j. Noble, and E. E. Prince. 1908. Report and recommendations (with appendices) of the Dominion Fisheries Commission appointed to enquire into the fisheries of Georgian Bay and adjacent waters. Govt. Print. Bur., Ottawa, Ont. 55 pp. (WALLEYE; COMMERCIAL FISHERIES; FISHING GEAR;).

264. Bishop, S. C. 1934. A biological survey of the Raquette watershed. III. The lakes of the Raquette River drainage basin. N.Y. Conserv. Dep., Suppl. 23rd Annu. Rep. (1933):109-135. (WALLEYE; INTRODUCTIONS; STOCKING;).

265. Bishop, S. C. 1936. A biological survey of the Delaware and Susquehanna watersheds. IV Fisheries investigations in the Delaware and Susquehanna Rivers. N.Y. Conserv. Dept., Suppl. 25th Annu. Rep. (1935):122-139. (WALLEYE; INTRODUCTIONS; STOCKING;).

266. Bishop, S. C., and R. E. James. 1938. A biological survey of the Allegheny and Chemung watersheds. VI. Fisheries investigation in the Allegheny and Chemung Rivers. N.Y. Conserv. Dept., Suppl. 27th Annu. Rep. (1937):102-112. (WALLEYE; ECOLOGY; STOCKING;).

267. Bissell, J. H. 1889. The Canadian and American fisheries of the Great Lakes. U.S. Fish Comm. Bull. 7(1887):7-10. (WALLEYE; COMMERCIAL FISHERIES; PROPAGATION;).

268. Black, J. J. 1983. Field and laboratory studies of environmental carcinogenesis in Niagara River fish. J. Great Lakes Research 9:326-334. (WALLEYE; HABITAT DEGRADATION; PATHOLOGY; TOXICANTS;).

269. Black, J. J. 1984. Environmental implications of neoplasia in Great Lakes fish. Mar. Envir. Res. 14:529-534. (SAUGER; WALLEYE; PATHOLOGY;).

270. Boad, W. A., R. W. Moshenko, and G. Low. 1978. An investigation of the walleye, *Stizostedion vitreum vitreum* from sport fishery of the Itay River, Northwest Territories, Canada 1975. Can. Fish. and Mar. Serv., Manuscript Rep. No. (1449), 1978 L-V1: 1-20. (WALLEYE; POPULATION STUDIES;).

271. Boaze, J. L., and R. T. Lackey. 1974. Age, growth, and utilization of landlocked alewives in Clayton Lake, Virginia. Prog. Fish-Cult. 36:163-164. (WALLEYE; FOOD STUDIES;).

272. Bodaly, R. A. 1980. Pre-and post spawning movements of walleye, *Stizostedion vitreum*, in Southern Indian Lake, Manitoba. Can. Tech. Rep. Fish. Aquatic Sci. No. 931: 30 pp. (WALLEYE; AGE AND GROWTH; BEHAVIOR; IMPOUNDMENTS; MOVEMENTS AND MIGRATIONS; SPAWNING STUDIES;).

273. Bodaly, R. A., R. E. Hecky, and R. J. P. Fudge. 1984. Increases in fish mercury levels in lakes flooded by the Churchill River diversion, northern Manitoba. Can. J. Fish. Aquat. Sci. 41:682-691. (WALLEYE; IMPOUNDMENTS; TOXICANTS;).

274. Boland, T., and G. Ackerman. 1980. Investigations of tailwater walleye and sauger fisheries of the Upper Mississippi River. Iowa

Cons. Comm., Job Comp. Rep. Proj. 80-II-C-7: 92-97. (SAUGER; WALLEYE; AGE AND GROWTH; MARKING;).

275. Boland, T., and G. Ackerman. 1981. Investigations of tailwater walleye and sauger fisheries of the Upper Mississippi River. Iowa Cons. Comm., Job Comp. Rep. Proj. 81-II-C-8: 81-94. (SAUGER; WALLEYE; AGE AND GROWTH; CREEL CENSUS; MARKING; MOVEMENT AND MIGRATIONS; POPULATION STUDIES;).

276. Boland, T., and G. Ackerman. 1982. Investigations of tailwater walleye and sauger fisheries of the Upper Mississippi River. Iowa Cons. Comm., Job Comp. Rep. Proj. 82-II-C-11: 120-148. (SAUGER; WALLEYE; AGE AND GROWTH; CREEL CENSUS; MARKING; MORTALITY; MOVEMENT AND MIGRATIONS; POPULATION STUDIES;).

277. Bond, C. E. 1961. Keys to Oregon freshwater fishes. Oreg. State Univ., Agr. Exp. Sta., Tech. Bull. 58: 42 pp. (WALLEYE; INTRODUCTIONS; TAXONOMY;).

278. Bond, L. J. 1974. Oba Lake creel census — 1974. Ont. Min. Nat. Res., Rep. 32 pp. (WALLEYE; CREEL CENSUS;).

279. Bond, W. A., R. W. Moshenko, and G. Low. 1978. An investigation of the walleye, *Stizostedion vitreum vitreum* (Mitchill), from the sport fishery of the Hay River, Northwest Territories, 1975. Can. Fish. Mar. Serv., Manuscript Rep. No. 1449: 19pp. (WALLEYE; AGE AND GROWTH; CREEL CENSUS; ECOLOGY; POPULATION STUDIES;).

280. Bonde, T. J. H. 1961. Determination of fishing success and satisfaction by means of a post card questionaire. Minn. Dept. Conserv., Invest. Rep. No. 231: 10 pp. (WALLEYE; CREEL CENSUS;).

281. Bonde, T. J. H. 1963. An investigation of the reproduction abundance and population of the walleye in the Whitefish Chain of Lakes. Minn. Dept. Conserv., Invest. Rep. No. 268: 24 pp. (WALLEYE; AGE AND GROWTH; GENETICS; SPAWNING STUDIES;).

282. Bonde, T. J. H. 1965. Comparison of two types of gillnets used for lake survey purposes in Minnesota-Ontario boundary waters. Minn. Dept. Conserv., Invest. Rep. No. 285: 11 pp. (SAUGER; WALLEYE; FISHING GEAR;).

283. Bonde, T. J. H., C. A. Elsey, and B. J. Caldwell. 1961. A preliminary investigation of Rainy Lake, 1959. Minn. Dept. Conserv., Invest. Rep. No. 234: 43 pp. (SAUGER; WALLEYE; AGE AND GROWTH; COMMUNITY DYNAMICS; CREEL CENSUS; MARKING; MOVEMENTS AND MIGRATIONS; POPULATION STUDIES; SPAWNING STUDIES;).

284. Bonde, T. J. H., C. A. Elsey, and B. Caldwell. 1964. A fisheries survey of Lac la Croix 1963. Minn. Dept. Conserv., Invest. Rep. No. 281: 10 pp. (SAUGER; WALLEYE; AGE AND GROWTH; COMMERCIAL FISHERIES; POPULATION STUDIES;).

285. Bonde, T. J. H., C. A. Elsey, and B. Caldwell. 1964. A fisheries survey of Namakan Lake 1962-1963. Minn. Dept. Conserv., Invest. Rep. No. 282: 27 pp. (WALLEYE; AGE AND GROWTH; COMMERCIAL FISHERIES; COMMUNITY DYNAMICS; FISHING GEAR; POPULATION STUDIES;).

286. Bonde, T. J. H., C. A. Elsey, and B. J. Caldwell. 1965. A second Rainy Lake report, 1957-1963. Minn. Dept. Conserv., Invest. Rep. No. 284: 42 pp. (SAUGER; WALLEYE; AGE AND GROWTH; COMMERCIAL FISHERIES; CREEL CENSUS; FISHING GEAR; MARKING; MOVEMENTS AND MIGRATIONS; POPULATION STUDIES;).

287. Bonde, T. J. H., and J. E. Maloney. 1960. Food habits of burbot. Trans. Am. Fish. Soc. 89:374-376. (WALLEYE; COMMUNITY DYNAMICS;).

288. Bonn, E. W., and J. H. Moczygemba. 1975. Cypress Springs walleye study. Tex. Parks Wildl. Dept., Fed. Aid Fish Wildl. Restor. Proj. F-31-R-1 Final Rep. Job IV: 34 pp. (WALLEYE; AGE AND GROWTH; COMMUNITY DYNAMICS; ECOLOGY; INTRODUCTIONS; MORTALITY; POPULATION STUDIES; PRODUCTIVITY; STOCKING;).

289. Borecky, R. A. 1980. Summary of the fishery monitoring program Shoal Lake 1979. Ont. Min. Nat. Res., Lake of the Woods — Rainy Lake Assess. Unit Rep. 1980-1: 105 pp. (WALLEYE; AGE AND GROWTH; COMMERCIAL FISHERIES; COMMUNITY

DYNAMICS; CREEL CENSUS; FOOD STUDIES; MARKING; PATHOLOGY; POPULATION STUDIES; SPAWNING STUDIES;).

290. Borecky, R. A. 1985. Status of the Lake Nipigon commercial walleye fishery, 1984. Ont. Min. Nat. Res., Lake Nipigon Fish. Assess. Unit Rep. 1985-1: 32 pp. (WALLEYE; AGE AND GROWTH; COMMERCIAL FISHERIES; POPULATION STUDIES; PRODUCTIVITY;).

291. Borges, H. M. 1950. Fish distribution studies, Niangua Arm of the Lake of the Ozarks, Missouri. J. Wildl. Manage. 14:16-33. (WALLEYE; ECOLOGY; IMPOUNDMENTS; MOVEMENT AND MIGRATIONS; POPULATION STUDIES; SAMPLING METHODS;).

292. Bouchard, B. 1984. Ecology and exploitation of walleye *(Stizostedion vitreum)* in Lake Opataca, Assinica Reserve. Que. Min. du Loisir, de la Chasse at de la Peche. 37 pp. (WALLEYE; AGE AND GROWTH; CREEL CENSUS; ECOLOGY; IMPOUNDMENTS;).

293. Boussu, M. F. 1954. Calculated growth at each annulus. S. D. Dept. Game Fish and Parks, Fed. Aid Fish Wildl. Restor. Proj. F-1-R-4, Job No. 2: 61-68. (WALLEYE; AGE AND GROWTH;).

294. Boussu, M. F. 1956. Lake fishery investigations, 1955-1956. Age and growth. S. D. Dept. Game Fish and Parks, Fed. Aid Fish Wildl. Restor. Proj. F-1-R-5, Job No. 1: 48-51. (WALLEYE; AGE AND GROWTH;).

295. Boussu, M. F. 1956. Lake fishery investigations, 1956. S. D. Dept. Game Fish and Parks, Fed. Aid Fish Wildl. Restor. Proj. F-1-R-6, Job No. 4: 34-36. (WALLEYE; AGE AND GROWTH;).

296. Boussu, M. F. 1957. Lake Alvin fishermen harvest study. S. D. Game, Fish Parks, Fed. Aid Fish Wildl. Restor. Proj. F-1-R-7, Job No. 15, Compl. Rep.: 19 pp. (WALLEYE; AGE AND GROWTH; COMMUNITY DYNAMICS; CREEL CENSUS; POPULATION STUDIES; STOCKING;).

297. Boussu, M. F. 1959. Southern lakes fishery investigations, 1959. Age and growth. S. D. Dept. Game Fish and Parks, Fed. Aid Fish Wildl. Restor. Proj. F-1-R-9, Job No. 2: 33-36. (WALLEYE; AGE AND GROWTH;).

298. Bowers, C. C., and M. Martin. 1956. Results of an opening week creel census and tagging study on three state-owned lakes. Ky. Dept. Fish Wildl. Res., Fish. Bull. 20: 13 pp. (WALLEYE; CREEL CENSUS; IMPOUNDMENTS; MARKING;).

299. Bradshaw, J., and B. S. Muir. 1960. The 1960 spawning run of yellow pickerel at Bobcaygeon in relation to water temperature. Ont. Dept. Lands For., Southeast. Reg., Spec. Fish. Wildl. Bull. 3:4-6. (WALLEYE; SPAWNING STUDIES;).

300. Branson, B. A. 1967. Fishes of the Neosho River system in Oklahoma. Am. Midl. Nat. 78:126-154. (SAUGER; WALLEYE; GEOGRAPHICAL DISTRIBUTION;).

301. Brege, D. A. 1981. Growth characteristics of young-of-the-year walleye, *Stizostedion vitreum vitreum*, in John Day Reservoir on the Columbia River, 1979. Fish. Bull. 79:567-569. (WALLEYE; AGE AND GROWTH; MORTALITY;).

302. Brehmer, M. L. 1953. Illinois and Mississippi Canal Fishery investigation. Ill. Dept. Conserv., Fed. Aid Fish Wildl. Restor. Proj. F-1-R-1: 89 pp. (SAUGER; WALLEYE; CREEL CENSUS; ECOLOGY; HABITAT DEGRADATION; IMPOUNDMENTS;).

303. Bross, M. G. 1967. Investigations of the reproduction of fishes in Canton Reservoir. Seining of young-of-the-year fishes. Okla. Dept. Wildl. Conserv., Fed. Aid Fish Wildl. Restor. Proj. F-16-R-3, Wk. Pl. 2, Job No. 2, Part 2: 19 pp. (WALLEYE; ECOLOGY; IMPOUNDMENTS; POPULATION STUDIES; SAMPLING METHODS;).

304. Brousseau, C. S., and E. R. Armstrong. 1987. The role of size limits in walleye management. Fisheries 12:2-5. (WALLEYE; POPULATION STUDIES; REGULATIONS;).

305. Brown, B. E. 1962. Occurrence of the walleye *Stizostedion vitreum* in Alabama south of the Tennessee Valley. Copeia 1962(2):469-471. (WALLEYE; AGE AND GROWTH; GEOGRAPHICAL DISTRIBUTION;).

306. Brown, C. J. D. 1962. A preliminary list of Montana fishes. Proc. Mont. Acad. Sci. 22:21-26. (SAUGER; WALLEYE; INTRODUCTIONS;).

307. Brown, C. J. D., and N. A. Thoreson. 1951. Ranch fish ponds in Montana, their construction and management. Mont. State Coll., Agr. Exp. Sta. Bull. 480: 30 pp. (WALLEYE; STOCKING;).

308. Brown, C. J. D., and N. A. Thoreson. 1952. Ranch fish ponds in Montana. J. Wildl. Manage. 16(3):275-278. (WALLEYE; INTRODUCTIONS;).

309. Brown, C. J. D., and N. A. Thoreson. 1958. Ranch fish ponds in Montana, their construction and management. Mont. State Coll., Agr. Exp. Sta. Bull. 544: 26 pp. (WALLEYE; STOCKING;).

310. Brown, G. 1980. Fly-in fishery creel census program. 1978-1979-1980. Ont. Min. Nat. Res., Rep. 83 pp. (WALLEYE; CREEL CENSUS;).

311. Brown, L., and K. Williams. 1985. Mid-Columbia walleye, fisheries, life history, management, 1979-1982. Wash. Dept. Game, 85-20: 39 pp. (WALLEYE; AGE AND GROWTH; CREEL CENSUS; INTRODUCTIONS; MOVEMENTS AND MIGRATIONS; REGULATIONS;).

312. Bruederlin, B. B. 1982. A creel census of Goose Lake 1979. Man. Dept. Nat. Res., Manuscript Rep. No. 82-13: 47 pp. (WALLEYE; CREEL CENSUS;).

313. Bruederlin, B. B., and B. H. Wright. 1981. A creel census of Reed Lake, 1979. Man. Dept. Nat. Res., Fish. Manuscript Rep. No. 81-25: 70 pp. (WALLEYE; AGE AND GROWTH; CREEL CENSUS;).

314. Brungs, W. A., and B. R. Jones. 1977. Temperature criteria for freshwater fish: protocol and procedures. U.S. Environ. Prot. Agency, EPA-600/3-77-061: 130 pp. (SAUGER; WALLEYE; AGE AND GROWTH; HABITAT DEGRADATION; MORTALITY; PHYSIOLOGY;).

315. Bryan, P., and H. H. Howell. 1946. Depth distribution of fish in lower Wheeler Reservoir, Alabama. Rep. Reelfoot Lake Biol. Sta. 10:4-9. (SAUGER; WALLEYE; MOVEMENTS AND MIGRATIONS;).

316. Bryan P., and L. F. Miller. 1947. Spring fishing on several TVA mainstream reservoirs, 1945-1946. J. Tenn. Acad. Sci. 22(1):70-78. (SAUGER; CREEL CENSUS;).

317. Bryant, V. S. 1888. List of fishes in the museum of the University of North Carolina, with description of a new species. J. Elisha Mitchell Sci. Soc. 5(1):16-18. (WALLEYE; TAXONOMY;).

318. Bryant, W. C. 1984. Status of the walleye in Michigan waters of Lake Erie and connecting waters, 1980-1983. Mich. Dept. Nat. Res., Fish. Research Rep. No. 1918: 30 pp. (WALLEYE; AGE AND GROWTH; CREEL CENSUS; GEOGRAPHICAL DISTRIBUTION; MARKING; MORTALITY; MOVEMENT AND MIGRATIONS; POPULATION STUDIES;).

319. Buck, H., and F. Cross. 1952. Early limnological and fish population conditions of Canton Reservoir, Oklahoma and fishery management recommendations. Okla. A. and M. Coll., Research Found. 110 pp. (WALLEYE; IMPOUNDMENTS; INTRODUCTIONS;).

320. Buck, W. O. 1911. Pike-perch notes and suggestions. Trans. Am. Fish. Soc. 40(1910):283-288. (WALLEYE; MORTALITY; PROPAGATION; STOCKING;).

321. Bulkley, R. V. 1970. Fluctuations in abundance and distribution of common Clear Lakes fishes as suggested by gillnet catch. Iowa State J. Sci. 44:413-422. (WALLEYE; FISHING GEAR; POPULATION STUDIES;).

322. Bulkley, R. V., V. L. Spykermann, and L. E. Inmon. 1976. Food of the pelagic young of walleye and five cohabiting fish species in Clear Lake, Iowa. Trans. Am. Fish. Soc. 105:77-83. (WALLEYE; FOOD STUDIES;).

323. Bulkowski, L., and J. W. Meade. 1983. Change in phototaxis during early development of walleye. Trans. Am. Fish. Soc. 112:445-447. (WALLEYE; BEHAVIOR; ECOLOGY;).

324. Bullen, W. H. 1986. Revised procedure for taking and handling walleye eggs in the field. Mich. Dept. Nat. Res., Tech. Rep. No. 86-7: 4 pp. (WALLEYE; PROPAGATION; SPAWNING STUDIES;).

325. Bumpus, H. C. 1898. The identification of adult fish that have been artificially hatched. Trans. Am. Fish. Soc. 27:70-83. (WALLEYE; MORPHOLOGY;).

326. Bur, M. T., D. M. Klarer, and K. A. Krieger. 1986. First records of a European cladoceran, *Bythotrephes cederstroemi*, in Lake Erie and Huron. J. Great Lakes Research 12:144-146. (WALLEYE; PATHOLOGY;).

327. Burkhardt, D. A. 1978. Responses and receptive-field organization of cones in perch retinas. J. Neurophysiol. 40:53-62. (WALLEYE; PHYSIOLOGY;).

328. Burkhardt, D. A., and G. Hassin. 1978. Influences of cones upon chromatic and luminosity-type horizontal cells in pikeperch retinas. J. Physiol. (London) 281:125-137. (SAUGER; WALLEYE; PHYSIOLOGY;).

329. Burkhardt, D. A., and G. Hassin. 1983. Quantitative relations between color-opponent response of horizontal cells and action spectra of cones. J. Neurol. 49:961-975. (SAUGER; WALLEYE; PHYSIOLOGY;).

330. Burkhardt, D. A., G. Hassin, J. S. Levine, and E. F. MacNichol, Jr. 1980. Electrical responses and photopigments of twin cones in the retina of the walleye. J. Physiol. 309:215-228. (WALLEYE; PHYSIOLOGY;).

331. Burnham, J. B. 1906. Report of the chief game protector for the year 1906. N.Y. Forest, Fish Game Comm., 12th Annu. Rep. (1906):241-244. (WALLEYE; SPAWNING STUDIES; STOCKING;).

332. Burrows, C. R. 1951. Status of the Lake of the Woods fisheries, 1938 through 1949, with special reference to the walleye. Minn. Dept. Conserv., Invest. Rep. No. 106: 20 pp. (SAUGER; WALLEYE; COMMERCIAL FISHERIES; POPULATION STUDIES;).

333. Burrows, C. R., and F. Bandow. 1970. Methods of increasing the growth rate of walleye fingerlings in ponds. Supplement feeding with forage fishes. Minn. Div. Game Fish., Fed. Aid Fish Wildl. Restor. Proj. F-26-R1, Wk. Pl. 2, Job 2: 8 pp. (WALLEYE; AGE AND GROWTH; FOOD STUDIES; PROPAGATION;).

334. Busch, W. D. N., R. L. Scholl, and W. L. Hartman. 1975. Environmental factors affecting the strength of walleye *(Stizostedion vitreum vitreum)* year-classes in western Lake Erie, 1960-70. J. Fish. Research Board Can. 32:1733-1743. (WALLEYE; AGE AND GROWTH; ECOLOGY; PRODUCTIVITY;

SPAWNING STUDIES;).

335. Butler, G. E. 1930. Fish culture in the prairie provinces, and some of its results. Trans. Am. Fish. Soc. 60:119-120. (WALLEYE; INTRODUCTIONS; STOCKING;).

336. Butler, G. E. 1937. Artificial propagation of walleyed pike. Trans. Am. Fish. Soc. 66:277-278. (WALLEYE; PROPAGATION;).

337. Butler, G. E. 1950. The lakes and lake fisheries of Manitoba. Trans. Am. Fish. Soc. 79:18-29. (WALLEYE; COMMERCIAL FISHERIES; CREEL CENSUS; GEOGRAPHICAL DISTRIBUTION;).

338. Butler, G. E. 1954. Sport fishing — commercial fishing relationships in Manitoba. Trans. 44th Convention Int. Ass. Game, Fish, Conserv. Comm. 29-35 pp. (WALLEYE; COMMERCIAL FISHERIES; CREEL CENSUS;).

339. Buynak, G. L., and A. J. Gurzynski. 1978. Lymphocystis disease in walleye *(Stizostedion vitreum)* captured in the Susquehanna River. Proc. Penn. Acad. Sci. 52(1):49-50. (WALLEYE; PATHOLOGY;).

340. Buynak, G. L., A. J. Gurzynski, and H. W. Mohr, Jr. 1980. Age and growth, food habits, and abundance of walleye *(Stizostedion vitreum)* in the Susquahanna River near Berwick, Pennsylvania. Proc. Penn. Acad. Sci. 54(2):136-140. (WALLEYE; AGE AND GROWTH; FOOD STUDIES;).

341. Buynak, G. L., H. W. Mohr, Jr., and A. J. Gurzynski. 1982. Some observations of food selectivity by small walleye *(Stizostedion vitreum)* under aquarium conditions. Proc. Penn. Acad. Sci. 56:26-28. (WALLEYE; COMMUNITY DYNAMICS; FOOD STUDIES;).

342. Byfold, R. D. 1972. Rice River creel census. Ont. Min. Nat. Res., Rep. 17 pp. (WALLEYE; CREEL CENSUS;).

343. Cady, E. R. 1945. Fish distribution, Norris Reservoir, Tennessee, 1943. I. Depth distribution of fish in Norris Reservoir. Reelfoot Lake Biol. Sta. Rep. No. 9:103-114. (SAUGER; WALLEYE; ECOLOGY; IMPOUNDMENTS;).

344. Cahn, A. R. 1927. An ecological study of certain southern Wisconsin fishes. Ill. Biol.

Monogr. 11(1):1-151. (SAUGER; WALL-
EYE; ECOLOGY; STOCKING;).

345. Cahn, A. R. 1929. The effect of carp on a small
lake: the carp as a dominant. Ecology
10:271-274. (WALLEYE; COMMUNITY
DYNAMICS;).

346. Caine, L. S. 1949. North American fresh water
sport fish. A. S. Barnes and Co., New York,
N. Y. 203 pp. (SAUGER; WALLEYE; LIFE
HISTORY;).

347. Calbert, H. E., S. E. Dunnick, and R. C. Lindsay. 1974. Taste panel detection of pollution-
related off-flavors in Flambeau River (Wisconsin) walleye pike. Envir. Letters
7:285-301. (WALLEYE; HABITAT DEG-
RADATION;).

348. Calbert, H. E., D. A. Stuiber, and H. T. Huh.
1974. Expanding man's protein supplies.
Fish farming with pike and perch. Univ.
Wisc. Agr. Bull. R 2632:4 pp. (WALLEYE;
FOOD STUDIES; PROPAGATION;).

349. Caldwell, B. 1960. Fort Frances District creel
census, 1956 to 1959. Ont. Dept. Lands Forest., Manuscript Rep. 12 pp. (SAUGER;
WALLEYE; CREEL CENSUS;).

350. Caldwell, B. 1961. Tagging of walleye Stizostedion vitreum vitreum (Mitchill) and lake
whitefish Coregonus clupeaformis clupeaformis (Mitchill) on Rainy Lake 1957-
1960. Ont. Dept. Lands Forest., Manuscript
Rep. 9 pp. (WALLEYE; MARKING;
MOVEMENT AND MIGRATIONS;).

351. Caldwell, B. 1962. Fort Frances District creel
census 1961. Ont. Dept. Lands Forest.,
Manuscript Rep. 4 pp. (WALLEYE;
CREEL CENSUS;).

352. Caldwell, B. 1963. An interim report concern-
ing fisheries in the North Arm of Rainy
Lake with particular reference to the 1962
tagging program. Ont. Dept. Lands Forest.,
Manuscript Rep. 6 pp. (SAUGER; WALL-
EYE; AGE AND GROWTH; COMMER-
CIAL FISHERIES; MARKING;).

353. Caldwell, B. 1964. A second interim report
concerning fisheries in the North Arm of
Rainy Lake. Ont. Dept. Lands Forest., Res.
Manage. Rep. 75:45-55. (WALLEYE; AGE
AND GROWTH; COMMERCIAL FISH-
ERIES; MARKING;).

354. Caldwell, B. 1972. Creel census — Quetico
Park. Ont. Min. Nat. Res., Rep. 18 pp.
(WALLEYE; CREEL CENSUS;).

355. Caldwell, B. 1975. Fly-in fisherman creel cen-
sus. Fort Frances and Rainy River. Ont.
Min. Nat. Res, Rep. 6 pp. (WALLEYE;
CREEL CENSUS;).

356. Caldwell, B., and P. R. Brown. 1973. Fly-in
fisherman creel census and checkout service
Fort Frances 1973. Ont. Min. Nat. Res.,
Rep. 6 pp. (WALLEYE; CREEL CEN-
SUS;).

357. Caldwell, B., and N. Galbraith. 1959. Fisheries
surveys of Lac la Croix — 1958 and 1959.
Ont. Dept. Lands Forsest., Manuscript
Rep. 7 pp. (SAUGER; WALLEYE; AGE
AND GROWTH; POPULATION STUD-
IES;).

358. Camden, R. M. 1973. Manitouwadge Lake
chain creel census report — 1972. Ont. Min.
Nat. Res., Rep. 29 pp. (WALLEYE; CREEL
CENSUS;).

359. Cameron, T. W. M. 1945. Fish-carried parasites
in Canada. (1) Parasites carried by fresh-water fish. Can. J. Comp. Med. 9:245-254, 283-
286, 302-311. (WALLEYE; PATHOLOGY;).

360. Campbell, J. S., and J. A. Babaluk. 1979. Age
determination of walleye, Stizostedion vitreum vitreum (Mitchill), based on the examination of eight different structures.
Can. Fish. & Mar. Serv. Tech. Rep. 849: 23
pp. (WALLEYE; AGE AND GROWTH;).

361. Campbell, J. S., and R. Craig. 1978. Small
Lakes creel census June 17 — September 4,
1978. Ont. Min. Nat. Res., Rep. 31 pp.
(WALLEYE; CREEL CENSUS;).

362. Campbell, J. S., and R. Craig. 1979. Trent-
Severn creel census June 4 to August 29,
1979. Ont. Min. Nat. Res., Rep. 33 pp.
(WALLEYE; CREEL CENSUS;).

363. Campbell, J. S., and K. R. Rowes. 1980.
Growth and survival of walleye, Stizoste-
dion vitreum vitreum (Mitchill) in rearing
ponds near Lake Winnipegosis, Manitoba.
Can. Tech. Rep. Fish. Aquat. Sci. No. 949: 17
pp. (WALLEYE; FOOD STUDIES; MOR-
TALITY; POPULATION STUDIES;
PROPAGATION; STOCKING;).

364. Campbell, W. J., E. Hayes, W. R. Chapman, and W. Seawell. 1976. Angling pressure and sport fish harvest in the predator-stocking-evaluation reservoirs. Proc. 30th Annu. Conf. Southeast Assoc. Fish Wildl. Agencies. 30:116-117. (WALLEYE; CREEL CENSUS; IMPOUNDMENTS;).

365. Carbine, W. F., and V. C. Applegate. 1946. Recaptures of tagged walleyes, *Stizostedion vitreum*, (Mitchill), in Houghton Lake and Muskegon River, Roscommon County, Michigan. Copeia 1946:97-100. (WALLEYE; MARKING; MOVEMENT AND MIGRATIONS;).

366. Carbine, W. F., and D. S. Shetter. 1945. Examples of the use of two-way fish weirs in Michigan. Trans. Am. Fish. Soc. 73(1943):70-89. (WALLEYE; MOVEMENT AND MIGRATIONS;).

367. Carl, G. C., and W. A. Clemens. 1953. The fresh-water fishes of British Columbia. B. C. Provincial Mus., Handbook 5. 136 pp. (WALLEYE; GEOGRAPHICAL DISTRIBUTION; LIFE HISTORY;).

368. Carlander, H. B. 1954. A history of fish and fishing in the upper Mississippi River. Upper Miss. River Conserv. Comm. Pub. 96 pp. (SAUGER; WALLEYE; COMMERCIAL FISHERIES; COMMUNITY DYNAMICS;).

369. Carlander, K. D. 1939. The fishes of Upper Red Lake, summer of 1939. Minn. Dept. Conserv., Invest. Rep. No. 4: 8 pp. (WALLEYE; AGE AND GROWTH; POPULATION STUDIES;).

370. Carlander, K. D. 1940. Preliminary report on the walleyed pike population of Lake of the Woods. Minn. Dept. Conserv., Invest. Rep. No. 5: 34 pp. (WALLEYE; AGE AND GROWTH; COMMERCIAL FISHERIES; FISHING GEAR; FOOD STUDIES; HABITAT DEGRADATION; PATHOLOGY; POPULATION STUDIES;).

371. Carlander, K. D. 1940. Sizes of wall-eyed pike in three spawning runs. Minn. Dept. Conserv., Invest. Rep. No. 12: 4 pp. (WALLEYE; SPAWNING STUDIES;).

372. Carlander, K. D. 1940. Experimental gill net catches from Lake Vermilion, St. Louis County. Minn. Dept. Conserv., Invest. Rep. No. 14: 12 pp. (WALLEYE; FISHING GEAR; SAMPLING METHODS;).

373. Carlander, K. D. 1941. Tagging returns on Lake Vermilion walleye, 1940. Minn. Dept. Conserv., Invest. Rep. No. 23: 8 pp. (WALLEYE; CREEL CENSUS; MARKING; MOVEMENT AND MIGRATIONS;).

374. Carlander, K. D. 1941. The species composition of the commercial fisheries of Lake of the Woods 1913-1940. Minn. Dept. Conserv., Invest. Rep. No. 32: 12 pp. (SAUGER; WALLEYE; COMMERCIAL FISHERIES;).

375. Carlander, K. D. 1941. Lake of the Woods and its commercial fisheries. Minn. Dept. Conserv., Invest. Rep. No. 33: 96 pp. (SAUGER; WALLEYE; AGE AND GROWTH; COMMERCIAL FISHERIES; FISHING GEAR;).

376. Carlander, K. D. 1941. Lake of the Woods report — some statistical analyses of gill-net data. I. The effect of leaving the nets set in the same location for several days. Minn. Dept. Conserv., Invest. Rep. No. 34: 20 pp. (SAUGER; WALLEYE; FISHING GEAR; MOVEMENT AND MIGRATIONS; SAMPLING METHODS;).

377. Carlander, K. D. 1941. Lake of the Woods report II. Some statistical analyses of gill net data. Fluctuations in the activity of fishes during various hours of the day. Minn. Dept. Conserv., Invest. Rep. No. 37: 10 pp. (SAUGER; WALLEYE; BEHAVIOR; FISHING GEAR; MOVEMENT AND MIGRATIONS;).

378. Carlander, K. D. 1941. The fishes of Lake of the Woods. Minn. Dept. Conserv., Invest. Rep. No. 39: 11 pp. (SAUGER; WALLEYE; GEOGRAPHICAL DISTRIBUTION;).

379. Carlander, K. D. 1942. An investigation of Lake of the Woods, Minnesota with particular reference to the commercial fisheries. Volume III. Management Recommendations. Minn. Dept. Conserv., Invest. Rep. No. 42:383-454. (SAUGER; WALLEYE; AGE AND GROWTH; COMMERCIAL FISHERIES; COMMUNITY DYNAMICS; FISHING GEAR; FOOD STUDIES; REGULATIONS; SOCIO-ECONOMICS OF FISHERIES;).

380. Carlander, K. D. 1942. Sizes of spawning walleye pike, *Stizostedion vitreum* (Mitchill) in

Minnesota. Minn. Dept. Conserv., Invest. Rep. No. 47: 9 pp. (WALLEYE; SPAWNING STUDIES;).

381. Carlander, K. D. 1943. The walleyes *Stizostedion vitreum* (Mitchell), of Lake of the Woods, with special reference to the commercial fisheries. Ph.D. Dissertation, Univ. Minn., St. Paul, Minn. 202 pp. (WALLEYE; COMMERCIAL FISHERIES; POPULATION STUDIES;).

382. Carlander, K. D. 1943. The use of the percentage increment index in comparisons of growth of certain Minnesota fishes. Minn. Dept. Conserv., Invest. Rep. No. 51: 10 pp. (WALLEYE; AGE AND GROWTH;).

383. Carlander, K. D. 1944. Relationship between scale radius and body-length of walleye pike, *Stizostedion vitreum vitreum* (Mitchill). Minn. Dept. Conserv., Invest. Rep. No. 15: 26 pp. (WALLEYE; AGE AND GROWTH;).

384. Carlander, K. D. 1944. Notes on the coefficient of conditions, K, of Minnesota fishes with an appended note on the coefficient of condition, C, of Minnesota fishes. Minn. Dept. Conserv., Invest. Rep. No. 41: 40 pp. (WALLEYE; AGE AND GROWTH;).

385. Carlander, K. D. 1944. Review of methods used in the study of fish growth at the Minnesota Bureau of Fisheries Research with suggestions for further work. Minn. Dept. Conserv., Invest. Rep. No. 56: 45 pp. (SAUGER; WALLEYE; AGE AND GROWTH;).

386. Carlander, K. D. 1944. Some factors to consider in the choice between standard, fork, or total lengths in fishery investigations. Minn. Dept. Conserv., Invest. Rep. No. 57: 9 pp. (SAUGER; WALLEYE; AGE AND GROWTH;).

387. Carlander, K. D. 1944. Some parasites of fish — a literature review. Minn. Dept. Conserv., Invest. Rep. No. 58: 14 pp. (SAUGER; WALLEYE; PATHOLOGY;).

388. Carlander, K. D. 1944. Average gill net ratios, using standard experimental gill nets in Minnesota lakes, 1941-1943. Minn. Dept. Conserv., Invest. Rep. No. 59: 4 pp. (SAUGER; WALLEYE; FISHING GEAR;).

389. Carlander, K. D. 1945. Age, growth, sexual maturity and population fluctuations of the yellow pike-perch, *Stizostedion vitreum vitreum* (Mitchill) with reference to the commercial fisheries, Lake of the Woods, Minnesota. Trans. Am. Fish. Soc. 73:90-103. (SAUGER; WALLEYE; AGE AND GROWTH; COMMERCIAL FISHERIES; FISHING GEAR; HABITAT DEGRADATION; PRODUCTIVITY; STOCKING;).

390. Carlander, K. D. 1945. Growth, length-weight relationship and population fluctuations of the tullibee, *Leucichthys artedi tullibee* (Richardson), with reference to the commercial fisheries, Lake of the Woods, Minnesota. Trans. Am. Fish. Soc. 73:125-135. (WALLEYE; COMMERCIAL FISHERIES;).

391. Carlander, K. D. 1948. Some changes in the fish population of Lake of the Woods, Minnesota, 1910 to 1945. Copeia 1948:271-274. (SAUGER; WALLEYE; ECOLOGY;).

392. Carlander, K. D. 1948. Growth of yellow pike-perch, *Stizostedion vitreum vitreum* (Mitchill), in some Iowa lakes, with a summary of growth rates reported in other areas. Iowa State Coll. J. Sci. 22:227-237. (WALLEYE; AGE AND GROWTH; ECOLOGY;).

393. Carlander, K. D. 1949. Some trends in the commercial fisheries of Lake of the Woods, Minnesota. Trans. Am. Fish. Soc. 77:13-25. (SAUGER; WALLEYE; COMMERCIAL FISHERIES; COMMUNITY DYNAMICS; FISHING GEAR; HABITAT DEGRADATION; WATER LEVELS;).

394. Carlander, K. D. 1950. Handbook of freshwater fishery biology. Wm. C. Brown Co., Dubuque, Iowa. 281 pp. (SAUGER; WALLEYE; AGE AND GROWTH; CREEL CENSUS; FISHING GEAR; GENETICS; PRODUCTIVITY;).

395. Carlander, K. D. 1950. Some considerations in the use of fish growth data based upon scale studies. Trans. Am. Fish. Soc. 79:187-194. (SAUGER; AGE AND GROWTH;).

396. Carlander, K. D. 1953. First supplement to handbook of freshwater fishery biology. Wm. C. Brown Co., Dubuque, Iowa. pp. 277-429. (SAUGER; WALLEYE; AGE AND GROWTH; CREEL CENSUS; FISHING GEAR; GENETICS; PRODUCTIVITY;).

397. Carlander, K. D. 1954. Use of gill nets in studying fish populations, Clear Lake, Iowa. Proc. Iowa Acad. Sci. 60:621-625. (WALLEYE; BEHAVIOR; FISHING GEAR;).

398. Carlander, K. D. 1955. Some simple mathematical models as an aid in interpreting the effect of fishing (with special reference to the walleyes of Clear Lake, Iowa). Iowa Coop. Fish. Research Unit, Proj. 39: 5 pp. (WALLEYE; MORTALITY; POPULATION STUDIES;).

399. Carlander, K. D. 1955. The standing crop of fish in lakes. J. Fish. Research Board Can. 12:543-570. (SAUGER; WALLEYE; PRODUCTIVITY;).

400. Carlander, K. D. 1956. Growth rates of Iowa fishes. Pages 254-256 in J. R. Harlan and E. B. Speaker, eds. Iowa fish and fishing. Iowa Conserv. Comm., Des Moines, Iowa. (WALLEYE; AGE AND GROWTH;).

401. Carlander, K. D. 1956. Appraisal of methods of fish population study — part 1. Fish growth rates studies: techniques and role in surveys and management. Trans. 21st. N. Am. Wildl. Conf. 21:262-274. (WALLEYE; AGE AND GROWTH;).

402. Carlander, K. D. 1958. Some simple mathematical models as aids in interpreting the effect of fishing. Iowa State Coll. J. Sci. 32:395-418. (WALLEYE; MORTALITY; POPULATION STUDIES;).

403. Carlander, K. D. 1958. Disturbance of the predator-prey balance as a management technique. Trans. Am. Fish. Soc. 87:34-38. (WALLEYE; COMMUNITY DYNAMICS; FOOD STUDIES; POPULATION STUDIES;).

404. Carlander, K. D. 1961. Variations on rereading walleye scales. Trans. Am. Fish. Soc. 90:230-231. (WALLEYE; AGE AND GROWTH;).

405. Carlander, K. D. 1971. Methods of evaluating stocking success. Proceedings of the North Central Warmwater Fish Culture — Management Workshop, Iowa Coop. Fish. Unit, Ames, Iowa. pp. 54-64. (WALLEYE; STOCKING;).

406. Carlander, K. D. 1977. Biomass, production, and yields of walleye (Stizostedion vitreum vitreum) and yellow perch (Perca flavescens) in North American Lakes. J. Fish. Research Board Can. 34:1602-1612. (WALLEYE; PRODUCTIVITY;).

407. Carlander, K. D. 1982. Standard intercepts of calculating lengths from scale measurements for some centrarchid and percid fishes. Trans. Am. Fish. Soc. 111:332-336. (WALLEYE; AGE AND GROWTH;).

408. Carlander, K. D., J. S. Campbell, and R. J. Muncy. 1978. Inventory of percid and esocid habitat in North America. Pages 27-38 in R.L. Kendall, ed. Selected coolwater fishes of North America. Am. Fish. Soc. Sp. Publ. No. 11, Washington, D.C. (SAUGER; WALLEYE; GEOGRAPHICAL DISTRIBUTION; IMPOUNDMENTS;).

409. Carlander, K. D., and R. E. Cleary. 1949. The daily activity patterns of some freshwater fishes. Am. Midl. Nat. 41:447-452. (SAUGER; WALLEYE; BEHAVIOR; ECOLOGY; MOVEMENT AND MIGRATIONS;).

410. Carlander, K. D., and S. Eddy. 1940. Selectivity of sampling methods and relation to fish growth studies. Minn. Dept. Conserv., Invest. Rep. No. 11: 11 pp. (WALLEYE; AGE AND GROWTH; CREEL CENSUS; FISHING GEAR; SAMPLING METHODS;).

411. Carlander, K. D., and L. E. Hiner. 1943. Fisheries investigation and management report for Lake Vermillion, St. Louis County. Minn. Dept. Conserv., Invest. Rep. No. 54: 175 pp. (WALLEYE; AGE AND GROWTH; COMMUNITY DYNAMICS; CREEL CENSUS; FOOD STUDIES; LIFE HISTORY; PATHOLOGY; SPAWNING STUDIES; STOCKING;).

412. Carlander, K. D., and P. M. Payne. 1977. Year-class abundance, population, and production of walleye (Stizostedion vitreum vitreum) in Clear Lake, Iowa, 1948-74, with varied fry stocking rates. J. Fish. Research Board Can. 34:1792-1799. (WALLEYE; AGE AND GROWTH; POPULATION STUDIES; PRODUCTIVITY; STOCKING;).

413. Carlander, K. D., and L. L. Smith, Jr. 1945. Some factors to consider in the choice between standard, fork, or total lengths in fishery investigations. Copeia 1945:7-12. (WALLEYE; AGE AND GROWTH; MORPHOLOGY;).

414. Carlander, K. D., and R. R. Whitney. 1961. Age and growth of walleyes in Clear Lake, Iowa, 1935-1957. Trans. Am. Fish. Soc. 90:130-138. (WALLEYE; AGE AND GROWTH;).

415. Carlander, K. D., R. R. Whitney, E. B. Speaker, and K. Madden. 1960. Evaluation of walleye fry stocking in Clear Lake, Iowa, by alternate-year planting. Trans. Am. Fish. Soc. 89:249-254. (WALLEYE; POPULATION STUDIES;).

416. Carline, R. F. 1986. Indices as predictors of fish community traits. Pages 46-56 in G. E. Hall and M. J. Van Den Avyle, eds. Reservoir fisheries management: strategies for the 80's. Reserv. Comm., S. Div. Am. Fish. Soc., Bethesda, Maryland. (WALLEYE; COMMUNITY DYNAMICS; ECOLOGY; POPULATION STUDIES;).

417. Carlson, E. 1980. Summer creel census on Stormer and Kirkness Lakes May — August 1980. Ont. Min. Nat. Res., Rep. 22 pp. (WALLEYE; CREEL CENSUS;).

418. Carlson, E., and C. Malinsky. 1980. Summer creel census on Coli Lake — May — August 1980. Ont. Min. Nat. Res., Rep. 14 pp. (WALLEYE; CREEL CENSUS;).

419. Carlson, R. M., and R. Caple. 1980. An evaluation of the possible detrimental effects by the introduction of the organic and second-order organics on commercial sport fishing in Lake Superior. Minn. Sea Grant Prog. Research Rep.: 49 pp. (WALLEYE; HABITAT DEGRADATION;).

420. Carpenter, K. E. 1930. A biological survey of the Champlain watershed. IX. Fish life in relation to pollution influences in the Lake Champlain watershed. N.Y. Conserv. Dept., Suppl. 19th Annu. Rep. (1929):186-209. (SAUGER; WALLEYE; ECOLOGY; HABITAT DEGRADATION;).

421. Carpenter, R. G., and H. R. Siegler. 1947. A sportsman's guide to the fresh-water fishes of New Hampshire. N.H. Fish Game Comm., 87 pp. (WALLEYE; INTRODUCTIONS; TAXONOMY;).

422. Carr, I. A. 1962. Distribution and seasonal movements of Saginaw Bay fishes. U.S. Fish Wildl. Serv., Spec. Sci. Rep. — Fish. 417: 13 pp. (SAUGER; WALLEYE; GEOGRAPHICAL DISTRIBUTION; MOVEMENTS AND MIGRATIONS;).

423. Carr, I. A. 1964. Lake Erie fisheries explorations, May-November 1960. Com. Fish. Rev. 26(4):1-8. (WALLEYE; FISHING GEAR;).

424. Carr, J. F. 1962. Dissolved oxygen in Lake Erie, past and present. Publ. Great Lakes Research Div., Inst. Sci. Tech., Univ. Mich. 9:1-14. (WALLEYE; ECOLOGY;).

425. Carroll, B. B., G. E. Hall, and R. D. Bishop. 1963. Three seasons of rough fish removal at Norris Reservoir, Tennessee. Trans. Am. Fish. Soc. 92:356-364. (SAUGER; WALLEYE; COMMERCIAL FISHERIES; IMPOUNDMENTS;).

426. Carson, R. L. 1943. Fishes of the Middle West. U.S. Fish Wildl. Serv., Conserv. Bull. 34: 44 pp. (SAUGER; WALLEYE; COMMERCIAL FISHERIES; LIFE HISTORY;).

427. Carter, B. T. 1954. The movement of fishes through navigation lock chambers in the Kentucky River. Trans. Ky. Acad. Sci. 15(3):48-56. (SAUGER; WALLEYE; MOVEMENT AND MIGRATIONS; SAMPLING METHODS;).

428. Carter, B. T., and W. M. Clay. 1962. General considerations and summary. Pages 121-128 in W.M. Clay, ed. Aquatic-life resources of the Ohio River. Ohio River Valley Water Sanitation Comm., Cincinnati, Ohio. (SAUGER; WALLEYE; ECOLOGY; HABITAT DEGRADATION;).

429. Carter, J. P. 1969. Pre- and post-impoundment surveys on Barren River. Ky. Dept. Fish Wildl. Res., Fish. Bull. 50: 33 pp. (SAUGER; ECOLOGY; IMPOUNDMENTS; POPULATION STUDIES;).

430. Carter, N. E., and R. L. Eley. 1968. Effects of a flood on fish distribution in Keystone Reservoir. Proc. Okla. Acad. Sci. 47(1966):382-385. (WALLEYE; IMPOUNDMENTS;).

431. Carufel, L. H. 1960. Evaluation of commercial fishing by use of a questionaire. Prog. Fish-Cult. 22:181-184. (SAUGER; WALLEYE; COMMERCIAL FISHERIES;).

432. Carver, D., G. E. Hall, and J. F. Hall. 1976. History and organization of predator-stocking-evaluation by the Reservoir Committee, Southern Division, American Fisheries Society. Proc. 30th Annu. Conf. Southeast Assoc. Fish Wildl. Agencies 30:103-107.

(WALLEYE; COMMUNITY DY-
NAMICS;).

433. Chambers, K. J. 1963. The Lake of the Woods
survey, Shoal Lake-1962 (Preliminary re-
port). Ont. Dept. Lands Forest., Manuscript
Rep. 43 pp. (SAUGER; WALLEYE; AGE
AND GROWTH; COMMERCIAL FISH-
ERIES;).

434. Chambers, K. J. 1963. Lake of the Woods survey northern sector-1963 (Preliminary report II). Ont. Dept. Lands Forest., Manuscript Rep. 65 pp. (SAUGER; WALLEYE;
AGE AND GROWTH; COMMERCIAL
FISHERIES;).

435. Chambers, K. J., and V. Macins. 1966. Lake of
the Woods survey southern section — 1965
(Preliminary Report IV). Ont. Dept. Lands
Forest., Manuscript Rep. 54 pp. (SAUGER;
WALLEYE; AGE AND GROWTH;
CREEL CENSUS; FOOD STUDIES;
MARKING; PATHOLOGY;).

436. Chance, C. J. 1958. History of fish and fishing
in Norris — a TVA tributary reservoir. Proc.
12th Annu. Conf. Southeast Assoc. Fish.
Wildl. Agencies. 12:116-127. (SAUGER;
WALLEYE; CREEL CENSUS; IM-
POUNDMENTS; MARKING; MORTAL-
ITY; MOVEMENT AND MIGRATIONS;).

437. Chance, C. J., and L. F. Miller. 1952. Fish sam-
pling with rotenone in TVA reservoirs. J.
Tenn. Acad. Sci. 27:214-222. (SAUGER;
WALLEYE; SAMPLING METHODS;).

438. Chapman, C. R. 1954. Six months creel census
on Sandusky Bay. Ohio Dept. Nat. Res.,
Rep. No. 269: 9 pp. (SAUGER; WALLEYE;
CREEL CENSUS;).

439. Chapman, C. R. 1955. Sandusky Bay report.
Ohio Dept. Nat. Res. 84 pp. (SAUGER;
WALLEYE; COMMERCIAL FISH-
ERIES; CREEL CENSUS; HABITAT
DEGRADATION; MOVEMENTS AND
MIGRATIONS; POPULATION STUD-
IES;).

440. Chapman, P., F. Cross, and W. Fish. 1983. Walleye investigation. Florida Game Fresh Water Fish Comm., Proj. No. 2082, Study No.
4: 12 pp. (WALLEYE; COMMUNITY DY-
NAMICS; FOOD STUDIES; INTRODUC-
TIONS; MORTALITY; STOCKING;).

441. Charles, J. J. K. 1979. Eagle Lake creel census
report — 1979. Ont. Min. Nat. Res., Rep. 47
pp. (SAUGER; WALLEYE; CREEL CEN-
SUS;).

442. Charles, J. R. 1962. Commercial fishing activi-
ties in the Kentucky waters of the Ohio
River. Pages 103-113, Append. 3: 184-188 in
W. M. Clay ed. Aquatic-life resources of the
Ohio River. Ohio River Valley Water Sanita-
tion Comm., Cincinnati, Ohio. (SAUGER;
WALLEYE; COMMERCIAL FISH-
ERIES;).

443. Charles, J. R. 1962. Creel census data for Kentucky waters of the Ohio River. Pages 91-
102, Append. 3: 181-183, Append. 4: 211-
213 in W. M. Clay, ed. Aquatic-life resources
on the Ohio River. Ohio River Valley Water
Sanitation Comm., Cincinnati, Ohio.
(SAUGER; WALLEYE; CREEL CEN-
SUS;).

444. Charles, K. 1977. Mistinikon Lake summer
creel census Kirkland Lake District. Ont.
Min. Nat. Res., Rep. 38 pp. (WALLEYE;
CREEL CENSUS;).

445. Chen, M. Y. 1972. Analysis of sampling Lake
Athabasca commercial fishery, 1972. Sask.
Dept. Nat. Res., Sask. Fish. Lab. Tech. Rep.
72-12: 54 pp. (WALLEYE; COMMERCIAL
FISHERIES;).

446. Chen, M. Y. 1973. Lake Athabasca commercial
fishery, 1973. Sask. Dept. Nat. Res., Sask.
Fish. Lab. Tech. Rep. 73-5: 33 pp. (WALL-
EYE; COMMERCIAL FISHERIES;).

447. Chen, M. Y. 1973. Lac la Ronge creel census,
1973. Sask. Dept. Nat. Res., Sask. Fish.
Lab. Tech. Rep. 73-6: 22 pp. (WALLEYE;
CREEL CENSUS;).

448. Chen, M. Y. 1974. Analysis of sampling Lake
Athabasca commercial fishery, 1974. Sask.
Dept. Tour. Renew. Res., Sask. Fish. Lab.
Tech. Rep. 74-10: 32 pp. (WALLEYE;
CREEL CENSUS;).

449. Chen, M. Y. 1976. An appraisal of the sport
fishery, Lac la Ronge, 1950-74. Sask. Dept.
Tour. Renew. Res., Sask. Fish. Lab. Tech.
Rep. 76-6: 25 pp. (WALLEYE; CREEL
CENSUS; PRODUCTIVITY;).

450. Chen, M. Y. 1977. 25 years sport-fishing — Lac
la Ronge record. Sask. Dept. Tour. Renew.
Res., Sask. Fish. Lab. Tech. Rep. 77-3: 61 pp.

(WALLEYE; COMMERCIAL FISH-ERIES; CREEL CENSUS; PRODUCTIV-ITY;).

451. Chen, M. Y. 1977. Lac la Ronge creel census, 1977. Sask. Dept. Tour. Renew. Res., Sask. Fish. Lab. Tech. Rep. 77-4: 13 pp. (WALL-EYE; CREEL CENSUS;).

452. Chen, M. Y. 1979. Lac la Ronge creel census, 1979. Sask. Dept. Tour. Renew. Res., Sask. Fish. Lab. Tech. Rep. 79-5: 9 pp. (WALL-EYE; CREEL CENSUS;).

453. Chen, M. Y. 1980. Walleye stocks in Lac la Ronge. Sask. Dept. Tour. Renew. Res., Sask. Fish. Lab. Tech. Rep. 80-4: 107 pp. (WALL-EYE; AGE AND GROWTH; COMMER-CIAL FISHERIES; CREEL CENSUS; FOOD STUDIES; MARKING; MORTAL-ITY; MOVEMENT AND MIGRATIONS; POPULATION STUDIES; SPAWNING STUDIES;).

454. Chen, M. Y. 1980. Walleye spawning and road construction, Highway Creek, La Ronge. Sask. Dept. Parks Renew. Res., Sask. Fish. Lab., Tech. Rep. 80-5: 101 pp. (WALLEYE; FISHWAYS; HABITAT DEGRADA-TION; SPAWNING STUDIES;).

455. Chen, M. Y. 1982. Evaluation of walleye cul-ture in Saskatchewan. Sask. Dept. Tour. Re-new. Res., Sask. Fish. Lab. Tech. Rep. 82-3: 66 pp. (WALLEYE; PROPAGATION;).

456. Chen, M. Y., J. J. Merkowsky, and L. A. Wall-ing. 1984. Walleye spawning run inventory in Saskatchewan. Sask. Dept. Parks Renew. Res., Sask. Fish. Lab., Tech. Rep. 1984-4: 95 pp. (WALLEYE; SPAWNING STUDIES;).

457. Chen, M. Y., and W. M. Whiting. 1984. Walleye culture report, 1983. Sask. Dept. Tour. Re-new. Res., Sask. Fish. Lab. Tech. Rep. 84-3: 31 pp. (WALLEYE; PROPAGATION;).

458. Chen, M. Y., W. M. Whiting, and J. R. Mar-chinko. 1984. The 1984 walleye culture pro-gram. Sask. Dept. Parks Renew. Res., Sask. Fish. Lab., Tech. Rep. 84-9: 52 pp. (WALL-EYE; PROPAGATION; SPAWNING STUDIES;).

459. Cheney, A. N. 1896. Commercial fisheries of the interior waters of the State. N.Y. Comm. Fish., Game, Forest., 1st Annu. Rep. (1895): 118-120. (WALLEYE; COMMERCIAL FISHERIES;).

460. Cheney, A. N. 1896. Mascalonge, pike, pickerel and pike-perch. N.Y. Comm. Fish., Game, Forest., 1st Annu. Rep. (1895):121-124. (SAUGER; WALLEYE; TAXONOMY;).

461. Cheney, A. N. 1897. The pike-perch *(Stizoste-dion vitreum)*. N.Y. Comm. Fish., Game, Forest., 2nd Annu. Rep. (1896) :203-206. (WALLEYE; INTRODUCTIONS; LIFE HISTORY; PROPAGATION;).

462. Cheney, A. N. 1897. Concerning the work of the Fisheries, Game, and Forest Commis-sion of the State of New York. Trans. Am. Fish. Soc. 25:112-120. (WALLEYE; PROP-AGATION;).

463. Cheney, A. N. 1898. A synopsis of the history of fish culture. N.Y. Comm. Fish., Game, Forest., 3rd Annu. Rep. (1897) :191-198. (WALLEYE; PROPAGATION;).

464. Cheney, A. N. 1901. Report of the state fish culturist. N. Y. Forest, Fish, Game Comm., 6th Annu. Rep. (1900): 47-56. (WALLEYE; STOCKING;).

465. Cheshire, W. F. 1962. A review of the biology and management of pickerel. Ont. Dept. Lands Forest., Res. Manage. Rep. No. 61:46-56. (WALLEYE; AGE AND GROWTH; ECOLOGY; GEOGRAPHI-CAL DISTRIBUTION; PRODUCTIV-ITY;).

466. Cheshire, W. F. 1965. Long term walleye study in the Tweed District, progress report. Ont. Dept. Lands Forest., Manuscript Rep. 39 pp. (WALLEYE; ECOLOGY; STOCK-ING;).

467. Cheshire, W. F. 1966. Preliminary data on the growth and survival of walleye fingerlings fed on a diet of beef liver and trout pellets. Ont. Dept. Lands Forest., Manuscript Rep. 11 pp. (WALLEYE; AGE AND GROWTH; FOOD STUDIES; INTRODUCTIONS; PROPAGATION;).

468. Cheshire, W. F. 1968. Long-term walleye study in the Tweed Forest District. Ont. Min. Nat. Res., Prog. Rep. No. 11: 71 pp. (WALLEYE; AGE AND GROWTH; CREEL CENSUS; POPULATION STUDIES; STOCKING;).

469. Cheshire, W. F., and K. L. Steele. 1963. Rearing walleye in bass ponds, 1962 progress report. Ont. Dept. Lands Forest., Res. Manage. Rep. No. 72:43-63. (WALLEYE; AGE AND

GROWTH; ECOLOGY; MORTALITY; PRODUCTIVITY; PROPAGATION;).

470. Cheshire, W. F., and K. L. Steele. 1963. Rearing pickerel in bass ponds, 1963 progress report. Ont. Dept. Lands For., Manuscript Rep. (1963): 27 pp. (WALLEYE; PROPAGATION;).

471. Cheshire, W. F., and K. L. Steele. 1967. Walleye rearing at the White Lake Station 1966 progress report. Ont. Dept. Lands Forest., Manuscript Rep. 14 pp. (WALLEYE; AGE AND GROWTH; ECOLOGY; MORTALITY; PRODUCTIVITY; PROPAGATION;).

472. Cheshire, W. F., and K. L. Steele. 1968. Survival and growth of walleye fry and fingerlings fed a diet of beef liver and trout pellets. Ont. Dept. Lands Forest., Manuscript Rep. 17 pp. (WALLEYE; AGE AND GROWTH; ECOLOGY; MORTALITY; PRODUCTIVITY; PROPAGATION;).

473. Cheshire, W. F., and K. L. Steele. 1972. Hatchery rearing of walleye using artificial food. Prog. Fish-Cult. 34:96-99. (WALLEYE; PROPAGATION;).

474. Chevalier, J. R. 1971. Cannibalism as a factor in first year survival of walleyes in Oneida Lake. M.S. Thesis. Cornell Univ., Ithaca, N.Y. 49 pp. (WALLEYE; COMMUNITY DYNAMICS; FOOD STUDIES; MORTALITY;).

475. Chevalier, J. R. 1973. Cannibalism as a factor in first year survival of walleye in Oneida Lake. Trans. Am. Fish. Soc. 102:739-744. (WALLEYE; COMMUNITY DYNAMICS; FOOD STUDIES; POPULATION STUDIES;).

476. Chevalier, J. R. 1975. Eagle Lake project final report — 1975. Ont. Min. Nat. Res., Rep. 192 pp. (SAUGER; WALLEYE; COMMERCIAL FISHERIES; COMMUNITY DYNAMICS; CREEL CENSUS; MARKING; MOVEMENTS AND MIGRATIONS; PATHOLOGY; POPULATION STUDIES; PRODUCTIVITY; SOCIO-ECONOMICS OF FISHERIES; STOCKING;).

477. Chevalier, J. R. 1977. Changes in walleye (Stizostedion vitreum vitreum) population in Rainy Lake and factors in abundance, 1924-75. J. Fish. Research Board Can. 34:1696-1702. (WALLEYE; AGE AND GROWTH; COMMERCIAL FISHERIES; POPULATION STUDIES; SPAWNING STUDIES; WATER LEVELS;).

478. Chovelon, A., L. George, C. Gulayets, Y. Hoyano, E. McGuinness, J. Moore, S. Ramamoorthy, S. Ramamoorthy, P. Singer, K. Smiley, and A. Wheatley. 1984. Pesticide and PCB levels in fish from Alberta (Canada). Chemosphere 13:19-32. (SAUGER; WALLEYE; TOXICANTS;).

479. Christensen, K. E. 1953. Fishing in twelve Michigan lakes under experimental regulations. Mich. Dept. Conserv., Misc. Pub. No. 7: 46 pp. (WALLEYE; CREEL CENSUS;).

480. Christenson, L. M., and L. L. Smith, Jr. 1965. Characteristics of fish populations in upper Mississippi River backwater area. U.S. Fish Wildl. Serv., Circ. 212: 53 pp. (SAUGER; WALLEYE; AGE AND GROWTH; PRODUCTIVITY;).

481. Christianson, J. 1975. Batch marking small finglerling (1-1.5") walleyes with fluorescent pigment. Iowa Conserv. Comm., 1975 Job Comp. Rep. Proj. 75-1-C-46: 30-32. (WALLEYE; MARKING;).

482. Christianson, J. 1978. Evaluation of fingerling walleye stocking in West Okoboji. Iowa Conserv. Comm., Job Comp. Rep. Proj. 78-I-C-1 (WALLEYE; MORTALITY; STOCKING;).

483. Christie, G. C. 1986. Measures of optimal thermal habitat and their relationship to yields for four commercial fish species. M.S. Thesis, Univ. Toronto, Ont., Can. 56 pp. (WALLEYE; COMMERCIAL FISHERIES; ECOLOGY; PRODUCTIVITY;).

484. Christie, W. J. 1964. Fishing in the Bay of Quinte. Ont. Dept. Lands Forest., Misc. Pub. : 12 pp. (WALLEYE; COMMERCIAL FISHERIES;).

485. Christie, W. J. 1965. Angling-commercial fishing relationships in the Great Lakes. Ont. Dept. Lands Forest., Fish Wildl. Branch 15 pp. (WALLEYE; COMMERCIAL FISHERIES; CREEL CENSUS; SOCIO-ECONOMICS OF FISHERIES;).

486. Christie, W. J. 1966. The Bay of Quinte walleye stock decline. Unpub. Manuscript in Great Lakes Inst. Libr., Univ. Toronto. 23 pp.

(WALLEYE; MARKING; POPULATION STUDIES;).

487. Christie, W. J. 1968. Possible influences of fishing in the decline of Great Lakes fish stocks. Proc. Int. Assoc. Great Lake Research 11:31-38. (WALLEYE; COMMERCIAL FISHERIES; POPULATION STUDIES;).

488. Christie, W. J. 1973. A review of the changes in the fish species composition of Lake Ontario. Great Lakes Fish. Comm., Tech. Rep. No. 23: 65 pp. (WALLEYE; COMMERCIAL FISHERIES; COMMUNITY DYNAMICS;).

489. Christie, W. J. 1974. Changes in the fish species composition of the Great Lakes. J. Fish. Research Board Can. 31:827-854. (SAUGER; COMMUNITY DYNAMICS;).

490. Christie, W. J., K. A. Scott, P. G. Sly, and R. H. Strus. 1987. Recent changes in the food web of eastern Lake Ontario. Can. J. Fish. Aquat. Sci. 44(Suppl. 2):37-52. (WALLEYE; COMMERCIAL FISHERIES; FOOD STUDIES;).

491. Christie, W. J., G. R. Spangler, K. H. Loftus, W. A. Hartman, P. J. Colby, M. A. Ross, and D. R. Talhelm. 1987. A perspective on Great Lakes fish community rehabilitation. Can. J. Fish. Aquat. Sci. 44(Suppl. 2):486-499. (WALLEYE; COMMUNITY DYNAMICS; ECOLOGY;).

492. Christir, W. J. 1973. A review of the changes in the fish species composition of Lake Ontario. Great Lakes Fish. Comm., Tech. Rep. 23: 65 pp. (WALLEYE; COMMUNITY DYNAMICS;).

493. Churchill, W. S. 1957. Conclusions from a ten year creel census on a lake with no angling restrictions. J. Wildl. Manage. 21:182-188. (WALLEYE; CREEL CENSUS; PRODUCTIVITY; REGULATIONS;).

494. Churchill, W. S. 1963. The effect of fin removal on survival, growth and vulnerability to capture of stocked walleye fingerlings. Trans. Am. Fish. Soc. 92:298-300. (WALLEYE; AGE AND GROWTH; MARKING; MORTALITY;).

495. Churchill, W. S., and H. Snow. 1964. Characteristics of the sport fishery in some northern Wisconsin lakes. Wis. Conserv. Dept.,

Tech. Bull. No. 32: 47 pp. (WALLEYE; CREEL CENSUS;).

496. Clady, M. D. 1978. Structure of fish communities in lakes that contain yellow perch, sauger, and walleye populations. Pages 100-108 in R.L. Kendall, ed. Selected coolwater fishes on North America. Am. Fish. Soc. Sp. Publ. No. 11, Washington, D.C. (SAUGER; WALLEYE; COMMUNITY DYNAMICS; IMPOUNDMENTS; POPULATION STUDIES; SPAWNING STUDIES;).

497. Clady, M. D., and L. Nielsen. 1978. Diversity of a community of small fishes as related to abundance of the dominant percid fishes. Pages 109-113 in R.L. Kendall, ed. Selected coolwater fishes of North America. Am. Fish. Soc. Sp. Publ. No. 11, Washington, D.C. (WALLEYE; COMMUNITY DYNAMICS;).

498. Clark, C. F. 1956. Sandusky River report. Ohio Dept. Nat. Res. 76 pp. (WALLEYE; HABITAT DEGRADATION; MOVEMENT AND MIGRATIONS; STOCKING;).

499. Clark, C. F. 1959. Experiments in the transportation of live fish in polyethylene bags. Prog. Fish-Cult. 21:177-182. (WALLEYE; PROPAGATION;).

500. Clark, C. F. 1970. Walleyes in Ohio and its management. Ohio Dept. Nat. Res. 38 pp. (WALLEYE; INTRODUCTIONS; PROPAGATION; STOCKING;).

501. Clark, C. F., and D. Allison. 1966. Fish population trends in the Maumee and Auglaize Rivers. Ohio Dept. Nat. Res., Pub. NRW-317: 51 pp. (WALLEYE; HABITAT DEGRADATION;).

502. Clark, F. N. 1883. Account of operations at the Northville Fish-hatching Station of the United States Fish Commission, from 1874-1882, inclusive. U.S. Fish. Comm., Bull. 2 (1882):355-372. (WALLEYE; PROPAGATION;).

503. Clarke, S. G. 1973. Walleye life history study. Tex. Parks Wildl. Dept., Fed. Aid Fish Wildl. Restor. Proj. F-7-R-21, Job No. 17a: 7 pp. (WALLEYE; FOOD STUDIES; POPULATION STUDIES; SPAWNING STUDIES;).

504. Clay, W. M. 1962. A field manual of Kentucky fishes. Ky. Dept. Fish Wildl. Res. 147 pp.

(SAUGER; WALLEYE; SPAWNING STUDIES; TAXONOMY;).

505. Clay, W. M. (ed.). 1962. Aquatic-life resources of the Ohio River. Ohio River Valley Water Sanitation Comm. Cincinnati, Ohio. 218 pp. (SAUGER; WALLEYE; COMMERCIAL FISHERIES; POPULATION STUDIES;).

506. Clayton, J. W., R. E. K. Harris, and D. N. Tretiak. 1973. Identification of supernatant and mitochondrial isozymes of malate dehydrogenase of electropherograms applied to the taxonomic discrimination of walleye *(Stizostedion vitreum vitreum)*, sauger *(S. canadense)* and suspected interspecific hybrid fishes. J. Fish. Research Board Can. 30:927-938. (SAUGER; WALLEYE; GENETICS;).

507. Clayton, J. W., R. E. K. Harris, and D. N. Tretiak. 1974. Geographical distribution of alleles for supernatant malate dehydrgense in walleye *(Stizostedion vitreum vitreum)* populations for Western Canada. J. Fish. Research Board Can. 31:342-345. (WALLEYE; GENETICS;).

508. Clayton, J. W., D. N. Tretiak, and A. H. Kooyman. 1971. Genetics of multiple malate dehydrogenase isozymes in skeletal muscle of walleye *(Stizostedion vitreum vitreum)*. J. Fish. Research Board Can. 28:1005-1008. (WALLEYE; GENETICS; GEOGRAPHICAL DISTRIBUTION;).

509. Cleary, R. E. 1948. Life history and management of the yellow pikeperch, *(Stizostedion vitreum vitreum)* (Mitchill), Clear Lake, Iowa. M.S. Thesis, Iowa State Univ., Ames, Iowa. 43 pp. (WALLEYE; AGE AND GROWTH; FISHING GEAR; LIFE HISTORY;).

510. Cleary, R. E. 1949. Life history and management of the yellow pikeperch, *Stizostedion v. vitreum* (Mitchill) of Clear Lake, Iowa. Iowa State Coll. J. Sci. 23:195-208. (WALLEYE; AGE AND GROWTH; FISHING GEAR; LIFE HISTORY;).

511. Cleary, R. E. 1958. Progress report on walleye and sauger in Mississippi River in Iowa. Iowa Conserv. Comm., Quart. Biol. Rep. 10(4):4-5. (SAUGER; WALLEYE; POPULATION STUDIES;).

512. Cleary, R. E., and J. K. Mayhew. 1961. An analysis of an alternate-year walleye fry stocking program in the Cedar River in Iowa. Proc. Iowa Acad. Sci. 68:254-259. (WALLEYE; POPULATION STUDIES; STOCKING;).

513. Clemens, H. P. 1951. The food of the burbot, *Lota lota maculosa* (Le Sueur), in Lake Erie. Trans. Am. Fish. Soc. 80:56-66. (WALLEYE; COMMUNITY DYNAMICS;).

514. Clemens, W. A., J. R. Dymond, and N. K. Bigelow. 1924. Food studies of Lake Nipigon fishes. Ont. Fish. Research Lab. Publ. 25:103-165. (SAUGER; WALLEYE; COMMUNITY DYNAMICS; FOOD STUDIES; MORTALITY;).

515. Clemens, W. A., J. R. Dymond, N. K. Bigelow, F. B. Adamstone, and W. J. K. Harkness. 1923. The food of Lake Nipigon fishes. Ont. Fish. Research, Lab. Publ. 16:173-188. (WALLEYE; FOOD STUDIES;).

516. Clemens, W. A., A. H. MacDonald, H. McAllister, A. Mansfield, and D. S. Rawson. 1947. Report of the Royal Commission on the Fisheries of the province of Saskatchewan. Kings's Printer, Regina, Sask. 131 pp. (SAUGER; WALLEYE; COMMERCIAL FISHERIES;).

517. Clifford, T. J. 1969. An estimate of the standing crop and angler harvest of the walleye sport fishery of Lake Poinsett, South Dakota. Proc. S. D. Acad. Sci. 48:151-156. (WALLEYE; CREEL CENSUS; GEOGRAPHICAL DISTRIBUTION; MARKING; WATER LEVELS;).

518. Close, T. L. 1978. A quantitative creel census of Upper Red Lake, Minnesota, 1976-77. Minn. Dept. Nat. Res., Fish Manage. Rep. No. 9: 16 pp. (WALLEYE; CREEL CENSUS;).

519. Clothier, W. D. 1953. Effects of Lake Madison bullhead removal. S. D. Dept. Game fish and Parks, Fed. Aid Fish Wildl. Restor. Proj. F-1-R-3, Job No. 1: 23-27. (WALLEYE; COMMUNITY DYNAMICS;).

520. Clothier, W. D., and M. F. Boussu. 1955. Creel and test net study, Angostura Reservoir, Fall River County, 1953. S. D. Dept. Game Fish Parks, Fed. Aid Fish Wildl. Restor. Proj. F-1-R-3, Job No. 2: 13 pp. (WALLEYE; CREEL CENSUS; IMPOUNDMENTS; POPULATION STUDIES; STOCKING;).

521. Cobb, E. W. 1923. Pike-perch propagation in northern Minnesota. Trans. Am. Fish. Soc. 53:95-105. (WALLEYE; PROPAGATION; SPAWNING STUDIES;).

522. Cobb, E. W. 1934. Division of fish restoration. Conn. State Bd. Fish. Game, 20th Bien. Rep. (1932-1934):25-144. (WALLEYE; INTRODUCTIONS;).

523. Cobb, J. N. 1898. The fisheries of Lake Ontario in 1897. N.Y. Comm. Fish. Game Forest., 3rd Annu. Rep. (1897):205-221. (WALLEYE; COMMERCIAL FISHERIES;).

524. Cobb, J. N. 1900. The commercial fisheries of Lake Erie, Lake Ontario, and the Niagara and St. Lawrence Rivers. N.Y. Comm. Fish. Game Forest., 5th Annu. Rep. (1899):189-239. (SAUGER; WALLEYE; COMMERCIAL FISHERIES;).

525. Cobb, J. N. 1904. The commercial fisheries of the interior lakes and rivers of New York and Vermont. U.S. Fish Comm., Annu. Rep. (1903):225-246. (WALLEYE; COMMERCIAL FISHERIES;).

526. Coble, D. W. 1966. Alkaline phosphatase in fish scales. J. Fish. Research Board Can. 23:149-152. (WALLEYE; AGE AND GROWTH; MORPHOLOGY;).

527. Coble, D. W. 1967. Effects of fin-clipping on mortality and growth of yellow perch with a review of similar investigations. J. Wildl. Manage., 31:173-180. (WALLEYE; AGE AND GROWTH; COMMUNITY DYNAMICS; MARKING; MORTALITY;).

528. Coble, D. W. 1982. Fish population in relation to dissolved oxygen in the Wisconsin River. Trans. Am. Fish. Soc. 111:612-623. (WALLEYE; ECOLOGY; HABITAT DEGRADATION;).

529. Cockerell, T. D. A. 1913. Observations on fish scales. U.S. Bur. Fish., Bull. 32(1912):119-174. (SAUGER; WALLEYE; MORPHOLOGY;).

530. Cohen, Y., and J. N. Stone. 1987. Multivariate time series analysis of the Canadian fisheries of Lake Superior. Can. J. Fish. Aquat. Sci. 44(Suppl. 2):171-181. (WALLEYE; COMMERCIAL FISHERIES; PRODUCTIVITY;).

531. Coker, R. E. 1930. Keokuk Dam and the fisheries of the upper Mississippi. U.S. Bur. Fish., Bull. 45(1929):87-139. (SAUGER; WALLEYE; COMMERCIAL FISHERIES; IMPOUNDMENTS;).

532. Colby, P. J. 1984. Appraising the status of fisheries: rehabilitation techniques. Pages 233-257 in V. W. Cairns and P. V. Hodson, eds. Contaminant effects on fisheries. John Wiley and Sons, Inc., New York, N. Y. (WALLEYE; COMMUNITY DYNAMICS; ECOLOGY; POPULATION STUDIES;).

533. Colby, P. J., R. E. McNicol, and R. A. Ryder. 1979. Synopsis of biological data on the walleye, Stizostedion vitreum (Mitchill 1818). FAO Fisheries Synopsis 119. Rome, Italy. 140 pp. (WALLEYE; AGE AND GROWTH; BEHAVIOR; COMMERCIAL FISHERIES; COMMUNITY DYNAMICS; CREEL CENSUS; ECOLOGY; EMBRYOLOGY; FISHING GEAR; FISHWAYS; FOOD STUDIES; GENETICS; TAXONOMY; HABITAT DEGRADATION; HABITAT IMPROVEMENT; IMPOUNDMENTS; INTRODUCTIONS; LIFE HISTORY; MARKING; MORPHOLOGY; MORTALITY; MOVEMENT AND MIGRATIONS; PATHOLOGY; PHYSIOLOGY; POPULATION STUDIES; PRODUCTIVITY; PROPAGATION; REGULATIONS; SAMPLING METHODS; SOCIO-ECONOMICS OF FISHERIES; SPAWNING STUDIES; STOCKING; TOXICANTS; WATER LEVELS;).

534. Colby, P. J., and S. J. Nepszy. 1981. Variation among stocks of walleye (Stizostedion vitreum vitreum): management implications. Can. J. Fish. Aquat. Sci. 38:1814-1831. (WALLEYE; AGE AND GROWTH; BEHAVIOR; COMMUNITY DYNAMICS; GENETICS; MOVEMENT AND MIGRATIONS; PATHOLOGY; PRODUCTIVITY; SPAWNING STUDIES;).

535. Colby, P. J., P. A. Ryan, D. H. Schupp, and S. L. Serns. 1987. Interactions in north-temperate lake fish communities. Can. J. Fish. Aquat. Sci. 44(Suppl. 2):104-128. (WALLEYE; COMMUNITY DYNAMICS; ECOLOGY; PRODUCTIVITY;).

536. Colby, P. J., and L. L. Smith, Jr. 1967. Survival of walleye eggs and fry on paper fiber sludge deposits in Rainy River, Minnesota. Trans. Am. Fish. Soc. 96:278-296. (WALLEYE;

ECOLOGY; INTRODUCTIONS; MOR-
TALITY; SPAWNING STUDIES;).

537. Cole, F. R. 1977. Rice River creel census. Ont.
Min. Nat. Res., Rep. 7 pp. (WALLEYE;
CREEL CENSUS;).

538. Cole, W. D. 1967. Fish population control.
Kans. Forest., Fish Game Comm., Fed. Aid
Fish Wildl. Restor. Proj. F-15-R-1, Job B-1:
54 pp. (WALLEYE; AGE AND GROWTH;
COMMUNITY DYNAMICS; IMPOUND-
MENTS; STOCKING;).

539. Cole, W. D., and L. D. Jones. 1969. Manage-
ment needs to improve fishing waters.
Kans. Forest., Fish Game Comm., Fed. Aid
Fish Wildl. Restor. Proj. F-15-R-4, Job B-1-
4: 19 pp. (WALLEYE; AGE AND
GROWTH; ECOLOGY; IMPOUND-
MENTS; STOCKING;).

540. Colesante, R. T., and A. Schiavone, Jr. 1980.
Walleye fry: shipping and stocking mortal-
ity. Prog. Fish-Cult. 42:238-239. (WALL-
EYE; MORTALITY;).

541. Colesante, R. T., and N. B. Youmans. 1983. Wa-
ter-hardening walleye eggs with tanic acid
in a production hatchery. Prog. Fish-Cult.
45:126-127. (WALLEYE; PROPAGA-
TION;).

542. Colesante, R. T., N. B. Youmans, and B.
Ziolkoski. 1986. Intensive culture of walleye
fry with live food and formulated diets.
Prog. Fish-Cult. 48:33-37. (WALLEYE;
FOOD STUDIES; MORTALITY; PROPA-
GATION;).

543. Collette, B. B. 1963. The subfamilies, tribes,
and genera of the Percidae (Teleostei). Copeia. :615-623. (SAUGER; WALLEYE;
MORPHOLOGY; TAXONOMY;).

544. Collette, B. B. 1965. Systematic significance
of breeding tubercles in fishes of the family
Percidae. Proc. U.S. Nat. Mus. 117
(3518):567-614. (SAUGER; WALLEYE;
TAXONOMY;).

545. Collette, B. B., M. A. Ali, K. E. F. Hokanson,
M. Nagiec, S. A. Smirnov, J. E. Thorpe, A.
H. Weatherly, and J. Willemsen. 1977. Biol-
ogy of the percids. J. Fish. Research Board
Can. 34:1890-1899. (SAUGER; WALL-
EYE; FOOD STUDIES; GEOGRAPHI-
CAL DISTRIBUTION; MORPHOLOGY;

MOVEMENT AND MIGRATIONS;
SPAWNING STUDIES; TAXONOMY;).

546. Collette, B. B., and P. Banarescu. 1977. Sys-
tematics and zoogeography of the fishes of
the family Percidae. J. Fish. Research
Board Can. 34:1450-1463. (SAUGER;
WALLEYE; GEOGRAPHICAL DISTRI-
BUTION; TOXICANTS;).

547. Colvin, M. A. 1975. The walleye population
and fishery in the Red Cedar River, Wiscon-
sin. M.S. Thesis, Univ. Wis., Stevens Point,
Wis. 94 pp. (WALLEYE; AGE AND
GROWTH; CREEL CENSUS; FOOD
STUDIES; MORTALITY; MOVEMENT
AND MIGRATIONS; POPULATION
STUDIES; PRODUCTIVITY;).

548. Congdon, J. C. 1968. Fish populations of channelized and unchannelized sections of Chari-
ton River, Missouri. Mo. Dept. of Conserv.
10 pp. (WALLEYE; HABITAT DEGRA-
DATION; COMMUNITY DYNAMICS;
PRODUCTIVITY;).

549. Congdon, J. C. 1979. Evaluation of Fox Lake
walleye fishery. Wis. Dept. Nat. Res., Rep.
14 pp. (WALLEYE; AGE AND GROWTH;
CREEL CENSUS; MORTALITY; POPU-
LATION STUDIES; SPAWNING STUD-
IES; STOCKING;).

550. Conover, M. C. 1986. Stocking cool-water species to meet management needs. Pages 31-
39 in R. H. Stroud, ed. Fish culture in fisheries management. Am. Fish. Soc.,
Bethesda, Maryland. (SAUGER; WALL-
EYE; STOCKING;).

551. Cook, F. A. 1959. Freshwater fishes in Missis-
sippi. Miss. Game Fish Comm., 239 pp.
(SAUGER; WALLEYE; COMMERCIAL
FISHERIES; SPAWNING STUDIES;
TAXONOMY;).

552. Cooper, A. R. 1917. A morphological study of
bothriocephalid cestodes from fishes. J.
Parasitol. 4:33-39. (WALLEYE; PATHOL-
OGY;).

553. Cooper, A. R. 1918. North American
pseudophyllidean cestodes from fishes. Ill.
Biol. Monogr 4(4):289-541. (SAUGER;
WALLEYE; PATHOLOGY;).

554. Cooper, C. L., M. R. Heniken, and C. F. Herdendorf. 1981. Limnetic larval fish in the
Ohio portion of the western basin of Lake

Erie 1975-1976. J. Great Lakes Research. 7:326-329. (WALLEYE; COMMUNITY DYNAMICS; HABITAT DEGRADATION; PRODUCTIVITY;).

555. Cooper, C. L., C. E. Herdendorf, J. J. Mizera, and A. M. White. 1983. Limnetic larval fish in the near shore zone of the south shore of the central basin of Lake Erie. Ohio J. Sci. 83:138-140. (SAUGER; WALLEYE; COMMUNITY DYNAMICS;).

556. Cooper, G. P. 1941. A biological survey of lakes and ponds of the Androscoggin and Kennebec River drainage systems in Maine. Maine Dept. Inland Fish Game, Fish Surv. Rep. 4; 225 pp. (WALLEYE; FOOD STUDIES; INTRODUCTIONS;).

557. Cooper, G. P. 1948. Fish stocking policies in Michigan. Trans. 13th N. Am. Wildl. Conf. 13:187-193. (WALLEYE; STOCKING;).

558. Cooper, G. P. 1952. Estimation of fish populations in Michigan lakes. Trans. Am. Fish. Soc. 81:4-16. (WALLEYE; MARKING; POPULATION STUDIES;).

559. Cope, E. D. 1877. Partial synopsis of the fishes of the fresh waters of North Carolina. Pages 448-495 in Proc. Am. Phil. Soc. 11 (1871). (SAUGER; WALLEYE; COMMUNITY DYNAMICS; FOOD STUDIES;).

560. Cope, E. D. 1885. Food fishes native to, or introduced into, the waters of Pennsylvania. Penn. State Comm. Fish., Rep. (1883 and 1884) :16-27. (WALLEYE; MORPHOLOGY; TAXONOMY;).

561. Corazza, L. 1980. Intensive culture of walleye: factors affecting the ability of juveniles to utilize a dry diet. Ph.D Thesis, Cornell Univ., Ithaca, N.Y. 86 pp. (WALLEYE; PROPAGATION;).

562. Corazza, L., and J. G. Nickum. 1981. Positive phototaxis during initial feeding stages of walleye larvae. Rapp. P.-v Reun. Cons. int. Explor. Mer. 178:492-494. (WALLEYE; BEHAVIOR; FOOD STUDIES; PROPAGATION;).

563. Corazza, L., and J. G. Nickum. 1981. Possible effects of phototactic behavior on initial feeding of walleye larvae. Pages 48-52 in L.J. Allen and E.C. Kirney, eds. Proc. Bioengineering. Symp. Fish Cult., Am. Fish.

Soc. pp. 48-52. (WALLEYE; BEHAVIOR; FOOD STUDIES; PROPAGATION;).

564. Corazza. L., and J. G. Nickum. 1983. Rate of food passage through the gastrointestinal tract of fingerling walleyes. Prog. Fish-Cult. 45:183-184. (WALLEYE; FOOD STUDIES;).

565. Corbett, B. W., and P. M. Powles. 1986. Spawning and larva drift of sympatric walleyes and white suckers in an Ontario stream. Trans. Am. Fish. Soc. 115:41-46. (WALLEYE; COMMUNITY DYNAMICS; ECOLOGY; SPAWNING STUDIES;).

566. Corbett, D. 1984. Creel survey of the early summer sport fishery on Mindemoya Lake May-June, 1984. Ont. Min. Nat. Res., Rep. 11 pp. (WALLEYE; CREEL CENSUS;).

567. Corbett, T. C. 1978. Kukukus and Press Lake creel census 1978. Ont. Min. Nat. Res., Rep. 15 pp. (WALLEYE; CREEL CENSUS;).

568. Costanzo, M. 1980. Wakami Lake creel survey report, 1979. Ont. Min. Nat. Res., Rep. 11 pp. (WALLEYE; CREEL CENSUS;).

569. Cotchefer, R. 1902. Report of the general foreman of hatcheries. N.Y. Forest, Fish Game Comm., 7th Annu. Rep. p. 58-62. (WALLEYE; STOCKING;).

570. Couey, F. M. 1935. Fish food studies of a number of northeastern Wisconsin lakes. Trans. Wis. Acad. Sci., Arts Letters 29:131-172. (WALLEYE; FOOD STUDIES;).

571. Coutant, C. C. 1972. Successful cold branding of nonsalmonids. Prog. Fish-Cult. 34:131-132. (SAUGER; MARKING;).

572. Coutant, C. C. 1977. Compilation of temperature preference data. J. Fish. Research Board Can. 34:739-746. (SAUGER; WALLEYE; BEHAVIOR;).

573. Covington, W. G. 1983. An indexed bibliography of literature pertaining to fish harvest regulations. Mo. Dept. of Conserv.; Fish Wildl. Research Center. 26 pp. (WALLEYE; REGULATIONS;).

574. Cox, U. O. 1897. A preliminary report on the fishes of Minnesota. Minn. Geol. Nat. Hist. Surv., Zool. Ser. 3: 93 pp. (SAUGER; WALLEYE; MORPHOLOGY; TAXONOMY;).

575. Crabtree, J. E. 1969. Walleye and northern pike study. Tex. Parks Wildl Dept., Fed. Aid Fish Wildl Restor. Proj. F-7-R-17, Job No. 17: 15 pp. (WALLEYE; AGE AND GROWTH; FOOD STUDIES; IMPOUND-MENTS; INTRODUCTIONS; MARK-ING; SPAWNING STUDIES;).

576. Craig, J. F., A. Sharma, and K. Smiley. 1986. The variability in catches from multi-mesh gillnets fished in three Canadian lakes. J. Fish. Biology 28:671-678. (WALLEYE; FISHING GEAR;).

577. Craig, J. F., and K. Smiley. 1986. Walleye, *Stizostedion vitreum* and northern pike, *Esox lucius*, populations in three Alberta lakes. J. Fish. Biol. 29:67-85. (WALLEYE; AGE AND GROWTH; COMMERCIAL FISH-ERIES; COMMUNITY DYNAMICS; CREEL CENSUS; FOOD STUDIES; POP-ULATION STUDIES;).

578. Craig, R. E., N. L. Buckingham, and R. G. Mulholland. 1976. Gravelly Bay fishery sur-vey 1976 creel census and population esti-mates. Ont. Min. Nat. Res., Rep. 20 pp. (WALLEYE; CREEL CENSUS; POPULA-TION STUDIES;).

579. Critchlow, D. 1988. 1986 summer creel census and an analysis of the walleye and northern pike sport fisheries of Nagagami Lake. Ont. Min. Nat. Res., Hearst Dist. (WALLEYE; MORTALITY; POPULATION STUDIES; PRODUCTIVITY;).

580. Crosby, J. 1980. A quantitative roving creel census and angler profile of the 1979-80 win-ter fishing season on the St. Louis estuary. Minn. Dept. Nat. Res., Fish Manage. Rep. No. 23: 19 pp. (WALLEYE; CREEL CEN-SUS; HABITAT DEGRADATION;).

581. Cross, F. B. 1967. Handbook of fishes of Kan-sas. Univ. Kans. Mus. Nat. Hist. Publ., 45: 357 pp. (SAUGER; WALLEYE; BEHAV-IOR; INTRODUCTIONS; MORPHOL-OGY; SPAWNING STUDIES; STOCK-ING; TAXONOMY;).

582. Cross, F. B., and M. Braasch. 1969. Qualitative changes in the fish-fauna of the upper Neosho River system, 1952-1967. Trans. Kans. Acad. Sci. 71(1968):350-360. (WALL-EYE; ECOLOGY; HABITAT DEGRADA-TION; INTRODUCTIONS;).

583. Cross, F. B., J. E. Deacon, and C. M. Ward. 1959. Growth data on sport fishes in twelve lakes in Kansas. Trans. Kans. Acad. Sci. 62:162-164. (WALLEYE; AGE AND GROWTH;).

584. Cross, F. B., and G. A. Moore. 1952. The fishes of Poteau River, Oklahoma and Arkansas. Am. Midl. Nat. 47:396-412. (SAUGER; GE-OGRAPHICAL DISTRIBUTION;).

585. Cross, J. E. 1964. Walleye distribution and movements in Berlin Reservoir, Ohio. Ohio Dept. Nat. Res., Pub. W337: 9 pp. (WALL-EYE; MOVEMENT AND MIGRATIONS; SPAWNING STUDIES;).

586. Cross, S. X. 1938. A study of the fish parasite relationships in the Trout Lake region of Wisconsin. Trans. Wis. Acad. Sci., Arts Let-ters 31:439-456. (WALLEYE; PATHOL-OGY;).

587. Crossman, E. J. 1962. Black spot parasite in fishes. Roy. Ont. Mus., Dept. Ichthyol. Her-petology, Information Leafl.; 5 pp. (WALL-EYE; PATHOLOGY;).

588. Crowe, J. M. E. 1969. Lake St. Martin water quality tests in 1968. Man. Dept. Mines Nat. Res., Manuscript Rep. 14: 13 pp. (WALLEYE; ECOLOGY;).

589. Crowe, W. R. 1953. An analysis of the fish pop-ulation of Big Bear Lake, Otsego County, Michigan. Papers Mich. Acad. Sci., Arts Letters 38 (1952):187-206. (WALLEYE; IN-TRODUCTIONS;).

590. Crowe, W. R. 1955. Numerical abundance and use of a spawning run of walleyes in the Muskegon River, Michigan. Trans. Am. Fish. Soc. 84:125-136. (WALLEYE; MARK-ING; MOVEMENT AND MIGRATIONS; POPULATION STUDIES;).

591. Crowe, W. R. 1957. Movements and harvest of native walleyes from impoundments on the Muskegon River. Mich. Dept. Conserv., In-vest. Fish. Research Rep. No. 1518: 9 pp. (WALLEYE; CREEL CENSUS; IM-POUNDMENTS; MARKING; MOVE-MENT AND MIGRATIONS;).

592. Crowe, W. R. 1958. Walleyes in the inland Wa-terway. Mich. Dept. Conserv., Invest. Fish. Research Rep. No. 1534: 20 pp. (WALL-EYE; AGE AND GROWTH; CREEL CEN-

SUS; MARKING; MOVEMENT AND MI-
GRATIONS; STOCKING;).

593. Crowe, W. R. 1962. Homing behavior in wall-
eyes. Trans. Am. Fish. Soc. 91:350-354.
(WALLEYE; MARKING; MOVEMENT
AND MIGRATIONS;).

594. Crowe, W. R. 1964. Fish populations. Walleyes
in Bay de Noc. Mich. Dept. Conserv., Fed.
Aid Fish Wildl. Restor. Proj. F-27-R-2, Wk.
Pl. 13, Job No. 2: 2 pp. (WALLEYE; COM-
MERCIAL FISHERIES; MARKING;
MOVEMENT AND MIGRATIONS; SAM-
PLING METHODS;).

595. Crowe, W. R. 1966. Fish populations. Walleyes
in Bay de Noc. Mich. Dept. Conserv., Fed.
Aid Fish Wildl. Restor. Proj. F-27-R-3, Wk.
Pl. 13, Job No. 2: 1 p. (WALLEYE; MARK-
ING;).

596. Crowe, W. R., E. Karvelis, and L. S. Joeris.
1963. The movement, heterogeneity, and
rate of exploitation of walleyes in northern
Green Bay, Lake Michigan, as determined
by tagging. Internat. Comm. N.W. Atlantic
Fish., Spec. Pub. 4:38-41. (WALLEYE;
COMMERCIAL FISHERIES; MARK-
ING; MOVEMENT AND MIGRATIONS;
SPAWNING STUDIES;).

609. Daiber, F. C. 1952. The food and feeding relationship of the freshwater drum, *Aplodinotus grunniens*, Rafinesque, in western Lake
Erie. Ohio J. Sci. 51:35-46. (SAUGER;
WALLEYE; FOOD STUDIES;).

610. Daley, S. A. 1960. Walleye and sauger study.
Minn. Dept. Conserv., Fed. Aid Fish Wildl.
Restor. Proj. F-15-R-4, Job No. 1: 9 pp.
(SAUGER; WALLEYE; MARKING;
MOVEMENTS AND MIGRATIONS;
POPULATION STUDIES;).

611. Daley, S. A. 1961. Notes on sauger and walleye
reproduction in the Mississippi River.
Minn. Dept. Conserv., Spec. Publ. No. 11: 12
pp. (SAUGER; WALLEYE; AGE AND
GROWTH; ECOLOGY; FOOD STUDIES;
SAMPLING METHODS;).

612. Daley, S. A., and J. Skrypek. 1964. Angler
creel census of Pools 4 & 5 of the Mississippi
River Goodhue and Wabasha Counties,
Minnesota in 1962-1963. Minn. Dept. Con-
serv., Invest. Rep. No. 277: 49 pp.
(SAUGER; WALLEYE; AGE AND

GROWTH; CREEL CENSUS; SOCIO-EC-
ONOMICS OF FISHERIES;).

613. Daly, R. 1954. Movement of tagged walleyes
(Stizostedion vitreum vitreum) Chequsme-
gon Bay 1947 — 1953. Wis. Conserv. Dept.,
Abstr. No. 11: 2 pp. (WALLEYE; MARK-
ING; MOVEMENT AND MIGRA-
TIONS;).

614. Daniel, K. L. 1984. Food habits, age and
growth, and forage value of the alewife in
Watauga Reservoir, Tennessee. Tenn. Wildl.
Res. Agency, Tech. Rep. No. 84-2: 93 pp.
(WALLEYE; AGE AND GROWTH; COM-
MUNITY DYNAMICS; FOOD STUD-
IES;).

615. Danzmann, R. G. 1979. The karyology of eight
species of fish belonging to the family Percidae. Can. J. Zool. 57:2055-2060. (WALL-
EYE; GENETICS;).

616. Davidoff, E. B. 1978. The Matheson Island
sauger fishery of Lake Winnipeg, 1972-
1976. Pages 308-312 *in* R. L. Kendall, ed. Selected coolwater fishes of North America.
Am. Fish. Soc. Spec. Publ. No. 11, Washington D.C. (SAUGER; WALLEYE; AGE
AND GROWTH; COMMERCIAL FISH-
ERIES; HABITAT DEGRADATION;).

617. Davidoff, E. B. 1978. The Matheson Island
sauger fishery of Lake Winnipeg 1972-1976.
Man. Dept. Renewable Res. Transpt. Sys.
Fish Research Sect., Fish Manage. Branch.
Manuscript Rep. No. 78-54: 21 pp.
(SAUGER; WALLEYE; AGE AND
GROWTH; COMMERCIAL FISHERIES;
HABITAT DEGRADATION; MORTAL-
ITY; POPULATION STUDIES; SPAWN-
ING STUDIES;).

618. Davies, J. H., P. J. Wingate, and W. R. Bonner.
1979. Evaluation of the removal of a minimum size limit on walleye in Glenville Reservoir, North Carolina. Proc. 33rd Annu.
Conf. Southeast Assoc. Fish Wildl. Agencies 33:518-522. (WALLEYE; AGE AND
GROWTH; CREEL CENSUS; PRODUC-
TIVITY; REGULATIONS;).

619. Davies, J. W. 1960. Canadian commercial fish
landings of eastern, central and western
Lake Erie 1870-1958. Ont. Dept. Lands Forest., 83 pp. (SAUGER; WALLEYE; COM-
MERCIAL FISHERIES;).

620. Davies, J. W. 1962. Statistical analysis of Canadian yellow pickerel landings, Lake Erie 1948 to 1961. Ont. Dept. Lands Forest. 15 pp. (WALLEYE; COMMERCIAL FISHERIES;).

621. Davis, H. S. 1940. Artificial propagation and the management of trout waters. Trans. Am. Fish. Soc. 69:158-168. (WALLEYE; MORTALITY; PROPAGATION;).

622. Davis, H. S. 1953. Culture and diseases of game fishes. Univ. Calif. Press, Berkeley, Calif. 332 pp. (WALLEYE; COMMUNITY DYNAMICS; PATHOLOGY; PRODUCTIVITY; SPAWNING STUDIES;).

623. Davis, R. A. 1975. Food habits of walleye in a southern Minnesota Lake. Minn. Dept. Nat. Res., Invest. Rep. No. 333: 15 pp. (WALLEYE; FOOD STUDIES;).

624. Davis, R. A. 1985. The role of research in Minnesota fisheries management. Minn. Dept. Nat. Res., Invest. Rep. No. 383: 15 pp. (WALLEYE; COMMUNITY DYNAMICS; CREEL CENSUS; PROPAGATION; STOCKING;).

625. Davis, R. A. 1987. Genetic stock description. Minn. Dept. Nat. Res., Fed. Aid Fish Wildl. Restor. Proj. F-26-R-18, Study No. 308: 12 pp. (WALLEYE; GENETICS; SPAWNING STUDIES;).

626. Davis, R. M. 1979. Life history and management of the walleye and yellow perch of Deep Creek Lake, Maryland. Md. Dept. Nat. Res., Fed. Aid Fish Wildl. Restor. Proj. F-28-R-3: 49 pp. (WALLEYE; AGE AND GROWTH; FOOD STUDIES; LIFE HISTORY; SPAWNING STUDIES; STOCKING;).

627. Dawson, F. N. 1987. 1985 summer creel survey Nagagami Lake. Ont. Min. Nat. Res. 23 pp. (WALLEYE; AGE AND GROWTH; CREEL CENSUS; MORTALITY; POPULATION STUDIES;).

628. Day, R. E., and K. O. Paxton. 1979. Development of an initial stocking program for new upground reservoirs. Ohio Dept. Nat. Res., Fed. Aid Fish Wildl. Restor. Proj. F-29-R: 107 pp. (WALLEYE; STOCKING;).

629. Day, R. E., F. Stevenson, K. O. Paxton, and M. R. Austin. 1983. Limnology and fish populations of Beaver Creek Reservoir, Ohio, 1972-1975. Ohio Dept. Nat. Res., Fish. Wildl. Rep. 9: 56 pp. (WALLEYE; AGE AND GROWTH; COMMUNITY DYNAMICS; CREEL CENSUS; ECOLOGY; FOOD STUDIES; POPULATION STUDIES;).

630. Daykin, P. N. 1965. Application of mass transfer theory to the problem of respiration of fish eggs. J. Fish. Research Board Can. 22:159-171. (WALLEYE; PHYSIOLOGY;).

631. Deary, C. 1980. Kabinakagami Lake creel census survey. Ont. Min. Nat. Res., Rep. 33 pp. (WALLEYE; CREEL CENSUS;).

632. Deason, H. J. 1933. Preliminary report on the growth rate, dominance, and maturity of the pike-perchs (Stizostedion) of Lake Erie. Trans. Am. Fish. Soc. 63:348-360. (SAUGER; WALLEYE; AGE AND GROWTH; POPULATION STUDIES;).

633. Dechtiar, A. O. 1972. New parasite records for Lake Erie fish. Great Lakes Fish. Comm., Tech. Rep. No. 17: 20 pp. (SAUGER; WALLEYE; PATHOLOGY;).

634. Dechtiar, A. O. 1972. Parasites of fish from Lake of the Woods, Ontario. J. Fish. Research Board Can. 29:275-283. (SAUGER; WALLEYE; PATHOLOGY;).

635. Degan, D. 1975. Stocking success of walleye in the Cedar River. Iowa Conserv. Comm., Job Comp. Rep. Proj. 75-II-C-120: 223-227. (WALLEYE; AGE AND GROWTH; STOCKING;).

636. Degan, D. 1978. Success of alternative year walleye fry stocking. Iowa Conserv. Comm., Job Comp. Rep. Proj. 78-II-C-11: 65-73:. (WALLEYE; AGE AND GROWTH; PRODUCTIVITY; STOCKING; WATER LEVELS;).

637. De Kay, J. E. 1842. Zoology of New York, or the New York fauna. Part IV: Fishes. D. Appleton and Co., New York, N.Y. 415 pp. (SAUGER; WALLEYE; MORPHOLOGY; MORTALITY; TAXONOMY;).

638. Dempsey, H. V. 1945. A biological examination of Isle Lake. Alta. Dept. Lands Mines, Fish. Serv., Manuscript Rep. 8 pp. (WALLEYE; COMMERCIAL FISHERIES;).

639. Dence, W. A. 1938. Hermaphrodism in a wall-eyed pike (Stizostedion vitreum). Copeia

(2):95. (WALLEYE; SPAWNING STUDIES;).

640. Dence, W. A. 1952. Establishment of white perch *(Morone americana)* in Central New York. Copeia 3:200-201. (WALLEYE; GEOGRAPHICAL DISTRIBUTION;).

641. Dence, W. A., and D. F. Jackson. 1959. Changing chemical and biological conditions in Oneida Lake, New York. School Sci. Math., April: 317-324. (WALLEYE; FOOD STUDIES; STOCKING;).

642. Dendy, J. S. 1945. Fish distribution, Norris Reservoir, Tennessee, 1943. II. Depth distribution of fish in relation to environmental factors, Norris Reservoir. J. Tenn. Acad. Sci. 21:94-104. (SAUGER; WALLEYE; ECOLOGY; GEOGRAPHICAL DISTRIBUTION; IMPOUNDMENTS;).

643. Dendy, J. S. 1946. Further studies of depth distribution of fish, Norris Reservoir, Tennessee. J. Tenn. Acad. Sci. 21:94-104. (SAUGER; WALLEYE; ECOLOGY; GEOGRAPHICAL DISTRIBUTION; IMPOUNDMENTS;).

644. Dendy, J. S. 1946. Food of several species of fish, Norris Reservoir, Tennessee. J. Tenn. Acad. Sci. 21:105-127. (SAUGER; WALLEYE; COMMUNITY DYNAMICS; FOOD STUDIES; IMPOUNDMENTS;).

645. Dendy, J. S. 1948. Predicting depth distribution of fish in three TVA storage type reservoirs. Trans. Am. Fish. Soc. 75:65-71. (SAUGER; WALLEYE; BEHAVIOR; ECOLOGY; GEOGRAPHICAL DISTRIBUTION; PHYSIOLOGY;).

646. Dendy, J. S., and R. H. Stroud. 1949. The dominating influence of Fontana Reservoir on temperature and dissolved oxygen in the Little Tennessee River and its impoundments. J. Tenn. Acad. Sci. 24:41-51. (WALLEYE; ECOLOGY; HABITAT IMPROVEMENT; IMPOUNDMENTS;).

647. Dentry, W. 1984. Sport fishing harvest from the upper Bay of Quinte, January to March, 1984. Ont. Min. Nat. Res., LOFAU Rep. 84.9: 54 pp. (WALLEYE; CREEL CENSUS;).

648. Dentry, W. 1984. Sport fishing in the Bay of Quite, summer of 1984. Ont. Min. Nat. Res.,

LOFAU Rep. 84.10: 30 pp. (WALLEYE; CREEL CENSUS;).

649. Denyes, N. 1980. Bob's Lake creel report, 1980. Ont. Min. Nat. Res., Rep. 35 pp. (WALLEYE; CREEL CENSUS;).

650. Derback, B. 1947. The adverse effect of cold weather upon the successful reproduction of pickerel, *Stizostedion vitreum,* at Heming Lake, Manitoba, in 1947. Can. Fish Cult. 2:22-23. (WALLEYE; ECOLOGY; SPAWNING STUDIES;).

651. Derksen, A. J. 1967. Variations in abundance of walleye, *Stizostedion vitreum vitreum* (Mitchill), in Cedar and Moose Lakes, Man. M.S. Thesis, Univ. Man., Winnipeg, Man. 98 pp. (WALLEYE; LIFE HISTORY; POPULATION STUDIES; WATER LEVELS;).

652. Derksen, A. J. 1975. Fisheries resource impact assessment of the upper Churchill River and Lower Hughes River, Manitoba. Man. Dept. Mines, Res. Envir. Manage., Envir. Manage. Div. 170 pp. (WALLEYE; AGE AND GROWTH; COMMERCIAL FISHERIES; MOVEMENTS AND MIGRATIONS; PRODUCTIVITY; WATER LEVELS;).

653. Derksen, A. J. 1978. Utilization of the Big Grass Marsh area by fish populations and proposals for fisheries enhancement 1978. Man. Dept. Mines, Nat. Res. Envir. Fisheries Research. Manuscript Rep. No. 78-77: 55 pp. (WALLEYE; COMMERCIAL FISHERIES; POPULATION STUDIES; SPAWNING STUDIES;).

654. Desjardine, R. L., and J. N. Lawrence. 1977. Summer creel census on Lake Simcoe. Ont. Min. Nat. Res., Rep. Lake Simcoe Fish. Assess. Unit 26 pp. (WALLEYE; CREEL CENSUS;).

655. Desjardine, R. L., C. Sutherland, and J. N. Lawrence. 1979. Summer creel census on Lake Lawrence. Ont. Min. Nat. Res., Rep. Lake Simcoe Fish. Assess. Unit 49 pp. (WALLEYE; CREEL CENSUS;).

656. Desrochers, R. 1953. Displacement of walleye *(Stizostedion vitreum)* (sic) liberated in Chambly Basin in spring 1952. Rev. Can. Biol. 11:502-505. (WALLEYE; MOVEMENT AND MIGRATIONS;).

657. DeVault, D. S. 1985. Contaminants in fish from the Great Lakes harbors and tributary

mouths. Arch. Environ. Contam. Toxicol. 14:587-594. (WALLEYE; HABITAT DEGRADATION; TOXICANTS;).

658. Devitt, O. E. 1959. The age and growth rates of Ontario game fishes for fish and wildlife management. Ont. Dept. Lands Forest., Fish Wildl. Manage. Rep. 45:65-74. (WALLEYE; AGE AND GROWTH;).

659. Devore, P. W., and J. R. Hargis. 1982. Spatial and temporal patterns of habitat utilization by young-of-year walleye *(Stizostedion v. vitreum)* in the St. Louis River Estuary. Minn. Sea Grant Prog., Research Rep. No. 6: 16 pp. (WALLEYE; ECOLOGY; FISHING GEAR; HABITAT IMPROVEMENT; LIFE HISTORY; MOVEMENT AND MIGRATIONS; SAMPLING METHODS;).

660. Deyne, G. 1983. Analysis and interpretation of Kenogamissi fish data, 1971-75. Ont. Min. Nat. Res., Manuscript Rep. 48 pp. (WALLEYE; CREEL CENSUS; IMPOUNDMENTS; MARKING; POPULATION STUDIES;).

661. Dick, T. A., and B. C. Poole. 1985. Identification of Diphyllobothrium-Dendriticum and Diphyllobothrium-Latum from some freshwater fishes of central Canada. Can. J. Zool. 63:196-201. (WALLEYE; PATHOLOGY;).

662. Dickinson, W. E. 1960. Handbook of Wisconsin fishes. Milwaukee Public Mus., Pop. Sci. Handbook Ser. 8: 83 pp. (SAUGER; WALLEYE; TAXONOMY;).

663. Dickson, I. 1963. Preliminary report on a pickerel spawning investigation — Red Deer River, May 1963. Man. Dept. Mines Nat. Res., Fish. Branch, Manuscript Rep. 13 pp. (WALLEYE; ECOLOGY; HABITAT IMPROVEMENT; MORTALITY; SPAWNING STUDIES;).

664. Dickson, I. 1964. A summary report on the Falcon River pickerel tagging-recapture project, 1964. Man. Dept. Mines Nat. Res., Fish. Branch, Manuscript Rep. 8 pp. (WALLEYE; MARKING; MOVEMENT AND MIGRATIONS; SPAWNING STUDIES;).

665. DiCostanzo, C. J. 1956. Clear Lake creel census and evaluation of sampling techniques. Pages 17-29 *in* K. D. Carlander, ed. Symposium on sampling problems in creel census.

Iowa State Coll., Ames, Iowa (WALLEYE; CREEL CENSUS;).

666. DiCostanzo, C. J., and R. L. Ridenhour. 1957. Angler harvest in the summers of 1953 to 1956 at Clear Lake, Iowa. Proc. Iowa Acad. Sci. 64:621-628. (WALLEYE; CREEL CENSUS;).

667. Disler, N. N., and S. A. Smirnov. 1977. Sensory organs of the lateral-line canal system in two percids and their importance in behavior. J. Fish. Research Board Can. 34:1492-1503. (WALLEYE; PHYSIOLOGY;).

668. Dixon, J. R. 1963. Periodic check and marked fisherman creel census of Caballo Lake. N. M. Dept. Game Fish, Fed. Aid Fish Wildl. Restor. Proj. F-22-R-4, Wk. Pl. 3, Job No. B-1-B: 13 pp. (WALLEYE; CREEL CENSUS;).

669. Doan, K. H. 1941. Relation of the sauger catch to turbidity in Lake Erie. Ohio J. Sci. 41(6):449-452. (SAUGER; COMMERCIAL FISHERIES; ECOLOGY; FOOD STUDIES; SPAWNING STUDIES;).

670. Doan, K. H. 1942. Some meteorological and limnological conditions as factors in the abundance of certain fishes in Lake Erie. Ecol. Monogr. 12:294-314. (SAUGER; WALLEYE; COMMERCIAL FISHERIES; ECOLOGY;).

671. Doan, K. H. 1944. The winter fishery in western Lake Erie, with a census of the 1942 catch. Ohio J. Sci. 44:69-74. (SAUGER; WALLEYE; COMMERCIAL FISHERIES; CREEL CENSUS;).

672. Doan, K. H. 1945. Catch of *Stizostedion vitreum* in relation to changes in lake level in western Lake Erie during the winter of 1943. Am. Midl. Nat. 33:455-459. (SAUGER; WALLEYE; COMMERCIAL FISHERIES; ECOLOGY;).

673. Doan, K. H., and R. R. Andrews. 1964. Experimental trawling in Lake Manitoba in October, 1964. Man. Dept. Mines Nat. Res., Fish. Branch, Manuscript Rep. 8 pp. (SAUGER; WALLEYE; PRODUCTIVITY; SAMPLING METHODS;).

674. Doan, K. H., and J. O. Edmister. 1940. Tagged fish in Lake Erie. Ohio Dept. Nat. Res., Rep. No. 2: 2 pp. (SAUGER; WALLEYE;

MARKING; MOVEMENT AND MIGRA-
TIONS;).

675. Doan, K. M. 1961. A sample of the commercial
pickerel catch at Duck Bay Lake Winnipe-
gosis, in Dec. 1960. Man. Dept. Mines Nat.
Res., Fish Branch 12 pp. (WALLEYE;
COMMERCIAL FISHERIES; POPULA-
TION STUDIES;).

676. Dobie, J. 1953. Walleye pike ponds 1952.
Minn. Dept. Conserv., Invest. Rep. No. 136:
18 pp. (WALLEYE; PROPAGATION;).

677. Dobie, J. 1956. Walleye pond management in
Minnesota. Prog. Fish-Cult. 18:51-57.
(WALLEYE; PROPAGATION;).

678. Dobie, J. 1956. Walleye ponds 1955. Minn.
Dept. Conserv., Invest. Rep. No. 169: 18 pp.
(WALLEYE; ECOLOGY;).

679. Dobie, J. 1957. Walleye ponds 1956. Minn.
Dept. Conserv., Invest. Rep. No. 179: 20 pp.
(WALLEYE; PROPAGATION;).

680. Dobie, J. 1958. Walleye rearing ponds 1957.
Minn. Dept. Conserv., Invest. Rep. No. 187:
13 pp. (WALLEYE; PROPAGATION;).

681. Dobie, J. 1966. Food and feeding habits of the
walleye, *Stizostedion v. vitreum*, and associated game and forage fishes in Lake Vermilion, Minnesota, with special reference to the
tullibee, *Coregonus (Leucichthys) artedi*.
Minn. Dept. Conserv., Invest. Rep. No.
293:39-71. (WALLEYE; AGE AND
GROWTH; ECOLOGY; FOOD STUD-
IES;).

682. Dobie, J. 1969. Growth of walleye and sucker
fingerlings in Minnesota rearing ponds.
Verh. Internat. Verein. Limnol 17:641-649.
(WALLEYE; AGE AND GROWTH; FOOD
STUDIES;).

683. Dobie, J., and J. Moyle. 1956. Methods used
for investigating productivity of fish-rear-
ing ponds in Minnesota. Minn. Dept. Conserv., Research Planning, Spec. Publ. No. 5:
62 pp. (WALLEYE; PRODUCTIVITY;).

684. Dobie, J. G. 1954. Analysis of conditions in
drainable walleye ponds — 1953. Minn.
Dept. Conserv., Invest. Rep. No. 150: 26 pp.
(WALLEYE; PROPAGATION;).

685. Dobie, J. G. 1955. Walleye ponds 1954. Minn.
Dept. Conserv., Invest. Rep. No. 154: 22 pp.
(WALLEYE; PROPAGATION;).

686. Dobie, J. G. 1959. walleye pike rearing ponds
— 1958. Minn. Dept. Conserv., Invest. Rep.
No. 211: 17 pp. (WALLEYE; PROPAGA-
TION;).

687. Doepke, P. A. 1970. An ecological study of the
walleye, *Stizostedion vitreum*, and its early
life history. Ph.D. Thesis, Univ. Wis., Madison, Wis. 202 pp. (WALLEYE; AGE AND
GROWTH; ECOLOGY; FOOD STUDIES;
POPULATION STUDIES; SAMPLING
METHODS; STOCKING;).

688. Dolley, J. S. 1933. Preliminary notes on the bi-
ology of the St. Joseph River. Am. Mildl.
Nat. 14:193-227. (WALLEYE; PATHOL-
OGY;).

689. Donetz, J. E., and V. Macins. 1981. An evalua-
tion of walleye movement in Lake of the
Woods, from tag returns 1962 to 1980. Ont.
Min. Nat. Res., Lake of the Woods — Rainy
Lake Fish. Assess. Unit Rep. 1981-4: 72 pp.
(WALLEYE; MARKING; MOVEMENT
AND MIGRATIONS; MORTALITY; POP-
ULATION STUDIES; SPAWNING STUD-
IES;).

690. Dosser, S. 1987. A summary of walleye and
muskellunge spawning site identification
and documentation, Bancroft District,
spring 1986. Ont. Min. Nat. Res., Bancroft
Dist. and Crowe Valley Conserv. Auth.,
Fish. Manage. Rep. 1987-02: 48 pp. (WALL-
EYE; SPAWNING STUDIES;).

691. Dotson, P. A. 1964. A revised list of the fishes
of North Dakota. N. D. Game Fish Dept. 15
pp. (SAUGER; WALLEYE; GEOGRAPH-
ICAL DISTRIBUTION;).

692. Downing, S. W. 1905. Collecting, hatching and
distribution of pike-perch: why the great
loss of eggs. Trans Am. Fish. Soc. 34:239-
255. (WALLEYE; PHYSIOLOGY; PROPA-
GATION; STOCKING;).

693. Downing, S. W. 1911. Some of the difficulties
encountered in collecting pike-perch eggs.
Trans. Am. Fish. Soc. 40:277-281. (WALL-
EYE; PROPAGATION;).

694. Downing, S. W. 1912. Are the hatcheries on the
Great Lakes of benefit to the commercial
fishermen? Trans. Am. Fish. Soc. 41:127-

133. (WALLEYE; PROPAGATION; STOCKING;).

695. Downing, S. W. 1917. Production and destruction of the food fishes of the Great Lakes. Trans. Am. Fish. Soc. 47:28-35. (SAUGER; WALLEYE; MORTALITY; PRODUCTIVITY; PROPAGATION; STOCKING;).

696. Doxtater, G. 1967. Experimental predator-prey relations in small ponds. Prog. Fish-Cult. 29:102-104. (WALLEYE; COMMUNITY DYNAMICS; MORTALITY; SPAWNING STUDIES;).

697. Driver, E. A. 1978. A biological survey of Burntwood Lake in 1965, with reference to the growth of walleye, *Stizostedion vitreum vitreum* (Mitchill). Man. Dept. Mines Nat. Res., Fish. Branch, Manuscript Rep. No. 78-86: 47 pp. (WALLEYE; AGE AND GROWTH; COMMERCIAL FISHERIES;).

698. Dryer, W. R. 1964. Movements, growth, and rate of recapture of whitefish tagged in the Apostle Islands area of Lake Superior. U.S. Fish Wildl. Serv., Fish. Bull. 63:611-618. (WALLEYE; AGE AND GROWTH;).

699. Dryer, W. R. 1966. Bathymetric distribution of fish in the Apostle Islands region, Lake Superior. Trans. Am. Fish. Soc. 95:248-259. (WALLEYE; SAMPLING METHODS;).

700. Drysdale, P. D. 1971. Lac Des Mille Lacs creel census. Ont. Min. Nat. Res., Rep. 8 pp. (WALLEYE; CREEL CENSUS;).

701. Drysdale, P. D. 1972. Lac Des Mille Lacs creel census. Ont. Min. Nat. Res., Rep. 6 pp. (WALLEYE; CREEL CENSUS;).

702. Drysdale, P. D. 1973. Lac Des Mille Lacs creel census. Ont. Min. Nat. Res., Rep. 16 pp. (WALLEYE; CREEL CENSUS;).

703. Drysdale, P. D. 1973. Lac Des Mille Lacs creel census summary 1958 — 1972. Ont. Min. Nat. Res., Rep. 9 pp. (WALLEYE; CREEL CENSUS;).

704. Drysdale, P. D. 1974. Lac Des Mille Lacs creel census 1974. Ont. Min. Nat. Res., Rep. 9 pp. (WALLEYE; CREEL CENSUS;).

705. Drysdale, P. D. 1975. Lac Des Mille Lacs creel census 1975. Ont. Min. Nat. Res., Rep. 17 pp. (WALLEYE; CREEL CENSUS;).

706. Duckworth, G. A. 1980. Lake Temiskaming summer creel census 1979. Ont. Min. Nat. Res., Rep. 87 pp. (WALLEYE; CREEL CENSUS;).

707. Duckworth, G. A. 1981. A yellow pickerel population study and creel census of the Lady Evelyn Lake summer fishery, 1980. Ont. Min. Nat. Res., Rep. 157 pp. (WALLEYE; AGE AND GROWTH; CREEL CENSUS; MARKING; MORTALITY; MOVEMENTS AND MIGRATIONS; PATHOLOGY; POPULATION STUDIES; SAMPLING METHODS; SPAWNING STUDIES;).

708. Duerre, D.C. 1966. Tagging studies on five North Dakota impoundments and one natural lake. N. D. Dept. Game Fish, Fed. Aid Fish Wildl. Restor. Proj. F-2-R-12, and F-2-R-13, Job No. 9: 7 pp. (WALLEYE; IMPOUNDMENTS; MARKING; MOVEMENT AND MIGRATIONS;).

709. Duff, D. A., and R. S. Wydoski. 1986. Indexed bibliography on stream habitat improvement. U.S.D.A. For. Serv. Intermountain Region. Wildl. Manage. Staff. Ogden, Utah. 99 pp. (WALLEYE; HABITAT IMPROVEMENT;).

710. Dumas, R. F., and J. S. Brand. 1972. Use of tannin solution in walleye and carp culture. Prog. Fish-Cult. 34:7. (WALLEYE; PROPAGATION;).

711. Dunn, C. L. 1983. Evaluation of the Kapeta vertical slot fishway. Sask. Fish. Lab. Tech. Rep. 1983-3: 90 pp. (WALLEYE; FISHWAYS; IMPOUNDMENTS;).

712. Dunning, P. 1884. Two hundred tons of dead fish, mostly perch, at Lake Mendota, Wisconsin. U.S. Fish Comm., Bull. 4:439-443. (WALLEYE; MORTALITY;).

713. Dupont, A., and M. Bernier. 1984. Summer creel survey North and South Tilley Lakes 1983. Ont. Min. Nat. Res., Rep. 43 pp. (WALLEYE; CREEL CENSUS;).

714. Dyke, R. D. 1977. Lake Scugog winter fishing 1976-1977. Ont. Min. Nat. Res., Rep. 3 pp. (WALLEYE; CREEL CENSUS;).

715. Dyke, R. D., C. A. Lewis, and J. H. Milford. 1981. Lake Scugog winter fishery: status and management recommendations. Ont. Min. Nat. Res., Kawartha Lakes Fish. As-

sess. Unit. Rep. 1981-1: 17 pp. (WALLEYE; CREEL CENSUS; SPAWNING STUDIES;).

716. Dymond, J. R. 1922. A provisional list of the fishes of Lake Erie. Ont. Fish. Res. Lab. 4: 57-72. (SAUGER; WALLEYE; GEOGRAPHICAL DISTRIBUTION;).

717. Dymond, J. R. 1923. A provisional list of the fishes of Lake Nipigon. Ont. Fish. Research Lab. Rep. No 12, Univ. Toronto Studies. pp. 35-73. (WALLEYE; GEOGRAPHICAL DISTRIBUTION;).

718. Dymond, J. R. 1926. The fishes of Lake Nipigon. Ont. Fish. Res. Lab., Publ. No. 27: 108 pp. (SAUGER; WALLEYE; LIFE HISTORY; TAXONOMY;).

719. Dymond, J. R. 1937. New records of Ontario fishes. Copeia 1:59. (WALLEYE; GEOGRAPHICAL DISTRIBUTION;).

720. Dymond, J. R. 1939. The fishes of the Ottawa region. Roy. Ont. Mus. Zool., Contrib. 15: 43 pp. (SAUGER; WALLEYE; COMMERCIAL FISHERIES; INTRODUCTIONS;).

721. Dymond, J. R. 1947. A list of the fresh water fishes of Canada east of the Rocky Mountains with keys. Roy. Ont. Mus. Zool., Misc. Publ. 1: 36 pp. (SAUGER; WALLEYE; TAXONOMY;).

722. Dymond, J. R. 1957. Artificial propagation in the management of Great Lakes fisheries. Trans. Am. Fish. Soc. 86:384-392. (WALLEYE; PROPAGATION; STOCKING;).

723. Dymond, J. R., and A. V. Delaporte. 1952. Pollution of the Spanish River. Ont. Dept. Lands Forest., Tech. Ser., Research Rep. 106 pp. (WALLEYE; HABITAT DEGRADATION;).

724. Dymond, J. R., and J. L. Hart. 1927. The fishes of Lake Abitibi (Ontario) and adjacent waters. Ont. Fish. Research Lab. Rep. No. 28, Univ. Toronto Studies. pp. 3-19. (SAUGER; WALLEYE; COMMERCIAL FISHERIES;).

725. Dymond, J. R., and W. B. Scott. 1941. Fishes of Patricia portion of the Kenora district, Ontario. Copeia 4:243-245. (SAUGER; WALLEYE; GEOGRAPHICAL DISTRIBUTION;).

726. Eales, J. G. 1969. A comparative study of purines responsible for silvering in several freshwater fishes. J. Fish. Research Board Can. 26:1927-1931. (WALLEYE; MORPHOLOGY;).

727. Eastgate, A. 1918. Planting fish in an alkali lake. Trans. Am. Fish. Soc. 47:89-91. (WALLEYE; ECOLOGY; PATHOLOGY; PHYSIOLOGY;).

728. Eaton, E. H. 1928. A biological survey of the Oswego River system. II. The Finger Lakes fish problem. N.Y. Conserv. Dept., Suppl. 17th Annu. Rep. (1927):40-66. (WALLEYE; FOOD STUDIES; STOCKING;).

729. Ebbers, M. A., and B. W. Hawkinson. 1978. Trapnetting survey of Pools 3-7 on the Mississippi River in 1957, 1963, 1970 and 1977. Minn. Dept. Nat. Res., Fish Manage. Rep. No. 12: 41 pp. (SAUGER; WALLEYE; ECOLOGY; POPULATION STUDIES;).

730. Economon, P. P. 1974. A survey of myofibrogranuloma in walleyes in Minnesota from thirty-two case reports 1959-1974. Minn. Dept. Nat. Res., Pathol. Arch. 19:25-47. (WALLEYE; PATHOLOGY;).

731. Economon, P. P. 1975. Myofibrogranuloma, a muscular dystrophy — like anomaly of walleye *(Stizostedion vitreum vitreum)*. Minn. Dept. Nat. Res., Spec. Publ. No. 113: 13 pp. (WALLEYE; PATHOLOGY;).

732. Economon, P. P. 1978. A muscular dystrophy-like anomaly of walleye. Pages 226-234 *in* R.L. Kendall, ed. Selected coolwater fishes of North America. Am. Fish. Soc. Sp. Publ. No.11, Washington, D.C. (WALLEYE; PATHOLOGY;).

733. Eddy, S. 1938. A classification of Minnesota lakes for fish propagation. Prog. Fish-Cult. 41:9-13. (WALLEYE; ECOLOGY;).

734. Eddy, S. 1938. Winter creel census 1937-38. Minn. Dept. Conserv., Invest. Rep. No. 1: 7 pp. (WALLEYE; CREEL CENSUS;).

735. Eddy, S. 1938. Report on the number of eggs produced by walleyed pike. Minn. Dept. Conserv., Invest. Rep. No. 2: 2 pp. (WALLEYE; SPAWNING STUDIES;).

736. Eddy, S. 1939. A report on the 1939 creel census for Lake Itasca. Minn. Dept. Conserv.,

Invest. Rep. No. 27: 6 pp. (WALLEYE; CREEL CENSUS;).

737. Eddy, S. 1940. Creel census of Minnesota waters. Minn. Dept. Conserv., Invest. Rep. No. 9: 12 pp. (WALLEYE; CREEL CENSUS;).

738. Eddy, S. 1940. Minnesota lake surveys and fish management. Proc. Minn. Acad. Sci. 8:9-14. (WALLEYE; COMMUNITY DYNAMICS; POPULATION STUDIES;).

739. Eddy, S. 1941. Minnesota fish yield studies for 1940. Prog. Fish-Cult. 53:39. (WALLEYE; CREEL CENSUS;).

740. Eddy, S. 1943. Limnological notes on Lake Superior. Proc. Minn. Acad. Sci. 11:34-39. (WALLEYE; ECOLOGY;).

741. Eddy, S. 1957. How to know the freshwater fishes. Wm. C. Brown Co., Dubuque, Iowa. 253 pp. (SAUGER; WALLEYE; MORPHOLOGY; TAXONOMY;).

742. Eddy, S., and K. Carlander. 1939. The growth rate of wall-eyed pike, *Stizostedion vitreum* (Mitchill) in various lakes of Minnesota. Proc. Minn. Acad. Sci. 7:44-48. (WALLEYE; AGE AND GROWTH; SAMPLING METHODS;).

743. Eddy, S., and K. D. Carlander. 1940. The problem of annual increments in fish growth studies. Minn. Dept. Conserv., Invest. Rep. No. 13: 5 pp. (WALLEYE; AGE AND GROWTH;).

744. Eddy, S., and K. D. Carlander. 1940. Correlations in the rates of growth of various species of fish from Minnesota lakes. Minn. Dept. Conserv., Invest. Rep. No. 16: 4 pp. (WALLEYE; AGE AND GROWTH;).

745. Eddy, S., and K. D. Carlander. 1940. Length-weight relationship of Minnesota fishes. Minn. Dept. Conserv., Invest. Rep. No. 17: 23 pp. (WALLEYE; AGE AND GROWTH;).

746. Eddy, S., and K. D. Carlander. 1940. The effects of environmental factors upon the growth rates of Minnesota fishes. Proc. Minn. Acad. Sci. 8:14-19. (WALLEYE; AGE AND GROWTH; ECOLOGY;).

747. Eddy, S., and K. D. Carlander. 1942. Growth rate studies of Minnesota fish. Minn. Dept. Conserv., Invest. Rep. No. 28: 64 pp. (WALLEYE; AGE AND GROWTH; SAMPLING METHODS;).

748. Eddy, S., and A. C. Hodson. 1964. Taxonomic keys to common animals of the north central states exclusive of the parasitic worms, insects, and birds. Burgess Publ. Co., Minneapolis, Minn. 162 pp. (SAUGER; WALLEYE; TAXONOMY;).

749. Eddy, S., J. B. Moyle, and J. C. Underhill. 1963. The fish fauna of the Mississippi River above St. Anthony Falls as related to the effectiveness of the falls as a migration barrier. Proc. Minn. Acad. Sci. 30:111-115. (SAUGER; WALLEYE; GEOGRAPHICAL DISTRIBUTION; MOVEMENT AND MIGRATIONS;).

750. Eddy, S., and T. Surber. 1960. Northern fishes with special reference to the upper Mississippi valley. Charles T. Banford Co., Newton Centre, Mass. 276 pp. (SAUGER; WALLEYE; INTRODUCTIONS; LIFE HISTORY; PROPAGATION;).

751. Eddy, S., and J. C. Underhill. 1974. Northern fishes. Univ. Minn. Press, Minneapolis, Minn, USA. 414 pp. (SAUGER; WALLEYE; ECOLOGY; TAXONOMY;).

752. Edminster, J. O. 1940. Report of Ohio Lake Erie commercial fisheries, 1939 season. Ohio Div. Conserv., 10 pp. (SAUGER; WALLEYE; COMMERCIAL FISHERIES;).

753. Edminster, J. O., and J. W. Gray. 1948. The toxicity thresholds for three chlorides and three acids to the fry of whitefish *(Coregonus clupeaformis)* and yellow pike *(Stizostedion v. vitreum)*. Prog. Fish-Cult. 10:105-106. (WALLEYE; HABITAT DEGRADATION; PHYSIOLOGY;).

754. Edrington, C. J., L. B. Starnes, and P. A. Hackney. 1979. Suitablility of Cherokee Reservoir and the Upper Holston River for sauger and walleye. Tenn. Valley Auth. (Norris) NP. 1903789: 29 pp. (SAUGER; WALLEYE; IMPOUNDMENTS; INTRODUCTIONS; SPAWNING STUDIES;).

755. Edsall, T. A., and T. G. Yocom. 1972. Review of recent technical information concerning the adverse effects of once-through cooling in Lake Michigan. U.S. Fish Wildl. Serv. Bur. Sports Fish Wildl. Publ. 86 pp. (WALLEYE; MORTALITY;).

756. Edwards, G. A., and W. N. Howard. 1980. Little Waterhen River fish movements and walleye tagging study, 1971-1972. Man. Dept. Nat. Res., Manuscript Rep. No. 80-8: 53 pp. (SAUGER; WALLEYE; COMMUNITY DYNAMICS; MARKING; MOVEMENT AND MIGRATIONS; POPULATION STUDIES;).

757. Edwards, P. 1978. English River creel census Sioux Lookout District 1978. Ont. Min. Nat. Res., Rep. 14 pp. (WALLEYE; CREEL CENSUS;).

758. Edwards, P., P. Ryan, and N. Ward. 1980. Further evaluation of the 1978 West Patricia creel census. Ont. Min. Nat. Res., Fish. Tech. Rep. No. 14, West Patricia Land Use Plan 36 pp. (SAUGER; WALLEYE; COMMUNITY DYNAMICS; CREEL CENSUS; PRODUCTIVITY; SOCIO-ECONOMICS OF FISHERIES;).

759. Eigenmann, C. H. 1895. Results of explorations in Western Canada and in Northwestern United States. U.S. Fish Comm., Bull. 14:101-132. (SAUGER; WALLEYE; GEOGRAPHICAL DISTRIBUTION;).

760. Eigenmann, C. H. 1896. First report of the biological station. Part II. The inhabitants of Turkey Lake. Fishes. Proc. Ind. Acad. Sci., 1895: 252-257. (SAUGER; WALLEYE; GEOGRAPHICAL DISTRIBUTION;).

761. Eigenmann, C. H., and C. H. Beeson. 1894. The fishes of Indiana. Proc. Ind. Acad. Sci., 1983: 76-108. (SAUGER; WALLEYE; GEOGRAPHICAL DISTRIBUTION;).

762. Eiler, P. D. 1987. Development of techniques for controlling the sex ratio of pond-reared walleye. Minn. Dept. Nat. Res., Fed. Aid Fish Wildl. Restor. Proj. F-26-R-18, Study No. 139: 8 pp. (WALLEYE; PROPAGATION; SPAWNING STUDIES;).

763. Einhouse, D. W. 1981. Summer-fall movements, habitat utilization, diel activity and feeding behavior of walleyes in Chautauqua Lake, New York. M.S. Thesis, State Univ. Coll., Fredonia, N.Y. 107 pp. (WALLEYE; BEHAVIOR; FOOD STUDIES; MOVEMENT AND MIGRATIONS; SPAWNING STUDIES;).

764. Einhouse, D. W., and J. Winter. 1981. Movement patterns and habitat utilization of radio-tagged walleye in Chautauqua Lake, New York. Underwat. Telem. Newsl. 11:1-3. (WALLEYE; BEHAVIOR; MOVEMENT AND MIGRATIONS;).

765. Eipper, A. W., and J. L. Forney. 1965. Evolution of partial fin clips for marking largemouth bass (Micropterus salmoides), walleyes (Stizostedion vitreum), and rainbow trout (Salmo gairdneri). N.Y. Fish Game J. 12:233-240. (WALLEYE; MARKING;).

766. Eklund, G. R. 1979. Summer creel census White Otter Lake 1978. Ont. Min. Nat. Res., Rep. 3 pp. (WALLEYE; CREEL CENSUS;).

767. Eley, R. L., N. E. Carter, and T. C. Dorris. 1967. Physicochemical limnology and related fish distribution of Keystone Reservoir. Pages 337-357 in Reservoir fishery resources symposium, Reservoir Comm., Southern Div., Am. Fish. Soc. (WALLEYE; ECOLOGY; IMPOUNDMENTS;).

768. Elkins, W. A. 1937. A fish yield study for certain lakes in the Chequamegon National Forest. Trans. Am. Fish. Soc. 66:306-312. (WALLEYE; CREEL CENSUS;).

769. Elliot, D. 1975. Summer creel census program Lake St. Francis-1975. Ont. Min. Nat. Res., Rep. 9 pp. (WALLEYE; CREEL CENSUS;).

770. Elliot, D. B. 1976. Ottawa and Nation Rivers creel census report winter — 1976. Ont. Min. Nat. Res., Rep. 14 pp. (WALLEYE; CREEL CENSUS;).

771. Elliot, R. E., and J. R. Brisbane. 1982. A summary of a winter creel census Whitefish and Clearwater Bays, Lake of the Woods 1982. Ont. Min. Nat Res., Rep. 34 pp. (WALLEYE; CREEL CENSUS;).

772. Ellis, D. V., and M. A. Giles. 1965. The spawning behavior of walleye (Stizostedion vitreum). Trans. Am. Fish. Soc. 94:358-362. (WALLEYE; BEHAVIOR; SPAWNING STUDIES;).

773. Ellis, J. M., G. B. Farabee, and J. B. Reynolds. 1979. Fish communities in three successional stages of side channels on the upper Mississippi River. Trans. Mo. Acad. Sci. 13:5-20. (SAUGER; WALLEYE; COMMUNITY DYNAMICS; ECOLOGY; HABITAT DEGRADATION;).

774. Ellis, M. M. 1914. Fishes of Colorado. Univ. Colo. Study 11: 136 pp. (WALLEYE; ECOLOGY; TAXONOMY;).

775. Elrod, J. H., and T. J. Hassler. 1969. Estimates of some vital statistics of northern pike, walleye, and sauger populations in Lake Sharpe, South Dakota. U.S. Fish Wildl. Serv., Tech. Paper No. 30:1-17. (SAUGER; WALLEYE; AGE AND GROWTH; IMPOUNDMENTS; MORTALITY; POPULATION STUDIES; SPAWNING STUDIES;).

776. Elrod, J. H., F. C. June, and L. G. Beckman. 1987. Biology of the walleye in Lake Sharp, South Dakota 1964-1975. U.S. Fish Wildl. Serv., Fish Wildl. Tech. Rep. 8:46-60. (WALLEYE; IMPOUNDMENTS; LIFE HISTORY;).

777. Elser, A. A. 1980. Southeastern Montana fisheries investigations-fish management surveys. Mont. Dept. Fish. Wildl. Parks, Fed. Aid Fish Wildl. Restor. Proj. F-30-R-16: 25 pp. (SAUGER; IMPOUNDMENTS; MARKING; MOVEMENT AND MIGRATIONS; SAMPLING METHODS;).

778. Elser, H. J. 1950. The common fishes of Maryland, and how to tell them apart. Md. Board Nat. Res., Dept. Research Educ., Publ. 88:45. (WALLEYE; TAXONOMY;).

779. Elser, H. J. 1960. Creel census results on the Northeast River, Maryland, 1958. Chesapeake Sci. 1:41-47. (WALLEYE; CREEL CENSUS;).

780. Elsey, C. A. 1959. The effects of distributing eyed whitefish (Coregonus clupeaformis) and yellow pike (Stizostedion vitreum) eggs on the commercial fisheries of Rainy Lake, Ontario. Ont. Dept. Lands Forests., Fish Wildl. Manage. Rep. No. 48:54-58. (WALLEYE; COMMERCIAL FISHERIES; STOCKING;).

781. Elsey, C. A., and B. Caldwell. 1964. A fishery survey of Lac La Croix, 1963. Minn. Dept. Conserv., Invest. Rep. No. 281: 10 pp. (WALLEYE; AGE AND GROWTH; POPULATION STUDIES;).

782. Elsey, C. A., and R. T. Thomson. 1977. Exploitation of walleye (Stizostedion vitreum vitreum) in Lac des Mille Lacs, northern Ontario, by commercial and sport fisheries, 1958-75. J. Fish. Research Board Can. 34:1769-1773. (WALLEYE; COMMERCIAL FISHERIES; CREEL CENSUS; FISHING GEAR;).

783. Elsey, C. A., R. E. Whitfield, and W. J. Christie. 1962. The present status of management and research on yellow pike (Stizostedion vitreum) in Ontario. Ont. Dept. Lands Forest., Fish Wildl. Branch 26 pp. (WALLEYE; COMMUNITY DYNAMICS; ECOLOGY; SPAWNING STUDIES;).

784. Elston, R., L. Corazza, and J. G. Nickum. 1981. Morphology and development of the olfactory organ in larval walleye, Stizostedion vitreum. Copeia 1981(4):890-893. (WALLEYE; EMBRYOLOGY; MORPHOLOGY;).

785. Embody, G. C. 1927. A biological survey of the Genesee River systems. I. Stocking policy for the Genesee River system. N.Y. Conserv. Dept., Suppl. 16th Annu. Rep. pp. 12-28, Append. 9-13: 88-98. (WALLEYE; ECOLOGY; IMPOUNDMENTS; INTRODUCTIONS; STOCKING;).

786. Embody, G. C. 1928. A biological survey of the Oswego River system. I. Stocking policy for the streams, smaller lakes and ponds of the Oswego watershed. N.Y. Conserv. Dept., Suppl. 17th Annu. Rep. pp. 17-39, Append. 3-11: 209-242. (WALLEYE; STOCKING;).

787. Embody, G. C. 1929. A biological survey of the Erie-Niagara system. I. Stocking policy for the streams, lakes and ponds of the Erie-Niagara watershed, exclusive of Lake Erie. N.Y. Conserv. Dept., Suppl. 18th Annu. Rep. pp. 19-39, Append. 3: 235-244. (WALLEYE; STOCKING;).

788. Erickson, C. M. 1979. Age differences among three hard tissue structures observed in fish populations experiencing various levels of exploitation. Man. Dept. Nat. Res., Manuscript Rep. No. 79-77: 31 pp. (SAUGER; WALLEYE; AGE AND GROWTH; POPULATION STUDIES;).

789. Erickson, C. M. 1982. The use of otolith section for determining ages and back calculating lengths of walleyes, Stizostedion vitreum. Man. Dept. Nat. Res. Manuscript Rep. No. 82-9: 31 pp. (WALLEYE; AGE AND GROWTH;).

790. Erickson, C. M. 1983. Age determination of Manitoban walleyes using otoliths, dorsal

spines, and scales. N. Am. J. Fish. Manage. 3:176-181. (WALLEYE; AGE AND GROWTH;).

791. Erickson, C. M., and W. Lysack. 1981. Seasonal and population growth parameters of southern Lake Winnipeg saugers. Man. Dept. Nat. Res., Manuscript Rep. No. 81-4: 56 pp. (SAUGER; AGE AND GROWTH; FISHING GEAR; FOOD STUDIES; POPULATION STUDIES;).

792. Erickson, J. 1965. Annual measurement of fish population levels in selected lakes. Ohio Dept. Nat. Res., Fed. Aid Fish Wildl. Restor. Proj. F-29-R-4, Job No. 2: 6 pp. (WALLEYE; IMPOUNDMENTS; POPULATION STUDIES; SAMPLING METHODS;).

793. Erickson, J. 1970. Evaluation of walleye spawning areas and reproductive success. Ohio Dept. Nat. Res., Fed. Aid Fish Wildl. Restor. Proj. F-29-R-9, Job No. 9: 21 pp. (WALLEYE; ECOLOGY; FOOD STUDIES; IMPOUNDMENTS; SPAWNING STUDIES;).

794. Erickson, J. 1972. Evaluation of environmental factors of Ohio reservoirs in relation to the success of walleye stocking. Ohio Dept. Nat. Res., Fed. Aid Fish Wildl. Restor. Proj. F-29-R-11, Job No. 9: 37 pp. (WALLEYE; CREEL CENSUS; IMPOUNDMENTS; POPULATION STUDIES; STOCKING; WATER LEVELS;).

795. Erickson, J., and F. Stevenson. 1967. An evaluation of Ohio's walleye stocking program. Ohio Dept. Nat. Res., Fed. Aid Fish Wildl. Restor. Proj. F-29-R-6, Job No. 9: 7 pp. (WALLEYE; STOCKING;).

796. Erickson, J., and F. Stevenson. 1967. Management consultation and experimental design. Ohio Dept. Nat. Res., Fed. Aid Fish Wildl. Restor. Proj. F-29-R-6, Job No. 12: 7 pp. (WALLEYE; AGE AND GROWTH; PATHOLOGY; PROPAGATION; SPAWNING STUDIES;).

797. Erkkila, L. F., B. R. Smith, and A. L. McClain. 1956. Sea lamprey control on the Great Lakes 1953 and 1954. U. S. Fish Wildl. Serv., Spec. Sci. Rep.-Fish. 175: 27 pp. (WALLEYE; SAMPLING METHODS;).

798. Ernst, D., and T. C. Osborn. 1980. The summer sportfishery in Voyageurs National Park and surrounding waters for 1977 and 1978.

Minn. Dept. Nat. Res., Invest. Rep. No. 370: 27 pp. (WALLEYE; AGE AND GROWTH; CREEL CENSUS;).

799. Eschmeyer, P. H. 1950. The life history of the walleye *(Stizostedion vitreum)* in Michigan. Mich. Dept. Conserv., Inst. Fish. Research, Bull. No. 3: 99 pp. (WALLEYE; AGE AND GROWTH; BEHAVIOR; ECOLOGY; FOOD STUDIES; LIFE HISTORY; MOVEMENT AND MIGRATIONS; SPAWNING STUDIES;).

800. Eschmeyer, P. H., and R. Crowe. 1955. Movement and recovery of tagged walleyes (Stizostedion vitreum) in Michigan, 1929-1953. Mich. Inst. Fish. Research, Misc. Publ. No. 8: 32 pp. (WALLEYE; AGE AND GROWTH; MARKING; MOVEMENT AND MIGRATIONS; POPULATION STUDIES;).

801. Eschmeyer, R. W. 1935. Analysis of the game fish catch in a Michigan lake. Trans. Am. Fish. Soc. 65:207-223. (WALLEYE; CREEL CENSUS;).

802. Eschmeyer, R. W. 1937. A second season of creel census on Fife Lake. Trans. Am. Fish. Soc. 66:324-334. (WALLEYE; CREEL CENSUS;).

803. Eschmeyer, R. W. 1939. Summary of a four-year creel census of Fife Lake, Michigan. Trans. Am. Fish. Soc. 68:354-358. (WALLEYE; CREEL CENSUS;).

804. Eschmeyer, R. W. 1940. Growth of fishes in Norris Lake, Tennessee. J. Tenn. Acad. Sci. 15:329-341. (SAUGER; WALLEYE; AGE AND GROWTH;).

805. Eschmeyer, R. W. 1942. The catch, abundance, and migration of fishes in Norris Reservoir, Tennessee, 1940. J. Tenn. Acad. Sci. 17:90-115. (SAUGER; WALLEYE; CREEL CENSUS; IMPOUNDMENTS; MARKING; MOVEMENTS AND MIGRATIONS; POPULATION STUDIES;).

806. Eschmeyer, R. W. 1943. Fish populations of a small Norris Reservoir bay. J. Tenn Acad. Sci. 18:47-48. (SAUGER; GEOGRAPHICAL DISTRIBUTION;).

807. Eschmeyer, R. W. 1944. Norris Lake fishing, 1944. Tenn. Dept. Conserv. 18 pp. (SAUGER; WALLEYE; SAMPLING METHODS;).

808. Eschmeyer, R. W. 1944. Fish migration into the Clinch River below Norris Dam, Tennessee. J. Tenn. Acad. Sci. 19:31-41. (SAUGER; MOVEMENT AND MIGRATIONS;).

809. Eschmeyer, R. W. 1945. The Norris Lake fishing experiment. Tenn. Dept. Conserv. 31 pp. (SAUGER; WALLEYE; CREEL CENSUS; ECOLOGY;).

810. Eschmeyer, R. W. 1950. Fish and fishing in TVA impoundments. Tenn. Dept. Conserv. 28 pp. (SAUGER; WALLEYE; AGE AND GROWTH; CREEL CENSUS; ECOLOGY; MARKING; MOVEMENTS AND MIGRATIONS;).

811. Eschmeyer, R. W., and O. F. Haslbauer. 1946. Utilization of the sauger (Stizostedion canadense) crop in Norris Reservoir, Tennessee. J. Tenn. Acad. Sci. 21:72-75. (SAUGER; WALLEYE; SAMPLING METHODS;).

812. Eschmeyer, R. W., and A. M. Jones. 1941. The growth of game fishes in Norris Reservoir during the first five years of impoundment. Trans. 6th N. Am. Wildl. Conf. 6:222-240. (SAUGER; WALLEYE; AGE AND GROWTH; MARKING;).

813. Eschmeyer, R. W., and D. E. Manges. 1945. Effect of a year-round open season on fishing in Norris Reservoir. J. Tenn. Acad. Sci. 20:20-34. (SAUGER; WALLEYE; CREEL CENSUS;).

814. Eschmeyer, R. W., and D. E. Manges. 1945. Fish migrations into the Norris Dam tailwater in 1943. J. Tenn. Acad. Sci. 20:92-97. (SAUGER; WALLEYE; MOVEMENT AND MIGRATIONS;).

815. Eschmeyer, R. W., D. E. Manges, and O. F. Haslbauer. 1946. Spring fishing on several TVA storage reservoir, 1945. J. Tenn. Acad. Sci. 21:78-88. (SAUGER; WALLEYE; CREEL CENSUS;).

816. Eschmeyer, R. W., D. E. Manges, and O. F. Haslbauer. 1947. Trends in fishing on TVA storage waters. J. Tenn. Acad Sci. 22:45-56. (SAUGER; WALLEYE; CREEL CENSUS;).

817. Eschmeyer, R. W., and C. G. Smith. 1943. Fish spawning below Norris Dam. J. Tenn. Acad. Sci. 18:4-5. (SAUGER; SPAWNING STUDIES;).

818. Eschmeyer, R. W., R. H. Stroud, and A. M. Jones. 1944. Studies of the fish populations on the shoal area of a TVA main stream reservoir. J. Tenn. Acad. Sci. 19:70-122. (SAUGER; AGE AND GROWTH; SAMPLING METHODS;).

819. Eschmeyer, R. W., and C. M. Tarzwell. 1941. An analysis of fishing in the TVA impoundments during 1939. J. Wildl. Manage. 5:15-41. (SAUGER; WALLEYE; AGE AND GROWTH; COMMERCIAL FISHERIES; CREEL CENSUS; POPULATION STUDIES;).

820. Eshenroder, R. L. 1977. Effects of intensified fishing, species changes, and spring water temperature on yellow perch (Perca flavescens) in Saginaw Bay. J. Fish. Research Board Can. 34:1830-1838. (WALLEYE; COMMUNITY DYNAMICS;).

821. Essex, H. E. 1928. On the life history of Bothriocephalus cuspidatus Cooper, 1917. Trans. Am. Microscop. Soc. 47:348-355. (WALLEYE; PATHOLOGY;).

822. Essex, Hiram E., and G. W. Hunter, III. 1926. A biological survey of fish parasites from the central states. Trans. Ill. Acad. Sci. 19:151-181. (WALLEYE; PATHOLOGY;).

823. Evans, D. O., and D. H. Loftus. 1987. Colonization of inland lakes in the Great Lakes region by rainbow smelt (Osmerus mordex): their freshwater niche and effects on indigenous fishes. Can. J. Fish. Aquat. Sci. 44(Suppl. 2):249-266. (WALLEYE; COMMUNITY DYNAMICS; FOOD STUDIES;).

824. Everhart, W. H. 1966. Fishes of Maine. Maine Dept. Inland Fish. Game. 96 pp. (WALLEYE; LIFE HISTORY;).

825. Evermann, B. W. 1902. List of species of fish known to occur in the Great Lakes or their connecting waters. U.S. Fish Comm.. Bull. 21:95-96. (SAUGER; WALLEYE; GEOGRAPHICAL DISTRIBUTION;).

826. Evermann, B. W. 1918. The fishes of Kentucky and Tennessee: a distributional catalogue of the known species. U. S. Bur. Fish.. Bull. 35:295-368. (SAUGER; WALLEYE; GEOGRAPHICAL DISTRIBUTION; TAXONOMY;).

827. Evermann, B. W., and C. H. Bollman. 1886. Notes on a collection of fishes from the Monogahela River. N.Y. Acad. Sci. 3:335-340. (WALLEYE; GEOGRAPHICAL DISTRIBUTION;).

828. Evermann, B. W., and H. W. Clark. 1920. Lake Maxinkuckee, a physical and biological survey. The fishes. Ind. Dept. Conserv., Publ. 7:238-452. (WALLEYE; LIFE HISTORY; SPAWNING STUDIES; TAXONOMY;).

829. Evermann, B. W., and E. L. Goldsborrugh. 1907. A check-list of the freshwater fishes of Canada. Proc. Bio. Soc. Wash. 20:89-120. (SAUGER; WALLEYE; GEOGRAPHICAL DISTRIBUTION;).

830. Evermann, B. W., and S. F. Hildebrand. 1916. Notes on the fishes of east Tennessee. U.S. Bur. Fish., Bull. 34:433-451. (SAUGER; WALLEYE; GEOGRAPHICAL DISTRIBUTION;).

831. Evermann, B. W., and W. C. Kendall. 1902. Notes on the fishes of Lake Ontario. U.S. Comm. Fish Fish., Annu. Rep. (1901):209-216. (SAUGER; WALLEYE; GEOGRAPHICAL DISTRIBUTION;).

832. Evermann, B. W., and W. C. Kendall. 1902. An annotated list of the fishes known to occur in Lake Champlain and its tributary waters. U.S. Comm. Fish Fish., 6th. Annu. Rep. (1901):217-225. (SAUGER; WALLEYE; GEOGRAPHICAL DISTRIBUTION;).

833. Evermann, B. W., and W. C. Kendall. 1902. An annotated list of the fishes known to occur in the St. Lawrence River. U.S. Comm. Fish Fish., Annu. Rep. (1901):227-240. (SAUGER; WALLEYE; GEOGRAPHICAL DISTRIBUTION;).

834. Evermann, B. W., and H. B. Latimer. 1910. The fishes of the Lake of the Woods and connecting waters. Proc. U. S. Nat. Mus. 39:121-136. (SAUGER; WALLEYE; COMMERCIAL FISHERIES;).

835. Ewers, L. A. 1933. Summary report of Crustacea used as food by the fishes of the western end of Lake Erie. Trans. Am. Fish Soc. 63:379-390. (SAUGER; WALLEYE; FOOD STUDIES;).

836. Faber, D. J. 1963. Larval fish from the pelagial region of two Wisconsin lakes. Ph.D. Thesis, Univ. Wis., Madison, Wis. 122 pp. (WALL-EYE; MORPHOLOGY; SAMPLING METHODS;).

837. Faber, D. J. 1967. Limnetic larval fish in northern Wisconsin lakes. J. Fish. Research Board Can. 24:927-937. (WALLEYE; BEHAVIOR; GEOGRAPHICAL DISTRIBUTION; SAMPLING METHODS;).

838. Faber, D. J. 1968. A net for catching limnetic fry. Trans. Am. Fish. Soc. 97:61-63. (WALLEYE; SAMPLING METHODS;).

839. Fago, D. 1982. Distribution and relative abundance of fishes in Wisconsin. I. Greater Rock River basin. Wis. Dept. Nat. Res., Tech. Bull. No. 136: 126 pp. (WALLEYE; GEOGRAPHICAL DISTRIBUTION;).

840. Fago, D. 1983. Distribution and relative abundance of fishes in Wisconsin. II. Black, Trempealeau, and Buffalo river basins. Wis. Dept. Nat. Res., Tech. Bull. No. 140: 120 pp. (SAUGER; WALLEYE; GEOGRAPHICAL DISTRIBUTION;).

841. Fago, D. 1984. Distribution and relative abundance of fishes in Wisconsin. III. Red Cedar River basin. Wis. Dept. Nat. Res., Tech. Bull. No. 143: 69 pp. (SAUGER; WALLEYE; GEOGRAPHICAL DISTRIBUTION;).

842. Fago, D. 1984. Distribution and relative abundance of fishes in Wisconsin. IV. Root, Milwaukee, Des Plaines, and Fox river basins. Wis. Dept. Nat. Res., Tech. Bull. No. 147: 128 pp. (WALLEYE; GEOGRAPHICAL DISTRIBUTION;).

843. Fago, D. 1985. Distribution and relative abundance of fishes in Wisconsin. V. Grant & Platte, Coon & Bad Axe, and La Crosse river basins. Wis. Dept. Nat. Res., Tech. Bull. No. 152: 112 pp. (SAUGER; WALLEYE; GEOGRAPHICAL DISTRIBUTION;).

844. Fago, D. 1985. Distribution and relative abundance of fishes in Wisconsin. VI. Sheboygan, Manitowoc, and Twin River basins. Wis. Dept. Nat. Res., Tech. Bull. No. 155: 100 pp. (WALLEYE; GEOGRAPHICAL DISTRIBUTION;).

845. Fago, D. 1986. Distribution and relative abundance of fishes in Wisconsin. VII. St. Croix River Basin. Wis. Dept. Nat. Res., Tech. Bull. No. 159: 112 pp. (SAUGER; WALL-

EYE; GEOGRAPHICAL DISTRIBU-
TION;).

846. Faigenbaum, H. M. 1934. A biological survey
of the Raquette watershed. V. Chemical investigation of the Raquette watershed. N.Y.
Conserv. Dept., Suppl. 23rd Annu. Rep.
(1933):164-208. (WALLEYE; ECOLOGY;).

847. Faigenbaum, H. M. 1936. A biological survey
of the Delaware and Susquehanna watersheds. V. Chemical investigation of the Susquehanna and Delaware watersheds. N.Y.
Conserv. Dept., Suppl. 25th Annu. Rep.
(1935):140-194. (WALLEYE; ECOLOGY;
IMPOUNDMENTS;).

848. Faigenbaum, H. M. 1938. A biological survey
of the Allegheny and Chemung watersheds.
V. Chemical investigation on the Allegheny
and Chemung watersheds. N.Y. Conserv.
Dept., Suppl. 27th Annu. Rep. (1937):113-
161. (WALLEYE; ECOLOGY;).

849. Faigenbaum, H. M. 1940. A biological survey
of the Lake Ontario watershed. V. Chemical
investigation of the Lake Ontario watershed. N.Y. Conserv. Dept., Suppl. 29th
Annu. Rep. (1939):117-146. (WALLEYE;
ECOLOGY; IMPOUNDMENTS;).

850. Faler, M. P. 1987. First year growth and sur-
vival of walleyes in power plant Evapora-
tion and Holding Reservoirs. M.S. Thesis,
S.D. State Univ., Brookings, S.D. 79 pp.
(WALLEYE; AGE AND GROWTH; COM-
MUNITY DYNAMICS; IMPOUND-
MENTS; MORTALITY; POPULATION
STUDIES; PRODUCTIVITY; STOCK-
ING;).

851. Falk, M. R., and L. W. Dahlke. 1975. Creel and
biological data from streams along the
south shore of Great Slave Lake, 1971-74.
Can. Dept. Environ. Fish. and Marine Serv.,
Data Rep. Series No.:CEN/D-75-8 87 pp.
(WALLEYE; CREEL CENSUS; MOVE-
MENTS AND MIGRATIONS;).

852. Falk, M. R., D. V. Gillman, and C. J. Read.
1980. Data on the Walleye, (Stizostedion vi-
treum Mitchill) and other fish species from
Mosquito Creek, Northwest Territories,
1973-78. Can. Data Rep. Fish. Aquat. Sci.
No. 186: 44 pp. (WALLEYE; AGE AND
GROWTH; CREEL CENSUS; MOVE-
MENT AND MIGRATIONS; POPULA-
TION STUDIES; SPAWNING STUD-
IES;).

853. Farabee, G. B. 1986. Fish species associated
with reverted and natural main channel border habitats in Pool 24 of the upper Mississippi River. N. Am. J. Fish. Manage. 6:504-
508. (SAUGER; WALLEYE; COM-
MUNITY DYNAMICS; POPULATION
STUDIES;).

854. Farell, M. A. 1933. A biological survey of the
Upper Hudson watershed. VI. Pollution
studies of the Upper Hudson watershed.
N.Y. Conserv. Dept., Suppl. 22nd Annu.
Rep. (1932):208-215. (WALLEYE; ECOL-
OGY; HABITAT DEGRADATION;).

855. Farmer, G. J., and F. W. H. Beamish. 1973. Sea
Lamprey (Petromyzon marinus) predation
on freshwater teleosts. J. Fish. Research
Board Can. 30:601-605. (WALLEYE; COM-
MUNITY DYNAMICS;).

856. Fast, A. W. 1966. Fisheries management of El
Capitan Reservoir, San Diego County, Cali-
fornia, 1960-1962. Calf. Dept. Fish Game,
Inland Fish. Admin. Rep. No. 66-5: 29 pp.
(WALLEYE; IMPOUNDMENTS; INTRO-
DUCTIONS; STOCKING;).

857. Fatora, J. R., and R. H. England. 1982. Evalu-
ation of predatory fish population of Lake
Burton. Ga. Game Fish Div., Fed. Aid Fish
Wildl. Restor. Proj. F-25-R-8: 67 pp. (WALL-
EYE; AGE AND GROWTH; CREEL CEN-
SUS; FOOD STUDIES; IMPOUND-
MENTS; INTRODUCTIONS; POPULA-
TION STUDIES; STOCKING;).

858. Fedoruk, A. N. 1966. Feeding relationship of
walleye and smallmouth bass. J. Fish. Research Board Can. 23:941-943. (WALLEYE;
COMMUNITY DYNAMICS; FOOD
STUDIES; MORTALITY;).

859. Fedoruk, A. N. 1969. Checklist of and key to
the freshwater fishes of Manitoba (Prelimi-
nary). Man. Dept. Mines Nat. Res., Can.
Land Inventory Proj., Rep. 6: 98 pp.
(SAUGER; WALLEYE; MORPHOLOGY;
TAXONOMY;).

860. Fehringer, N. V., S. M. Walters, R. J. Ayers, R.
J. Kozora, J. D. Ogger, and L. F. Schneider.
1985. A survey of 2,3,7,8-TCDD residue in
fish from the Great Lakes and selected
Michigan rivers. Chemosphere 14:909-912.
(WALLEYE; TOXICANTS;).

861. Feiler, E. L. 1980. An electrofishing survey of a portion of Pool 2, Mississippi River from Lock and Dam No. 2 (R.M. 815) to Upper Gray Cloud Island (R.M. 827). Minn. Dept. Nat. Res., Fish Manage. Rep. No. 21: 31 pp. (SAUGER; WALLEYE; POPULATION STUDIES;).

862. Feldmann, R. M. 1963. Distribution of fish in the Forest River of North Dakota. Proc. N. D. Acad. Sci. 17:11-19. (WALLEYE; GEOGRAPHICAL DISTRIBUTION;).

863. Ferguson, R. G. 1955. Lake Erie commercial fisheries: a preliminary appraisal. Ont. Dept. Lands Forest., Tech. Ser. 20 pp. (SAUGER; WALLEYE; COMMERCIAL FISHERIES;).

864. Ferguson, R. G. 1957. Fish tagging studies in Lakes Erie, St. Clair and Huron. Ont. Dept. Lands Forest., Prel. Rep. 12 pp. (WALLEYE; MOVEMENT AND MIGRATIONS; POPULATION STUDIES;).

865. Ferguson, R. G. 1958. The preferred temperature of fish and their midsummer distribution in temperate lakes and streams. J. Fish Research Board Can. 15:607-624. (SAUGER; WALLEYE; BEHAVIOR; GEOGRAPHICAL DISTRIBUTION; PHYSIOLOGY;).

866. Ferguson, R. G., and A. J. Derksen. 1971. Migrations of adult and juvenile walleyes *(Stizostedion vitreum vitreum)* in southern Lake Huron, Lake St. Clair, Lake Erie, and connecting waters. J. Fish. Research Board Can. 28:1133-1142. (WALLEYE; MARKING; MOVEMENT AND MIGRATIONS; SPAWNING STUDIES;).

867. Fiedler, R. H. 1928. Trade in fresh and frozen fishery products and related marketing considerations in greater St. Louis, Missouri. U.S. Bur. Fish., Annu. Rep. 1927 (Append. 6):485-514. (SAUGER; WALLEYE; COMMERCIAL FISHERIES;).

868. Fiedler, R. H. 1928. Trade in fresh and frozen fishery products and related marketing considerations in Atlanta, Georgia. U.S. Bur. Fish., Annu. Rep. 1928 (Append. 3):43-60. (WALLEYE; COMMERCIAL FISHERIES;).

869. Fiedler, R. H., J. R. Manning, and F. F. Johnson. 1934. Fishery industries of the United States 1933. U.S. Bur. Fish., Annu. Rep. 1934 (Append.1):1-235. (SAUGER; WALLEYE; COMMERCIAL FISHERIES;).

870. Fielder, R. H., and J. H. Matthews. 1926. Wholesale trade in fresh and frozen fishery products and related marketing considerations in New York city. U.S. Bur. Fish., Annu. Rep. 1925 (Append. 6):183-217. (SAUGER; WALLEYE; COMMERCIAL FISHERIES;).

871. Fierstine, H. L., J. L. Geis, and S. P. Gustafson. 1978. A statistical comparison of incomplete and complete angler trip catch rates. Minn. Dept. Nat. Res., Invest. Rep. No. 360: 8 pp. (SAUGER; WALLEYE; CREEL CENSUS;).

872. Fillmore, R. 1977. Nagagami Lake creel census report. Ont. Min. Nat. Res., Rep. 26 pp. (WALLEYE; CREEL CENSUS;).

873. Fillmore, R. 1978. Pickerel fishery Nagagami Lake. Ont. Min. Nat. Res., Rep. 9 pp. (WALLEYE; CREEL CENSUS;).

874. Fimreite, N., W. N. Holsworth, J. A. Keith, P. A. Pearce, and I. M. Gruchy. 1971. Mercury in fish and fish-eating birds near sites of industrial contamination in Canada. Can. Field Nat. July-Sept. 85:211-220. (WALLEYE; HABITAT DEGRADATION;).

875. Finnell, J. C., R. M. Jenkins, and G. E. Hall. 1956. The fishery resources of the Little River system, McCurtain County, Oklahoma. Okla. Dept. Nat. Res., Fish. Research Lab., Rep. 55: 82 pp. (WALLEYE; IMPOUNDMENTS; STOCKING;).

876. Finnell, L. M. 1981. Warm water fisheries investigation, walleye studies. Colo. Div. Wildl., Fed. Aid Fish Wildl. Restor. Proj. F-34-R, Job No. 1: 16 pp. (WALLEYE; IMPOUNDMENTS; POPULATION STUDIES; STOCKING;).

877. Finnell, L. M., and R. Taliaferro. 1959. 1958 creel census. Colo. Dept. Game Fish. 21 pp. (WALLEYE; CREEL CENSUS; STOCKING;).

878. Finnell, L. M., and R. Taliaferro. 1961. 1960 creel census report. Colo. Dept. Game Fish. 18 pp. (WALLEYE; CREEL CENSUS; STOCKING;).

879. Fischthal, J. H. 1945. Parasites of northwest Wisconsin fishes. I. The 1944 survey. Trans.

Wis. Acad. Sci., Arts Letters 37:157-220. (WALLEYE; PATHOLOGY;).

880. Fischthal, J. H. 1949. Grubs in fishes. Wis. Conserv. Dept., Biol. Bull. 32: 8 pp. (WALLEYE; PATHOLOGY;).

881. Fischthal, J. H. 1950. Parasites of northwest Wisconsin fishes. II. The 1945 survey. Trans. Wis. Acad. Sci., Arts Letters 40:87-113. (WALLEYE; PATHOLOGY;).

882. Fischthal, J. H. 1952. Parasites of northwest Wisconsin fishes. III. The 1946 survey. Trans. Wis. Acad. Sci., Arts Letters 41:17-58. (WALLEYE; PATHOLOGY;).

883. Fischthal, J. H. 1953. Parasites of northwest Wisconsin fishes. IV. Summary and limnological relationships. Trans. Wis. Acad. Sci., Arts Letters 42:83-108. (WALLEYE; ECOLOGY; PATHOLOGY;).

884. Fish, M. P. 1929. Contributions to the early life histories of Lake Erie fishes. Buffalo Soc. Nat. Sci. 14(3):136-187. (SAUGER; MORPHOLOGY; TAXONOMY;).

885. Fish, M. P. 1929. A biological survey of the Erie-Niagara system. II. A preliminary report on the joint survey of Lake Erie. 6. Contributions to the early life histories of Lake Erie fishes. N.Y. Conserv. Dept., Suppl. 18th Annu. Rep. (1928):76-95. (SAUGER; MORPHOLOGY; TAXONOMY;).

886. Fish, M. P. 1932. Contributions to the early life histories of sixty-two species of fishes from Lake Erie and its tributary waters. U.S. Bur. Fish., Bull. 47:293-398. (SAUGER; WALLEYE; MORPHOLOGY; TAXONOMY;).

887. Fisher, H. J. 1962. Some fishes of the lower Missouri River. Am. Midl. Nat. 68:424-429. (SAUGER; WALLEYE; IMPOUNDMENTS; SAMPLING METHODS;).

888. Fish Nutrition Laboratory. 1978. Nutrition of walleye: experiments at White Lake Fish Culture Station. Pages 179-186 in Aquaculture with emphasis on fish nutrition and diet formulation. 1977 annual report of the Fish Nutrition Laboratory, Univ. Guelph, Guelph, Ont. (WALLEYE; PROPAGATION;).

889. Fitz, R. B. 1968. Fish habitat and population changes resulting from impoundment of Clinch River by Melton Hill Dam. J. Tenn. Acad. Sci. 43:7-15. (SAUGER; WALLEYE; AGE AND GROWTH; ECOLOGY; IMPOUNDMENTS;).

890. Fitz, R. B., and J. A. Holbrook, II. 1978. Sauger and walleye in Norris Reservoir, Tennessee. Pages 82-88 in R.L. Kendall, ed. Selected coolwater fishes of North America. Am. Fish. Soc. Sp. Publ. No. 11, Washington, D.C. (SAUGER; WALLEYE; AGE AND GROWTH; BEHAVIOR; CREEL CENSUS; FISHING GEAR; FOOD STUDIES; IMPOUNDMENTS; POPULATION STUDIES;).

891. Flannagan, J. F., J. A. Mathias, and W. G. Franzin. 1984. Fisheries rehabilitation research — the Dauphlin Lake walleye rehabilitation pilot project. Fed. Dept. Fish. Oceans, Freshwater Inst., Man. 42 pp. (WALLEYE; AGE AND GROWTH; COMMERCIAL FISHERIES; COMMUNITY DYNAMICS; MORTALITY; POPULATION STUDIES; SOCIO-ECONOMICS OF FISHERIES; SPAWNING STUDIES; STOCKING;).

892. Fleener, G. G. 1965. Life history of the walleye in Current River, Missouri. Mo. Conserv. Comm., Fed. Aid Fish Wildl. Restor. Proj. F-1-R-14, Wk. Pl. 9, Job No. 4: 4 pp. (WALLEYE; CREEL CENSUS;).

893. Fleener, G. G. 1966. Life history of the walleye in Current River, Missouri. Mo. Conserv. Comm., Fed. Aid Fish Wildl. Restor. Proj. F-1-R-15, Wk. Pl. 9, Job No. 4: 9 pp. (WALLEYE; CREEL CENSUS;).

894. Fleener, G. G. 1967. Life history of the walleye in Current River, Missouri. Mo. Conserv. Comm., Fed. Aid Fish Wildl. Restor. Proj. F-1-R-16, Wk. Pl. No. 9, Job No. 4: 3 pp. (WALLEYE; LIFE HISTORY; SPAWNING STUDIES; STOCKING;).

895. Fleener, G. G. 1968. A quantitative creel census of the Current River. Mo. Conserv. Comm., Fed. Aid Fish Wildl. Restor. Proj. F-1-R-17, Wk. Pl. No. 9, Job No. 1: 11 pp. (WALLEYE; CREEL CENSUS; STOCKING;).

896. Fleener, G. G. 1968. A quantitative creel census of pool 26, Mississippi River. Mo. Conserv. Comm., Fed. Aid Fish Wildl. Restor. Proj. F-1-R-18, Wk. Pl. 22, Job No. 1: 38 pp.

(SAUGER; WALLEYE; AGE AND GROWTH; CREEL CENSUS;).

897. Fleener, G. G. 1969. A quantitative creel census of the Current River. Mo. Conserv. Comm., Fed. Aid Fish Wildl. Restor. Proj. F-1-R-18, Wk. Pl. No. 9, Job No. 1: 10 pp. (WALLEYE; CREEL CENSUS; STOCKING;).

898. Fleener, G. G. 1971. Harvest of fish from the Current River. Mo. Dept. Conserv., Fed. Aid Fish Wildl. Restor. Proj. F-1-R-20, Study S-10, Job No. 1: 10 pp. (WALLEYE; CREEL CENSUS; STOCKING;).

899. Fleming, R. 1973. 1973 Winter Fishing Survey on Lake Nipissing. Ont. Min. Nat. Res., Lake Nipissing Fish. Assess. Unit Rep. 26 pp. (WALLEYE; CREEL CENSUS;).

900. Fletcher, D. H. 1981. Warm water fishery investigations in Washington State 1981. Wash. State Game Dept., Fed. Aid Fish Wildl. Restor. Proj. F-71-R: 351 pp. (WALLEYE; AGE AND GROWTH; CREEL CENSUS; IMPOUNDMENTS; LIFE HISTORY;).

901. Fletcher, D. H. 1982. Warm water fishery investigations in Washington State. Washington State Game Dept., Fed. Aid Fish Wildl. Restor. Proj. F-71-R: 309 pp. (WALLEYE; CREEL CENSUS; PROPAGATION;).

902. Fletcher, D. H. 1987. Hooking mortality of walleyes captured in Porcupine Bay, Washington. N. Am. J. Fish. Manage. 7:594-596. (WALLEYE; MORTALITY; REGULATIONS;).

903. Fletcher, D. H. 1987. Columbia River walleye creel survey, March 29, 1986. Wash. State Dept. Game 7 pp. (WALLEYE; CREEL CENSUS;).

904. Fogle, N. E. 1961. Report of fisheries investigations during the third year of impoundment of Oahe Reservoir, South Dakota, 1960. S. D. Dept. Game, Fish Parks, Fed. Aid Fish Wildl. Restor. Proj. F-1-R-10, Jobs No. 9, 10, 11, & 12: 61 pp. (SAUGER; WALLEYE; AGE AND GROWTH; CREEL CENSUS; MARKING; MOVEMENT AND MIGRATIONS; SPAWNING STUDIES; WATER LEVELS;).

905. Fogle, N. E. 1961. Report of fisheries investigations during the second year of impound-ment of Oahe Reservoir, South Dakota, 1959. S. D. Dept. Game, Fish Parks, Fed. Aid Fish Wildl. Restor. Proj. F-1-R-9, Jobs No. 12, 13, 14: 55 pp. (SAUGER; WALLEYE; AGE AND GROWTH; CREEL CENSUS; MARKING; MOVEMENT AND MIGRATIONS; SPAWNING STUDIES; WATER LEVELS;).

906. Fogle, N. E. 1963. Report of fisheries investigations during the fourth year of impoundment of Oahe Reservoir, South Dakota, 1961. S. D. Dept. Game, Fish Parks, Fed. Aid Fish Wildl. Restor. Proj. F-1-R-11, Jobs No. 10, 11, 12: 36 pp. (SAUGER; WALLEYE; AGE AND GROWTH; CREEL CENSUS; MARKING; MOVEMENT AND MIGRATIONS; SPAWNING STUDIES; WATER LEVELS;).

907. Fogle, N. E. 1964. Summation of four years of creel census on Oahe tailwaters, July 1959 through June 1963. S. D. Dept. Game, Fish Parks, Fed. Aid Fish Wildl. Restor. Proj. F-1-R-3, Job No. 12-A: 20 pp. (SAUGER; WALLEYE; CREEL CENSUS; IMPOUNDMENTS; POPULATION STUDIES;).

908. Fogle, N. E. 1964. Estimation of reproductive success in Fort Randall Reservoir, 1963. S. D. Dept. Game, Fish Parks, Fed. Aid Fish Wildl. Restor. Proj. F-1-R-13, Job No. 29: 8 pp. (SAUGER; WALLEYE; IMPOUNDMENTS; POPULATION STUDIES;).

909. Foote, C. J., J. E. Donetz, and J. R. Brisbane. 1981. An examination of the fish communities of the eastern sector, Lake of the Woods, with special reference to walleye, northern pike and sauger. Lake of the Woods — Rainy Lake Fish. Assess. Unit Rep. 1981-3: 120 pp. (SAUGER; WALLEYE; AGE AND GROWTH; COMMUNITY DYNAMICS; CREEL CENSUS; ECOLOGY; FOOD STUDIES; POPULATION STUDIES; SPAWNING STUDIES;).

910. Forbes, S. A. 1878. The food of Illinois fishes. Ill. State Lab. Nat. Hist., Bull. 2 (5): 71-89. (SAUGER; WALLEYE; FOOD STUDIES;).

911. Forbes, S. A. 1888. Notes on the food of the fishes of the Mississippi Valley. Trans. Am. Fish. Soc. 17:37-59. (SAUGER; WALLEYE; COMMUNITY DYNAMICS; FOOD STUDIES;).

912. Forbes, S. A. 1888. On the food relations of fresh-water fishes: a summary and discussion. Ill. State Lab. Nat. Hist., Bull. 2 (8): 475-538. (SAUGER; WALLEYE; COMMUNITY DYNAMICS; FOOD STUDIES;).

913. Forbes, S. A. 1890. Preliminary report upon the invertebrate animals inhabiting Lake Geneva and Mendota, Wisconsin, with an account of the fish epidemic in Lake Mendota in 1884. U.S. Fish Comm., Bull. 8 (1888): 473-487. (WALLEYE; MORTALITY;).

914. Forbes, S. A. 1903. The food of fishes: Acanthopteri. Ill. State lab. Nat. Hist., Bull. 1 (3) (2nd edition): 19-70. (1st ed. published 1880, p. 18-65.) (SAUGER; WALLEYE; FOOD STUDIES; LIFE HISTORY;).

915. Forbes, S. A. 1909. On the general and interior distribution of Illinois fishes. Ill. State Lab. Nat. Hist., Bull. 8 (3): 381-437. (SAUGER; WALLEYE; ECOLOGY; GEOGRAPHICAL DISTRIBUTION;).

916. Forbes, S. A., and R. E. Richardson. 1913. Studies on the biology of the upper Illinois River. Ill. State Lab. Nat. Hist., Bull. 9 (10): 481-574. (WALLEYE; ECOLOGY; HABITAT DEGRADATION;).

917. Forbes, S. A., and R. E. Richardson. 1919. Some recent changes in Illinois River biology. Ill. Nat. Hist. Surv., Bull. 13 (6): 139-156. (WALLEYE; COMMERCIAL FISHERIES; HABITAT DEGRADATION;).

918. Forbes, S. A., and R. E. Richardson. 1920. The fishes of Illinois. Ill. Nat. Hist. Surv. 342 pp. (2nd edition). (SAUGER; WALLEYE; FOOD STUDIES; LIFE HISTORY; MORPHOLOGY; PROPAGATION; SPAWNING STUDIES; TAXONOMY;).

919. Forelle, F. 1857. On the classification of fishes. With particular reference to the fishes of Canada. Can. Nat. Geol. 1(43):275-283. (SAUGER; WALLEYE; TAXONOMY;).

920. Forney, J. L. 1955. Life history of the black bullhead, *Ameiurus melas* (Rafinesque), of Clear lake, Iowa. Iowa State Coll. J. Sci. 30 (1):145-162. (WALLEYE; FOOD STUDIES;).

921. Forney, J. L. 1961. Year-class distribution of walleyes collected by five types of gear. Trans. Am. Fish. Soc. 90:308-311. (WALLEYE; FISHING GEAR; POPULATION STUDIES; SPAWNING STUDIES;).

922. Forney, J. L. 1963. Distribution and movement of marked walleyes in Oneida Lake, New York. Trans Am. Fish. Soc. 92:47-52. (WALLEYE; MARKING; MOVEMENT AND MIGRATIONS; SAMPLING METHODS; SPAWNING STUDIES;).

923. Forney, J. L. 1965. Factors affecting growth and maturity in a walleye population. N.Y. Fish Game J. 12:217-232. (WALLEYE; AGE AND GROWTH; POPULATION STUDIES; SPAWNING STUDIES;).

924. Forney, J. L. 1966. Factors affecting first-year growth of walleye in Oneida Lake, New York. N.Y. Fish Game J. 13:146-167. (WALLEYE; AGE AND GROWTH; ECOLOGY; FOOD STUDIES;).

925. Forney, J. L. 1967. Estimates of biomass and mortality rates in a walleye population. N.Y. Fish Game J. 14:176-192. (WALLEYE; AGE AND GROWTH; MORTALITY; POPULATION STUDIES; PRODUCTIVITY;).

926. Forney, J. L. 1971. Development of dominant year classes in a yellow perch population. Trans. Am. Fish. Soc. 100:739-749. (WALLEYE; COMMUNITY DYNAMICS; FOOD STUDIES;).

927. Forney, J. L. 1974. Interaction between yellow perch abundance, walleye predation, and survival of alternate prey in Oneida Lake, New York. Trans. Am. Fish. Soc. 103:15-24. (WALLEYE; AGE AND GROWTH; COMMUNITY DYNAMICS; FOOD STUDIES; MORTALITY; POPULATION STUDIES;).

928. Forney, J. L. 1975. Abundance of larval walleye *(Stizostedion vitreum)* estimated from the catch in high-speed nets. Symposium on the methodology for the survey, monitoring and appraisal of fishery resources in lakes and large rivers. European Inland Fisheries Advisory Commission, FAO, U.N., Tech. Paper 23 (Suppl. 1):581-588. (WALLEYE; POPULATION STUDIES; SAMPLING METHODS;).

929. Forney, J. L. 1975. Contribution of stocked fry to walleye fry populations in New York Lakes. Prog. Fish-Cult. 37:20-24. (WALLEYE; STOCKING;).

930. Forney, J. L. 1976. Year-class formation in the walleye *(Stizostedion vitreum vitreum)* population of Oneida lake, New York, 1966-73. J. Fish. Research Board Can. 33:783-792. (WALLEYE; COMMUNITY DYNAMICS; MORTALITY; POPULATION STUDIES; PRODUCTIVITY; STOCKING;).

931. Forney, J. L. 1977. Reconstruction of yellow perch *(Perca flavescens)* cohorts from examination of walleye *(Stizostedion vitreum vitreum)* stomachs. J. Fish. Research Board Can. 34:925-932. (WALLEYE; COMMUNITY DYNAMICS; FOOD STUDIES;).

932. Forney, J. L. 1977. Evidence of inter- and intraspecific competition as factors regulating walleye *(Stizostedion vitreum vitreum)* biomass in Oneida Lake, New York. J. Fish. Research Board Can. 34:1812-1820. (WALLEYE; AGE AND GROWTH; COMMERCIAL FISHERIES; COMMUNITY DYNAMICS; CREEL CENSUS; POPULATION STUDIES;).

933. Forney, J. L. 1978. Prepare walleye policy statement for New York waters. N.Y. Div. Fish Wildl., Fed. Aid Fish Wildl. Restor. Proj. F-17-R-22 Wk. Pl. 4, Job A: 36 pp. (WALLEYE; AGE AND GROWTH; HABITAT IMPROVEMENT; LIFE HISTORY; POPULATION STUDIES; REGULATIONS; SPAWNING STUDIES; STOCKING;).

934. Forney, J. L. 1980. Evolution of a management strategy for the walleye in Oneida Lake, New York. N.Y. Fish Game J. 27:105-141. (WALLEYE; AGE AND GROWTH; COMMUNITY DYNAMICS; CREEL CENSUS; FOOD STUDIES; MORTALITY; REGULATIONS; STOCKING;).

935. Forsythe, T. D. 1977. Predator-prey interactions among crustacean plankton, young bluegill *(Lepomis macrochirus)* and walleye *(Stizostedion vitreum)* in experimental ecosystems. Ph.D Thesis, Mich. State Univ., East Lansing, Mich. 104 pp. (WALLEYE; COMMUNITY DYNAMICS; ECOLOGY; MORTALITY; PRODUCTIVITY;).

936. Forsythe, T. D., and W. B. Wrenn. 1979. Predator — prey relationships among walleye and bluegill. Pages 475-482 *in* H. Clapper, ed. Predator — prey systems in fisheries management. Sport. Fish. Inst., Washington, D.C. (WALLEYE; AGE AND GROWTH; COMMUNITY DYNAMICS; FOOD STUDIES; POPULATION STUDIES;).

937. Fortin, R. 1975. Studies on the walleye *Stizostedion vitreum vitreum* (Mitchill) and the sauger *Stizostedion canadense* (Smith) in certain water areas near Montreal. Nat. Can. 102:305-316. (SAUGER; WALLEYE; POPULATION STUDIES;).

938. Fossum, J. D. 1975. Age and growth, food habit analysis, and movement patterns of walleyes *(Stizostedion vitreum vitreum* (Mitchill)) in pools 3 and 4 of the upper Mississippi River. M.S. Thesis, St. Mary's College, Winona, Minn. 144 pp. (WALLEYE; AGE AND GROWTH; FOOD STUDIES; MOVEMENT AND MIGRATIONS;).

939. Fowler, H. W. 1906. Notes on Pennsylvania Fishes. Am. Nat. 40:595-596. (WALLEYE; GEOGRAPHICAL DISTRIBUTION;).

940. Fowler, H. W. 1913. Records of fishes for the Middle Atlantic States and Virginia. Proc. Phil. Acad. Nat. Sci. 64:34-59. (SAUGER; WALLEYE; GEOGRAPHICAL DISTRIBUTION;).

941. Fowler, H. W. 1919. A list of the fishes of Pennsylvania. Proc. Biol. Soc. Washington 32:49-74. (SAUGER; WALLEYE; GEOGRAPHICAL DISTRIBUTION; INTRODUCTIONS;).

942. Fowler, H. W. 1921. The fishes of Buck's County, Pennsylvania. Copeia 1921:62-68. (WALLEYE; GEOGRAPHICAL DISTRIBUTION;).

943. Fowler, H. W. 1945. A study of the fishes of the Southern Piedmont and coastal plain. Phil. Acad. Nat. Sci. 7: 408 pp. (WALLEYE; GEOGRAPHICAL DISTRIBUTION;).

944. Fowler, H. W. 1948. A list of the fishes recorded from Pennsylvania (revised edition). Penn. Board Fish Comm., Bull. 7: 26 pp. (SAUGER; WALLEYE; GEOGRAPHICAL DISTRIBUTION; INTRODUCTIONS;).

945. Fowler, H. W. 1950. The fishes of Lancaster County, Pennsylvania. Penn. Fish Comm., Bien. Rep. (1948-1950): 89-99. (WALLEYE; GEOGRAPHICAL DISTRIBUTION;).

946. Fowler, H. W. 1952. A list of the fishes of New Jersey, with off-shore species. Proc. Acad.

Nat. Sci., Philadelphia 104:89-151. (WALL-EYE; GEOGRAPHICAL DISTRIBUTION; INTRODUCTIONS;).

947. Frank, R., A. G. Carpentier, and D. L. Mackenzie. 1987. Monitoring for 2 4-D residues in fish species resident in treated lakes in east central Ontario, Canada 1977-80. Environ. Monit. Assess. 9:71-82. (WALLEYE; TOXICANTS;).

948. Frank, R., M. Van Hove Holdrinet, R. L. Desjardine, and D. P. Dodge. 1978. Organochlorine and mercury residues in fish from Lake Simcoe, Ontario 1970-1976. Envir. Biol. Fish. 3:275-286. (WALLEYE; HABITAT DEGRADATION;).

949. Franklin, D. R. 1951. Notes on the use of median growth indices for comparisons of fish growth. Minn. Dept. Conserv., Invest. Rep. No. 117: 3 pp. (WALLEYE; AGE AND GROWTH;).

950. Franklin, D. R., C. R. Burrows, R. E. Schumacher, J. E. Maloney, D. W. Kelley, F. H. Johnson, J. G. Erickson, E. J. Longtin, R. G. Lorenz, W. J. Scidmore, and D. E. Olson. 1952. Creel census of 23 Minnesota Lakes — 1952. Minn. Dept. Conserv., Invest. Rep. No. 135: 71 pp. (WALLEYE; CREEL CENSUS;).

951. Fraser, J. M. 1954. Investigation of pickerel spawning in Melville Creek and in Consecon Lake. Ont. Dept. Lands Forests Fish Wildl., Manage. Rep. No. 19:31-34. (WALLEYE; SPAWNING STUDIES;).

952. Fraune, J. W., and W. J. Scidmore. 1963. Observations on the walleye spawning run in the Tamarac River and its tributaries, Upper Red Lake, Minnesota. Minn. Dept. Conserv., Invest. Rep. No. 269: 12 pp. (WALLEYE; SPAWNING STUDIES;).

953. Frazer, K. J. 1985. Evaluation of the fishery in the Fort Peck tailwater/dredge cut area and assessment of potential impacts from increased hydropower production at Fort Peck Dam on this fishery. Mont. Dept. Fish, Wildl, Parks. 145 pp. (SAUGER; WALLEYE; ECOLOGY; HABITAT DEGRADATION; IMPOUNDMENTS; MOVEMENT AND MIGRATIONS; POPULATION STUDIES; SAMPLING METHODS; SPAWNING STUDIES;).

954. Frazer, K. J. 1986. Fort Peck fishery habitat evaluation and improvement study. Mont.

Dept. Fish, Wildl., Parks. 42 pp. (SAUGER; WALLEYE; HABITAT IMPROVEMENT; IMPOUNDMENTS; POPULATION STUDIES; SPAWNING STUDIES; WATER LEVELS;).

955. Fredenberg, W. A. 1985. South central Montana fisheries investigations, Bighorn Lake and Bighorn River post-impoundment study. Mont. Dept. Fish Wildl. Parks, Fed. Aid Fish Wildl. Restor. Proj. F-20-R-29, Job No. IV-a: 80 pp. (WALLEYE; AGE AND GROWTH; CREEL CENSUS; FOOD STUDIES; IMPOUNDMENTS; INTRODUCTIONS; POPULATION STUDIES; STOCKING; WATER LEVELS;).

956. Fredenberg, W. A. 1987. Inventory of waters of the project area. Mont. Dept. Fish, Wildl. Parks, Fed. Aid Fish Wildl. Restor. Proj. F-20-R-31, Job I-a:. (WALLEYE; AGE AND GROWTH; IMPOUNDMENTS; POPULATION STUDIES; STOCKING;).

957. Fredenberg, W. A. 1987. Bighorn Lake and Bighorn River post-impoundment study. Mont. Dept. Fish, Wildl. Parks, Fed. Aid Fish Wildl. Restor. Proj. F-20-R-31, Job IV:. (WALLEYE; CREEL CENSUS; MARKING; POPULATION STUDIES; SPAWNING STUDIES;).

958. Fredenberg, W. A., S. E. Swedberg, and S. L. McMullin. 1985. Inventory of waters of the project area, South Central Montana fisheries study. Mont. Dept. Fish Wildl. Parks, Fed. Aid Fish Wildl. Restor. Proj. F-20-R-29, Job No. I-a: 19 pp. (WALLEYE; IMPOUNDMENTS; INTRODUCTIONS;).

959. French, J. L. 1984. Rye Patch Reservoir. Nevada Fish Game, Fed. Aid Fish Wildl. Restor. Proj. F-20-20, Job No. 106: 15 pp. (WALLEYE; COMMUNITY DYNAMICS; CREEL CENSUS; IMPOUNDMENTS; MARKING; POPULATION STUDIES;).

960. Frey, D. G. (ed.). 1963. Limnology in North America. Univ. Wis. Press, Madison, Wis. 734 pp. (SAUGER; WALLEYE; ECOLOGY; GEOGRAPHICAL DISTRIBUTION; LIFE HISTORY; MOVEMENT AND MIGRATIONS;).

961. Frey, D. G., H. Pedracine, and L. Vike. 1939. Results of a summer creel census of Lakes Waubesa and Kegonsa, Wisconsin. J. Wildl. Manage. 3:243-254. (WALLEYE; CREEL CENSUS;).

962. Frey, D. G., and L. Vike. 1941. A creel census on Lakes Waubesa and Kegonsa, Wisconsin, in 1939. Trans. Wis. Acad. Sci., Arts Letters 33:339-362. (WALLEYE; CREEL CENSUS; ECOLOGY; POPULATION STUDIES; STOCKING;).

963. Friedrich, G. W. 1933. A catalog of the fishes of central Minnesota. Copeia 1:27-30. (WALLEYE; GEOGRAPHICAL DISTRIBUTION;).

964. Fukano, K. G. 1966. The Michigan general creel census for 1963. Mich. Dept. Conerv., Inst. Fish. Research Rep. 1726: 27 pp. (SAUGER; WALLEYE; CREEL CENSUS;).

965. Fullerton, S. F. 1906. Protection as an aid to propagation. Trans. Am. Fish. Soc. 35:59-86. (WALLEYE; COMMERCIAL FISHERIES;).

966. Funk, J. L. 1953. The Black River studies. Management and utilization of the fishery of Black River, Missouri. Univ. Mo. Stud. 26(2):113-122. (SAUGER; WALLEYE; CREEL CENSUS;).

967. Funk, J. L. 1956. Study of migration of stream fishes. Mo. Conserv. Comm., Fed. Aid Fish Wildl. Restor. Proj. F-1-R-5, Wk. Pl. 2, Job No. 2: 5 pp. (SAUGER; WALLEYE; MARKING; MOVEMENTS AND MIGRATIONS;).

968. Funk, J. L. 1959. Study of the species composition and relative abundance of fishes present in the Current River. Mo. Conserv. Comm., Fed. Aid Fish Wildl. Restor. Proj. F-1-R-8, Wk. Pl. 9, Job No. 2: 7 pp. (SAUGER; WALLEYE; POPULATION STUDIES;).

969. Gabel, J. A. 1974. Species and age composition of trap net catches in Lake Oahe, South Dakota, 1963-67. U.S. Fish Wildl. Serv., Tech. Paper 75: 21 pp. (SAUGER; WALLEYE; AGE AND GROWTH; COMMUNITY DYNAMICS; FISHING GEAR; POPULATION STUDIES;).

970. Gabel, J. A. 1974. An experimental trap net fishery, Lake Oahe, South Dakota, 1965. U.S. Fish Wildl. Serv., Tech. Paper 82: 9 pp. (SAUGER; WALLEYE; COMMERCIAL FISHERIES; SAMPLING METHODS;).

971. Gabelhouse, D. W., Jr. 1984. A length-categorization system to assess fish stocks. N.

Am. J. Fish. Manage. 4:273-285. (SAUGER; WALLEYE; POPULATION STUDIES;).

972. Gaboury, M. N. 1982. Fish stock assessment of Burntwood Lake, 1980. Man. Dept. Nat. Res., Fish. Manuscript Rep. 82-15: 71 pp. (SAUGER; WALLEYE; AGE AND GROWTH; COMMERCIAL FISHERIES; FOOD STUDIES; POPULATION STUDIES;).

973. Gaboury, M. N. 1985. A fisheries survey of the Valley River Manitoba, with particular reference to walleye (Stizostedion vitreum) reproductive success. Man. Dept. Nat. Res., Fish., Manuscript Rep. 85-02: 149 pp. (WALLEYE; COMMUNITY DYNAMICS; ECOLOGY; LIFE HISTORY; MOVEMENTS AND MIGRATIONS; POPULATION STUDIES; SPAWNING STUDIES; WATER LEVELS;).

974. Gaboury, M. N., and J. W. Patalas. 1982. The fisheries of Cross, Pipestone, and Walker Lakes, and effects of hydroelectric development. Man. Dept. Nat. Res., Fish. Manuscript Rep. 82-14: 198 pp. (WALLEYE; AGE AND GROWTH; COMMUNITY DYNAMICS; HABITAT DEGRADATION; POPULATION STUDIES; WATER LEVELS;).

975. Gaboury, M. N., and J. W. Patalas. 1984. Influence of water level drawdown on the fish populations of Cross Lake, Manitoba. Can. J. Fish. Aquat. Sci. 41:118-125. (WALLEYE; AGE AND GROWTH; ECOLOGY; MORTALITY; MOVEMENT AND MIGRATIONS; POPULATION STUDIES; SPAWNING STUDIES; WATER LEVELS;).

976. Gage, J. F. 1964. Angler success survey Lake Nipissing, 1963. Ont. Dept. Lands Forest., Res. Manage. Rep. 73:46-52. (WALLEYE; CREEL CENSUS;).

977. Gale, D. D. 1980. Red Lake system creel census — 1980. Ont. Min. Nat. Res., Rep. 45 pp. (WALLEYE; CREEL CENSUS;).

978. Gale, P., J. O'Malley, and G. Brown. 1979. Fly-in fishery creel census — 1979. Ont. Min. Nat. Res., Rep. 39 pp. (WALLEYE; CREEL CENSUS;).

979. Gale, W. F., and H. W. Mohr, Jr. 1978. Larval fish drift in a large river with a comparison

of sampling methods. Trans. Am. Fish. Soc. 107:46-55. (WALLEYE; FISHING GEAR; MOVEMENT AND MIGRATIONS; SAMPLING METHODS;).

980. Galligan, J. P. 1960. Winter food habits of pike-perch in Oneida Lake. N.Y. Fish Game J. 7:156-157. (WALLEYE; FOOD STUDIES;).

981. Galloway, R. L. 1975. Opasatika Lake Complex Kapuskasing District creel survey report 1973 and 1974. Ont. Min. Nat. Res., Rep. 31 pp. (WALLEYE; CREEL CENSUS;).

982. Gammon, J. R. 1973. The responses of fish populations in the Wabash River to heated effluents. Proc. 3rd Natl. Symp. Radioecol. AEC Symp. Ser., CONF-710501: 513-523. (SAUGER; HABITAT DEGRADATION; POPULATION STUDIES;).

983. Gardner, W. M. 1986. Middle Missouri River Basin — instream flow studies. Mont. Dept. Fish, Wildl. Parks, Fed. Aid Fish Wildl. Restor. Proj. F-2-R-15, Job No. 1-B: 11 pp. (SAUGER; WALLEYE; POPULATION STUDIES; SPAWNING STUDIES;).

984. Gardner, W. M. 1987. Middle Missouri River Basin — instream flow studies, planning inventory, fisheries. Mont. Dept. Fish, Wildl. Parks, Fed. Aid Fish Wildl. Restor. Proj. F-2-R-16, Job I-b:. (SAUGER; WALLEYE; ECOLOGY; POPULATION STUDIES; SPAWNING STUDIES;).

985. Gardner, W. M., and P. A. Stewart. 1987. The fishery of the Lower Missouri River, Montana. Mont. Dept. Fish, Wildl. Parks, Fed. Aid Fish Wildl. Restor. Proj. FW-2-R, Job I-b:. (SAUGER; AGE AND GROWTH; COMMUNITY DYNAMICS; FOOD STUDIES; IMPOUNDMENTS; LIFE HISTORY; POPULATION STUDIES; SPAWNING STUDIES;).

986. Garside, E. T., A. J. Derksen, and W. M. Howard. 1973. Summer food relations and aspects of the distribution of the principal percid fishes of the Saskatchewan River delta prior to 1965 impoundment. Man. Dept. Mines Res., Envirn. Manage. Div. No. 73-18: 17 pp. (SAUGER; WALLEYE; COMMUNITY DYNAMICS; FOOD STUDIES;).

987. Gasaway, C. R. 1967. The sport fishery of Tenkiller Ferry Reservoir, Oklahoma. Okla Dept. Wildl. Conserv., Fish. Research Lab. Bull. No. 7: 21 pp. (SAUGER; WALLEYE; CREEL CENSUS; IMPOUNDMENTS; PRODUCTIVITY;).

988. Gasaway, C. R. 1970. Changes in the fish populations in Lake Francis Case in South Dakota in the first 16 years of inpoundment. U.S. Fish. Wildl. Serv., Tech. Papers 56: 30 pp. (SAUGER; WALLEYE; AGE AND GROWTH; IMPOUNDMENTS; POPULATION STUDIES; SPAWNING STUDIES;).

989. Gasaway, C. R., and V. W. Lambou. 1968. A simple surface-midwater trawl. Prog. Fish-Cult. 30:178-180. (WALLEYE; FISHING GEAR; SAMPLING METHODS;).

990. Gauthier, C. W. 1887. Fish transported from Duck Island to Detroit. U.S. Fish. Comm. Bull. 6:408. (WALLEYE; COMMERCIAL FISHERIES;).

991. Gaylord, W. E., and B. R. Smith. 1966. Treatment of East Bay, Alger County, Michigan with toxaphene for control of sea lampreys. U.S. Fish Wildl. Serv., Invest. Fish Control 7: 7 pp. (WALLEYE; COMMUNITY DYNAMICS;).

992. Gebken, D. F., and K. J. Wright. 1972. Walleye and sauger spawning areas study, Pool 7, Mississippi River 1960-1970. Wis. Dept. Nat. Res., Manage. Rep. No. 60: 27 pp. (SAUGER; WALLEYE; AGE AND GROWTH; SPAWNING STUDIES;).

993. Gee, J. H., R. F. Tallman, and H. J. Smart. 1978. Reactions of some great plains fishes to progressive hypoxia. Can. J. Zool. 56:1962-1966. (WALLEYE; HABITAT DEGRADATION; PHYSIOLOGY;).

994. Geer, W. H. 1977. Characterization and evaluation of Utah Division of Wildlife Resources fish hatchery water. Utah Div. Wildl. Res., Publ. No. 77-11 110 pp. (WALLEYE; PROPAGATION;).

995. Gehres, R. E., and R. L. Scholl. 1969. Walleye sampling. Ohio Dept. Nat. Res., Fed. Aid Fish Wildl. Restor. Proj. F-35-R-8, Job 2: 21 pp. (WALLEYE; ECOLOGY; GEOGRAPHICAL DISTRIBUTION; MOVEMENT AND MIGRATIONS; POPULATION STUDIES;).

996. Gemeroy, D. G. 1943. On the relationship of some common fishes as determined by the precipitation reaction. Zoologica 28(15):109-123. (WALLEYE; PHYSIOLOGY; TAXONOMY;).

997. Gennings, R. M. 1966. Investigations of the reproduction of fishes in Canton Reservoir — reproduction of walleye. Okla. Dept. Wildl. Conserv., Fed. Aid Fish Wildl. Restor. Proj. F-16-R-1, Wk. Pl. 2, Job No. 2-B: 6 pp. (WALLEYE; AGE AND GROWTH; ECOLOGY; IMPOUNDMENTS; MORTALITY; SAMPLING METHODS; SPAWNING STUDIES;).

998. Gennings, R. M. 1966. Investigations of the reproduction of fishes in Canton Reservoir. Reproduction of walleye. Okla. Dept. Wildl. Conserv., Fed. Aid Fish Wildl. Restor. Proj. F-16-R-2, Wk. Pl. 2, Job No. 2, Part 3: 3 pp. (WALLEYE; IMPOUNDMENTS; SAMPLING METHODS; SPAWNING STUDIES;).

999. Gennings, R. M. 1967. Investigations of the reproduction of fishes in Canton Reservoir. Reproduction of the walleye. Okla. Dept. Wildl. Conserv., Fed. Aid Fish Wildl. Restor. Proj. F-16-R-3, Wk. Pl. 2, Job No. 2, Part 3: 12 pp. (WALLEYE; ECOLOGY; IMPOUNDMENTS; INTRODUCTIONS; SAMPLING METHODS; SPAWNING STUDIES;).

1000. Gerking, S. D. 1945. The distribution of the fishes of Indiana. Invest. Ind. Lakes Streams 3(1):1-137. (SAUGER; WALLEYE; ECOLOGY;).

1001 Gerking, S. D. 1950. Populations and exploitation of fishes in a marl lake. Invest. Ind. Lakes Streams 3(11):389-434. (WALLEYE; STOCKING;).

1002. Gerking, S. D. 1955. Key to the fishes of Indiana. Invest. Ind. Lakes Streams 4(2):49-86. (SAUGER; WALLEYE; STOCKING; TAXONOMY;).

1003. Gerking, S. D. 1957. Fish behavior as related to stable stream populations. Pages 3-18 in K .D. Carlander ed. Symposium on evaluation of fish populations in warm-water streams. Iowa State Coll., Ames, Iowa. (WALLEYE; MOVEMENT AND MIGRATIONS;).

1004. Gerking, S. D. 1959. The restricted movement of fish populations. Biol. Rev. 34:221-242. (WALLEYE; MOVEMENT AND MIGRATIONS; SPAWNING STUDIES;).

1005. Gibson, R. J. 1969. Spawning of walleye, Stizostedion vitreum vitreum (Mitchill) in Hamilton's Creek, 1967 and 1968. Man. Dept. Mines Nat. Res., Fish. Branch., Manuscript Rep. No. 69-11: 121 pp. (WALLEYE; AGE AND GROWTH; BEHAVIOR; FOOD STUDIES; MOVEMENT AND MIGRATIONS; SPAWNING STUDIES;).

1006. Gibson, R. J., and W. R. Cuff. 1967. Vital staining of walleye fry, Stizostedion vitreum vitreum (Mitchill). Man. Dept. Mines Nat. Res., Fish Branch, Manuscript Rep. 7 pp. (WALLEYE; MARKING;).

1007. Gibson, R. J., and C. E. Hughes. 1977. A walleye (Stizostedion vitreum) stream spawning study on Hamilton's Creek. Man. Dept. Renew. Res. Trans. Serv., Research Branch, Manuscript Rep. 77-31: 57 pp. (WALLEYE; HABITAT IMPROVEMENT; SPAWNING STUDIES;).

1008. Gibson, R. J., and E. J. Schindler. 1969. "Barrow pits" as rearing ponds for muskellunge and walleye. Man. Dept. Mines Nat. Res., Fish. Research. Manuscript Rep. No. 69-5: 37 pp. (WALLEYE; PROPAGATION;).

1009. Gilbertson, B. 1979. A creel census and water surface use study of four Washington County lakes. Minn. Dept. Nat. Res., Fish Manage. Rep. No. 13: 47 pp. (WALLEYE; CREEL CENSUS;).

1010. Gilbertson, B. 1980. A creel census and water use study of Waconia Lake, Carver County. Minn. Dept. Nat. Res., Fish Manage. Rep. No. 18: 37 pp. (WALLEYE; CREEL CENSUS;).

1011. Gilderhus, P. A., B. L. Berger, and R. E. Lennon. 1969. Field trials of antimycin A as a fish toxicant. U.S. Fish Wildl. Serv., Invest. Fish Control 27: 21 pp. (WALLEYE; TOXICANTS;).

1012. Giles, M. A., and M. Foster. 1987. Design construction and field testing of a mobile hatchery for thirty million walleye eggs. Can. Tech. Rep. Fish Aquat. Sci. 1533: 28 pp. (WALLEYE; PROPAGATION;).

1013. Gill, T. 1857. On the fishes of New York. Smithsonian Inst., Annu. Rep. 1856:253-269. (WALLEYE; COMMERCIAL FISHERIES;).

1014. Gill, T. 1894. On the relations and nomenclature of *Stizostedion* or *Lucioperca.* Proc. U.S. Nat. Mus. 17:123-128. (SAUGER; WALLEYE; TAXONOMY;).

1015. Gillies, D. G., and A. J. Derksen. 1979. Preliminary results in the development of a photoelectric method for enumerating live whitefish and walleye fry. Man. Dept. Renewable Res. Transport. Svs. Research Branch Planning Manage. Support Div. Manuscript Rep. No. 77-10: 73 pp. (WALLEYE; STOCKING;).

1016. Gillies, D. G., and D. J. Green. 1980. An interim report on food and growth of walleyes, *Stizostedion vitreum vitreum* (Mitchill), from four rearing ponds bordering on Lake Winnipegosis, Manitoba, in 1978 and 1979. Man. Dept. Nat. Res., Fish. Branch, Manuscript Rep No. 80-38: 62 pp. (WALLEYE; AGE AND GROWTH; FOOD STUDIES; PROPAGATION; STOCKING;).

1017. Gilliland, G. 1987. Evaluation of YOY walleye and striped bass x white bass hybrid sampling methods. Okla. Dept. Wildl. Conserv., Fed. Aid Fish Wildl. Restor. Proj. F-37-R, Job No. 11: 28 pp. (WALLEYE; SAMPLING METHODS; STOCKING;).

1018. Girard, C. 1858. Notice upon new genera and new species of marine and fresh-water fishes from western North America. Proc. Phil. Acad. Sci. 9:200-202. (SAUGER; MORPHOLOGY; TAXONOMY;).

1019. Girling, F. 1948. Fish parasites of Lake Erie. Unpub. Manuscript in Roy. Ont. Mus., Ichthyol. Libr. 12 pp. (WALLEYE; PATHOLOGY;).

1020. Glazer, R. 1975. Annual report of mercury levels in fish from the Mississippi, Red and St. Louis Rivers, Minnesota, 1975. Minn. Dept. Nat. Res., Invest. Rep. No. 358: 23 pp. (SAUGER; WALLEYE; HABITAT DEGRADATION;).

1021. Glazer, R. 1977. Mercury levels in fish collected in Rainy and Crane Lakes in August, 1976. Minn. Dept. Nat. Res., Invest. Rep. No. 356: 22 pp. (WALLEYE; HABITAT DEGRADATION;).

1022. Glazer, R. 1977. Annual report of mercury levels in fish in the Mississippi, Red and St. Louis Rivers, Minnesota 1976. Minn. Dept. Nat. Res., Invest. Rep. No. 357: 20 pp. (SAUGER; WALLEYE; HABITAT DEGRADATION;).

1023. Glazer, R. 1978. Annual report of mercury levels in the Mississippi, Red and St. Louis Rivers, Minnesota, 1977. Minn. Dept. Nat. Res., Invest. Rep. No. 359: 28 pp. (SAUGER; WALLEYE; HABITAT DEGRADATION;).

1024. Glazer, R., and D. Bohlander. 1978. Mercury levels in fish from eleven northeastern Minnesota lakes, 1977. Minn. Dept. Nat. Res., Invest. Rep. No. 355: 35 pp. (WALLEYE; HABITAT DEGRADATION;).

1025. Glenn, C. L. 1970. Seasonal rates of growth within a population of walleye, *Stizostedion vitreum vitreum* (Mitchill), in West Blue Lake, Manitoba, during 1966-67. M.S. Thesis, Univ. of Man., Winnipeg, Man. 63 pp. (WALLEYE; AGE AND GROWTH;).

1026. Glenn, C. L., and J. A. Mathias. 1985. Circuli development on body scales of young pond reared walleye *(Stizostedion vitreum).* Can. J. Zool. 63:912-915. (WALLEYE; AGE AND GROWTH;).

1027. Glenn, C. L., and F. J. Ward. 1968. "Wet" weight as a method for measuring stomach contents of walleye, *Stizostedion vitreum vitreum.* J. Fish. Research Board Can. 25:1505-1507. (WALLEYE; FOOD STUDIES;).

1028. Glover, R. C. 1960. Fish culture in Pennsylvania. Penn. Fish Comm. 12 pp. (WALLEYE; PROPAGATION;).

1029. Goddard, J. A., and L. C. Redmond. 1978. Northern pike, tiger muskellunge, and walleye populations in Stockton Lake, Missouri: a management evaluation. Pages 313-319 *in* R.L. Kendall, ed. Selected coolwater fishes of North America. Am. Fish. Soc. Sp. Publ. No. 11, Washington, D.C. (WALLEYE; AGE AND GROWTH; COMMUNITY DYNAMICS; CREEL CENSUS; IMPOUNDMENTS; MARKING; REGULATIONS; STOCKING;).

1030. Goddard, J. A., and L. C. Redmond. 1986. Stockton Lake: prolonging the "boom," managing a new large reservoir with minimum length limits,. Pages 203-210 *in* G. E. Hall and M. J. Van Den Avyle, eds. Reservoir fisheries management: strategies for the 80's. Reserv. Comm., S. Div. Am. Fish. Soc., Bethesda, Maryland. (WALLEYE; CREEL CENSUS; IMPOUNDMENTS; REGULATIONS; STOCKING;).

1031. Goeman, T. J. 1984. Fish survival at a cooling water intake designed to minimize mortality. Prog. Fish-Cult. 46:279-281. (SAUGER; WALLEYE; MORTALITY;).

1032. Goettl, J. P., Jr., and M. S. Jones. 1984. Evaluation of fish forage organisms. Colo. Div. Wildl., Fed. Aid Fish. Wildl. Restor. Proj. F-53-R, Job No. 1: 27 pp. (WALLEYE; AGE AND GROWTH; COMMUNITY DYNAMICS; FOOD STUDIES; POPULATION STUDIES;).

1033. Goetz, F. W., and H. L. Bergman. 1978. The in vitro effects of mammalian and piscine gonadotropin and pituitary preparations on final maturation in yellow perch *(Perca flavescens)* and walleye *(Stizostedion vitreum).* Can. J. Zool. 56:348-350. (WALLEYE; SPAWNING STUDIES;).

1034. Goode, G. B. 1887. American fishes. A popular treatise upon the game and food fishes of North America with special reference to the habits and methods of capture. Estes and Lauriat, Boston, Mass. 496 pp. (SAUGER; WALLEYE; COMMERCIAL FISHERIES; LIFE HISTORY; SPAWNING STUDIES; TAXONOMY;).

1035. Goodson, L. F., Jr. 1966. Walleye. Pages 423-426 *in* A. Calhoun, ed. Inland fisheries management. Calif. Dept. Fish Game, Sacramento, Calif. (WALLEYE; INTRODUCTIONS;).

1036. Gopsill, B. 1977. Clayton and Taylor creel census summer 1977. Ont. Min. Nat. Res., Rep. 21 pp. (WALLEYE; CREEL CENSUS;).

1037. Goyan, M. A., B. A. Towson, and R. Hamilton. 1976. Whitefish Lake creel census May 15 — August 6, 1976. Ont. Min. Nat. Res., Rep. 31 pp. (WALLEYE; CREEL CENSUS;).

1038. Graham, I. D. 1885. Preliminary list of Kansas fish. Trans. Kan. Acad. Sci. 9:69-78. (SAUGER; WALLEYE; GEOGRAPHICAL DISTRIBUTION;).

1039. Graham, R. J. 1959. Age and growth, bottom sample and miscellaneous studies. Mont. Fish Game Dept., Fed. Aid Fish Wildl. Restor. Proj. F-23-R-2, Job No. 1-3: 4 pp. (SAUGER; AGE AND GROWTH;).

1040. Graham, R. J., R. W. Larimore, and W. F. Dimond. 1984. Recreational fishing in the Kankakee River, Illinois. Ill. Nat. Hist. Surv., Biol. Notes 120:3-13. (WALLEYE; CREEL CENSUS;).

1041. Gravel, Y., and G. Pageau. 1976. The biological and recreational resources of the St. Lawrence: are they inexhaustible? L'ingenieur 314:21-36. (WALLEYE; CREEL CENSUS; POPULATION STUDIES;).

1042. Gray, G. A., D. E. Palmer, B. L. Hilton, P. J. Connolly, H. C. Hansel, J. M. Beyer, and G. M. Sonnevil. 1984. Feeding activity, rate of consumption, daily ration and prey selection of major predators in the John Day Pool. Annual Rep. (1983) to Bonneville Power Admin., U.S.F.W.S., Nat. Fish. Research Cent., Cook, Wash. 65 pp. (WALLEYE; COMMUNITY DYNAMICS; FOOD STUDIES; IMPOUNDMENTS;).

1043. Gray, G. A., D. E. Palmer, B. J. Hilton, P. J. Connolly, H. C. Hansel, J. M. Beyer, P. T. Lofy, D. D. Duke, M. J. Parsley, M. G. Mesa, G. M. Sonnevil, and L. A. Prendergast. 1984. Feeding activity, rate of consumption, daily ration and prey selection of major predators in John Day Reservoir. Annual Rep. to Bonneville Power Admin., U.S.F.W.S., Nat. Fish. Research Center, Cook, Wash. 163 pp. (WALLEYE; COMMUNITY DYNAMICS; FOOD STUDIES; IMPOUNDMENTS;).

1044. Gray, G. A., and D. W. Rondorf. 1986. Predation on juvenile salmonids in Columbia basin reservoirs. Pages 178-185 *in* G. E. Hall and M. J. Van Den Avyle, eds. Reservoir fisheries management: strategies for the 80's. Reserv. Comm., S. Div. Am. Fish. Soc., Bethesda, Maryland. (WALLEYE; COMMUNITY DYNAMICS; FOOD STUDIES; IMPOUNDMENTS; STOCKING;).

1045. Gray, G. A., G. M. Sonnevil, H. C. Hansel, C. W. Huntington, and D. E. Palmer. 1982. Feeding activity, rate of consumption, daily ration and prey selection of major predators in the John Day Pool. Annual Rep. (1982) to Bonneville Power Admin., U.S.F.W.S., Nat. Fish. Research Cent., Cook, Wash. 81 pp.

(WALLEYE; AGE AND GROWTH; COMMUNITY DYNAMICS; FOOD STUDIES; IMPOUNDMENTS;).

1046. Gray, P. D. 1971. Mistinikon Lake creel census summer 1971. Ont. Min. Nat. Res., Rep. 6 pp. (WALLEYE; CREEL CENSUS;).

1047. Gray, P. D. 1972. Mistinikon Lake creel census summer 1972. Ont. Min. Nat. Res., Rep 3 pp. (WALLEYE; CREEL CENSUS;).

1048. Greeley, J. R. 1927. A biological survey of the Genesee River system. IV. Fishes of the Genesee region with annotated list. N.Y. Conserv. Dept., Suppl. 16th Annu. Rep. (1926):47-66. (WALLEYE; FOOD STUDIES; INTRODUCTIONS;).

1049. Greeley, J. R. 1929. A biological survey of the Erie-Niagara watershed. N.Y. Conserv. Dept., Suppl. 18th Annu. Rep. (1928):150-179. (SAUGER; WALLEYE; COMMERCIAL FISHERIES; ECOLOGY;).

1050. Greeley, J. R. 1930. A biological survey of the Champlain watershed. II. Fishes of the Lake Champlain watershed. N.Y. Conserv. Dept., Suppl. 19th Annu. Rep. (1929):44-87. (SAUGER; WALLEYE; INTRODUCTIONS;).

1051. Greeley, J. R. 1934. A biological survey of the Raquette watershed. II. Fishes of the Raquette watershed with annotated list. N.Y. Conserv. Dept., Suppl. 23rd Annu. Rep. (1933):53-108. (WALLEYE; GEOGRAPHICAL DISTRIBUTION;).

1052. Greeley, J. R. 1936. A biological survey of the Delaware and Susquehanna watersheds. II. Fishes of the area with annotated list. N.Y. Conserv. Dept., Suppl. 25th Annu. Rep. (1935):45-88. (WALLEYE; INTRODUCTIONS; STOCKING;).

1053. Greeley, J. R. 1939. A biological survey of the fresh waters of Long Island. II. The freshwater fishes of Long Island and Staten Island with annotated list. N.Y. Conserv. Dept., Suppl. 28th Annu. Rep. (1938):29-44. (WALLEYE; INTRODUCTIONS; STOCKING;).

1054. Greeley, J. R. 1940. A biological survey of the Lake Ontario watershed. II. Fishes of the watershed with annotated list. N.Y. Conserv. Dept., Suppl. 29th Annu. Rep. (1939):42-81. (SAUGER; WALLEYE; MOVEMENT AND MIGRATIONS; TAXONOMY;).

1055. Greeley, J. R., and S. C. Bishop. 1932. A biological survey of the Osegatchie and Black River systems. II. Fishes of the area with annotated list. N.Y. Conserv. Dept., Suppl. 21st Annu. Rep. (1931):54-93. (SAUGER; WALLEYE; ECOLOGY; INTRODUCTIONS; SPAWNING STUDIES;).

1056. Greeley, J. R., and S. C. Bishop. 1933. A biological survey of the Upper Hudson watershed. II. Fishes of the Upper Hudson watershed with annotated list. N.Y. Conserv. Dept., Suppl. 22nd Annu. Rep. (1932):64-101. (WALLEYE; INTRODUCTIONS;).

1057. Green, D. J. 1980. An interim report on walleye, *Stizostedion v. vitreum* (Mitchill), stocking and survival data from five rearing ponds in the vicinity of Lake Winnipegosis, Manitoba 1978 and 1979. Man. Dept. Nat. Res., Fish. Branch. Manuscript Rep. No. 80-9: 32 pp. (WALLEYE; MARKING; MORTALITY; POPULATION STUDIES; PRODUCTIVITY; STOCKING;).

1058. Green, D. J. 1986. Summary of fish mercury data collected from Lakes on the Rat-Burntwood and Nelson River systems, 1983-1985. Man. Dept. Nat. Res., Fish Branch Manuscript Rep. No. 86-06: 359 pp. (SAUGER; WALLEYE; HABITAT DEGRADATION; TOXICANTS;).

1059. Green, D. J., and A. J. Derksen. 1982. An assessment of the Lake Winnipegosis walleye rearing ponds and their contributions to the Lake Winnipegosis commercial fishery. Man. Dept. Nat. Res., Fish. Branch Manuscript Rep. No. 82-25: 96 pp. (WALLEYE; AGE AND GROWTH; FOOD STUDIES; MARKING; PRODUCTIVITY; STOCKING;).

1060. Green, D. J., and A. J. Derksen. 1984. The past, present and projected demands on Manitoba's freshwater fish resources. Man. Dept. Nat. Res., Manuscript Rep. No. 84-4: 179 pp. (WALLEYE; SOCIO-ECONOMICS OF FISHERIES;).

1061. Green, D. M. 1978. Importance of yellow perch in the food of predator fish in Canadarago Lake. N.Y. Div. Fish Wildl., Fed. Aid Fish Wildl. Restor. Proj. F-29-R-6, Job No. 1E: 20 pp. (WALLEYE; FOOD STUDIES; STOCKING;).

1062. Green, D. M. 1986. Post-stocking survival of walleye fingerlings in Canadarago Lake, New York. Pages 381-389 *in* R. H. Stroud, ed. Fish culture in fisheries management. Am. Fish. Soc., Bethesda, Maryland. (WALLEYE; AGE AND GROWTH; COMMUNITY DYNAMICS; MORTALITY; POPULATION STUDIES; STOCKING;).

1063. Green, S. 1874. Experiences of a practical fish culturist. Proc. Am. Fish. Cult. Assoc. 3:22-24. (WALLEYE; PROPAGATION;).

1064. Greenbank, J. 1936. A biological survey of the Delaware and Susquehanna watersheds. I. Stocking policy for the waters of the Delaware and Susquehanna watersheds and discussion of fish management polices. N.Y. Conserv. Dept., Suppl. 25th Annu. Rep. (1935):19-44, Append. 2: 251, Append. 3:252-356. (WALLEYE; STOCKING;).

1065. Greenbank, J. 1947. A brief discussion of the characteristics of commercial fishing devices used in the Minnesota-Wisconsin-Iowa section of the Mississippi River. Upper Miss. River Conserv. Comm., Tech. Comm. Fish., 3rd Prog. Rep. Append. 7: 46-55. (WALLEYE; COMMERCIAL FISHERIES; FISHING GEAR;).

1066. Greenbank, J. 1956. Movement of fish under the ice. Copeia 1956(3):158-162. (WALLEYE; MOVEMENT AND MIGRATIONS;).

1067. Greenbank, J. 1957. Creel census on the upper Mississippi River. U.S. Fish Wildl. Serv., Spec. Sci. Rep. — Fish. 202: 59 pp. (SAUGER; WALLEYE; CREEL CENSUS;).

1068. Greene, C. W. 1926. An ichthyological survey of Wisconsin. Mich. Acad. Sci. 7:299-310. (SAUGER; WALLEYE; GEOGRAPHICAL DISTRIBUTION;).

1069. Greene, C. W. 1930. A biological survey of the Champlain watershed. IV. The smelts of Lakes Champlain with supplementary material from the Finger Lakes, the Saranac chain, and the Cold Spring Harbour Hatchery, Long Island, N.Y. N.Y. Conserv. Dept., Suppl. 19th Annu. Rep. (1929):105-129. (SAUGER; WALLEYE; COMMUNITY DYNAMICS; FOOD STUDIES;).

1070. Greene, C. W. 1937. A biological survey of the lower Hudson watershed. I. Stocking policy for the lower Hudson area and discussion of some fish management policies. N.Y. Conserv. Dept., Suppl. 26th Annu. Rep. (1936):20-44, Append. 2: 280, Append. 3:281-373. (WALLEYE; STOCKING;).

1071. Greene, C. W. 1938. A biological survey of the Allegheny and Chemung watersheds. I. Stocking policy for the Allegheny and Chemung watersheds and discussion of some fish management policies. N.Y. Conserv. Dept., Suppl. 27th Annu. Rep. (1937):22-47, Append. 1: 236, Append. 2:237-287. (WALLEYE; STOCKING;).

1072. Greene, C. W. 1940. A biological survey of the Lake Ontario watershed. I. Stocking policy for the Ontario watershed with suggestions for other fish management methods. N.Y. Conserv. Dept., Suppl. 29th Annu. Rep. (1939):20-41, Append. 1: 232, Append. 2:233-261. (WALLEYE; STOCKING;).

1073. Greene, C. W. 1942. New York states's fish yield and suggestions for increasing freshwater yields in wartime. Trans. 7th N. Am. Wildl. Conf. 7:417-423. (WALLEYE; COMMERCIAL FISHERIES; ECOLOGY;).

1074. Greene, C. W., R. P. Hunter, and W. C. Senning. 1932. A biological survey of the Oswegatchie and Black River systems. I. Stocking policy for streams, lakes and ponds in the Oswegatchie and Black River systems. N.Y. Conserv. Dept., Suppl. 21st Annu. Rep. (1931):18-53, Append. 3:295-343. (WALLEYE; STOCKING;).

1075. Greene, W. C., R. P. Hunter, and W. C. Senning. 1933. A biological survey of the upper Hudson watershed. I. Stocking policy for streams, lakes and ponds in the upper Hudson watershed. N.Y. Conserv. Dept., Suppl. 22nd Annu. Rep. (1932):26-63, Append. 3:270-341. (WALLEYE; STOCKING;).

1076. Greene, W. C., R. P. Hunter, and W. C. Senning. 1934. A biological survey of the Raquette watershed. I. Stocking policy for streams, lakes and ponds in the Raquette watershed. N.Y. Conserv. Dept., Suppl. 23rd Annu. Rep. (1933):20-52, Append. 3:268-301. (WALLEYE; STOCKING;).

1077. Gregory, R. W. 1970. Physical and chemical properties of walleye sperm and seminal plasma. Trans. Am. Fish. Soc. 99:518-525. (WALLEYE; PHYSIOLOGY;).

1078. Gregory, R. W., and T. G. Powell. 1969. Walleye fry stocking. Colo. Dept. Game, Fish Parks, Fed. Aid Fish Wildl. Restor. Proj. F-34-R-4, Job No. 4:8-19. (WALLEYE; AGE AND GROWTH; CREEL CENSUS; IMPOUNDMENTS; STOCKING;).

1079. Grice, F. 1961. An attempt to use sodium sulphite to facilitate the recovery of pond-reared walleyes. Prog. Fish-Cult. 23:189. (WALLEYE; PROPAGATION;).

1080. Griffiths, J. S. 1981. Potential effects of fluctuating thermal regimes on incubation of walleye (Stizostedion vitreum) eggs. Ont. Hydro. Res. Div., Rep. 81-77-K: 61 pp. (SAUGER; WALLEYE; EMBRYOLOGY; MORTALITY; PHYSIOLOGY; SPAWNING STUDIES;).

1081. Griffiths, J. S. 1987. Simulation studies of potential effects from Atikokan TGS on walleye eggs. Ont. Hydro Research Div. Rep. No. 86-290-K 15 pp. (WALLEYE; HABITAT DEGRADATION; IMPOUNDMENTS; SPAWNING STUDIES;).

1082. Grinstead, B. G. 1971. Reproductive success of young-of-the-year, life history and ecology studies. Reproduction and some aspects of the early life history of walleye, Stizostedion vitreim vitreum (Mitchell), in Canton Resvoir, Oklahoma. Okla. Dept. Wildl. Conserv., Fed. Aid Fish Wildl. Restor. Proj. F-16-R-8: 33 pp. (WALLEYE; AGE AND GROWTH; IMPOUNDMENTS; INTRODUCTIONS; LIFE HISTORY; MOVEMENTS AND MIGRATIONS; SPAWNING STUDIES; STOCKING;).

1083. Grinstead, B. G. 1971. Reproduction and some aspects of the early life history of walleye, Stizostedion vitreum (Mitchill) in Canton Reservoir, Oklahoma. Pages 41-51 in G.E. Hall, ed. Reservoir fisheries and limnology. Am. Fish. Soc. Sp. Publ. No. 8, Washington D.C. (WALLEYE; AGE AND GROWTH; ECOLOGY; EMBRYOLOGY; FISHING GEAR; IMPOUNDMENTS; LIFE HISTORY; MOVEMENT AND MIGRATIONS; SPAWNING STUDIES; STOCKING;).

1084. Grinstead, B. G., R. M. Gennings, G. R. Hooper, C. A. Schultz, and D. A. Whorton. 1976. Estimation of standing crop of fishes in the predator-stocking-evaluation reservoirs. Proc. 30th Annu. Conf. Southeast Assoc. Fish Wild. Agencies. 30:120-130. (WALLEYE; COMMUNITY DYNAMICS; IMPOUNDMENTS; PRODUCTIVITY; STOCKING;).

1085. Groebner, J. F. 1959. A three year creel census of Lake Mazaska, Rice County, with evaluation of the harvest of stocked year-classes of walleyes. Minn. Dept. Nat. Res., Invest. Rep. No. 212: 13 pp. (WALLEYE; CREEL CENSUS; INTRODUCTIONS; STOCKING;).

1086. Groebner, J. F. 1960. Appraisal of the sport fishery catch in a bass-panfish lake of southern Minnesota, Lake Francis, LeSueur County, 1952-1957. Minn. Dept. Conserv., Invest. Rep. No. 225: 17 pp. (WALLEYE; CREEL CENSUS; INTRODUCTIONS;).

1087. Groen, C. L., and J. C. Schmulback. 1978. The sport fishery of the unchannelized and channelized middle Missouri River. Trans. Am. Fish. Soc. 107:412-418. (SAUGER; WALLEYE; CREEL CENSUS; HABITAT DEGRADATION;).

1088. Groen, C. L., and T. A. Schroeder. 1978. Effects of water level management on walleye and other coolwater fishes in Kansas reservoirs. Pages 278-283 in R.L. Kendall, ed. Selected coolwater fishes of North America. Am. Fish Soc. Sp. Publ. No. 11, Washington D.C. (WALLEYE; CREEL CENSUS; HABITAT IMPROVEMENT; IMPOUNDMENTS; POPULATION STUDIES;).

1089. Grosslein, M. D. 1961. Estimation of angler harvest in Oneida Lake, New York. Ph.D. Thesis, Cornell Univ., Ithaca, N.Y. 296 pp. (WALLEYE; CREEL CENSUS;).

1090. Grosslein, M. D., and L. L. Smith, Jr. 1959. The goldeye, Amphiodon alosoides (Rafinesque), in the commercial fishery of the Red Lakes, Minnesota. U.S. Fish Wildl. Serv., Fish. Bull. 60:33-41. (WALLEYE; COMMUNITY DYNAMICS; FOOD STUDIES;).

1091. Gunn, J. M. 1979. A study of the walleye (Stizostedion vitreum) population at the mouth of the French River. Ont. Min. Nat. Res., French River Proj. 1974-78: 88 pp. (WALLEYE; AGE AND GROWTH; COMMERCIAL FISHERIES; COMMUNITY DYNAMICS; CREEL CENSUS; FISHING GEAR; MARKING; MORTALITY;

MOVEMENT AND MIGRATIONS;
SPAWNING STUDIES;).

1092. Hackney, P. A., and J. A. Holbrook, II. 1978. Sauger, walleye, and yellow perch in the southeastern United States. Pages 74-81 *in* R.L. Kendall, ed. Selected coolwater fishes of North America. Am. Fish. Soc. Sp. Publ. No. 11, Washington D.C. (SAUGER; WALLEYE; AGE AND GROWTH; ECOLOGY; GEOGRAPHICAL DISTRIBUTION; IMPOUNDMENTS; MORTALITY; SPAWNING STUDIES;).

1093. Hagan, R. J. 1978. Length-weight relationship, population structure, and diet of the walleye, *Stizostedion vitreum vitreum* (Mitchill), in the Grand Rapids area of Lake Winnipeg, 1977. Man. Dept. Mines Nat. Res. Environ., Manuscript Rep. No. 78-85: 33 pp. (WALLEYE; AGE AND GROWTH; FOOD STUDIES; PATHOLOGY; POPULATION STUDIES;).

1094. Hagen, W., and J. P. O'Connor. 1959. Public fish culture in the United States, 1958. U. S. Fish Wildl. Serv., Circ. 58:44. (WALLEYE; PROPAGATION; STOCKING;).

1095. Hagenson, I., and J. F. O'Connor. 1978. A creel census of Gods Lake, 1974 & 1975. Man. Dept. Northern Affairs, Fish. Manuscript Rep. No. 78-57: 66 pp. (SAUGER; WALLEYE; AGE AND GROWTH; POPULATION STUDIES;).

1096. Hagenson, I., and J. F. O'Connor. 1979. A fisheries inventory of Obukowin and Aikens Lakes, 1978. Man. Dept. Nat. Res., Manuscript Rep. No. 79-75: 60 pp. (WALLEYE; STOCKING;).

1097. Hagenson, I., and J. F. O'Connor. 1980. A fisheries inventory of Dogskin, Family, Viking, and Vickers Lakes, 1978. Man. Dept. Nat. Res., Fish. Manuscript Rep. No. 80-32: 64 pp. (WALLEYE; AGE AND GROWTH; ECOLOGY; PRODUCTIVITY;).

1098. Hagenson, I., and J. F. O'Connor. 1981. A fisheries inventory of Harrop, Eardley, Weaver, and Wrong Lakes, 1978. Man. Dept. Nat. Res., Fish. Manuscript Rep. No. 81-24: 68 pp. (WALLEYE; AGE AND GROWTH; POPULATION STUDIES;).

1099. Hair, E. M. 1972. Effects of dieldrin on walleye egg development, hatching and fry survival. Ph.D. Dissertation, Ohio St. Univ., Columbus, Ohio. 52 pp. (WALLEYE; TOXICANTS;).

1100. Halkett, A. 1913. Check lists of the fishes of the Dominion of Canada and Newfoundland. King's Printer, Ottawa, Ont. 138 pp. (SAUGER; WALLEYE; GEOGRAPHICAL DISTRIBUTION;).

1101. Hall, C. B. 1982. Movement and behavior of walleye, *Stizostedion vitreum vitreum* (Mitchill) in Jamestown Reservoir, North Dakota, as determined by biotelemetry. M.S. Thesis. Univ. N.D., Grand Forks, N.D. 115 pp. (WALLEYE; IMPOUNDMENTS; MARKING; MOVEMENTS AND MIGRATIONS;).

1102. Hall, G. E. 1954. Observations on the fishes of Fort Gibson and Tenkiller Reservoir areas, 1952. Proc. Okla. Acad. Sci. 33:55-63. (SAUGER; IMPOUNDMENTS;).

1103. Hall, G. E. 1956. Additions to the fish fauna of Oklahoma with a summary of introduced species. Southwestern Nat. 1:16-26. (WALLEYE; AGE AND GROWTH; INTRODUCTIONS; STOCKING;).

1104. Halnon, L. C. 1960. A study of the Lake Champlain walleyes. Vt. Fish Game Serv., Fed. Aid Fish Wildl. Restor. Proj. F-1-R-8, Job No. 1, Job Completion Rep. 34 pp. (WALLEYE; AGE AND GROWTH; CREEL CENSUS; ECOLOGY; MARKING; MOVEMENTS AND MIGRATIONS; PATHOLOGY; POPULATION STUDIES; SPAWNING STUDIES;).

1105. Halnon, L. C. 1963. Historical survey of Lake Champlain's fishery. Vt. Fish Game Serv., Fed. Aid Fish Wildl. Restor. Proj. F-1-R-10, Job No. 6: 95 pp. (SAUGER; WALLEYE; COMMERCIAL FISHERIES; COMMUNITY DYNAMICS; MARKING; PROPAGATION; REGULATIONS; SPAWNING STUDIES; STOCKING;).

1106. Halnon, L. C. 1963. A study of the walleye fishery in Lake Champlain (including a report summarizing ten years of walleye tagging). Vt. Fish Game Serv., Fed. Aid Fish Wildl. Restor. Proj. F-1-R-11, Job No. 1: 41 pp. (WALLEYE; AGE AND GROWTH; CREEL CENSUS; ECOLOGY; MARKING; MOVEMENTS AND MIGRATIONS; PATHOLOGY; SPAWNING STUDIES;).

1107. Halnon, L. C. 1967. A study of the Lake Champlain walleye. Vt. Fish Game Serv., Fed. Aid Fish Wildl. Restor. Proj. F-1-R-16, Job No. 1: 38 pp. (WALLEYE; AGE AND GROWTH; MARKING; PATHOLOGY; POPULATION STUDIES; SPAWNING STUDIES;).

1108. Hamilton, J. G. 1979. Bennett Lake overview — 1979. Ont. Min. Nat. Res., Rep. 30 pp. (WALLEYE; AGE AND GROWTH; CREEL CENSUS; HABITAT DEGRADATION; POPULATION STUDIES; STOCKING;).

1109. Hamilton, J. G. 1979. 1977-1978 winter creel census and aerial survey, Black, Christie, Clayton, Pike, Taylor and White Lakes. Ont. Min. Nat. Res., Rep. 7 pp. (WALLEYE; CREEL CENSUS;).

1110. Hamilton, J. G. 1979. Mississippi Lake Management Report — 1979. Ont. Min. Nat. Res., Rep. 25 pp. (WALLEYE; AGE AND GROWTH; CREEL CENSUS; HABITAT DEGRADATION; POPULATION STUDIES;).

1111. Hamley, J. M. 1971. Gillnet selectivity to walleyes *(Stizostedion vitreum)*. Univ. Toronto, Dept. Zool. 9 pp. (WALLEYE; FISHING GEAR;).

1112. Hamley, J. M., and H. A. Regier. 1973. Direct estimates of gillnet selectivity to walleye *(Stizostedion vitreum vitreum)*. J. Fish. Research Board Can. 30:817-830. (WALLEYE; FISHING GEAR;).

1113. Hancock, H. M. 1954. Investigations and experimentation relative to winter aggregations of fishes in Canton Reservoir, Oklahoma. Okla. Agr. Mech. Coll., Research Found. Publ. 58: 104 pp. (WALLEYE; ECOLOGY;).

1114. Hancock, H. M. 1955. Age and growth of some of the principal fishes in Canton Reservoir, Oklahoma, 1951, with particular emphasis on the white crappie *(Pomoxis annularis)*. Okla. Fish Game Council, Rep. Part II: 55-60. (WALLEYE; AGE AND GROWTH;).

1115. Hancock, H. M. 1957. Creel census Fort Gibson Reservoir. Okla. Dept. Wildl. Conserv., Fed. Aid Fish Wildl. Restor. Proj. F-4-R-1, Job No. 1-B: 7 pp. (SAUGER; CREEL CENSUS; IMPOUNDMENTS;).

1116. Hankinson, T. L. 1911. Ecological notes on the fishes of Walnut Lake, Michigan. Trans. Am. Fish. Soc. 40:195-206. (WALLEYE; ECOLOGY; GEOGRAPHICAL DISTRIBUTION;).

1117. Hankinson, T. L. 1913. Distribution of fish in the streams about Charleston, Illinois. Trans. Ill. Acad. Sci. 6:102-113. (SAUGER; WALLEYE; GEOGRAPHICAL DISTRIBUTION;).

1118. Hankinson, T. L. 1929. Fishes of North Dakota. Mich. Acad. Sci. 10:439-460. (SAUGER; WALLEYE; GEOGRAPHICAL DISTRIBUTION;).

1119. Hankinson, T. L. 1933. Distribution of the fishes in the inland lakes of Michigan. Papers Mich. Acad. Sci., Arts Letters 17:553-574. (WALLEYE; ECOLOGY; GEOGRAPHICAL DISTRIBUTION;).

1120. Hansen, D. R. 1982. Beneficial aspects of various walleye fry stocking densities in lakes with reproducing walleye populations. S.D. Dept. Game Fish Parks, Fed. Aid Fish Wildl. Restor. Proj. F-15-R-17, Jobs No. 2 & 3: 14 pp. (WALLEYE; CREEL CENSUS; POPULATION STUDIES; STOCKING;).

1121. Hansen, D. R. 1983. Beneficial aspects of various walleye fry stocking densities in lakes with reproducing walleye populations. S.D. Dept. Game Fish Parks, Fed. Aid Fish Wildl. Restor. Proj. F-15-R-18, Study No. XIV, Jobs No. 2 & 3: 14 pp. (WALLEYE; CREEL CENSUS; STOCKING;).

1122. Hanson, W. D. 1960. Fish tagging program for the large impoundments of Missouri. Mo. Conserv. Comm., Fed. Aid Fish Wildl. Restor. Proj. F-1-R-9, Wk. Pl. 5, Job No. 4: 15 pp. (WALLEYE; AGE AND GROWTH; CREEL CENSUS; IMPOUNDMENTS; MARKING;).

1123. Hanson, W. D. 1966. Harvest of fish in Pomme de Terre Reservoir, it tailwater, and Bagnell Dam tailwater. Mo. Conserv. Comm., Fed. Aid Fish Wildl. Proj. F-1-R-13, Wk. Pl. 18, Job No. 3: 13 pp. (WALLEYE; CREEL CENSUS; IMPOUNDMENTS;).

1124. Hanson, W. D. 1968. Harvest of fish in Lake of the Ozarks and its tailwater. Mo. Conserv. Comm., Fed. Aid Fish Wildl. Proj. F-1-R-17, Wk. Pl. 23, Job No. 1: 12 pp. (WALL-

EYE; CREEL CENSUS; IMPOUND-
MENTS;).

1125. Hanson, W. D., and R. S. Campbell. 1963. The
effects of pool size and beaver activity on
the distribution and abundance of warmwater fishes in a north Missouri stream.
Am. Midl. Nat. 69:136-149. (SAUGER;
WALLEYE; ECOLOGY;).

1126. Harkness, W. J. K. 1929. Report on Lac Seul,
Ontario. Manuscript Rep. in Univ. Toronto,
Great Lakes Inst. Libr. 9 pp. (WALLEYE;
AGE AND GROWTH; FOOD STUDIES;
INTRODUCTIONS;).

1127. Harkness, W. J. K. 1936. Commercial fishing
effects studied in Lake Nipissing. North
Bay Nugget, Feb. 14. p. 11. (WALLEYE;
COMMERCIAL FISHERIES;).

1128. Harkness, W. J. K. 1945. Rate of growth of
game fish. Univ. Toronto, Dept. Zool. 6 pp.
(WALLEYE; AGE AND GROWTH;).

1129. Harkness, W. J. K., and J. R. Dymond. 1961.
The lake sturgeon. Ont. Dept. Lands For-
est., Fish Wildl. Branch. 121 pp. (WALL-
EYE; SPAWNING STUDIES;).

1130. Harkness, W. J. K., and J. L. Hart. 1927. The
fishes of Long Lake, Ontario. Univ. Toronto,
Ont. Fish. Research Lab. 29:23-31. (WALL-
EYE; GEOGRAPHICAL DISTRIBU-
TION;).

1131. Harlan, J. R., and E. B. Speaker. 1956. Iowa
fish and fishing (3rd edition). Iowa State
Conserv. Comm. Des Moines. 377 pp.
(SAUGER; WALLEYE; LIFE HISTORY;
TAXONOMY;).

1132. Harlon, L. C. 1967. A study of the Lake
Champlain walleye. Vt. Fish Game Serv.,
Fed. Aid Fish Wildl. Restor. Proj. F-1-R-15,
Job No. 1: 32 pp. (WALLEYE; POPULA-
TION STUDIES;).

1133. Harper, J. L. 1978. Advanced fry stocking.
Okla. Dept. Wildl. Conserv., Fed. Aid Fish
Wildl. Restor. Proj. F-25-R, Job No. 4 (C) 11
pp. (WALLEYE; COMMUNITY DY-
NAMICS; IMPOUNDMENTS;).

1134. Harrison, H. M. 1948. Use by fish of the mod-
ified Denil fishway in the Des Moines River.
Proc. Iowa Acad. Sci. 55:367-373. (WALL-
EYE; FISHWAYS; MOVEMENT AND
MIGRATIONS;).

1135. Harrison, H. M. 1949. An annotated list of
the fishes of the upper Des Moines River basin in Iowa. Proc. Iowa Acad. Sci. 56:333-
342. (WALLEYE; GEOGRAPHICAL DIS-
TRIBUTION;).

1136. Harrison, H. M. 1956. Creel census on the
Des Moines River and its important tribu-
taries, 1953-1955. Pages 42-43 in K. D.
Carlander, ed. Symposium on sampling
problems in creel census. Iowa State Coll.,
Ames, Iowa. (WALLEYE; CREEL CEN-
SUS;).

1137. Harrison, H. M. 1962. Creel census of the Des
Moines River fishermen in Boone, Dallas,
and Polk counties, Iowa. Proc. Iowa Acad.
Sci. 69:277-285. (WALLEYE; ·CREEL
CENSUS;).

1138. Harrison, H. M., and E. B. Speaker. 1950.
Further studies of the modified Denil fish-
way in Des Moines River. Proc. Iowa Acad.
Sci. 57:409-456. (WALLEYE; FISHWAYS;
MOVEMENT AND MIGRATIONS;).

1139. Hart, J. L. 1928. Data on the growth of pike-
perch *(Stizostedion vitreum)* and sauger
(Stizostedion canadense) in Ontario. Univ.
Toronto Stud. Biol. Serv. No. 31, Publ. Ont.
Fish. Research Lab. 34:45-55. (SAUGER;
WALLEYE; AGE AND GROWTH;).

1140. Hart, L. G. 1978. Smith Mountain Reservoir
research study. Virginia Comm. Game In-
land Fish., Fed. Aid Fish Wildl. Restor.
Proj. F-30-R, Compl. Rep.: 121 pp. (WALL-
EYE; AGE AND GROWTH; COMMU-
NITY DYNAMICS; CREEL CENSUS;
IMPOUNDMENTS;   POPULATION
STUDIES; PRODUCTIVITY; REGULA-
TIONS; STOCKING;).

1141. Hart, M. L. 1973. Ottawa River creel census
summer — 1973. Ont. Min. Nat. Res., Rep.
15 pp. (WALLEYE; CREEL CENSUS;).

1142. Hart, M. L. 1973. Ottawa River creel census
1973. Ont. Min. Nat. Res., Rep. 17 pp.
(WALLEYE; CREEL CENSUS;).

1143. Hart, M. L. 1974. Pickerel spawning area, re-
habilitation study in Lake Nipissing 1974.
Ont. Min. Nat. Res., Lake Nipissing Fish.
Assess. Unit Rep. 35 pp. (WALLEYE;
SPAWNING STUDIES;).

1144. Hart, M. L. 1976. Lake Nipissing creel census, fall 1976. Ont. Min. Nat. Res., Lake

Nipissing Fish. Assess. Unit. Rep. 13 pp. (WALLEYE; CREEL CENSUS;).

1145. Hart, M. L. 1976. Lake Nipissing creel census, winter 1976. Ont. Min. Nat. Res., Lake Nipissing Fish. Assess. Unit Rep. 39 pp. (WALLEYE; CREEL CENSUS;).

1146. Hart, M. L. 1977. Lake Nipissing creel census, winter 1977. Ont. Min. Nat. Res., Lake Nipissing Fish. Assess. Unit Rep. 28 pp. (WALLEYE; CREEL CENSUS;).

1147. Hart, M. L. 1978. Lake Nipissing creel census, fall 1977. Ont. Min. Nat. Res., Lake Nipissing Fish. Assess. Unit. Rep. 17 pp. (WALLEYE; CREEL CENSUS;).

1148. Hartman, W. L. 1958. The use of sedatives to reduce manipulative error in measuring fish. N.Y. Fish Game J. 5:1-8. (WALLEYE; SAMPLING METHODS;).

1149. Hartman, W. L. 1970. Effect of different incubation temperatures on the embryonic development of walleye *(Stizostedion vitreum)* eggs. Bur. Comm. Fish., Biol. Lab., Sandusky, Ohio. 12 pp. (WALLEYE; EMBRYOLOGY;).

1150. Hartman, W. L. 1973. Effects of exploitation, environmental changes, and new species on the fish habitats and resources of Lake Erie. Great Lakes Fish. Comm., Tech. Rep. No. 22: 43 pp. (WALLEYE; COMMERCIAL FISHERIES; HABITAT DEGRADATION;).

1151. Hartmann, R. F. 1968. Fish stocking needs. Kan. Forest, Fish and Game Comm., Fed. Aid Fish and Wildl. Restor. Proj. F-15-R-3, Job C-1-3: 31 pp. (WALLEYE; IMPOUNDMENTS; INTRODUCTIONS;).

1152. Harvey, H. H. 1975. Fish populations in a large group of acid-stressed lakes. Pages 2406-2417 *in* V. Sladecek ed., Congress in Canada 1974. (WALLEYE; ECOLOGY; HABITAT DEGRADATION;).

1153. Harvey, H. H. 1978. Fish communities of the Manitoulin Island lakes. Verh. Internat. Verein. Limnol. 20:2031-2038. (WALLEYE; COMMUNITY DYNAMICS; ECOLOGY;).

1154. Harvey, H. H. 1981. Fish communities of the lakes of the Bruce Peninsula. Verh. Internat. Verein. Limnol. 21:1222-1230.

(WALLEYE; COMMUNITY DYNAMICS; ECOLOGY;).

1155. Haskell, D. C., D. Geduldig, and E. Snoek. 1955. An electric trawl. N.Y. Fish Game J. 2:120-125. (WALLEYE; SAMPLING METHODS;).

1156. Haskell, D. C., and R. C. Zilliox. 1941. Further developments of the electrical method of collecting fish. Trans. Am. Fish. Soc. 70:404-409. (WALLEYE; SAMPLING METHODS;).

1157. Haslbauer, O. F. 1945. Fish distribution, Norris Reservoir, Tennessee 1943. III. Relation of the bottom of fish distribution, Norris Reservoir. Rep. Reelfoot Lake Biol. Stat. 9:135-138. (SAUGER; WALLEYE; ECOLOGY; GEOGRAPHICAL DISTRIBUTION;).

1158. Hassler, W. W. 1957. Age and growth of the sauger, *Stizostedion canadense* (Smith) in Norris Reservoir, Tennessee. J. Tenn. Acad. Sci. 32:55-76. (SAUGER; AGE AND GROWTH; ECOLOGY;).

1159. Hassler, W. W. 1958. The fecundity, sex ratio, and maturity of the sauger, *Stizostedion canadense* (Smith) in Norris Reservoir, Tennessee. J. Tenn. Acad. Sci. 33:32-38. (SAUGER; AGE AND GROWTH; SPAWNING STUDIES;).

1160. Hatch, R. W., S. J. Nepszy, K. M. Muth, and C. T. Baker. 1987. Dynamics of the recovery of the western Lake Erie walleye *(Stizostedion vitreum vitreum)* stock. Can. J. Fish. Aquat. Sci. 44(Suppl. 2):15-22. (WALLEYE; AGE AND GROWTH; COMMERCIAL FISHERIES; POPULATION STUDIES;).

1161. Hauber, A. B. 1983. Two methods for evaluating fingerling walleye stocking success and natural year-class densities in Seven Island Lake, Wisconsin, 1977-1981. N. Am. J. Fish. Manage. 3:152-155. (WALLEYE; FISHING GEAR; POPULATION STUDIES; STOCKING;).

1162. Hawkinson, B. W., and H. F. Krosch. 1972. Annual report of the statewide creel census on 80 lakes and 38 trout streams in Minnesota, May 1971-February 1972. Minn. Dept. Nat. Res., Invest. Rep. No. 319: 73 pp. (WALLEYE; CREEL CENSUS;).

1163. Hay, O. P. 1894. The lampreys and fishes of Indiana. Ind. Dept. Geol. Nat. Res., 19th Annu. Rep. pp. 146-296. (SAUGER; WALLEYE; GEOGRAPHICAL DISTRIBUTION; TAXONOMY;).

1164. Hay, O. P. 1896. On some collections of fishes made in the Kankakee and Illinois Rivers. Field Columbian Mus., Zool. Serv. 1:83-97. (WALLEYE; GEOGRAPHICAL DISTRIBUTION;).

1165. Hayes, F. R. 1957. On the variation in bottom fauna and fish yield in relation to trophic level and lake dimensions. J. Fish. Research Board Can. 14:1-32. (WALLEYE; ECOLOGY; PRODUCTIVITY;).

1166. Haymes, G. T. 1986. Atikokan GS preoperational aquatic survey three-year summary, 1981-1983. Ont. Hydro Res. Div. Rep. No. 86-38-K:. (WALLEYE; AGE AND GROWTH; COMMUNITY DYNAMICS; ECOLOGY; MORTALITY;).

1167. Hayne, D. W., G. E. Hall, and H. M. Nichols. 1967. An evaluation of cove sampling of fish populations in Douglas Reservoir, Tennessee. Reservoir Fishery Resour. Symposium, Reservoir Comm., Southern Div., Am. Fish. Soc., Bethesda, Md. pp. 244-297. (SAUGER; IMPOUNDMENTS; MOVEMENTS AND MIGRATIONS;).

1168. Hazel, P. P., and R. Fortin. 1986. The walleye (Stizostedion vitreum Mitchill) in Quebec: biology and management. Univ. of Quebec at Montreal, Preliminary 415 pp. (WALLEYE; ECOLOGY; GEOGRAPHICAL DISTRIBUTION; POPULATION STUDIES; PRODUCTIVITY; REGULATIONS;).

1169. Hazzard, A. S. 1930. A biological survey of Lake Champlain watershed. I. Stocking policy for the streams, lakes and ponds of the Champlain watershed. N.Y. Conserv. Dept., Suppl. 19th Annu. Rep. pp. 22-43, Append. 3: 289-321. (WALLEYE; STOCKING;).

1170. Hazzard, A. S., and R. W. Eschmeyer. 1937. A comparison of summer and winter fishing in Michigan lakes. Trans. Am. Fish. Soc. 66:87-97. (WALLEYE; CREEL CENSUS;).

1171. Hazzard, A. S., and R. W. Eschmeyer. 1938. Analysis of the fish catch for one year in the Waterloo project area. Papers Mich. Acad. Sci., Arts Letters 23:633-643. (WALLEYE; IMPOUNDMENTS;).

1172. Hearn, M. C. 1980. Ovulation of pond-reared walleyes in response to various injection levels of human chorionic gonadotropin. Prog. Fish-Cult. 42:228-230. (WALLEYE; PROPAGATION;).

1173. Hearn, M. C. 1986. Reproductive viability of sauger-walleye hybrids. Prog. Fish-Cult. 48:149-150. (SAUGER; WALLEYE; GENETICS;).

1174. Heartwell, C. M. 1970. Walleye life history studies. W. Va. Div. Game Fish, Fed. Aid Fish Wildl. Restor. Proj. F-10-R-12, Wk. Pl. 4: 12 pp. (WALLEYE; AGE AND GROWTH; CREEL CENSUS; IMPOUNDMENTS; MARKING; SPAWNING STUDIES;).

1175. Heaton, J. R. 1962. Age and growth studies and analysis of bottom samples in connection with pollution studies. Mont. Fish Game Dept., Fed. Aid Fish Wildl. Restor. Proj. F-23-R-5, Jobs No. 1 and 2: 7 pp. (WALLEYE; AGE AND GROWTH; HABITAT DEGRADATION;).

1176. Heckmann, R. A., C. W. Thompson, and D. A. White. 1981. Fishes of Utah Lake. Great Basin Nat. Mem. pp. 107-127. (WALLEYE; LIFE HISTORY;).

1177. Hector, D. G. 1978. Summer creel census in the Canadian waters of the western basin of Lake Erie 1977. Ont. Min. Nat. Res., Lake Erie Fish. Assess. Unit. Rep. 105 pp. (WALLEYE; CREEL CENSUS;).

1178. Hector, D. G. 1979. Fall pound net program, Lake St. Clair, 1978. Ont. Min. Nat. Res., Lake St. Clair Fish. Assess. Unit Rep. 1979-1: 25 pp. (WALLEYE; AGE AND GROWTH; POPULATION STUDIES;).

1179. Hector, D. G. 1979. Winter creel census in the Canadian waters of Lake St. Clair and the lower Thames River 1979. Ont. Min. Nat. Res., Lake St. Clair Fish. Assess. Unit Rep. 1979-2: 35 pp. (WALLEYE; AGE AND GROWTH; CREEL CENSUS;).

1180. Hector, D. G. 1979. Summer creel census in the Canadian waters of Lake St. Clair, 1979. Ont. Min. Nat. Res., Lake St. Clair Fish. Assess. Unit Rep. 1979-8: 25 pp. (WALLEYE; AGE AND GROWTH; CREEL CENSUS;).

1181. Hector, D. G. 1979. Fall pound net program Lake St. Clair, 1979. Ont. Min. Nat. Res.,

Lake St. Clair Fish. Assess. Unit Rep. 1979-10: 11 pp. (WALLEYE; AGE AND GROWTH; POPULATION STUDIES;).

1182. Hector, D. G. 1979. Summer creel census in the Canadian waters of Lake St. Clair, 1978. Ont. Min. Nat. Res., Lake St. Clair Fish. Assess. Unit Rep. 1979-11: 25 pp. (WALLEYE; AGE AND GROWTH; CREEL CENSUS;).

1183. Hector, D. G. 1979. Winter creel census in the Canadian waters of Lake St. Clair and Lower Thames River, 1978. Ont. Min. Nat. Res., Lake St. Clair Fish. Assess. Unit Rep. 1979-12: 32 pp. (WALLEYE; AGE AND GROWTH; CREEL CENSUS;).

1184. Hector, D. G. 1979. Winter creel census in the Canadian waters of Lake St. Clair and Lower Thames River, 1977. Ont. Min. Nat. Res., Lake St. Clair Fish. Assess. Unit Rep. 1979-13: 32 pp. (WALLEYE; AGE AND GROWTH; CREEL CENSUS;).

1185. Hector, D. G. 1980. Winter creel census in the Canadian waters of Lake St. Clair and the lower Thames River, 1980. Ont. Min. Nat. Res., Lake St. Clair Fish. Assess. Unit Rep. 1980-1: 33 pp. (WALLEYE; AGE AND GROWTH; CREEL CENSUS;).

1186. Hector, D. G. 1980. Summer creel census in the Canadian waters of Lake St. Clair, 1980. Ont. Min. Nat. Res., Lake St. Clair Fish Assess. Unit Rep. 1980-3: 31 pp. (WALLEYE; AGE AND GROWTH; CREEL CENSUS;).

1187. Hector, D. G. 1980. Fall pound net program, Lake St. Clair, 1980. Ont. Min. Nat. Res., Lake St. Clair Fish Assess. Unit Rep. 1980-5: 23 pp. (WALLEYE; POPULATION STUDIES;).

1188. Hector, D. G. 1981. Winter creel census in the Canadian waters of Lake St. Clair and the lower Thames River 1981. Ont. Min. Nat. Res., Lake St. Clair Fish. Assess. Unit Rep. 1981-1: 21 pp. (WALLEYE; AGE AND GROWTH; CREEL CENSUS;).

1189. Hector, D. G. 1981. Summer creel census in the Canadian waters of Lake St. Clair, 1981. Ont. Min. Nat. Res., Lake St. Clair Fish. Assess. Unit Rep. 1981-3: 30 pp. (WALLEYE; AGE AND GROWTH; CREEL CENSUS;).

1190. Hector, D. G. 1981. Fall pound net program, Lake St. Clair, 1981. Ont. Min. Nat. Res.,

Lake St. Clair Fish. Assess. Unit Rep. 1981-4: 10 pp. (WALLEYE; POPULATION STUDIES;).

1191. Hector, D. G. 1982. Winter creel census in the Canadian waters of Lake St. Clair and the Lower Thames River, 1982. Ont. Min. Nat. Res., Lake St. Clair Fish. Assess. Unit Rep. 1982-1: 38 pp. (WALLEYE; AGE AND GROWTH; CREEL CENSUS;).

1192. Hector, D. G. 1982. Summer creel census in the Canadian waters of Lake St. Clair, 1982. Ont. Min. Nat. Res., Lake St. Clair Fish. Assess. Unit Rep. 1982-2: 50 pp. (WALLEYE; AGE AND GROWTH; CREEL CENSUS;).

1193. Hector, D. G. 1982. Fall pound net program, Lake St. Clair, 1982. Ont. Min. Nat. Res., Lake St. Clair Fish. Assess. Unit Rep. 1982-4: 28 pp. (WALLEYE; AGE AND GROWTH; POPULATION STUDIES;).

1194. Hector, D. G. 1983. Summer creel census in the Canadian waters of Lake St. Clair, 1983. Ont. Min. Nat. Res., Lake St. Clair Fish. Assess. Unit Rep. 1983-1: 52 pp. (WALLEYE; CREEL CENSUS;).

1195. Hector, D. G. 1983. Fall pound net program, Lake St. Clair, 1983. Ont. Min. Nat. Res., Lake St. Clair Fish. Assess. Unit Rep. 1983-5: 46 pp. (WALLEYE; AGE AND GROWTH; POPULATION STUDIES;).

1196. Hector, D. G. 1984. Winter angler survey in the Canadian waters of Lake St. Clair and the Lower Thames River, 1984. Ont. Min. Nat. Res., Lake St. Clair Fish. Assess. Unit Rep. 1984-1: 56 pp. (WALLEYE; AGE AND GROWTH; CREEL CENSUS;).

1197. Hector, D. G. 1984. Fall pound net program, Lake St. Clair, 1984. Ont. Min. Nat. Res., Lake St. Clair Fish. Assess. Unit Rep. 1984-5: 57 pp. (WALLEYE; AGE AND GROWTH; POPULATION STUDIES;).

1198. Hector, D. G. 1985. Fall pound net program, Lake St. Clair, 1985. Ont. Min. Nat. Res., Lake St. Clair Fish. Assess. Unit Rep. 1985-5: 52 pp. (WALLEYE; AGE AND GROWTH; POPULATION STUDIES;).

1199. Heidinger, R. C., and K. Clodfelter. 1987. Validity of the otolith for determining age and growth of walleye, striped bass, and smallmouth bass in power plant cooling ponds. Pages 241-251 *in* R.C. Summerfelt and G.E. Hall, eds. Age and growth of fish. Iowa St. Univ. Press, Ames, Iowa. (WALLEYE; AGE AND GROWTH;).

1200. Heidinger, R. C., D. R. Helms, T. I. Hiebert, and P. H. Howe. 1983. Operational comparison of three electrofishing systems. N. Am. J. Fish. Manage. 3:254-257. (WALLEYE; FISHING GEAR; SAMPLING METHODS;).

1201. Heidinger, R. C., and B. L. Tetzlaff. 1985. Illinois Walleye research: Investigation of intensive Walleye rearing techniques and evaluation of the relative survival of larval vs. fingerling Walleye stocked in two Illinois reservoirs. S. Illinois Univ., Co-op Fish. Research Lab., Carbondale, Ill.: 83 pp. (WALLEYE; FOOD STUDIES; IMPOUNDMENTS; MORTALITY; PROPAGATION; STOCKING;).

1202. Heidinger, R. C., B. L. Tetzlaff, and J. H. Waddell. 1984. Illinois walleye research. Ill. Dept. Conserv. and South. Ill. Univ., Carbondale, Ill., Fed. Aid Fish Wildl. Restor. Proj. F-41-R-3, Study No. 101, 102: 18 pp. (WALLEYE; FOOD STUDIES; PROPAGATION;).

1203. Helfman, G. S. 1981. Twilight activities and temporal structure in a freshwater fish community. Can. J. Fish. Aquat. Sci. 38:1405-1420. (WALLEYE; BEHAVIOR; COMMUNITY DYNAMICS; MOVEMENT AND MIGRATIONS;).

1204. Henderson, J. P. 1971. Food habits of the walleye, *Stizostedion vitreum vitreum* (Mitchill), in Canton Reservoir, Oklahoma. M.S. Thesis. Univ. Okla., Norman, Okla. 90 pp. (WALLEYE; FOOD STUDIES; IMPOUNDMENTS;).

1205. Henderson, N. E., and R. E. Peter. 1969. Distribution of fishes of southern Alberta. J. Fish. Research Board Can. 26:325-338. (SAUGER; WALLEYE; GEOGRAPHICAL DISTRIBUTION;).

1206. Henderson, P. 1967. Investigations of the food habits of walleye in Canton Reservoir. Okla. Dept. Wildl. Conserv., Fed. Aid Fish Wildl. Restor. Proj. F-16-R-3, Wk. Pl. 2, Job No. 1, Part 2: 21 pp. (WALLEYE; AGE AND GROWTH; COMMUNITY DYNAMICS; FOOD STUDIES; IMPOUNDMENTS;).

1207. Hendry, M. J. 1977. Bay of Quinte creel census report — 1976. Ont. Min. Nat. Res., LO-FAU Rep. (76.1): 36 pp. (WALLEYE; CREEL CENSUS;).

1208. Henegar, D. L. 1966. Minimum lethal levels of toxaphene as a pesticide in North Dakota lakes. U.S. Fish Wildl. Serv., Invest. Fish Control 3:16. (WALLEYE; TOXICANTS;).

1209. Henshall, J. A. 1884. Comparative excellence of food fishes. Trans. Am. Fish Cult. 13:115-122. (WALLEYE; FOOD STUDIES;).

1210. Henshall, J. A. 1889. Contributions to the ichthyology of Ohio. J. Cincinnati Soc., Nat. Hist. 11:76-80. (SAUGER; WALLEYE; GEOGRAPHICAL DISTRIBUTION;).

1211. Henshall, J. A. 1891. On the teeth of fishes as a guide to their food habits. Trans. Am. Fish. Soc. 20:24-30. (WALLEYE; FOOD STUDIES;).

1212. Henshall, J. A. 1919. Bass, Pike, perch and other game fishes of America. Stewart and Kidd Co., Cincinnati, Ohio. 410 pp. (SAUGER; WALLEYE; BEHAVIOR; LIFE HISTORY; TAXONOMY;).

1213. Hepworth, D., and S. P. Gloss. 1976. Food habits and age-growth of walleye in Lake Powell, Utah-Arizona, with reference to introduction of threadfin shad. Utah State Div. Wildl. Res. Publ. No. 76-15: 13 pp. (SAUGER; WALLEYE; AGE AND GROWTH; FOOD STUDIES; IMPOUNDMENTS;).

1214. Herdendorf, C. F., C. E. Raphael, and E. Jaworski. 1986. The ecology of Lake St. Clair wetlands: a community profile. U.S. Fish Wildl. Serv. Biol. Rep. 85(7.7): 187 pp. (WALLEYE; SPAWNING STUDIES;).

1215. Hesse, L. W., C. R. Wallace, and L. Lehman. 1976. Age-growth, length-frequency, length-weight, coefficient of condition, catch curves and mortality of 25 species of channelized Missouri River fishes. Neb. Game Parks Comm., Fed. Aid Fish Wildl. Restor. Proj. F-4-R: 59 pp. (WALLEYE; AGE AND GROWTH; MORTALITY;).

1216. Hesse, L. W., C. R. Wallace, and L. Lehman. 1978. Fishes of the channelized Missouri. Age-growth, length-frequency, length-weight, coefficient of condition, catch curves and mortality of 25 species of channelized Missouri River fishes. Neb. Game Parks Comm., Tech. Series No. 4: 61 pp. (SAUGER; AGE AND GROWTH; COMMUNITY DYNAMICS; HABITAT DEGRADATION; MORTALITY;).

1217. Hewson, L. C. 1951. A comparison of nylon and cotton gill nets used in the Lake Winnipeg winter fishery. Can. Fish. Cult. 11:1-3. (SAUGER; WALLEYE; FISHING GEAR; SAMPLING METHODS;).

1218. Hewson, L. C. 1955. Age, maturity, spawning and food of burbot *(Lota lota)*, in Lake Winnipeg. J. Fish. Research Board Can. 12:930-940. (SAUGER; WALLEYE; COMMUNITY DYNAMICS;).

1219. Hewson, L. C. 1959. A seven year study of the fishery for lake whitefish *(Coregonus clupeaformis)* on Lake Winnipeg. J. Fish. Research Board Can. 16:107-120. (SAUGER; WALLEYE; COMMERCIAL FISHERIES;).

1220. Hewson, L. C. 1959. A study of six winter seasons of commercial fishing on Lake Winnipeg, 1950-1955. J. Fish. Research Board Can. 16:131-145. (SAUGER; WALLEYE; AGE AND GROWTH; COMMERCIAL FISHERIES; FISHING GEAR;).

1221. Heyerdahl, E. G., and L. L. Smith, Jr. 1971. Annual catch of yellow perch from Red Lakes, Minnesota, in relation to the growth rate and fishing effort. Univ. Minn., Agri. Exp. Sta., Tech. Bull. No. 285: 51 pp. (WALLEYE; AGE AND GROWTH;).

1222. Heyerdahl, E. G., and L. L. Smith, Jr. 1972. Fishery resources for Lake of the Woods, Minnesota. Univ. Minn., Agri. Exp. Sta., Tech. Bull. 288: 145 pp. (SAUGER; WALLEYE; AGE AND GROWTH; COMMERCIAL FISHERIES; COMMUNITY DYNAMICS; FISHING GEAR; MORTALITY; REGULATIONS;).

1223. Hickman, G. D., and K. W. Hevel. 1986. Effect of a hypolimnetic discharge on reproductive success and growth of warmwater fish in a downstream impoundment. Pages 286-293 in G. E. Hall and M. J. Van Den Avyle, eds. Reservoir fisheries management: strategies for the 80's. Reserv. Comm., S. Div. Am. Fish. Soc., Bethesda, Maryland. (SAUGER; WALLEYE; IMPOUNDMENTS; POPULATION STUDIES; SPAWNING STUDIES;).

1224. Hicks, D. E. 1963. Utilization of trap nets for the capture of walleye. Okla. Dept. Wildl. Conserv., Fed. Aid Fish Wildl. Restor. Proj. F-7-R-3, Job No. 1: 3 p. (WALLEYE; IMPOUNDMENTS; POPULATION STUDIES; SAMPLING METHODS; STOCKING;).

1225. Higgins, E. 1942. Can the fisheries supply more food during a national emergency? Trans. Am. Fish. Soc. 71:61-73. (SAUGER; WALLEYE; COMMUNITY DYNAMICS;).

1226. Hile, R. 1936. Age and growth of the cisco *(Coregonus artedi)* in lakes of the northeastern highlands, Wisconsin. U.S. Bur. Fish., Bull. 48:211-317. (SAUGER; WALLEYE; GEOGRAPHICAL DISTRIBUTION;).

1227. Hile, R. 1937. The increase in the abundance of the yellow pike perch *(Stizostedion vitreum)* (Mitchill) in Lake Huron and Michigan, in relation to the artificial propagation of the species. Trans. Am. Fish. Soc. 66:143-159. (WALLEYE; COMMERCIAL FISHERIES; POPULATION STUDIES; PROPAGATION; STOCKING;).

1228. Hile, R. 1954. Fluctuations in growth and year class strength of the walleyes in Saginaw Bay. U.S. Fish Wildl. Serv., Fish. Bull. 91:5-59. (WALLEYE; AGE AND GROWTH; COMMERCIAL FISHERIES; PATHOLOGY; SPAWNING STUDIES;).

1229. Hile, R. 1955. The walleye problem in Green Bay. Prog. Fish-Cult. 17:44. (WALLEYE; CREEL CENSUS;).

1230. Hile, R. 1962. Collection and analysis of commercial fishery statistics in the Great Lakes. Great Lakes Fish. Comm., Tech. Rep. No. 5:31. (SAUGER; WALLEYE; COMMERCIAL FISHERIES; SAMPLING METHODS;).

1231. Hile, R., and H. J. Buetter. 1959. Fluctuations in the commercial fisheries of Saginaw Bay, 1885-1956. U.S. Fish Wildl. Serv., Research Rep. 51:38. (SAUGER; WALLEYE; COMMERCIAL FISHERIES;).

1232. Hile, R., and W. R. Duden. 1933. Methods for the investigation of statistics of the commercial fisheries of the Great Lakes. Trans. Am. Fish. Soc. 63:292-305. (WALLEYE; COMMERCIAL FISHERIES;).

12.. Hile R., and F. W. Jobes. 1941. Age, growth, and production of the yellow perch *(Perca flavescens)* of Saginaw Bay. Trans. Am. Fish. Soc. 70:102-122. (WALLEYE; COMMERCIAL FISHERIES;).

1234 Hile. R., and R. W. Jobes. 1942. Age and growth of the yellow perch *(Perca flavescens)* in the Wisconsin waters of Green Bay and northern Lake Michigan. Mich. Acad. Sci., Arts Letters 27:241-266. (WALLEYE; CREEL CENSUS;).

1235 Hile. R., and C. Judy. 1941. Bathymetric distribution of fish in lakes of the northeastern highlands, Wisconsin. Trans. Wis. Acad. Sci., Arts Letter 33:147-187. (WALLEYE; ECOLOGY; GEOGRAPHICAL DISTRIBUTION; SAMPLING METHODS;).

1236. Hile. R., G. E. Luger, and H. J. Buettner. 1953. Fluctuations in the fisheries of Michigan waters of Green Bay. U.S. Fish Wildl. Serv., Fish. Bull. 54:1-34. (WALLEYE; COMMERCIAL FISHERIES;).

1237. Hill, C. W. 1961. Northeast Montana fisheries study. General investigations. Mont. Fish Game Dept., Fed. Aid Fish Wildl. Restor. Proj. F-11-R-8, Job No. 1-E: 6 pp. (SAUGER; WALLEYE; AGE AND GROWTH; ECOLOGY; IMPOUNDMENTS; SAMPLING METHODS; STOCKING;).

1238. Hill, W. J., and A. H. Wipperman. 1985. Inventory and survey of waters in the western half of Region Four. Mont. Dept. Fish Wildl. Parks, Fed. Aid Fish Wildl. Restor. Proj. F-5-R-34, Job No. I-a: 17 pp. (WALLEYE; FOOD STUDIES; MARKING; MORTALITY;).

1239. Hill, W. J., and A. H. Wipperman. 1986. Inventory and survey of waters in the western half of Region Four. Mont. Dept. Fish Wildl. Parks, Fed. Aid Fish Wildl. Restor. Proj. F-5-R-35, Job No. I-a: 15 pp. (WALLEYE; CREEL CENSUS; MARKING; MORTALITY; POPULATION STUDIES;).

1240. Hill, W. J., and A. H. Wipperman. 1987. Inventory and development of warm/cool fish populations in Region Four waters. Mont. Dept. Fish, Wildl. Parks, Fed. Aid Fish Wildl. Restor. Proj. F-5-R-36, Job III:. (WALLEYE; COMMUNITY DYNAMICS; IMPOUNDMENTS; MARKING; POPULATION STUDIES; STOCKING;).

1241. Hilsenhoff, W. L. 1962. Toxicity of granular malathion to walleye *(Stizostedion vitreum)* fingerlings. Mosquito News 22:14-15. (WALLEYE; HABITAT DEGRADATION; MORTALITY; TOXICANTS;).

1242. Hiltner, R. J. 1983. Comparison of walleye, *Stizostedion vitreum vitreum* (Mitchill), ecology and biology from three discrete areas of Lake Sakakawea, North Dakota. M.S. Thesis, Univ. N.D., Grand Forks, N.D.: 111 pp. (WALLEYE; COMMUNITY DYNAMICS; ECOLOGY; MOVEMENTS AND MIGRATIONS;).

1243. Hiner, L. E. 1943. A creel census on Minnesota lakes, 1938-1942. Minn. Dept. Conserv., Invest. Rep. No. 44: 20 pp. (WALLEYE; CREEL CENSUS; STOCKING;).

1244. Hiner, L. E. 1947. Creel census summary 1946. Minn. Dept. Conserv., Invest. Rep. No. 68: 9 pp. (WALLEYE; CREEL CENSUS;).

1245. Hinks, D. 1943. The fishes of Manitoba. Man. Dept. Mines Nat. Res. 102 pp. (SAUGER; WALLEYE; LIFE HISTORY; TAXONOMY;).

1246. Hinton, D. E., E. R. Walker, C. A. Pinkstaff, and E. M. Zuchelkowski. 1984. Morphological survey of teleost organs important in carcinogenesis with attention to fixation. Pages 291-320 *in* K.L. Hoover, ed. Use of small fish species in carcinogenicity testing. National Cancer Institute Monograph No. 65, Bethesda, Maryland. (WALLEYE; MORPHOLOGY;).

1247. Hnath, J. G. 1975. A summary of the fish diseases and treatments administered in a cool water diet testing program. Prog. Fish-Cult. 37:106-107. (WALLEYE; PATHOLOGY;).

1248. Hoff, J. G., and M. Chittenden. 1969. Oxygen requirements of the walleye *(Stizostedion vitreum)*. N.Y. Fish Game J. 16:125-126. (WALLEYE; MORTALITY; PHYSIOLOGY;).

1249. Hoffman, G. L. 1956. The life cycle of *Crassiphiala bulboglossa* (Trematoda: Strigeida). Development of the metacercaria and cyst, and the effects on the fish hosts. J. Parasitology. 42:435-444. (WALLEYE; PATHOLOGY;).

1250. Hoffman, G. L. 1960. Synopsis of Strigeoidea (Trematoda) of fishes and their life cycles. U.S. Fish Wildl. Serv., Fish. Bull. 60:439-469. (SAUGER; WALLEYE; PATHOLOGY;).

1251. Hoffman, G. L. 1967. Parasites of North American freshwater fishes. Univ. Calif. Press, Berkeley, Calif. 486 pp. (SAUGER; WALLEYE; PATHOLOGY;).

1252. Hofmann, P. 1969. Growth of walleye in Oneida Lake and its relation to food supply. N.Y. Coop. Fish. Res. Unit, Fed. Aid Fish Wildl. Restor. Proj. F-17-R-13, Job No. 1-F: 19 pp. (WALLEYE; AGE AND GROWTH; COMMUNITY DYNAMICS; FOOD STUDIES;).

1253. Hofmann, P. 1972. Consumption of young yellow perch (Perca flavescens) by a walleye (Stizostedion vitreum vitreum) population in Oneida Lake. Ph.D. Dissertation, Cornell Univ., Ithaca, N.Y. 76 pp. (WALLEYE; AGE AND GROWTH; COMMUNITY DYNAMICS; FOOD STUDIES; PRODUCTIVITY;).

1254. Hogan, J. 1941. The effects of high vacuum on fish. Trans. Am. Fish. Soc. 70:469-474. (WALLEYE; IMPOUNDMENTS; MORTALITY; MOVEMENT AND MIGRATIONS;).

1255. Hogg, D. M. 1974. Results of Port Severn creel census spring 1974. Ont. Min. Nat. Res., Rep. 19 pp. (WALLEYE; CREEL CENSUS;).

1256. Hohn, M. H. 1966. Analysis of plankton ingested by Stizostedion vitreum vitreum (Mitchill) fry and concurrent vertical plankton tows from southwestern Lake Erie, May, 1961 and May, 1962. Ohio J. Sci. 66:193-197. (WALLEYE; FOOD STUDIES;).

1257. Hokanson, K. E. F. 1977. Temperature requirements of some percids and adaptations to the seasonal temperature cycle. J. Fish. Research Board Can. 34:1524-1550. (SAUGER; WALLEYE; ECOLOGY; MORTALITY; SPAWNING STUDIES;).

1258. Hokanson, K. E. F., and W. M. Koenst. 1986. Revised estimates of growth requirements and lethal temperature limits of juvenile walleyes. Prog. Fish-Cult. 48:90-94. (WALL-EYE; AGE AND GROWTH; MORTALITY; PHYSIOLOGY;).

1259. Hokanson, K. E. F., and G. J. Lien. 1985. Effects of organic contaminants in ova upon growth and survival of larval walleye from the Lower Fox River and Sturgeon Bay Areas of Green Bay, Wisconsin. Environ. Protection Agency — Duluth, Minnesota, In-house Rep. 45 pp. (WALLEYE; EMBRYOLOGY; HABITAT DEGRADATION; MORTALITY; TOXICANTS;).

1260. Hokanson, K. E. F., and G. J. Lien. 1986. Effects of diet on growth and survival of larval walleyes. Prog. Fish-Cult. 48:250-258. (WALLEYE; FOOD STUDIES; MORTALITY; PROPAGATION;).

1261. Holanov, S. H., and J. C. Tash. 1976. Walleye management program in Arizona (with a bibliography on walleyes). Ariz. Coop. Fish. Research Unit, Research Rep. Series No. 76-1: 26 pp. (WALLEYE; AGE AND GROWTH; IMPOUNDMENTS; INTRODUCTIONS; STOCKING;).

1262. Holland, L. E. 1987. Effect of brief navigation-related dewaterings on fish eggs and larvae. N. Am. J. Fish. Manage. 7:145-147. (WALLEYE; ECOLOGY; HABITAT DEGRADATION; MORTALITY; SPAWNING STUDIES;).

1263. Hollingsworth, R. 1967. Clear Lake walleye (Stizostedion vitreum) population estimate. Iowa State Conserv. Comm., Quart. Biol. Rep. 19:27-32. (WALLEYE; POPULATION STUDIES;).

1264. Holloway, H. L., Jr., and N. T. Hagstrom. 1981. Comparison of four North Dakota impoundments and factors affecting the development of impoundments parasite fauna. The Prairie Nat. 13:85-93. (WALLEYE; IMPOUNDMENTS; PATHOLOGY;).

1265. Holloway, H. L., Jr., and C. E. Smith. 1978. Muscular necrosis of Stizostedion vitreum in North Dakota. Am. Zool. 18:611. (WALLEYE; PHYSIOLOGY;).

1266. Holloway, H. L., Jr., and C. E. Smith. 1982. A myopathy in North Dakota walleye, Stizostedion vitreum (Mitchill). J. Fish Dis. 5:527-530. (WALLEYE; PATHOLOGY;).

1267. Holmbeck, D. G., and W. G. Johnson. 1978. The summer sport fishery Big Splithand

Lake, Itasca County, Minnesota 1975-77 with comparison to the 1955-56 fishery. Minn. Dept. Nat. Res., Fish Manage. Rep. No. 5: 15 pp. (WALLEYE; CREEL CENSUS;).

1268. Holmbeck, D. G., and W. G. Johnson. 1978. The summer sport fishery Big Moose Lake, Itasca County, Minnesota 1975-77 with comparison to the 1952-56 fishery. Minn. Dept. Nat. Res., Fish Manage. Rep. No. 6: 13 pp. (WALLEYE; CREEL CENSUS;).

1269. Holt, C. S., G. D. S. Grant, G. P. Oberstar, C. C. Oakes, and D. W. Bradt. 1977. Movement of walleye, *Stizostedion vitreum vitreum*, in Lake Bemidji, Minnesota as determined by radio-biotelemetry. Trans. Am. Fish. Soc. 106:163-169. (WALLEYE; BEHAVIOR; ECOLOGY; MOVEMENTS AND MIGRATIONS;).

1270. Holzer, J. A., and K. L. Von Ruden. 1981. Determining walleye *(Stizostedion vitreum)* movement and exploitation rates in the Upper Mississippi River. Miss. River Work Unit Annu. Rep. pp. 73-81. (WALLEYE; MOVEMENT AND MIGRATIONS;).

1271. Hood, S. 1968. Walleye culture in Pennsylvania. Penn. Fish. Comm. 7 pp. (WALLEYE; PROPAGATION;).

1272. Hooper, F. F., and K. G. Fukano. 1960. Summary of experimental lake treatments with toxaphene 1954-1958. Mich. Dept. Conserv., Inst. Fish. Research, Rep. 1584: 18 pp. (WALLEYE; HABITAT IMPROVEMENT; TOXICANTS;).

1273. Hope, D. 1972. Summer creel census for Gowganda Lake, Management Unit 7, Swastika District. Ont. Min. Nat. Res., Rep. 15 pp. (WALLEYE; CREEL CENSUS;).

1274. Hopky, G. E. 1982. A comparison of yellow perch *(Perca flavescens)*, walleye *(Stizostedion vitreum)*, and northern pike *(Esox lucious)* populations characteristics in two saline-eutrophic lakes of southwestern Manitoba. M.S. Thesis, Univ. Man., Winnipeg, Man. 174 pp. (WALLEYE; AGE AND GROWTH; POPULATION STUDIES;).

1275. Horn, M. H. 1966. Analysis of plankton ingested by *Stizostedion vitreum vitreum* (Mitchill) fry and concurrent vertical plankton tows from southwestern Lake Erie, May 1961 and May 1962. Ohio J. Sci. 66:193-197. (WALLEYE; FOOD STUDIES;).

1276. Horrall, R. M., and J. D. Bruin. 1965. Population dynamics of yellow walleye in lakes. Wis. Conserv. Dept., Fed. Aid Fish Wildl. Restor. Proj. F-83-R-1, Wk. Pl. 18, Job C: 2 pp. (WALLEYE; POPULATION STUDIES; SPAWNING STUDIES; STOCKING;).

1277. Houde, E. D. 1967. Food of pelagic young of the walleye, *Stizostedion vitreum vitreum* in Oneida Lake, New York. Trans. Am. Fish. Soc. 96:17-24. (WALLEYE; FOOD STUDIES;).

1278. Houde, E. D. 1968. The relation of water currents and zooplankton abundance to distribution of larval walleyes *(Stizostedion vitreum)*, in Oneida Lake, New York. Ph.D. Dissertation, Cornell Univ., Ithaca, N.Y. 164 pp. (WALLEYE; ECOLOGY; GEOGRAPHICAL DISTRIBUTION; SAMPLING METHODS;).

1279. Houde, E. D. 1969. Distribution of larval walleye and yellow perch in a bay of Oneida Lake and its relation to water currents and zooplankton. N.Y. Fish Game J. 16:184-205. (WALLEYE; BEHAVIOR; MOVEMENT AND MIGRATIONS;).

1280. Houde, E. D. 1969. Sustained swimming ability of larvae of walleye *(Stizostedion vitreum)* and yellow perch *(Perca flavescens)*. J. Fish. Research Board Can. 26:1647-1659. (WALLEYE; ECOLOGY; PHYSIOLOGY;).

1281. Houde, E. D., and J. L. Forney. 1970. Effects of water currents on distribution of walleye larvae in Oneida Lake, New York. J. Fish. Research Board Can. 27:445-456. (WALLEYE; ECOLOGY; MOVEMENT AND MIGRATIONS; STOCKING;).

1282. Houde, L. 1984. Characteristics of a walleye population, Lac Vincennes, Centre of Quebec. Que. Min. du Loisir, de la Chasse at de la Peche. 30 pp. (WALLEYE; AGE AND GROWTH; POPULATION STUDIES;).

1283. Howard, W. M. 1971. Fall sauger sampling in 1967 and assorted sampling of pickerel and sauger 1964-1967. Man. Dept. Mines Nat. Res., Fish. Branch Manuscript Rep. 70-17: 16 pp. (SAUGER; POPULATION STUDIES;).

1284. Howard, W. M. 1980. Experimental seining and netting in the North Basin of Lake Winnipeg, 1963 to 1967, with special reference to sauger and whitefish. Man. Dept. Nat. Res., Manuscript Rep. No. 80-7: 58 pp. (SAUGER; WALLEYE; AGE AND GROWTH; FISHING GEAR; FOOD STUDIES; POPULATION STUDIES;).

1285. Howey, R. G., G. L. Theis, and P. B. Haines. 1980. Intensive culture of walleye (Stizostedion vitreum vitreum). Lamar Fish Culture Development Center, Lamar, PA, Leaflet No. 80-5:1-10. (WALLEYE; PROPAGATION;).

1286. Huang, C., and P. H. Cleveland, Jr. 1968. Binding of inorganic iodide to the plasma proteins of teleost fishes. J. Fish. Research Board Can. 25:1651-1666. (WALLEYE; PHYSIOLOGY;).

1287. Hubay, J. 1983. A comparative summary of Remi Lake creel surveys Kapuskasing District (1971, 1975, 1976, 1982 and 1983 surveys). Ont. Min. Nat. Res., Rep. 42 pp. (WALLEYE; CREEL CENSUS;).

1288. Hubbell, G. G. 1966. The Michigan general creel census for 1964. Mich. Dept. Conserv., Inst. Fish. Research Rep. 1727: 28 pp. (SAUGER; WALLEYE; CREEL CENSUS;).

1289. Hubbs, C. 1954. Corrected distributional records for Texas fresh-water fishes. Tex. J. Sci. 6:277-291. (SAUGER; GEOGRAPHICAL DISTRIBUTION;).

1290. Hubbs, C. 1961. A checklist of Texas freshwater fishes (revised edition). Tex. Game Fish Comm., I. F. SER.3: 14 pp. (SAUGER; GEOGRAPHICAL DISTRIBUTION;).

1291. Hubbs, C. 1971. Survival of intergroup percid hybrids. Jap. J. Ichthyol. 18:65-75. (WALLEYE; GENETICS; MORTALITY;).

1292. Hubbs, C. L. 1926. A check-list of the fishes of the Great Lakes and tributary waters, with nomenclatorial notes and analytical keys. Univ. Mich. Museum Zool., Misc. Pub. 15: 77 pp. (SAUGER; WALLEYE; TAXONOMY;).

1293. Hubbs, C. L. 1955. Hybridization between fish species in nature. Syst. Zool. 4:1-20. (WALLEYE; GENETICS;).

1294. Hubbs, C. L., and D. E. S. Brown. 1929. Materials for a distributional study of Ontario fishes. Trans. Roy. Can. Inst. 17:1-56. (SAUGER; WALLEYE; GEOGRAPHICAL DISTRIBUTION;).

1295. Hubbs, C. L., and R. W. Eschmeyer. 1938. The improvement of lakes for fishing. A method of fish management. Mich. Inst. Fish. Research Bull. 2:44-45, 105. (WALLEYE; SPAWNING STUDIES;).

1296. Hubbs, C. L., and W. I. Follett. 1953. Manuscript list of the fishes of California. Manuscript Rep. 22 pp. (WALLEYE; INTRODUCTIONS;).

1297. Hubbs, C. L., and C. W. Greene. 1928. Further notes on the fishes of the Great Lakes and tributary waters. Mich. Acad. Sci., Arts Letters 8:371-392. (SAUGER; WALLEYE; GEOGRAPHICAL DISTRIBUTION;).

1298. Hubbs, C. L., and K. F. Lagler. 1939. Keys for the identification of the fishes of the Great Lakes and tributary waters. Published by the authors, Ann Arbor, Mich. 37 pp. (SAUGER; WALLEYE; TAXONOMY;).

1299. Hubbs, C. L., and K. F. Lagler. 1941. Guide to the fishes of the Great Lakes and tributary waters. Cranbrook Inst. Sci., Bull. 18: 100 pp. (SAUGER; WALLEYE; TAXONOMY;).

1300. Hubbs, C. L., and K. F. Lagler. 1943. Annotated list of the fishes of Foots Pond, Gibson County, Indiana. Invest. Ind. Lakes and Streams 2:73-83. (SAUGER; TAXONOMY;).

1301. Hubbs, C. L., and K. F. Lagler. 1947. Fishes of the Great Lakes region. Cranbrook Inst. Sci., Bull. 26: 186 pp. (SAUGER; WALLEYE; MORPHOLOGY; TAXONOMY;).

1302. Hubbs, C. L., and K. F. Lagler. 1949. Fishes of Isle Royale, Lake Superior, Michigan. Papers Mich. Acad. Sci., Arts Letters 33:73-133. (WALLEYE; ECOLOGY;).

1303. Hubbs, C. L., and K. F. Lagler. 1957. List of fishes of the Great Lakes and tributary waters. Univ. Mich., Dept. Fish., Mich. Fish. 1: 6 pp. (SAUGER; WALLEYE; GEOGRAPHICAL DISTRIBUTION;).

1304. Hubbs, C. L., and K. F. Lagler. 1958. Fishes of the Great Lakes region. Univ. Mich. Press,

Ann Arbor, Mich. 213 pp. (SAUGER; WALLEYE; MORPHOLOGY; TAXONOMY;).

1305. Hubbs, C. L., and T. E. B. Pope. 1937. The spread of the sea lamprey through the Great Lakes. Trans. Am. Fish. Soc. 66:173-176. (WALLEYE; POPULATION STUDIES;).

1306. Hubert, W. A., and D. N. Schmit. 1982. Factors influencing catches of drifted trammel nets in a pool of the Upper Mississippi River. Proc. Iowa Acad. Sci. 89:153-154. (WALLEYE; ECOLOGY;).

1307. Hubley, R. C., Jr. 1961. Incidence of lamprey scarring on fish in the upper Mississippi River, 1956-58. Trans. Am. Fish. Soc. 90:83-85. (WALLEYE; POPULATION STUDIES;).

1308. Hubley, R. C., Jr. 1963. The second year of the walleye and sauger tagging on the upper Mississippi River. Wis. Conserv. Dept., Invest. Memo. 16: 4 pp. (SAUGER; WALLEYE; MARKING; MOVEMENTS AND MIGRATIONS;).

1309. Hubley, R. C., Jr., and J. G. Brasch. 1959. First progress report of the effects of commercial gill netting and seining upon spring populations of game fish and migratory waterfowl on the upper Mississippi River. Wis. Conserv. Dept., Invest. Mem. 3: 3 pp. (WALLEYE; COMMERCIAL FISHERIES; MORTALITY;).

1310. Hubley, R. C., Jr., and G. D. Jergens. 1959. Walleye and sauger tagging investigations on the upper Mississippi River. Wis. Conserv. Dept., Invest. Rep. No. 1: 9 pp. (SAUGER; WALLEYE; MARKING; MOVEMENTS AND MIGRATIONS;).

1311. Huet, M. 1970. Textbook of fish culture — breeding and cultivation of fish. Eyre and Spottiswoods Ltd. at Thante Press, Margate, England. 435 pp. (WALLEYE; PROPAGATION;).

1312. Hugg, J. B., D. F. Reid, and E. E. Prince. 1911. Report and recommendations (with appendices) of the Manitoba Fisheries Commission, 1910-11. Government Printing Bureau, Ottawa, Ont. 43 pp. (WALLEYE; COMMERCIAL FISHERIES; MOVEMENTS AND MIGRATIONS; PROPAGATION; STOCKING;).

1313. Hughson, D. R. 1966. Report on Panache (Penage) Lake winter angling success, 1965. Ont. Dept. Lands Forest., Res. Manage. Rep. 85:39-42. (WALLEYE; CREEL CENSUS;).

1314. Hughson, D. R., and J. M. Sheppard. 1962. Some observations on fish behavior and the environmental relationships of fish in selected Sudbury District lakes by the use of self-contained underwater breathing apparatus. Ont. Dept. Lands Forest., Res. Management Rep. 64:48-53. (WALLEYE; BEHAVIOR; ECOLOGY;).

1315. Huh, H. T. 1975. Bioenergetics of food conversion and growth of yellow perch (Perca flavescens) and walleye (Stizostedion vitreum vitreum) using formulated diets. Ph.D. Dissertation, Univ. Wis., Madison, Wis. 213 pp. (WALLEYE; AGE AND GROWTH; FOOD STUDIES; PROPAGATION;).

1316. Huh, H. T., H. E. Calbert, and D. A. Stuiber. 1976. Effects of temperature and light on growth of yellow perch and walleye using formulated feed. Trans. Am. Fish. Soc. 105:254-258. (WALLEYE; AGE AND GROWTH; ECOLOGY; FOOD STUDIES;).

1317. Hulsman, P. F. 1982. Incubation and egg survival of walleye (Stizostedion vitreum vitreum) in Lake Nipissing. Ont. Min. Nat. Res., Lake Nipissing Fish. Assess. Unit Rep. 27 pp. (WALLEYE; SPAWNING STUDIES;).

1318. Hulsman, P. F., P. M. Powles, and J. M. Gunn. 1983. Mortality of walleye eggs and rainbow trout yolk-sac larvae in low-pH waters of the La Cloche Mountain Area, Ontario. Trans. Am. Fish. Soc. 112:680-688. (WALLEYE; ECOLOGY; HABITAT DEGRADATION; MORTALITY; SPAWNING STUDIES;).

1319. Humphreys, M., J. L. Wilson, and D. C. Peterson. 1984. Growth and food habits of young of year walleye X sauger hybrids in Cherokee Reservoir, Tennessee. Proc. 38th Annu. Conf. Southeast. Assoc. Fish. Wildl. Agencies 38:413-420. (SAUGER; WALLEYE; AGE AND GROWTH; FOOD STUDIES;).

1320. Hunn, J. B. 1972. Blood chemistry values for some fishes of the Upper Mississippi River.

J. Minn. Acad. Sci. 38:19-20. (WALLEYE; PHYSIOLOGY;).

1321. Hunn, J. B., R. A. Schoettger, and E. W. Whealdon. 1968. Observations on the handling and maintenance of bioassay fish. Prog. Fish-Cult. 30:164-167. (WALLEYE; PHYSIOLOGY; PROPAGATION;).

1322. Hunninen, A. V. 1936. A biological survey of the Delaware and Susquehanna watersheds. IX. Studies of fish parasites in the Delaware and Susquehanna watersheds. N.Y. Conserv. Dept., Suppl. 25th Annu Rep. pp. 235-245. (WALLEYE; PATHOLOGY;).

1323. Hunter, G. W., III, and W. S. Hunter. 1929. A biological survey of the Erie-Niagara system. IX. Further experimental studies on the bass tapeworm, *Proteocephalus ambloplitis.* N.Y. Conserv. Dept., Suppl. 18th Annu. Rep. pp. 198-207. (SAUGER; WALLEYE; PATHOLOGY;).

1324. Hunter, G. W., III, and W. S. Hunter. 1932. A biological survey of the Oswegatchie and Black River system. X. Studies on the parasites of fish and fish-eating birds. N.Y. Conserv. Dept., Suppl. 21st Annu. Rep. pp. 252-271. (WALLEYE; PATHOLOGY;).

1325. Huntsman, A. G. 1922. The Quill Lakes of Saskatchewan and their fishery possibilities. Contribution Can. Biol. 1:127-141. (WALLEYE; ECOLOGY; INTRODUCTIONS;).

1326. Hurley, D. A. 1972. Observations on incubating walleye eggs. Prog. Fish-Cult. 34:49-54. (WALLEYE; PROPAGATION;).

1327. Hurley, D. A. 1986. Fish populations of the Bay of Quinte, Lake Ontario, before and after phosphorus control. Pages 201-214 *in* C.K. Minns, D.A. Hurley, and H. Nicholls, eds. Project Quinte: point-source phosphorous control and ecosystem response in the Bay of Quinte, Lake Ontario. Can. Spec. Publ. Fish. Aquat. Sci. 86: 270 pp. (WALLEYE; COMMUNITY DYNAMICS; HABITAT DEGRADATION; POPULATION STUDIES;).

1328. Hurley, D. A. 1986. Effect of nutrient reduction on the diets of four fish species in the Bay of Quinte, Lake Ontario. Pages 237-246 *in* C.K. Minns, D.A. Hurley, and H. Nicholls, eds. Project Quinte: point-source phosphorous control and ecosystem response in the Bay of Quinte, Lake Ontario. Can. Spec. Publ. Fish. Aquat. Sci. 86: 270 pp. (WALLEYE; FOOD STUDIES; HABITAT DEGRADATION;).

1329. Hurley, D. A. 1986. Growth, diet, and food consumption of walleye *(Stizostedion vitreum vitreum):* an application of bioenergetics modelling to the Bay of Quinte, Lake Ontario, population. Pages 224-236 *in* C.K. Minns, D.A. Hurley, and H. Nicholls, eds. Project Quinte: point-source phosphorous control and ecosystem response in the Bay of Quinte, Lake Ontario. Can. Spec. Publ. Fish. Aquat. Sci. 86: 270 pp. (WALLEYE; FOOD STUDIES; PHYSIOLOGY; POPULATION STUDIES;).

1330. Hurley, D. A., and W. J. Christie. 1977. Depreciation of the warmwater fish community in the Bay of Quinte, Lake Ontario. J. Fish. Research Board Can. 34:1849-1860. (WALLEYE; COMMUNITY DYNAMICS; ECOLOGY; HABITAT DEGRADATION;).

1331. Hurley, S. T., and M. R. Austin. 1987. Evaluation of walleye stocking in Caesar Creek Lake. Ohio Dept. Nat. Res., Fed. Aid Fish Wildl. Restor. Proj. F-29-R, Study No. 19: 90 pp. (WALLEYE; AGE AND GROWTH; COMMUNITY DYNAMICS; CREEL CENSUS; ECOLOGY; FOOD STUDIES; MORTALITY; MOVEMENTS AND MIGRATIONS; POPULATION STUDIES; SPAWNING STUDIES; STOCKING;).

1332. Hushah, L. J., G. W. Morse, and K. K. Appahu. 1986. Regional impacts of fishery allocation to sport and commercial interests: a case study of Ohio's portion of Lake Erie. N. Am. J. Fish. Manage. 6:472-480. (WALLEYE; COMMERCIAL FISHERIES; CREEL CENSUS; SOCIO-ECONOMICS OF FISHERIES;).

1333. Hutson, B. 1985. Detour Lake Road creel survey 1985. Ont. Min. Nat. Res., Rep. 32 pp. (WALLEYE; CREEL CENSUS;).

1334. Hyatt, R. A. 1982. Summer creel census in the Canadian waters of the western basin of Lake Erie, 1981. Ont. Min. Nat. Res., Lake Erie Fish. Assess. Unit Rep. 1982-1 53 pp. (WALLEYE; AGE AND GROWTH; CREEL CENSUS;).

1335. Hyatt. R. A. 1983. Summer creel census in the Canadian waters of the western basin of Lake Erie, 1982. Ont. Min. Nat. Res., Lake Erie Fish. Assess. Unit Rep. 1984-1: 54 pp. (WALLEYE; CREEL CENSUS;).

1336. Hyatt, R. A. 1984. Summer creel census in the Canadian waters of the western basin of Lake Erie, 1983. Ont. Min. Nat. Res., Lake Erie Fish. Assess. Unit Rep. 1984-1: 66 pp. (WALLEYE; CREEL CENSUS;).

1337. Hyatt, R. A. 1985. Summer creel census in the Canadian waters of the western basin of Lake Erie, 1984. Ont. Min. Nat. Res., Lake Erie Fish. Assess. Unit Rep. 1985-1: 63 pp. (WALLEYE; AGE AND GROWTH; CREEL CENSUS;).

1338. Hyatt, R. A. 1986. Summer creel census in the Canadian waters of the western basin of Lake Erie, 1985. Ont. Min. Nat. Res., Lake Erie Fish. Assess. Unit Rep. 1986-1: 72 pp. (WALLEYE; CREEL CENSUS;).

1339. Hyatt, R. A. 1986. Summer creel census of the Wheatley, Leamington and Kingsville Docks, 1985. Ont. Min. Nat. Res., Lake Erie Fish. Assess. Unit Rep. 1986-5: 40 pp. (WALLEYE; CREEL CENSUS;).

1340. Imler, R. L. 1974. Fluorescent pigment marking techniques. Colo. Div. Wildl., Fish. Infor. Leaflet No. 28: 2 pp. (WALLEYE; MARKING;).

1341. Inmon, L. E. 1974. Feeding interaction between pelagic larvae of walleye, Stizostedion vitreum vitreum (Mitchill), and associated fish species in Clear Lake. M.S. Thesis, Iowa State Univ., Ames, Iowa. 54 pp. (WALLEYE; COMMUNITY DYNAMICS; FOOD STUDIES; STOCKING;).

1342. Inskip, P. D., and J. J. Magnuson. 1983. Changes in fish populations over an 80-year period: Big Pine Lake, Wisconsin. Trans. Am. Fish. Soc. 112:378-389. (WALLEYE; COMMUNITY DYNAMICS; CREEL CENSUS; POPULATION STUDIES;).

1343. Irwin, K., and J. Brisbane. 1985. A summary of walleye and maskinonge spawning site identification and documentation, Bancroft District, spring 1985. Ont. Min. Nat. Res., Bancroft Dis. and Sir Sanford Flemming College, Fish. Manage. Rep. 1985-13: 80 pp. (WALLEYE; SPAWNING STUDIES;).

1344. Isfort, L. G. 1949. A partial bibliography of natural history in the Chicago region. Am. Midl. Nat. 42:406-410, 451-455. (WALLEYE; GEOGRAPHICAL DISTRIBUTION;).

1345. Jacknow, J., J. L. Ludke, and N. C. Coon. 1986. Monitoring fish and wildlife for environmental contaminants the national contaminant biomonitoring program. U.S. Fish Wildl. Serv., Fish Wildl. Leafl. 4:1-15. (WALLEYE; HABITAT DEGRADATION;).

1346. Jackson, D. F. 1962. Historical notes on fish fauna. Pages 1-19 in W.M. Clay, ed. Aquatic-life resources of the Ohio River, Ohio River Valley Water Sanitation Comm., Cincinnati, Ohio. (SAUGER; WALLEYE; COMMERCIAL FISHERIES;).

1347. Jackson, R. V. 1984. Ohio River sport fishery investigation. Ky. Dept. Fish Wildl. Res., Fed. Aid Fish Wildl. Restor. Proj. F-40-R-6, Subsection III: 47 pp. (WALLEYE; CREEL CENSUS;).

1348. Jackson, S. W. 1963. Canton Reservoir creel census," Hess " method. Okla. Dept. Wildl. Conserv., Fed. Aid Fish Wildl. Restor. Proj. F-7-R-2, Job No. 4: 8 pp. (WALLEYE; CREEL CENSUS; IMPOUNDMENTS; STOCKING;).

1349. Januschka, M. M., D. A. Burkhardt, S. L. Erlandsen, and R. L. Purple. 1987. The ultrastructure of cones in the walleye retina. Vision Res. 27:327-342. (WALLEYE; PHYSIOLOGY;).

1350. Jardine, C. G., and J. S. Sigurdson. 1981. A sport fisheries investigation of Sasaginnigak and Fishing Lakes, 1979. Man. Dept. Nat. Res., Fish. Branch, Manuscript Rep. 81-2: 68 pp. (WALLEYE; AGE AND GROWTH; CREEL CENSUS; POPULATION STUDIES;).

1351. Jarvis, R. S., H. F. Klodowski, and S. P. Sheldon. 1978. New method of quantifying scale shape and an application to stock identification in walleye (Stizostedion vitreum vitreum). Trans. Am. Fish. Soc. 107:528-534. (WALLEYE; GENETICS; MORPHOLOGY;).

1352. Jeffries, P. J., Jr. 1974. Food habits of selected game fishes related to composition and distribution of resident and anadromous fish populations in the Connecticut River below Holyoke Dam, Massachusetts. M.S. Thesis, Univ. Mass., Amherst, Mass. 89 pp. (WALLEYE; COMMUNITY DYNAMICS; FOOD STUDIES;).

1353. Jenkins, R. M. 1953. Growth histories of the principal fishes in Grand Lake, Oklahoma, through thirteen years of impoundment. Okla. Fish. Research Lab., Rep. 34: 87 pp. (WALLEYE; IMPOUNDMENTS; INTRODUCTIONS;).

1354. Jenkins, R. M. 1970. The influence of engineering design and operation and other environmental factors on reservoir fishery resources. Water Resource Bull. 6:110-118. (WALLEYE; ECOLOGY; IMPOUNDMENTS;).

1355. Jenkins, R. M., and J. C. Finnell. 1957. The fishery resources of the Verdigris River in Oklahoma. Okla. Fish. Research Lab., Rep. 59: 46 pp. (SAUGER; GEOGRAPHICAL DISTRIBUTION;).

1356. Jenkins, R. M., E. M. Leonard, and G. E. Hall. 1952. An investigation of the fisheries resources of the Illinois River and pre-impoundment study of Tenkiller Reservoir, Oklahoma. Okla. Fish. Research Lab., Rep. 26: 136 pp. (SAUGER; AGE AND GROWTH; IMPOUNDMENTS;).

1357. Jenkins, R. M., and D. I. Morais. 1976. Prey-predator relations in the predator-stocking-evaluation reservoirs. Proc. 30th Annu. Conf. Southeast Assoc. Fish Wild. Agencies. 30:141-157. (WALLEYE; COMMUNITY DYNAMICS; PRODUCTIVITY; STOCKING;).

1358. Jenness, R. A. 1963. Great Slave Lake fishing industry. Can. Dept. Northern Affairs Nat. Res., Northern Coordination Research Center, Ottawa, Ont. 41 pp. (WALLEYE; COMMERCIAL FISHERIES;).

1359. Jennings, T. 1968. Summary of 22 consecutive years of creel census on Spirit Lake. Proc. Iowa Acad. Sci. 75:159-163. (WALLEYE; CREEL CENSUS;).

1360. Jennings, T. 1968. Spirit Lake walleye studies. Iowa State Conserv. Comm., Quart. Biol. Rep. 20(3):51-54. (WALLEYE; CREEL CENSUS; POPULATION STUDIES;).

1361. Jennings, T. 1969. Summary of 23 consecutive years of creel census on West Okoboji. Proc. Iowa Acad. Sci. 76:206-210. (WALLEYE; CREEL CENSUS;).

1362. Jennings, T. 1969. Spirit Lake walleye studies. Iowa State Conserv. Comm., Quart. Biol. Rep. 21(2):73-76. (WALLEYE; MARKING; POPULATION STUDIES;).

1363. Jennings, T. 1969. Progress report on Spirit Lake walleye studies, natural reproduction. Iowa Conserv. Comm., Quart. Rep. 21:10-14. (WALLEYE; MORTALITY; SPAWNING STUDIES;).

1364. Jennings, T. 1970. Spirit Lake walleye studies. Iowa State Conserv. Comm., Quart. Biol. Rep. 22(2):4-10. (WALLEYE; MARKING; POPULATION STUDIES; SPAWNING STUDIES;).

1365. Jernejcic, F. 1986. Walleye migration through Tygart Dam and angler utilization of the resulting tailwater and lake fisheries. Pages 294-300 in G.E. Hall and M.J. Van Den Avyle, eds. Reservoir fisheries management: strategies for the 80's. Reserv. Comm., S. Div. Am. Fish. Soc., Bethesda, Maryland. (WALLEYE; AGE AND GROWTH; CREEL CENSUS; IMPOUNDMENTS; MARKING; MORTALITY; MOVEMENT AND MIGRATIONS;).

1366. Jernejcic, F. A. 1969. Use of emetics to collect stomach contents of walleye (Stizostedion vitreum) and largemouth bass (Micropterus salmoides). Trans. Am. Fish. Soc. 98:698-702. (WALLEYE; FOOD STUDIES;).

1367. Jernejcic, F. A. 1969. Prey selectivity of Clear Lake walleye. M.S. Thesis, Iowa State Univ., Ames, Iowa. 52 pp. (WALLEYE; COMMUNITY DYNAMICS; FOOD STUDIES;).

1368. Jessop, C. S. 1980. Summer creel census of Mesomikenda, Minisinakwa and Mattagami Lakes in 1975, 1976 and 1977. Ont. Min. Nat. Res., Rep. 54 pp. (WALLEYE; CREEL CENSUS;).

1369. Jester, D. B. 1972. Effects of commercial fishing, species introduction and draw-down control on fish populations in Elephant Butte Reservoir, New Mexico. Pages 265-285 in G.E. Hall, ed. Reservoir fisheries and limnology. Am. Fish. Soc. Sp. Publ. No. 8, Washington D.C. (WALLEYE; COMMER-

CIAL FISHERIES; COMMUNITY DYNAMICS; IMPOUNDMENTS; INTRODUCTIONS; POPULATION STUDIES; STOCKING; WATER LEVELS;).

1370. Jester, D. B. 1973. Variations in catchability of fishes with color of gillnets. Trans. Am. Fish. Soc. 102:109-115. (WALLEYE; FISHING GEAR;).

1371. Jester, D. B. 1977. Effects of color, mesh size, and fishing in seasonal concentrations, and baiting on catch rates of fishes in gill nets. Trans. Am. Fish. Soc. 106:43-56. (WALLEYE; FISHING GEAR; IMPOUNDMENTS; POPULATION STUDIES; SAMPLING METHODS;).

1372. Jester, D. B., C. Sanchez, D. E. Jennings, and T. M. Moody. 1969. A study of game fish reproduction and rough fish problems in Elephant Butte Lake. N. M. Dept. Game Fish, Fed. Aid Fish Wildl. Restor. Proj. F-22-R-9, Wk. Pl. 3, Job No. F-1: 73 pp. (WALLEYE; AGE AND GROWTH; FOOD STUDIES; IMPOUNDMENTS; INTRODUCTIONS; POPULATION STUDIES; SPAWNING STUDIES; STOCKING;).

1373. Johnson, B. L. 1981. First year growth, survival, habitat preference, and food habits of stocked walleye and walleye X sauger hybrids in Pleasant Hill Reservoir, Ohio. M.S. Thesis. Ohio State Univ., Columbus, Ohio. (SAUGER; WALLEYE; AGE AND GROWTH; COMMUNITY DYNAMICS; FOOD STUDIES; MORTALITY;).

1374. Johnson, B. L., and R. F. Carline. 1980. Evaluation of saugeye stocking in selected Ohio lakes. Ohio Div. Wildl., Fed. Aid Fish Wildl. Restor. Proj. F-57-R-2: (SAUGER; WALLEYE; STOCKING;).

1375. Johnson, B. L., D. L. Smith, and R. F. Carline. 1988. Habitat preference, survival, growth, foods, and harvest of walleyes and walleye x sauger hybrids. N. Am. J. Fish Manage. 8(2):. (SAUGER; WALLEYE; AGE AND GROWTH; CREEL CENSUS; ECOLOGY; FOOD STUDIES; GENETICS; MORTALITY; STOCKING;).

1376. Johnson, D. C. 1980. A quantitative creel census of Upper Red Lake, Minnesota, 1978 and 1979. Minn. Dept. Nat. Res., Fish Manage. Rep. No. 19: 12 pp. (WALLEYE; CREEL CENSUS;).

1377. Johnson, D. C., and T. L. Close. 1979. A quantitative creel census of Upper Red Lake, Minnesota, 1977-78. Minn. Dept. Nat. Res., Fish Manage. Rep. No. 17: 9 pp. (WALLEYE; AGE AND GROWTH; CREEL CENSUS;).

1378. Johnson, F. H. 1953. Size of harvest and present status of the walleye (Stizostedion vitreum) fishery in Cutfoot Sioux, Itasca County, Minnesota. Minn. Dept Conserv., Invest. Rep. No. 138: 7 pp. (WALLEYE; AGE AND GROWTH; CREEL CENSUS; POPULATION STUDIES; PRODUCTIVITY;).

1379. Johnson, F. H. 1953. Notes on mortality of walleye (Stizostedion vitreum) fingerlings during and following fin-clipping. Minn. Dept. Conserv., Invest. Rep. No. 145: 6 pp. (WALLEYE; MARKING; MORTALITY; STOCKING;).

1380. Johnson, F. H. 1957. Survival of stocked walleye fingerlings in Moose Lake, Itasca County, Minnesota. Minn. Dept. Conserv., Invest. Rep. No. 215: 6 pp. (WALLEYE; CREEL CENSUS; POPULATION STUDIES; STOCKING;).

1381. Johnson, F. H. 1960. Some observations on hatchery survival of walleye (Stizostedion vitreum) eggs collected from early, mid, and late run fish of three size-groups at Little Cutfoot Sioux Lake in 1960. Minn. Dept. Nat. Res., Internal Rep. No. 145: 6 pp. (WALLEYE; SPAWNING STUDIES;).

1382. Johnson, F. H. 1961. Walleye egg survival during incubation on several types of bottom in Lake Winnibigoshish, Minnesota, and connecting waters. Trans. Am. Fish. Soc. 90:312-322. (WALLEYE; MORTALITY; SPAWNING STUDIES;).

1383. Johnson, F. H. 1967. Status of the Rainy Lake walleye fishery, 1966. Minn. Dept. Conserv., Invest. Rep. No. 295: 16 pp. (WALLEYE; COMMERCIAL FISHERIES; POPULATION STUDIES; SPAWNING STUDIES; WATER LEVELS;).

1384. Johnson, F. H. 1968. Status of the fish population of Lake Vermilion in 1968 with special emphasis on the walleye, Stizostedion vitreum. Minn. Dept. Conserv., Invest. Rep. No. 300: 16 pp. (WALLEYE; AGE AND

GROWTH; COMMUNITY DYNAMICS;
POPULATION STUDIES;).

1385. Johnson, F. H. 1969. Environmental and spe-
cies associations of the walleye in Lake Win-
nibigoshish and connected waters, includ-
ing observations on food habits and
predator-prey relationships. Minn. Dept.
Conserv., Fish. Invest. No. 5:5-36. (WALL-
EYE; AGE AND GROWTH; COMMU-
NITY DYNAMICS; ECOLOGY; FOOD
STUDIES; MOVEMENTS AND MIGRA-
TIONS; POPULATION STUDIES;).

1386. Johnson, F. H. 1971. Survival of stocked wall-
eye fingerlings in northern Minnesota
Lakes as estimated from the age-composi-
tion of experimental gill net catches. Minn.
Dept. Nat. Res., Invest. Rep. No. 314: 12 pp.
(WALLEYE; AGE AND GROWTH; FISH-
ING GEAR; POPULATION STUDIES;
STOCKING;).

1387. Johnson, F. H. 1971. Numerical abundance,
sex ratios, and size-age composition of the
walleye spawning run at Little Cut Foot
Sioux Lake, Minnesota 1942-1969, with
data on fecundity and incidence of *Lymphocystis*. Minn. Dept. Nat. Res., Invest. Rep.
No. 315: 9 pp. (WALLEYE; AGE AND
GROWTH; PATHOLOGY; SPAWNING
STUDIES;).

1388. Johnson, F. H. 1975. An analysis of past and
current data on walleye populations and
catch for Minnesota lakes with an estimate
of the possible effects of a size limit. Minn.
Dept. Nat. Res., Div. Fish Game Staff Rep.
24 pp. (WALLEYE; AGE AND GROWTH;
CREEL CENSUS; MORTALITY; POPU-
LATION STUDIES; REGULATIONS;
SPAWNING STUDIES;).

1389. Johnson, F. H. 1975. Interspecific relation-
ships of walleye, white sucker and associ-
ated species in a northeastern Minnesota
lake with an evaluation of white sucker re-
moval for increased walleye yield. Minn.
Dept. Nat. Res., Invest Rep. No. 338: 46 pp.
(WALLEYE; AGE AND GROWTH; COM-
MUNITY DYNAMICS; CREEL CENSUS;
FOOD STUDIES; LIFE HISTORY; MOR-
TALITY; POPULATION STUDIES;
SPAWNING STUDIES;).

1390. Johnson, F. H. 1977. Responses of walleye
(Stizostedion vitreum vitreum) and yellow
perch *(Perca flavescens)* populations to removal of white sucker *(Catostomus commer-*

soni) from a Minnesota lake, 1966. J. Fish.
Research Board Can. 34:1633-1642. (WALL-
EYE; AGE AND GROWTH; COMMU-
NITY DYNAMICS; FOOD STUDIES;
POPULATION STUDIES;).

1391. Johnson, F. H., and J. G. Hale. 1977. Interre-
lations between walleye *(Stizostedion vi-
treum vitreum)* and smallmouth bass *(Mi-
cropterus dolomieui)* in four northeastern
Minnesota lakes, 1948-69. J. Fish. Research
Board Can. 34:1626-1632. (WALLEYE;
AGE AND GROWTH; COMMUNITY DY-
NAMICS; FOOD STUDIES; POPULA-
TION STUDIES; SPAWNING STUD-
IES;).

1392. Johnson, F. H., and M. W. Johnson. 1971.
Characteristics of the 1957-1958 and 1939
sport fishery of Lake Winnibigoshish and
connecting waters with special emphasis on
the walleye population and catch. Minn.
Dept. Nat. Res., Invest. Rep. No. 312: 31 pp.
(WALLEYE; AGE AND GROWTH;
CREEL CENSUS; MARKING; MORTAL-
ITY; MOVEMENTS AND MIGRA-
TIONS;).

1393. Johnson, F. H., and T. C. Osborn. 1977. Ex-
perimental management of a small re-
claimed lake in northern Minnesota for wall-
eye, *Stizostedion vitreum vitreum*
(Mitchell). Minn. Dept. Nat. Res., Invest.
Rep. No. 346: 41 pp. (WALLEYE; AGE
AND GROWTH; COMMUNITY DY-
NAMICS; CREEL CENSUS; FOOD
STUDIES; HABITAT IMPROVEMENT;
MORTALITY; POPULATION STUDIES;
STOCKING;).

1394. Johnson, F. H., R. D. Thomasson, and B.
Caldwell. 1966. Status of the Rainy Lake
walleye fishery, 1965. Minn. Dept. Conserv.,
Invest. Rep. No. 292: 22 pp. (SAUGER;
WALLEYE; AGE AND GROWTH; COM-
MERCIAL FISHERIES; CREEL CEN-
SUS; FOOD STUDIES; POPULATION
STUDIES; SPAWNING STUDIES; WA-
TER LEVELS;).

1395. Johnson, J. H. 1958. Surface-current studies
of Saginaw Bay and Lake Huron, 1956. U.S.
Fish Wildl. Serv., Spec. Sci. Rep.-Fish. 267:
84 pp. (WALLEYE; COMMERCIAL
FISHERIES; HABITAT DEGRADA-
TION;).

1396. Johnson, L. 1975. Distribution of fish species
in Great Bear Lake, Northwest Territories,

with reference to zooplankton, benthic invertebrates, and environmental conditions. J. Fish. Research Board Can. 32:1989-2004. (WALLEYE; GEOGRAPHICAL DISTRIBUTION; MOVEMENT AND MIGRATIONS;).

1397. Johnson, M. G. 1987. Trace element loadings of sediments of fourteen Ontario lakes and correlations with concentrations in fish. Can. J. Fish. Aquat. Sci. 44:3-13. (WALLEYE; HABITAT DEGRADATION; TOXICANTS;).

1398. Johnson, M. G., J. H. Leach, C. K. Minns, and C. H. Olver. 1977. Limnological characteristics of Ontario Lakes in relation to associations of walleye *(Stizostedion vitreum vitreum)*, northern pike *(Esox lucius)*, lake trout *(Salvelinus namaycush)*, and smallmouth bass *(Micropterus dolomieui)*. J. Fish. Research Board Can. 34:1592-1601. (WALLEYE; COMMUNITY DYNAMICS; ECOLOGY; GEOGRAPHICAL DISTRIBUTION;).

1399. Johnson, M. W. 1957. Annual report of statewide creel census of fourteen Minnesota lakes. Minn. Dept. Conserv., Invest. Rep. No. 183: 34 pp. (WALLEYE; CREEL CENSUS;).

1400. Johnson, M. W. 1964. A five-year study of the sport fishery of Mille Lacs Lake, Minnesota, 1958-1962. Minn. Dept. Conserv., Invest. Rep. No. 273: 16 pp. (WALLEYE; CREEL CENSUS;).

1401. Johnson, M. W., and J. H. Kuehn. 1956. Annual report of statewide creel census of fourteen Minnesota lakes. Minn. Dept. Conserv., Invest. Rep. No. 174: 32 pp. (WALLEYE; CREEL CENSUS;).

1402. Johnson, M. W., and L. Wroblewski. 1962. Errors associated with a systematic sampling creel census. Trans. Am. Fish. Soc. 91:201-207. (WALLEYE; SAMPLING METHODS;).

1403. Johnson, R. E. 1949. Investigation of catches made by nets during tullibee and herring season, 1948. Minn. Dept. Conserv., Invest. Rep. No. 85: 16 pp. (WALLEYE; COMMUNITY DYNAMICS;).

1404. Johnson, R. E. 1949. Natural reproduction in Minnesota game fish lakes during 1949. Minn. Dept. Conserv., Invest. Rep. No. 90: 12 pp. (WALLEYE; POPULATION STUDIES; SAMPLING METHODS;).

1405. Johnson, R. L. 1965. Southeast Montana fisheries study. Inventory of the waters of the project area. Mont. Fish Game Dept., Fed. Aid Fish Wildl. Restor. Proj. F-30-R-1, Job No.1: 4 pp. (SAUGER; IMPOUNDMENTS;).

1406. Johnson, R. L. 1966. Southeast Montana fisheries study. Inventory of the waters of the project area. Mont. Fish Game Dept., Fed. Aid Fish Wildl. Restor. Proj. F-30-R-2, Job No. 1: 4 pp. (SAUGER; IMPOUNDMENTS;).

1407. Johnson, R. P. 1963. Studies of the life history and ecology of the bigmouth buffalo, *Ictiobus cyprinellus*. J. Fish. Research Board Can. 20:1397-1429. (WALLEYE; ECOLOGY;).

1408. Johnson, R. P. 1965. Lac la Ronge creel census, 1964. Sask. Fish. Lab. Tech. Rep. 1965-3: 3 pp. (WALLEYE; CREEL CENSUS;).

1409. Johnson, R. P. 1970. Puskwakau River creel census, 1965-1970. Sask. Dept. Nat. Res. 12: 13 pp. (WALLEYE; CREEL CENSUS;).

1410. Johnson, R. P. 1971. Limnology and fishery biology of Black Lake northern Saskatchewan. Sask. Dept. Nat. Res., Fish Rep. No. 9: 46 pp. (WALLEYE; AGE AND GROWTH; CREEL CENSUS; FOOD STUDIES; POPULATION STUDIES;).

1411. Johnson, R. P. 1972. Analysis of sampling Lake Athabasca commercial fishery, 1969, 1970, 1971. Sask. Fish. Lab. Tech. Rep. 1972-2: 76 pp. (WALLEYE; COMMERCIAL FISHERIES;).

1412. Johnson R. S. 1916. The distribution of fish and fish eggs during the fiscal year 1915. U.S. Bureau Fish., Annu. Rep. 1915: 1-138. (WALLEYE; PROPAGATION; STOCKING;).

1413. Johnston, D. A. 1977. Population dynamics of walleye *(Stizostedion vitreun vitreun)* and yellow perch *(Perca flavescens)* in Lake St. Clair, especially during 1970-76. J. Fish. Research Board Can. 34:1869-1877. (SAUGER; WALLEYE; AGE AND GROWTH; COMMERCIAL FISHERIES; COMMUNITY DYNAMICS; CREEL

CENSUS; POPULATION STUDIES; PRODUCTIVITY;).

1414. Jones, B. R. 1961. Report on a survey of the Pine River, Cass and Crow Wing Counties, April and May, 1957. Minn. Dept. Conserv., Invest. Rep. No. 232: 13 pp. (WALLEYE; HABITAT DEGRADATION; POPULATION STUDIES; SPAWNING STUDIES;).

1415. Jones, B. R., and J. E. Maloney. 1956. Preliminary report on possible influence of pollution on walleye pike reproduction in the Pine River, Cass and Crow Wing Counties. Minn. Dept. Conserv., Invest. Rep. No. 175: 4 pp. (WALLEYE; AGE AND GROWTH; HABITAT DEGRADATION; SPAWNING STUDIES;).

1416. Jones, D. 1963. Statistical methods for fishery studies. Neb. Game Forest. Parks Comm., Fed Aid Fish. Wildl. Restor. Proj. F-4-R-8, Job No. 16: 29 pp. (WALLEYE; PROPAGATION;).

1417. Jones, D. R., J. W. Kiceniuk, and O. S. Bamford. 1974. Evaluation of the swimming performance of several fish species from the MacKenzie River. J. Fish. Research Board Can. 31:1641-1647. (WALLEYE; ECOLOGY; MOVEMENTS AND MIGRATIONS;).

1418. Jones, M. S. 1985. Fish forage evaluations. Colo. Div. Wildl., Fed. Aid Fish Wildl. Restor. Proj. F-53-R, Job No. 1: 76 pp. (WALLEYE; AGE AND GROWTH; COMMUNITY DYNAMICS; FOOD STUDIES; POPULATION STUDIES;).

1419. Jones, T. W. 1986. Establishment of a walleye population by stocking in Gaston Reservoir. Page 312 in G.E. Hall and M.J. Van Den Avyle, eds. Reservoir fisheries management: strategies for the 80's. Reserv. Comm., S. Div. Am. Fish. Soc., Bethesda, Maryland. (WALLEYE; IMPOUNDMENTS; STOCKING;).

1420. Jordon, D. S. 1877. Concerning the fishes of the Ichthyologia Ohiensis. Buffalo Soc. Nat. Hist., Bull. 3:91-97. (WALLEYE; TAXONOMY;).

1421. Jordon, D. S. 1877. Notes on Cottidae, Etheostomidae, Percidae, Centrarchidae, Aphododeridae, Umbridae, Esocoidae, Dorysomatidae, Cyprinidae, Catastomidae, and Hyodontidae, with revisions of the genera and descriptions of new or little known species. N. Am. Ichthyology, U.S. Nat. Mus. Bull. 10:1-68. (SAUGER; WALLEYE; MORPHOLOGY; TAXONOMY;).

1422. Jordon, D. S. 1877. A partial synopsis of the fishes of Upper Georgia. Annu. Lyceum Nat. Hist. N.Y. 11:307-377. (WALLEYE; GEOGRAPHICAL DISTRIBUTION;).

1423. Jordon, D. S. 1877. On the distribution of fresh-water fish. Am. Nat. 11:607-613. (SAUGER; WALLEYE; GEOGRAPHICAL DISTRIBUTION;).

1424. Jordon, D. S. 1888. A manual of the vertebrate animals of the northern United States including the district north and east of the Ozark Mountains, south of the Laurentian Hills, north of the southern boundary of Virginia, and east of the Missouri River, inclusive of marine species. A.C. McClurg and Co., Chicago, Ill., 5th edition pp. 121, 135. (SAUGER; WALLEYE; TAXONOMY;).

1425. Jordon, D. S. 1929. A manual of the vertebrate animals of the northeastern United States inclusive of marine species. World Book Co., Yonkers-On-Hudson, N.Y. 13th edition pp. 170-171, 446. (SAUGER; WALLEYE; MORPHOLOGY; TAXONOMY;).

1426. Jordon, D. S., and H. E. Copeland. 1876. Check list of the fishes of the fresh waters of North America. Buffalo Soc. Nat. Hist., Bull. 3:133-164. (SAUGER; WALLEYE; TAXONOMY;).

1427. Jordon, D. S., and B. W. Everman. 1902. American food and game species. A popular account of all the species found in America north of the equator, with keys for ready identification, life histories and methods of capture. Doubleday, Page and Co., New York, N.Y. 573 pp. (SAUGER; WALLEYE; PROPAGATION; SPAWNING STUDIES; TAXONOMY;).

1428. Jordon, D. S., and C. H. Gilbert. 1877. On the genera of North American fresh-water fishes. Proc. Phil. Acad. Nat. Sci. 29:83-104. (SAUGER; WALLEYE; TAXONOMY;).

1429. Jordon, D. S., and C. H. Gilbert. 1882. A synopsis of the fishes of North America. U.S. Nat. Mus., Bull. 16: 1018 pp. (SAUGER;

WALLEYE; MORPHOLOGY; TAXON-
OMY;).

1430. Jordon, D. S., and S. E. Meek. 1886. List of
fishes collected in Iowa and Missouri in August 1884, with descriptions of three new
species. Proc. U.S. Nat. Mus. 8: 17 pp.
(SAUGER; GEOGRAPHICAL DISTRI-
BUTION;).

1431. Jorgensen, C. R. 1974. The discreteness of
populations of pickerel (Stizostedion sp.) in
Lake Nipissing. Ont. Min. Nat. Res., Lake
Nipissing Fish. Assess. Unit Rep. 17 pp.
(WALLEYE; AGE AND GROWTH; GE-
NETICS; PATHOLOGY;).

1432. Jorgensen, C. R. 1977. Lake Nipissing creel
survey, open water season, 1960-1976. Ont.
Min. Nat. Res., Lake Nipissing Fish. Assess. Unit. Rep. 92 pp. (WALLEYE; AGE
AND GROWTH; CREEL CENSUS;).

1433. Jorgensen, C. R. 1979. The five year interim
report on the fisheries of Lake Nipissing for
the period 1974-1978. Ont. Min. Nat. Res.,
Lake Nipissing Fish. Assess. Unit Rep. 200
pp. (WALLEYE; AGE AND GROWTH;
COMMERCIAL FISHERIES; COMMU-
NITY DYNAMICS; CREEL CENSUS;
MARKING; MORTALITY; POPULA-
TION STUDIES; SOCIO-ECONOMICS
OF FISHERIES;).

1434. Jorgensen, C. R. 1980. Summer creel census
survey on Lake Nipissing 1979. Ont. Min.
Nat. Res., Lake Nipissing Fish. Assess.
Unit Rep. 1980-3: 69 pp. (WALLEYE; AGE
AND GROWTH; COMMUNITY DY-
NAMICS; CREEL CENSUS;).

1435. Jorgensen, C. R. 1980. Summer creel census
on Lake Nipissing, 1980. Ont. Min. Nat.
Res., Rep. 74 pp. (WALLEYE; CREEL
CENSUS;).

1436. Jorgensen, C. R. 1981. Lake Nipissing pick-
erel study, 1968-1978. Ont. Min. Nat. Res.,
Lake Nipissing Fish., Assess. Unit Rep.
1981-1: 15 pp. (WALLEYE; AGE AND
GROWTH; CREEL CENSUS; MARK-
ING; MORTALITY;).

1437. Jorgensen, C. R. 1982. Assessment of the
North Bay Nipissing Pickerel Tournament
June 12-13, 1982. Ont. Min. Nat. Res., Lake
Nipissing Fish. Assess. Unit Rep. 8 pp.
(WALLEYE; CREEL CENSUS; MORTAL-
ITY;).

1438. Jorgensen, C. R. 1983. The effects of a change
in the angling season on the pickerel (Stizostedion vitreum sp.) of Lake Nipissing
and recommendations for management.
Ont. Min. Nat. Res., Lake Nipissing Fish.
Assess. Unit. 72 pp. (WALLEYE; POPU-
LATION STUDIES; REGULATIONS;).

1439. Jorgensen, C. R. 1986. A history of the Lake
Nipissing creel survey areas, 1960 to 1984.
Ont. Min. Nat. Res., Lake Nipissing Fish.
Assess. Unit Rep. 42 pp. (WALLEYE;
COMMUNITY DYNAMICS; CREEL
CENSUS;).

1440. Joseph, T. W. 1976. Populations of invertebrate organisms and their consumption by
rainbow trout (Salmo gairdneri Richardson)
and walleye (Stizostedion vitreum Mitchill)
in Gravel Lake, Rolette County, North
Dakota. Ph.D. Dissertation, Univ. N.D.,
Grand Forks, N.D. 123 pp. (WALLEYE;
FOOD STUDIES;).

1441. Josephson, D. B., R. C. Lindsay, and D. A.
Stuiber. 1984. Variation in the occurrences
of enzymically derived volatile aroma com-
pounds in salt-water and fresh water fish. J.
Agric. Food Chem. 32:1344-1347. (WALL-
EYE; PHYSIOLOGY;).

1442. Jovanovic, M. 1970. Comparative life histo-
ries of the North American and European
walleye. Mich. Dept. Nat. Res., Rep. No.
201: 71 pp. (WALLEYE; AGE AND
GROWTH; BEHAVIOR; COMMUNITY
DYNAMICS; FOOD STUDIES; GEO-
GRAPHICAL DISTRIBUTION; MOR-
TALITY; MOVEMENT AND MIGRA-
TIONS; SPAWNING STUDIES;
TAXONOMY;).

1443. Joy, E. T., Jr. 1975. The walleye Stizostedion
vitreum (Mitchill), population and sport
fishery of the Big Eau Plaine, a fluctuating,
central-Wisconsin reservoir. M.S. Thesis,
Univ. Wis., Stevens Point, Wis. 97 pp.
(WALLEYE; AGE AND GROWTH;
CREEL CENSUS; FOOD STUDIES; IM-
POUNDMENTS; MARKING; POPULA-
TION STUDIES;).

1444. Juday, C. 1938. Fish records for Lake Win-
gra. Trans. Wis. Acad. Sci., Arts Letters
31:533-534. (WALLEYE; GEOGRAPHI-
CAL DISTRIBUTION;).

1445. Juday, C., and C. L. Schloemer. 1938. Growth
of game fish in Wisconsin waters — fifth Re-

port. Wis. Geol. Nat. Hist. Surv., Notes Limnol. Lab. 26 pp. (WALLEYE; AGE AND GROWTH;).

1446. Juday, C., and E. Schneberger. 1930. Growth studies of game fish in Wisconsin waters. Wis. Geol. Nat. Hist. Surv., Notes Biol. Lab. 7 pp. (WALLEYE; AGE AND GROWTH;).

1447. Juday, C., and E. Schneberger. 1933. Growth studies of game fish in Wisconsin waters-Second Report. Wis. Geol. Nat. Hist. Surv., Notes Limnol. Lab. 10 pp. (WALLEYE; AGE AND GROWTH;).

1448. Juday, C., and L. E. Vike. 1938. A census of the fish caught by anglers in Lake Kegonsa. Trans. Wis. Acad. Sci., Arts Letters 31:527-532. (WALLEYE; GEOGRAPHICAL DISTRIBUTION;).

1449. Juday, C. C., C. Livingston, and H. Pedracine. 1937. A census of the fish caught by anglers in Lake Waubesa in 1937. Wis. Geol. Nat. Hist. Surv., Notes Limnol. Lab. 7 pp. (WALLEYE; GEOGRAPHICAL DISTRIBUTION;).

1450. June, F. C. 1977. Reproductive patterns in seventeen species of warmwater fishes in a Missouri River Reservoir. Envir. Biol. Fish. 2:285-296. (SAUGER; WALLEYE; IMPOUNDMENTS; SPAWNING STUDIES; WATER LEVELS;).

1451. June, F. C., L. G. Beckman, J. H. Elrod, G. K. O'Bryan, and D. A. Vogel. 1987. Limnological and fishery studies on Lake Sharpe, a main-stem Missouri River reservoir, 1964-1975. U.S. Fish Wildl. Serv., Fish Wildl. Tech. Rep. No. 8: 83 pp. (WALLEYE; AGE AND GROWTH; COMMUNITY DYNAMICS; ECOLOGY; FOOD STUDIES; IMPOUNDMENTS; MORTALITY; MOVEMENT AND MIGRATIONS; SPAWNING STUDIES;).

1452. Jurgens, T. J. 1964. Investigations of walleye reproduction and stocking success in eastern lakes, 1963. S. D. Dept. Game Fish Parks, Fed. Aid Fish Wildl. Restor. Proj. F-1-R-13, Job No. 19: 17 pp. (WALLEYE; POPULATION STUDIES; SAMPLING METHODS; STOCKING;).

1453. Jurgens, T. J. 1965. Summary of five years of investigation on walleye reproduction and stocking success in eastern South Dakota. S. D. Dept. Game, Fish, Parks, Fed. Aid Fish and Wildl. Restor. Proj. F-1-R-14, Job No. 19-A: 20 pp. (WALLEYE; AGE AND GROWTH; MORPHOLOGY; POPULATION STUDIES; SAMPLING METHODS; STOCKING;).

1454. Kallemeyn, L. 1987. Correlations of regulated lake levels and climatic factors with abundance of young-of-the-year walleye and yellow perch in four lakes in Voyageurs National Park. N. Am. J. Fish. Manage. 7:513-521. (WALLEYE; COMMUNITY DYNAMICS; ECOLOGY; IMPOUNDMENTS; POPULATION STUDIES; SPAWNING STUDIES; WATER LEVELS;).

1455. Kathrein, J. W. 1953. An intensive creel census on Clearwater Lake, Missouri during its first four years of impoundment, 1949-1952. Trans. 18th N. Am. Wildl. Conf. 18:282-295. (WALLEYE; CREEL CENSUS; IMPOUNDMENTS;).

1456. Katz, M., and A. R. Gaufin. 1953. The effects of sewage pollution on the fish population of a midwestern stream. Trans. Am. Fish. Soc. 82:156-165. (WALLEYE; GEOGRAPHICAL DISTRIBUTION; HABITAT DEGRADATION;).

1457. Keeton, D. 1965. Application of Stoeltzner's method to determine growth of fish scales. Trans. Am. Fish. Soc. 94:93-94. (WALLEYE; AGE AND GROWTH;).

1458. Kehoe, D., and J. Strachan. 1977. 1977 creel census report, Bennett, White and Fagan. Ont. Min. Nat. Res., Rep. 80 pp. (WALLEYE; CREEL CENSUS;).

1459. Keleher, J. J. 1961. Comparison of largest Great Slave Lake fish with North American records. J. Fish. Research Board Can. 18:417-421. (WALLEYE; AGE AND GROWTH;).

1460. Keleher, J. J. 1963. The movement of tagged Great Slave Lake fish. J. Fish. Research Board Can. 20:319-326. (WALLEYE; MARKING; MOVEMENT AND MIGRATIONS;).

1461. Keleher, J. J. 1966. A survey of Great Slave Lake fishing. North 13:50-53. (WALLEYE; AGE AND GROWTH; COMMERCIAL FISHERIES; CREEL CENSUS;).

1462. Keleher, J. J., and B. Kooyman. 1957. Supplement to Hink's The Fishes of Manitoba.. Man. Dept. Mines Nat. Res. pp. 103-117. (WALLEYE; GEOGRAPHICAL DISTRIBUTION;).

1463. Keller, M. 1964. Lake Erie sport fishing survey. Ohio Dept. Nat. Res., Div. Wildl. Publ. W-316: 19 pp. (WALLEYE; CREEL CENSUS;).

1464. Keller, M. 1964. Walleye fry sampling (Sandusky Bay). Ohio Dept. Nat. Res., Fed. Aid Fish Wildl. Restor. Proj. F-35-R-1 & 2, Job No. 2: 25 pp. (WALLEYE; POPULATION STUDIES;).

1465. Keller, M. 1965. The winter fishery of South Bass Island with a census of the 1963 catch. Ohio J. Sci. 65:327-334. (SAUGER; WALLEYE; COMMERCIAL FISHERIES; CREEL CENSUS;).

1466. Keller, M., and J. V. Manz. 1963. Walleye spawning study area in western Lake Erie. Ohio Dept. Nat. Res., Fed. Aid Fish Wildl. Restor. Proj. F-35-R-1, Job No. 1: 29 pp. (WALLEYE; SPAWNING STUDIES;).

1467. Keller, M., J. C. Schneider, L. E. Mrozinski, R. C. Haas, and J. R. Weber. 1987. History, status, and management of fishes in Saginaw Bay, Lake Huron, 1891-1986. Mich. Dept. Nat. Res., Tech. Rep. No. 87-2: 42 pp. (WALLEYE; AGE AND GROWTH; COMMERCIAL FISHERIES; CREEL CENSUS; HABITAT DEGRADATION; MARKING; MORTALITY; PATHOLOGY; STOCKING;).

1468. Kelley, D. W. 1952. Fishing success on Koronis and Osakis Lakes during the summer of 1951. Minn. Dept. Conserv., Invest. Rep. No. 119: 5 pp. (WALLEYE; CREEL CENSUS;).

1469. Kelley, D. W. 1953. Fluctuations in trap net catches in the upper Mississippi River. U.S. Fish Wildl. Serv., Spec. Sci. Rep. Fish 101: 38 pp. (WALLEYE; COMMUNITY DYNAMICS; ECOLOGY; POPULATION STUDIES;).

1470. Kelley, D. W., and J. Greenbank. 1948. Census of Miller Lake, a Mississippi River backwater. Upper Miss. River Conserv. Comm., Tech. Comm. Fish., Progr. Rep. 4:17-25. (SAUGER; WALLEYE; FISHING GEAR;).

1471. Kelly, R. K., J. F. Klaverkamp, R. V. Hunt, and O. Nielsen. 1987. Chemical analysis of muscle from walleye (Stizostedion vitreum vitreum) with myofibrogranuloma, a chronic myopathy. Can. J. Fish. Aquat. Sci. 44:1425-1431. (WALLEYE; PATHOLOGY; PHYSIOLOGY;).

1472. Kelly, R. K., H. R. Miller, O. Nielsen, and J. W. Clayton. 1980. Fish cell culture: characteristics of a continuous fibroblastic cell line from walleye (Stizostedion vitreum vitreum). Can. J. Fish. Aquat. Sci. 37:1070-1075. (WALLEYE; PATHOLOGY;).

1473. Kelly, R. K., O. Nielsen, S. C. Mitchell, and T. Yamamoto. 1983. Characterization of Herpesvitus vitreum isolated from hyperplastic epidermal tissue of walleye, Stizostedion vitreum vitreum (Mitchill). J. Fish Dis. 6:249-260. (WALLEYE; PATHOLOGY;).

1474. Kelly, T. M., J. D. Jones, and G. R. Smith. 1975. Historical changes in mercury contamination in Michigan walleyes (Stizostedion vitreum vitreum). J. Fish. Research Board Can. 32:1745-1754. (WALLEYE; HABITAT DEGRADATION; TOXICANTS;).

1475. Kelso, J. R. M. 1972. Population parameters and bioenergetic demands of walleye, Stizostedion vitreum vitreum (Mitchill) in relation to their trophic dynamic ecology, West Blue Lake, Manitoba. Ph.D. Dissertation, Univ. Manitoba, Winnipeg, Man. 146 pp. (WALLEYE; ECOLOGY; FOOD STUDIES; POPULATION STUDIES;).

1476. Kelso, J. R. M. 1972. Conversion, maintenance, and assimilation for walleye (Stizostedion vitreum vitreum), as affected by size, diet, and temperature. J. Fish. Research Board Can. 29:1181-1183. (WALLEYE; FOOD STUDIES;).

1477. Kelso, J. R. M. 1973. Seasonal energy changes in walleye and their diet in West Blue Lake, Manitoba. Trans. Am. Fish. Soc. 102:363-368. (WALLEYE; FOOD STUDIES;).

1478. Kelso, J. R. M. 1976. Diel movement of walleye, Stizostedion vitreum vitreum, in West Blue Lake, Manitoba, as determined by ultrasonic tracking. J. Fish. Research Board Can. 33:2070-2072. (WALLEYE; BEHAVIOR; MOVEMENT AND MIGRATIONS;).

1479. Kelso, J. R. M. 1978. Diel rhythm in activity of walleye, *Stizostedion vitreum vitreum.* J. Fish. Biol. 12:593-599. (WALLEYE; BEHAVIOR; MOVEMENT AND MIGRATIONS;).

1480. Kelso, J. R. M., and T. B. Bagenal. 1977. Percids in unperturbed ecosystems. J. Fish. Research Board Can. 34:1959-1963. (WALLEYE; AGE AND GROWTH; MORTALITY; PRODUCTIVITY;).

1481. Kelso, J. R. M., H. R. MacCrimmon, and D. J. Ecobichon. 1970. Seasonal insecticide residue changes in tissues of fish from the Grand River, Ontario. Tran. Am. Fish. Soc. 99:423-426. (WALLEYE; TOXICANTS;).

1482. Kelso, J. R. M., and F. J. Ward. 1972. Vital statistics, biomass, and seasonal production of an unexploited walleye *(Stizostedion vitreum vitreum)* population in West Blue Lake, Manitoba during 1969-70. J. Fish. Research Board Can. 29:1043-1052. (WALLEYE; AGE AND GROWTH; MARKING; MORTALITY; POPULATION STUDIES; PRODUCTIVITY;).

1483. Kelso, J. R. M., and F. J. Ward. 1977. Unexploited percid populations of West Blue Lake, Manitoba, and their interactions. J. Fish. Research Board Can. 34:1655-1669. (WALLEYE; BEHAVIOR; FOOD STUDIES; POPULATION STUDIES; PRODUCTIVITY;).

1484. Kempinger, J. J. 1968. Impact of underwater spearfishing on a mixed warmwater fish population. Wis. Dept. Nat. Res., Research Rep. No. 30: 10 pp. (WALLEYE; ECOLOGY; POPULATION STUDIES;).

1485. Kempinger, J. J. 1977. Cost of stocked walleyes caught by anglers in Escanaba Lake. Wis. Dept. Nat. Res., Research Rep. No. 91: 5 pp. (WALLEYE; COMMUNITY DYNAMICS; CREEL CENSUS; STOCKING;).

1486. Kempinger, J. J., and Carline. R. F. 1977. Dynamics of the walleye *(Stizostedion vitreum vitreum)* population in Escanaba Lake, Wisconsin, 1955-72. J. Fish. Research Board Can. 34:1800-1811. (WALLEYE; AGE AND GROWTH; COMMUNITY DYNAMICS; CREEL CENSUS; MORTALITY; POPULATION STUDIES; PRODUCTIVITY; REGULATIONS;).

1487. Kempinger, J. J., and L. M. Christenson. 1978. Population estimates and standing crops of fish in Nebish Lake. Wis. Dept. Nat. Res., Research Rep. No. 96: 12 pp. (WALLEYE; COMMUNITY DYNAMICS; POPULATION STUDIES; PROPAGATION;).

1488. Kempinger, J. J., and W. S. Churchill. 1972. Contribution of native and stocked walleye fingerlings of the anglers' catch, Escanaba Lake, Wisconsin. Trans. Am. Fish. Soc. 101:644-649. (WALLEYE; AGE AND GROWTH; CREEL CENSUS; MORTALITY; POPULATION STUDIES; STOCKING;).

1489. Kempinger, J. J., W. S. Churchill, G. R. Priegel, and L. M. Christenson. 1975. Estimate of abundance, harvest, and exploitation of the fish population of Escanaba Lake, Wisconsin, 1946-69. Wis. Dept. Nat. Res., Tech. Bull. No. 84: 30 pp. (WALLEYE; AGE AND GROWTH; COMMUNITY DYNAMICS; CREEL CENSUS; POPULATION STUDIES; REGULATIONS; STOCKING;).

1490. Kendall, W. C. 1908. Fauna of New England. 8. List of the Pisces. Occ. Papers Boston Soc. Nat. Hist. 7: 512 pp. (SAUGER; WALLEYE; GEOGRAPHICAL DISTRIBUTION;).

1491. Kendall, W. C. 1921. The relationship of so-called blue pike and yellow pike of Lake Erie and Lake Ontario. Trans. Am. Fish. Soc. 50:257-267. (WALLEYE; MORPHOLOGY; TAXONOMY;).

1492. Kendall, W. C. 1927. The smelts. U. S. Bureau Fish., Bull. 42:217-375. (WALLEYE; COMMUNITY DYNAMICS; FOOD STUDIES;).

1493. Kennedy, W. 1947. Some information on the minimum adult stock of fish needed to provide adequate natural spawning. Can. Fish Cult. 1:14-15. (WALLEYE; ECOLOGY; MORTALITY; SPAWNING STUDIES;).

1494. Kennedy, W. 1948. Recent increases in growth rate in two species of Lake Manitoba fish. Can. Fish Cult. 3:18-19. (SAUGER; WALLEYE; AGE AND GROWTH; COMMERCIAL FISHERIES; COMMUNITY DYNAMICS; ECOLOGY;).

1495. Kennedy, W. 1951. The relationship of fishing effort by gill nets to the interval between lifts. J. Fish. Research Board Can. 8:264-274. (WALLEYE; COMMERCIAL FISHERIES; FISHING GEAR;).

1496. Kennedy, W. 1956. The first ten years of commercial fishing on Great Slave Lake. Fish. Research Board Can., Bull. 107: 58 pp. (WALLEYE; COMMERCIAL FISHERIES;).

1497. Kennedy, W. A. 1935. Report on the migration of Pickerel due to temperature changes. Unpubl. typescript, Univ. Toronto, Great Lakes Inst. Libr. 15 pp. (WALLEYE; BEHAVIOR; ECOLOGY; MOVEMENT AND MIGRATIONS;).

1498. Kennedy, W. A. 1949. Relationship of length, weight, and sexual maturity to age in three species of Lake Manitoba fish. Fish. Research Board Can., Bull. 81: 5 pp. (SAUGER; WALLEYE; AGE AND GROWTH;).

1499. Kennedy, W. A. 1950. The determination of optimum size of mesh for gill nets in Lake Manitoba. Trans. Am. Fish. Soc. 79:167-179. (SAUGER; WALLEYE; AGE AND GROWTH; COMMERCIAL FISHERIES; SPAWNING STUDIES;).

1500. Kennedy, W. A. 1961. Daily catch records of Crewe Brothers fishery Lake Erie-1904 to 1956. Fish. Research Board Can., Manuscript Rep. 706: 411 pp. (SAUGER; WALLEYE; COMMERCIAL FISHERIES;).

1501. Kernen, L. 1979. Walleye assessment, Lake Michigan (Green Bay). Wis. Dept. Nat. Res., AFC-14: 15 pp. (WALLEYE; MORTALITY; POPULATION STUDIES; SPAWNING STUDIES; STOCKING;).

1502. Kerr, S. J. 1982. 1981 summer creel census program Dog Lake. Ont. Min. Nat. Res., Rep. 58 pp. (WALLEYE; CREEL CENSUS;).

1503. Kerr, S. J. 1982. 1982 winter creel survey — Esnagi Lake. Ont. Min. Nat. Res., Rep. 23 pp. (WALLEYE; CREEL CENSUS;).

1504. Kerr, S. J. 1987. Proposed walleye management strategies and implementation schedule for the Alymer District waters of the Thames Rivers, 1987-1990. Ont. Min. Nat. Res., Aylmer Dist. 15 pp. (WALLEYE; REGULATIONS;).

1505. Kerr, S. R., and R. A. Ryder. 1977. Niche theory and percid community structure. J. Fish. Research Board Can. 34:1952-1958. (SAUGER; WALLEYE; COMMUNITY DYNAMICS; ECOLOGY; FOOD STUDIES;).

1506. Ketola, H. G. 1978. Nutritional requirements and feeding of selected coolwater fishes: a review. Prog. Fish-Cult. 40:127-132. (WALLEYE; FOOD STUDIES; PROPAGATION;).

1507. Keyes, C. M. 1894. The fishing industry of Lake Erie, past and present. U.S. Fish. Comm., Bull. 13:349-353. (SAUGER; WALLEYE; COMMERCIAL FISHERIES;).

1508. Kidd, P. E. 1927. The food of Minnesota fishes with special reference to the algae. Trans. Am. Fish. Soc. 57:85-91. (WALLEYE; FOOD STUDIES;).

1509. King, W. 1947. Important food and game fishes of North Carolina. N. C. Dept. Conserv. Development, Div. Game Inland Fish. 54 pp. (WALLEYE; HABITAT DEGRADATION; INTRODUCTIONS;).

1510. Kinman, B. T. 1982. An evaluation of walleye introductions at Nolin River Lake, Kentucky. Ky. Dept. Fish Wildl. Res., Spec. Rep. No. 4: 21 pp. (WALLEYE; AGE AND GROWTH; CREEL CENSUS; FISHING GEAR; IMPOUNDMENTS; INTRODUCTIONS; POPULATION STUDIES; SPAWNING STUDIES; STOCKING;).

1511. Kinman, B. T. 1984. Sport fishery investigation. Ky. Dept. Fish Wildl. Res., Fed. Aid Fish Wildl. Restor. Proj. F-40-R-6, Subsection I: 62 pp. (WALLEYE; POPULATION STUDIES;).

1512. Kirsch, P. H. 1893. Notes on a collection of fishes from the southern tributaries of Cumberland River in Kentucky and Tennessee. U.S. Fish. Comm., Bull. 11:259-268. (WALLEYE; GEOGRAPHICAL DISTRIBUTION;).

1513. Kirsch, P. H. 1895. A report upon investigations in the Maumee River Basin during the summer of 1893. U.S. Fish. Comm., Bull. 14:315-337. (SAUGER; WALLEYE; GEOGRAPHICAL DISTRIBUTION;).

1514. Kitchell, J. F., M. G. Johnson, K. C. Minns, K. H. Loftus, L. Greig, and C. H. Olver. 1977. Percid habitat: The river analogy. J. Fish. Research Board Can. 34:1936-1940. (WALLEYE; ECOLOGY;).

1515. Kitchell, J. F., D. J. Stewart, and D. Weininger. 1977. Applications of a bioenergetics model to yellow perch *(Perca flavescens)* and walleye *(Stizostedion vitreum vitreum)*. J. Fish. Research Board Can. 34:1922-1935. (WALLEYE; ECOLOGY; FOOD STUDIES;).

1516. Kleinert, S. J. 1967. Delafield studies. Annual progress report for the period of January 1-December 31, 1966. Wis. Conserv. Dept. 15 pp. (WALLEYE; ECOLOGY; HABITAT DEGRADATION; SAMPLING METHODS; STOCKING;).

1517. Kleinert, S. J. 1967. Survival of walleyes *(Stizostedion vitreum)* from eggs of known DDT and dieldrin residues in three southeastern Wisconsin Lakes. Wis. Conserv. Dept., Research Rep. 21: 9 pp. (WALLEYE; HABITAT DEGRADATION; MORTALITY;).

1518. Kleinert, S. J., and P. E. Degurse. 1968. Survival of walleye eggs and fry of known DDT residue levels from ten Wisconsin waters in 1967. Wis. Dept. Nat. Res., Research Rep. 37: 30 pp. (WALLEYE; EMBRYOLOGY; HABITAT DEGRADATION; MORTALITY; TOXICANTS;).

1519. Kleinert, S. J., P. E. Degurse, and T. L. Wirth. 1968. Occurrence and significance of DDT and Dieldrin residues in Wisconsin fish. Wis. Dept. Nat. Res., Tech Bull. No. 41: 43 pp. (SAUGER; WALLEYE; ECOLOGY; HABITAT DEGRADATION; TOXICANTS;).

1520. Kleinert, S. J., P. E. Degurse, T. L. Wirth, and L. C. Hall. 1967. DDT and Dieldrin residue found in Wisconsin fishes from the survey of 1966. Wis. Conserv. Dept., Research Rep. 23: 29 pp. (SAUGER; WALLEYE; ECOLOGY; HABITAT DEGRADATION; TOXICANTS;).

1521. Kleinert, S. J., and D. Mraz. 1966. Delafield studies. Annual progress report for the period of January 1-December 31, 1965. Wis. Conserv. Dept., Prog. Rep. (1965): 45 pp. (WALLEYE; ECOLOGY; MORPHOLOGY; POPULATION STUDIES; SAMPLING METHODS; SPAWNING STUDIES; STOCKING;).

1522. Klingbiel, J. 1969. Management of walleye in the upper Midwest. Wis. Dept. Nat. Res., Fish Manage. Rep. No. 18: 14 pp. (WALLEYE; CREEL CENSUS; HABITAT IMPROVEMENT; POPULATION STUDIES; PROPAGATION; REGULATIONS;).

1523. Klingbiel, J. 1983. Fish management species workshop — walleye. Wis. Dept. Nat. Res., Rep. 83 pp. (WALLEYE; POPULATION STUDIES; REGULATIONS;).

1524. Kmiotek, S. 1952. Observations on spawning walleyes in the Wolf River including creel census and growth studies. Wis. Conserv. Dept., Invest. Rep. 658: 22 pp. (WALLEYE; AGE AND GROWTH; CREEL CENSUS; ECOLOGY; POPULATION STUDIES; SPAWNING STUDIES;).

1525. Knapp, F. T. 1953. Fishes found in the freshwaters of Texas. Ragland Studio and Litho Printing Co., Brunswick, Ga. 156 pp. (SAUGER; TAXONOMY;).

1526. Knight, R. L. 1982. Piscivory by walleye and yellow perch in western Lake Erie. M.S. Thesis. Ohio State Univ., Columbus, Ohio (WALLEYE; FOOD STUDIES;).

1527. Knight, R. L., and F. J. Margraf. 1982. Estimating stomach fullness in fishes. N. Am. J. Fish. Manage. 2:413-414. (WALLEYE; FOOD STUDIES;).

1528. Knight, R. L., F. J. Margraf, and R. F. Carline. 1982. Predation by walleye *(Stizostedion viteum)* and yellow perch *(Perca flavescens)* on forage fishes in western Lake Erie. Ohio J. Sci. 82:. (WALLEYE; COMMUNITY DYNAMICS;).

1529. Knight, R. L., F. J. Margraf, and R. F. Carline. 1984. Piscivory by walleyes and yellow perch in western Lake Erie. Trans. Am. Fish. Soc. 113:677-693. (WALLEYE; COMMUNITY DYNAMICS; FOOD STUDIES;).

1530. Koch, E. A., W. C. Dolowy, R. H. Spitzer, S. Greenberg, and E. R. Brown. 1976. Postulated developmental forms in the life cycle of the lymphocystis virus. Cancer Biochem. Biophys. 1:163-166. (WALLEYE; PATHOLOGY;).

1531. Koelz, W. 1926. Fishing industry of the Great Lakes. U.S. Bureau Fish., Annu. Rep. (1925):553-617. (SAUGER; WALLEYE; COMMERCIAL FISHERIES; PROPAGATION; STOCKING;).

1532. Koenst, W. M., and L. L. Smith, Jr. 1976. Thermal requirements of the early life history stages of walleye, *Stizostedion vitreum vitreum*, and sauger, *Stizostedion canadense*. J. Fish. Research Board Can. 33:1130-1138. (SAUGER; WALLEYE; ECOLOGY; LIFE HISTORY;).

1533. Kohler, C. C., and J. J. Ney. 1981. Consequences of an alewife die-off to fish and zooplankton in a reservoir. Trans. Am. Fish. Soc. 110:360-369. (WALLEYE; FOOD STUDIES;).

1534. Kohler, C. C., J. J. Ney, and W. E. Kelso. 1986. Filling the void: development of a pelagic fishery and its consequences to littoral fishes in a Virginia mainstream reservoir. Pages 166-177 in G.E. Hall and M.J. Van Den Avyle, eds. Reservoir fisheries management: strategies for the 80's. Reserv. Comm., S. Div. Am. Fish. Soc., Bethesda, Maryland. (WALLEYE; AGE AND GROWTH; COMMUNITY DYNAMICS; CREEL CENSUS; POPULATION STUDIES; STOCKING;).

1535. Koonce, J. E., and B. J. Shuter. 1987. Influence of various sources of error and community interactions on quota management of fish stocks. Can. J. Fish. Aquat. Sci. 44(Suppl. 2):61-67. (WALLEYE; PRODUCTIVITY;).

1536. Koonce, J. F., T. B. Bagenal, R. F. Carline, K. E. F. Hokanson, and M. Nagiec. 1977. Factors influencing year-class strength of percids: A summary and model of temperature effects. J. Fish. Research Board Can. 34:1900-1909. (WALLEYE; EMBRYOLOGY; LIFE HISTORY; PRODUCTIVITY;).

1537. Kooyman, B. 1952. Pickerel-sauger investigation-Lake Winnipeg fall season, 1952. Man. Dept. Mines Nat. Res., Fish. Branch, Manuscript Rep. 19 pp. (SAUGER; WALLEYE; COMMERCIAL FISHERIES; FISHING GEAR; POPULATION STUDIES;).

1538. Koshinsky, G. D. 1965. Limnology and fisheries of five precambrian headwater lakes near Lac La Rogue, Saskatchewan. Sask. Dept. Nat. Res., Fish. Rep. 7: 52 pp. (WALLEYE; AGE AND GROWTH; COMMERCIAL FISHERIES; ECOLOGY; FOOD STUDIES; PRODUCTIVITY;).

1539. Koshinsky, G. D. 1967. Report on the Lac la Ronge creel census, 1965, 1966, and 1967. Sask. Dept. Nat. Res., Fish. Lab. Tech. Rep. 1967-9: 16 pp. (WALLEYE; CREEL CENSUS;).

1540. Koshinsky, G. D. 1968. Report on the Lac la Ronge creel census, 1968. Sask. Dept. Nat. Res., Fish. Lab. Tech. Rep. 1968-6: 18 pp. (WALLEYE; CREEL CENSUS;).

1541. Koshinsky, G. D. 1969. Report on the Lac la Ronge and Hunter Bay creel census, 1969. Sask. Dept. Nat. Res., Fish. Lab. Tech. Rep. 1969-8: 5 pp. (WALLEYE; CREEL CENSUS;).

1542. Koshinsky, G. D. 1971. The Lac la Ronge creel census, 1970. Sask. Dept. Nat. Res., Fish. Lab. Tech. Rep. 1971-6: 6 pp. (WALLEYE; CREEL CENSUS;).

1543. Koski, K. J. 1985. Lake Timiskaming winter creel census Temagami District 1985. Ont. Min. Nat. Res., Rep. 33 pp. (SAUGER; WALLEYE; CREEL CENSUS;).

1544. Koster, W. J. 1957. Guide to the fishes of New Mexico. Univ. N. Mex. Press, Albuquerque, N. Mex. 116 pp. (WALLEYE; INTRODUCTIONS; MORPHOLOGY; TAXONOMY;).

1545. Kraai, J. E., and J. A. Prentice. 1974. Walleye life history study. Tex. Parks Wildl. Dept., Fed. Aid Fish Wildl. Restor. Proj. F-7-R-23, Job No. 17a: 28 pp. (WALLEYE; AGE AND GROWTH; FOOD STUDIES; IMPOUNDMENTS; INTRODUCTIONS; MOVEMENT AND MIGRATIONS; PATHOLOGY;).

1546. Kraai, J. E., W. C. Provine, and J. A. Prentice. 1983. Case histories of three walleye stocking techniques with cost-to-benefit considerations. Proc. 37th Annu. Conf. Southeast Assoc. Fish Wildl. Agencies. 37:395-400. (WALLEYE; CREEL CENSUS; IMPOUNDMENTS; STOCKING;).

1547. Kraft, T. W., and D. A. Burkhardt. 1986. Telodendrites of cone photoreceptors structure and proble function. J. Comp. Neurol. 249:13-27. (WALLEYE; PHYSIOLOGY;).

1548. Kramer, R. H., and L. L. Smith, Jr. 1966. Survival of walleye eggs in suspended wood fibers. Prog. Fish-Cult 28:79-82. (WALLEYE; HABITAT DEGRADATION; MORTALITY;).

1549. Kreil, A. 1969. Air agua system research in Rolette County. N.D. Game Fish Dept., Fed. Aid Fish Wildl. Restor. Proj. F-2-R-15, Job No. 8: 28 pp. (WALLEYE; HABITAT IMPROVEMENT;).

1550. Kreil, A. 1973. Evaluation of air induced circulation to alleviate winter kill. N.D. Game Fish Dept., Fed. Aid Fish Wildl. Restor. Proj. F-2-R-20, Study 3: 27 pp. (WALLEYE; HABITAT IMPROVEMENT;).

1551. Krise, W. F., L. Bulkowski-Cummings, A. D. Shellman, K. A. Kraus, and R. W. Gould. 1986. Increased walleye egg hatch and larval survival after protease treatment of eggs. Prog. Fish-Cult. 48:95-100. (WALLEYE; PROPAGATION;).

1552. Krise, W. F., and J. W. Meade. 1986. Review of the intensive culture of walleye fry. Prog. Fish-Cult. 48:81-89. (WALLEYE; PROPAGATION;).

1553. Kristensen, D. R. 1983. Creel census survey for the Hearst "Chain of Lakes," 1982 — Pivabishka Lake, Wolverine Lake, Hanlan Lake, Fushimi Lake. Ont. Min. Nat. Res., Rep. 40 pp. (WALLEYE; CREEL CENSUS;).

1554. Kristensen, J., and S. A. Summers. 1979. Fish populations in the Peace Athabasca Delta, Canada and the effects of water control structures on fish movements. Can. Fish. Marine Serv., Manuscript Rep. No. 1465: 62 pp. (WALLEYE; AGE AND GROWTH; FISHING GEAR; MARKING; MORTALITY; MOVEMENTS AND MIGRATIONS; POPULATION STUDIES; SAMPLING METHODS; WATER LEVELS;).

1555. Kristofferson, H. K. 1985. Year class strength assessments of walleye, *Stizostedion v. vitreum*, and sauger, *S. canadense*, cohorts as determined from trawl and fyke net catches from the south basin and channel areas of Lake Winnipeg, 1976-1983. Man. Dept. Nat. Res., Manuscript Rep. No. 85-18: 182 pp. (WALLEYE; LIFE HISTORY; MORTALITY; MOVEMENT AND MIGRATIONS; POPULATION STUDIES; SAMPLING METHODS;).

1556. Krum, R. L. 1979. Chemical renovation of Lake Louise, Hand County, South Dakota. S.D. Game Fish Parks, Fed. Aid Fish Wildl. Restor. Proj. F-31-R-1: 9 pp. (WALLEYE; HABITAT IMPROVEMENT;).

1557. Krumholz, L. A. 1945. Fillet weights and loss on filleting of yellow pikeperch *(Stizostedion vitreum)* from Saginaw Bay. Mich. Dept. Conserv., Inst. Fish. Research, Misc. Pub. 3: 12 pp. (WALLEYE; AGE AND GROWTH; COMMERCIAL FISHERIES;).

1558. Krumholz, L. A., J. R. Charles, and W. L. Minckley. 1962. The fish population of the Ohio River. Aquatic-life Resources of the Ohio River pp. 49-89, Append. 2: 143-152, Append. 3: 166-180, Append. 4: 200-210. Ohio River Valley Water Sanitation Comm., Cincinnati, Ohio. (SAUGER; WALLEYE; ECOLOGY; HABITAT DEGRADATION; POPULATION STUDIES;).

1559. Kucera, T. A., and B. L. Torp. 1976. Annual report of the statewide creel census program on 83 lakes and 36 trout streams in Minnesota, April 27, 1973-February 28, 1974. Minn. Dept. Nat. Res., Invest. Rep. No. 342: 112 pp. (WALLEYE; CREEL CENSUS;).

1560. Kucera, T. A., and B. L. Torp. 1976. Annual report of the statewide creel census on 90 lakes and 32 trout streams in Minnesota, May 5 1974-February 28, 1975. Minn. Dept. Nat. Res., Invest. Rep. No. 344: 124 pp. (WALLEYE; CREEL CENSUS;).

1561. Kucera, T. A., B. L. Torp, and G. M. Clymer. 1976. Annual report of the statewide creel census on 75 lakes and 30 trout streams in Minnesota, May 3, 1974-September 28, 1975. Minn. Dept. Nat. Res., Invest. Rep. No. 343: 111 pp. (WALLEYE; CREEL CENSUS;).

1562. Kudo, R. 1920. Studies on Myxosporidia. A synopsis of genera and species of Myxosporidia. Ill. Biol. Monogr. 5:1-265. (WALLEYE; PATHOLOGY;).

1563. Kuehl, D. W., H. L. Kopperman, G. D. Veith, and G. E. Glass. 1976. Isolation and identification of polychlorinated styrenes in Great

Lakes fish. Bull. Environ. Contam. Toxicol. 16:127-132. (WALLEYE; TOXICANTS;).

1564 Kuehn, J. H. 1948. A reconnaissance of the Blue Earth River to determine present status of smallmouth bass and to evaluate present environmental conditions. Minn. Dept. Conserv., Invest. Rep. No. 81: 7 pp. (WALLEYE; IMPOUNDMENTS;).

1565. Kuehn, J. H. 1948. A reconnaissance of the Cottonwood River to determine present status of smallmouth bass *(Micropterus dolomieui)*. Minn. Dept. Conserv., Invest. Rep. No. 82: 5 pp. (WALLEYE; ECOLOGY;).

1566. Kuehn, J. H. 1949. Fish population estimates based on 1948-49 winter rough fish seining operations. Minn. Dept. Conserv., Invest. Rep. No. 86: 47 pp. (WALLEYE; POPULATION STUDIES;).

1567. Kuehn, J. H. 1950. Experimental testnetting at various times of year in two Anoka County lakes containing "know" fish population. Minn. Dept. Conserv., Invest. Rep. No. 91: 12 pp. (WALLEYE; FISHING GEAR; POPULATION STUDIES;).

1568. Kuehn, J. H., and M. W. Johnson. 1956. Semi-annual report of statewide creel census of 14 Minnesota lakes. Minn. Dept. Conserv., Invest. Rep. No. 184: 21 pp. (WALLEYE; CREEL CENSUS;).

1569. Kuehn, J. H., W. Niemuth, and A. R. Peterson. 1961. A biological reconnaissance of the Upper St. Croix River. Minn. Dept. Conserv., Invest. Rep. No. 239: 47 pp. (SAUGER; WALLEYE; ECOLOGY; POPULATION STUDIES;).

1570. Kuhne, E. R. 1939. A guide to fishes of Tennessee and the mid-south. Tenn. Dept. Conserv. 123 pp. (SAUGER; WALLEYE; LIFE HISTORY; MORPHOLOGY; TAXONOMY;).

1571. Kuhne, E. R. 1939. Preliminary report on the productivity of some Tennessee waters. J. Tenn. Acad. Sci. 14:54-60. (WALLEYE; CREEL CENSUS; IMPOUNDMENTS; PRODUCTIVITY;).

1572. Kuhne, E. R. 1939. Tennessee's fisheries program. Trans. Am. Fish. Soc. 68:240-245. (WALLEYE; TAXONOMY;).

1573. Kumlien, L. 1887. The fisheries of the Great Lakes. The fisheries and fishery industries of the United States. Sec. 5. History and methods of the fisheries 2:757-769. (WALLEYE; COMMERCIAL FISHERIES; FISHING GEAR;).

1574. Kumlien, L., and F. W. True. 1887. The fishing grounds of the Great Lakes. The fisheries and fishery industries of the United States. Sec. 3. The fishing grounds of North America. pp. 117-131. (WALLEYE; COMMERCIAL FISHERIES; GEOGRAPHICAL DISTRIBUTION;).

1575. Kutkuhn, J. H. 1955. Food and feeding habits of some fishes in a dredged Iowa lake. Proc. Iowa Acad. Sci. 62:576-588. (WALLEYE; FOOD STUDIES;).

1576. Kutkuhn, J. H. 1958. Utilization of gizzard shad by game fishes. Proc. Iowa Acad. Sci. 65:571-579. (WALLEYE; COMMUNITY DYNAMICS; FOOD STUDIES;).

1577. Kutkuhn, J. H. 1981. Stock definition as a necessary basis for cooperative management of Great Lakes fish resources. Can. J. Fish Aquat. Sci. 38:1476-1478. (WALLEYE; ECOLOGY;).

1578. Laarman, P. W. 1971. Separation of genetic strains of Great Lake fishes. Mich. Dept. Conserv., Fed. Aid Fish Wildl. Restor. Proj. F-32-R-1, Study No. IV, Job No. 1 & 2: 10 pp. (WALLEYE; GENETICS; POPULATION STUDIES;).

1579. Laarman, P. W. 1978. Case histories of stocking walleyes in inland lakes, impoundments, and the Great Lakes — 100 years with walleyes. Pages 254-260 *in* R.L. Kendall, ed. Selected coolwater fishes of North America. Am. Fish. Soc. Sp. Publ. No. 11, Washington, D.C. (WALLEYE; IMPOUNDMENTS; STOCKING;).

1580. Laarman, P. W. 1979. Evaluation of a chemical reclamation and restocking program on the Huron River in the Detroit Metropolitan Area. Mich. Dept. Nat. Res., Fish. Research Rep. No. 1866: 34 pp. (WALLEYE; AGE AND GROWTH; COMMUNITY DYNAMICS; CREEL CENSUS; HABITAT IMPROVEMENT; IMPOUNDMENTS; POPULATION STUDIES; PRODUCTIVITY; STOCKING; TOXICANTS;).

1581. Laarman, P. W. 1980. Vital statistics of the fish population in Manistee Lake, Kalkaska County, with special emphasis on mortality and exploitation of stocked 15-cm walleye fingerlings. Mich. Dept. Nat. Res., Fish. Research Rep. No. 1881: 37 pp. (WALLEYE; AGE AND GROWTH; CREEL CENSUS; MORTALITY; POPULATION STUDIES; STOCKING;).

1582. Laarman, P. W. 1981. Vital statistics on a Michigan fish population, with special emphasis on the effectiveness of stocking 15-cm walleye fingerlings. N. Am. J. Fish. Manage. 1:177-185. (WALLEYE; AGE AND GROWTH; CREEL CENSUS; MORTALITY; POPULATION STUDIES; SOCIO-ECONOMICS OF FISHERIES; STOCKING;).

1583. Laarman, P. W., and D. E. Reynolds. 1974. Methods for propagation of walleye fingerlings in Michigan. Mich. Dept. Nat. Res., Tech. Rep. 74-5: 14 pp. (WALLEYE; PROPAGATION;).

1584. Laarman, P. W., and J. R. Ryckman. 1980. Size selectivity of trap nets for eight species of fish. Mich Dept. Nat. Res., Fish. Research Rep. No. 1880: 16 pp. (WALLEYE; FISHING GEAR;).

1585. Laarman, P. W., and J. R. Ryckman. 1982. Relative size selectivity of trap nets for eight species of fish. N. Am. J. Fish. Manage. 2:33-37. (WALLEYE; FISHING GEAR; POPULATION STUDIES;).

1586. Laarman, P. W., and J. C. Schneider. 1986. Walleye stocking experiments and fish population studies at Manistee Lake, 1972-84. Mich. Dept. Nat. Res., Fish. Research Rep. No. 1938: 43 pp. (WALLEYE; AGE AND GROWTH; COMMUNITY DYNAMICS; ECOLOGY; INTRODUCTIONS; MORTALITY; POPULATION STUDIES; PRODUCTIVITY; SPAWNING STUDIES; STOCKING;).

1587. LaBar, G. W., and S. Parren. 1983. A comprehensive examination of data and data analysis on walleye from Lake Champlain: 1903 to the present. Vt. Fish Game Dept. 57 pp. (WALLEYE; AGE AND GROWTH; COMMUNITY DYNAMICS; CREEL CENSUS; MARKING; MORTALITY; POPULATION STUDIES; SPAWNING STUDIES; STOCKING;).

1588. Lacarte, L. 1978. Kirkland Lake District Gowanda Lake creel census summer 1978. Ont. Min. Nat. Res., Rep. 37 pp. (WALLEYE; CREEL CENSUS;).

1589. Lacarte, L., and K. Charles. 1978. Kirkland Lake District Skeleton Lake creel census summer 1978. Ont. Min. Nat. Res., Rep. 34 pp. (WALLEYE; CREEL CENSUS;).

1590. Lachner, E. A. 1956. The changing fish fauna of the Upper Ohio Basin. Univ. Pittsburgh, Pymatuning Lab. Field Biol., Spec. Pub. 1:64-78. (SAUGER; ECOLOGY; HABITAT DEGRADATION;).

1591. Lafrance, W. 1973. Summer creel census report Dalhousie, Silver and Christie Lakes. Ont. Min. Nat. Res., Rep. 70 pp. (WALLEYE; CREEL CENSUS;).

1592. Lagler, K. F. 1947. Lepidological studies. 1. Scale characters of the families of Great Lakes fishes. Trans. Am. Micros. Soc. 66:149-171. (SAUGER; MORPHOLOGY; TAXONOMY;).

1593. Lagler, K. F. 1949. Fish and fishing in Michigan. Follett's Bookstore, Ann Arbor, Mich. 91 pp. (WALLEYE; LIFE HISTORY;).

1594. Lagler, K. F. 1956. Freshwater fishery biology. Wm. C. Brown Co. Publ. Dubuque, Iowa. 421 pp. (WALLEYE; LIFE HISTORY;).

1595. Lagler, K. F., and M. J. Lagler. 1944. Natural enemies of crayfishes in Michigan. Paper Mich. Acad. Sci., Arts Letters 29:293-303. (SAUGER; WALLEYE; FOOD STUDIES;).

1596. Lake Erie Fish Management Committee. 1955. Report of committee on methods for the more efficient use of fishery statistics. Great Lakes Fish. Comm. 33 pp. (SAUGER; WALLEYE; COMMERCIAL FISHERIES;).

1597. La Monte, F. 1945. North American game fishes. Doubleday, Doran and Co. Inc., Garden City, N.Y. 202 pp. (SAUGER; WALLEYE; TAXONOMY;).

1598. Langlois, T. H. 1937. Lake Erie fisheries-Ohio commercial catch for 1936. Franz Theodore Stone Biol. Lab. 2 pp. (SAUGER; WALLEYE; COMMERCIAL FISHERIES;).

1599. Langlois, T. H. 1941. Two processes operating for the reduction in abundance or elimination of fish species from certain types of water areas. Trans. 6th N. Am. Wildl. Conf. 6:189-201. (SAUGER; WALLEYE; ECOLOGY; MORTALITY; POPULATION STUDIES;).

1600. Langlois, T. H. 1941. Trends of shifting abundance of Lake Erie fishes in 1941. Ohio Div. Conserv. Nat. Res. 5 pp. (SAUGER; WALLEYE; ECOLOGY; POPULATION STUDIES;).

1601. Langlois, T. H. 1945. Ohio's fish program. Ohio Div. Conserv. Nat. Res. 40 pp. (SAUGER; WALLEYE; AGE AND GROWTH; PROPAGATION; SPAWNING STUDIES;).

1602. Langlois, T. H. 1945. Water, fishes, and cropland management. Trans. 10th N. Am. Wildl. Conf. 6:190-196. (SAUGER; WALLEYE; ECOLOGY;).

1603. Langlois, T. H. 1946. Statement of basis for the Ohio point of view regarding management of the Great Lakes fisheries. Ohio Div. Conserv. Nat. Res. 12 pp. (WALLEYE; ECOLOGY; HABITAT DEGRADATION;).

1604. Langlois, T. H. 1946. The herring fishery of Lake Erie. Inland Seas, Quart. Bull. Great Lakes Hist. Soc. 2:101-104. (SAUGER; WALLEYE; COMMERCIAL FISHERIES;).

1605. Langlois, T. H. 1954. The western end of Lake Erie and its ecology. J.W. Edwards, Pub., Inc., Ann Arbor, Mich. 479 pp. (SAUGER; WALLEYE; COMMERCIAL FISHERIES; FOOD STUDIES;).

1606. Langlois, T. H. 1965. Portage River watershed and fishery. Ohio Dept. Nat. Res. W-130: 22 pp. (WALLEYE; ECOLOGY;).

1607. Langlois, T. H., and M. H. Langlois. 1948. South Bass Islands and islanders. Contrib. Franz Theodore Stone Lab. 10: 139 pp. (SAUGER; WALLEYE; COMMERCIAL FISHERIES; PROPAGATION;).

1608. Lapham, I. A. 1876. Oconomowoc Lake, and other small lakes of Wisconsin, considered with reference to their capacity for fish-production. Trans. Wis. Acad. Sci., Arts Letters 3:31-36. (WALLEYE; GEOGRAPHICAL DISTRIBUTION;).

1609. Lapworth, E. D. 1953. Investigation of pickerel destruction at Healey Falls, 1952. Ont. Dept. Lands Forest., Fish Wildl. Manage. Rep. 11:1-6. (WALLEYE; IMPOUNDMENTS; MORTALITY;).

1610. Larimore, R. W. 1967. Ecology of the fish of the Kaskasia River. Ill. Dept. Conserv., Fed. Aid Fish Wildl. Restor. Proj. F-16-R-5, Wk. Pl. 2: 5 pp. (SAUGER; WALLEYE; AGE AND GROWTH; FOOD STUDIES; IMPOUNDMENTS; POPULATION STUDIES;).

1611. Larimore, R. W., and P. W. Smith. 1963. The fishes of Champaign County, Illinois, as affected by 60 years of stream changes. Ill. Nat. Hist. Surv. Bull. 28:299-382. (SAUGER; GEOGRAPHICAL DISTRIBUTION;).

1612. La Rivers, I. 1962. Fishes and fisheries of Nevada. Nev. State Fish Game Comm. 782 pp. (WALLEYE; INTRODUCTIONS;).

1613. Larkin, P. A. 1964. Canadian lakes. Verh. Int. Verein. Limnol. 15:76-90. (WALLEYE; ECOLOGY;).

1614. Larrabee, A. P. 1926. An ecological study of the fishes of the Lake Okoboji region. Univ. Iowa Stud. Nat. Hist. 11:1-35. (SAUGER; WALLEYE; ECOLOGY; STOCKING;).

1615. Larson, G. 1959. A study of the walleye catch in two west-central Minnesota panfish lakes. Minn. Dept. Conserv., Invest. Rep. No. 202: 7 pp. (WALLEYE; CREEL CENSUS; POPULATION STUDIES;).

1616. Larson, G. 1961. A creel census of Lake Andrew, Douglas County. Minn. Dept. Conserv., Invest. Rep. No. 229: 3 pp. (WALLEYE; CREEL CENSUS;).

1617. Larson, G. 1961. A creel census of Lake Mina, Douglas County. Minn. Dept. Conserv., Invest. Rep. No. 228: 3 pp. (WALLEYE; CREEL CENSUS;).

1618. Larson, G. 1961. A six-year study of the population and catch on a west-central Minnesota bass-panfish lake, Maple Lake, Douglas County. Minn. Dept. Conserv., Invest. Rep. No. 236: 15 pp. (WALLEYE; CREEL CENSUS; STOCKING;).

1619. Larson, O. R. 1966. Some helminths of Itasca Park fishes. J. Minn. Acad. Sci. 33:99-101. (WALLEYE; PATHOLOGY;).

1620. Latta, W. C. 1975. Effects of "trophy" and "fish-for-fun" regulations on fish populations in Lakes of Sylvania. Mich. Dept. Nat. Res., Fish. Research Report No. 1826: 15 pp. (WALLEYE; AGE AND GROWTH; CREEL CENSUS; POPULATION STUDIES; REGULATIONS;).

1621. Lawler, G. H. 1950. *Triaenophorus* studies at Heming Lake, 1950. Fish. Research Board Can., Centr. Fish. Research Sta., Annu. Rep. (1950):24-28. (WALLEYE; PATHOLOGY;).

1622. Lawler, G. H. 1954. Observations on trout-perch *(Percopsis omiscomaycus)* at Heming Lake, Manitoba. J. Fish. Research Board Can. 11:1-4. (WALLEYE; FOOD STUDIES; PATHOLOGY;).

1623. Lawler, G. H. 1960. A history of an intensive fishery on Heming Lake, Manitoba. Fish. Research Board Can. 4 pp. (WALLEYE; COMMUNITY DYNAMICS; MORTALITY; POPULATION STUDIES;).

1624. Lawler, G. H. 1965. Fluctuations in the success of year-classes of whitefish populations with special reference to Lake Erie. J. Fish. Research Board Can. 22:1197-1227. (SAUGER; WALLEYE; COMMUNITY DYNAMICS; ECOLOGY; POPULATION STUDIES;).

1625. Lawler, G. H. 1965. The food of the pike, *Esox lucius*, in Heming Lake, Manitoba. J. Fish. Research Board Can. 22:1357-1377. (WALLEYE; COMMUNITY DYNAMICS;).

1626. Lawler, G. H. 1969. Activity periods of some fishes in Heming Lake, Canada. J. Fish. Research Board Can. 26:3266-3267. (WALLEYE; BEHAVIOR; MOVEMENT AND MIGRATIONS;).

1627. Lawler, G. H., and W. B. Scott. 1954. Notes on the geographical distribution and hosts of cestode genus *Triaenophorus* in North America. J. Fish. Research Board Can. 11:884-893. (SAUGER; WALLEYE; PATHOLOGY;).

1628. Lawler, G. H., L. A. Sunde, and J. Whitaker. 1974. Trout production in prairie ponds. J. Fish. Research Board Can. 31:929-936. (WALLEYE; PROPAGATION;).

1629. Lawler, G. H., and N. H. F. Watson. 1958. Limnological studies of Heming Lake, Manitoba and two adjacent lakes. J. Fish. Research Board Can. 15:203-218. (WALLEYE; PATHOLOGY;).

1630. Lawrence, J. D. 1907. Report of the deputy commissioner of the state hatcheries for the year 1904. N.Y. Forest, Fish, Game Comm., 10th Annu. Rep. (1904):139-145. (WALLEYE; PROPAGATION;).

1631. Lawrie, A. H. 1978. The fish community of Lake Superior. International Assoc. Great Lakes Res., J. Great Lakes Res. 4:513-549. (WALLEYE; COMMERCIAL FISHERIES; HABITAT DEGRADATION; PRODUCTIVITY;).

1632. Leach, G. C. 1927. Artificial propagation of pike perch *(Stizostedion vitreum)*, yellow perch *(Perca flavescens)*, and pike *(Esox lucious)*. U.S. Bur. Fish. Rep. (1927):1-27. (SAUGER; WALLEYE; LIFE HISTORY; MORTALITY; PHYSIOLOGY; PROPAGATION; SPAWNING STUDIES; STOCKING;).

1633. Leach, J. F. 1964. The Georgian Bay walleye (yellow pickerel) study. A progress report, 1962. Res. Manage. Rep. Ont. 73: 53-68. (WALLEYE; POPULATION STUDIES;).

1634. Leach, J. H., M. G. Johnson, J. R. M. Kelso, J. Hartmann, W. Numann, and B. Entz. 1977. Responses of percid fishes and their habitats to eutrophication. J. Fish. Research Board Can. 34:1964-1971. (SAUGER; WALLEYE; AGE AND GROWTH; FOOD STUDIES; HABITAT DEGRADATION; PATHOLOGY;).

1635. Leach, J. H., and S. J. Nepszy. 1976. The fish community in Lake Erie. J. Fish. Research Board Can. 33:622-639. (SAUGER; WALLEYE; COMMERCIAL FISHERIES; COMMUNITY DYNAMICS; HABITAT DEGRADATION;).

1636. Lealos, J. M., and G. G. Bever. 1982. The Flambeau Flowage Fishery. Wis. Dept. Nat. Res., Fish Manage. Rep. No. 110: 17 pp. (WALLEYE; AGE AND GROWTH; CREEL CENSUS; MARKING; MOVEMENTS AND MIGRATIONS; POPULATION STUDIES; SPAWNING STUDIES;).

1637. Leering, G. M. 1983. Bay Lake — Montreal River creel census summer 1982. Ont. Min. Nat. Res., Rep. 45 pp. (WALLEYE; CREEL CENSUS;).

1638. Legendre, V. 1951. List of the freshwater fishes of the Province of Quebec. Que. Game Fish. Dept., Biol. Bur. 4 pp. (SAUGER; WALLEYE; TAXONOMY;).

1639. Legendre, V. 1953. The freshwater fishes of the Province of Quebec.: List of species, ecological groups, history, nomenclature, annotations. Que. Game Fish. Dept., Biol. Bur., 9th Rep. (1951-1952):190-295. (SAUGER; WALLEYE; TAXONOMY;).

1640. Legendre, V. 1954. Key to game and commercial fishes of the Province of Quebec. Que. Game Fish Dept., Quebec, Quebec. 180 pp. (SAUGER; WALLEYE; MORPHOLOGY; TAXONOMY;).

1641. Lennon, R. E. 1954. Feeding mechanism of the sea lamprey and its effect on host fishes. U.S. Fish Wildl. Serv., Fish. Bull. 56:247-293. (WALLEYE; COMMUNITY DYNAMICS; MORTALITY;).

1642. Lennon, R. E. 1962. An annotated list of the fishes of Great Smoky Mountains National Park. J. Tenn. Acad. Sci. 37:5-7. (SAUGER; GEOGRAPHICAL DISTRIBUTION;).

1643. Lennon, R. E., and P. S. Parker. 1959. Reclamation of Indian and Abrams Creeks in Great Smoky Mountains National Park. U.S. Dept. Int., Fish Wildl. Serv., Spec. Sci. Rep.-Fish. 306: 22 pp. (SAUGER; TOXICANTS;).

1644. Lennon, R. E., and C. R. Walker. 1964. Laboratories and methods for screening fish-control chemicals. Bur. Sport Fish. Wildl., Circ. 185: 15 pp. (WALLEYE; TOXICANTS;).

1645. Leong, T. S., and J. C. Holmes. 1981. Communities of metazoan parasites in open water fishes of Cold Lake, Alberta, Canada. J. Fish. Biol. 18:693-714. (WALLEYE; PATHOLOGY;).

1646. Lere, M. 1986. Mid-Missouri Reservoirs study. Mont. Dept. Fish, Wildl. Parks, Fed. Aid Fish Wildl. Restor. Proj. F-36-R-2, Job II-f:. (WALLEYE; ECOLOGY; FOOD STUDIES; IMPOUNDMENTS; POPULATION STUDIES;).

1647. Leroux, D. 1984. An assessment of the fish stocks in Rocky Lake, 1981. Man. Dept. Nat. Res., Manuscript Rep. No. 84-20: 45 pp. (WALLEYE; AGE AND GROWTH; POPULATION STUDIES;).

1648. Leslie, J. K., R. Kozopas, and W. H. Hyatt. 1979. Considerations of entrainment of larval fish by a St. Clair River, Ontario, power station. Can. Fish. Marine Serv., Tech. Rep. No. 868: 25 pp. (WALLEYE; LIFE HISTORY; MORTALITY;).

1649. Lessman, C. A. 1978. Effects of gonadotropin mixtures and two steroids on inducing ovulation in the walleye. Prog. Fish-Cult. 40:3-5. (WALLEYE; SPAWNING STUDIES;).

1650. Letendre, G. C., and C. P. Schneider. 1969. Age and growth of male walleyes in spawning runs from Black Lake, New York. N.Y. Fish Game J. 16:136-144. (WALLEYE; AGE AND GROWTH; SPAWNING STUDIES;).

1651. Leung, S. T. 1979. Effect of impounding a river on the pesticide concentration in warmwater fish. Ph.D. Dissertation, Iowa State Univ., Ames, Iowa. 166 pp. (WALLEYE; HABITAT DEGRADATION; TOXICANTS;).

1652. Leung, S. T., R. V. Bulkley, and J. J. Richard. 1981. Influence of a new impoundment on pesticide concentrations in warm water fish Saylorville Reservoir, Des Moines River, Iowa 1977-1978. Pestic. Monit. J. 15:117-122. (WALLEYE; HABITAT DEGRADATION; TOXICANTS;).

1653. Levere, R. 1970. 1970 creel census report Upper Rideau, Upper Beverely, Redhorse Lakes. Ont. Min. Nat. Res., Rep. 42 pp. (WALLEYE; CREEL CENSUS;).

1654. Levine, J. S., and E. F. Mac Nichol, Jr. 1982. Color vision in fishes. Sci. Am. 246:140-149. (WALLEYE; PHYSIOLOGY;).

1655. Lewis, C. A. 1964. Some current fisheries problems in Patricia lakes and recommendations for future work of the inventory programme, 1964. Ont. Dept. Lands Forest., Manuscript Rep. 11 pp. (WALLEYE; AGE AND GROWTH; COMMERCIAL FISHERIES; FISHING GEAR; SPAWNING STUDIES;).

1656. Lewis, C. A. 1977. 1977 creel census report —
Lake Scugog and Sturgeon Lake. Ont. Min.
Nat. Res., Rep. 34 pp. (WALLEYE; CREEL
CENSUS;).

1657. Lewis, C. A. 1978. 1978 creel census report —
Balsam Lake. Ont. Min. Nat. Res., Kawar-
tha Lakes Fish. Assess. Unit Rep. 30 pp.
(WALLEYE; CREEL CENSUS;).

1658. Lewis, C. A. 1979. Cameron Lake creel census
— 1978. Ont. Min. Nat. Res., Kawartha
Lakes Fish. Assess. Unit Rep. 25 pp.
(WALLEYE; CREEL CENSUS;).

1659. Lewis, C. A. 1980. 1979 creel census Rice
Lake and the Otonabee River. Ont. Min.
Nat. Res., Kawartha Lakes Fish. Assess.
Unit 48 pp. (WALLEYE; CREEL CEN-
SUS;).

1660. Lewis, C. A. 1981. Report of 1980 trap-netting Lake Scugog. Ont. Min. Nat. Res., Kawartha Lakes Fish. Assess. Unit Rep. 1981-
3: 28 pp. (WALLEYE; AGE AND
GROWTH; COMMUNITY DYNAMICS;
POPULATION STUDIES;).

1661. Lewis, C. A. 1981. Report of 1980 trap-netting Balsam Lake. Ont. Min. Nat. Res., Kawartha Lakes Fish. Assess. Unit Rep. 1981-
4: 27 pp. (WALLEYE; AGE AND
GROWTH; COMMUNITY DYNAMICS;
POPULATION STUDIES;).

1662. Lewis, C. A. 1981. 1981 fall creel census of
Kawartha Lakes shore anglers. Ont. Min.
Nat. Res., Kawartha Lakes Fish. Assess.
Unit Rep. 1981-5: 19 pp. (WALLEYE;
CREEL CENSUS;).

1663. Lewis, C. A. 1981. Bobcaygeon River creel
census May 9-15, 1981. Ont. Min. Nat. Res.,
Kawartha Lakes Fish. Assess. Unit Rep.
1981-6: 21 pp. (WALLEYE; CREEL CEN-
SUS;).

1664. Lewis, C. A. 1981. Lake Scugog creel census,
1980. Ont. Min. Nat. Res., Kawartha Lakes
Fish. Assess. Unit Rep. 48 pp. (WALLEYE;
CREEL CENSUS;).

1665. Lewis, C. A. 1982. 1981 creel census of Pigeon, Buckhorn and Chemung Lakes. Ont.
Min. Nat. Res., Kawartha Lakes Fish. Assess. Unit Rep. 1982-3: 64 pp. (WALLEYE;
CREEL CENSUS;).

1666. Lewis, C. A. 1982. Report of 1981 trapnetting
Pigeon, Buckhorn and Chemung Lakes.
Ont. Min. Nat. Res., Kawartha Lakes Fish.
Assess. Unit Rep. 1982-4: 27 pp. (WALL-
EYE; AGE AND GROWTH; COMMU-
NITY DYNAMICS; POPULATION
STUDIES;).

1667. Lewis, C. A. 1982. Report of 1981 trapnetting
Rice Lake. Ont. Min. Nat. Res., Kawartha
Lakes Fish. Assess. Unit Rep. 1982-5: 28 pp.
(WALLEYE; AGE AND GROWTH; COM-
MUNITY DYNAMICS; POPULATION
STUDIES;).

1668. Lewis, C. A. 1982. Report of 1982 trapnetting
Lake Scugog. Ont. Min. Nat. Res., Kawar-
tha Lakes Fish. Assess. Unit Rep. 1982-8:
28 pp. (WALLEYE; AGE AND GROWTH;
COMMUNITY DYNAMICS; POPULA-
TION STUDIES;).

1669. Lewis, C. A. 1982. 1982 spring walleye tag-
ging at Coboconk, Balsam Lake. Ont. Min.
Nat. Res., Kawartha Lakes Fish. Assess.
Unit Rep. 1982-10: 27 pp. (WALLEYE;
AGE AND GROWTH; MARKING; PA-
THOLOGY; SPAWNING STUDIES;).

1670. Lewis, C. A. 1983. 1982 creel census of Bal-
sam Lake. Ont. Min. Nat. Res., Kawartha
Lakes Fish. Assess. Unit Rep. 1983-1: 48 pp.
(WALLEYE; CREEL CENSUS;).

1671. Lewis, C. A. 1983. Report of the 1981-82 win-
ter creel survey of Lake Scugog. Ont. Min.
Nat. Res., Kawartha Lakes Fish. Assess.
Unit Rep. 1983-2: 27 pp. (WALLEYE; AGE
AND GROWTH; CREEL CENSUS;).

1672. Lewis, C. A. 1983. Report of 1979 trap-netting Buckhorn Lake. Ont. Min. Nat. Res.,
Kawartha Lakes Fish. Assess. Unit. Rep.
1983-3: 24 pp. (WALLEYE; COMMUNITY
DYNAMICS; POPULATION STUDIES;).

1673. Lewis, C. A. 1984. Report of 1977 fall trap-
netting Lake Scugog. Ont. Min. Nat. Res.,
Kawartha Lakes Fish. Assess. Unit Rep.
1984-1: 23 pp. (WALLEYE; COMMUNITY
DYNAMICS; MARKING; POPULATION
STUDIES;).

1674. Lewis, C. A. 1984. Report of 1977 spring trap-
netting Lake Scugog. Ont. Min. Nat. Res.,
Kawartha Lakes Fish. Assess. Unit Rep.
1984-2: 25 pp. (WALLEYE; COMMUNITY
DYNAMICS; MARKING; POPULATION
STUDIES;).

1675. Lewis, C. A. 1984. Report of the 1983-84 winter creel survey on Lake Scugog. Ont. Min. Nat. Res., Kawartha Lakes Fish. Assess. Unit Rep. 1984-7: 18 pp. (WALLEYE; AGE AND GROWTH; CREEL CENSUS;).

1676. Lewis, C. A. 1985. 1984 spring walleye tagging at Coboconk, Balsam Lake. Ont. Min. Nat. Res., Kawartha Lakes Fish. Assess. Unit Rep. 1985-1: 21 pp. (WALLEYE; AGE AND GROWTH; MARKING; PATHOLOGY; POPULATION STUDIES;).

1677. Lewis, C. A. 1986. The walleye stocking and stocking assessment program of the Ontario Ministry of Natural Resources Program Review. Ont. Min. Nat. Res., Rep. 16 pp. (WALLEYE; MARKING; STOCKING;).

1678. Lewis, C. A., C. H. Olver, W. A. West, and F. J. Atkinson. 1964. Progress report #2 of the fisheries inventory work in the Patricias 1961-63. Ont. Dept. Lands Forest., Manuscript Rep. 135 pp. (WALLEYE; AGE AND GROWTH; PRODUCTIVITY;).

1679. Lewis, L. D., and J. E. Tilton. 1965. Walleye stocking Lakes Meredith and Canyon. Tex. Dept. Parks Wildl., Fed. Aid Fish Wildl. Restor. Proj. F-14-D-8, Wk. Pl. 18, Job No. 22: 1p. (WALLEYE; IMPOUNDMENTS; MORTALITY; STOCKING;).

1680. Lewis, S. A. 1970. Age and growth of walleye, *Stizostedion vitreum vitreum* (Mitchill), in Canton Reservoir, Oklahoma. Proc. Okla. Acad. Sci. 50:84-86. (WALLEYE; AGE AND GROWTH; IMPOUNDMENTS;).

1681. Lewis, S. A., K. D. Hopkins, and T. F. White. 1971. Average growth rates and length-weight relationships of sixteen species of fish in Canton Reservoir, Oklahoma. Okla. Dept. Wildl. Conserv., Bull. No. 9: 66 pp. (WALLEYE; AGE AND GROWTH; IMPOUNDMENTS;).

1682. Lewis, W. M. 1955. The fish population of the main stream of the Big Muddy River. Trans. Ill. Acad. Sci. 47:20-24. (SAUGER; WALLEYE; GEOGRAPHICAL DISTRIBUTION;).

1683. Li, S., and G. B. Ayles. 1981. An investigation of feeding habits of walleye *(Stizostedion vitreum vitreum)* fingerlings in constructed earthen ponds in the Canadian Prairies. Can. Tech. Rep. Fish. Aqua. Sci. No. 1040: 10 pp. (WALLEYE; FOOD STUDIES; PROPAGATION;).

1684. Li, S., and G. B. Ayles. 1981. Preliminary experiments on growth, survival, production and interspecific interactions of walleye *(Stizostedion vitreum vitreum)* fingerlings in constructed ponds in the Canadian prairies. Can. Tech. Rep. Fish. Aqua. Sci. No. 1041: 14 pp. (WALLEYE; AGE AND GROWTH; COMMUNITY DYNAMICS; MORTALITY; PRODUCTIVITY; PROPAGATION; STOCKING;).

1685. Li, S., and J. A. Mathias. 1982. Causes of high mortality among cultured larval walleyes. Trans. Am. Fish. Soc. 111:710-721. (WALLEYE; FOOD STUDIES; MORTALITY; PROPAGATION;).

1686. Liaw, W. K. 1984. Pond rearing of walleye *(Stizostedion vitreum vitreum)* fingerlings in Saskatchewan. Sask. Dept. Parks Renew. Res., Fish. Lab. Tech. Rep. 1984-1: 80 pp. (WALLEYE; PROPAGATION;).

1687. Liaw, W. K. 1985. Size at maturity and gillnet selectivity of walleye culture program. Sask. Fish. Lab. Tech. Rep. 1985-3: 31 pp. (WALLEYE; AGE AND GROWTH; COMMERCIAL FISHERIES; FISHING GEAR;).

1688. Libbey, J. E. 1969. Certain aspects of the life history of the walleye, *Stizostedion vitreum vitreum* (Mitchill), in Dale Hollow Reservoir, Tennessee, Kentucky, with emphasis on spawning. M.S. Thesis, Tenn. Tech. Univ., Cookeville, Tenn. 55 pp. (WALLEYE; AGE AND GROWTH; FOOD STUDIES; LIFE HISTORY; SPAWNING STUDIES;).

1689. Liebelt, J. E. 1976. Development of commercial fishing management practices in large impoundments. Mont. Dept. Fish. Game, Compl. Rep. No. 1 88-D: (WALLEYE; COMMERCIAL FISHIES; IMPOUNDMENTS;).

1690. Liegey, F., E. H. Donahue, and S. W. Eaton. 1955. The fishes of Olean Creek, Cattaraugus County, New York. St. Bonaventure Univ., Sci. Stud. 17:5-25. (WALLEYE; GEOGRAPHICAL DISTRIBUTION;).

1691. Lincicome, D. R., and H. J. Van Cleave. 1949. Distribution of *Leptorhynchoides thecatus*, a common Acanthocephalan parastic in fishes. Am. Midl. Nat. 41:421-431. (SAUGER; WALLEYE; PATHOLOGY;).

1692. Lindeborg, R. G. 1941. Records of fishes from the Quetico Provincial Park of Ontario, with comments on the growth of the yellow pike-perch. Copeia 1941 3:159-161. (WALLEYE; AGE AND GROWTH;).

1693. Lindsey, C. C. 1956. Distribution and taxonomy of fishes in the Mackenzie Drainage of British Columbia. J. Fish. Research Board Can. 13:759-789. (WALLEYE; GEOGRAPHICAL DISTRIBUTION;).

1694. Lindsey, C. C. 1957. Possible effects of water diversions on fish distribution in British Columbia. J. Fish. Research Board Can. 14:651-668. (WALLEYE; GEOGRAPHICAL DISTRIBUTION;).

1695. Little, J. F. 1975. Wabatongushi Lake creel census — 1973. Ont. Min. Nat. Res., Rep. 59 pp. (WALLEYE; CREEL CENSUS;).

1696. Loadman, N. L., G. E. E. Moodie, and J. A. Mathias. 1986. Significance of cannibalism in larval walleye (Stizostedion vitreum). Can. J. Fish. Aquat. Sci. 43:613-618. (WALLEYE; BEHAVIOR; COMMUNITY DYNAMICS; FOOD STUDIES; MORTALITY; PRODUCTIVITY;).

1697. Loch, J. S., A. J. Derksen, M. E. Hora, and R. B. Oetting. 1979. Potential effects of exotic fishes on Manitoba: an impact assessment of the Garrison Diversion Unit. Can. Fish. Marine Serv., Tech. Rep. No. 838: 38 pp. (WALLEYE; COMMUNITY DYNAMICS; GEOGRAPHICAL DISTRIBUTION; INTRODUCTIONS;).

1698. Lockhart, S., V. Macins, and T. Mosindy. 1986. An interim assessment of the Shoal Lake fishery. 1985. Ont. Min. Nat. Res., Lake of the Woods Fish. Assess. Unit Rep. 1986-01: 19 pp. (WALLEYE; AGE AND GROWTH; POPULATION STUDIES; SPAWNING STUDIES;).

1699. Lockhart, W. L., and D. A. Metner. 1978. Methocychlor residues in fish tissues following treatment of the Athabasca River, Alberta, Canada and following experimental exposures. Proc. Can. Fed. Biol. Soc. 21:158. (WALLEYE; TOXICANTS;).

1700. Lockhart, W. L., D. A. Metner, F. J. Ward, and G. M. Swanson. 1985. Population and cho-

linesterase responses in fish exposed to malathion sprays. Pestic. Biochem. Physiol. 24:12-18. (WALLEYE; TOXICANTS;).

1701. Loftus, D. H., C. H. Olver, E. H. Brown, P. J. Colby, W. L. Hartmen, and D. H. Schupp. 1987. Partitioning potential fish yields from the Great Lakes. Can. J. Fish. Aquat. Sci. 44(Suppl. 2):417-424. (WALLEYE; PRODUCTIVITY;).

1702. Loftus, K. H. 1976. Science for Canada's fisheries rehabilitation needs. J. Fish. Research Board Can. 33:1822-1857. (SAUGER; WALLEYE; COMMERCIAL FISHERIES; GENETICS; HABITAT IMPROVEMENT; PROPAGATION;).

1703. Longtin, E. J. 1953. Report of investigations on walleye (Stizostedion vitreum) egg survival and fish populations Rainy River and tributaries in 1953. Minn. Dept. Conserv., Invest. Rep. No. 144: 13 pp. (WALLEYE; HABITAT DEGRADATION; MORTALITY; POPULATION STUDIES;).

1704. Lopinot, A. C. 1968. Inventory of the fishes of nine river basins in Illinois 1967. Ill. Dept. Conserv., Spec. Fish. Rep. 25: 173 pp. (SAUGER; WALLEYE; GEOGRAPHICAL DISTRIBUTION;).

1705. Lorz, H. W. 1964. Distribution of fishes in British Columbia. 15th B.C. Nat. Res. Conf. (1963): 4 pp. (WALLEYE; GEOGRAPHICAL DISTRIBUTION;).

1706. Lound, R., and J. Dobie. 1958. A study of mortality associated with walleye rearing pond harvest and stocking operations. Minn. Dept. Conserv., Invest. Rep. No. 194: 6 pp. (WALLEYE; MORTALITY; PROPAGATION; STOCKING;).

1707. Lovejoy, S. 1903. Fish on the farm-what species to select, with a discussion of Samuel Lovejoy's paper. Trans. Am. Fish. Soc. 32:116-121. (WALLEYE; COMMERCIAL FISHERIES; ECOLOGY; PROPAGATION;).

1708. Luebke, R. W. 1978. Evaluation of a multipredator introduction. Tex. Parks Wildl. Dept., Fed. Aid Fish Wildl. Restor. Proj. F-31-R-4, Wk. Pl. 28: 23 pp. (WALLEYE; COMMUNITY DYNAMICS; IMPOUNDMENTS; POPULATION STUDIES; STOCKING;).

1709. Lux, F. E., and L. L. Smith, Jr. 1960. Some factors influencing seasonal changes in angler catch in a Minnesota lake. Trans. Am. Fish. Soc. 89:67-79. (WALLEYE; CREEL CENSUS;).

1710. Lychwick, T. J. 1983. Walleye assessment, Lake Michigan (Green Bay). Wis. Dept. Nat. Res., Proj. AFC 15-4: 70 pp. (WALLEYE; AGE AND GROWTH; CREEL CENSUS; MARKING; MOVEMENTS AND MIGRATIONS; POPULATION STUDIES; STOCKING;).

1711. Lychwick, T. J. 1984. Status of walleye in Wisconsin waters of Lake Michigan (Green Bay). Wis. Dept. Nat. Res., Proj. AFC 15-5: 50 pp. (WALLEYE; COMMERCIAL FISHERIES; CREEL CENSUS; MOVEMENT AND MIGRATIONS; POPULATION STUDIES; SAMPLING METHODS;).

1712. Lychwick, T. J. 1986. Status of walleye in Wisconsin waters of Lake Michigan (Green Bay). Wis. Dept. Nat. Res., Proj. AFC 16-3: 40 pp. (WALLEYE; AGE AND GROWTH; CREEL CENSUS; MARKING; POPULATION STUDIES;).

1713. Lydell, D. 1923. Brief notes on fish culture in Michigan. Trans. Am. Fish. Soc. 52:184-185. (WALLEYE; PROPAGATION;).

1714. Lynch, T. M. 1955. A progress and evaluation report on the success of the walleye (Stizostedion vitreum) in Colorado waters. Colo. Game Fish Dept., Spec. Purpose Rep. 31: 7pp. (WALLEYE; AGE AND GROWTH; COMMUNITY DYNAMICS; IMPOUNDMENTS; INTRODUCTIONS; MORTALITY;).

1715. Lynch, T. M. 1957. Exotic fish study. Colo. Dept. Game, Fish, Parks, Prog. Rep. 3 pp. (WALLEYE; INTRODUCTIONS;).

1716. Lynch, T. M. 1957. The average growth and weight of two members each of the perch and catfish families. Colo. Game Fish Dept., Fish. Leafl. No. 39: 1 p. (WALLEYE; AGE AND GROWTH;).

1717. Lynch, T. M. 1957. Growth data on fourteen fish species collected from warm water regions of Colorado. Colo. Dept. Game, Fish Parks, Spec. Purp. Rep. No. 48: 16 pp. (WALLEYE; AGE AND GROWTH;).

1718. Lynch, W. E., D. L. Johnson, and S. A. Schell. 1983. Survival, growth, and food habits of walleye x sauger hybrids (saugeye) in ponds. N. Am. J. Fish. Manage. 2:381-387. (SAUGER; WALLEYE; AGE AND GROWTH; COMMUNITY DYNAMICS; FOOD STUDIES; MORTALITY; STOCKING;).

1719. Lyons, J. 1984. Walleye predation, yellow perch abundance, and the population dynamics of an assemblage of littoral-zone fishes in Sparkling Lake, Wisconsin. Ph.D. Dissertation, Univ. Wis., Madison, Wis. 205 pp. (WALLEYE; COMMUNITY DYNAMICS; ECOLOGY; FOOD STUDIES; POPULATION STUDIES;).

1720. Lyons, J. 1987. Prey choice among piscivorous juvenile walleyes (Stizostedion vitreum). Can. J. Fish. Aquat. Sci. 44:758-764. (WALLEYE; FOOD STUDIES;).

1721. Lyons, J., and J. J. Magnuson. 1987. Effects of walleye predation on the population dynamics of small littoral-zone fishes in a northern Wisconsin lake. Trans. Am. Fish. Soc. 116:29-39. (WALLEYE; COMMUNITY DYNAMICS; FOOD STUDIES; POPULATION STUDIES; PRODUCTIVITY;).

1722. Lysack, W. 1980. 1979 Lake Winnipeg fish stock assessment program. Man. Dept. Nat. Res., Manuscript Rep. No. 80-30: 118 pp. (SAUGER; WALLEYE; AGE AND GROWTH; COMMERCIAL FISHERIES; MORTALITY; SAMPLING METHODS; SPAWNING STUDIES;).

1723. Lysack, W. 1980. 1980 Cedar Lake fish stock assessment program. Man. Dept. Nat. Res., Fish. Branch. Manuscript Rep. No. 80-22: 41 pp. (SAUGER; WALLEYE; AGE AND GROWTH; COMMERCIAL FISHERIES; COMMUNITY DYNAMICS; MORTALITY; POPULATION STUDIES;).

1724. Lysack, W. 1981. 1980 Lake Winnipeg fish stock assessment program. Man. Dept. Nat. Res., Fish. Branch. Manuscript Rep. No. 81-20: 67 pp. (SAUGER; WALLEYE; AGE AND GROWTH; COMMERCIAL FISHERIES; COMMUNITY DYNAMICS; FISHING GEAR; MORTALITY; POPULATION STUDIES; SPAWNING STUDIES;).

1725. Lysack, W. 1982. Fish stock assessment of Lakes in the Pulse Fishing Project. Man. Dept. Nat. Res., Manuscript Rep. No. 82-5: 307 pp. (SAUGER; WALLEYE; AGE AND GROWTH; COMMERCIAL FISHERIES; CREEL CENSUS; FISHING GEAR; GEOGRAPHICAL DISTRIBUTION; HABITAT DEGRADATION; POPULATION STUDIES; SOCIO-ECONOMICS OF FISHERIES; SPAWNING STUDIES;).

1726. Lysack, W. 1982. 1981 Lake Winnipeg fish stock assessment program. Man. Dept. Nat. Res., Manuscript Rep. 82-28: 99 pp. (SAUGER; WALLEYE; AGE AND GROWTH; COMMERCIAL FISHERIES; FISHING GEAR; MORTALITY; SPAWNING STUDIES;).

1727. Lysack, W. 1983. 1981 and 1982 Cedar Lake fish stock assessment and changes in stock dynamics from 1979-1982. Man. Dept. Nat. Res., Fish. Branch. Manuscript Rep. No. 83-3: 83 pp. (WALLEYE; AGE AND GROWTH; COMMERCIAL FISHERIES; FISHING GEAR; MORTALITY; POPULATION STUDIES; SPAWNING STUDIES;).

1728. Lysack, W. 1983. Data from the 1982 Lake Winnipeg fish stock assessment program. Man. Dept. Nat. Res., Manuscript Rep. No. 83-20: 112 pp. (SAUGER; WALLEYE; AGE AND GROWTH; COMMERCIAL FISHERIES; FISHING GEAR; MORTALITY; POPULATION STUDIES; SPAWNING STUDIES;).

1729. Lysack, W. 1984. Data from the 1983 Lake Winnipeg stock assessment program. Man. Dept. Nat. Res., Fish. Branch. Manuscript Rep. No. 84-7: 121 pp. (SAUGER; WALLEYE; AGE AND GROWTH; COMMERCIAL FISHERIES; FISHING GEAR; MORTALITY; POPULATION STUDIES; SPAWNING STUDIES;).

1730. Lysack, W. 1986. Towards a predictive capability for management of the Lake Winnipeg fishery. Man. Dept. Nat. Res., Fish. Branch. Manuscript Rep. No. 86-15: 236 pp. (SAUGER; WALLEYE; AGE AND GROWTH; COMMERCIAL FISHERIES; HABITAT DEGRADATION; MORTALITY; POPULATION STUDIES; SPAWNING STUDIES;).

1731. Lysack, W. 1987. The bait fishery of the Lower Red River. Man. Dept. Nat. Res., Manuscript Rep. No. 87-13: 265 pp. (WALLEYE; COMMUNITY DYNAMICS; SAMPLING METHODS;).

1732. Lysack, W., and L. Ebbeling. 1980. Differences in sauger growth regimes among three major areas of Lake Winnipeg. Man. Dept. Nat. Res., Manuscript Rep. No. 80-15: 23 pp. (SAUGER; AGE AND GROWTH; COMMERCIAL FISHERIES; FISHING GEAR; POPULATION STUDIES;).

1733. Lyster, L. L. 1939. Parasites of freshwater fish. I. Internal trematodes of commercial fish in the central St. Lawrence watershed. Can. J. Research 17:154-168. (WALLEYE; PATHOLOGY;).

1734. Maa, R. 1974. Northern Light Lake creel census. Ont. Min. Nat. Res., Rep. 14 pp. (WALLEYE; CREEL CENSUS;).

1735. MacCallum, G. A. 1894. The assimilation of the fishery laws of the Great Lakes. U.S. Fish. Comm., Bull. 13:17-20. (WALLEYE; COMMERCIAL FISHERIES;).

1736. MacCallum, W. R., and J. H. Selgeby. 1987. Lake Superior revisited 1984. Can. J. Fish. Aquat. Sci. 44(Suppl. 2):23-36. (WALLEYE; CREEL CENSUS; POPULATION STUDIES;).

1737. MacCrimmon, H. R., and E. Skobe. 1970. The fisheries of Lake Simcoe. Ont. Dept. Lands Forests, Fish Wildl. Branch 140 pp. (WALLEYE; COMMERCIAL FISHERIES; CREEL CENSUS; MOVEMENT AND MIGRATIONS; REGULATIONS; STOCKING;).

1738. MacDonald, W. H. 1951. Fishing in Alberta. Alta. Dept. Lands Forests 36 pp. (WALLEYE; GEOGRAPHICAL DISTRIBUTION;).

1739. Machniak, K. 1975. The effects of hydroelectric development on the biology of northern fishes (reproduction and population dynamics). III. Yellow walleye Stizostedion vitreum vitreum (Mitchill). A literature review and bibliography. Can. Fish. Mar. Serv. Res. Dev. Tech. Rep. 529: 68 pp. (WALLEYE; AGE AND GROWTH; FOOD STUDIES; HABITAT IMPROVEMENT; IMPOUNDMENTS; LIFE HISTORY; MOVEMENTS AND MIGRATIONS; POPULATION STUDIES; SPAWNING STUDIES; WATER LEVELS;).

1740. Macins, V. 1967. Combined air and boat creel census Lake of the Woods — 1967. Ont. Min. Nat. Res., Rep. 25 pp. (WALLEYE; CREEL CENSUS;).

1741. Macins, V. 1979. Fisheries of Shoal Lake: A case in overfishing. Ont. Min. Nat. Res., Lake of the Woods Fish. Assess. Unit Rep. 1979-2: 18 pp. (WALLEYE; AGE AND GROWTH; COMMERCIAL FISHERIES; CREEL CENSUS; POPULATION STUDIES; SPAWNING STUDIES;).

1742. Macins, V. 1981. Walleye (Stizostedion vitreum) spawning bed rehabilitation. Rep., Lake of the Woods Assess. Unit. 5 pp. (WALLEYE; HABITAT IMPROVEMENT; SPAWNING STUDIES;).

1743. MacKay, H. H. 1930. The present status of fish culture in the Province of Ontario. Trans. Am. Fish. Soc. 60:33-44. (WALLEYE; PROPAGATION;).

1744. MacKay, H. H. 1930. Pollution problems in Ontario. Trans. Am. Fish. Soc. 60:297-305. (SAUGER; WALLEYE; HABITAT DEGRADATION;).

1745. MacKay, H. H. 1947. Rearing fish in Ontario. Sylva 8:1-7. (WALLEYE; PROPAGATION;).

1746. MacKay, H. H. 1958. Yellow pike perch (Stizostedion vitreum). Sylva 14:24-31. (WALLEYE; AGE AND GROWTH; COMMERCIAL FISHERIES; ECOLOGY; LIFE HISTORY; SPAWNING STUDIES; STOCKING;).

1747. MacKay, H. H. 1963. Fishes of Ontario. Ont. Dept. Lands Forests., Toronto, Ont. xi ⅓ 300 pp. (WALLEYE; AGE AND GROWTH; COMMERCIAL FISHERIES; ECOLOGY; LIFE HISTORY; STOCKING;).

1748. Mackenthun, K. M., E. H. Herman, and A. F. Bartsch. 1948. A heavy mortality of fishes resulting from the decomposition of algae in Yahara River, Wisconsin. Trans. Am. Fish. Soc. 75:175-180. (WALLEYE; HABITAT DEGRADATION; MORTALITY;).

1749. MacLean, J., and J. J. Magnuson. 1977. Species interactions in percid communities. J. Fish. Research Board Can. 34:1941-1951. (WALLEYE; COMMUNITY DYNAMICS; ECOLOGY;).

1750. Maclean, N. G., and D. A. Schlesinger. 1982. The sport fisheries of the Big Clear, Big Rideau, Big Salmon, Charleston and Devil Lakes, 1981. Ont. Min. Nat. Res., Rideau Lakes Fish. Assess. Unit, Rep. No. 4: 117 pp. (WALLEYE; CREEL CENSUS;).

1751. MacLeod, J. C., L. L. Smith, Jr., and R. H. Kramer. 1965. Effects of pulpwood fibers on fathead minnows and walleye fingerlings. J. Water Pollut. Control Fed. 37:130-140. (WALLEYE; HABITAT DEGRADATION;).

1752. MacMartin, J. M. 1954. Population studies. Vt. Fish Game Serv., Fed. Aid Fish Wildl. Restor. Proj., Job Comp. Rep. F-2-R-1, and 2, Wk. Pl. 4-B, Job No. 2: 26 pp. (WALLEYE; GEOGRAPHICAL DISTRIBUTION;).

1753. Madden, K.M. 1956. Annual meeting reports on fisheries techniques (reference to shallow freeze-out lakes as walleye nurseries). Iowa Conserv. Comm. 3 pp. (WALLEYE; PROPAGATION; SPAWNING STUDIES;).

1754. Maddux, H.R., and R.L. Applegate, 1984. Differential infection of walleyes by Contracaecum Spp. in heated and nonheated reservoirs. The Prairie Nat. 16:44-45 (WALLEYE; IMOUNDMENTS; PATHOLOGY;).

1755. Magath, T. B., and H. E. Essex. 1931. Concerning the distribution of Diphyllobothrium latum in North America. J. Preventive Med. 5:227-242. (SAUGER; WALLEYE; PATHOLOGY;).

1756. Magnin, E., and G. Beaulieu. 1968. Displacement of yellow walleye Stizostedion vitreum (Mitchill) in the St. Lawrence River after marking. Nat. Can. 95:897-905. (WALLEYE; MARKING; MOVEMENTS AND MIGRATIONS;).

1757. Magnuson, J. L., and L. L. Smith. 1963. Some phases of the life history of the trout-perch. Ecology 44:83-95. (WALLEYE; FOOD STUDIES;).

1758. Mai, J., J. K. Shetty, T-M Kan, and J. E. Kinsella. 1980. Protein and amino acid composition of selected freshwater fish. J. Agr. Food Chem. 28:884-885. (WALLEYE; MORPHOLOGY; PHYSIOLOGY;;).

1759. Maloney, J. E. 1953. Survival, growth and food of fin-clipped walleye pike fingerlings in Maloney Pond, Cass County, Minnesota. Minn. Dept. Conserv., Invest. Rep. No. 137: 5 pp. (WALLEYE; AGE AND GROWTH; FOOD STUDIES; MARKING; MORTALITY; PROPAGATION;).

1760. Maloney, J. E. 1956. Development of an introduced fish population in a small northern Minnesota lake with notes on the survival of stocked walleye pike young-of-the-year. Minn. Dept. Conserv., Invest. Rep. No. 172: 7 pp. (WALLEYE; COMMUNITY DYNAMICS; MARKING; MORTALITY; POPULATION STUDIES; STOCKING;).

1761. Maloney, J. E. 1978. A qualitative and quantitative census of Mille Lacs, 1976 — 1977. Minn. Dept. Nat. Res., Fish Manage. Rep. No. 7: 18 pp. (WALLEYE; CREEL CENSUS;).

1762. Maloney, J.E., and F.H. Johnson. 1955. Life histories and inter-relationships of walleye (Stizostedion vitreum) and yellow perch (Perca flavescens) especially during their first summer, in two Minnesota Lakes. Trans. Am. Fish. Soc. 85:191-202. (WALLEYE; AGE AND GROWTH; BEHAVIOR; ECOLOGY; FOOD STUDIES; LIFE HISTORY; SAMPLING METHODS; SPAWNING STUDIES;).

1763. Manges, D. E. 1950. Fish tagging studies in TVA storage reservoirs, 1947-1949. J. Tenn. Acad. Sci. 25:126-140. (SAUGER; WALLEYE; MARKING; MOVEMENT AND MIGRATIONS; POPULATION STUDIES;).

1764. Manohar, S. V., D. L. Rigby, and L. C. Dugal. 1973. Effect of sodium tripolyphosphate on thaw drip and taste of fillets of some freshwater fish. J. Fish. Research Board Can. 30:685-688. (SAUGER; WALLEYE; COMMERCIAL FISHERIES;).

1765. Mansueti, R. J. 1961. Ecology of eggs, larvae, and young of game fishes in the Chesapeake Bay. Univ. Md. Chesapeake Biol. Lab. 61: 2 pp. (WALLEYE; HABITAT DEGRADATION; SPAWNING STUDIES;).

1766. Mansueti, R. J. 1962. Checklist of fishes of the Patuxent River drainage and of Chesapeake Bay of Clavert County, Maryland. Univ. Md., Chesapeake Biol. Lab. 62: 5 pp. (WALLEYE; INTRODUCTIONS;).

1767. Mansueti, R. J. 1964. Eggs, larvae, and young of the white perch, Roccus americanus, with comments on its ecology in the estuary. Chesapeake Sci. 5:3-45. (WALLEYE; EMBRYOLOGY; MORPHOLOGY; TAXONOMY;).

1768. Manter, H. W. 1926. Some North American fish trematodes. Ill. Biol. Monogr. 10:1-138. (WALLEYE; PATHOLOGY;).

1769. Manz, J. V. 1961. A preliminary survey of walleye pike (Stizostedion vitreum) spawning sites in western Lake Erie-1960. Ohio Dept. Nat. Res. 21 pp. (SAUGER; WALLEYE; ECOLOGY; SPAWNING STUDIES;).

1770. Manz, J. V. 1963. Walleye fry sampling. Ohio Dept. Nat. Res., Fed. Aid Fish Wildl. Restor. Proj. F-35-R-1, Job No. 1: 156 pp. (WALLEYE; AGE AND GROWTH; ECOLOGY; FOOD STUDIES; PRODUCTIVITY; SAMPLING METHODS;).

1771. Manz, J. V. 1964. A pumping device used to collect walleye eggs from off-shore spawning areas in western Lake Erie. Trans. Am. Fish. Soc. 93:204-206. (WALLEYE; SAMPLING METHODS; SPAWNING STUDIES;).

1772. Maraldo, D. 1986. Effects of water level fluctuation on walleye reproduction at Lock 19 Peterborough and recommendations for rehabilitation. Ont. Min. Nat. Res., Kawartha Lakes Fish. Assess. Unit Rep. 1986-1: 62 pp. (WALLEYE; HABITAT DEGRADATION; MARKING; MOVEMENT AND MIGRATIONS; SPAWNING STUDIES; WATER LEVELS;).

1773. Marcuson, P. E. 1981. South Central Montana fisheries study — Musselshell River study. Mont. Dept. Fish Wildl. Parks, Fed. Aid Fish. Wildl. Restor. Proj. F-20-R-25, Job No. III-a: 12 pp. (SAUGER; ECOLOGY; MARKING; POPULATION STUDIES;).

1774. Margenau, T. L. 1982. Modified procedure for aging walleyes by using dorsal spine sections. Prog. Fish-Cult. 44:204. (WALLEYE; AGE AND GROWTH;).

1775. Marking, L. L. 1967. Toxicity of MS-222 to selected fishes. U.S. Fish Wildl. Serv., Invest. Fish Control 12: 10 pp. (WALLEYE; HABITAT DEGRADATION; MORTALITY; PHYSIOLOGY; TOXICANTS;).

1776. Marking, L. L. 1969. Toxicity of methylpentynol to selected fishes. U.S. Fish Wildl. Serv., Invest. Fish Control 30: 7 pp. (WALLEYE; GEOGRAPHICAL DISTRIBUTION;).

1777. Marking, L. L. 1969. Toxicity of quinaldine to selected fishes. U.S. Fish Wildl. Serv., Invest. Fish Control 23: 10 pp. (WALLEYE; GEOGRAPHICAL DISTRIBUTION;).

1778. Marking, L. L. 1972. Salicylanilide I, an effective non-persistent candidate piscicide. Trans. Am. Fish. Soc. 101:526-533. (WALLEYE; TOXICANTS;).

1779. Marking, L. L. 1974. Toxicity of 2-(digeranylamino)-ethanol, a candidate selective fish toxicant. Trans. Am. Fish. Soc. 103:736-742. (WALLEYE; TOXICANTS;).

1780. Markus, H. C. 1933. The effects of tags upon fresh water fishes. Trans. Am. Fish. Soc. 63:319-325. (SAUGER; MARKING; MOVEMENT AND MIGRATIONS;).

1781. Marshall, I. 1981. Creel census Vermilion River Road 1981. Ont. Min. Nat. Res., Rep. 17 pp. (WALLEYE; CREEL CENSUS;).

1782. Marshall, T. L., and R. P. Johnson. 1971. History and results of fish introductions in Saskatchewan 1900-1969. Sask. Dept. Nat. Res., Fish. Rep. No. 8: 30 pp. (WALLEYE; INTRODUCTIONS; STOCKING;).

1783. Marshall, T. R. 1977. Morphological. physiological, and ethological difference between walleye (Stizostedion vitreum vitreum) and pikeperch (S. lucioperca). J. Fish. Research Board Can. 34:1515-1523. (WALLEYE; BEHAVIOR; HABITAT DEGRADATION; IMPOUNDMENTS; MORPHOLOGY; PHYSIOLOGY; SPAWNING STUDIES;).

1784. Marshall, T. R., and P. A. Ryan. 1987. Abundance patterns and community attributes of fishes relative to environmental gradients. Can. J. Fish. Aquat. Sci. 44(Suppl. 2):198-215. (WALLEYE; COMMERCIAL FISHERIES; ECOLOGY;).

1785. Martin, A. 1973. Northern Ligth Lake creel census — 1973. Ont. Min. Nat. Res., Spec. Rep. 15 pp. (WALLEYE; CREEL CENSUS;).

1786. Martin, L. R. G. 1987. Economic impact analysis of a sport fishery on Lake Ontario: an appraisal of method. Trans. Am. Fish. Soc. 116:461-468. (WALLEYE; SOCIO-ECONOMICS OF FISHERIES;).

1787. Martin, M. 1959. Walleye hatching, rearing, and transportation techniques as practiced in Kentucky. Proc. 12th Annu. Conf. Southeast Assoc. Game Fish Comm. 12:78-91. (WALLEYE; PROPAGATION;).

1788. Martin, N. V., and D. C. Scott. 1959. Use of tricaine methanesulfonate (M.S. 222) in the transport of live fish without water. Prog. Fish-Cult. 21:183-184. (WALLEYE; STOCKING;).

1789. Martin, R. 1975. Dry diet tests results on walleye fry and fingerlings. Proc. 6th Interstate Muskellunge Workshop 6:25-27. (WALLEYE; FOOD STUDIES; PROPAGATION;).

1790. Marvin, A. 1973. Winter creel census report 1972 — 1973. Ont. Min. Nat. Res., Rep. 11 pp. (WALLEYE; CREEL CENSUS;).

1791. Marvin, A. 1973. Creel census program Lake St. Francis winter-1973. Ont. Min. Nat. Res., Rep. 14 pp. (WALLEYE; CREEL CENSUS;).

1792. Marvin, A. 1974. Creel census program Lake St. Francis winter-1974. Ont. Min. Nat. Res., Rep. 12 pp. (WALLEYE; CREEL CENSUS;).

1793. Mason, M. B. 1978. Winter creel census report 1978. Ont. Min. Nat. Res., Rep. 29 pp. (WALLEYE; CREEL CENSUS;).

1794. Masterson, M. F. 1984. Effect of feed color on growth and feed acceptance parameters of walleye fry and fingerlings. M.S. Thesis, Mich. State Univ., East Lansing, Mich. 91 pp. (WALLEYE; PROPAGATION;).

1795. Mate, S. M., and H. R. Gibson. 1976. Salmon Falls Creek Reservoir fisheries investigations. Idaho Dept. Fish Game, Fed. Aid Fish Wildl. Restor. Proj. F-53-R-11, Job No. XVII: 46 pp. (WALLEYE; COMMUNITY DYNAMICS; CREEL CENSUS; FOOD STUDIES; IMPOUNDMENTS; POPULATION STUDIES;).

1796. Materson, M. F., and D. L. Garling. 1986. Effect of feed color on feed acceptance and growth of walleye fingerlings. Prog. Fish-

Cult. 48:306-309. (WALLEYE; PROPAGA-TION;).

1797. Mather, F. 1890. Eggs of pike-perch — *Sti-zostedion vitreum*. Trans. Am. Fish. Soc. 19:15-16. (WALLEYE; PROPAGATION;).

1798. Mathers, A. 1987. Eastern Region walleye stocking assessment 1984 annual report. Ont. Min. Nat. Res., White Lake Complex, Carlton Place Dist. 98 pp. (WALLEYE; CREEL CENSUS; POPULATION STUD-IES; STOCKING;).

1799. Mathers, A., R. R. Claytor, and N. G. Ma-clean. 1986. The fish communities and popu-lations of Long, Mica, Opinicon, Sydenham and Upper Rideau Lakes, 1982. Ont. Min. Nat. Res., Rideau Lakes Fish. Assess. Unit Rep. No. 12: 83 pp. (WALLEYE; AGE AND GROWTH; COMMUNITY DYNAMICS; POPULATION STUDIES; SPAWNING STUDIES;).

1800. Mathers, R. A., and P. H. Johansen. 1985. The effects of feeding ecology on mercury accumulations in walleye *(Stizostedion vi-treum)* and pike *(Esox lucious)* in Lake Sim-coe. Can. J. Zool. 63:2006-2012. (WALL-EYE; FOOD STUDIES; HABITAT DEGRADATION;).

1801. Mathias, J. A., J. A. Babaluk, and K. D. Rowes. 1985. An analysis of the 1984 wall-eye, *Stizostedion vitreum vitreum*, (Mit-chill), run at Crean Lake in Prince Albert National Park, Saskatchewan with refer-ence to the impact of spawn-taking. Can. Tech. Rep. Fish. Aqua. Sci. No. 1407: 38 pp. (WALLEYE; GENETICS; MOVEMENTS AND MIGRATIONS; PATHOLOGY; POP-ULATION STUDIES; PROPAGATION; SPAWNING STUDIES; STOCKING;).

1802. Mathias, J. A., J. Babuluk, and K. D. Rowes. 1985. A description of 1984 walleye spawn-ing activities in Prince Albert National Park, with reference to benefits and poten-tial impacts. Fed. Dept. Fish. Oceans, Freshwater Inst., Man. 55 pp. (WALLEYE; AGE AND GROWTH; GENETICS; MARKING; MOVEMENT AND MIGRA-TIONS; PATHOLOGY; POPULATION STUDIES; PROPAGATION; SPAWNING STUDIES;).

1803. Mathias, J. A., and S. Li. 1982. Feeding habits of walleye larvae and juveniles: com-parative laboratory and field studies. Trans.

Am. Fish. Soc. 111:722-735. (WALLEYE; FOOD STUDIES;).

1804. Mathur, D., R. M. Schutsky, E. J. Purdy, Jr., and C. A. Silver. 1983. Simularities in avoid-ance temperatures of freshwater fishes. Can. J. Fish. Aquat. Sci. 40:2144-2152. (WALLEYE; BEHAVIOR; ECOLOGY;).

1805. Matuszek, J. E. 1978. Empirical predictions of fish yields of large North American lakes. Trans. Am. Fish. Soc. 107:385-394. (SAUGER; WALLEYE; ECOLOGY; PRO-DUCTIVITY;).

1806. Maule, A. G. 1982. The spring diets of wall-eye in the lower Columbia River, 1980-1981. Pages 205-210 *in* G.M. Cailliet and C.A. Si-mensted, eds. Gutshop '81, fish food habit studies. Proceeding of the Third Pacific Workshop. Washington Sea Grant Prog., WSG-WO-82-2, Univ. Wash., Seattle. (WALLEYE; FOOD STUDIES;).

1807. Maule, A. G. 1983. Aspects of the life history and feeding ecology of walleye (Stizostedion vitreum vitreum) in the mid-Columbia River. M.S. Thesis, Oreg. State Univ., Cor-vallis, Oreg. 43 pp. (WALLEYE; AGE AND GROWTH; COMMUNITY DYNAMICS; ECOLOGY; FOOD STUDIES; IM-POUNDMENTS; INTRODUCTIONS; LIFE HISTORY; POPULATION STUD-IES; SPAWNING STUDIES;).

1808. Maule, A. G., and H. F. Horton. 1984. Feed-ing ecology of walleye, *Stizostedion vitreum vitreum*, in the mid-Columbia River. with emphasis on the interactions between wall-eye and juvenile anadromous fishes. Fish. Bull. 82:411-418. (WALLEYE; COMMU-NITY DYNAMICS; FOOD STUDIES;).

1809. Maule, A. G., and H. F. Horton. 1985. Proba-ble causes of the rapid growth and high fe-cundity of walleye, *Stizostedion vitreum vi-treum*, in the Mid-Columbia River. Fish. Bull. 83:701-706. (WALLEYE; AGE AND GROWTH; ECOLOGY; SPAWNING STUDIES;).

1810. Mavor, J. W. 1916. Studies on the protozoan parasites of the fishes of the Georgian Bay. Trans. Roy. Soc. Can. 10:63-73. (WALL-EYE; PATHOLOGY;).

1811. Mavor, J. W., and S. M. Feinburg. 1918. *Lym-phocystis vitrel*. A new sporozoan from pike-perch, *Stizostedion vitreum*. Trans.

Wis. Acad. Sci., Arts Letters 19:559-561. (WALLEYE; PATHOLOGY;).

1812. May, B. E., and S. P. Gloss. 1979. Depth distribution of Lake Powell fishes. Utah Div. Wildl. Res., Publ. No. 78-1: 19 pp. (WALLEYE; ECOLOGY; MOVEMENT AND MIGRATIONS;).

1813. May, E. B., and C. R. Gasaway. 1967. A preliminary key to the identification of larval fishes of Oklahoma, with particular reference to Canton Reservoir, including a selected bibliography. Okla. Fish. Research Lab. Bull. 5: 42 pp. (WALLEYE; IMPOUNDMENTS; MORPHOLOGY; TAXONOMY;).

1814. May, T. W., and G. L. McKinney. 1981. Cadmium, lead, mercury, arsenic, and selenium concentrations in freshwater fish, 1976-77. National Pesticide Monitoring Program. Pestic. Monit. J. 15:14-38. (SAUGER; WALLEYE; HABITAT DEGRADATION; TOXICANTS;).

1815. Mayes, M. A., H. C. Alexander, D. L. Hopkins, and P. B. Latvaitis. 1986. Acute and chronic toxicity of ammonia to freshwater fish: a site-specific study. Environ. Toxicol. Chem. 5:437-442. (WALLEYE; HABITAT DEGRADATION;).

1816. Mayhew, J. 1963. An evaluation of introducing the walleye (Stizostedion vitreum) into a southern Iowa artificial lake. Part II. Age and growth. Iowa State Conserv. Comm., Quart. Biol. Rep. 16:58-66. (WALLEYE; AGE AND GROWTH; IMPOUNDMENTS; INTRODUCTIONS;).

1817. McAuley, R. W. 1970. Automatic food pellet dispenser for walleyes. Prog. Fish-Cult. 32:42. (WALLEYE; PROPAGATION;).

1818. McBride, F. T., R. L. Curry, and S. L. Van Horn. 1986. Evaluation of walleye fry introductions in Lake Gaston. N. Car. Wildl. Res. Comm., Fish Invest. Proj. No. F-23-S: 11 pp. (WALLEYE; STOCKING;).

1819. McBride, S. I., and D. Tarter. 1983. Foods and feeding behavior of sauger, Stizostedion canadense (Smith) (Pisces:Percidae), from Gallipolis Locks and Dam, Ohio River. Brimleyana 9:123-134. (WALLEYE; FOOD STUDIES; IMPOUNDMENTS;).

1820. McCabe, B. C. 1946. Fisheries report for the lakes of central Massachusetts 1944-1945. Mass. Dept. Conserv. 254 pp. (WALLEYE; CREEL CENSUS;).

1821. McCann, J. A., and K. D. Carlander. 1970. Mark and recovery estimates of fish populations in Clear Lake, Iowa, 1958 and 1959. Iowa State J. Sci. 44:369-403. (WALLEYE; FISHING GEAR; MARKING; POPULATION STUDIES; PRODUCTIVITY;).

1822. McCauley, D. J., L. T. Brooke, and M. D. Balcer. 1985. Ecological assessment of factors affecting walleye ova survival in the lower Fox River. Proc. 28th Conf. on Great Lakes Research. 54 pp. (WALLEYE; EMBRYOLOGY; MORTALITY; SPAWNING STUDIES;).

1823. McCay, C. M. 1929. A biological survey of the Erie-Niagara system. V. Studies upon fish blood and its relation to water pollution. N.Y. Conserv. Dept., Suppl. 18th Annu. Rep. (1928):140-149. (WALLEYE; HABITAT DEGRADATION; PHYSIOLOGY;).

1824. McConville, D. R., and J. D. Fossum. 1981. Movement patterns of walleye (Stizostedion v. vitreum) in pool 3 of the upper Mississippi River as determined by ultrasonic telemetry. J. Freshwater Ecol. 1:279-286. (WALLEYE; BEHAVIOR; MARKING; MOVEMENTS AND MIGRATIONS;).

1825. McCormick, W. 1976. Opasatika Lake complex creel census report 1975. Ont. Min. Nat. Res., Rep. 32 pp. (WALLEYE; CREEL CENSUS;).

1826. McCrimmon, H. R. 1956. Fishing in Lake Simcoe. Ont. Dept. Land Forest. Fish Wildl. Branch 137 pp. (WALLEYE; AGE AND GROWTH; COMMERCIAL FISHERIES; FOOD STUDIES; LIFE HISTORY; MOVEMENT AND MIGRATIONS; SPAWNING STUDIES; STOCKING;).

1827. McCrimmon, H. R. 1958. Observations on the spawning of lake trout, Salvelinus namaycush, and the post-spawning movement of adult trout in Lake Simcoe. Can. Fish Cult. 23:3-11. (WALLEYE; ECOLOGY;).

1828. McCutcheon, A. 1984. Lac la Ronge creel census, 1982. Sask. Fish. Lab. Tech. Rep. 1984-7: 31 pp. (WALLEYE; CREEL CENSUS;).

1829. McDonald, J. W. 1973. Rice River creel survey. Ont. Min. Nat. Res., Rep. 11 pp. (WALLEYE; CREEL CENSUS;).

1830. McDonald, P. 1971. Lake of the Woods creel census report. Ont. Min. Nat. Res., Rep. 20 pp. (WALLEYE; CREEL CENSUS;).

1831. McDonough, T. A., and W. C. Barr. 1977. An analysis of fish associations in Tennessee and Cumberland drainage impoundments. Proc. 31st Annu. Conf. Southeast Assoc. Fish Wildl. Agencies. 31:555-557. (SAUGER; WALLEYE; GEOGRAPHICAL DISTRIBUTION;).

1832. McDowall, J. E., C. J. Foote, J. E. Donetz, and J. R. Brisbane. 1981. An assessment of the fishery in central sector Lake of the Woods 1980. Ont. Min. Nat. Res., Lake of the Woods — Rainy Lake Fish. Assess. Unit Rep. 1981-2: 80 pp. (SAUGER; WALLEYE; AGE AND GROWTH; COMMERCIAL FISHERIES; COMMUNITY DYNAMICS; CREEL CENSUS; FOOD STUDIES;).

1833. McElman, J. F. 1978. Early ontogeny of the walleye *Stizostedion vitreum* and the white sucker *Catostomus commersoni:* ecomorphological features of embryonic development. M.S. Thesis, Univ. Guelph, Guelph, Ont. 218 pp. (WALLEYE; EMBRYOLOGY; MORPHOLOGY;).

1834. McElman, J. F. 1983. Comparative embryonic ecomorphology and the reproductive guild classification of walleye, *Stizostedion vitreum*, white sucker, *Catostomus commerconi.* Copeia. 1983:246-250. (WALLEYE; EMBRYOLOGY; SPAWNING STUDIES;).

1835. McElman, J. F., and E. K. Balon. 1979. Early ontogeny of walleye, *Stizostedion vitreum*, with steps of saltatory development. Environ. Biol. Fish. 4:309-349. (WALLEYE; EMBRYOLOGY; LIFE HISTORY; PHYSIOLOGY;).

1836. McGee, M. V., J. S. Griffith, and R. B. McLean. 1977. Prey selection by sauger in Watts Bar Reservoir, Tennessee, as affected by cold-induced mortality of threadfin shad. Proc. 31st Annu. Conf. Southeast. Assoc. Fish Wildl. Agencies 31:404-411. (SAUGER; FOOD STUDIES; IMPOUNDMENTS;).

1837. McGee, M. V., J. S. Griffith, and R. B. McLean. 1978. Aspects of the winter predator-prey relationship between sauger and threadfin shad in Watts Bar Reservoir, Tennessee. Oak Ridge Nat. Lab., Envir. Sci. Div. Publ. 1192, ORNL/NUREG/TM-222: 61 pp. (WALLEYE; ECOLOGY; FOOD STUDIES; HABITAT DEGRADATION;).

1838. McGovern, S. P. 1979. A summary of angling activity within the Ignace District, 1978. Ont. Min. Nat. Res., Rep. 17 pp. (WALLEYE; CREEL CENSUS;).

1839. McGovern, S. P. 1981. Creel survey — Sowden Lake. Ont. Min. Nat. Res., Rep. 8 pp. (WALLEYE; CREEL CENSUS;).

1840. McGregor, D. B. 1970. Creel census of Rainy Lake south arm 1970. Redgut Bay and North Arm 1970. Ont. Min. Nat. Res., Rep. 73 pp. (WALLEYE; CREEL CENSUS;).

1841. McGuire, S. 1980. Mesomikenda Lakes — fishery rehabilitation project 1980. Ont. Min. Nat. Res., Rep. 61 pp. (WALLEYE; AGE AND GROWTH; FISHING GEAR; PRODUCTIVITY; WATER LEVELS;).

1842. McIntyre, E. J. 1980. Summary of the fishery monitoring program north and central sectors Lake of the Woods 1979. Ont. Min. Nat. Res., Lake of the Woods — Rainy Lake Assess. Unit Rep. 1980-2: 67 pp. (WALLEYE; AGE AND GROWTH; COMMERCIAL FISHERIES; COMMUNITY DYNAMICS; CREEL CENSUS; FOOD STUDIES; POPULATION STUDIES; SPAWNING STUDIES;).

1843. McIntyre, E. J., and L. Thurston. 1983. Assessment of 3 years of planting fall and summer fingerling walleye at the Moon River, Eastern Georgian Bay. Ont. Min. Nat. Res., Parry Sound Dist., Manuscript Rep. 34 pp. (WALLEYE; STOCKING;).

1844. McKenzie, R. A. 1930. The reported decrease in fish life and the pollution of the Winnipeg River, Kenora, Ontario. Trans. Am. Fish. Soc. 60:311-323. (SAUGER; WALLEYE; HABITAT DEGRADATION;).

1845. McKenzie, R. A. 1931. The fish trade of southern Ontario. Biol. Board Can., Bull. 23: 37 pp. (SAUGER; WALLEYE; COMMERCIAL FISHERIES;).

1846. McKeown, W. J., M. R. Wolfe, and R. R. Tremblay. 1983. Summer creel survey on Marten and Wicksteed Lakes. Ont. Min. Nat. Res., Rep. 10 pp. (WALLEYE; CREEL CENSUS;).

1847. McKim, J. M., G. M. Christensen, J. H. Tucker, D. A. Benoit, and M. J. Lewis. 1974. Effects of pollution of freshwater fish. J. Water Pollution Control Federation, June 1974 46:1540-1591. (WALLEYE; HABITAT DEGRADATION; PHYSIOLOGY;).

1848. McKnight, D., and D. Payne. 1985. Detour Lake Road creel survey 1984. Ont. Min. Nat. Res., Rep. 31 pp. (WALLEYE; CREEL CENSUS;).

1849. McKnight, T. C. 1975. Artificial walleye spawning reefs in Jennie Weber Lake, Oneida County. Wis. Dept. Nat. Res., Fish Manage. Rep. No. 81: 16 pp. (WALLEYE; HABITAT IMPROVEMENT; SPAWNING STUDIES; STOCKING;).

1850. McLain, A. L., and F. H. Dahl. 1968. An electric beam trawl for the capture of larval lampreys. Trans. Am. Fish. Soc. 97:289-293. (SAUGER; WALLEYE; SAMPLING METHODS;).

1851. McLain, A. L., B. R. Smith, and H. H. Moore. 1965. Experimental control of sea lampreys with electricity on the south shore of Lake Superior, 1953-60. Great Lakes Fish. Comm., Tech. Rep. 10: 48 pp. (WALLEYE; SAMPLING METHODS;).

1852. McLean, R. B., J. S. Griffith, and M. V. McGee. 1985. Threadfin shad, *Dorosoma petenense* Gunther, mortality: causes and ecological implications in a South-eastern United States reservoir. J. Fish. Biol. 27:1-12. (SAUGER; COMMUNITY DYNAMICS; ECOLOGY; FOOD STUDIES;).

1853. McLeod, A. M., and P. Nemenyi. 1940. An investigation of fishways. Univ. Iowa Stud. Eng., Bull. 24: 72 pp. (WALLEYE; FISHWAYS;).

1854. McLeod, D. 1984. Fort Francis District Rainy Lake creel survey 1983. Ont. Min. Nat. Res., Rep. 53 pp. (WALLEYE; CREEL CENSUS;).

1855. McMahon, T. E., J. W. Terrell, and P. C. Nelson. 1984. Habitat suitability information: walleye. U.S. Fish Wildl. Serv., FWS/OBS-82/10.56. 44 pp. (WALLEYE; ECOLOGY; HABITAT DEGRADATION; HABITAT IMPROVEMENT;).

1856. McMillan, J. 1984. Evaluation and enhancement of the trout and walleye fishes in the North Platte River System of Wyoming with emphasis on Seminoe Reservoir. Wy. Game Fish Dept., Fed. Aid Fish Wildl. Restor. Proj. F-44-R, Completion Rep.: 169 pp. (WALLEYE; AGE AND GROWTH; COMMUNITY DYNAMICS; FOOD STUDIES; IMPOUNDMENTS; LIFE HISTORY; MOVEMENTS AND MIGRATIONS; POPULATION STUDIES; SPAWNING STUDIES; STOCKING;).

1857. McNaught, D. C. 1963. The fishes of Lake Mendota. Trans. Wis. Acad. Sci., Arts Letters 52:37-55. (WALLEYE; STOCKING;).

1858. McPhail, J. D., and C. Lindsey, C,. 1970. Freshwater fishes of northwestern Canada and Alaska. Fish. Research Board Can. Bull. 173: 381 pp. (SAUGER; WALLEYE; ECOLOGY; LIFE HISTORY;).

1859. McWilliams, R. H. 1972. Sport fishery harvest at Spirit Lake, 1971. Iowa Conserv. Comm., Job Comp. Rep. 72-2: 13 pp. (WALLEYE; CREEL CENSUS;).

1860. McWilliams, R. H. 1973. Sport fishery harvest at Spirit Lake, 1972-73. Iowa Conserv. Comm., Job Comp. Rep. 102-3: 8 pp. (WALLEYE; COMMUNITY DYNAMICS; CREEL CENSUS;).

1861. McWilliams, R. H. 1974. Sport fishery harvest at Spirit Lake, 1973. Iowa Conserv. Comm., Job Comp. Rep. 102-4: 8 pp. (WALLEYE; COMMUNITY DYNAMICS; CREEL CENSUS;).

1862. McWilliams, R. H. 1975. 0-age fish production and survival in Spirit lake. Pages 1-4 Study 101-3. *in* A compendium of fisheries research in Iowa. Iowa Conserv. Comm., Fish. Sect., Des Moines. (WALLEYE; MORTALITY; PRODUCTIVITY; STOCKING;).

1863. McWilliams, R. H. 1976. Larval walleye and yellow perch population dynamics in Spirit Lake and the contribution of stocked sac-fry to the larval walleye density. Iowa Conserv. Comm., Tech. Series 76-1: 40 pp. (WALLEYE; AGE AND GROWTH; FOOD STUDIES; MORTALITY; MOVEMENTS

AND MIGRATIONS; POPULATION STUDIES; STOCKING;).

1864. McWilliams, R. H. 1982. Natural lakes investigations: large natural lakes. Iowa Conserv. Comm., Fed. Aid Fish Wildl. Restor. Proj. F-95-R-1: 48 pp. (WALLEYE; AGE AND GROWTH; COMMUNITY DYNAMICS; CREEL CENSUS; MARKING; MORTALITY; MOVEMENTS AND MIGRATIONS; POPULATION STUDIES;).

1865. McWilliams, R. H. 1983. Natural lakes investigation: large natural lakes. Iowa Conserv. Comm., Fed. Aid Fish Wildl. Restor. Proj. F-95-R-2: 42 pp. (WALLEYE; AGE AND GROWTH; CREEL CENSUS; LIFE HISTORY; MARKING; POPULATION STUDIES;).

1866. McWilliams, R. H. 1984. Natural lakes investigations: large natural lakes. Iowa Conserv. Comm., Fed. Aid Fish Wildl. Restor. Proj. F-95-R-3: 117 pp. (WALLEYE; CREEL CENSUS; MARKING; MORTALITY; MOVEMENTS AND MIGRATIONS; POPULATION STUDIES;).

1867. McWilliams, R. H. 1985. Natural lakes investigations. Iowa Conserv. Comm., Fed. Aid Fish Wildl. Restor. Proj. F-95-R, Study No. 1, Job No. 4 & 5: 1-12. (WALLEYE; COMMUNITY DYNAMICS; POPULATION STUDIES; STOCKING;).

1868. McWilliams, R. H. 1986. Natural lakes investigations. Iowa Conserv. Comm., Fed. Aid Fish Wildl. Restor. Proj. F-95-R, Study No. 1, Job No. 4 & 5: 1-15. (WALLEYE; COMMUNITY DYNAMICS; POPULATION STUDIES; STOCKING;).

1869. McWilliams, R. H., L. Mitzner, and J. Mayhew. 1974. An evaluation of several types of gear for sampling fish populations. Iowa Conserv. Comm., Tech. Series 74-2: 35 pp. (WALLEYE; COMMUNITY DYNAMICS; FISHING GEAR; POPULATION STUDIES;).

1870. Meade, J. W., J. T. Fuss, and C. B. Mitchell. 1983. Design of small, low cost rearing unit. Prog. Fish-Cult. 45:181-182. (WALLEYE; PROPAGATION;).

1871. Meehan, W. E. 1902. The fishing industry of Lake Erie. Penn. State Fish Comm., Annual Rep. pp. 101-109. (WALLEYE; COMMERCIAL FISHERIES;).

1872. Meek, S. E. 1889. Notes on the fishes of Cayuga Lake basin. Annu. N.Y. Acad. Sci. 4:297-316. (SAUGER; WALLEYE; GEOGRAPHICAL DISTRIBUTION;).

1873. Meek, S. E. 1895. Notes on the fishes of western Iowa and eastern Nebraska. U.S. Fish. Comm., Bull. 14:133-138. (SAUGER; WALLEYE; GEOGRAPHICAL DISTRIBUTION;).

1874. Meek, S. E., and H. W. Clark. 1902. Notes on a collection of cold-blooded vertebrates from Ontario. Field Columbian Mus., Pub. 67:131-140. (WALLEYE; HABITAT DEGRADATION; GEOGRAPHICAL DISTRIBUTION;).

1875. Meek, S. E., and S. F. Hildebrand. 1910. A synoptic list of the fishes known to occur within 50 miles of Chicago. Field Mus. Nat. Hist., Pub. 142:223-338. (SAUGER; WALLEYE; MORPHOLOGY; TAXONOMY;).

1876. Meester, R. J. 1985. An evaluation of northern pike and walleye spawn taking effort in South Dakota Lakes, 1981-1984. S.D. Dept. Game Fish and Parks, Fed. Aid Fish Wildl. Restor. Proj. F-15-R-18, Study No. 1700, Jobs No. 1, 2, & 3: 21 pp. (WALLEYE; POPULATION STUDIES; SPAWNING STUDIES;).

1877. Mendis, A. S. 1956. A limnological comparison of four lakes in central Saskatchewan. Sask. Dept. Nat. Res., Fish. Rep. 2: 23 pp. (WALLEYE; AGE AND GROWTH; FOOD STUDIES; POPULATION STUDIES;).

1878. Menhinick, E. F., and T. M. Burton. 1974. An annotated checklist of freshwater fishes of North Carolina. Rep. J. Elisha Mitchell Sci. Soc. 90:23-50. (SAUGER; WALLEYE; GEOGRAPHICAL DISTRIBUTION;).

1879. Merna, J. W. 1977. Food selection by walleye fry. Mich. Dept. Nat. Res., Research Rep. No. 1847: 12 pp. (WALLEYE; FOOD STUDIES; PROPAGATION;).

1880. Merriam, C. H. 1884. The fish of Lake Champlain. U.S. Fish Comm., Bull. 4:287-288. (WALLEYE; COMMERCIAL FISHERIES;).

1881. Merz, E. A., and K. J. Wright. 1974. Mississippi River special fall tailwaters sport fishing creel census, pools 7, 8, and 9, October 1, 1973 — November 30, 1973. Wis. Dept. Nat.

Res., Publ. No. 70: 59 pp. (SAUGER; WALLEYE; CREEL CENSUS;).

1882. Messer, J. B. 1967. Ecology of the kokanee in North Carolina waters. N. Car. Wildl. Res. Comm., Fed. Aid Fish Wildl. Restor. Proj. F-16-R, Wk. Pl. V., Job V-A: 10 pp. (WALLEYE; IMPOUNDMENTS; POPULATION STUDIES;).

1883. Metcalf, A. L. 1966. Fishes of the Kansas River system in relation to zoogeography of the Great Plains. Univ. Kansas. Pub., Mus Nat. Hist. 17:23-189. (SAUGER; WALLEYE; INTRODUCTIONS; MORPHOLOGY; TAXONOMY;).

1884. Meyer, M. C. 1946. Further notes on the leeches (Piscicolidae) living on fresh-water fishes of North America. Trans. Am. Micros. Soc. 65:237-249. (WALLEYE; PATHOLOGY;).

1885. Michaletz, P. H. 1984. Utilization of rip-rap by spawning walleyes in Lake Francis Case near Chamberlain, South Dakota. S.D. Dept. Game Fish and Parks, Report No. 84-6: 31 pp. (WALLEYE; HABITAT IMPROVEMENT; IMPOUNDMENTS; POPULATION STUDIES; SPAWNING STUDIES; WATER LEVELS;).

1886. Michaletz, P. H., B. Johnson, J. Riis, C. Stone, D. Unkenholz, and D. Warnick. 1986. Annual fisheries surveys on the Missouri River Reservoirs, 1981-1985. S.D. Dept. Game Fish and Parks, Prog. Rep. No. 86-11: 67 pp. (SAUGER; WALLEYE; AGE AND GROWTH; COMMUNITY DYNAMICS; IMPOUNDMENTS; MORTALITY; POPULATION STUDIES;).

1887. Michaletz, P. H., D. G. Unkenholz, and C. C. Stone. 1987. Prey size selectivity and food partitioning among zooplanktivorous age-0 fishes in Lake Francis Case, South Dakota. Am. Mid. Nat. 117:126-138. (WALLEYE; FOOD STUDIES; IMPOUNDMENTS;).

1888. Michlus, R. C. 1959. A four-year creel census of Pike Lake, Cook County (1954-1957). Minn. Dept. Conserv., Invest. Rep. No. 199: 7 pp. (WALLEYE; COMMUNITY DYNAMICS; CREEL CENSUS; ECOLOGY; PRODUCTIVITY;).

1889. Michlus, R. C. 1959. A three year creel census of soft-water walleye population in northeastern Minnesota, Caribou Lake, Cook

County. Minn. Dept. Conserv., Invest. Rep. No. 220: 5 pp. (WALLEYE; CREEL CENSUS; STOCKING;).

1890. Michlus, R. C. 1961. A comparison of sport fisheries of 1937 and 1957 on Seagull Lake, Cook County. Minn. Dept. Conserv., Invest. Rep. No. 203:43-50. (WALLEYE; COMMUNITY DYNAMICS; CREEL CENSUS; FOOD STUDIES;).

1891. Michlus, R. C., and H. C. Clementson. 1960. A three year study of the fish population and catch in Splithand Lake, Itasca County. Minn. Dept. Conserv., Invest. Rep. No. 226: 6 pp. (WALLEYE; AGE AND GROWTH; CREEL CENSUS; POPULATION STUDIES;).

1892. Middendorf, R., and R. Gent. 1980. Evaluation of the walleye population in Lake Macbride. Iowa Conserv. Comm., Job Comp. Rep. Proj. 80-III-C-8: 98-102. (WALLEYE; AGE AND GROWTH; FOOD STUDIES; IMPOUNDMENTS; POPULATION STUDIES; STOCKING;).

1893. Miklovics, M. H., E. Kovacs-Gayer, and J. Szakolczai. 1985. Accumulation and effect of heavy metals in the fishes on Lake Balaton. Symposia Biologica Hungarica 29:111-118. (WALLEYE; TOXICANTS;).

1894. Miles, P. H. 1915. Hatching the wall-eye pike. Bienn. Rep. Comm. Fish. Game, Indiana. (1913-1914):39-48. (WALLEYE; PROPAGATION;).

1895. Miller, F. 1952. Walleyed pike fingerling production in drainable constructed ponds in Minnesota. Prog. Fish-Cult. 14:173-176. (WALLEYE; PRODUCTIVITY; PROPAGATION;).

1896. Miller, L., and J. Hudson. 1977. Evaluation of walleye fry stocking in the Little Sioux River. Iowa Conserv. Comm., Job Comp. Rep. Proj. 77-I-C-4: 37-39. (WALLEYE; AGE AND GROWTH; STOCKING;).

1897. Miller, L., and J. Hudson. 1978. Evaluation of walleye fry stocking in the Little Sioux River. Iowa Conserv. Comm., Job Comp. Rep. Proj. 78-I-C-6: 47-49. (WALLEYE; AGE AND GROWTH; STOCKING;).

1898. Miller, L. F. 1945. A comparison of the hoopnet catches in several fish habitats of Wheeler Reservoir. Trans. Am. Fish. Soc.

73:37-40. (SAUGER; FISHING GEAR; MOVEMENT AND MIGRATIONS;).

1899. Miller, L. F. 1954. Spring fishing on two TVA mainstream reservoirs (1945-1953). Prog. Fish-Cult. 16:114-121. (SAUGER; WALLEYE; CREEL CENSUS;).

1900. Miller, L. F., and C. J. Chance. 1954. Fishing in the tailwaters of TVA dams. Prog. Fish-Cult. 16:3-9. (SAUGER; WALLEYE; CREEL CENSUS;).

1901. Miller, L. W. 1967. The introduction, growth, diet, and depth distribution of walleye, (Stizostedion vitreum) (Mitchell), in El Capitan Reservoir, San Diego County. Calf. Res. Agency, Dept. Fish Game, Inland Fish. Admin. Rep. 67-10: 14 pp. (WALLEYE; AGE AND GROWTH; BEHAVIOR; CREEL CENSUS; FOOD STUDIES; GEOGRAPHICAL DISTRIBUTION; POPULATION STUDIES;).

1902. Miller, M., and D. Maenpae. 1983. Birch Lake creel census summer 1983. Ont. Min. Nat. Res., Rep. 14 pp. (WALLEYE; CREEL CENSUS;).

1903. Miller, M., and D. Maenpae. 1983. La Cloche Lake creel census summer 1983. Ont. Min. Nat. Res., Rep. 16 pp. (WALLEYE; CREEL CENSUS;).

1904. Miller, M. D., and R. R. Andrews. 1972. An investigation into the sport fishery of Nutimik Lake, summer 1968. Man. Dept. Mines, Research & Environ. Manage., Manuscript Rep. No. 72- 17: 112 pp. (SAUGER; WALLEYE; CREEL CENSUS; POPULATION STUDIES; SOCIO-ECONOMICS OF FISHERIES;).

1905. Miller, R. B. 1945. Studies on cestodes of the genus Triaenophorus from fish of Lesser Slave Lake, Alberta. V. Description and life history of Triaenophorus stizostedionis. Can. J. Research, Part D 23:117-127. (WALLEYE; PATHOLOGY;).

1906. Miller, R. B. 1947. Northwest Canadian fisheries surveys in 1944-1945. IV. Great Bear Lake. Fish. Research Board Can., Bull. 72:31-44. (WALLEYE; ECOLOGY; GEOGRAPHICAL DISTRIBUTION;).

1907. Miller, R. B. 1947. The effects of different intensities of fishing on the whitefish populations of two Alberta lakes. J. Wildl. Man-

age. 11:289-301. (WALLEYE; GEOGRAPHICAL DISTRIBUTION;).

1908. Miller, R. B. 1952. A review of the Triaenophorus problem in Canadian lakes. Fish. Research Board Can., Bull. 95: 42 pp. (WALLEYE; PATHOLOGY;).

1909. Miller, R. B. 1956. The collapse and recovery of a small whitefish fishery. J. Fish. Research Board Can. 13:135-146. (WALLEYE; GEOGRAPHICAL DISTRIBUTION;).

1910. Miller, R. B. 1959. The effects of power, irrigation, and stock water developments on the fisheries of the south Saskatchewan River. Can. Fish Cult. 25:13-26. (WALLEYE; ECOLOGY;).

1911. Miller, R. B. 1960. Systematics and biology of gizzard shad (Dorosoma cepedianum) and related fishes. U.S. Fish Wildl. Serv., Fish. Bull. 60:371-392. (SAUGER; WALLEYE; COMMUNITY DYNAMICS; FOOD STUDIES;).

1912. Miller, R. B., and W. H. MacDonald. 1950. Preliminary biological surveys of Alberta watersheds, 1947-1949. Alta. Dept. Lands Forest. 140 pp. (WALLEYE; COMMERCIAL FISHERIES;).

1913. Miller, R. B., and M. J. Paetz. 1953. Preliminary biological surveys of Alberta watersheds, 1950-1952. Alta. Dept. Lands Forest. 114 pp. (WALLEYE; ECOLOGY;).

1914. Miller, S. J., and B. L. Tetzlaff. 1985. Daily growth increments in otoliths of larval walleye Stizostedion vitreum. Trans. Ill. State Acad. Sci. 78:115-120. (WALLEYE; AGE AND GROWTH;).

1915. Millikin, M. R. 1982. Qualitative and quantitative nutrient requirements of fishes: a review. Fish. Bull. 80:655-686. (WALLEYE; FOOD STUDIES;).

1916. Mills, E. L., and A. Schiavone, Jr. 1982. Evaluation of fish communities through assessment of zooplankton populations and measures of lake productivity. N. Am. J. Fish. Manage. 2:14-27. (WALLEYE; COMMUNITY DYNAMICS; ECOLOGY; FOOD STUDIES;).

1917. Milner, J. W. 1874. The progress of fish culture in the United States. U.S. Comm. Fish Fish., Rep. (1872-1873):523-55* WALL-

EYE; INTRODUCTIONS; PROPAGA-
TION;).

1918. Milton. M. L. 1962. A preliminary report on
the White Lake fishery. Ont. Dept. Land
Forest., Res. Manage. Rep. 61:27-45.
(WALLEYE; AGE AND GROWTH;
CREEL CENSUS; MARKING;).

1919. Minckley, W. L. 1973. Fishes of Arizona. Sims
Printing Co., Inc., Phoenix, Ariz., USA. 293
pp. (WALLEYE; PRODUCTIVITY;).

1920. Minns, C. K. 1986. A model of bias in lake se-
lection for survey. Can. Tech. Rep. Fish
Aquatic. Sci. 1496: 21 pp. (WALLEYE;
POPULATION STUDIES;).

1921. Minns, C. K., E. S. Millard, J. M. Cooley, M.
G. Johnson, D. A. Hurley, K. H. Nicholls, G.
W. Robinson, G. E. Owens, and A. Crowder.
1987. Production and biomass size-spectra
in the Bay of Quinte, an eutrophic ecosystem. Can. J. Fish. Aquat. Sci. 44 (Suppl.
2):148-155. (WALLEYE; COMMUNITY
DYNAMICS; PRODUCTIVITY;).

1922. Minor, J. D. 1980. Seasonal movements and
postulated spawning locations of walleyes
(Stizostedion v. vitreum, Mitchill) in Lake
Scugog, Ontario, as determined by radiote-
lemetry. Ont. Min. Nat. Res., Kawartha
Lakes Fish. Assess. Unit Rep. 1980-3: 70 pp.
(WALLEYE; BEHAVIOR; MARKING;
MOVEMENT AND MIGRATIONS;
SPAWNING STUDIES;).

1923. Minor, J. D. 1980. Location and seasonal
movements of walleye (Stizostedion v. vi-
treum, Mitchell) in the Nottawasaga River,
Ontario as determined by radiotelemtry.
Ont. Min. Nat. Res., Huronia Dist. 55 pp.
(WALLEYE; MOVEMENT AND MIGRA-
TIONS; SPAWNING STUDIES;).

1924. Minton, J. W., and R. B. McLean. 1982. Measurements of growth and consumption of
sauger (Stizostedion canadense): implication for fish energetics studies. Can. J. Fish.
Aquat. Sci. 39:1396-1403. (SAUGER; AGE
AND GROWTH; FOOD STUDIES; IN-
TRODUCTIONS; PHYSIOLOGY;).

1925. Mitchell, L. G., J. G. Nickum, and M. T. Long.
1986. Histochemical localization of some digestive enzymes in larval walleyes. Prog.
Fish-Cult. 48:279-281. (WALLEYE; LIFE
HISTORY; PHYSIOLOGY;).

1926. Mitchill, S. L. 1818. Memoir on ichthyology.
The fishes of New York described and ar-
ranged. Am. Month. Mag. Crit. Rev. 1817-
1818:241-248, 321-328. (WALLEYE; TAX-
ONOMY;).

1927. Mitzner, L. 1970. Growth and length-weight
relationship of walleye in Lake McBride.
Iowa Conserv. Comm. Quar. Biol. Rep.
22:11-19. (WALLEYE; AGE AND
GROWTH;).

1928. Mitzner, L. 1978. Utilization of the forage
fish population by predators in Lake
Rathbun. Iowa Conserv. Comm., Fed. Aid
Fish Wildl. Restor. Proj. F-91-R-1, Wk. Pl.
57, Job No. 3: 9 pp. (WALLEYE; COMMU-
NITY DYNAMICS; FOOD STUDIES;).

1929. Mitzner, L. 1978. Utilization of the forage
fish population by predators in Lake
Rathbun. Iowa Conserv. Comm., Fed. Aid
Fish Wildl. Restor. Proj. F-91-R-2, Job No. 2:
10 pp. (WALLEYE; COMMUNITY DY-
NAMICS; FOOD STUDIES;).

1930. Mitzner, L. 1978. Predator population abun-
dance in Lake Rathbun. Iowa Conserv.
Comm., Fed. Aid Fish Wildl. Restor. Proj. F-
91-R-1, Wk. Pl. 57, Job No. 2: 10 pp. (WALL-
EYE; COMMUNITY DYNAMICS; POPU-
LATION STUDIES;).

1931. Mitzner, L. 1980. Inter-relationships of for-
age fish species and predator populations in
Lake Rathbun. Iowa Conserv. Comm., Fed.
Aid Fish Wildl. Restor. Proj. F-91-R, Study
507, Job No. 1-3: 49 pp. (WALLEYE; COM-
MUNITY DYNAMICS; FOOD STUDIES;
IMPOUNDMENTS; POPULATION
STUDIES;).

1932. Mitzner, L. 1985. Assessment of population
dynamics and fish stocking methods of
walleye at Rathbun Lake. Iowa Conserv.
Comm., Fed. Aid Fish Wildl. Restor. Proj. F-
94-R-5, Study No. 4:22-43. (WALLEYE;
AGE AND GROWTH; CREEL CENSUS;
FOOD STUDIES; IMPOUNDMENTS;
MORTALITY; POPULATION STUDIES;
PRODUCTIVITY; STOCKING;).

1933. Mitzner, L. 1986. Assessment of population
dynamics and fish stocking methods of
walleye at Rathbun Lake. Iowa Conserv.
Comm., Fed. Aid Fish Wildl. Restor. Proj. F-
94-R-6, Study No. 4:19-40. (WALLEYE;
AGE AND GROWTH; CREEL CENSUS;
FOOD STUDIES; IMPOUNDMENTS;

MORTALITY; POPULATION STUDIES; PRODUCTIVITY; STOCKING;).

1934. Mizera, J. J., C. L. Cooper, and C. E. Herdendorf. 1981. Limnetic larval fish in the nearshore zone of the western basin of Lake Erie. J. Great Lakes Research 7:62-64. (WALLEYE; POPULATION STUDIES;).

1935. Moeller, D., and S. Schutte. 1974. Evaluation of a walleye fishery. Iowa Conserv. Comm., 1974 Job Comp. Rep. Proj. 74-I-C-18: 47-48. (WALLEYE; MORTALITY; POPULATION STUDIES;).

1936. Moen, T. 1951. Hydra in an Iowa nursery lake. Proc. Iowa Acad. Sci. 58:501-505. (WALLEYE; MORTALITY; PROPAGATION;).

1937. Moen, T. 1956. The 45-day creel census of several Iowa lakes. Pages 4-7 in K.D. Carlander, ed. Symposium on sampling problems in creel census. Iowa State Col., Ames, Iowa. (WALLEYE; CREEL CENSUS;).

1938. Moen, T. 1959. Sexing of channel catfish. Trans. Am. Fish. Soc. 88(2):149. (WALLEYE; MORPHOLOGY;).

1939. Moen, T. 1962. Walleye population studies, Spirit Lake. Iowa Conserv. Comm., Fed. Aid Fish Wildl. Restor. Proj. F-68-R-1, Job No. 2: 8 pp. (WALLEYE; MARKING; POPULATION STUDIES;).

1940. Moen, T. 1962. Age and growth studies. Iowa Conserv. Comm., Fed. Aid Fish Wildl. Restor. Proj. F-68-R-1, Job No. 3: 6 pp. (WALLEYE; AGE AND GROWTH;).

1941. Moen, T. 1963. Walleye population studies, Spirit Lake. Iowa Conserv. Comm., Fed. Aid Fish Wildl. Restor. Proj. F-68-R-2, Job No. 2: 9 pp. (WALLEYE; MARKING; POPULATION STUDIES;).

1942. Moen, T. 1963. Age and growth studies. Iowa Conserv. Comm., Fed. Aid Fish Wildl. Restor. Proj. F-68-R-2, Job No.3: 7 pp. (WALLEYE; AGE AND GROWTH;).

1943. Moen, T. 1964. Walleye population studies, Spirit Lake. Iowa Conserv. Comm., Fed. Aid Fish Wildl. Restor. Proj. F-68-R-3, Job No. 2: 19 pp. (WALLEYE; POPULATION STUDIES;).

1944. Moen, T. 1964. Age and growth studies. Iowa Conserv. Comm., Fed. Aid Fish Wildl. Restor. Proj. F-68-R-3, Job No. 3: 10 pp. (WALLEYE; AGE AND GROWTH;).

1945. Moenig, J. T. 1975. Dynamics of an experimentally exploited walleye population in Dexter Lake, Ontario. M.S. Thesis, Univ. Toronto, Toronto, Ont. 198 pp. (WALLEYE; FISHING GEAR; POPULATION STUDIES;).

1946. Moffett, J. W. 1954. A research program for Lake Erie. Fisherman 22:7, 11-12, 14 pp. (WALLEYE; COMMERCIAL FISHERIES;).

1947. Moffett, J. W. 1957. Recent changes in the deep-water fish populations of Lake Michigan. Trans. Am. Fish. Soc. 86:393-408. (WALLEYE; GEOGRAPHICAL DISTRIBUTION;).

1948. Momot, W. T., J. Erickson, and F. Stevenson. 1977. Maintenance of a walleye, *Stizostedion vitreum vitreum*, fishery in a eutrophic reservoir. J. Fish. Research Board Can. 34:1725-1733. (WALLEYE; ECOLOGY; HABITAT DEGRADATION; IMPOUNDMENTS; SPAWNING STUDIES; STOCKING;).

1949. Monk, C. E. 1966. Northern Light Lake-Survey (1964). Ont. Dept. Land Forest., Res. Manage. Rep. 85:20-32. (WALLEYE; AGE AND GROWTH; FOOD STUDIES;).

1950. Mooradian, S. R., J. L. Forney, and M. D. Staggs. 1986. Response of muskellunge to establishment of walleye in Chautaugus Lake, New York. Pages 168-175 in G.E. Hall, ed. Managing muskies. Am. Fish. Soc. Sp. Publ. No. 15, Washington D.C. (WALLEYE; AGE AND GROWTH; COMMUNITY DYNAMICS; MARKING; MORTALITY; POPULATION STUDIES; STOCKING;).

1951. Moore, A. 1983. Crypreservation of walleye and muskellunge sperm. Iowa Conserv. Comm., Fed. Aid Fish Wildl. Restor. Proj. F-98-R, Study No. 2, Job No. 1 & 2:12-28. (WALLEYE; PHYSIOLOGY; PROPAGATION;).

1952. Moore, A. 1984. Cryopreservation of walleye and muskellunge sperm. Iowa Conserv. Comm., Fed. Aid Fish Wildl. Restor. Proj.,

Study No. 2, Job No. 2:14-24. (WALLEYE; PHYSIOLOGY; PROPAGATION;).

1953. Moore, E. 1929. A biological survey of the Erie-Niagara system. Introduction. N.Y. Conserv. Dept., Suppl. 18th Annu. Rep. (1928):9-18. (WALLEYE; STOCKING;).

1954. Moore, E. 1930. A biological survey of the Champlain watershed. Introduction. N.Y. Conserv. Dept., Suppl. 19th Annu. Rep. (1929):9-21. (WALLEYE; STOCKING;).

1955. Moore, E. 1931. A biological survey of the St. Lawrence watershed. Introduction. N.Y. Conserv. Dept., Suppl. 20th Annu. Rep. (1930):7-13. (WALLEYE; STOCKING;).

1956. Moore, E. 1933. A biological survey of the upper Hudson watershed. Introduction. N.Y. Conserv. Dept., Suppl. 22nd Annu. Rep. (1932):9-25. (WALLEYE; IMPOUND-MENTS; STOCKING;).

1957. Moore, E. 1934. A biological survey of the Raquette watershed. Introduction. N.Y. Conserv. Dept., Suppl. 23rd Annu. Rep. (1933):9-19. (WALLEYE; STOCKING;).

1958. Moore, E. 1936. A biological survey of the Delaware and Susquehanna watersheds. Introduction. N.Y. Conserv. Dept., Suppl. 25th Annu. Rep. (1935):9-18. (WALLEYE; STOCKING;).

1959. Moore, E. 1937. A biological survey of lower Hudson watershed. Introduction. N.Y. Conserv. Dept., Suppl. 26th Annu. Rep. (1936):9-19. (WALLEYE; STOCKING;).

1960. Moore, E. 1938. A biological survey of the Allegheny and Chemung watersheds. Introduction. N.Y. Conserv. Dept., Suppl. 27th Annu. Rep. (1937):9-21. (WALLEYE; STOCKING;).

1961. Moore, E. 1939. A biological survey of the fresh waters of Long Island. Introduction. N.Y. Conserv. Dept., Suppl. 28th Annu Rep. (1938):9-15. (WALLEYE; STOCKING;).

1962. Moore, G. A. 1944. The retinae of two North American teleosts with special reference to their tapeta lucida. J. Comp. Neurol. 80:369-370. (SAUGER; WALLEYE; ECOLOGY; MORPHOLOGY; PHYSIOLOGY;).

1963. Moore, G. A. 1952. Fishes of Oklahoma. Pub. Okla. Fish Game Dept. 11 pp. (SAUGER; WALLEYE; GEOGRAPHICAL DISTRIBUTION;).

1964. Moore, H. H., and R. A. Braem. 1965. Distribution of fishes in U.S. streams tributary to Lake Superior. U.S. Fish Wildl. Serv., Spec. Sci. Rep. Fish. 516: 61 pp. (WALLEYE; GEOGRAPHICAL DISTRIBUTION;).

1965. Moore, W. D. 1975. Walleye culture in Wyoming. Wyo. Game Fish Comm., Admin. Rep. 9 pp. (WALLEYE; IMPOUND-MENTS; PROPAGATION; SPAWNING STUDIES;).

1966. Moraal, G. J. 1978. Wakami Lake creel census 1978. Ont. Min. Nat. Res., Rep. 41 pp. (WALLEYE; CREEL CENSUS;).

1967. Morgan, A. H. 1948. Food of game and pan fishes of the 1944 biological survey. Pages 63-69 in Fisheries report for lakes of central Massachusetts 1944-1945. Mass. Div. Fish Game. (WALLEYE; FOOD STUDIES;).

1968. Morgan, A. H. 1948. Food of game and pan fishes of the 1945 biological survey. In Fisheries report for lakes of Central Massachusetts 1944-1945. Mass. Div. Fish. Game. 3 pp. (WALLEYE; FOOD STUDIES;).

1969. Morris, L. A. 1968. Sauger and walleye investigations in the Missouri River. Neb. Game, Forest. and Parks Comm., Fed. Aid Fish Wildl. Restor. Proj. F-4-R-13, Job No. 21: 4 pp. (SAUGER; WALLEYE; MARKING; POPULATION STUDIES;).

1970. Morris, L. A. 1969. Sauger and walleye investigations in the Missouri River. Neb. Game, Forest. and Parks Comm., Fed. Aid Fish Wildl. Restor. Proj., F-4-R-14, Job No. 2: 6 pp. (SAUGER; WALLEYE; CREEL CENSUS; IMPOUNDMENTS; MARKING; POPULATION STUDIES;).

1971. Morris, L. A. 1970. Sauger and walleye investigations in the Missouri River. Neb. Game, Forests, Parks Comm., Fed. Aid Fish Wildl. Restor. Proj. F-4-R-15, Job No. I-a: 5 pp. (SAUGER; WALLEYE; IMPOUND-MENTS; MARKING; MOVEMENT AND MIGRATIONS; POPULATION STUDIES; SPAWNING STUDIES;).

1972. Morris, W. K. 1977. Evaluation of methods of attaching simulated ultrasonic transmitters to adult male walleye, *Stizostedion vitreum vitreum* (Mitchill) under adverse environmental conditions. M.S. Thesis, Univ. Okla., Norman, Okla. 128 pp. (WALLEYE; MARKING;).

1973. Morsell, J. W. 1970. Food habits and growth of young-of-the-year walleyes from Escanaba lake (Preliminary report). Wis. Dept. Nat. Res., Research Rep. No. 56: 14 pp. (WALLEYE; AGE AND GROWTH; FOOD STUDIES;).

1974. Morsell, J. W., and J. J. Kempinger. 1971. Walleye fry-plankton relationships in Escanaba Lake. Wis. Conserv. Dept., Fed. Aid Fish Wildl. Restor. Proj. F-83-R-6: 18 pp. (WALLEYE; ECOLOGY; FOOD STUDIES; POPULATION STUDIES;).

1975. Moser, B. B. 1967. Dynamics of the fish population in Canton Reservoir. Creel survey of Canton Reservoir. Okla. Dept. Wildl. Conserv., Fed. Aid Fish Wildl. Restor. Proj. F-16-R-3, Wk. Pl. 2, Job No. 1, Part 1: 15 pp. (WALLEYE; AGE AND GROWTH; CREEL CENSUS; IMPOUNDMENTS; INTRODUCTIONS;).

1976. Moser, B. B. 1967. Investigations of the reproduction of fishes in Canton Reservoir. Meter net, surface-midwater trawl and bottom trawl sampling. Okla. Dept. Wildl. Conserv., Fed. Aid Fish Wildl. Restor. Proj. F-16-R-3, Wk. Pl. 2, Job No. 2, Part 5: 44 pp. (WALLEYE; IMPOUNDMENTS; POPULATION STUDIES; SAMPLING METHODS;).

1977. Moser, B. B., and D. Hicks. 1970. Fish populations of the Stilling Basin below Canton Reservoir. Proc. Okla Acad. Sci. 50:69-74. (WALLEYE; COMMUNITY DYNAMICS; IMPOUNDMENTS; POPULATION STUDIES;).

1978. Moshenko, R. W., and G. Low. 1980. The walleye sport fishery on the Hay River, Northwest Territories, 1978. Can. Data Rep. Fish. Aquat. Sci. 16 pp. (WALLEYE; CREEL CENSUS;).

1979. Mosher, A. A. 1885. Notes on fish culture in Iowa. U.S. Fish Comm., Bull. 5: 312 pp. (WALLEYE; PROPAGATION;).

1980. Mosher, T. D. 1987. An assessment of walleye populations in small Kansas lakes with recommendations for future stocking. Kans. Fish Game Comm., Fish, I&D No. 87-4: 39 pp. (WALLEYE; COMMUNITY DY-
NAMICS; CREEL CENSUS; ECOLOGY; IMPOUNDMENTS; MORTALITY; POPULATION STUDIES; STOCKING;).

1981. Mosindy, T. E. 1982. A preliminary examination of the fish community in Lac des Mille Lacs, Ontario, 1981. Ont. Min. Nat. Res., Quetico-Mille Lacs Fish. Assess. Unit Rep. 1982-2: 52 pp. (WALLEYE; AGE AND GROWTH; COMMUNITY DYNAMICS; MORTALITY;).

1982. Mosindy, T. E. 1982. Age verification of walleye from Lac des Mille Lacs, Ontario based on the examination of scales and dorsal fin spines. Ont. Min. Nat. Res., Quetico-Mille Lacs Fish. Assess. Unit Rep. 1982-1: 17 pp. (WALLEYE; AGE AND GROWTH;).

1983. Mosindy, T. E. 1983. An assessment of the south sector fishery, Lake of the Woods, 1982. Ont. Min. Nat. Res., Lake of the Woods Fish. Assess. Unit Rep. 1983-2: 114 pp. (SAUGER; WALLEYE; AGE AND GROWTH; COMMERCIAL FISHERIES; COMMUNITY DYNAMICS; CREEL CENSUS; FOOD STUDIES; POPULATION STUDIES; SPAWNING STUDIES;).

1984. Mosindy, T. E. 1984. Lake of the Woods creel survey — 1983. Ont. Min. Nat. Res., Lake of the Woods Fish. Assess. Unit Rep. 1984-02: 45 pp. (SAUGER; WALLEYE; AGE AND GROWTH; CREEL CENSUS;).

1985. Mosindy, T. E., W. T. Momot, and P. J. Colby. 1987. Impact of angling on the production and yield of mature walleyes and northern pike in a small boreal lake in Ontario. N. Am. J. Fish. Manage. 7:493-501. (WALLEYE; AGE AND GROWTH; CREEL CENSUS; IMPOUNDMENTS; MARKING; MORTALITY; POPULATION STUDIES; PRODUCTIVITY; REGULATIONS;).

1986. Mossier, J. N. 1971. The effect of salinity on the eggs and sac fry of the fathead minnow (Pimephales primelas promelas), northern pike (Esox lucius) and walleye (Stizostedion vitreum vitreum). Ph.D. Dissertation. N. D. St. Univ., Fargo, N.D. 56 pp. (WALLEYE; EMBRYOLOGY; PHYSIOLOGY;).

1987. Mottley, C. M., and T. K. Chamberlain. 1948. Management of game fish of Conchas Reservoir. Prog. Fish-Cult. 10:177-186. (WALLEYE; INTRODUCTIONS;).

1988. Mount, D. I. 1961. Development of a system for controlling dissolved oxygen content of water. Trans. Am. Fish. Soc. 90:323-327. (WALLEYE; BEHAVIOR; PHYSIOLOGY;).

1989. Moyle, J. B. 1940. A biological survey of the upper Mississippi River system. Minn. Dept. Conserv., Invest. Rep. No. 10: 69 pp. (SAUGER; WALLEYE; PROPAGATION; STOCKING;).

1990. Moyle, J. B. 1945. Further considerations on yield, fertilization, and natural chemical fertility of Minnesota pike-perch ponds. Minn. Dept. Conserv., Invest. Rep. No. 63: 9 pp. (WALLEYE; ECOLOGY; PRODUCTIVITY; PROPAGATION;).

1991. Moyle, J. B. 1947. Indices of lake productivity. Minn. Dept. Conserv., Invest. Rep. No. 71: 17 pp. (WALLEYE; ECOLOGY; PRODUCTIVITY; PROPAGATION;).

1992. Moyle, J. B. 1949. Fish population concepts and management of Minnesota lakes for sport fishing. Trans. 14th N. Am. Wildl. Conf. 14:283-294. (WALLEYE; HABITAT IMPROVEMENT; POPULATION STUDIES;).

1993. Moyle, J. B. 1949. Some indices of lake productivity. Trans. Am. Fish. Soc. 76:322-334. (WALLEYE; PRODUCTIVITY; PROPAGATION;).

1994. Moyle, J. B. 1950. Gill nets for sampling fish populations in Minnesota waters. Trans. Am. Fish. Soc. 79:195-204. (WALLEYE; FISHING GEAR; SAMPLING METHODS;).

1995. Moyle, J. B. 1950. Notes on the present status of the walleye in Minnesota waters. Minn. Dept. Conserv., Invest. Rep. No. 95: 9 pp. (WALLEYE; AGE AND GROWTH; CREEL CENSUS; MORTALITY; POPULATION STUDIES; SPAWNING STUDIES; STOCKING;).

1996. Moyle, J. B. 1951. Weeds and weed control in state walleye ponds. Minn. Dept. Conserv., Invest. Rep. No. 114: 13 pp. (WALLEYE; PROPAGATION;).

1997. Moyle, J. B. 1954. Records of fishing success by members of the Monmouth Miltona Club in Douglas County, Minnesota, during the years 1894 to 1897. Minn. Dept. Conserv.,
Invest. Rep. No. 147: 19 pp. (WALLEYE; CREEL CENSUS;).

1998. Moyle, J. B. 1954. Some aspects of the chemistry of Minnesota surface waters as related to game and fish management. Minn. Dept. Conserv., Invest. Rep. No. 151: 36 pp. (WALLEYE; ECOLOGY; PRODUCTIVITY; PROPAGATION; STOCKING;).

1999. Moyle, J. B. 1955. Summary of some aspects of the 1946 test netting operations northern section. Minn. Dept. Conserv., Invest. Rep. No. 156: 23 pp. (SAUGER; WALLEYE; POPULATION STUDIES;).

2000. Moyle, J. B. 1955. Sport fishing trends in Minnesota. Prog. Fish-Cult. 17:136-137. (WALLEYE; COMMUNITY DYNAMICS; CREEL CENSUS; STOCKING;).

2001. Moyle, J. B. 1955. Notes on the 1948 test netting northern section. Minn. Dept. Conserv., Invest. Rep. No. 161: 7 pp. (SAUGER; WALLEYE; POPULATION STUDIES;).

2002. Moyle, J. B. 1956. Relationship between the chemistry of Minnesota surface waters and wildlife management. J. Wildl. Manage. 20:303-320. (WALLEYE; ECOLOGY; PRODUCTIVITY;).

2003. Moyle, J. B. 1963. Notes on experiment on dissolved oxygen levels and survival and hatching of walleye eggs. Minn. Conserv. Dept., Invest. Rep. No. 261: 2 pp. (WALLEYE; PROPAGATION;).

2004. Moyle, J. B., and W. D. Clothier. 1959. Effects of management and winter oxygen levels on the fish populations of a prairie lake. Trans. Am. Fish. Soc. 88:178-185. (WALLEYE; ECOLOGY; HABITAT IMPROVEMENT; MORTALITY; PHYSIOLOGY; SAMPLING METHODS; STOCKING;).

2005. Moyle, J. B., and D. R. Franklin. 1953. Creel census of 23 Minnesota lakes-1952. Minn. Dept. Conserv., Invest. Rep. No. 135: 71 pp. (WALLEYE; CREEL CENSUS;).

2006. Moyle, J. B., and D. R. Franklin. 1954. Creel census of 12 Minnesota lakes December 1, 1952-December 1, 1953. Minn. Dept. Conserv., Invest. Rep. No. 146: 36 pp. (WALLEYE; CREEL CENSUS;).

2007. Moyle, J. B., and D. R. Franklin. 1955. Creel census of 12 Minnesota Lakes December 1, 1953 to December 1, 1954. Minn. Dept. Conserv., Invest. Rep. No. 159: 35 pp. (WALLEYE; CREEL CENSUS;).

2008. Moyle, J. B., and D. R. Franklin. 1957. Quantitative creel census on 12 Minnesota lakes. Trans. Am. Fish. Soc. 85:28-38. (WALLEYE; CREEL CENSUS;).

2009. Moyle, J. B., J. H. Kuehn, and C. R. Burrows. 1950. Fish populations and catch data from Minnesota lakes. Trans Am. Fish. Soc. 78:163-175. (WALLEYE; COMMUNITY DYNAMICS; FISHING GEAR; POPULATION STUDIES;).

2010. Moyle, J. B., and R. Lound. 1960. Confidence limits associated with means and medians of series of net catches. Trans. Am. Fish. Soc. 89:53-58. (WALLEYE; FISHING GEAR;).

2011. Mraz, D. 1964. Age, growth, sex ratio, and maturity of the whitefish in central Green Bay and adjacent waters of Lake Michigan. U.S. Fish Wildl. Serv., Fish. Bull. 63:619-634. (WALLEYE; POPULATION STUDIES;).

2012. Mraz, D. 1968. Recruitment, growth, exploitation and management of walleyes in a southeastern Wisconsin Lake. Wis. Dept. Nat. Res., Tech. Bull. No. 40: 38 pp. (WALLEYE; AGE AND GROWTH; LIFE HISTORY; MARKING; POPULATION STUDIES; SPAWNING STUDIES; STOCKING;).

2013. Mrozinski, L. E., R. E. Sheperd, J. Webes, and J. C. Schneider. 1985. Growth, mortality, and movement of walleyes in Saginaw River system. Mich. Dept. Nat. Res., Fed Aid Fish Wildl. Restor. Proj. F-35-R-10: 64-78. (WALLEYE; AGE AND GROWTH; COMMERCIAL FISHERIES; HABITAT DEGRADATION; MORTALITY; MOVEMENT AND MIGRATIONS; SPAWNING STUDIES;).

2014. Mueller, J. F. 1934. Part IV. Additional notes on parasites of Oneida Lake fishes, including descriptions of new species. N.Y. State Coll. Forest., Roosevelt Wildl. Annu. Bull. 3:335-373. (WALLEYE; PATHOLOGY;).

2015. Mueller, J. W. 1968. Walleye spawning operations on Keyhole Reservoir, 1967. Wyo.

Game Fish Comm., Admin. Rep., Proj. 0367-06-6702: 5 pp. (WALLEYE; IMPOUNDMENTS; PROPAGATION; SPAWNING STUDIES;).

2016. Mueller, J. W. 1972. Walleye predation on planted rainbow trout Keyhole Reservoir, 1972. Wyo. Game Fish Dept., Proj. No. 3-06-371: 3 pp. (WALLEYE; COMMUNITY DYNAMICS; FOOD STUDIES;).

2017. Mueller, J. W. 1985. Walleye spawning operation, Keyhole Reservoir, 1985. Wyo. Game Fish Dept., Admin. Rep., Proj. 3085-06-6502: 3 pp. (WALLEYE; IMPOUNDMENTS; SPAWNING STUDIES;).

2018. Mueller, J. W., L. C. Rockett, and B. Ditton. 1968. Use of radio tags in tracking walleye in Keyhole Reservoir. Wyo. Game Fish Comm., Admin Rep., Proj. 0368-17-6601: 2 pp. (WALLEYE; IMPOUNDMENTS; MARKING; MOVEMENTS AND MIGRATIONS; SPAWNING STUDIES;).

2019. Muench, K. A. 1966. Certain aspects of the life history of the walleye, *Stizostedion vitreum vitreum,* in Center Hill Reservoir, Tennessee. M.S. Thesis, Tenn. Tech. Univ., Cookeville, Tenn. 66 pp. (WALLEYE; AGE AND GROWTH; FOOD STUDIES; IMPOUNDMENTS; LIFE HISTORY; MOVEMENTS AND MIGRATIONS; SPAWNING STUDIES;).

2020. Muldoon, J. A. 1982. Summer creel census in the Bay of Quinte 1980-81. Ont. Min. Nat. Res., LOFAU Rep. 82-1: 56 pp. (WALLEYE; CREEL CENSUS;).

2021. Mulholland, H., and L. Bond. 1975. Lanark District 1975, summer creel census report, Bennett, Dalhousie and Patterson Lakes. Ont. Min. Nat. Res., Rep. 55 pp. (WALLEYE; CREEL CENSUS;).

2022. Mulholland, H., and B. Gopsill. 1978. 1978 co-operative creel census report on Christie Lake. Ont. Min. Nat. Res., Rep. 16 pp. (WALLEYE; CREEL CENSUS;).

2023. Muncy, R. J., and A. P. D'Silva. 1981. Marking walleye eggs and fry. Trans. Am. Fish. Soc. 110:300-305. (WALLEYE; MARKING;).

2024. Munro, J. A. 1927. Observations on the double-crested cormorant *(Phalacrocorax auritus)* on Lake Manitoba. Can. Field Nat.

41:102-108. (SAUGER; WALLEYE; COMMUNITY DYNAMICS;).

2025. Murphy, B. R. 1981. Genetic evaluation of walleye *(Stizostedion vitreum vitreum)* stock structure and recruitment in Clayton Lake, Virginia. Ph.D. Dissertation, Virginia Polytechnic Institute and State University, Blacksburg, Virginia. 116 pp. (WALLEYE; GENETICS; GEOGRAPHICAL DISTRIBUTION;).

2026. Murphy, B. R., L. A. Nielsen, and B. J. Turner. 1983. Use of genetic tags to evaluate stocking success for reservoir walleyes. Trans. Am. Fish. Soc. 112:457-463. (WALLEYE; GENETICS; IMPOUNDMENTS; STOCKING;).

2027. Muth, K. M. 1978. Allocating percid resources in the Great Lakes: biological, institutional, political, social, and economic ramifications: — a panel. Pages 428-435 *in* R.L. Kendall, ed. Selected coolwater fishes of North America. Am. Fish. Soc. Sp. Publ. No. 11, Washington, D.C. (WALLEYE; COMMERCIAL FISHERIES; CREEL CENSUS; SOCIO-ECONOMICS OF FISHERIES;).

2028. Muth, K. M., and D. R. Wolfert. 1986. Changes in growth and maturity of walleyes associated with stock rehabilitation in western Lake Erie, 1964-1983. N. Am. J. Fish Manage. 6:168-175. (WALLEYE; AGE AND GROWTH; FOOD STUDIES; SPAWNING STUDIES;).

2029. Myers, R. W. 1977. Wolfe-Howe Islands creel census report. Ont. Min. Nat. Res., Lake Ont. Fish. Assess. Unit Rep. 33 pp. (WALLEYE; CREEL CENSUS;).

2030. Nagel, T. O. 1974. Rearing of walleye fingerlings in an intensive culture using Oregon moist pellets as an artificial diet. Prog. Fish-Cult. 36:59-61. (WALLEYE; FOOD STUDIES; PROPAGATION;).

2031. Nagel, T. O. 1976. Intensive culture of fingerling walleye on formulated feeds. Prog. Fish-Cult. 38:90-91. (WALLEYE; FOOD STUDIES; PROPAGATION;).

2032. Nagel, T. O. 1985. Development of a domestic walleye broodstock. Prog. Fish-Cult. 47:121-122. (WALLEYE; PROPAGATION;).

2033. Nash, C. B. 1950. Associations between fish species in tributaries and shore waters of western Lake Erie. Ecology 31:561-566. (SAUGER; ECOLOGY;).

2034. Nash, C. W. 1908. Vertebrates of Ontario. Ont. Dept. Educ., Toronto, Ont. 229 pp. (SAUGER; WALLEYE; ECOLOGY; LIFE HISTORY; MORPHOLOGY;).

2035. Nash, C. W. 1913. Fishes. Pages 249-271 *in* J.H. Faull, ed. The Natural History of the Toronto Region, Ontario, Canada (SAUGER; WALLEYE; GEOGRAPHICAL DISTRIBUTION;).

2036. Neal, M. 1938. A faunal survey of the Favourable Lake area, Patricia District Ontario. Manuscript in Univ. Toronto, Great Lakes Inst. Libr., Toronto, Ont. 12 pp. (SAUGER; WALLEYE; GEOGRAPHICAL DISTRIBUTION;).

2037. Needham, R. G., and K. W. Gilge. 1985. Inventory and survey of waters of the project area, Northeast Montana. Mont. Dept. Fish Wildl. Parks, Fed. Aid Fish Wildl. Restor. Proj. F-11-R-32, Job No. I-a: 35 pp. (SAUGER; WALLEYE; AGE AND GROWTH; CREEL CENSUS; IMPOUNDMENTS; POPULATION STUDIES; SPAWNING STUDIES; STOCKING;).

2038. Needham, R. G., and K. W. Gilge. 1986. Northeast Montana fisheries study: inventory and survey of waters of the project area. Mont. Dept. Fish, Wildl., Parks. 30 pp. (SAUGER; WALLEYE; IMPOUNDMENTS; POPULATION STUDIES; SPAWNING STUDIES;).

2039. Needham, R. G., and K. W. Gilge. 1987. Inventory and survey of waters of the project area. Mont. Dept. Fish, Wildl. Parks, Fed. Aid Fish Wildl. Restor. Proj. F-11-R-34, Job I-a:. (WALLEYE; IMPOUNDMENTS; POPULATION STUDIES; SPAWNING STUDIES;).

2040. Nelson, D. J. 1878. Fisheries of Chicago and vicinity. U.S. Comm. Fish Fish., Annu. Rep. (1875-1876):783-800. (WALLEYE; COMMERCIAL FISHERIES;).

2041. Nelson, D. J. 1967. Ecological behavior of radionuclides in the Clinch and Tennessee Rivers. Pages 169-187 *in* Reservoir Fishery Symposium, Reservoir Comm., Southern

Div., Am. Fish. Soc. (SAUGER; WALL-EYE; HABITAT DEGRADATION; IM-POUNDMENTS; MARKING;).

2042. Nelson, K. K. 1980. A qualitative and quantitative roving creel census with a modification of the Weitman-Anderson methodology. Minn. Dept. Nat. Res., Fish Manage. Rep. No. 25: 37 pp. (WALLEYE; CREEL CENSUS;).

2043. Nelson, W. R. 1961. Report of fisheries investigations during the eighth year of impoundment of Fort Randall Reservoir, South Dakota, 1960. S.D. Dept. Game, Fish Parks, Fed. Aid Fish Wildl. Restor. Proj. F-1-R-10, Jobs 3-B, 4-B, 5, 6, 7, 8: 34 pp. (SAUGER; WALLEYE; AGE AND GROWTH; CREEL CENSUS; FOOD STUDIES; IMPOUNDMENTS; PRO-DUCTIVITY;).

2044. Nelson, W. R. 1961. Report of fisheries investigations during the 6th year of impoundments of Gavins Point Reservoir, South Dakota, 1960. S.D. Dept. Game Fish Parks, Fed. Aid Fish Wildl. Restor. Proj. F-1-R-10, Jobs 2, 3, 4: 63 pp. (SAUGER; WALLEYE; AGE AND GROWTH; ECOLOGY; FOOD STUDIES; IMPOUNDMENTS; POPU-LATION STUDIES;).

2045. Nelson, W. R. 1962. Report of fisheries investigations during the seventh year of impoundment of Gavins Point Reservoir, South Dakota, 1961. S.D. Dept. Game Fish Parks, Fed. Aid Fish Wildl. Restor. Proj. F-1-R-11, Job 1, 2, 3, 7: 40 pp. (SAUGER; WALLEYE; AGE AND GROWTH; CREEL CENSUS; FOOD STUDIES; IM-POUNDMENTS; POPULATION STUD-IES;).

2046. Nelson, W. R. 1968. Embryo and larval characteristics of sauger, walleye and their reciprocal hybrids. Trans. Am. Fish. Soc. 97:167-174. (SAUGER; WALLEYE; GENETICS; MORPHOLOGY; TAXONOMY;).

2047. Nelson, W. R. 1968. Reproduction and early life history of sauger (Stizostedion canadense) in Lewis and Clark Lake. Trans. Am. Fish. Soc. 97:159-166. (SAUGER; AGE AND GROWTH; ECOLOGY; FOOD STUDIES; MORTALITY; POPULATION STUDIES; SPAWNING STUDIES;).

2048. Nelson, W. R. 1969. Biological characteristics of sauger populations in Lewis and

Clark Lake. Bureau of Sport Fish. Wildl., Tech. Paper 21: 11 pp. (SAUGER; AGE AND GROWTH; IMPOUNDMENTS; MARKING; POPULATION STUDIES; SPAWNING STUDIES;).

2049. Nelson, W. R. 1974. Age, growth, and maturity of thirteen species of fish from Lake Oahe during the early years of impoundment, 1963-1968. U.S. Fish Wildl. Serv., Tech. Paper 77: 29 pp. (SAUGER; WALL-EYE; AGE AND GROWTH; ECOLOGY; SPAWNING STUDIES;).

2050. Nelson, W. R. 1978. Implications of water management in Lake Oahe for the spawning success of coolwater fishes. Pages 154-158 in R.L. Kendall, ed. Selected coolwater fishes of North America. Am. Fish. Soc. Sp. Publ. No. 11, Washington, D.C. (SAUGER; WALLEYE; ECOLOGY; IMPOUND-MENTS; SPAWNING STUDIES; WATER LEVELS;).

2051. Nelson, W. R. 1980. Ecology of larval fishes in Lake Oahe, South Dakota. U.S. Fish Wildl. Serv., Tech. Paper 101: 18 pp. (SAUGER; WALLEYE; IMPOUND-MENTS; MORTALITY; POPULATION STUDIES; SPAWNING STUDIES;).

2052. Nelson, W. R., and M. F. Boussa. 1974. Evaluation of trawls for monitoring and harvesting fish populations in Lake Oahe, South Dakota. U.S. Fish Wildl. Serv., Tech. Paper 76: 15 pp. (SAUGER; WALLEYE; FISH-ING GEAR; POPULATION STUDIES;).

2053. Nelson, W. R., N. R. Hines, and L. G. Beckman. 1965. Artificial propagation of saugers and hybridization with walleyes. Prog. Fish-Cult. 27:216-218. (SAUGER; WALLEYE; GENETICS; PROPAGA-TION;).

2054. Nelson, W. R., R. E. Seifert, and D. V. Swedberg. 1967. Studies of the early life history of reservoir fishes. Pages 374-385 in Reservoir Fishery Symposium, Reservoir Comm., Southern Div., Am. Fish. Soc. pp. 374-385. (SAUGER; WALLEYE; ECOLOGY; IM-POUNDMENTS; POPULATION STUD-IES;).

2055. Nelson, W. R., and C. A. Walburg. 1977. Population dynamics of yellow perch (Perca flavescesns), sauger (Stizostedion canadense), and walleye (Stizostedion vitreum vitreum) in four main stem Missouri River reservoirs. J. Fish. Research Board Can. 34:1748-1763. (SAUGER; WALLEYE; AGE AND GROWTH; CREEL CENSUS; ECOLOGY; IMPOUNDMENTS; POPULATION STUDIES; SPAWNING STUDIES; WATER LEVELS;).

2056. Nepszy, S. J. 1977. Changes in percid populations and species interactions in Lake Erie. J. Fish. Research Board Can. 34:1861-1868. (SAUGER; WALLEYE; COMMERCIAL FISHERIES; COMMUNITY DYNAMICS; HABITAT DEGRADATION; POPULATION STUDIES;).

2057. Nepszy, S. J. 1985. Walleye (Stizostedion vitreum) in western Lake Erie: Responses to change in predator and prey. Great Lakes Fish. Comm., Spec. Pub. 85-3:57-76. (WALLEYE; AGE AND GROWTH; COMMERCIAL FISHERIES; COMMUNITY DYNAMICS; POPULATION STUDIES;).

2058. Nevin, J. 1887. Hatching the wall-eyed pike. Trans. Am. Fish. Soc. 16:14-16. (WALLEYE; PROPAGATION;).

2059. Nevin, J. 1897. Wall-eyed pike. Trans. Am. Fish. Soc. 26:126-127. (WALLEYE; ECOLOGY; MORTALITY; PROPAGATION;).

2060. Nevin, J. 1911. Reminiscences of forty-one years' work in fish culture. Trans. Am. Fish. Soc. 40:313-318. (WALLEYE; PROPAGATION;).

2061. Newburg, H. J. 1969. Investigation of Douglas County, Minnesota, bass lakes conducted during the summer of 1968. Minn. Dept. Nat. Res., Invest. Rep. No. 305: 26 pp. (WALLEYE; POPULATION STUDIES; STOCKING;).

2062. Newburg, H. J. 1973. Evaluation of potential use of pulsed direct current electrofishing gear in some fish management activities. Minn. Dept. Nat. Res., Invest. Rep. No. 321: 18 pp. (WALLEYE; SAMPLING METHODS;).

2063. Newburg, H. J. 1974. Planarians as a mortality factor on spawned fish eggs. Prog. Fish-Cult. 36:227-230. (WALLEYE; MORTALITY; SPAWNING STUDIES;).

2064. Newburg, H. J. 1975. Evaluation of an improved walleye (Stizostedion vitreum) spawning shoal with criteria for design and placement. Minn. Dept. Nat. Res., Invest. Rep. No. 340: 39 pp. (WALLEYE; HABITAT IMPROVEMENT; SPAWNING STUDIES;).

2065. Newell, A. E. 1960. Biological survey of the lakes and ponds in Coos, Grafton and Carroll Counties. N.H. Fish Game Dept. 295 pp. (WALLEYE; INTRODUCTIONS;).

2066. Newell, A. E. 1963. Biological survey of the lakes and ponds in Sullivan, Merrimack, Belknap and Strafford Counties. N.H. Fish Game Dept., Surv. Rep. 8B: 276 pp. (WALLEYE; INTRODUCTIONS;).

2067. Newton, M. V. B. 1933. The biology of Triaenophorus tricuspidatus in western Canada. Can. Biol. Fish., NS No. 7:341-360. (SAUGER; WALLEYE; PATHOLOGY;).

2068. Ney, J. J. 1978. A synoptic review of yellow perch and walleye biology. Pages 1-12 in R.L. Kendall, ed. Selected coolwater fishes of North America. Am. Fish. Soc. Sp. Publ. No. 11, Washington, D.C. (WALLEYE; AGE AND GROWTH; BEHAVIOR; COMMUNITY DYNAMICS; FOOD STUDIES; LIFE HISTORY; MORTALITY; SPAWNING STUDIES; TAXONOMY;).

2069. Ney, J. J., and D. J. Orth. 1986. Coping with future shock: matching predator stocking programs to prey abundance. Pages 81-92 in R. H. Stroud, ed. Fish culture in fisheries management. Am. Fish. Soc., Bethesda, Maryland. (WALLEYE; COMMUNITY DYNAMICS; FOOD STUDIES; STOCKING;).

2070. Nicholson, A. J., and H. M. Borges. 1955. Creel census and expenditure studies, Missouri River basin. U.S. Fish Wildl. Serv., Spec. Sci. Rep., Fish. 141:28. (SAUGER; WALLEYE; CREEL CENSUS;).

2071. Nickum, J. C. 1978. Intensive culture of walleyes: the state of the art. Pages 187-194 in R.L. Kendall, ed. Selected coolwater fishes of North America. Am. Fish. Soc. Sp. Publ. No. 11, Washington, D.C. (WALLEYE; PROPAGATION;).

2072. Nickum, J. G. 1986. Walleye. Pages 115-126 in R. R. Stickney, ed. Culture of non-salmonid freshwater fishes. CRC Press, Inc., Boca Raton, FL. (WALLEYE; PROPAGATION;).

2073. Nielsen, J. R. 1975. Investigation of the walleye fishery in Franklin D. Roosevelt Lake. Wash. Dept. Game, Fed. Aid Fish Wildl. Restor. Proj. F-64-R-2, Job No. 2:28-50. (WALLEYE; AGE AND GROWTH; CREEL CENSUS; IMPOUNDMENTS; REGULATIONS; WATER LEVELS;).

2074. Nielsen, L. A. 1980. Effect of walleye (Stizostedion vitreum vitreum) predation on juvenile mortality and recruitment of yellow perch (Perca flavescens) in Oneida Lake, New York. Can. J. Fish. Aquat. Sci. 37:11-19. (WALLEYE; COMMUNITY DYNAMICS; FOOD STUDIES; MORTALITY;).

2075. Niemuth, W., W. Churchill, and T. Wirth. 1959. The walleye, its life history, ecology and management. Wis. Dept. Nat. Res., Publ. No. 227: 14 pp. (WALLEYE; AGE AND GROWTH; ECOLOGY; LIFE HISTORY;).

2076. Niemuth, W., and J. Klingbiel. 1962. The evaluation of the boom shocker in the study of the fish population of Big Sand Lake, Sawyer County. Wis. Conserv. Dept., Invest. Rep. No. 6: 18 pp. (WALLEYE; AGE AND GROWTH; MOVEMENT AND MIGRATIONS; POPULATION STUDIES; SAMPLING METHODS;).

2077. Nigrelli, R. F. 1952. Virus and tumors in fishes. N.Y. Acad. Sci. 54:1076-1092. (WALLEYE; PATHOLOGY;).

2078. Nigrelli, R. F. 1954. Tumors and other atypical cell growths in temperate freshwater fishes of North America. Trans. Am. Fish. Soc. 83:262-296. (SAUGER; WALLEYE; PATHOLOGY;).

2079. Nigrelli, R. F., and G. D. Ruggieri. 1965. Studies on virus diseases of fishes. Spontaneous and experimentally induced cellular hypertrophy (Lymphocystis disease) in fishes of the New York Aquarium, with a report of new cases and annotated bibliography (1874-1965). Zoologica 50:83-95. (SAUGER; WALLEYE; PATHOLOGY;).

2080. Niimi, A. J., and S. L. Morgan. 1980. Morphometric examination of the gills of walleye, Stizostedion vitreum vitreum (Mitchill) and rainbow trout, Salmo gairderi Richarson. J. Fish Biol. 16:685-692. (WALLEYE; MORPHOLOGY;).

2081. Noble, R. L. 1968. Mortality rates of pelagic fry of yellow perch, Perca flavescens in Oneida Lake, New York, and an analysis of the sampling problem. Ph.D. Dissertation, Cornell Univ., Ithaca, N.Y. 104 pp. (WALLEYE; COMMUNITY DYNAMICS;).

2082. Noble, R. L. 1970. Evaluation of the Miller high-speed sampler for sampling yellow perch and walleye fry. J. Fish. Research Board Can. 27:1033-1044. (WALLEYE; FISHING GEAR; SAMPLING METHODS;).

2083. Noble, R. L. 1970. Parasites of yellow perch in Oneida Lake, New York. N.Y. Fish Game J. 17:95-101. (WALLEYE; PATHOLOGY;).

2084. Noble, R. L. 1971. An evaluation of the meter net for sampling fry of yellow perch, Perca flavescens, and walleye, Stizostedion v. vitreum. Chesapeake Sci. 12:47-48. (WALLEYE; FISHING GEAR; SAMPLING METHODS;).

2085. Noble, R. L. 1972. Distribution of walleye and yellow perch fry in a bay of Oneida Lake. N.Y. Fish Game J. 19:168-177. (WALLEYE; COMMUNITY DYNAMICS; MOVEMENT AND MIGRATIONS;).

2086. Noble, R. L. 1972. Mortality rates of walleye fry in a bay of Oneida Lake, New York. Trans. Am. Fish. Soc. 101:720-723. (WALLEYE; ECOLOGY; MORTALITY; MOVEMENTS AND MIGRATIONS; POPULATION STUDIES;).

2087. Norcross, J. J. 1986. The walleye fishery of Michigan's Lake Gogebic. Mich. Dept. Nat. Res., Tech. Rep. No. 86-9: 26 pp. (WALLEYE; AGE AND GROWTH; INTRODUCTIONS; POPULATION STUDIES; REGULATIONS; SPAWNING STUDIES;).

2088. Nord, R. C. 1964. The 1962-1963 sport fishery survey of the upper Mississippi River. Upper Miss. River Conserv. Comm. 209 pp. (SAUGER; WALLEYE; CREEL CENSUS;).

2089. Nord, R. C. 1967. A compendium of fishery information on the Upper Mississippi River. Upper Miss. River Conserv. Comm. 238 pp. (SAUGER; WALLEYE; AGE AND GROWTH; ECOLOGY; MARKING; MOVEMENT AND MIGRATIONS; SPAWNING STUDIES;).

2090. Norden, C. R. 1961. The identification of larval yellow perch *(Perca flavescens),* and walleye *(Stizostedion vitreum).* Copeia 1961 3:282-288. (WALLEYE; MORPHOLOGY; TAXONOMY;).

2091. Nordqvist, O. 1894. Some notes about American fish culture. U.S. Fish. Comm., Bull. 13:197-200. (WALLEYE; PROPAGATION;).

2092. Nowak, A. 1985. Computer analysis of the Opasatika Complex creel survey 1973-1981, Kapuskasing District. Ont. Min. Nat. Res., Rep. 13 pp. (WALLEYE; CREEL CENSUS;).

2093. Nunan, C. P. 1982. Initial effects of the exploitation of walleye *(Stizostedion vitreum)* on the boreal percid community of Henderson Lake, Northwestern Ontario. M.S. Thesis, Lakehead Univ., Ont. 127pp. (WALLEYE; COMMUNITY DYNAMICS; ECOLOGY; MORTALITY; POPULATION STUDIES;).

2094. Nurnberger, P. K. 1930. The plant and animal food of the fishes of Big Sandy Lake. Trans. Am. Fish. Soc. 60:253-259. (WALLEYE; COMMUNITY DYNAMICS; FOOD STUDIES;).

2095. Nursall, J. R., and M. E. Pinsent. 1969. Aggregations of spottail shiners and yellow perch. J. Fish. Research Board Can. 26:1672-1676. (WALLEYE; BEHAVIOR; COMMUNITY DYNAMICS; ECOLOGY;).

2096. Nutting, C. C. 1893. Report on zoological explorations on the Lower Saskatchewan River. Iowa State Univ., Lab. Nat. Hist., Bull. 2:231-383. (WALLEYE; GEOGRAPHICAL DISTRIBUTION;).

2097. O'Donnell, D. J. 1935. Annotated list of fishes of Illinois. Ill. Nat. Hist. Surv., Bull. 20:473-500. (SAUGER; WALLEYE; GEOGRAPHICAL DISTRIBUTION;).

2098. O'Donnell, D. J. 1942. A study of the natural propagation of walleyed pike in Devil's Lake Burnett County, Wisconsin. Wis. Conserv. Dept., Progress Rep. 1: 5 pp. (WALLEYE; SPAWNING STUDIES;).

2099. O'Donnell, D. J. 1943. The fish population in three small lakes in northern Wisconsin. Trans. Am. Fish. Soc. 72:187-196. (WALLEYE; TOXICANTS;).

2100. O'Donnell, D. J., and W. S. Churchill. 1954. Certain physical, chemical and biological aspects of the Brule River, Douglas County, Wisconsin. Brule River survey report No. 11. Trans. Wis. Acad. Sci., Arts Letters 43:201-255. (WALLEYE; STOCKING;).

2101. O'Malley, H. 1917. The distribution of fish and fish eggs during the fiscal year 1916. U.S. Bur. Fish., Annu. Rep. (1916):1-111. (WALLEYE; PROPAGATION; STOCKING;).

2102. O'Malley, H. 1918. The distribution of fish and fish eggs during the fiscal year 1917. U.S. Bur. Fish., Annu. Rep. (1917):1-97. (WALLEYE; PROPAGATION; STOCKING;).

2103. O'Malley, H. 1919. The distribution of fish and fish eggs during the fiscal year 1918. U.S. Bur. Fish., Annu. Rep. (1918):1-76. (WALLEYE; PROPAGATION; STOCKING;).

2104. Odell, T. T. 1930. A biological survey of the Champlain watershed. V. The fishes of Lake Champlain. N.Y. Conserv. Dept., Suppl. 19th Annu. Rep. (1929):130-138. (SAUGER; WALLEYE; ECOLOGY; SAMPLING METHODS;).

2105. Odell, T. T. 1932. A biological survey of the Oswegatchie and Black River systems. III. Lakes of the Oswegatchie and Black River systems. N.Y. Conserv. Dept., Suppl. 21st Annu. Rep. (1931):94-119. (WALLEYE; ECOLOGY; IMPOUNDMENTS;).

2106. Odell, T. T. 1932. The depth distribution of certain species of fish in some of the lakes of New York. Trans. Am. Fish. Soc. 62:331-335. (WALLEYE; BEHAVIOR; ECOLOGY; GEOGRAPHICAL DISTRIBUTION; PHYSIOLOGY;).

2107. Odell, T. T. 1933. A biological survey of the Upper Hudson watershed. III. Lakes of the Upper Hudson watershed. N.Y. Conserv. Dept., Suppl. 22nd Annu. Rep. (1932):102-129. (WALLEYE; STOCKING;).

2108. Odell, T. T. 1934. The life history and ecological relationship of the alewife *(Pomolobus pseudoharaengus)* in Seneca Lake, New York. Trans. Am. Fish. Soc. 64:118-126. (WALLEYE; FOOD STUDIES;).

2109. Odell, T. T. 1940. A biological survey of the Lake Ontario watershed. III. Bays and ponds of the shore area. N.Y. Conserv. (1939):82-97. (WALLEYE; GEOGRAPHICAL DISTRIBUTION;).

2110. Odell, T. T., and W. C. Senning. 1936. A biological survey of the Delaware and Susquehana watersheds. III. Lakes and ponds of the Delaware and Susquehanna watersheds. N.Y. Conserv. Dept., Suppl. 25th Annu. Rep. (1935):89-121. (WALLEYE; INTRODUCTIONS; STOCKING;).

2111. Odell, T. T., and W. C. Senning. 1937. A biological survey of the lower Hudson watershed. III. Lakes and ponds of the lower Hudson area. N.Y. Conserv. Dept., Suppl. 26th Annu. Rep. (1936):45-103. (WALLEYE; STOCKING;).

2112. Odell, T. T., and W. C. Senning. 1938. A biological survey of the Allegheny and Chemung watersheds. III. Lakes and ponds of the Allegheny and Chemung watersheds. N.Y. Conserv. Dept., Suppl. 27th Annu. Rep. (1937):74-101. (WALLEYE; IMPOUNDMENTS; STOCKING;).

2113. Odlaug, T. O. 1956. Helminth parasites reported from vertebrates in Minnesota. Flicker 28:138-148. (WALLEYE; PATHOLOGY;).

2114. Olgesby, R. T., J. H. Leach, and J. L. Forney. 1987. Potential *Stizostedion* yield as a function of chlorophyll concentration with special reference to Lake Erie. Can. J. Fish. Aquat. Sci. 44(Suppl. 2):166-170. (WALLEYE; PRODUCTIVITY;).

2115. Oliver, D. R. 1960. The macroscopic bottom fauna of Lac la Rongee Saskatchewan. J. Fish. Research Board Can. 17:607-624. (WALLEYE; COMMUNITY DYNAMICS; PATHOLOGY;).

2116. Olsen, E. 1968. Population dynamics of the walleye in lakes. Wis. Conserv. Dept., Fed. Aid Fish Wildl. Restor. Proj. F-83-R-3, Job No. VII-B: 12 pp. (WALLEYE; ECOLOGY; MOVEMENT AND MIGRATIONS; SAMPLING METHODS;).

2117. Olsen, E. K. 1979. Distribution of pelagic yellow perch and walleye fry in two northern Wisconsin lakes. Ph.D. Dissertation, Univ. Wis., Madison, Wis. 100 pp. (WALLEYE; MOVEMENT AND MIGRATIONS;).

2118. Olson, D. E. 1955. Notes on the size, structure and mortality rates of the walleye *(Stizostedion vitreum)* population of Lake Sallie. Minn. Dept. Conserv., Invest. Rep. No. 158: 7 pp. (WALLEYE; AGE AND GROWTH; MARKING; MORTALITY; POPULATION STUDIES; SPAWNING STUDIES;).

2119. Olson, D. E. 1958. Statistics of a walleye *(Stizostedion vitreum)* sport fishery in a Minnesota lake. Trans. Am. Fish. Soc. 87:52-72. (WALLEYE; AGE AND GROWTH; CREEL CENSUS; MARKING; MOVEMENT AND MIGRATIONS; POPULATION STUDIES; STOCKING;).

2120. Olson, D. E. 1963. Role of the white sucker in Minnesota waters. Proc. Minn. Acad. Sci. 31:68-73. (WALLEYE; COMMUNITY DYNAMICS; FOOD STUDIES; HABITAT IMPROVEMENT;).

2121. Olson, D. E. 1966. Physical characteristics of fertilized and unfertilized walleye eggs during early stages of development. Minn. Dept. Conserv., Invest. Rep. No. 4:31-38. (WALLEYE; EMBRYOLOGY;).

2122. Olson, D. E. 1968. Sex ratio of young-of-the-year walleye in Minnesota rearing ponds and lakes. Prog. Fish-Cult. 30:196-202. (WALLEYE; AGE AND GROWTH; ECOLOGY; GENETICS; PROPAGATION;).

2123. Olson, D. E. 1971. An improved method of artificial fertilization of walleye eggs. Minn. Dept. Nat. Res., Invest. Rep. No. 310: 10 pp. (WALLEYE; PROPAGATION;).

2124. Olson, D. E. 1974. Effects of elevated temperature and fry density on initiation of feeding by walleye fry. Minn. Dept. Nat. Res., Invest. Rep. No. 327: 7 pp. (WALLEYE; BEHAVIOR; ECOLOGY; FOOD STUDIES; MORTALITY;).

2125. Olson, D. E. 1980. Comparison of marks on scales and dorsal spine sections as indicators of walleye age. Minn. Dept. Nat. Res., Invest. Rep. No. 371: 17 pp. (WALLEYE; AGE AND GROWTH;).

2126. Olson, D. E. 1981. Experimental incubation of fish eggs in a moist-air environment. Minn. Dept. Nat. Res., Invest. Rep. No. 373: 13 pp. (WALLEYE; PROPAGATION;).

2127. Olson, D. E., D. H. Schupp, and V. Macins. 1978. An hypothesis of homing behavior of walleyes as related to observed patterns of passive and active movements. Pages 52-57 in R.L. Kendall, ed. Selected coolwater fishes of North America. Am. Fish. Soc. Sp. Publ. No. 11, Washington, D.C. (WALL-EYE; FOOD STUDIES; MARKING; MOVEMENTS AND MIGRATIONS; SPAWNING STUDIES;).

2128. Olson, D. E., and W. J. Scidmore. 1962. Homing behavior of spawning walleyes. Trans. Am. Fish. Soc. 91:355-361. (WALLEYE; BEHAVIOR; ECOLOGY; MARKING; MOVEMENT AND MIGRATIONS; POPULATION STUDIES;).

2129. Olson, D. E., and W. J. Scidmore. 1963. Homing tendency of spawning white suckers in Many Point Lake, Minnesota. Trans. Am. Fish. Soc. 92:13-16. (WALLEYE; COMMUNITY DYNAMICS;).

2130. Olson, D. E., and M. Wesloh. 1962. A record of six years of angling on Many Point Lake, Becker County, Minnesota, with special reference to the effects of walleye (Stizostedion vitreum) fingerling stocking. Minn. Dept. Conserv., Invest. Rep. No. 247: 7 pp. (WALLEYE; COMMUNITY DYNAMICS; CREEL CENSUS; LIFE HISTORY; STOCKING;).

2131. Olson, S. T., and W. H. Marshall. 1952. The common loon in Minnesota. Univ. Minn. Mus. Nat. Hist., Occasional paper 5: 77 pp. (WALLEYE; COMMUNITY DYNAMICS;).

2132. Olver, C. H. 1966. Selection of a mesh size for the commercial gill-net fishery of the walleye, Stizostedion vitreum vitreum (Mitchill), in Sachigo Lake, Ontario. M.S. Thesis, Univ. Mich., Ann Arbor, Mich. 81 pp. (WALLEYE; AGE AND GROWTH; COMMERCIAL FISHERIES; FISHING GEAR; MORTALITY; POPULATION STUDIES; SPAWNING STUDIES;).

2133. Olver, C. H., J. M. Casselman, P. J. Colby, and N. R. Payne. 1982. Report of the Georgian Bay walleye (Stizostedion vitreum) review committee. Ont. Min. Nat. Res., Sept. 1982: 68 pp. (WALLEYE; AGE AND GROWTH; COMMERCIAL FISHERIES; CREEL CENSUS; ECOLOGY; HABITAT DEGRADATION; MOVEMENTS AND MIGRATIONS; POPULATION STUDIES; SPAWNING STUDIES; STOCKING; WATER LEVELS;).

2134. Olynyk, J. P. R. 1980. An analysis of sauger maturity regimes in southern Lake Winnipeg. Man. Dept. Nat. Res., Manuscript Rep. No. 80-36: 52 pp. (SAUGER; WALLEYE; AGE AND GROWTH; POPULATION STUDIES; SPAWNING STUDIES;).

2135. Olynyk, J. P. R. 1982. Lake Winnipeg walleye fecundity. Man. Dept. Nat. Res., Manuscript Rep. No. 82-27: 21 pp. (WALLEYE; POPULATION STUDIES; SPAWNING STUDIES;).

2136. Ontario Ministry of Natural Resources, Tourism and Recreation, Minnesota Department of Natural Resources. 1984. Minnesota-Ontario boundary waters fisheries atlas for Lake of the Woods, Rainy Lake and the Rainy River. Minn. Dept. Nat. Res. 103 pp. (SAUGER; WALLEYE; COMMERCIAL FISHERIES; CREEL CENSUS; MARKING; MOVEMENT AND MIGRATIONS; REGULATIONS; SOCIO-ECONOMICS OF FISHERIES;).

2137. Ontario Ministry of Natural Resources. 1970. An indexed bibliography of North American Stizostedion. Ont. Dept. Lands. & Forests. Res Info. Pap. 38 pp. (SAUGER; WALLEYE; ECOLOGY; LIFE HISTORY;).

2138. Ontario Ministry of Natural Resources. 1972. Creel census Beaverhouse Lake Quetico Park 1971 and 1972. Ont. Min. Nat. Res., Rep. 4 pp. (WALLEYE; CREEL CENSUS;).

2139. Ontario Ministry of Natural Resources. 1977. Gravelly Bay and Point Abino fishery survey. Ont. Min. Nat. Res., Rep. 20 pp. (WALLEYE; CREEL CENSUS;).

2140. Ontario Ministry of Natural Resources. 1977. Onaman Lake creel census — 1977. Ont. Min. Nat. Res., Rep. 16 pp. (WALLEYE; AGE AND GROWTH; CREEL CENSUS;).

2141. Ontario Ministry of Natural Resources. 1978. Onaman Lake creel census — 1978. Ont. Min. Nat. Res., Rep. 10 pp. (WALLEYE; CREEL CENSUS;).

2142. Ontario Ministry of Natural Resources. 1980. Lake Scugog winter fishing 1979-

1980. Ont. Min. Nat. Res., Rep. 6 pp. (WALLEYE; CREEL CENSUS;).

2143. Ontario Ministry of Natural Resources. 1981. Lake St. Clair fisheries report 1980. Ont. Min. Nat. Res., Lake St. Clair Fish. Assess. Unit Rep. 16 pp. (WALLEYE; AGE AND GROWTH; COMMERCIAL FISHERIES; CREEL CENSUS; REGULATIONS;).

2144. Ontario Ministry of Natural Resources. 1982. A public information package concerning the Shoal Lake walleye fishery. Ont. Min. Nat. Res., Lake of the Woods Assess. Unit Rep. 13 pp. (WALLEYE; AGE AND GROWTH; COMMERCIAL FISHERIES; CREEL CENSUS; POPULATION STUDIES; SPAWNING STUDIES;).

2145. Ontario Ministry of Natural Resources. 1982. Lake St. Clair fisheries report 1981. Ont. Min. Nat. Res., Lake St. Clair Fish. Assess. Unit. 22 pp. (WALLEYE; AGE AND GROWTH; COMMERCIAL FISHERIES; CREEL CENSUS; REGULATIONS;).

2146. Ontario Ministry of Natural Resources. 1983. A summer creel survey of seven area lakes in the Temagami District. Ont. Min. Nat. Res., Rep. 36 pp. (WALLEYE; CREEL CENSUS;).

2147. Ontario Ministry of Natural Resources. 1983. Lake St. Clair fisheries report 1982. Ont. Min. Nat. Res., Lake St. Clair Fish. Assess. Unit 25 pp. (WALLEYE; AGE AND GROWTH; COMMERCIAL FISHERIES; CREEL CENSUS; REGULATIONS;).

2148. Ontario Ministry of Natural Resources. 1984. Lake St. Clair fisheries report 1983. Ont. Min. Nat. Res., Lake St. Clair Fish. Assess. Unit 24 pp. (WALLEYE; AGE AND GROWTH; COMMERCIAL FISHERIES; CREEL CENSUS; REGULATIONS;).

2149. Ontario Ministry of Natural Resources. 1984. Report of the Lake Huron fisheries assessment unit Ontario Ministry of Natural Resources to the Lake Huron committee. Ont. Min. Nat. Res. 31 pp. (WALLEYE; COMMERCIAL FISHERIES; POPULATION STUDIES;).

2150. Ontario Ministry of Natural Resources. 1985. Annual report to the Great Lakes Fishery Commission's Lake Ontario Committee. Ont. Min. Nat. Res., LOFAU Rep.

(84.11): 66 pp. (WALLEYE; COMMERCIAL FISHERIES; CREEL CENSUS; MOVEMENT AND MIGRATIONS; POPULATION STUDIES; REGULATIONS;).

2151. Ontario Ministry of Natural Resources. 1985. Bay of Quinte summer creel census 1985. Ont. Min. Nat. Res., LOFAU Rep. (85.1): 63 pp. (WALLEYE; CREEL CENSUS;).

2152. Ontario Ministry of Natural Resources. 1985. Lake Erie fisheries report 1984. Ont. Min. Nat. Res. 31 pp. (WALLEYE; AGE AND GROWTH; COMMERCIAL FISHERIES; CREEL CENSUS;).

2153. Ontario Ministry of Natural Resources. 1985. Lake St. Clair fisheries report 1984. Ont. Min. Nat. Res., Lake St. Clair Fish. Assess. Unit 22 pp. (WALLEYE; AGE AND GROWTH; COMMERCIAL FISHERIES; CREEL CENSUS; REGULATIONS;).

2154. Ontario Ministry of Natural Resources. 1985. Walleye stocking assessment five year operational plan. Ont. Min. Nat. Res., Eastern Region, File Rep. No. 1: 14 pp. (WALLEYE; STOCKING;).

2155. Ontario Ministry of Natural Resources. 1986. 1985 annual report to the Great Lakes Fishery Commission's Lake Ontario Committee. Ont. Min. Nat. Res., LOFAU Rep. (85.30): 115 pp. (WALLEYE; COMMERCIAL FISHERIES; CREEL CENSUS; POPULATION STUDIES; REGULATIONS;).

2156. Ontario Ministry of Natural Resources. 1986. Lake St. Clair fisheries report 1985. Ont. Min. Nat. Res., Lake St. Clair Fish. Assess. Unit 32 pp. (WALLEYE; AGE AND GROWTH; COMMERCIAL FISHERIES; CREEL CENSUS; REGULATIONS;).

2157. Osborn, T. C. 1974. Fish population dynamics in Mabel Lake. Minn. Dept. Nat. Res., Fed. Aid Fish Wildl. Restor. Proj. F-26-R-05, Job No. 104.2: 16 pp. (WALLEYE; AGE AND GROWTH; COMMUNITY DYNAMICS; CREEL CENSUS; FISHING GEAR; MARKING; POPULATION STUDIES;).

2158. Osborn, T. C. 1974. Walleye (Stizostedion vitreum) food habits. Minn. Dept. Nat. Res., Fed. Aid Fish Wildl. Rest. Proj. F-26-R-05, Job No. 104.3: 11 pp. (WALLEYE; FOOD STUDIES;).

2159. Osborn, T. C., D. B. Ernst, and Schupp. D. H. 1981. The effects of water levels and other factors on walleye and northern pike reproduction and abundance in Rainy and Namakan Reservoirs. Minn. Dept. Nat. Res., Invest. Rep. No. 374: 32 pp. (SAUGER; WALLEYE; COMMERCIAL FISHERIES; POPULATION STUDIES; SPAWNING STUDIES; WATER LEVELS;).

2160. Osborn, T. C., and D. H. Schupp. 1985. Long-term changes in the Lake Winnibigoshish walleye sport fishery. Minn. Dept. Nat. Res., Invest. Rep. No. 381: 41 pp. (WALLEYE; AGE AND GROWTH; CREEL CENSUS; MARKING; MOVEMENTS AND MIGRATIONS; SPAWNING STUDIES;).

2161. Osburn, R. C. 1901. The fishes of Ohio. Ohio State Acad. Sci., Spec. Paper 4: 105 pp. (SAUGER; WALLEYE; MORPHOLOGY; TAXONOMY;).

2162. Osburn, R. C., E. L. Wickliff, and M. B. Trautman. 1930. A revised list of the fishes of Ohio. Ohio J. Sci. 30:169-176. (SAUGER; WALLEYE; GEOGRAPHICAL DISTRIBUTION;).

2163. Oseid, D. M. 1977. Control of fungus growth on fish eggs by *Asellus militaris* and *Gammarus pseudolimnaeus*. Trans. Am. Fish. Soc. 106:192-195. (WALLEYE; PROPAGATION;).

2164. Oseid, D. M., and L. L. Smith, Jr. 1971. Survival and hatching of walleye eggs at various dissolved oxygen levels. Prog. Fish-Cult. 33:81-85. (WALLEYE; ECOLOGY; SPAWNING STUDIES;).

2165. Osterberg, D. 1979. Food consumption, feeding habits, and growth of walleye *(Stizostedion vitreum)* and sauger *(Stizostedion canadense)* in the Ottawa River near Ottawa-Hull. Ph.D. Dissertation, Univ. Ottawa, Canada (SAUGER; WALLEYE; AGE AND GROWTH; FOOD STUDIES;).

2166. Otto, G. R., and T. L. Jahn. 1943. Internal myxosporidian infections in some fishes of the Okoboji region. Proc. Iowa Acad. Sci. 50:323-335. (WALLEYE; PATHOLOGY;).

2167. Ouellette, J., B. Jolkowski, and E. Armstrong. 1984. Detour Lake Road fisheries studies VI. winter creel survey 1984. Ont. Min. Nat. Res., Rep. 13 pp. (WALLEYE; CREEL CENSUS;).

2168. Oughton, J. P. 1930. Game fish of the Trent Canal system. Roy. Ont. Mus., Ichthyol. Libr., Manuscript 11 pp. (WALLEYE; INTRODUCTIONS; MOVEMENT AND MIGRATIONS; STOCKING;).

2169. Owen, J. B., and F. G. Duerr. 1974. Nutrient sources and lake nutrient dynamics as affected by commercial and sport fishery harvests in Lake Ashtabula, North Dakota. N.D. State Game Fish Dept., Rep. No. 1322: 93 pp. (WALLEYE; COMMUNITY DYNAMICS; CREEL CENSUS; HABITAT DEGRADATION; IMPOUNDMENTS;).

2170. Paetz, M. J. 1958. The sauger a newly discovered game fish in Alberta. Alta. Dept. Lands Forests, Lands Forest Wildl., Pub. 1:24-26. (SAUGER; WALLEYE; MORPHOLOGY; TAXONOMY;).

2171. Pageau, G., Y. Gravel, and L. Levesque. 1971. The ichthyofauna and flora of Lake St. Louis on the St. Lawrence River near Montreal, Quebec: general features and recent changes. Proc, 14th Conf. Great Lakes Research. 14:79-89. (WALLEYE; GEOGRAPHICAL DISTRIBUTION;).

2172. Palmer, D. E., H. C. Hansel, J. M. Beyer, S. C. Vigg, W. T. Yasutake, P. T. Lofy, S. D. Duke, M. J. Parsley, M. G. Mesa, L. A. Prendergast, R. Burkhart, C. Burley, D. W. Eib, and T. P. Poe. 1985. Feeding activity, rate of consumption, daily ration and prey selection of major predators in John Day Reservoir, 1985. Annual Rep. (1985) to Bonneville Power Admin., U.S.F.W.S., Nat. Fish. Research Cent., Cook, Wash. 105 pp. (WALLEYE; COMMUNITY DYNAMICS; FOOD STUDIES; IMPOUNDMENTS;).

2173. Palmer, E. L. 1950. Fish and fishing. Cornell Rural School leafl. 44:1-32. (WALLEYE; TAXONOMY;).

2174. Panek, F. M. 1981. The warmwater sport fishery of eastern Lake Ontario. N.Y. Fish Game J. 28:178-190. (WALLEYE; CREEL CENSUS;).

2175. Pankhurst, N. W., G. Van Der Kraak, and R. E. Peter. 1986. Effects of human chorionic gonadotropin, DES-GLY[10] (D-ALA[6]) LHRH-ethylamide and pimozide on oocyte final maturation, ovulation and levels of plasma sex steroids in the walleye *(Stizostedion vitreum)*. Fish Physiol. Biochem. 1:45-54. (WALLEYE; PHYSIOLOGY;).

2176. Paragamian, V. L. 1977. Fish population development in two Iowa flood control reservoirs and the impact of fish stocking and floodwater management. Iowa Conserv. Comm., Tech. Series 77-1: 64 pp. (WALLEYE; AGE AND GROWTH; COMMUNITY DYNAMICS; CREEL CENSUS; IMPOUNDMENTS; POPULATION STUDIES; STOCKING; WATER LEVELS;).

2177. Paragamian, V. L. 1984. Diversity and standing stocks of stream fishes. Iowa Conserv. Comm., Fish. Sec., Federal Aid Fish Wildl. Restoration Proj. F-99-R, Job 1, 2 & 3: 66 pp. (WALLEYE; AGE AND GROWTH; COMMUNITY DYNAMICS; POPULATION STUDIES;).

2178. Parker, R. A. 1958. Some effects of thinning on a population of fishes. Ecology 39:304-317. (WALLEYE; GEOGRAPHICAL DISTRIBUTION;).

2179. Parmalee, P. W. 1962. The faunal complex of the fisher site, Illinois. Am. Midl. Nat. 68:399-408. (WALLEYE; GEOGRAPHICAL DISTRIBUTION;).

2180. Parmalee, P. W. 1964. Vertebrate remains from an historic archaeological site in Rock Island County, Illinois. Trans. Ill. Acad. Sci. 57:167-174. (WALLEYE; GEOGRAPHICAL DISTRIBUTION;).

2181. Parnell, I. W. 1934. Fish parasites and their importance. Trans. Am. Fish. Soc. 64:390-400. (SAUGER; WALLEYE; PATHOLOGY;).

2182. Parsons, B. 1987. Population dynamics and harvest of maintained walleye populations in southern Minnesota lakes. Minn. Dept. Nat. Res., Fed. Aid Fish Wildl. Restor. Proj. F-26-R-18,Study No. 134: 10 pp. (WALLEYE; MARKING; POPULATION STUDIES; STOCKING;).

2183. Parsons, J. W. 1958. Fishery management problems and possibilities of large southeastern reservoirs. Trans. Am. Fish. Soc. 87:333-355. (SAUGER; WALLEYE; IMPOUNDMENTS;).

2184. Parsons, J. W. 1967. Contributions of year-classes of blue pike to the commercial fishery of Lake Erie, 1943-59. J. Fish. Research Board Can. 24:1035-1066. (WALLEYE; AGE AND GROWTH; COMMERCIAL FISHERIES; POPULATION STUDIES;).

2185. Parsons, J. W. 1970. Walleye fishery of Lake Erie in 1943-62 with emphasis on contributions of the 1942-61 year class. J. Fish. Research Board Can. 27:1475-1489. (WALLEYE; AGE AND GROWTH; COMMERCIAL FISHERIES; ECOLOGY; COMMERCIAL FISHERIES;).

2186. Parsons, J. W. 1971. Selected food preferences of walleyes of the 1959 year class in Lake Erie. Trans. Am. Fish. Soc. 100:474-485. (WALLEYE; COMMUNITY DYNAMICS; FOOD STUDIES;).

2187. Parsons, J. W. 1972. Life history and production of walleyes of the 1959 year-class in western Lake Erie, 1959-62. Trans. Am. Fish. Soc. 101:655-661. (WALLEYE; AGE AND GROWTH; COMMERCIAL FISHERIES; MARKING; MOVEMENTS AND MIGRATIONS; SPAWNING STUDIES;).

2188. Pasko, D. G. 1957. Carry Falls Reservoir investigations. N.Y. Fish Game J. 4:1-31. (WALLEYE; AGE AND GROWTH; CREEL CENSUS; IMPOUNDMENTS; INTRODUCTIONS;).

2189. Passino, D. R. M., and S. B. Smith. 1987. Acute bioassays and hazard evaluation of representative contaminants detected in Great lakes fish. Environ. Toxicol. Chem. 6:901-907. (WALLEYE; HABITAT DEGRADATION; TOXICANTS;).

2190. Pate, V. S. L. 1933. A biological survey of the Upper Hudson watershed. IV. Studies on fish food in selected areas. N.Y. Conserv. Dept., Suppl. 22nd Annu. Rep. (1932):130-155. (WALLEYE; FOOD STUDIES;).

2191. Pate, V. S. L. 1934. A biological survey of the Raquette watershed. IV. Studies of the fish food supply in selected areas of the Raquette watershed. N.Y. Conserv. Dept., Suppl. 23rd Annu. Rep. (1933):136-157. (WALLEYE; FOOD STUDIES;).

2192. Patriarche, M. H., and R. S. Campbell. 1958. The development of the fish population in a new flood-control reservoir in Missouri, 1948-54. Trans. Am. Fish. Soc. 87:240-258.

(SAUGER; WALLEYE; IMPOUND-
MENTS; POPULATION STUDIES;).

2193. Patterson, D. L. 1953. The walleye *(Stizoste-
dion vitreum)* population in Escanaba Lake,
Vilas County, Wisconsin. Trans. Am. Fish.
Soc. 82:34-41. (WALLEYE; AGE AND
GROWTH; CREEL CENSUS; INTRO-
DUCTIONS; MARKING; POPULATION
STUDIES;).

2194. Patterson, R. L., and K. D. Smith. 1982. Impact of power plant entrainment of ichthyo-
plankton on juvenile recruitment of four
fishes in western Lake Erie in 1975-77. J.
Great Lakes Research 8:558-569. (WALL-
EYE; ECOLOGY; MORTALITY;).

2195. Paulus, R. D. 1969. Walleye fry food habits in
Lake Erie. Ohio Dept. Nat. Res., Fish.
Monogr. No. 2: 45 pp. (WALLEYE; ECOL-
OGY; FOOD STUDIES; SPAWNING
STUDIES;).

2196. Paxton, K. O. 1975. Effects of ice fishing on
yellow perch in an Ohio upground reservoir.
Ohio Dept. Nat. Res., Fish Wildl. Rep. No. 5:
11 pp. (WALLEYE; CREEL CENSUS; IM-
POUNDMENTS;).

2197. Paxton, K. O., and R. E. Day. 1974. Evalua-
tion of the fishery of upground reservoirs in
Ohio. Ohio Dept. Nat. Res., Fed. Aid Fish
Wildl. Restor. Proj. F-29-R-13, Study No. 3:
144 pp. (WALLEYE; ECOLOGY; FOOD
STUDIES; IMPOUNDMENTS; POPU-
LATION STUDIES; SPAWNING STUD-
IES;).

2198. Paxton, K. O., and R. E. Day. 1974. Ecological study of the experimental Killdeer Reservoir. Ohio Dept. Nat. Res., Fed. Aid Fish
Wildl. Restor. Proj. F-29-R-13, Study No. 4:
83 pp. (WALLEYE; AGE AND GROWTH;
COMMUNITY DYNAMICS; ECOLOGY;
FOOD STUDIES; IMPOUNDMENTS;).

2199. Paxton, K. O., and R. E. Day. 1979. The devel-
opment of an initial stocking program for
new upground reservoirs. Ohio Dept. Nat.
Res., Fed. Aid Fish Wildl. Restor. Proj. F-
29-R, Study No. 7: 106 pp. (WALLEYE;
ECOLOGY; FOOD STUDIES; IM-
POUNDMENTS; POPULATION STUD-
IES; STOCKING; WATER LEVELS;).

2200. Paxton, K. O., and R. E. Day. 1981. An evaluation of supplemental stocking as a method
of stabilizing yellow perch recruitment and

harvest in upground reservoirs. Ohio Dept.
Nat. Res., Fed. Aid Fish Wildl. Restor. Proj.
F-29-R, Study 8: 27 pp. (WALLEYE; COM-
MUNITY DYNAMICS;).

2201. Paxton, K. O., R. E. Day, M. R. Austin, and F.
Stevenson. 1980. Evaluation of the fishery
of upground reservoirs in Ohio. Ohio Dept.
Nat. Res., Fed. Aid Fish Wildl. Restor. Proj.
F-29-R, Study No. 3: 59 pp. (WALLEYE;
AGE AND GROWTH; COMMUNITY DY-
NAMICS; CREEL CENSUS; ECOLOGY;
FOOD STUDIES; IMPOUNDMENTS;
POPULATION STUDIES; SPAWNING
STUDIES; WATER LEVELS;).

2202. Paxton, K. O., R. E. Day, and F. Stevenson.
1981. Limnology and fish populations of
Ferguson Reservoir, Ohio, from 1971-1975.
Ohio Dept. Nat. Res., Fish Wildl. Rep No. 8:
53 pp. (WALLEYE; AGE AND GROWTH;
COMMUNITY DYNAMICS; ECOLOGY;
FOOD STUDIES; IMPOUNDMENTS;
POPULATION STUDIES; SPAWNING
STUDIES;).

2203. Paxton, K. O., and F. Stevenson. 1978. Food,
growth, and exploitation of percids in Ohio's
upground reservoirs. Pages 270-277 *in* R.L.
Kendall, ed. Selected coolwater fishes of
North America. Am. Fish. Soc. Sp. Publ.
No. 11, Washington, D.C. (WALLEYE;
AGE AND GROWTH; CREEL CENSUS;
FOOD STUDIES;).

2204. Paxton, K. O., and F. Stevenson. 1979. Influence of artificial structures on angler harvest from Killdeer Reservoir, Ohio. Ohio
Dept. Nat. Res., Fed. Aid Fish Wildl. Restor. Proj. F-29-R-6: 70-76. (WALLEYE;
CREEL CENSUS; HABITAT IMPROVE-
MENT;).

2205. Payer, R. D., D. L. Pereira, M. L. Larson, J. A.
Younk, R. V. Frie, D. H. Schupp, and T. C.
Osborn. 1987. Status and simulation model
of Lake of the Woods, Minnesota, walleye
fishery. Minn. Dept. Nat. Res., Invest. Rep.
No. 389: 160 pp. (SAUGER; WALLEYE;
AGE AND GROWTH; COMMERCIAL
FISHERIES; COMMUNITY DY-
NAMICS; CREEL CENSUS; FISHING
GEAR; MARKING; MORTALITY; POPU-
LATION STUDIES; PRODUCTIVITY;
REGULATIONS;).

2206. Payer, R. D., R. B. Pierce, and D. L. Pereira.
1987. Hooking mortality of walleye caught
on live and artificial baits. Minn. Dept. Nat.

Res., Invest. Rep. No. 390: 15 pp. (WALLEYE; CREEL CENSUS; MORTALITY; REGULATIONS;).

2207. Payne, N. R. 1964. A preliminary report on the Mississagi River walleye study, Sault St. Marie District. Ont. Dept. Lands Forest., Manuscript Rep. 24 pp. (WALLEYE; AGE AND GROWTH; COMMERCIAL FISHERIES; CREEL CENSUS; ECOLOGY; MARKING; POPULATION STUDIES;).

2208. Payne, N. R. 1964. Progress report on the Bright Lake fisheries investigation, Sault St. Marie District. Ont. Dept. Lands Forest., Manuscript Rep. 8 pp. (WALLEYE; AGE AND GROWTH; CREEL CENSUS;).

2209. Payne, N. R. 1964. The life history of the walleye, *Stizostedion vitreum*, in the Bay of Quinte. M.A. Thesis, Univ. Toronto, Toronto, Ont. 40 pp. (WALLEYE; AGE AND GROWTH; ECOLOGY; FOOD STUDIES; MARKING; MOVEMENT AND MIGRATIONS; POPULATION STUDIES; SPAWNING STUDIES;).

2210. Payne, N. R. 1965. A progress report on the Mississagi River walleye *(Stizostedion vitreum)* study, Sault Ste. Marie District. Ont. Dept. Lands Forest., Manuscript Rep. 29 pp. (WALLEYE; AGE AND GROWTH; COMMERCIAL FISHERIES; CREEL CENSUS; ECOLOGY; FOOD STUDIES; MARKING; MOVEMENT AND MIGRATIONS; POPULATION STUDIES;).

2211. Payne, N. R. 1967. The Mississagi walleye study in 1966. Ont. Dept. Lands Forest., Manuscript Rep. 4 pp. (WALLEYE; COMMERCIAL FISHERIES; CREEL CENSUS; MARKING; POPULATION STUDIES;).

2212. Payne, P. M. 1975. Year class abundance of walleyes in Clear Lake, Iowa (1958-1974) with particular reference to fry stocking. M.S. Thesis, Iowa State Univ., Ames, Iowa. 44 pp. (WALLEYE; AGE AND GROWTH; POPULATION STUDIES; STOCKING;).

2213. Payne, P. M. 1978. Methods in determining annual production in walleye, 1948-1974 in Clear Lake, Iowa. Iowa Coop. Fish. Research Unit, Iowa St. Univ., Ames, Project No. 2076: 69 pp. (WALLEYE; AGE AND GROWTH; FISHING GEAR; MORTALITY; POPULATION STUDIES; PRODUCTIVITY;).

2214. Pearse, A. S. 1918. The food of the shore fishes of certain Wisconsin lakes. U.S. Bur. Fish., Bull. 35:247-292. (WALLEYE; FOOD STUDIES;).

2215. Pearse, A. S. 1921. Fishing in Lake Michigan. Sci. Monthly. July pp. 81-91. (WALLEYE; COMMERCIAL FISHERIES;).

2216. Pearse, A. S. 1921. The distribution and food of three Wisconsin lakes in summer. Univ. Wis. Stud. Sci. 3:5-61. (SAUGER; WALLEYE; ECOLOGY; FOOD STUDIES; GEOGRAPHICAL DISTRIBUTION;).

2217. Pearse, A. S. 1924. The parasites of lake fishes. Trans. Wis. Acad. Sci., Arts, Letters 21:161-194. (WALLEYE; PATHOLOGY;).

2218. Pearse, A. S., and H. Achtenberg. 1920. Habits of yellow perch in Wisconsin lakes. U.S. Bur. Fish., Bull. 36:294-336. (WALLEYE; FOOD STUDIES;).

2219. Pellegrini, M. 1979. Woman River creel census 1979. Ont. Min. Nat. Res., Rep. 20 pp. (WALLEYE; CREEL CENSUS;).

2220. Pellegrini, M. 1984. 1982 summer creel census — Esnagi Lake. Ont. Min. Nat. Res., Rep. 63 pp. (WALLEYE; AGE AND GROWTH; CREEL CENSUS;).

2221. Pepin, S. 1986. Biometric analysis for the study of the growth of yellow perch walleye *Stizostedion vitreum vitreum* (Mitchill) in Lake St. Louis and Lake of Two Mountains (Montreal Region). Que. Min. du Loisir. de la Chasse at de la Peche. 60 pp. (WALLEYE; AGE AND GROWTH;).

2222. Pepin, S., and F. Levesque. 1985. Techniques for aging walleye applicable to populations of this species in Quebec. Que. Min. du Loisir, de la Chasse at de la Peche. 34 pp. (WALLEYE; AGE AND GROWTH;).

2223. Personius, R. G., and S. Eddy. 1955. Fishes of the Little Missouri River. Copeia 1:41-43. (SAUGER; GEOGRAPHICAL DISTRIBUTION;).

2224. Peterka, J. J. 1978. Fishes and fisheries of the Cheyenne River, North Dakota. N.D. Acad. Sci. 32:29-44. (SAUGER WALL-

EYE; GEOGRAPHICAL DISTRIBU-
TION;).

2225. Peters, J. C. 1964. Age and growth studies and analysis of bottom samples in connection with pollution studies. Mont. Fish Game Dept., Fed. Aid Fish Wildl. Restor. Proj. F-23-R-6, Jobs No. 1 and 2: 76 pp. (SAUGER; WALLEYE; AGE AND GROWTH;).

2226. Peters, L., D. Cavis, and J. Robertson. 1978. Is *Diphyllobothrium latum* currently present in northern Michigan. J. Parasitology 64:947-949. (WALLEYE; PATHOLOGY;).

2227. Peterson, A. R. 1962. A biological reconnaissance of the Upper Mississippi River. Minn. Dept. Nat. Res., Invest. Rep. No. 255: 50 pp. (WALLEYE; POPULATION STUDIES;).

2228. Peterson, A. R. 1975. Analysis of the composition of fish populations in Minnesota's rivers and streams. Minn. Dept. Nat. Res., Invest. Rep. No. 335: 34 pp. (WALLEYE; COMMUNITY DYNAMICS; POPULATION STUDIES;).

2229. Peterson, A. R. 1978. Analysis and summary of the statewide creel census that extended from 1971-75. Minn. Dept. Nat. Res., Invest. Rep. No. 349: 46 pp. (WALLEYE; CREEL CENSUS;).

2230. Peterson, J. H. 1976. Rearing of walleye pike in the Moss Lake Borrow Pit, Delta County, 1975. Mich. Dept. Nat. Res., Tech. Rep. No. 76-4: 9 pp. (WALLEYE; PROPAGATION;).

2231. Peterson, J. H. 1976. Rearing of walleye pike in the Rapid River Borrow Pit, Delta County, 1975. Mich. Dept. Nat. Res., Tech. Rep. No. 76-3: 6 pp. (WALLEYE; PROPAGATION;).

2232. Petit, G. D. 1973. Effects of dissolved oxygen on survival and behavior of selected fishes of western Lake Erie. Ohio Biol. Surv., Bull. 4: 85 pp. (WALLEYE; POPULATION STUDIES;).

2233. Pettengill, T. D. 1975. Evaluation of a walleye, *Stizostedion vitreum vitreum* (Mitchill), stocking program, Fish Lake, Michigan. M.S. Thesis, Cent. Mich. Univ., Mt. Pleasant, Mich. 36 pp. (WALLEYE; STOCKING;).

2234. Pflieger, W. L. 1975. The fishes of Missouri. Mo. Dept. Conserv., 343 pp. (SAUGER; WALLEYE; ECOLOGY; LIFE HISTORY; TAXONOMY;).

2235. Phenicie, C. K. 1950. The Fort Peck Reservoir fishing survey. Mont. Fish Game Comm., Bull. 3:19. (SAUGER; GEOGRAPHICAL DISTRIBUTION; IMPOUNDMENTS; SAMPLING METHODS;).

2236. Phillips, G. R., T. E. Lenhart, and R. W. Gregory. 1980. Relation between tropic position and mercury accumulation among fishes from the Tongue River Reservoir, Montana. Environ. Res. 22:73-80. (SAUGER; TOXICANTS;).

2237. Pikitch, E. K. 1983. Feeding ecology of the walleye in western Lake Erie and its potential consequences. Ph.D. Dissertation, Ind. Univ., Bloomington, Ind. 122 pp. (WALLEYE; AGE AND GROWTH; COMMUNITY DYNAMICS; MORTALITY;).

2238. Pilcher, K. S., and J. L. Fryer. 1980. Viral diseases of fish, a review through 1978. Diseases in which a viral etiology is suspected but unproven. Critical Reviews Microbiology 8:1-24. (WALLEYE; PATHOLOGY;).

2239. Pitlo, J. M., Jr. 1978. Walleye movement and behavior in West Lake Okoboji, Iowa. M.S. Thesis. Iowa State Univ., Ames, Iowa. 87 pp. (WALLEYE; BEHAVIOR; ECOLOGY; MARKING; MOVEMENT AND MIGRATIONS;).

2240. Pitlo, J. M., Jr. 1985. Wing and closing dam investigations. Iowa Conserv. Comm., Fed. Aid Fish Wildl. Restor. Proj. F-96-R: 56 pp. (SAUGER; WALLEYE; CREEL CENSUS; ECOLOGY; MARKING; MOVEMENT AND MIGRATIONS; SPAWNING STUDIES;).

2241. Ploskey, G. R., L. R. Aggus, W. M. Bivin, and R. M. Jenkins. 1986. Regression equations for predicting fish standing crop, angler use, and sport fish yield for United States Reservoirs. U.S. Fish Wildl. Serv., Admin. Rep. No. 86-5: 92 pp. (WALLEYE; CREEL CENSUS; ECOLOGY; IMPOUNDMENTS; PRODUCTIVITY;).

2242. Poe, T. P., D. E. Palmer, H. C. Hansel, S. Vigg, P. T. Lofy, S. D. Duke, M. J. Parsley, L. A.

Prendergast, R. Burkhart, and C. Burley. 1986. Feeding activity, rate of consumption, daily ration and prey selection of major predators in John Day Reservoir, 1986. Annual report to Bonneville Power Admin. U.S.F.W.S. Nat. Fish. Research Cent., Cook, Washington. 50 pp. (WALLEYE; COMMUNITY DYNAMICS; FOOD STUDIES; IMPOUNDMENTS;).

2243. Poole, B. C., and T. A. Dick. 1985. Parasite recruitment by stocked walleye, *Stizostedion vitreum vitreum* (Mitchill), fry in a small boreal lake in central Canada. J. Wildl. Dis. 21:371-376. (WALLEYE; PATHOLOGY;).

2244. Poole, B. C., and T. A. Dick. 1986. *Raphidascaris acus* (Boch, 1779) in northern pike, *Esox lucius* L., walleye, *Stizostedion vitreum vitreum* (Mitchill), and yellow perch, *Perca flavescens* (Mitchill), from central Canada. J. Wildl. Dis. 22:435-436. (WALLEYE; PATHOLOGY;).

2245. Posewitz, J. A. 1962. Fish population investigation in the Marias River below Tiber Dam. Mont. Fish Game Dept., Fed. Aid Fish Wildl. Restor. Proj. F-5-R-11, Job No. 2-A: 9 pp. (SAUGER; AGE AND GROWTH; FOOD STUDIES; SAMPLING METHODS;).

2246. Posewitz, J. A. 1963. Missouri River fish population study. Mont. Fish Game Dept., Fed. Aid Fish Wildl. Restor. Proj. F-11-R-10, Job No. 3: 9 pp. (SAUGER; AGE AND GROWTH; MARKING; MOVEMENT AND MIGRATIONS; SAMPLING METHODS;).

2247. Posewitz, J. A. 1964. Missouri River fish population study. Mont. Fish Game Dept., Fed. Aid Fish Wildl. Restor. Proj. F-11-R-11, Job No. 3:9 pp. (SAUGER; AGE AND GROWTH;).

2248. Posewitz, J. A. 1964. Northeast Montana fisheries study. Inventory of waters of the project area. Mont. Fish Game Dept., Fed. Aid Fish Wildl. Restor. Proj. F-11-R-11, Job No. 1: 5 pp. (SAUGER; WALLEYE; IMPOUNDMENTS; POPULATION STUDIES; STOCKING;).

2249. Posewitz, J. A. 1965. Northeast Montana fisheries study. Inventory of the waters of the project area. Mont. Fish Game Dept., Fed. Aid Fish Wildl. Restor. Proj. F-11-R-12,

Job No. 1: 17 pp. (SAUGER; IMPOUNDMENTS; POPULATION STUDIES;).

2250. Posewitz, J. A. 1967. Northeast Montana fisheries study. Inventory of the waters of the project area. Mont. Fish Game Dept., Fed. Aid Fish Wildl. Restor. Proj. F-11-R-13, Job No. 1: 11 pp. (SAUGER; WALLEYE; ECOLOGY; IMPOUNDMENTS; SAMPLING METHODS;).

2251. Post, H. 1894. Fish-culture in Michigan. U.S. Fish. Comm., Bull. 13:201-211. (WALLEYE; PROPAGATION;).

2252. Pothier, F., and M. A. Ali. 1978. Scotopic visual pigments in three Percidae, *Perca flavescens, Stizostedion vitreum,* and *Stizostedion canadense.* Can. Biol. 37:91-100. (SAUGER; WALLEYE; PHYSIOLOGY;).

2253. Potter, B. 1980. Canal Lake creel census 1980. Ont. Min. Nat. Res., Rep. 39 pp. (WALLEYE; CREEL CENSUS;).

2254. Powell, M. J. 1983. The effects of exploitation on the pickerel *(Stizostedion vitreum),* pike *(Esox lucius)* and perch *(Perca flavescens)* of Lake Nipissing. Ont. Min. Nat. Res., Lake Nipissing Fish. Assess. Unit Rep. 65 pp. (WALLEYE; AGE AND GROWTH; CREEL CENSUS; ECOLOGY; FOOD STUDIES; MARKING; MORTALITY; POPULATION STUDIES; SPAWNING STUDIES;).

2255. Power, G. J., and J. B. Owen. 1984. Comparison of plankton populations in three discrete regions of Lake Sakakawea, North Dakota. The Prairie Nat. 16:123-129. (WALLEYE; COMMUNITY DYNAMICS;).

2256. Pratt, J. H. 1907. Fishes of North Carolina; A review. J. Elisha Mitchell Sci. Soc. 23:175-183. (WALLEYE; GEOGRAPHICAL DISTRIBUTION;).

2257. Pratt, J. H. 1917. The fisheries of North Carolina. J. Elisha Mitchell Sci. Soc. 32:149-153, 165, 175. (WALLEYE; GEOGRAPHICAL DISTRIBUTION;).

2258. Pratt, L. C. 1972. Summer creel census report Bennett, Fagan, Mississippi, and White Lakes. Ont. Min. Nat. Res., Rep. 73 pp. (WALLEYE; CREEL CENSUS;).

2259. Pratt, L. C. 1973. 1973 summer creel census report Black, Pike and Westport Lakes. Ont. Min. Nat. Res., Rep. 50 pp. (WALLEYE; CREEL CENSUS;).

2260. Prentice, J. A. 1976. Walleye-white crappie study, Greenbelt Reservoir. Tex. Parks Wildl. Dept., Fed. Aid Fish Wildl. Restor. Proj. F-31-R-22: 25 pp. (WALLEYE; COMMUNITY DYNAMICS; CREEL CENSUS; IMPOUNDMENTS; POPULATION STUDIES; STOCKING;).

2261. Prentice, J. A. 1977. Statewide walleye stocking evaluation. Tex. Parks Wildl. Dept., Fed. Aid Fish Wildl. Restor. Proj. F-31-R-3, Obj. 11, Final Rep,: 47 pp. (WALLEYE; AGE AND GROWTH; COMMUNITY DYNAMICS; MORTALITY; POPULATION STUDIES; PRODUCTIVITY; SPAWNING STUDIES; STOCKING;).

2262. Prentice, J. A. 1983. A systems approach to walleye fishery management in Texas — an update. Pages 1-8 *in* Fisheries and computer practical applications, northeast warmwater workshop. Am. Fish. Soc., New York Chapter. (WALLEYE; IMPOUNDMENTS; INTRODUCTIONS; LIFE HISTORY;).

2263. Prentice, J. A. 1985. Texas statewide walleye fishery management program. Tex. Parks Wildl. Dept., Fed. Aid Fish Wildl. Restor. Proj. F-31-R-11, Final Rep., Job L1:21 pp. (WALLEYE; IMPOUNDMENTS; INTRODUCTIONS; LIFE HISTORY; PRODUCTIVITY; STOCKING;).

2264. Prentice, J. A., and R. D. Clark, Jr. 1978. Walleye fishery management program in Texas — a systems approach. Pages 408-416 *in* R.L. Kendall, ed. Selected coolwater fishes of North America. Am. Fish. Soc. Sp. Publ. No. 11, Washington, D.C. (WALLEYE; AGE AND GROWTH; CREEL CENSUS; INTRODUCTIONS; LIFE HISTORY; PRODUCTIVITY; SPAWNING STUDIES; STOCKING;).

2265. Prentice, J. A., R. D. Clark, Jr., and N. E. Carter. 1977. Walleye acceptance — a national review. Fisheries 2:15-17. (WALLEYE; INTRODUCTIONS;).

2266. Prentice, J. A., and W. J. Dean, Jr. 1977. Effect of temperature on walleye egg hatch rate. Proc. 31st Annu. Conf. Southeast Assoc. Fish Wildl. Agencies 31:458-462. (WALLEYE; PROPAGATION; SPAWNING STUDIES;).

2267. Preston, G. R. 1978. Lake Nipissing trawl netting project, 1978. Ont. Min. Nat. Res., Lake Nipissing Fish. Assess. Unit Rep. 50 pp. (WALLEYE; COMMUNITY DYNAMICS; FISHING GEAR; POPULATION STUDIES;).

2268. Preston, G. R. 1979. Trap netting, 1979. Ont. Min. Nat. Res., Lake Nipissing Fish. Assess. Unit Rep. 19 pp. (WALLEYE; AGE AND GROWTH; COMMUNITY DYNAMICS; MARKING; MORTALITY; POPULATION STUDIES;).

2269. Preston, G. R. 1980. Winter creel survey on Lake Nipissing 1978-79. Ont. Min. Nat. Res., Lake Nipissing Fish. Assess. Unit Rep. 1980-2: 27 pp. (WALLEYE; COMMUNITY DYNAMICS; CREEL CENSUS;).

2270. Preston, G. R. 1984. Results of M.N.R. tagging program on angler caught yellow pickerel entered in the Lake Nipissing live release pickerel tournament 1982-1983. Ont. Min. Nat. Res., Lake Nipissing Fish. Assess. Unit Rep. 4 pp. (WALLEYE; CREEL CENSUS; MORTALITY;).

2271. Preston, G. R., and C. Hill. 1978. Summary of trap, seine and gill netting, Lake Nipissing, 1978. Ont. Min. Nat. Res., Lake Nipissing Fish. Assess. Unit Rep. 28 pp. (WALLEYE; COMMUNITY DYNAMICS; MARKING; MORTALITY; POPULATION STUDIES;).

2272. Price, J. W. 1959. A study of the food habits of some Lake Erie fish. Ohio State Univ., Research Found. Rep. 837:107. (WALLEYE; FOOD STUDIES;).

2273. Price, J. W. 1963. A study of the food habits of some Lake Erie fish. Ohio Biol. Surv., Bull. 11:1-89. (WALLEYE; FOOD STUDIES;).

2274. Price, L. R. 1972. White Lake creel census — 1972. Ont. Min. Nat. Res., Rep. 19 pp. (WALLEYE; CREEL CENSUS;).

2275. Priegel, G. R. 1962. Food of walleye and sauger in Lake Winnebago. Wis. Conserv. Dept., Misc. Research Rep. 6:10. (SAUGER; WALLEYE; FOOD STUDIES;).

2276. Priegel, G. R. 1963. Food of walleyes and sauger in Lake Winnebago, Wisconsin. Trans. Am. Fish. Soc. 92:312-313. (SAUGER; WALLEYE; COMMUNITY DYNAMICS; FOOD STUDIES;).

2277. Priegel, G. R. 1964. Early scale development in the walleye. Trans. Am. Fish. Soc. 93:199-200. (WALLEYE; AGE AND GROWTH; MORPHOLOGY;).

2278. Priegel, G. R. 1965. Relative effectiveness of day and night trawling in Lake Winnebago. Wis. Conserv. Dept., Research Rep. No. 14: 7 pp. (SAUGER; WALLEYE; BEHAVIOR; MOVEMENT AND MIGRATIONS; SAMPLING METHODS;).

2279. Priegel, G. R. 1966. Lake Puckaway walleye. Wis. Conserv. Dept., Research Rep. No. 19: 22 pp. (WALLEYE; AGE AND GROWTH; ECOLOGY; IMPOUNDMENTS; MARKING; MORTALITY; MOVEMENT AND MIGRATIONS; POPULATION STUDIES; SPAWNING STUDIES;).

2280. Priegel, G. R. 1967. A list of the fishes of Lake Winnebago. Wis. Conserv. Dept., Research Rep. No. 27: 6pp. (SAUGER; WALLEYE; SPAWNING STUDIES;).

2281. Priegel, G. R. 1967. Evaluation of dredged channels, lagoons and marinas as fish habitat. Wis. Dept. Nat. Res., Fed. Aid Fish Wildl. Restor. Proj. F-83-R-2, Wk. Pl. 5, Job E: 17-35. (WALLEYE; ECOLOGY; INTRODUCTIONS;).

2282. Priegel, G. R. 1967. Food of the freshwater drum, *Aplodinotus grunions*, in Lake Winnebago, Wisconsin. Trans. Am. Fish. Soc. 96:218-220. (SAUGER; WALLEYE; COMMUNITY DYNAMICS; FOOD STUDIES;).

2283. Priegel, G. R. 1967. Identification of young walleyes and saugers in Lake Winnebago, Wisconsin. Prog. Fish-Cult. 29:108-109. (SAUGER; WALLEYE; TAXONOMY;).

2284. Priegel, G. R. 1967. Movements of adult tagged walleye stocked in Big Butte des Morts and Spochr's Marsh, Wolf River. Wis. Dept. Nat. Res., Research Rep. No. 28: 4 pp. (WALLEYE; BEHAVIOR; COMMUNITY DYNAMICS; MARKING; MOVEMENT AND MIGRATIONS; STOCKING;).

2285. Priegel, G. R. 1968. The movements, rate of exploitation and homing behavior of walleyes in Lake Winnebago and connecting waters, Wisconsin, as determined by tagging. Trans. Wis. Acad. Sci., Arts Letters 56:207-223. (WALLEYE; AGE AND GROWTH; MARKING; MOVEMENT AND MIGRATIONS; POPULATION STUDIES; SAMPLING METHODS;).

2286. Priegel, G. R. 1969. Age and growth of the walleye in Lake Winnebago. Trans. Wis. Acad. Sci., Arts Letters 57:121-133. (WALLEYE; AGE AND GROWTH;).

2287. Priegel, G. R. 1969. Food and growth of the young walleye in Lake Winnebago, Wisconsin. Trans. Am. Fish. Soc. 98:121-124. (WALLEYE; AGE AND GROWTH; FOOD STUDIES;).

2288. Priegel, G. R. 1969. The Lake Winnebago sauger. Age, growth, reproduction, food habits and early life history. Wis. Dept. Nat. Res., Tech. Bull. No. 43: 63 pp. (SAUGER; WALLEYE; AGE AND GROWTH; ECOLOGY; FOOD STUDIES; MORPHOLOGY; SPAWNING STUDIES;).

2289. Priegel, G. R. 1970. Reproduction and early life history of the walleye in the Lake Winnebago region. Wis. Dept. Nat. Res., Tech. Bull. No. 45: 105 pp. (WALLEYE; AGE AND GROWTH; ECOLOGY; FISHING GEAR; FOOD STUDIES; MORTALITY; MOVEMENTS AND MIGRATIONS; POPULATION STUDIES; SPAWNING STUDIES;).

2290. Priegel, G. R. 1971. Evaluation of intensive freshwater drum removal in Lake Winnebago, Wisconsin, 1955-1966. Wis. Dept. Nat. Res., Tech. Bull. No. 47: 28 pp. (WALLEYE; COMMUNITY DYNAMICS;).

2291. Priegel, G. R. 1971. Walleye fry stocking in relation to zooplankton densities in southeastern Wisconsin lakes. Wis. Conserv. Dept., Fed. Aid Fish Wildl. Restor. Proj. F-83-R-7: 13 pp. (WALLEYE; MORTALITY; STOCKING;).

2292. Prince, E. E. 1897. A concise account of fishes' eggs. Can. Dept Marine Fish., Fish. Branch, 29th Annu. Rep., Suppl. 1:17-28. (WALLEYE; PROPAGATION;).

2293. Prince, E. E. 1899. Neglected structural features in young fry. Can. Dept. Marine Fish., Fish. Branch, Annu. Rep., Spec. Append. Rep. 2:27-30. (WALLEYE; PHYSIOLOGY; PROPAGATION;).

2294. Prince, E. E. 1899. Water pollutions as affecting fisheries. Can. Dept. Marine Fish., Fish Branch, Annu. Rep., Spec. Append. Rep. 1:7-26. (WALLEYE; FOOD STUDIES; HABITAT DEGRADATION;).

2295. Prince, E. E. 1901. The vernacular names of fishes. Can. Dept. Marine Fish., Fish. Branch, Annu. Rep., Spec. Append. Rep. 2:12-23. (SAUGER; WALLEYE; TAXONOMY;).

2296. Prince, E. E. 1902. The propagation and planting of predacious fish. Can. Dept. Marine Fish., Fish Branch, 34th Annu. Rep., Spec. Rep. 2:7-19. (SAUGER; WALLEYE; COMMUNITY DYNAMICS; ECOLOGY; STOCKING;).

2297. Prince, E. E. 1904. The maximum size of fishes and its causes. Can. Dept. Marine Fish., Fish. Branch, Annu. Rep., Spec. Rep. 2:19-27. (WALLEYE; AGE AND GROWTH;).

2298. Prince, E. E. 1905. Report on fish-breeding operations in Canada, 1904. Can. Dept. Marine Fish., Fish. Branch, Annu. Rep. (1904):35-36. (WALLEYE; PROPAGATION; STOCKING;).

2299. Prince, E. E. 1909. The fish and fisheries of Manitoba. Can. Dept. Marine Fish., Fish. Branch, Spec. Rep. 8 pp. (SAUGER; WALLEYE; COMMERCIAL FISHERIES;).

2300. Prince, E. E., A. Halkett, W. S. Odell, and E. E. Lemieux. 1906. Zoological report: 1905-1906. Ottawa Nat. 20:56-61. (WALLEYE; GEOGRAPHICAL DISTRIBUTION;).

2301. Prince, E. E., A. Halkett, W. S. Odell, and E. E. Lemieux. 1908. Report on the zoological branch, 1907 to the council of the Ottawa Naturalists' Club. Ottawa Nat. 21:198-201. (WALLEYE; GEOGRAPHICAL DISTRIBUTION;).

2302. Pritchard, D. L., O. D. May, Jr., and L. Rider. 1976. Stocking of predators in the predator-stocking-evaluation reservoirs. Proc. 30th Annu. Conf. Southeast Fish Wildl. Agencies 30:108-113. (WALLEYE; COMMUNITY DYNAMICS; STOCKING;).

2303. Propst, D. L., and C. A. Carlson. 1986. The distribution and status of warmwater fishes in the Platte River drainage Colorado, USA. Southwest Nat. 31:149-168. (WALLEYE; GEOGRAPHICAL DISTRIBUTION;).

2304. Publow, J. 1972. Creel census Newboro, Loon, Benson, Mosquito, Indian and Clear Lakes. Ont. Min. Nat. Res., Rep. 65 pp. (WALLEYE; CREEL CENSUS;).

2305. Pugsley, R. W. 1983. Yellow pickerel, Stizostedion vitreum in the Talbot River of Lake Simcoe, 1982. Ont. Min. Nat. Res., Rep. 83-2: 74 pp. (WALLEYE; AGE AND GROWTH; HABITAT DEGRADATION; MARKING; MOVEMENT AND MIGRATIONS; POPULATION STUDIES; SPAWNING STUDIES;).

2306. Purkett, C. A., Jr. 1958. Growth rates of Missouri stream fishes. Mo. Conserv. Comm., D-J Ser. 1: 46 pp. (WALLEYE; AGE AND GROWTH;).

2307. Puttmann, S. J., and L. Finnell. 1980. Walleye studies. Colo. Div. Wildl., Fed. Aid. Fish Wildl. Restor. Proj. F-34-R-12, Job No 1:1-28. (WALLEYE; COMMUNITY DYNAMICS; FOOD STUDIES; IMPOUNDMENTS; POPULATION STUDIES; STOCKING;).

2308. Puttmann, S. J., and D. T. Weber. 1980. Variable walleye fry stocking rates in Boyd Reservoir, Colorado. Colo. Div. Wildl., Tech. Publ. No. 33: 47 pp. (WALLEYE; AGE AND GROWTH; CREEL CENSUS; FOOD STUDIES; IMPOUNDMENTS; POPULATION STUDIES; STOCKING;).

2309. Pycha, R. L. 1961. Recent changes in the walleye (Stizostedion vitreum) fishery of northern Green Bay and history of the 1943 year class. Trans. Am. Fish. Soc. 90:475-488. (WALLEYE; COMMERCIAL FISHERIES; POPULATION STUDIES;).

2310. Qadri, S. U., and D. E. Mcallister. 1967. Fish remains from a 700-year-old southern Ontario Archeological site. Nat. Mus. Can., Nat. Hist. Papers 34: 6pp. (WALLEYE; GEOGRAPHICAL DISTRIBUTION;).

2311. Rada, R. G., J. E. Findley, and J. G. Wiener. 1986. Environmental fate of mercury discharged into the Upper Wisconsin River. Water Air Soil Pollut. 29:57-76. (WALLEYE; HABITAT DEGRADATION; TOXICANTS;).

2312. Radforth, I. 1944. Some considerations on the distribution of fishes in Ontario. Contrib. Ont. Mus. Zool. 25: 116 pp. (WALLEYE; GEOGRAPHICAL DISTRIBUTION;).

2313. Rafinesque, C. S. 1820. Ichthyologia Ohiensis or natural history of the fishes inhabiting the river Ohio and its tributary streams, preceded by a physical description of the Ohio and its branches. Pages in R.E. Call (1899). A vertbatim et literatim reprint of the original work with a sketch of the life, the ichthyologic work, and the ichthyologic bibliography of Rafinesque. 175 pp. (WALLEYE; GEOGRAPHICAL DISTRIBUTION;).

2314. Ragan, J. E. 1970. Management surveys of the Missouri River and its mainstream reservoirs in North Dakota. N.D. State Game Fish Dept., Fed. Aid Fish Wildl. Restor. Proj. F-2-R-17, Job No. 1: 75-80;98-102. (SAUGER; WALLEYE; AGE AND GROWTH; IMPOUNDMENTS;).

2315. Ragan, J. E. 1972. Mortality and movement of adult walleye and pike. N.D. Fish Game Dept., Fed. Aid Fish Wildl. Restor. Proj. F-2-R-19, Study 4: 16 pp. (WALLEYE; AGE AND GROWTH; GEOGRAPHICAL DISTRIBUTION; MOVEMENTS AND MIGRATIONS; POPULATION STUDIES;).

2316. Ragan, J. E. 1975. Mortality and movement of adult walleye (Stizostedion vitreum) and pike (Esox lucius). N.D. State Game Fish Dept., Fed. Aid Fish Wildl. Restor. Proj. F-2-R-21, Study No. 4: 27 pp. (WALLEYE; AGE AND GROWTH; IMPOUNDMENTS; MARKING; MOVEMENTS AND MIGRATIONS; SPAWNING STUDIES;).

2317. Ragan, J. E. 1977. Mortality and movement of adult walleye (Stizostedion vitreum) and pike (Esox lucius). N.D. State Fish Dept., Fed. Aid Fish Wildl. Restor. Proj. F-2-R-23, Study No. 4: 21 pp. (WALLEYE; AGE AND GROWTH; IMPOUNDMENTS; MARKING; MOVEMENTS AND MIGRATIONS; SPAWNING STUDIES;).

2318. Raine, G. E. 1970. 1969-70 winter fishing report Kemptville Administrative District. Ont. Min. Nat. Res., Rep. 26 pp. (WALLEYE; CREEL CENSUS;).

2319. Raine, G. E. 1970. An analysis of the Upper Rideau Lake yellow pickerel fishery. Ont. Min. Nat. Res., Rep. 38 pp. (WALLEYE; AGE AND GROWTH; COMMUNITY DYNAMICS; CREEL CENSUS; MARKING; POPULATION STUDIES; SPAWNING STUDIES; STOCKING; WATER LEVELS;).

2320. Raine, G. E. 1971. Upper Rideau Lake Trap Net Study. Ont. Min. Nat. Res., Rep. 26 pp. (WALLEYE; AGE AND GROWTH; CREEL CENSUS; POPULATION STUDIES; PROPAGATION; SAMPLING METHODS; SPAWNING STUDIES; STOCKING; TOXICANTS; WATER LEVELS;).

2321. Raine, G. E. 1976. A proposal for the construction of an artificial yellow pickerel (Stizostedion vitreum) spawning and incubation channel. Ont. Min. Nat. Res., Brockville Dist. Rep. 38 pp. (WALLEYE; HABITAT IMPROVEMENT;).

2322. Raisanen, G. A. 1982. Survival, growth, food selection, and alimentary canal development of intensively reared walleye (Stizostedion vitreum) and yellow perch (Perca flavéscens). M.S. Thesis, S.D. State Univ., Brookings, S.D. (WALLEYE; PROPAGATION;).

2323. Raisanen, G. A., and R. L. Applegate. 1983. Prey selection of walleye fry in an experimental system. Prog. Fish-Cult. 45: 209-214. (WALLEYE; FOOD STUDIES; LIFE HISTORY;).

2324. Raleigh, R. F., D. H. Bennett, L. O. Mohn, and O. E. Maughan. 1978. Changes in fish stocks after major fish kills in the Clinch River near St. Paul, Virginia. Am. Midl. Nat. 99: 1-9. (SAUGER; WALLEYE; COMMUNITY DYNAMICS; HABITAT DEGRADATION; POPULATION STUDIES;).

2325. Raney, E. C. 1959. Some young fresh water fishes of New York. N.Y. State Conser. 1959, Aug-Sept. pp. 22-28. (WALLEYE; SPAWNING STUDIES;).

2326. Raney, E. C., and E. A. Lachner. 1942. Studies of the summer food, growth, and movements of young yellow pike-perch, *Stizostedion v. vitreum,* in Oneida Lake, New York. J. Wildl. Manage. 6:1-16. (WALLEYE; AGE AND GROWTH; COMMUNITY DYNAMICS; ECOLOGY; FOOD STUDIES; GEOGRAPHICAL DISTRIBUTION;).

2327. Range, J. D. 1971. Possible effects of threadfin shad, *Dorosoma petenense,* on the growth of five species of game fish in Dale Hollow Reservoir. M.S. Thesis, Tenn. Tech. Univ., Cookeville, Tenn. 61 pp. (WALLEYE; AGE AND GROWTH; COMMUNITY DYNAMICS;).

2328. Range, J. D. 1973. Growth of five species of game fishes before and after introduction of the thread fin shad into Dale Hollow Reservoir. Proc. Annu. Conf. Southeast Assoc. Fish Wild. Agencies. 26: 510-518. (WALLEYE; AGE AND GROWTH; IMPOUNDMENTS; STOCKING;).

2329. Ranthum, R. G. 1975. Five-year summary of Mississippi River special tailwater creel census in Pool 7, 1969-1973. Wis. Dept. Nat. Res., Fish Manage. Rep. No. 90: 37 pp. (SAUGER; WALLEYE; AGE AND GROWTH; CREEL CENSUS;).

2330. Rawson, D. S. 1930. The bottom fauna of Lake Simcoe and its role in the ecology of the lake. Ont. Fish. Res. Lab., Pub. 183 pp. (WALLEYE; STOCKING;).

2331. Rawson, D. S. 1945. The experimental introduction of smallmouth black bass *(Micropterus dolomieui)* into lakes of Prince Albert National Park, Saskatchewan. Trans. Am. Fish. Soc. 73:19-31. (WALLEYE; ECOLOGY; POPULATION STUDIES;).

2332. Rawson, D. S. 1946. Successful introduction of fish in a large saline lake. Can. Fish Cult. 1:5-8. (WALLEYE; ECOLOGY; INTRODUCTIONS;).

2333. Rawson, D. S. 1947. Northwest Canadian fisheries surveys in 1944-1945. V. Great Slave Lake. Fish. Research Board Can., Bull. 72:45-68. (WALLEYE; COMMERCIAL FISHERIES; ECOLOGY; PATHOLOGY;).

2334. Rawson, D. S. 1947. Northwest Canadian fisheries surveys in 1944-1945. V. Lake Athabaska. Fish. Research Board Can., Bull. 72:69-85. (WALLEYE; COMMER-CIAL FISHERIES; ECOLOGY; FOOD STUDIES; PATHOLOGY;).

2335. Rawson, D. S. 1949. Estimating the fish production of Great Slave Lake. Trans. Am. Fish. Soc. 77:81-92. (WALLEYE; COMMERCIAL FISHERIES; PRODUCTIVITY;).

2336. Rawson, D. S. 1949. A check list of the fishes of Saskatchewan. Sask. Dept. Nat. Res., Indust. Dev., Roy. Comm. on the Fish of Sask. 9 pp. (SAUGER; WALLEYE; GEOGRAPHICAL DISTRIBUTION;).

2337. Rawson, D. S. 1951. Studies of the fish of Great Slave Lake. J. Fish. Research Board Can. 8:207-240. (WALLEYE; AGE AND GROWTH; ECOLOGY; FOOD STUDIES; GEOGRAPHICAL DISTRIBUTION; PATHOLOGY; SAMPLING METHODS;).

2338. Rawson, D. S. 1953. The bottom fauna of Great Slave Lake. J. Fish. Research Board Can. 10:486-520. (WALLEYE; FOOD STUDIES;).

2339. Rawson, D. S. 1957. Limnology and fisheries of five lakes in the upper Churchill Drainage, Saskatchewan. Sask. Dept. Nat. Res., Fish. Rep. 3: 61 pp. (WALLEYE; AGE AND GROWTH; COMMERCIAL FISHERIES; FOOD STUDIES; PATHOLOGY; POPULATION STUDIES;).

2340. Rawson, D. S. 1957. The life history and ecology of the yellow walleye *Stizostedion vitreum,* in Lac La Ronge, Saskatchewan. Trans. Am. Fish. Soc. 86:15-37. (WALLEYE; AGE AND GROWTH; CREEL CENSUS; LIFE HISTORY; MARKING; MOVEMENTS AND MIGRATIONS; POPULATION STUDIES; SPAWNING STUDIES;).

2341. Rawson, D. S. 1959. Limnology and fisheries of Cree and Wollaston Lakes in northern Saskatchewan. Sask. Dept. Nat. Res., Fish. Rep. 4: 73 pp. (WALLEYE; AGE AND GROWTH; COMMERCIAL FISHERIES; FOOD STUDIES; PRODUCTIVITY;).

2342. Rawson, D. S. 1960. Five lakes on the Churchill River near Stanley, Saskatchewan. Sask. Dept. Nat. Res., Fish. Rep. 5: 38 pp. (SAUGER; WALLEYE; AGE AND GROWTH; COMMERCIAL FISHERIES; FOOD STUDIES; PATHOLOGY; PRODUCTIVITY;).

2343. Rawson, D. S. 1960. A limnological comparison of twelve large lakes in northern Saskatchewan. Limno. Oceanogr. 5:195-211. (WALLEYE; ECOLOGY;).

2344. Rawson, D. S. 1961. The lake trout of Lac la Ronge, Saskatchewan. J. Fish. Research Board Can. 18:423-462. (WALLEYE; COMMUNITY DYNAMICS; POPULATION STUDIES;).

2345. Rawson, D. S., and F. M. Atton. 1951. Fisheries investigation of Lac la Ronge, Saskatchewan, 1948, 1949. Sask. Dept. Nat. Res. Fish. Lab. Tech. Rep. 1951-1 54 pp. (WALLEYE; AGE AND GROWTH; ECOLOGY; FOOD STUDIES; POPULATION STUDIES;).

2346. Rawson, D. S., and F. M. Atton. 1953. Biological investigation and fisheries management at Lac la Ronge, Saskatchewan. Sask. Dept. Nat. Res., Fish Rep 1: 39 pp. (WALLEYE; AGE AND GROWTH; COMMERCIAL FISHERIES; COMMUNITY DYNAMICS; ECOLOGY; FOOD STUDIES; PRODUCTIVITY;).

2347. Rawson, D. S., E. C. Hope, J. Mitchell, and E. W. Tisdale. 1943. The Big River Survey. A comprehensive study of natural resources as an aid to improved utilization. Univ. Sask., Saskatoon, Sask. 33 pp. (WALLEYE; COMMERCIAL FISHERIES;).

2348. Rawson, D. S., and J. E. Moore. 1944. The saline lakes of Saskatchewan. Can. J. Res., Sect. D 22:141-201. (WALLEYE; AGE AND GROWTH; COMMUNITY DYNAMICS; ECOLOGY; INTRODUCTIONS; PHYSIOLOGY; STOCKING;).

2349. Rawson, D. S., and R. A. Ruttan. 1952. Pond fish studies in Saskatchewan. J. Wildl. Manage. 16:283-288. (WALLEYE; ECOLOGY; IMPOUNDMENTS; INTRODUCTIONS;).

2350. Rawson, D. S., and R. A. Wheaton. 1950. Studies of *Triaenophorus crassus* in Nesslin Lake, Saskatchewan, 1950. Fish. Research Board Can., Central Fish. Research Station Annu. Rep. 4:18-21. (WALLEYE; PATHOLOGY;).

2351. Rawson, M. R., and R. L. Scholl. 1978. Reestablishment of sauger in Western Lake Erie. Pages 261-265 in R.L. Kendall, ed. Selected coolwater fishes of North America. Am. Fish. Soc. Spec. Publ. No. 11, Washington, D.C. (SAUGER; WALLEYE; AGE AND GROWTH; COMMUNITY DYNAMICS; FOOD STUDIES; INTRODUCTIONS; MARKING; MOVEMENTS AND MIGRATIONS; SPAWNING STUDIES; STOCKING;).

2352. Ray, J., and W. D. Cole. 1967. Fish stocking needs. Kans. Forest., Fish Game Comm., Fed. Aid Fish Wildl. Restor. Proj. F-5-R-1, Job C-1:18 pp. (WALLEYE; ECOLOGY; IMPOUNDMENTS; INTRODUCTIONS;).

2353. Ray, J., and G. Coslett. 1968. Fish stocking needs. Kans. Forest., Fish Game Comm., Fed. Aid Fish Wildl. Restor. Proj. F-15-R-3, Job C 1-3: 40 pp. (WALLEYE; AGE AND GROWTH; ECOLOGY; IMPOUNDMENTS;).

2354. Read, D. 1978. Lake Temiskaming creel census winter 1978. Ont. Min. Nat. Res., Rep. 71 pp. (SAUGER; WALLEYE; AGE AND GROWTH; CREEL CENSUS;).

2355. Read, D. 1982. Lake Temiskaming winter creel census 1982. Ont. Min. Nat. Res., Rep. 47 pp. (SAUGER; WALLEYE; AGE AND GROWTH; CREEL CENSUS;).

2356. Redmond, L. C. 1986. The history and development of warmwater fish harvest regulations. Pages 186-195 in G.E. Hall and M.J. Van Den Avyle, eds. Reservoir fisheries management: strategies for the 80's. Reserv. Comm., Southern Div. Am. Fish. Soc., Bethesda, Maryland. (WALLEYE; IMPOUNDMENTS; REGULATIONS;).

2357. Reed, E. B. 1962. Limnology and fisheries of the Saskatchewan River in Saskatchewan. Sask. Dept. Nat. Res., Fish. Rep. 6: 48 pp. (SAUGER; WALLEYE; AGE AND GROWTH; COMMERCIAL FISHERIES; FOOD STUDIES; HABITAT DEGRADATION;).

2358. Reed, H. D., and A. H. Wright. 1909. The vertebrates of the Cayuga Lake Basin, N.Y. Proc. Am. Philosophical Soc. 48:370-459. (SAUGER; WALLEYE; GEOGRAPHICAL DISTRIBUTION;).

2359. Reedstrom, D. C. 1964. A biological reconnaissance of the Snake River. Minn. Dept. Nat. Res., Invest. Rep. No. 275: 66 pp. (WALLEYE; POPULATION STUDIES;).

2360. Regier, H. A. 1966. A perspective on research on the dynamics of fish populations in the Great Lakes. Prog. Fish-Cult. 28:3-18. (WALLEYE; COMMERCIAL FISHERIES;).

2361. Regier, H. A. 1968. Concepts of species segregation and desegregation related to Great Lake fishery management. Proc. Int. Assn. Great Lakes Research 11:124-129. (SAUGER; WALLEYE; COMMERCIAL FISHERIES; GENETICS;).

2362. Regier, H. A., V. C. Applegate, and R. A. Ryder. 1969. The ecology and management of the walleye (Stizostedion vitreum) in western Lake Erie. Great Lakes Fish. Comm., Tech. Rep. 15: 101 pp. (SAUGER; WALLEYE; BEHAVIOR; COMMERCIAL FISHERIES; COMMUNITY DYNAMICS; ECOLOGY; FOOD STUDIES; GENETICS; HABITAT DEGRADATION; LIFE HISTORY; POPULATION STUDIES; SPAWNING STUDIES;).

2363. Regier, H. A., and W. L. Hartman. 1973. Lake Erie fish community: 150 years of culture stresses. Science. 180: 1248-1255. (SAUGER; WALLEYE; COMMERCIAL FISHERIES; ECOLOGY; HABITAT DEGRADATION;).

2364. Reid, D. M. 1985. Effects of an episodic removal scheme on a walleye Stizostedion vitreum vitreum population. M.S. Thesis, Lakehead Univ., Thunder Bay, Ont. 247 pp. (WALLEYE; ECOLOGY; FISHING GEAR; MORTALITY; POPULATION STUDIES; REGULATIONS; SAMPLING METHODS;).

2365. Reid, D. M. 1986. Lake Nipigon experimental walleye netting program, 1980-1985. Ont. Min. Nat. Res., Lake Nipigon Fish. Assess. Unit Rep. 1986-1: 55 pp. (SAUGER; WALLEYE; AGE AND GROWTH; COMMUNITY DYNAMICS; FOOD STUDIES; MORTALITY; POPULATION STUDIES; SPAWNING STUDIES;).

2366. Reid, D. M., and W. T. Momot. 1985. Evaluation of pulse fishing for the walleye, Stizostedion vitreum vitreum, in Henderson Lake, Ontario. J. Fish Biol. 27(Suppl. A):235-251. (WALLEYE; AGE AND GROWTH; CREEL CENSUS; POPULATION STUDIES; PRODUCTIVITY;).

2367. Reid, H. 1979. Trent River creel report summer 1979. Ont. Min. Nat. Res., Rep. 15 pp. (WALLEYE; AGE AND GROWTH; CREEL CENSUS;).

2368. Reighard, J. 1890. The development of the wall-eyed pike (Stizostedion vitreum). A popular introduction to the development of bony fishes. Mich. Fish. Comm., Bull. 1: 66 pp. (WALLEYE; EMBRYOLOGY; MORPHOLOGY;).

2369. Reighard, J. 1894. A biological examination of Lake St. Clair. Mich. Fish. Comm., Bull. 4:1-60. (SAUGER; WALLEYE; PATHOLOGY;).

2370. Reighard, J. 1914. Improvement of fishing through a knowledge of the breeding habits of fishes. Trans. Am. Fish. Soc. 43:97-130. (WALLEYE; SPAWNING STUDIES; STOCKING;).

2371. Reigle, N. J., Jr. 1969. Bottom trawl explorations in Lake Superior, 1963-65. U.S. Fish Wildl. Serv., Circ. 294:25 pp. (WALLEYE; FISHING GEAR;).

2372. Reigle, N. J., Jr. 1969. Bottom trawl explorations in Green Bay of Lake Michigan, 1963-65. U.S. Fish Wildl. Serv., Circ. 297: 14 pp. (WALLEYE; COMMERCIAL FISHERIES; SAMPLING METHODS;).

2373. Reinert, R. E. 1970. Pesticide concentrations in Great Lakes fish. Pesticides Monitoring J. 3:233-240. (WALLEYE; HABITAT DEGRADATION;).

2374. Reinert, R. E., and H. L. Bergman. 1974. Residue of DDT in Lake trout (Salvelinus namaycush) and coho salmon (Oncorhynchus kisutch) from the Great Lakes. J. Fish. Research Board Can. 31:191-199. (WALLEYE; COMMERCIAL FISHERIES; GENETICS; HABITAT DEGRADATION;).

2375. Reinitz, G., and R. Austin. 1980. Practical diets for intensive culture of walleyes. Prog. Fish Cult. 42: 212-214. (WALLEYE; PROPAGATION;).

2376. Renyard, T. S., and R. Hilborn. 1986. Sports angler preferences for alternative regulatory methods. Can. J. Fish. Aquat. Sci. 43:240-242. (WALLEYE; CREEL CENSUS; REGULATIONS;).

2377. Reutter, J. M., C. E. Herdendorf, M. D. Barnes, and W. E. Carey. 1980. Response of fish and invertebrates to the heated discharge from the Davis-Besse nuclear power station, Lake Erie, Ohio. Ohio Dept. Nat. Res., Fed. Aid Fish Wildl. Restor. Proj. F-41-R-1: 308 pp. (SAUGER; WALLEYE; ECOLOGY; FISHING GEAR; HABITAT DEGRADATION; PHYSIOLOGY;).

2378. Reynolds, J. B. 1965. Life history of the smallmouth bass (Micropterus dolomieui) in the Des Moines River, Boone County, Iowa. Iowa State J. Sci. 39:417-436. (WALLEYE; GEOGRAPHICAL DISTRIBUTION;).

2379. Reynolds, J. B., and P. W. Laarman. 1970. Estimation of total mercury in Lake St. Clair walleyes. Mich. Dept. Nat. Res., Research and Develop. Rep. No. 220: 19 pp. (WALLEYE; HABITAT DEGRADATION; TOXICANTS;).

2380. Reynolds. L. M. 1972. Pesticide residue analysis in the presence of polychlorobiphenyls (PCB's). Pestic. Rev. 34: 27-57. (WALLEYE; PATHOLOGY;).

2381. Rice, D. J. 1964. Report on the White Lake fishery project, 1963. Ont. Dept. Lands For., Res. Manage. Rep. 78:50-58. (WALLEYE; CREEL CENSUS;).

2382. Rice, V. J., and T. L. Jahn. 1943. Myxosporidian parasites from the gills of some fishes of the Okoboji region. Proc. Iowa Acad. Sci. 50:313-321. (WALLEYE; PATHOLOGY;).

2383. Richards, J. S. 1976. Changes in fish species composition in the Au Sable River, Michigan from the 1920's to 1972. Trans. Am. Fish. Soc. 105:32-40. (WALLEYE; ECOLOGY;).

2384. Richards, K. R., R. J. Dent, Jr., and W. H. Dieffenbach. 1986. Fisheries problems associated with the Truman Dam pumped storage hydroelectric project in west central Missouri. Pages 247-254 in G.E. Hall and M.J. Van Den Avyle, eds. Reservoir fisheries management: strategies for the 80's. Reserv. Comm., Southern Div. Am. Fish. Soc., Bethesda, Maryland. (WALLEYE; IMPOUNDMENTS; MORTALITY; SPAWNING STUDIES;).

2385. Richardson, L. R. 1942. The parasites of the fishes of Lake Wakonichi, central northern Quebec. Trans. Am. Fish. Soc. 71:286-289. (WALLEYE; PATHOLOGY;).

2386. Richardson, L. R. 1944. Brief record of fishes from central northern Quebec. Copeia 4:205-208. (WALLEYE; GEOGRAPHICAL DISTRIBUTION;).

2387. Ricker, W. E. 1949. Mortality rates in some little-exploited populations of fresh-water fishes. Trans. Am. Fish. Soc. 77:114-128. (SAUGER; MORTALITY; POPULATION STUDIES;).

2388. Ricker, W. E. 1958. Handbook of computations for biological statistics of fish populations. Fish Research Board Can., Bull. 119: 300pp. (WALLEYE; AGE AND GROWTH; POPULATION STUDIES;).

2389. Ricker, W. E. 1962. Productive capacity of Canadian Fisheries. Fish. Research Board Can., Circ. 64: 79 PP. (SAUGER; WALLEYE; COMMERCIAL FISHERIES; PRODUCTIVITY;).

2390. Ricker, W. E., and J. Gottschalk. 1941. An experiment in removing coarse fish from a lake. Trans. Am. Fish. Soc. 70:382-390. (WALLEYE; HABITAT IMPROVEMENT; SAMPLING METHODS;).

2391. Ridenhour, R. L. 1960. Abundance, growth and food of young game fish in Clear Lake, Iowa, 1949 to 1957. Iowa State J. Sci. 35:1-23. (WALLEYE; AGE AND GROWTH; COMMUNITY DYNAMICS; ECOLOGY; FOOD STUDIES; POPULATION STUDIES;).

2392. Ridenhour, R. L. 1960. Development of a program to sample young fish in a lake. Trans. Am. Fish. Soc. 89:185-192. (WALLEYE; FISHING GEAR; SAMPLING METHODS;).

2393. Ridenhour, R. L., and C. L. DiCostanzo. 1956. Nylon vs. linen gillnets at Clear Lake, Iowa. Proc. Iowa Acad. Sci. 63:700-704. (WALLEYE; FISHING GEAR; SAMPLING METHODS;).

2394. Riggs, V. L., and R. W. Gregory. 1980. Environmental effects of western coal surface mining. Part 5: Age and growth of walleyes and saugers in the Tongue River Reservoir, Montana 1975-1977. Mont. State Univ., Coop. Fish. Res. Unit, Bozeman, Mont. 54 pp. (SAUGER; WALLEYE; AGE AND

GROWTH; HABITAT DEGRADATION; IMPOUNDMENTS; MARKING; MOVE-MENTS AND MIGRATIONS; POPULA-TION STUDIES;).

2395. Riis, J. C. 1979. Beneficial aspects of various walleye fry stocking densities in lakes with reproducing walleye populations. S.D. Dept. Game Fish and Parks, Fed. Aid Fish Wildl. Restor. Proj. F-15-R-15, Job No. 2 & 3: 29 pp. (WALLEYE; CREEL CENSUS; POPULATION STUDIES; STOCKING;).

2396. Riis, J. C. 1980. Beneficial aspects of various walleye fry stocking densities in lakes with reproducing walleye populations. S.D. Dept. Game Fish and Parks, Fed. Aid Fish Wildl. Restor. Proj. F-15-R-16, Job No. 2 & 3: 12 pp. (WALLEYE; CREEL CENSUS; POPULATION STUDIES; STOCKING;).

2397. Riis, J. C. 1985. Walleye movement, harvest and angler use on Lake Oahe, South Dakota, 1981-84. S.D. Dept. Game Fish and Parks, Completion Rep. No. 84-4: 68 pp. (WALL-EYE; CREEL CENSUS; IMPOUND-MENTS; MARKING; MOVEMENTS AND MIGRATIONS; SPAWNING STUD-IES;).

2398. Riis, J. C. 1986. Angler use and sport fishing harvest survey of Lake Sharpe, South Dakota, 1984 — 1985. S.D. Dept. Game Fish and Parks, Completion Rep. 86-8: 34 pp. (WALLEYE; AGE AND GROWTH; CREEL CENSUS; IMPOUNDMENTS;).

2399. Riklik, L., and W. T. Momot. 1982. Produc-tion ecology of *Hexagenia limbata* in Savanne Lake, Ontario. Can. J. Zool. 60:2317-2323. (WALLEYE; FOOD STUD-IES;).

2400. Riley, L. M. 1981. Applicability of quantified scale shape for the identification of Lake Erie walleye *(Stizostedion vitreum)* stocks. M.S. Thesis, Ohio St. Univ., Ohio Coop. Fish. Res. Unit, Columbus, Ohio. 41 pp. (WALLEYE; MORPHOLOGY;).

2401. Riley, L. M., and R. F. Carline. 1982. Evalua-tion of scale shape for the identification of walleye stocks of western Lake Erie. Trans. Am. Fish. Soc. 111: 736-741. (WALLEYE; GENETICS; MORPHOLOGY;).

2402. Rimsky-korsakoff, V. N. 1930. A biological survey of the Champlain watershed. III.

The food of certain fishes of the Lake Cham-plain watershed. N.Y. Conserv. Dept., Suppl. 19th Annu. Rep. (1929):88-104. (SAUGER; WALLEYE; FOOD STUD-IES;).

2403. Riordan, T. 1979. Walleye introductions in the Chapleau District. Ont. Min. Nat. Res., Rep. 14 pp. (WALLEYE; STOCKING;).

2404. Robbins, R. M. 1981. Creel census report for the Opasatika Lake complex 1979, 1980, 1981. Ont. Min. Nat. Res., Rep. 10 pp. (WALLEYE; CREEL CENSUS;).

2405. Roberge, M. M., G. Low, and C. J. Read. 1986. An assessment of the commercial fish-ery and population structure of walleye in Kakisa Lake, Northwest Territories, 1977-1985. Can. Tech. Rep. Fish. Aquatic Sci. No. 1435: 59 pp. (WALLEYE; COMMERCIAL FISHERIES; POPULATION STUDIES;).

2406. Robins, G. L. 1970. A bibliography of the pike perch of the genus *Stizostedion* (includ-ing the genus known as *Lucioperca*). Fish. Research Board Can. Tech. Rep. 161: 67 pp. (SAUGER; WALLEYE; ECOLOGY;).

2407. Rock, L. F. 1963. 1962 Mississippi River sport fishing creel census. Ill. Dept. Con-serv. 92 pp. (SAUGER; WALLEYE; CREEL CENSUS;).

2408. Rock, L. F. 1968. The Edwards River and Henderson Creek basins. Pages 53-69 *in* A.C. Lopinot, ed. Inventory of the Fishes of Nine River Basins in Illinois 1967. (SAUGER; WALLEYE; ECOLOGY;).

2409. Rock, L. F. 1969. The history of the 1959 wall-eye year class in the Rock Nine River, Illi-nois. Ill. Dept. Conserv., Spec. Fish Rep. 29: 56 pp. (WALLEYE; LIFE HISTORY;).

2410. Rockett, L. C. 1967. Life history of walleye in Keyhole Reservoir. Wyo. Game Fish Comm., Admin. Rep., Proj. 0366-23-6502: 27 pp. (WALLEYE; AGE AND GROWTH; ECOLOGY; FOOD STUDIES; IM-POUNDMENTS; INTRODUCTIONS; LIFE HISTORY; MOVEMENTS AND MI-GRATIONS; POPULATION STUDIES;).

2411. Rodd, J. A. 1924. Sketch of the development of fish culture in Canada. Trans. Am. Fish. Soc. 54:148-160. (WALLEYE; PROPAGA-TION;).

2412. Rogers, D. W., T. A. Watson, J. S. Langan, and T. J. Wheaton. 1987. Effects of pH and feeding regime on methylmercury accumulation within aquatic microcosms. Environ. Pollut. 45:261-274. (WALLEYE; TOXICANTS;).

2413. Roos, J. A., J. R. Brisbane, and V. Macins. 1982. An assessment of the Shoal Lake fishery, 1981. Ont. Min. Nat. Res., Lake of the Woods — Rainy Lake Fish. Assess. Unit Rep. 1982-01: 93 pp. (WALLEYE; AGE AND GROWTH; COMMERCIAL FISHERIES; CREEL CENSUS; FISHING GEAR; MOVEMENT AND MIGRATIONS; SPAWNING STUDIES;).

2414. Roos, J. A., C. J. Foote, J. E. Donetz, and J. R. Brisbane. 1981. An evaluation of the Shoal Lake fishery 1980. Ont. Min. Nat. Res., Lake of the Woods — Rainy Lake Fisheries Assess. Unit Rep. 1981-1: 92 pp. (WALLEYE; AGE AND GROWTH; COMMERCIAL FISHERIES; COMMUNITY DYNAMICS; CREEL CENSUS; FISHING GEAR; FOOD STUDIES; PATHOLOGY; POPULATION STUDIES; SPAWNING STUDIES;).

2415. Roos, J. A., V. Macins, and T. Mosindy. 1983. An assessment of the Shoal Lake fishery, 1982. Ont. Min. Nat. Res., Lake of the Woods Fish. Assess. Unit Rep. 1983-01: 95 pp. (WALLEYE; AGE AND GROWTH; COMMERCIAL FISHERIES; COMMUNITY DYNAMICS; CREEL CENSUS; FOOD STUDIES; PATHOLOGY; SPAWNING STUDIES;).

2416. Roos, J. A., V. Macins, and T. Mosindy. 1984. An interim report of the Shoal Lake Monitoring program 1983. Ont. Min. Nat. Res., Lake of the Woods Fish. Assess. Unit Rep. 1984-01: 9 pp. (WALLEYE; AGE AND GROWTH; COMMUNITY DYNAMICS; HABITAT IMPROVEMENT; MORTALITY; SPAWNING STUDIES;).

2417. Roosevelt, R. B. 1874. Remarks of Hon. Robert B. Roosevelt at the third annual meeting. Proc. Am. Fish Cult. Assoc. 3:7-9. (WALLEYE; PROPAGATION; STOCKING;).

2418. Roosevelt, R. B. 1879. President's remarks as reported at the eighth annual meeting. Trans. Am. Fish Cult. Assoc. 8:3 pp. (WALLEYE; TAXONOMY;).

2419. Rose, E. T. 1949. A fish population of Storm Lake. Proc. Iowa Acad. Sci. 56:385-395. (WALLEYE; MARKING; POPULATION STUDIES; STOCKING;).

2420. Rose, E. T. 1949. The population of yellow pike-perch (Stizostedion vitreum) in Spirit Lake, Iowa. Trans. Am. Fish. Soc. 77:32-41. (WALLEYE; AGE AND GROWTH; MARKING; POPULATION STUDIES;).

2421. Rose, E. T. 1951. Notes on the age and growth of Spirit Lake yellow pike-perch (Stizostedion v. vitreum). Proc. Iowa Acad. Sci. 58:517-525. (WALLEYE; AGE AND GROWTH; MARKING;).

2422. Rose, E. T. 1955. The fluctuation in abundance of walleye in Spirit Lake, Iowa. Proc. Iowa Acad. Sci. 62:567-575. (WALLEYE; COMMUNITY DYNAMICS; MARKING; POPULATION STUDIES; STOCKING;).

2423. Rose, E. T. 1956. The year-around creel census of Spirit and Okoboji Lakes. Pages 8-13 in K.D. Carlander, ed. Symposium on sampling problems in creel census. Iowa State College, Ames, Iowa. (WALLEYE; CREEL CENSUS;).

2424. Rose, E. T. 1956. Catch record variance in completed and uncompleted fishing trips. Pages 14-16 in K.D. Carlander, ed. Symposium on sampling Problems in creel census. Iowa State College, Ames, Iowa. (WALLEYE; CREEL CENSUS;).

2425. Rose, E. T. 1957. The recapture of tagged walleye (Stizostedion vitreum) from Dickinson County Lakes. Iowa Conserv. Comm., Biol. Rep. 9:32-35. (WALLEYE; MARKING; MOVEMENT AND MIGRATIONS;).

2426. Rose, E. T., and T. Moen. 1951. Results of an increased fish harvest in Lost Island Lake. Trans. Am. Fish. Soc. 80:50-55. (WALLEYE; CREEL CENSUS; POPULATION STUDIES;).

2427. Rose, E. T., and T. Moen. 1953. The increase in game fish population in east Okoboji Lake, Iowa following intensive removal of rough fish. Trans. Am. Fish. Soc. 82:104-114. (WALLEYE; HABITAT IMPROVEMENT; POPULATION STUDIES; SAMPLING METHODS;).

141

2428. Rose, G. A. 1984. The Goulais River walleye population — an account of the demise of a fishery. Ont. Min. Nat. Res., Rep. 23 pp. (WALLEYE; COMMUNITY DYNAMICS; ECOLOGY; HABITAT DEGRADATION; LIFE HISTORY; MORTALITY; MOVEMENT AND MIGRATIONS; SPAWNING STUDIES; TOXICANTS;).

2429. Rose, G. A., and M. F. Bernier. 1984. An inventory of fish habitat and populations of the Lower Goulais River during 1984. Ont. Min. Nat. Res., Rep. 49 pp. (WALLEYE; COMMUNITY DYNAMICS; ECOLOGY; MOVEMENT AND MIGRATIONS; SAMPLING METHODS; SPAWNING STUDIES;).

2430. Rose, G. A., and G. Kruppert. 1984. An assessment of the walleye fishery and migratory patterns of other species — Goulais River, Spring of 1984. Ont. Min. Nat. Res., Rep. 18 pp. (WALLEYE; CREEL CENSUS; MOVEMENT AND MIGRATIONS; POPULATION STUDIES; SPAWNING STUDIES;).

2431. Roseberry, D. A. 1950. Fishery management of Clayton Lake, an impoundment of the New River in Virginia. Trans. Am. Fish. Soc. 80:194-209. (WALLEYE; AGE AND GROWTH; CREEL CENSUS; FOOD STUDIES; IMPOUNDMENTS; POPULATION STUDIES; STOCKING;).

2432. Roseborough, J. D. 1958. Yellow pickerel tagging program, Lake Erie District, 1957. Ont. Dept. Lands Forest., Fish Wildl. Manage. Rep. 44:40-44. (SAUGER; WALLEYE; MARKING; MORTALITY; MOVEMENT AND MIGRATIONS;).

2433. Ross, M. J., and C. F. Kleiner. 1982. Shielded needle technique for surgically implanting radio frequency transmitters in fish. Prog. Fish-Cult. 44:41-43. (WALLEYE; MARKING;).

2434. Ross, M. J., and D. B. Siniff. 1980. Spatial distribution and temperature selection of fish near the thermal outfall of a power plant during fall, winter and spring. U.S. Environ. Prot. Agency, Environ. Research Lab., Duluth, Mn, EPA-600/3-80-009: 117 pp. (WALLEYE; BEHAVIOR; MARKING; MOVEMENTS AND MIGRATIONS;).

2435. Ross, M. J., and J. D. Winter. 1981. Winter movements of four fish species near a thermal plume in northern Minnesota. Trans. Am. Fish. Soc. 110:14-18. (WALLEYE; BEHAVIOR; MOVEMENT AND MIGRATIONS;).

2436. Rostlund, E. 1952. Freshwater fish and fishing in native North America. Univ. Calif., Publ. Geogr. 9:242. (SAUGER; WALLEYE; GEOGRAPHICAL DISTRIBUTION;).

2437. Rottiers, D. V., and C. A. Lemm. 1985. Movement of underyearling walleyes in response to odor and visual cues. Prog. Fish-Cult. 47:34-41. (WALLEYE; BEHAVIOR; PROPAGATION;).

2438. Rounsefell, G. A., and W. H. Everhart. 1953. Fishery science, its methods and applications. John Wiley and Sons, New N.Y. xii + p. 444. (WALLEYE; COMMUNITY DYNAMICS; ECOLOGY;).

2439. Roussow, G. 1953. Rearing and pathology of maskinonge, yellow pikeperch and carp, and other works. Que. Game Fish Dept., Biol. Bur., 9th Rep. pp. 377-383. (WALLEYE; PROPAGATION;).

2440. Rowes, K. D., and J. A. Mathias. 1986. A report to Parks Canada. Fed. Dept. Fish. Oceans, Freshwater Inst., Man. 13 pp. (WALLEYE; AGE AND GROWTH; COMMUNITY DYNAMICS; MARKING; MORTALITY; POPULATION STUDIES; REGULATIONS; SPAWNING STUDIES;).

2441. Royer, L. M. 1967. Evaluation of walleye reproduction and hatchery stocking in Greenwater Lake, 1961-1966. Sask. Dept. Nat. Res., Fish. Lab. Tech. Rep. 1967-2: 13 pp. (WALLEYE; SPAWNING STUDIES; STOCKING;).

2442. Rudd, J. W. M., A. Furatani, and M. A. Turner. 1980. Mercury methylation by fish intestinal contents. Applied Environ. Microbiology 40:777-782. (WALLEYE; TOXICANTS;).

2443. Rudstram, L. G. 1984. Long-term comparison of the population structure of cisco *Coregonus artedii* in smaller lakes. Trans. Wis. Acad. Sci., Arts Letters 72:185-200. (WALLEYE; COMMUNITY DYNAMICS; STOCKING;).

2444. Ruggles, C. P. 1959. Biological and fisheries survey of Dore Lake, 1956. Sask. Dept. Nat. Res., Fish. Lab. Tech. Rep. 59-3:44 pp. (WALLEYE; AGE AND GROWTH; COMMERCIAL FISHERIES; ECOLOGY; FOOD STUDIES; POPULATION STUDIES;).

2445. Russell, T. R. 1966. Fish population of the Current River. Mo. Conserv. Comm., Fed. Aid Fish Wildl. Restor. Proj. F-1-R-15, Wk. Pl. 9, Job No. 2: 16 pp. (SAUGER; WALLEYE; POPULATION STUDIES;).

2446. Russell, T. R. 1973. Walleye population in Current River. Mo. Dept. Conserv., Fed. Aid Fish Wildl. Restor. Proj. F-1-R-21, Study S-10, Job No. 2:20 pp. (WALLEYE; MARKING; MOVEMENTS AND MIGRATIONS; POPULATION STUDIES;).

2447. Ruthven, A. G. 1911. A biological survey of the sand dune region on the south shore of Saginaw Bay, Michigan. Mich. Geol. Biol. Surv., Pub. 4, Biol. Serv. 2: 256 pp. (WALLEYE; COMMERCIAL FISHERIES;).

2448. Rutledge, W. P., and S. G. Clarke. 1972. Walleye (Stizostedion vitreum) life history. Tex. Parks Wildl. Dept., Fed. Aid Fish Wild. Restor. Proj. F-7-R-20, Job No. 17a: 10 pp. (WALLEYE; PATHOLOGY; POPULATION STUDIES; SPAWNING STUDIES;).

2449. Ryan, P. 1975. Creel survey report Nagagami Lake. Ont. Min. Nat. Res., Rep. 36 pp. (WALLEYE; CREEL CENSUS;).

2450. Rybicki, R. W. 1962. Results of the small otter trawl trials, September, 1961. Man. Dept. Mines Nat. Res., Fish Branch, Manuscript Rep. 12 pp. (SAUGER; WALLEYE; SAMPLING METHODS;).

2451. Rybicki, R. W. 1962. Pickerel tag returns, Lake Winnipeg, 1959-1962. Man. Dept. Mines Nat. Res, Fish. Branch, Manuscript Rep. 15 pp. (WALLEYE; MARKING; MOVEMENT AND MIGRATIONS;).

2452. Ryckman, J. R. 1986. A creel survey of sportfishing in Saginaw Bay, Lake Huron, 1983-84. Mich. Dept. Nat. Res., Fish. Tech. Rep. 86-4: 35 pp. (WALLEYE; CREEL CENSUS;).

2453. Ryckman, J. R. 1986. Effectiveness of fish ladders in the Grand River. Mich. Dept. Nat. Res., Research Rep. 1937: 23 pp. (WALLEYE; FISHWAYS;).

2454. Ryckman, J. R., and R. N. Lockwood. 1985. On-site creel surveys in Michigan 1975-82. Mich. Dept. Nat. Res., Fish. Research Rep. No. 1922: 96 pp. (WALLEYE; CREEL CENSUS;).

2455. Ryder, R. A. 1956. A creel census of the Black Sturgeon area, 1956. Ont. Dept. Land Forest., Manuscript Rep. 14 pp. (WALLEYE; CREEL CENSUS;).

2456. Ryder, R. A. 1960. Comparative tagging returns employing three different anaesthetics. Can. Fish Cult. 26:23-25. (WALLEYE; MARKING; POPULATION STUDIES;).

2457. Ryder, R. A. 1961. Lymphocystis as a mortality factor in walleye population. Prog. Fish-Cult. 23:183-186. (WALLEYE; MORTALITY; PATHOLOGY;).

2458. Ryder, R. A. 1961. Preliminary report of fisheries inventory work in the Patricias 1959-1960. Limnological aspects of Patricia Lakes. Ont. Dept. Land Forests., Manuscript Rep. 25p. (WALLEYE; PRODUCTIVITY;).

2459. Ryder, R. A. 1965. A method for estimating the potential fish production of north-temperate lakes. Trans. Am. Fish. Soc. 94:214-218. (WALLEYE; COMMERCIAL FISHERIES; COMMUNITY DYNAMICS; HABITAT DEGRADATION; MARKING; MOVEMENT AND MIGRATIONS; POPULATION STUDIES; SPAWNING STUDIES;).

2460. Ryder, R. A. 1968. Dynamics and exploitation of mature walleyes, (Stizostedion vitreum vitreum) in the Nipigon Bay region of Lake Superior. J. Fish. Research Board Can. 25:1347-1376. (WALLEYE; COMMERCIAL FISHERIES; COMMUNITY DYNAMICS; CREEL CENSUS; HABITAT DEGRADATION; MARKING; MORTALITY; MOVEMENTS AND MIGRATIONS; POPULATION STUDIES; SPAWNING STUDIES;).

2461. Ryder, R. A. 1973. Major advances in fisheries management in North American Glacial lakes. Pages 115-127 in N.G. Benson, ed. A Century of fisheries in North America. Am. Fish. Soc. Sp. Publ. No. 7, Washington,

D.C. (WALLEYE; ECOLOGY; STOCK-ING;).

2462. Ryder, R. A. 1977. Effects of ambient light variations on behavior of yearling, subadult, and adult walleyes *(Stizostedion vitreum vitreum)*. J. Fish. Research Board Can. 34:1481-1491. (WALLEYE; BEHAVIOR;).

2463. Ryder, R. A., and S. R. Kerr. 1978. The adult walleye in the percid community — a niche definition based on feeding behavior and food specificity. Pages 39-51 *in* R.L. Kendall, ed. Selected coolwater fishes of North America. Am. Fish. Soc. Sp. Publ. No. 11, Washington D.C. (WALLEYE; COMMUNITY DYNAMICS; ECOLOGY;).

2464. Ryder, R. A., S. R. Kerr, K. H. Loftus, and H. A. Regier. 1974. The morphoedaphic index, a fish yield estimator — review and evaluation. J. Fish. Research Board Can. 31:663-686. (WALLEYE; PRODUCTIVITY;).

2465. Ryder, R. A., W. B. Scott, and E. J. Crossman. 1964. Fishes of northern Ontario, north of the Albany River. Roy. Ont. Mus. Contrib. 60:30 pp. (SAUGER; WALLEYE; GEOGRAPHICAL DISTRIBUTION;).

2466. Sadoswky, J. A. 1983. Winter creel census report. Ont. Min. Nat. Res., Rep. 44 pp. (WALLEYE; CREEL CENSUS;).

2467. Sakamote, C. J., and D. A. White. 1974. A growth and fecundity study in Utah Lake walleye spawning on the Provo River, spring, 1974. Utah Acad. Proc. 51:69-72. (WALLEYE; AGE AND GROWTH; SPAWNING STUDIES;).

2468. Sandhu, J. S. 1979. Annual production and population dynamics of a relatively unexploited walleye *(Stizostedion vitreum)* population in Savanne Lake, Ontario. M.S. Thesis, Lakehead Univ.,Thunder Bay, Ont. 139 pp. (WALLEYE; COMMUNITY DYNAMICS; ECOLOGY; POPULATION STUDIES;).

2469. Sauter, S., K. S. Burton, K. J. Macek, and S. R. Petrocelli. 1976. Effects of exposure to heavy metals on selected freshwater fish. U.S. Environ. Prot. Agency, Natl. Environ. Research Cent. Ecol. Research Ser. EPA-600/3-76-105.x + 75 pp. (WALLEYE; TOXICANTS;).

2470. Savoie, P. J. 1983. Exploratory fishing for y.o.y. walleye in the Bay of Quinte, summer, 1982. Ont. Min. Nat. Res., LOFAU Rep. 83-1: 95 pp. (WALLEYE; POPULATION STUDIES; SAMPLING METHODS;).

2471. Savoie, P. J. 1984. Spawning and early life history assessment of walleye in the Bay of Quinte area. Ont. Min. Nat. Res., LOFAU Rep. 84-1: 46 pp. (WALLEYE; ECOLOGY; LIFE HISTORY; SAMPLING METHODS; SPAWNING STUDIES;).

2472. Sawyko, P. M. 1985. Fishes in the barge canal and tributary waters of central and western New York 1979-1980. Proc. Rochester Acad. Sci. 15:192-199. (WALLEYE; POPULATION STUDIES;).

2473. Schachow, H. 1973. Creel census survey Nagagamisis Lake. Ont. Min. Nat. Res., Rep. 22 pp. (WALLEYE; CREEL CENSUS;).

2474. Schachow, H. 1976. Nagagamisis Lake creel survey. Ont. Min. Nat. Res., Rep. 35 pp. (WALLEYE; AGE AND GROWTH; CREEL CENSUS;).

2475. Schademann, R. 1987. Food habits, growth and distribution of walleye in Clinton Reservoir, Kansas. Kans. Fish Game Comm., Fish. I & D No. 87-2: 63 pp. (WALLEYE; AGE AND GROWTH; FOOD STUDIES; IMPOUNDMENTS; MOVEMENTS AND MIGRATIONS; STOCKING;).

2476. Schaeffer, F. S., and F. J. Margraf. 1987. Predation of fish eggs by white perch, *Morone americana*, in western Lake Erie. Environ. Biol. Fish. 18:77-80. (WALLEYE; COMMUNITY DYNAMICS;).

2477. Schainost, S. 1983. Harvest and population dynamics of the walleye in Branched Oak Lake, Nebraska. Neb. Game Parks Comm., Tech. Serv. 12: 35pp. (WALLEYE; AGE AND GROWTH; CREEL CENSUS; MARKING; MORTALITY; POPULATION STUDIES;).

2478. Schainost, S., and S. Satra. 1986. Reservoir investigations: population dynamics of the fishes in Branched Oak, Pawnee, and East Twin lakes, Nebraska. Neb. Game Parks Comm., Fed. Aid Fish Wildl. Restor. Proj. F-51-R: 123 pp. (WALLEYE; AGE AND GROWTH; FOOD STUDIES; POPULATION STUDIES;).

2479. Schaner, T. 1986. Sports fisheries in the Bay of Quinte, 1981-1986. Ont. Min. Nat. Res., Internal Rep. LOFAU (86.11): 80 pp. (WALLEYE; CREEL CENSUS;).

2480. Scheftel, Z. 1958. An economic evaluation of the sport fishery in Minnesota. Trans. 23rd N. Am. Wildl. Conf. 23:262-268. (WALLEYE; CREEL CENSUS; SOCIO-ECONOMICS OF FISHERIES;).

2481. Scheftel, Z. 1958. An economic evaluation of the sport fishery in Minnesota-Part One. Minn. Fish Game Invest., Fish. Ser. 1:26-34. (WALLEYE; CREEL CENSUS; SOCIO-ECONOMICS OF FISHERIES;).

2482. Scheider, W. A., D. S. Jeffries, and P. J. Dillon. 1979. Effects of acidic precipitation on Precambrian freshwaters in southern Ontario. J. Great Lakes Research 5:45-51. (WALLEYE; HABITAT DEGRADATION;).

2483. Schelske, C. L. 1957. An ecological study of the fishes of Fall and Verdigris Rivers in Wilson and Montgomery Counties, Kansas, March 1954 to February 1955. M.S. Thesis, Kans. State Teacher's Coll., Emporia, Kans. 153 pp. (WALLEYE; GEOGRAPHICAL DISTRIBUTION; LIFE HISTORY;).

2484. Scherer, E. 1971. Effects of oxygen depletion and of carbon dioxide buildup on the photic behavior of the walleye (Stizostedion vitreum vitreum). J. Fish. Research Board Can. 28:1303-1307. (WALLEYE; BEHAVIOR; ECOLOGY;).

2485. Scherer, E. 1976. Overhead-light intensity and vertical positioning of the walleye, Stizostedion vitreum vitreum. J. Fish. Research Board Can. 33:289-292. (WALLEYE; BEHAVIOR; ECOLOGY;).

2486. Scherer, E. 1979. Testing responsiveness to overhead-light stimulation. From Scherer, E. 1979. Toxicity Tests for Freshwater Organisms. Can. Spec. Publ., Fish. Aquat. Sci. 44:171-178. (WALLEYE; BEHAVIOR; PHYSIOLOGY; TOXICANTS;).

2487. Scherer, E., F. A. J. Armstrong, and S. H. Nowak. 1975. Effects of mercury-contaminated diet upon walleyes, Stizostedion vitreum vitreum (Mitchill). Fish. Marine Serv., Can. Tech. Rep. No. 597: 21 pp. (WALLEYE; HABITAT DEGRADATION; TOXICANTS;).

2488. Schiavone, A., Jr. 1981. Decline of the walleye population in Black Lake. N.Y. Fish Game J. 28:68-72. (WALLEYE; AGE AND GROWTH; COMMUNITY DYNAMICS; POPULATION STUDIES;).

2489. Schiavone, A., Jr. 1983. The Black Lake fish community: 1931 to 1979. N.Y. Fish Game J. 30:78-90. (WALLEYE; AGE AND GROWTH; COMMUNITY DYNAMICS; POPULATION STUDIES;).

2490. Schiavone, A., Jr. 1984. Rates of exploitation and survival of walleyes in Black Lake, 1953-1971. N.Y. Fish Game J. 31: 112-115. (WALLEYE; COMMUNITY DYNAMICS; MARKING; MORTALITY; POPULATION STUDIES; SPAWNING STUDIES;).

2491. Schiavone, A., Jr. 1985. Response of walleye populations to the introduction of the black crappie in the Indian River Lakes. N.Y. Fish Game J. 32:114-140. (WALLEYE; AGE AND GROWTH; COMMUNITY DYNAMICS; ECOLOGY; POPULATION STUDIES; STOCKING;).

2492. Schlagenhaft, T. W., and B. R. Murphy. 1985. Habitat use and overlap between adult largemouth bass and walleye in a west Texas Reservoir. N. Am. J. Fish. Manage. 5:465-470. (WALLEYE; COMMUNITY DYNAMICS; ECOLOGY; IMPOUNDMENTS; MARKING; MOVEMENTS AND MIGRATIONS;).

2493. Schlesinger, D. A., and N. G. Maclean. 1983. The winter sport fisheries of Big Clear, Big Rideau, Big Salmon, Charleston and Devil Lakes, 1982. Ont. Min. Nat. Res., Rideau Lakes Fish. Assess. Unit, Rep. No. 6: 70 pp. (WALLEYE; CREEL CENSUS;).

2494. Schlesinger, D. A., and A. M. McCombie. 1983. An evaluation of climatic, morphoedaphic, and effort data as predictors of yields from Ontario sport fisheries. Ont. Min. Nat. Res., Ont. Fish. Tech. Rep. No. 10: 14 pp. (WALLEYE; CREEL CENSUS; PRODUCTIVITY;).

2495. Schlesinger, D. A., and H. A. Regier. 1983. Relationship between environmental temperature and yields of subarctic and temperate zone fish species. Can. J. Fish. Aquat. Sci. 40:1829-1837. (WALLEYE; AGE AND GROWTH; ECOLOGY; POPULATION STUDIES;).

2496. Schlesinger, D. A., G. E. Ridout, and N. G. Maclean. 1984. The sport fisheries of Long, Mica, Opinicon, Sydenham and Upper Rideau Lakes, 1982. Ont. Min. Nat. Res., Rideau Lakes Fish. Assess. Unit Rep. 60 pp. (WALLEYE; CREEL CENSUS;).

2497. Schlick, R. O. 1968. A survey of Sipiwesk Lake in 1966. Man. Dept. Mines Nat. Res., Fish. Branch, Manuscript Rep. 68-5:17 pp. (SAUGER; WALLEYE; AGE AND GROWTH; COMMERCIAL FISHERIES; PRODUCTIVITY;).

2498. Schlick, R. O. 1968. A survey of Setting Lake in 1967. Man. Dept. Mines Nat. Res., Fish. Branch Manuscript Rep. 68-6:17 pp. (SAUGER; WALLEYE; AGE AND GROWTH; COMMERCIAL FISHERIES; PRODUCTIVITY;).

2499. Schlick, R. O. 1973. Paint Lake creel census 1968. Man. Mines Res. Environ. Manage. Research Board Manuscript Rep. 73-14: 15 pp. (WALLEYE; CREEL CENSUS;).

2500. Schlick, R. O. 1978. A history of sauger (Stizostedion canadense) and walleye (S. vitreum vitreum) harvests, South Basin, Lake Winnipeg and literature review of ecological influences on these species. Man. Dept. Min. Nat. Res. Envir., Fish. Manage. Branch, Manuscript Rep. No. 78-78: 36 pp. (SAUGER; WALLEYE; COMMERCIAL FISHERIES; ECOLOGY; SOCIO-ECONOMICS OF FISHERIES;).

2501. Schlick, R. O. 1978. Management for walleye or sauger, South Basin, Lake Winnipeg. Pages 266-269 in R.L. Kendall, ed. Selected coolwater fishes of North America. Am. Fish. Soc. Sp. Publ. No. 11, Washington, D.C. (SAUGER; WALLEYE; COMMERCIAL FISHERIES; HABITAT DEGRADATION; PRODUCTIVITY; SOCIO-ECONOMICS OF FISHERIES;).

2502. Schloemer, C. L., and R. Lorch. 1942. The rate of growth of walleyed pike, Stizostedion vitreum (Mitchill), in Wisconsin's inland waters with special reference to the growth characteristics of the Trout Lake population. Trans. Am. Fish. Soc. 81:179-196. (WALLEYE; AGE AND GROWTH;).

2503. Schmidt, P. J. 1949. Analyses of freshwater fishes from Canadian interior provinces. Fish. Research Board Can., Ind. Mem. 12: 10 pp. (WALLEYE; GEOGRAPHICAL DISTRIBUTION;).

2504. Schmidt, P. J. 1950. Analyses of freshwater fishes from Canadian interior provinces. Fish. Research Board Can., Ind. Mem. 13:8 pp. (WALLEYE; GEOGRAPHICAL DISTRIBUTION;).

2505. Schmitt, C. J., M. A. Ribick, J. L. Ludke, and T. W. May. 1983. National pesticide monitoring program: organochlorine residues in freshwater fish, 1976-1979. U.S. Fish and Wildl. Serv., Res. Publ. 152:62 pp. (SAUGER; WALLEYE; HABITAT DEGRADATION; TOXICANTS;).

2506. Schmulbach, J. C. 1959. Factors affecting the harvest of fish in the Des Moines River, Boone County, Iowa. Ph.D. Dissertation, Iowa State Univ., Ames, Iowa. 195 pp. (WALLEYE; CREEL CENSUS;).

2507. Schmulbach, J. C. 1959. Growth of the walleye in the Des Moines River, Boone County, Iowa. Iowa Acad. Sci. 66:523-533. (WALLEYE; AGE AND GROWTH; ECOLOGY; STOCKING;).

2508. Schneider, J. C. 1969. Results of experimental stocking of walleye fingerlings, 1951-1963. Mich. Dept. Nat. Res., Fish. Research Rep. 1753: 31 pp. (WALLEYE; AGE AND GROWTH; CREEL CENSUS; POPULATION STUDIES; STOCKING;).

2509. Schneider, J. C. 1974. Growth, survival, and food habits of walleyes, related to food. Mich. Dept. Nat. Res., Fed. Aid Fish Wildl. Restor. Proj. F-29-R-8, Study 14, Job No. 2: 6 pp. (WALLEYE; AGE AND GROWTH; FOOD STUDIES; MORTALITY; PROPAGATION;).

2510. Schneider, J. C. 1975. Typology and fisheries potential of Michigan Lakes. Mich. Acad. Science. 8:59-84. (WALLEYE; ECOLOGY; GEOGRAPHICAL DISTRIBUTION;).

2511. Schneider, J. C. 1975. Survival, growth and food of 4 inch walleyes in ponds with invertebrates, sunfishes or minnows. Mich. Dept. Nat. Res., Fish Research Rep. No. 1833:18 pp. (WALLEYE; AGE AND GROWTH; FOOD STUDIES; MORTALITY; PRODUCTIVITY; STOCKING;).

2512. Schneider, J. C. 1977. Pilot study on Muskegon River walleyes. Mich. Dept. Nat. Res., Fed. Aid Fish Wildl. Restor. Proj. F-35-R-3 (Study Group 2) Study No. 18: 115-137. (WALLEYE; AGE AND GROWTH; CREEL CENSUS; MARKING; MOVEMENTS AND MIGRATIONS; SPAWNING STUDIES;).

2513. Schneider, J. C. 1977. History of the walleye fisheries of Saginaw Bay, Lake Huron. Mich. Dept. Nat. Res., Fish. Research Rep. No. 1850: 16 pp. (WALLEYE; COMMERCIAL FISHERIES; COMMUNITY DYNAMICS; ECOLOGY; HABITAT DEGRADATION; SPAWNING STUDIES;).

2514. Schneider, J. C. 1978. Selection of minimum size limits for walleye fishing in Michigan. Pages 398-407 in R.L. Kendall, ed. Selected coolwater fishes of North America. Am. Fish. Soc. Sp. Publ. No. 11, Washington, D.C. (WALLEYE; AGE AND GROWTH; MORTALITY; PRODUCTIVITY; REGULATIONS; SPAWNING STUDIES;).

2515. Schneider, J. C. 1979. Survival, growth, and vulnerability to angling of walleyes stocked as fingerlings in a small lake with yellow perch and minnows. Mich. Dept. Nat. Res., Fish. Research Rep. No. 1875: 20 pp. (WALLEYE; AGE AND GROWTH; COMMUNITY DYNAMICS; CREEL CENSUS; FOOD STUDIES; MORTALITY; PRODUCTIVITY; STOCKING;).

2516. Schneider, J. C. 1981. Fish communities in warm water lakes. Mich. Dept. Nat. Res., Fish. Research Rep. No. 1890: 22 pp. (WALLEYE; COMMUNITY DYNAMICS; ECOLOGY; POPULATION STUDIES;).

2517. Schneider, J. C. 1983. Experimental walleye-perch management in a small lake. Mich. Dept. Nat. Res., Research Rep. No. 1905: 30 pp. (WALLEYE; COMMUNITY DYNAMICS; CREEL CENSUS; MORTALITY;).

2518. Schneider, J. C. 1984. Pilot study to evaluate status of Jewett Lake fish community. Mich. Dept. Nat. Res., Fed. Aid Fish Wildl. Restor. Proj. F-35-R-9 Final Report: 6 pp. (WALLEYE; COMMUNITY DYNAMICS; CREEL CENSUS; POPULATION STUDIES;).

2519. Schneider, J. C., and W. R. Crowe. 1977. A synopsis of walleye tagging experiments in Michigan, 1929-1965. Mich. Dept. Nat. Res., Fish. Research Rep. No. 1844: 29 pp. (WALLEYE; AGE AND GROWTH; MARKING; MORTALITY; MOVEMENTS AND MIGRATIONS;).

2520. Schneider, J. C., P. H. Eschmeyer, and W. R. Crowe. 1976. Longevity, survival and harvest of tagged walleyes in Lake Gogebic, Michigan. Mich. Dept. Nat. Res., Fish. Research Rep. No. 1842: 8 pp. (WALLEYE; AGE AND GROWTH; MARKING;).

2521. Schneider, J. C., P. H. Eschmeyer, and W. R. Crowe. 1977. Longevity, survival, and harvest of tagged walleyes in Lake Gogebic, Michigan. Trans. Am. Fish. Soc. 106:566-568. (WALLEYE; AGE AND GROWTH; MARKING; MORTALITY;).

2522. Schneider, J. C., and T. M. Kelly. 1973. Additional observations on growth rate and food habits of the walleye in Michigan waters. Mich. Dept. Nat. Res., Fish. Research Rep. No. 1796: 10 pp. (WALLEYE; AGE AND GROWTH; FOOD STUDIES;).

2523. Schneider, J. C., and J. H. Leach. 1977. Walleye (Stizostedion vitreum vitreum) fluctuations in the Great Lakes and possible causes, 1800-1975. J. Fish. Research Board Can. 34:1878-1889. (SAUGER; WALLEYE; COMMERCIAL FISHERIES; CREEL CENSUS; HABITAT DEGRADATION; PRODUCTIVITY;).

2524. Schneider, J. C., and J. H. Leach. 1979. Walleye stocks in the Great Lakes, 1800-1975: Fluctuations and possible causes. Great Lakes Fish. Comm., Tech. Rep. No. 31: 51 pp. (SAUGER; WALLEYE; AGE AND GROWTH; COMMERCIAL FISHERIES; CREEL CENSUS; HABITAT DEGRADATION; MARKING; POPULATION STUDIES;).

2525. Schneider, J. C., and R. N. Lockwood. 1979. Effects of regulations on the fisheries of Michigan lakes, 1946-65. Mich. Dept. Nat. Res., Fish. Research Rep. No. 1872: 247 pp. (WALLEYE; REGULATIONS;).

2526. Schneider, J. C., and R. J. Spiter. 1987. A study of walleye in Belleville Lake, Wayne County, 1976-80. Mich. Dept. Nat. Res., Tech. Rep. No. 87-4: 9 pp. (WALLEYE; AGE AND GROWTH; IMPOUNDMENTS; MARKING; MOVEMENT AND

MIGRATIONS; POPULATION STUD-
IES; SPAWNING STUDIES;).

2527. Schneider, R. W., W. K. Wilson, and B. L.
Evenhuis. 1977. Migration of sauger past a
thermal discharge in Melton Hill Reservoir.
Proc. 31st Annu. Conf. Southeast. Assoc.
Fish Wildl. Agencies 31:538-545.
(SAUGER; ECOLOGY; IMPOUND-
MENTS; MARKING; MOVEMENTS
AND MIGRATIONS;).

2528. Schnerberger, E. 1948. Natural propagation
of fishes. Trans. 13th N. Am. Wildl. Conf.
13:198-206. (WALLEYE; STOCKING;).

2529. Schoettger, R. A., and E. W. Steucke, Jr.
1970. Quinaldine and MS-222 as spawning
aids for northern pike, muskellunge, and
walleyes. Prog. Fish-Cult. 32:199-201.
(WALLEYE; PHYSIOLOGY; PROPAGA-
TION; SPAWNING STUDIES;).

2530. Scholl, R. L., and G. L. Rudolph. 1970. Walleye spawning area study in western Lake
Erie. Ohio Dept. Nat. Res., Fed. Aid Fish
Wildl. Restor. Proj. F-35-R-9, Job No. 1:24
pp. (WALLEYE; SPAWNING STUDIES;).

2531. Schoonover, R., and W. H. Thompson. 1954.
A post-impoundment study of the fisheries
resources of Fall River Reservoir, Kansas.
Trans. Kans. Acad. Sci. 57:172-179. (WALL-
EYE; AGE AND GROWTH; INTRODUC-
TIONS;).

2532. Schoumacher, R. 1963. A summary of an in-
tensive creel census on pools 11 and 18 of
the Mississippi River. Iowa State Conserv.
Comm., Quart. Biol. Rep. 16:51-54.
(SAUGER; WALLEYE; CREEL CEN-
SUS;).

2533. Schoumacher, R. 1965. Movement of walleye
and sauger in the upper Mississippi River.
Trans. Am. Fish. Soc. 94:270-271.
(SAUGER; WALLEYE; MARKING;
MOVEMENT AND MIGRATIONS;).

2534. Schrader, F., and S. H. Schrader. 1922. Mor-
tality in pike-perch eggs in hatcheries. U.S.
Bur. Fish., Annu Rep. Append. 5 :1-11.
(WALLEYE; EMBRYOLOGY; MORTAL-
ITY; PROPAGATION;).

2535. Schraeder, H., and B. Walroth. 1984. An investigation into the status of transplanted
walleye populations in two Nipigon District
lakes. Ont. Min. Nat. Res., Manuscript Rep.

50 pp. (WALLEYE; AGE AND GROWTH;
COMMUNITY DYNAMICS; ECOLOGY;
POPULATION STUDIES; STOCKING;).

2536. Schrenkeisen, R. 1938. Field book of fresh-
water fishes of North America north of
Mexico. G. P. Putnam's Sons, New York,
N.Y. 312 pp. (SAUGER; WALLEYE; TAX-
ONOMY;).

2537. Schreyer, F. 1967. Fish population control.
Kans. Forest. Fish Game Comm., Fed. Aid
Fish Wildl. Restor. Proj. F-15-R-1, Job B-
1:41 pp. (WALLEYE; AGE AND
GROWTH; IMPOUNDMENTS; MOR-
TALITY; STOCKING;).

2538. Schreyer, F. 1967. Fish stocking needs. Kans.
Forest., Fish Game Comm., Fed. Aid Fish
Wildl. Restor. Proj. F-15-R-1, Job C-1:21 pp.
(WALLEYE; AGE AND GROWTH;
ECOLOGY; IMPOUNDMENTS; INTRO-
DUCTIONS; STOCKING;).

2539. Schuiling, W. C. 1939. Incidence of infection
of fish with Clinostomum marginatum in
northern Minnesota. Proc. Minn. Acad. Sci.
7:49-52. (WALLEYE; PATHOLOGY;).

2540. Schultz, C. A. 1971. Survey of the walleye
population and related parameters in the
Tombigee River system in Mississippi.
Miss. Game Fish Comm., Fed. Aid Fish
Wildl. Restor. Proj. F-23(Final Report), Job
No. 1-4: 47 pp. (WALLEYE; AGE AND
GROWTH; COMMERCIAL FISHERIES;
COMMUNITY DYNAMICS; CREEL
CENSUS; ECOLOGY; GEOGRAPHICAL
DISTRIBUTION; HABITAT DEGRADA-
TION; POPULATION STUDIES;
SPAWNING STUDIES;).

2541. Schultz, F. H. 1956. Transfer of anaesthetized
pike and yellow walleye. Can. Fish. Cult.
18:1-5. (WALLEYE; STOCKING;).

2542. Schulz, R. L. 1970. Walleye tagging in Lake
Kampeska. S.D. Dept. Game Fish Parks,
Fed. Aid Fish Wildl. Restor. Proj. F-20-R-3,
Job No. 3:7 pp. (WALLEYE; MARKING;
MOVEMENT AND MIGRATIONS;).

2543. Schumacher, R. E. 1964. Preliminary results
from experimental introduction of rainbow
trout as an additional game fish in large
Minnesota lakes. Minn. Dept. Conserv., Invest. Rep. No. 279:42 pp. (WALLEYE;
AGE AND GROWTH; COMMUNITY DY-

NAMICS; POPULATION STUDIES; STOCKING;).

2544. Schumann, G. O. 1963. Artificial light to attract young perch: a new method of augmenting the food supply of predacious fish fry in hatcheries. Prog. Fish-Cult. 25:171-174. (WALLEYE; BEHAVIOR;).

2545. Schumann, G. O. 1964. The effect of abnormal temperature on the spawning and developmental success of eggs from the North American walleye *(Stizostedion vitreum)*. Osterreichs Fishcerei 5:1-5. (WALLEYE; BEHAVIOR; ECOLOGY; SPAWNING STUDIES;).

2546. Schupp, D. H. 1959. A five-year study of the population and catch of a central Minnesota bass-panfish lake, Nokay Lake, Crow Wing County. Minn. Dept. Conserv., Invest. Rep. No. 206: 18 pp. (WALLEYE; CREEL CENSUS;).

2547. Schupp, D. H. 1959. Three years of creel census on White Sand Lake, Crow Wing County. Minn. Dept. Conserv., Invest. Rep. No. 213: 6 pp. (WALLEYE; CREEL CENSUS;).

2548. Schupp, D. H. 1959. A qualitative creel census of Mille Lacs Lake, April 1958 — March 1959. Minn. Dept. Conserv., Invest. Rep. No. 217: 11 pp. (WALLEYE; AGE AND GROWTH; CREEL CENSUS; POPULATION STUDIES;).

2549. Schupp, D. H. 1964. A method of creel census applicable to large lakes. Minn. Dept. Conserv., Invest. Rep. No. 274:10 pp. (WALLEYE; CREEL CENSUS;).

2550. Schupp, D. H. 1972. The walleye fishery of Leech Lake, Minnesota. Minn. Dept. Nat. Res., Invest. Rep. No. 317:11 pp. (WALLEYE; AGE AND GROWTH; COMMUNITY DYNAMICS; CREEL CENSUS; MORTALITY; MOVEMENTS AND MIGRATIONS;).

2551. Schupp, D. H. 1974. The fish population structure and angling harvest of Lake of the Woods, Minnesota 1968-70. Minn. Dept. Nat. Res., Invest. Rep. No. 324:33 pp. (SAUGER; WALLEYE; AGE AND GROWTH; CREEL CENSUS; FISHING GEAR; MORTALITY; MOVEMENTS AND MIGRATIONS; POPULATION STUDIES;).

2552. Schupp, D. H. 1978. Walleye abundance, growth, movement, and yield in disparate environments within a Minnesota Lake. Pages 58-65 *in* R.L. Kendall, ed. Selected coolwater fishes of North America. Am. Fish. Soc. Sp. Publ. No. 11, Washington, D.C. (WALLEYE; AGE AND GROWTH; CREEL CENSUS; MORTALITY; POPULATION STUDIES;).

2553. Schupp, D. H., and V. Macins. 1977. Trends in percid yields from Lake of the Woods, 1888-1973. J. Fish. Research Board Can. 34:1784-1791. (SAUGER; WALLEYE; COMMERCIAL FISHERIES; CREEL CENSUS; POPULATION STUDIES;).

2554. Schutte, S. L. 1975. Evaluation of a walleye fishery. Iowa Conserv. Comm., 1975 Job Comp. Rep. Proj. 75-I-C-18:68-69. (WALLEYE; POPULATION STUDIES;).

2555. Schwalme, K., W. C. Mackay, and D. Lindner. 1985. Suitability of vertical slot and Denil fishways for passing north-temperate, non-salmonid fish. Can. J. Fish. Aquat. Sci. 42:1815-1822. (WALLEYE; FISHWAYS;).

2556. Schwartz, F. J., and C. A. Tryon, Jr. 1954. Comparisons of small fish populations in Pymatuning Lake, Pennsylvania. J. Wildl. Manage. 18:286-288. (WALLEYE; GEOGRAPHICAL DISTRIBUTION;).

2557. Schwartz, J. J. 1974. Prevalence of pathogenic pseudomonad bacteria isolated from fish in a warmwater lake. Trans. Am. Fish. Soc. 103:114-116. (WALLEYE; PATHOLOGY;).

2558. Schweigert, J. F., F. J. Ward, and J. W. Clayton. 1977. Effects of fry and fingerling introductions on walleye *(Stizostedion vitreum vitreum)* production in West Blue Lake, Manitoba. J. Fish. Research Board Can. 34:2142-2150. (WALLEYE; MARKING; POPULATION STUDIES; STOCKING;).

2559. Scidmore, W. J. 1955. Notes of the fish population structure of a typical rough fish-crappie lake of southern Minnesota. Minn. Dept. Conserv., Invest. Rep. No. 162: 11 pp. (WALLEYE; INTRODUCTIONS; STOCKING;).

2560. Scidmore, W. J. 1955. Notes of trapnet catches in two ponds and their populations present. Minn. Dept. Conserv., Invest. Rep.

No. 166: 3 pp. (WALLEYE; POPULATION STUDIES;).

2561. Scidmore, W. J. 1961. A test of the compressed air technique for marking fish. Minn. Dept. Conserv., Invest. Rep. No. 240: 8 pp. (WALLEYE; MARKING;).

2562. Scidmore, W. J. 1962. Report on first season's operation of a trawl fishery in Lake of the Woods, 1961. Minn. Dept. Conserv., Invest. Rep. No. 243: 8 pp. (SAUGER; WALLEYE; COMMERCIAL FISHERIES; COMMUNITY DYNAMICS; FISHWAYS;).

2563. Scidmore, W. J. 1963. Experimental commercial trawl fishing Lake of the Woods, Minnesota, 1961-62. Minn. Dept. Conserv., Invest. Rep. No. 266: 24 pp. (SAUGER; WALLEYE; AGE AND GROWTH; COMMERCIAL FISHERIES; FISHING GEAR;).

2564. Scidmore, W. J. 1970. Using winterkill to advantage. Pages 47-51 in E. Schneberger, ed. A symposium on the management of midwestern winterkill lakes. Am. Fish. Soc., N. Cent. Div. Sp. Publ., Bethesda, Md. (WALLEYE; ECOLOGY; STOCKING;).

2565. Scidmore, W. J., C. A. Elsey, and B. Caldwell. 1961. A fisheries survey of Basswood Lake 1961. Minn. Dept. Conserv., Invest. Rep. No. 241:12 pp. (WALLEYE; AGE AND GROWTH; FOOD STUDIES; POPULATION STUDIES; PRODUCTIVITY;).

2566. Scidmore, W. J., and D. E. Olson. 1969. Marking walleye fingerlings with oxytetracycline antibiotic. Prog. Fish-Cult. 31:213-216. (WALLEYE; MARKING;).

2567. Scidmore, W. J., and Z. Scheftel. 1958. Relative efficiency and selectivity of experimental gill nets of linen and nylon. Minn. Dept. Conserv., Fish Game Invest., Fish Ser. 1:46-53. (WALLEYE; FISHING GEAR; SAMPLING METHODS;).

2568. Scidmore, W. J., and D. E. Woods. 1960. Some observations on the competition between several species of fish for summer foods in four southern Minnesota lakes in 1955, 1956, and 1957. Minn. Dept. Conserv., Fish Game Invest., Fish. Ser. 2:13-24. (WALLEYE; COMMUNITY DYNAMICS; FOOD STUDIES;).

2569. Scidmore, W. J., and D. E. Woods. 1961. Changes in the fish populations of four southern Minnesota lakes subjected to rough fish removal. Minn. Dept. Conserv., Fish Game Invest., Fish. Ser. 3:19 pp. (WALLEYE; GEOGRAPHICAL DISTRIBUTION;).

2570. Scidmore, W. J., and L. Wroblewski. 1973. Mail survey of Minnesota resident fishermen — 1972. Minn. Dept. Nat. Res., Invest. Rep. No. 320:10 pp. (WALLEYE; CREEL CENSUS;).

2571. Scott, D. P. 1974. Mercury concentration of white muscle in relation to age, growth, and condition in four species of fishes from Clay Lake, Ontario. J. Fish. Research Board Can. 31:1723-1729. (WALLEYE; HABITAT DEGRADATION; TOXICANTS;).

2572. Scott, E. M., Jr. 1976. Dynamics of the Center Hill walleye population. Tenn. Wildl. Res. Agency, Tech. Rep. No. 76-55:86 pp. (WALLEYE; AGE AND GROWTH; FOOD STUDIES; IMPOUNDMENTS; MOVEMENTS AND MIGRATIONS; PROPAGATION; SPAWNING STUDIES; TAXONOMY;).

2573. Scott, K. R., and H. J. Ballon. 1983. Hydraulic automatic lift-gate mechanism for controlled release of walleye into Lake Winnipegosis. Can. Manuscript Rep. Fish. Aquat. Sci. Rep. No.1704: 15 pp. (WALLEYE; STOCKING;).

2574. Scott, W. B., and E. J. Crossman. 1961. A list of Ontario fishes. Roy. Ont. Mus., Dept. Fish. 6 pp. (SAUGER; WALLEYE; GEOGRAPHICAL DISTRIBUTION;).

2575. Scott, W. B., and E. J. Crossman. 1969. Checklist of Canadian freshwater fishes with keys for identification. Roy. Ont. Mus., Life Sci. Misc. Publ. 103 pp. (SAUGER; WALLEYE; MORPHOLOGY; TAXONOMY;).

2576. Scott, W. B., and E. J. Crossman. 1973. Freshwater fishes of Canada. Fish. Research Board Can. Bull. 184:966 pp. (SAUGER; WALLEYE; LIFE HISTORY;).

2577. Scriba, G. F. 1910. Oneida hatchery. N.Y. Forest, Fish Game Comm., 15th Annu. Rep. pp. 322-323. (WALLEYE; COMMUNITY DYNAMICS; MORTALITY; PROPAGATION; STOCKING;).

2578. Seaburg, K. G. 1957. A stomach sampler for live fish. Minn. Dept. Conserv., Invest. Rep. No. 193:9 pp. (WALLEYE; FOOD STUDIES;).

2579. Seaburg, K. G., and J. B. Moyle. 1964. Feeding habits, digestive rates, and growth of some Minnesota warmwater fishes. Trans. Am. Fish. Soc. 93:269-285. (WALLEYE; COMMUNITY DYNAMICS; FOOD STUDIES; PHYSIOLOGY;).

2580. Seehorn, M. E. 1975. Fishes of southeastern national forests. Proc. 29th Annu. Conf. Southeast Assoc. Fish Wild. Agencies 29:10-27. (SAUGER; WALLEYE; GEOGRAPHICAL DISTRIBUTION;).

2581. Seelye, J. G., L. L. Marking, E. L. King, Jr., L. H. Hanson, and T. D. Bills. 1987. Toxicity of TFM lampricide to early life stages of walleye. N. Am. J. Fish. Manage. 7:598-601. (WALLEYE; MORTALITY; TOXICANTS;).

2582. Selbig, W. 1970. Chemical rehabilitation of chronic winterkill lakes. Pages 27-30 in E. Schneberger, ed. A symposium on the management of midwestern winterkill lakes. Am. Fish. Soc., N. Cent. Div. Sp. Publ. (WALLEYE; ECOLOGY; STOCKING; TOXICANTS;).

2583. Sequin, L. 1958. Missisquoi Bay — A natural walleye nursery. Paper, Northeast Wildl. Conf. 11 pp. (WALLEYE; SPAWNING STUDIES; STOCKING;).

2584. Serns, S. L. 1978. Effects of a minimum size limit on the walleye population of a northern Wisconsin lake. Pages 390-397 in R.L. Kendall, ed. Selected coolwater fishes of North America. Am. Fish. Soc. Sp. Publ. No. 11, Washington, D.C. (WALLEYE; AGE AND GROWTH; CREEL CENSUS; PATHOLOGY; POPULATION STUDIES; PRODUCTIVITY; REGULATIONS;).

2585. Serns, S. L. 1979. Relationship of walleye fingerling density and electrofishing catch per effort in northern Wisconsin Lakes. Wis. Dept. Nat. Res., Fish Manage. Rep. No. 104:8 pp. (WALLEYE; POPULATION STUDIES;).

2586. Serns, S. L. 1981. Occurrence of accessory checks on the scales of walleye fingerlings stocked in mid-August. Prog. Fish-Cult.

43:46-47. (WALLEYE; AGE AND GROWTH;).

2587. Serns, S. L. 1981. Effects of a minimum length limit on the walleye population of Wolf Lake, Vilas County, Wisconsin. Wis. Dept. Nat. Res., Fish Manage. Rep. No. 106: 11 pp. (WALLEYE; AGE AND GROWTH; CREEL CENSUS; MORTALITY; POPULATION STUDIES; PRODUCTIVITY; REGULATIONS;).

2588. Serns, S. L. 1982. Relationship of walleye fingerling density and electrofishing catch per effort in northern Wisconsin lakes. N. Am. J. Fish. Manage. 2:38-44. (WALLEYE; FISHING GEAR; POPULATION STUDIES;).

2589. Serns, S. L. 1982. Walleye fecundity, potential egg deposition, and survival from egg to fall young-of-year in Escanaba Lake, Wisconsin, 1979-1981. N. Am. J. Fish. Manage. 2:388-394. (WALLEYE; AGE AND GROWTH; MORTALITY; SPAWNING STUDIES;).

2590. Serns, S. L. 1982. Influence of formalin on size of walleye eggs. Prog. Fish-Cult. 44:149. (WALLEYE; MORPHOLOGY; SPAWNING STUDIES;).

2591. Serns, S. L. 1982. Influence of various factors on density and growth of age-0 walleyes in Escanaba Lake, Wisconsin, 1958-1980. Trans. Am. Fish. Soc. 111:299-306. (WALLEYE; AGE AND GROWTH; ECOLOGY; POPULATION STUDIES; WATER LEVELS;).

2592. Serns, S. L. 1983. Relationship between electrofishing catch per unit effort and density of walleye yearlings. N. Am. J. Fish. Manage. 3:451-452. (WALLEYE; POPULATION STUDIES; SPAWNING STUDIES;).

2593. Serns, S. L. 1984. Walleye growth in relation to water temperature, food availability, and population density in Escanaba lake, 1956-1962. Wis. Dept. Nat. Res., Research Rep. No. 130: 16 pp. (WALLEYE; AGE AND GROWTH; CREEL CENSUS; ECOLOGY; FOOD STUDIES; POPULATION STUDIES;).

2594. Serns, S. L. 1985. Proportional stock density index — is it a useful tool for assessing fish populations in northern latitudes? Wis. Dept. Nat. Res., Research Rep. No. 132: 11 pp. (WALLEYE; CREEL CENSUS; FISHING GEAR; POPULATION STUDIES; SAMPLING METHODS;).

2595. Serns, S. L. 1986. Cohort analysis as an indication of walleye year-class strength in Escanaba Lake, Wisconsin. Trans. Am. Fish. Soc. 115:849-852. (WALLEYE; AGE AND GROWTH; CREEL CENSUS; POPULATION STUDIES; PRODUCTIVITY;).

2596. Serns, S. L. 1986. Impact of an artificial spawning operation on the walleye population of Escanaba lake, Wisconsin. Pages 263-270 in R.H. Stroud, ed. Fish culture in fisheries management. Am. Fish. Soc., Bethesda, Maryland. (WALLEYE; POPULATION STUDIES; SPAWNING STUDIES;).

2597. Serns, S. L. 1987. Relationship between the size of several walleye year classes and the percent harvested over the life of each cohort in Escanaba Lake, Wisconsin. N. Am. J. Fish. Manage. 7:305-306. (WALLEYE; CREEL CENSUS; LIFE HISTORY; POPULATION STUDIES;).

2598. Serns, S. L., and J. J. Kempinger. 1981. Relationship of angler exploitation to the size, age, and sex of walleyes in Escanaba Lake, Wisconsin. Trans. Am. Fish. Soc. 110:216-220. (WALLEYE; AGE AND GROWTH; CREEL CENSUS; FOOD STUDIES; MORTALITY; REGULATIONS;).

2599. Serns, S. L., and T. C. McKnight. 1974. A summer creel census of Stormy Black Oak, and Laura Lakes, Vilas County. Wis. Dept. Nat. Res., Fish. Manage. Sec. Rep. 71: 27 pp. (WALLEYE; CREEL CENSUS;).

2600. Shapovalov, L., and W. A. Dill. 1950. A check list of fresh-water and anadromous fishes of California. Calif. Fish Game J. 36:382-391. (WALLEYE; INTRODUCTIONS;).

2601. Shapovalov, L., W. A. Dill, and A. J. Cordone. 1959. A revised check list of the fresh-water and anadromous fishes of California. Calif. Fish Game J. 45:159-180. (WALLEYE; INTRODUCTIONS;).

2602. Sharp, R. W. 1941. Report of the investigation of biological conditions of Lake Kabetogama, Namakan and Crane, as influenced by fluctuating water levels. Minn. Dept.

Conserv., Invest. Rep. No. 30:58 pp. (SAUGER; WALLEYE; POPULATION STUDIES;).

2603. Sharp, R. W. 1942. Some studies of the distribution and ecology of german carp in Minnesota with suggested control measures. Minn. Dept. Conserv., Invest. Rep. No. 45:25 pp. (WALLEYE; COMMUNITY DYNAMICS; ECOLOGY; HABITAT IMPROVEMENT;).

2604. Shebley, W, H. 1917. History of the introduction of food and game fishes into the waters of California. Calif. Fish Game J. 3:1-10. (WALLEYE; INTRODUCTIONS;).

2605. Shelford, V. E., and M. W. Boesel. 1942. Bottom animal communities of the island area of western Lake Erie in the summer of 1937. Ohio J. Sci. 42:179-190. (SAUGER; WALLEYE; ECOLOGY;).

2606. Shetter, D. S. 1949. A brief history of the sea lamprey problem in Michigan waters. Trans. Am. Fish. Soc. 76:160-176. (WALLEYE; COMMUNITY DYNAMICS; MOVEMENT AND MIGRATIONS; PATHOLOGY;).

2607. Shields, J. T. 1955. Report of fisheries investigations during the second year of impoundment of Fort Randall Reservoir, South Dakota, 1954. S.D. Dept. Game, Fish Parks, Fed. Aid Fish Wildl. Restor. Proj. F-1-R-4, Jobs No. 4 and 5: 114 pp. (SAUGER; WALLEYE; AGE AND GROWTH; CREEL CENSUS; ECOLOGY; IMPOUNDMENTS; MARKING; POPULATION STUDIES;).

2608. Shields, J. T. 1956. Report of fisheries investigations during the third year of impoundment of Fort Randall Reservoir, South Dakota, 1955. S.D. Dept. Game, Fish Parks, Fed. Aid Fish Wildl. Restor. Proj. F-1-R-5, Jobs No. 4 and 5: 100 pp. (SAUGER; WALLEYE; AGE AND GROWTH; ECOLOGY; IMPOUNDMENTS; POPULATION STUDIES; PRODUCTIVITY;).

2609. Shields, J. T. 1957. Report of fisheries investigations during the fourth year of impoundment of Fort Randall Reservoir, South Dakota, 1956. S.D. Dept. Game, Fish Parks, Fed. Aid Fish Wildl. Restor. Proj. F-1-R-6, Job No. 5-A: 66 pp. (SAUGER; WALLEYE; AGE AND GROWTH; COMMUNITY DYNAMICS; CREEL CENSUS; IMPOUND-

MENTS; MARKING; MOVEMENT AND MIGRATIONS; POPULATION STUDIES; SPAWNING STUDIES; STOCKING; WATER LEVELS;).

2610. Shields, J. T. 1958. Report of fisheries investigations during the fifth year of impoundment of Fort Randall Reservoir, South Dakota, 1957. S.D. Dept. Game, Fish Parks, Fed. Aid Fish Wildl. Restor. Proj. F-1-R-7, Jobs No. 2, 3, 4-A, 5: 33 pp. (SAUGER; WALLEYE; AGE AND GROWTH; IMPOUNDMENTS; MARKING; POPULATION STUDIES; PRODUCTIVITY;).

2611. Shipman, S. T. 1985. Evaluation of the stocking of small walleye fingerlings in two natural lakes: 1984 Progress Report. Ind. Dept. Nat. Res. 30 pp. (WALLEYE; CREEL CENSUS; POPULATION STUDIES; STOCKING;).

2612. Shockley, C. H. 1949. Fish and invertebrate populations of an Indiana bass stream. Invest. of Ind. Lakes and Streams. 3:247-270. (SAUGER; GEOGRAPHICAL DISTRIBUTION;).

2613. Shodeen, D. 1965. Fisheries survey of Lake St. Croix from Oak Park Heights, Minnesota to vicinity of Hudson, Wisconsin 1964. Minn. Dept. Conserv., Invest. Rep. No. 283: 23 pp. (SAUGER; WALLEYE; POPULATION STUDIES;).

2614. Shodeen, D., and F. Tureson. 1975. A creel census of eighteen metropolitan lakes. Minn. Dept. Nat. Res., Fish Manage. Rep. No. 1: 48 pp. (WALLEYE; CREEL CENSUS;).

2615. Shoup, C. S., J. H. Peyton, and G. Gentry. 1941. A limited biological survey of the Obey River and adjacent streams in Tennessee. J. Tenn. Acad. Sci. 16:48-76. (SAUGER; GEOGRAPHICAL DISTRIBUTION;).

2616. Shuter, B. J., and J. F. Koonce. 1977. A dynamic model of the Western Lake Erie walleye (Stizostedion vitreum vitreum) population. J. Fish. Research Board Can. 34:1972-1982. (WALLEYE; AGE AND GROWTH; ECOLOGY; MORTALITY; POPULATION STUDIES; PRODUCTIVITY;).

2617. Shuter, B. J., J. F. Koonce, and H. A. Regier. 1979. Modeling the western Lake Erie wall-

eye population: a feasibility study. Great Lakes Fish. Comm., Tech. Rep. No. 32:40 pp. (WALLEYE; AGE AND GROWTH; ECOLOGY; MORTALITY; POPULATION STUDIES; PRODUCTIVITY;).

2618. Sibley, C. K. 1929. A biological survey of the Erie-Niagara system. VII. The Food of certain fishes of the Lake Erie drainage basin. N.Y. Conserv. Dept., Suppl. 18th Annu. Rep. (1928):180-188. (WALLEYE; FOOD STUDIES;).

2619. Sibley, C. K. 1932. A biological survey of the Oswegatchie and Black River systems. IV. Fish food studies. N.Y. Conserv. Dept., Suppl. 21st Annu. Rep. (1931):120-132. (WALLEYE; FOOD STUDIES;).

2620. Sibley, C. K., and V. Rimsky-korsakoff. 1931. A biological survey of the St. Lawrence watershed. IV. Food of certain fishes in the watershed. N.Y. Conserv. Dept., Suppl. 20th Annu. Rep. (1930):109-120. (WALLEYE; FOOD STUDIES;).

2621. Siefert, R. E., and W. A. Spoor. 1974. Effects of reduced oxygen on embryos and larvae of the white sucker, coho salmon, brook trout, and walleye. Pages 487-495 in J.H.S. Blaxter, ed. The early life history of fish. Springer — Verlag, 1974. (WALLEYE; ECOLOGY; EMBRYOLOGY; MORTALITY;).

2622. Sieh, J. G., and J. Parsons. 1950. Activity patterns of some Clear Lake, Iowa fishes. Proc. Iowa Acad. Sci. 57:511-518. (WALLEYE; BEHAVIOR; ECOLOGY; GEOGRAPHICAL DISTRIBUTION; MOVEMENT AND MIGRATIONS;).

2623. Sigler, W. F., and R. R. Miller. 1963. Fishes of Utah. Utah State Dept. Fish Game. 203 pp. (WALLEYE; INTRODUCTIONS; LIFE HISTORY; TAXONOMY;).

2624. Simon, J. R. 1946. Wyoming fishes. Wyo. Game Fish Dept., Bull. 4:124 pp. (SAUGER; WALLEYE; INTRODUCTIONS; LIFE HISTORY; TAXONOMY;).

2625. Sinclair, S., S. Trachtenburg, and M. L. Beckford. 1967. Physical and economic organization of the fisheries of the District of Mackenzie, Northwest Territories. Fish. Research Board Can., Bull. 158:70 pp. (WALLEYE; COMMERCIAL FISHERIES;).

2626. Skaptason, J. B. 1926. The fish resources of Manitoba. Man. Ind. Development Board, Bull. 3:43 pp. (WALLEYE; COMMERCIAL FISHERIES; STOCKING;).

2627. Skrypek, J. L. 1969. Differences in the composition of the fish population in Pool 2 and other areas of the Mississippi River as related to waste from the Twin City Metropolitan Area-1964. Minn. Dept. Conserv., Invest. Rep. No. 307:17 pp. (SAUGER; WALLEYE; HABITAT DEGRADATION; POPULATION STUDIES;).

2628. Slastenenko, E. P. 1956. The growth of yellow pikeperch, *Stizostedion vitreum* (Mitchill) in Three Mile Lake, Ontario. Can. Fish-Cult. 19:17-24. (WALLEYE; AGE AND GROWTH;).

2629. Slastenenko, E. P. 1958. The distribution of freshwater fishes in the Provinces and main water basins of Canada. Shebchenko Sci. Soc. Bull. 1(6):3-11 pp. (SAUGER; WALLEYE; GEOGRAPHICAL DISTRIBUTION;).

2630. Slastenenko, E. P. 1958. The freshwater fishes of Canada. Kiev Printers, Toronto, Ont. 385 pp. (SAUGER; WALLEYE; LIFE HISTORY; MORPHOLOGY; TAXONOMY;).

2631. Small, H. B. 1883. Fishes of the Ottawa district. Trans. Field Nat. Club. 4:31-49. (SAUGER; WALLEYE; GEOGRAPHICAL DISTRIBUTION;).

2632. Smiley, C. W. 1882. Changes in the fisheries of the Great Lakes during the decade, 1870-1880. U.S. Fish Comm., Bull. 1:252-258. (WALLEYE; ECOLOGY; POPULATION STUDIES;).

2633. Smith, C. G. 1941. Egg production of walleyed pike and sauger. Norris Reservoir fish differ from some species in other localities. Prog. Fish-Cult. 54:32-34. (SAUGER; WALLEYE; AGE AND GROWTH; IMPOUNDMENTS; SPAWNING STUDIES;).

2634. Smith, C. G., and L. F. Miller. 1943. A comparison of the hoop-net catch on several waters in the Tennessee valley before and after impoundment. Trans. Am. Fish. Soc. 72:212-219. (SAUGER; IMPOUNDMENTS; SAMPLING METHODS;).

2635. Smith, C. L., and R. M. Bailey. 1961. Evolution of the dorsal fin supports of percoid fishes. Paper, Mich. Acad. Sci., Arts, Letters 46:345-363. (SAUGER; WALLEYE; MORPHOLOGY;).

2636. Smith, C. L., and R. M. Bailey. 1962. The subocular shelf of fishes. J. Morphol. 110:1-18. (SAUGER; WALLEYE; MORPHOLOGY;).

2637. Smith, D. Q. 1965. Stocking of walleye in Possum Kingdom Lake. Tex. Parks Wildl. Dept., Fed. Aid Fish Wild. Restor. Proj. F-4-R-11, Wk. Pl. F, Job No. 3: 3 pp. (WALLEYE; AGE AND GROWTH; IMPOUNDMENTS; INTRODUCTIONS; MORTALITY; STOCKING;).

2638. Smith, D. Q. 1966. Walleye stocking in Possum Kingdom Lake. Tex. Dept. Parks Wildl., Fed. Aid Fish Wildl. Restor. Proj. F-4-R-12, Wk. Pl. F, Job No. 3:2 pp. (WALLEYE; AGE AND GROWTH; IMPOUNDMENTS; INTRODUCTIONS; POPULATION STUDIES; STOCKING;).

2639. Smith, D. Q. 1967. Evaluation of walleye fry stocked in Possum Kingdom Lake. Tex. Parks Wildl. Dept., Fed. Aid Fish Wildl. Restor. Proj. F-4-R-13, Wk. Pl. B, Job No. 35:5 pp. (WALLEYE; AGE AND GROWTH; IMPOUNDMENTS; STOCKING;).

2640. Smith, H. M. 1892. Report on an investigation of the fisheries of Lake Ontario. U.S. Fish. Comm., Bull. 10:177-215. (SAUGER; WALLEYE; AGE AND GROWTH; COMMERCIAL FISHERIES; ECOLOGY; FOOD STUDIES; MOVEMENT AND MIGRATIONS;).

2641. Smith, H. M. 1893. Report on a collection of fishes from the Albemarle region of North Carolina. U.S. Fish. Comm., Bull. 11:185-200. (WALLEYE; COMMERCIAL FISHERIES; INTRODUCTIONS;).

2642. Smith, H. M. 1894. Statistics of the fisheries of the United States. U.S. Fish Comm., Bull. 13:389-404. (WALLEYE; COMMERCIAL FISHERIES;).

2643. Smith, H. M. 1896. A review of the history and results of attempts to acclimatize fish and other water animals in the Pacific states. U.S Fish Comm., Bull. 15:379-472. (WALLEYE; INTRODUCTIONS;).

2644. Smith, H. M. 1898. Statistics of the fisheries of the interior waters of the United States. U.S. Fish Comm., Annu. Rep. (1896):489-574. (SAUGER; WALLEYE; COMMERCIAL FISHERIES; FISHING GEAR;).

2645. Smith, H. M. 1904. Report on the inquiry respecting food-fishes and the fishing-grounds. River and lake investigations. U.S. Fish. Comm., Great Lakes Biol. Surv., Annu. Rep (1902):127-128. (WALLEYE; TAXONOMY;).

2646. Smith, H. M. 1910. The United States Bureau of Fisheries: its establishment, functions, organization, resources, operations, and achievements. U.S. Bur. Fish., Bull. 28:1365-1410. (WALLEYE; PROPAGATION; STOCKING;).

2647. Smith, H. M. 1920. Some biological problems in the Yellowstone Park. J. Wash. Acad. Sci. 10:583-585. (WALLEYE; INTRODUCTIONS;).

2648. Smith, H. M., and M. Snell. 1891. Review of the fisheries of the Great Lakes in 1885. U.S. Comm. Fish., Annu. Rep. (1887):1-333. (SAUGER; WALLEYE; COMMERCIAL FISHERIES; FISHING GEAR;).

2649. Smith, L. 1937. Observations on natural versus artificial propagation of commercial species of fish in the Great Lakes region. Trans. Am. Fish. Soc. 66:56-62. (WALLEYE; PROPAGATION; STOCKING;).

2650. Smith, L. L., Jr. 1948. Effectiveness of modern fish management practices: planting. Proc. 38th Conv. Int. Assn. Game, Fish, Conserv. Comm. 38:42-48. (WALLEYE; COMMERCIAL FISHERIES; PROPAGATION; STOCKING;).

2651. Smith, L. L., Jr. 1963. Effect of pollution on aquatic populations. Wildl. Dis. 63:157-165. (WALLEYE; HABITAT DEGRADATION; MORTALITY;).

2652. Smith, L. L., Jr. 1977. Walleye (Stizostedion vitreum vitreum) and yellow perch (Perca flavescens) populations and fisheries of the Red Lakes, Minnesota, 1930-75. J. Fish. Research Board Can. 34:1774-1783. (WALLEYE; AGE AND GROWTH; COMMERCIAL FISHERIES; POPULATION STUDIES; PRODUCTIVITY;).

2653. Smith, L. L., Jr., and R. H. Kramer. 1963. Survival of walleye eggs in relation to wood fibers and Sphaerotilus natans in the Rainy River, Minnesota. Trans. Am. Fish. Soc. 92:220-234. (WALLEYE; ECOLOGY; HABITAT DEGRADATION; MORTALITY; PATHOLOGY; SPAWNING STUDIES;).

2654. Smith, L. L., Jr., and R. H. Kramer. 1964. The spottail shiner in lower Red Lake, Minnesota. Trans. Am. Fish. Soc. 93:35-45. (WALLEYE; FOOD STUDIES;).

2655. Smith, L. L., Jr., and R. H. Kramer. 1964. Some effects of paper fibres in fish eggs and small fish. Proc. 19th Ind. Waste Conf., Purdue Univ., Engng Extn. Ser. No. 117:369-378. (WALLEYE; HABITAT DEGRADATION; MORTALITY;).

2656. Smith, L. L., Jr., and R. H. Kramer. 1965. Survival of walleye fingerlings in conifer groundwood fiber. Trans. Am. Fish. Soc. 94:402-404. (WALLEYE; HABITAT DEGRADATION; MORTALITY; PHYSIOLOGY;).

2657. Smith, L. L., Jr., R. H. Kramer, and P. J. Colby. 1967. Survival of walleye eggs and fry on paper-fibre sludge deposits in Rainy River, Minnesota. Trans. Am. Fish. Soc. 96:278-296. (WALLEYE; HABITAT DEGRADATION; SPAWNING STUDIES;).

2658. Smith, L. L., Jr., R. H. Kramer, and J. C. Macleod. 1965. Effects of pulpwood fibers on fathead minnows and walleye fingerlings. J. Water Poll. Con. Fed. 37:130-140. (WALLEYE; HABITAT DEGRADATION; MORTALITY;).

2659. Smith, L. L., Jr., R. H. Kramer, and D. M. Oseid. 1966. Long-term effects of conifer-groundwood paper fiber on walleyes. Trans. Am. Fish. Soc. 95:60-70. (WALLEYE; AGE AND GROWTH; HABITAT DEGRADATION; PHYSIOLOGY;).

2660. Smith, L. L., Jr., and L. W. Krefting. 1954. Fluctuations in production and abundance of commercial species in the Red Lakes, Minnesota, with special reference to changes in the walleye population. Trans. Am. Fish. Soc. 83:131-160. (WALLEYE; COMMERCIAL FISHERIES; ECOLOGY; POPULATION STUDIES; STOCKING;).

2661. Smith. L. L., Jr., L. W. Krefting, and R. L. Butler. 1952. Movements of marked walleye. *Stizostedion vitreum vitreum* (Mitchill) in the fishery of the Red Lakes, Minnesota. Trans. Am. Fish. Soc. 81:179-196. (WALLEYE; AGE AND GROWTH; COMMERCIAL FISHERIES; MARKING; MOVEMENT AND MIGRATIONS; SPAWNING STUDIES;).

2662. Smith, L. L., Jr., and J. B. Moyle. 1945. Factors influencing production of yellow pikeperch, *Stizostedion vitreum vitreum*, in Minnesota rearing ponds. Trans. Am. Fish. Soc. 73:243-261. (WALLEYE; AGE AND GROWTH; COMMUNITY DYNAMICS; ECOLOGY; FOOD STUDIES; PRODUCTIVITY; PROPAGATION;).

2663. Smith, L. L., Jr., and D. M. Oseid. 1972. Effects of hydrogen sulfide on fish eggs and fry. Water Res. 6:711-720. (WALLEYE; HABITAT DEGRADATION;).

2664. Smith, L. L., Jr., and D. M. Oseid. 1974. Effect of hydrogen sulfide on development and survival of eight freshwater fish species. Pages 417-430 *in* J. H. S. Blaxter, ed. The early life history of fish. Springer-Verlag, New York. (WALLEYE; TOXICANTS;).

2665. Smith, L. L., Jr., and D. M. Oseid. 1977. Toxic effects of hydrogen sulfide to juvenile fish and fish eggs. Minn. Agric. Exp. Stn., Sci. J. Series. 7 pp. (WALLEYE; TOXICANTS;).

2666. Smith, L. L., Jr., D. M. Oseid, I. R. Adelman, and S. J. Broderius. 1976. Effect of hydrogen sulfide on fish and invertebrates Part I — acute and chronic toxicity studies. U.S. Environ. Prot. Agency, Nat. Environ. Research Cent., Ecol. Research Ser. EPA-600/3-76-062a:286 pp. (WALLEYE; AGE AND GROWTH; FOOD STUDIES; MORTALITY; HABITAT DEGRADATION;).

2667. Smith, L. L., Jr., and R. L. Pycha. 1960. First-year growth of the walleye, *Stizostedion vitreum*, and associated factors in the Red Lakes, Minnesota. Limnol. Oceanogr. 5:281-290. (WALLEYE; AGE AND GROWTH; ECOLOGY; FOOD STUDIES; SPAWNING STUDIES;).

2668. Smith, L. L., Jr., and R. L. Pycha. 1961. Factors related to commercial production of the walleye in the Red Lakes, Minnesota. Trans. Am. Fish. Soc. 90:190-217. (WALLEYE; AGE AND GROWTH; COMMERCIAL FISHERIES; FISHING GEAR; MORTALITY; POPULATION STUDIES;).

2669. Smith, L. L. Jr., and W. M. Koenst. 1975. Temperature effects on eggs and fry of percoid fishes. U.S. Environ. Prot. Agency, Proj. EPA-660/3-75-017 67 pp. (SAUGER; WALLEYE; ECOLOGY; MORTALITY; SPAWNING STUDIES;).

2670. Smith, P. W. 1965. A preliminary annotated list of the lampreys and fishes of Illinois. Ill. Nat. Hist. Surv., Biol. Notes 54:3-12. (SAUGER; WALLEYE; GEOGRAPHICAL DISTRIBUTION;).

2671. Smith, S. H. 1968. Species succession and fishery exploitation in the Great Lakes. J. Fish. Research Board Can. 25:667-693. (WALLEYE; COMMUNITY DYNAMICS;).

2672. Smith, S. H. 1972. Factors of ecologic succession in oligotrophic fish communities of the Laurentian Great Lakes. J. Fish. Research Board Can. 29:717-730. (SAUGER; WALLEYE; ECOLOGY;).

2673. Smith, S. L., R. E. Twillman, and J. E. Thomerson. 1969. The fishes of Piasa Creek, west central Illinois. Trans. Ill. Acad. Sci. 62:70-79. (WALLEYE; GEOGRAPHICAL DISTRIBUTION;).

2674. Smith, W. G., and M. J. Hendry. 1979. Winter creel census of Consecon, East, and West Lakes 1978. Ont. Min. Nat. Res., Lake Ont. Fish. Assess. Unit Rep. 46 pp. (WALLEYE; AGE AND GROWTH; CREEL CENSUS;).

2675. Smith, W. G., and M. J. Hendry. 1979. Summer creel census of Consecon, East, and West Lakes 1978. Ont. Min. Nat. Res., Lake Ont. Fish. Assess. Unit Rep. 93 pp. (WALLEYE; AGE AND GROWTH; CREEL CENSUS;).

2676. Snow, H. E. 1968. Stocking of muskellunge and walleye as a panfish control practice in Clear Lake, Sawyer County. Wis. Dept. Nat. Res., Research Rep. 38: 18 pp. (WALLEYE; STOCKING;).

2677. Snow, H. E. 1969. Comparative growth of eight species of fish in thirteen northern Wisconsin lakes. Wis. Dept. Nat. Res., Research Rep. No. 46: 23 pp. (WALLEYE; AGE AND GROWTH;).

2678. Sobchuk, M. 1981. Estimated abundance, harvest and exploitation of a river spawning walleye population. Ont. Min. Nat. Res., Rep. 54 pp. (WALLEYE; AGE AND GROWTH; CREEL CENSUS; FISHING GEAR; HABITAT DEGRADATION; MARKING; MOVEMENT AND MIGRATIONS; POPULATION STUDIES; PRODUCTIVITY; REGULATIONS; SPAWNING STUDIES;).

2679. Somers, K. M., and H. H. Harvey. 1984. Alteration of fish communities in lakes stressed by acid deposition and heavy metals near Wawa, Ontario. Can. J. Fish. Aquat. Sci. 41:20-29. (WALLEYE; COMMUNITY DYNAMICS; ECOLOGY; HABITAT DEGRADATION;).

2680. Sommerfeldt, T. E. 1984. Initial assessment of the introduction of spottail shiner *(Notropis hudsonius)* and delta smelt *(Hypomesus transpacificus)* into Willard Bay Reservoir, Utah. M.S. Thesis, Utah State Univ., Logan, Utah 106 pp. (WALLEYE; AGE AND GROWTH; FOOD STUDIES; IMPOUNDMENTS;).

2681. Sopuck, R. D. 1979. The commercial fishery of Moose Lake, Manitoba with special emphasis on the walleye *(Stizostedion vitreum)* and the whitefish *(Coregonus clupeaformis)*. Man. Dept. Nat. Res. Envir., Fish. Branch Manuscript Rep. No. 79-5:56 pp. (WALLEYE; AGE AND GROWTH; COMMERCIAL FISHERIES; MORTALITY; POPULATION STUDIES;).

2682. Sowards, C. L. 1985. Results of the South Dakota field office Ecological Services Fish and Wildlife Service 1984 research contaminant assessment program. U.S. Fish Wildl. Serv., Ecol. Serv. S.D. Field Off. SD-IR-85-02:14 pp. (WALLEYE; TOXICANTS;).

2683. Spacie, A. 1975. The bioconcentration of trifluralin from a manufacturing effluent of fish in the Wabash River. Ph.D. Dissertation, Purdue Univ., West Lafayette, Ind. 149 pp. (SAUGER; HABITAT DEGRADATION;).

2684. Spangler, G. R., N. R. Payne, J. E. Thorpe, J. M. Byrne, H. A. Regier, and W. J. Christie. 1977. Responses of percids to exploitation. J. Fish. Research Board Can. 34:1983-1988. (WALLEYE; AGE AND GROWTH; COMMUNITY DYNAMICS; GENETICS; POPULATION STUDIES; SPAWNING STUDIES;).

2685. Spangler, G. R., N. R. Payne, and G. K. Winterton. 1977. Percids in the Canadian waters of Lake Huron. J. Fish. Research Board Can. 34:1839-1848. (SAUGER; WALLEYE; AGE AND GROWTH; COMMERCIAL FISHERIES; ECOLOGY; FOOD STUDIES; GEOGRAPHICAL DISTRIBUTION; HABITAT DEGRADATION; MORTALITY; MOVEMENTS AND MIGRATIONS; POPULATION STUDIES; PRODUCTIVITY; SPAWNING STUDIES;).

2686. Speaker, E. B. 1936. Growth of bass and pike-perch in ponds. Prog. Fish-Cult. 24:27. (WALLEYE; AGE AND GROWTH; PROPAGATION;).

2687. Speaker, E. B. 1938. Pond rearing of walleyed pike. Prog. Fish-Cult. 36:1-6. (WALLEYE; AGE AND GROWTH; COMMUNITY DYNAMICS; PROPAGATION;).

2688. Speaker, E. B. 1942. The administration of fishery programs. Trans. Am. Fish. Soc. pp. 318-320. (WALLEYE; AGE AND GROWTH; PROPAGATION;).

2689. Speirs, J. M. 1953. History of the original descriptions of Great Lakes fishes. Res. Council Ont., Tech. Sess. 1951. 38 pp. (SAUGER; WALLEYE; TAXONOMY;).

2690. Sprague, J. W. 1959. Report of fisheries investigations during the fourth year of impoundment of Gavins Point Reservoir, South Dakota, 1958. S.D. Dept. Game. Fish Parks, Fed. Aid Fish Wildl. Restor. Proj. F-1-R-8, Jobs No. 2, 4 and 5:44 pp. (SAUGER; WALLEYE; COMMUNITY DYNAMICS; IMPOUNDMENTS; MOVEMENT AND MIGRATIONS; POPULATION STUDIES; SPAWNING STUDIES; STOCKING; WATER LEVELS;).

2691. Sprague, J. W. 1961. Report of fisheries investigations during the seventh year of impoundment of Fort Randall Reservoir, South Dakota, 1959. S.D. Dept. Game. Fish Parks, Fed. Aid Fish Wildl. Restor. Proj. F-1-R-9, Jobs No. 5, 6, 7 and 8:49 pp. (SAUGER; WALLEYE; AGE AND GROWTH; COMMUNITY DYNAMICS; CREEL CENSUS; IMPOUNDMENTS; MOVEMENT AND MIGRATIONS; POP

ULATION STUDIES; SPAWNING STUDIES; STOCKING; WATER LEVELS;).

2692. Sprague, J. W. 1963. Investigations of artificially created walleye spawning areas, 1961 and 1962. N.D. Dept. Fish Game, Fed. Aid Fish Wildl. Restor. Proj. F-2-R-9 and F-2-R-10, Job No. 11:6 pp. (WALLEYE; HABITAT IMPROVEMENT; IMPOUNDMENTS; SPAWNING STUDIES;).

2693. Sprigings, R. 1976. Lake St. Francis summer creel census report. Ont. Min. Nat. Res., Rep. 10 pp. (WALLEYE; CREEL CENSUS;).

2694. Sprigings, R. M. 1975. Lake St. Francis creel census report winter — 1975. Ont. Min. Nat. Res., Rep. 9 pp. (WALLEYE; CREEL CENSUS;).

2695. Sprigings, R. M. 1975. Summer creel census program Lake St. Francis — 1974. Ont. Min. Nat. Res., Rep. 8 pp. (WALLEYE; CREEL CENSUS;).

2696. Sprules, W. M. 1946. Goldeye flushing experiment. Fish. Research Board Can., Manuscript Rep. 466:11 pp. (SAUGER; WALLEYE; FOOD STUDIES;).

2697. Sprules, W. M. 1949. A report of the Lake Claire goldeye fishery for 1948. Fish. Research Board Can., Manuscript Rep. 469:21 pp. (WALLEYE; COMMERCIAL FISHERIES;).

2698. Sprules, W. M. 1950. A report of the Lake Claire goldeye fishery for 1949. Fish. Research Board Can., Manuscript Rep. 470:21 pp. (WALLEYE; COMMERCIAL FISHERIES;).

2699. Sprules, W. M. 1954. The goldeye fishery of the Big Sandy Lake area, Ontario. Can. Dept. Fish. 15 pp. (SAUGER; WALLEYE; COMMERCIAL FISHERIES; COMMUNITY DYNAMICS;).

2700. Spykerman, V. L. 1973. Food habits, growth, and distribution of larval walleye, *Stizostedion vitreum vitreum* (Mitchill), in Clear Lake, Iowa. M.S. Thesis, Iowa State Univ., Ames, Iowa. 49 pp. (WALLEYE; AGE AND GROWTH; FOOD STUDIES; MOVEMENT AND MIGRATIONS;).

2701. Spykerman, V. L. 1974. Food habits, growth, and distribution of larval walleye, *Stizoste-dion vitreum vitreum* (Mitchill), in Clear Lake, Iowa. Proc. Iowa Acad. Sci. 81:143-149. (WALLEYE; AGE AND GROWTH; FOOD STUDIES; MOVEMENTS AND MIGRATIONS; SPAWNING STUDIES;).

2702. Sriprasert, R. 1974. Length-weight relationships of walleye, *Stizostedion vitreum*, in Clear lake, Iowa. M.S. Thesis. Iowa State Univ., Ames, Iowa. 30 pp. (WALLEYE; AGE AND GROWTH;).

2703. Stafford, J. A. 1975. Construction of an artificial spawning bed for walleye at Glen Elder Reservoir. Kans. For. Fish Game Comm. 7 pp. (WALLEYE; HABITAT IMPROVEMENT; IMPOUNDMENTS; SPAWNING STUDIES;).

2704. Stang, D. L. 1982. Habitat partitioning and utilization of adult and juvenile fish in Clear Lake, Iowa. M.S. Thesis, Iowa State Univ., Ames, Iowa. 121 pp. (WALLEYE; COMMUNITY DYNAMICS; POPULATION STUDIES;).

2705. Stang, D. L., and W. A. Hubert. 1984. Spatial separation of fishes captured in passive gear in a turbid prairie lake. Environ. Biol. Fish. 11:309-314. (WALLEYE; COMMUNITY DYNAMICS; ECOLOGY; FISHING GEAR;).

2706. Stansby, M. E., and A. S. Hall. 1967. Chemical composition of commercially important fish of the United States. U.S. Fish Wildl. Serv., Fish. Ind. Res. 3:29-46. (WALLEYE; GEOGRAPHICAL DISTRIBUTION;).

2707. Starrett, W. C. 1950. Distribution of the fishes of Boone County, Iowa, with special reference to the minnows and darters. Am. Midl. Nat. 43:112-127. (WALLEYE; GEOGRAPHICAL DISTRIBUTION;).

2708. Starrett, W. C., and P. G. Barnickol. 1955. Efficiency and selectivity of commercial fishing devices used on the upper Mississippi River. Ill. Nat. Hist. Surv., Bull. 26:325-366. (SAUGER; WALLEYE; COMMERCIAL FISHERIES; FISHING GEAR;).

2709. Starrett, W. C., and A. W. Fritz. 1965. A biological investigation of the fishes of Lake Chautaugua, Illinois. Ill. Nat. Hist. Surv., Bull. 29:104 pp. (SAUGER; GEOGRAPHICAL DISTRIBUTION;).

2710. Steinwand, T. 1986. Movement of walleye within Lake Sakakawea. N.D. Game Fish Dept., Fed. Aid Fish Wildl. Restor. Proj. F-2-R-32, Job 4-A:10 pp. (WALLEYE; AGE AND GROWTH; MARKING; MOVEMENTS AND MIGRATIONS; SPAWNING STUDIES;).

2711. Stephenson, M. 1977. Walleye in Cedar lake, 1977. Ont. Min. Nat. Res., Rep. 4 pp. (WALLEYE; AGE AND GROWTH; MARKING;).

2712. Sterba, G. 1962. Freshwater fishes of the world. Vista Books, London pp. 626-640. (WALLEYE; MORPHOLOGY; TAXONOMY;).

2713. Sterling, E. 1883. On the impropriety of depositing whitefish minnows off the harbor of Cleveland, Ohio-fishing for saugers. U.S. Fish Comm., Bull. 3:302-303. (SAUGER; WALLEYE; COMMERCIAL FISHERIES; COMMUNITY DYNAMICS; POPULATION STUDIES;).

2714. Sterling, E. 1884. Notes on the Great Lakes fisheries, depletion of black bass, etc. U.S. Fish Comm., Bull. 4:218-219. (WALLEYE; COMMERCIAL FISHERIES; COMMUNITY DYNAMICS;).

2715. Sternberg, R. B. 1969. Angler creel census of Pools 4 and 5 of the Mississippi River, Goodhue and Wabasha Counties, Minnesota in 1967-1968. Minn. Dept. Conserv., Invest. Rep. No. 306: 53 pp. (SAUGER; WALLEYE; CREEL CENSUS;).

2716. Sternberg, R. B. 1971. Mississippi River spring creel census in the tailwaters of Pools 4 and 5, 1968-1970. Minn. Dept. Nat. Res., Invest. Rep. No. 311:31 pp. (SAUGER; WALLEYE; CREEL CENSUS; SPAWNING STUDIES;).

2717. Sternberg, R. B. 1974. Assessment of continuous walleye-sauger fishing at Lock Dam No. 3 and 4 of the Mississippi River, 1968-74. Minn. Dept. Nat. Res., Invest Rep. No. 332:27 pp. (SAUGER; WALLEYE; CREEL CENSUS;).

2718. Sternberg, R. B. 1974. Angler creel census of Pools 4 and 5 of the Mississippi River, 1972-73. Minn. Dept. Nat. Res., Invest. Rep. No. 331:15 pp. (SAUGER; WALLEYE; CREEL CENSUS;).

2719. Steuche, E. W. 1968. Optimum temperatures for hatching northern pike and walleye eggs. Proc. North Central Warm-water Fish Culture Workshop, Ames, Iowa Coop. Fish. Unit, February 15-16, 1968. pp. 32-34. (WALLEYE; PROPAGATION;).

2720. Stevenson, F., R. E. Day, M. R. Austin, and K. O. Paxton. 1981. An evaluation of the physical structure incorporated into Killdeer Reservoir. Ohio Dept. Nat. Res., Fed. Aid Fish Wildl. Restor. Proj. F-29-R-11-20, Job No. 4:142 pp. (WALLEYE; AGE AND GROWTH; CREEL CENSUS; ECOLOGY; FOOD STUDIES; HABITAT IMPROVEMENT; IMPOUNDMENTS; POPULATION STUDIES; SPAWNING STUDIES;).

2721. Stevenson, J., and A. H. Hulsey. 1958. Appraisal and management recommendations resulting from a three-year comparative study of Lake Catherine, Lake Hamilton and Lake Ouachita, Arkansas. Proc. 12th Annu. Conf. Southeast Assoc. Fish Wildl. Agencies 12:183-198. (WALLEYE; STOCKING;).

2722. Stewart, K. 1964. Million dollar fish from Manitoba. Can. Dept. Fish., Trade News 17:5-6. (SAUGER; COMMERCIAL FISHERIES; LIFE HISTORY;).

2723. Stewart, P. A. 1979. Lower Missouri River basin investigations. Planning inventory, fisheries. Mont. Dept. Fish Game, Fed. Aid Fish Wildl. Restor. Proj. FW-2-R-8, Job No. 1-b:44 pp. (WALLEYE; ECOLOGY; MARKING; MOVEMENT AND MIGRATIONS; POPULATION STUDIES; SPAWNING STUDIES;).

2724. Stewart, P. A. 1985. Southeastern Montana fisheries investigation, fish management surveys. Mont. Dept. Fish Wildl. Parks, Fed. Aid Fish Wildl. Restor. Proj. F-30-R-21, Job No. I-B:10 pp. (SAUGER; WALLEYE; MOVEMENT AND MIGRATIONS; PROPAGATION; SPAWNING STUDIES;).

2725. Stewart, P. A. 1986. Southeast Montana fisheries study: inventory of the waters of the project area. Mont. Dept. Fish, Wildl., Parks, Fed. Aid Fish Wildl. Restor. Proj. F-30-R-22, Job No. I-a: 14 pp. (WALLEYE; IMPOUNDMENTS; POPULATION STUDIES;).

2726. Stewart, P. A. 1986. Southeast Montana fisheries study: fish management surveys. Mont. Dept. Fish, Wildl., Parks, Fed. Aid Fish Wildl. Restor. Proj. F-30-R-22, Job No. I-b: 9 pp. (SAUGER; WALLEYE; IMPOUNDMENTS; POPULATION STUDIES; SPAWNING STUDIES; WATER LEVELS;).

2727. Stewart, P. A. 1987. Inventory of the waters of the project area. Mont. Dept. Fish, Wildl. Parks, Fed. Aid Fish Wildl. Restor. Proj. F-30-R-23, Job I-a:. (WALLEYE; IMPOUNDMENTS; POPULATION STUDIES;).

2728. Stewart, P. A. 1987. Fish management surveys. Mont. Dept. Fish, Wildl. Parks, Fed. Aid Fish Wildl. Restor. Proj. F-30-R-23, Job I-b:. (WALLEYE; FISHWAYS; MARKING; MOVEMENT AND MIGRATIONS; SPAWNING STUDIES;).

2729. Stewart, R. R. 1970. Creel census — Lac Des Mille Lacs Thunder Bay District. Ont. Min. Nat. Res., Rep. 6 pp. (WALLEYE; CREEL CENSUS;).

2730. Stieber, S. F., and V. A. Cvancara. 1977. Tissue decimation of L-amino acids in the Teleost Stizostedion vitreum (Mitchill). Comp. Biochem. Physiol. B. Comp. Biochem 56:285-287. (WALLEYE; PHYSIOLOGY;).

2731. Stiles, C. W. 1894. Reports on a parasitic protozoan observed on fish in the aquarium. U.S. Fish Comm., Bull. 13:173-190. (WALLEYE; PATHOLOGY;).

2732. Stinauer, R. 1968. Honey-Bear Creek basin. Ill. Dept. Conserv., Spec. Fish. Rep., Inventory of the fishes of Nine River Basins in Illinois, 1967 25:70-84. (WALLEYE; ECOLOGY;).

2733. Stone, C. C. 1985. Angler use and sport fishing harvest survey on Lake Francis Case, South Dakota, 1984. S.D. Dept. Game Fish and Parks, Completion Report 85-1:26 pp. (SAUGER; WALLEYE; CREEL CENSUS; IMPOUNDMENTS;).

2734. Stone, C. C. 1985. Lewis and Clark Lake fishing and hunting use survey 1984. S.D. Dept. Game Fish and Parks, Completion Report 85-2:44 pp. (WALLEYE; CREEL CENSUS; IMPOUNDMENTS; SOCIO-ECONOMICS OF FISHERIES;).

2735. Stone, D. 1963. Lake St. Martin fish production and water control. Man. Mines Res. Envir. Manage. Research Branch, Manuscript Rep. 8 pp. (WALLEYE; PRODUCTIVITY;).

2736. Stone, D. 1966. Pesticide residues in Manitoba fish and water. Man. Dept. Mines Nat. Res., Fish. Branch, Manuscript Rep. 13 pp. (SAUGER; HABITAT DEGRADATION;).

2737. Stone, F. L. 1949. A study of the taxonomy of the blue and yellow pikeperches (Stizostedion) of Lake Erie and Lake Ontario. Ph.D. Dissertation, Univ. Rochester, Rochester, N.Y. 164 pp. (WALLEYE; MORPHOLOGY; TAXONOMY;).

2738. Stone, U. B. 1938. Growth, habits, and fecundity of the ciscoes of Irondequoit Bay, New York. Trans. Am. Fish. Soc. 67:234-245. (WALLEYE; ECOLOGY;).

2739. Stone, U. B. 1947. A study of the deep-water cisco fishery of Lake Ontario with particular reference to the bloater Leucichthys hoyi (Gill). Trans. Am. Fish. Soc. 74:230-249. (WALLEYE; BEHAVIOR; MOVEMENT AND MIGRATIONS;).

2740. Storck, T., B. Dimond, and S. Miller. 1982. Determination of factors affecting the survival of larval fish and an evaluation of their utilization as food by predators. Ill. Nat. Hist. Surv., Fed. Aid Fish Wildl. Restor. Proj. F-31-R-1, Job No. 8:70 pp. (WALLEYE; SPAWNING STUDIES; STOCKING;).

2741. Storck, T. W., D. W. Dufford, and K. T. Clement. 1978. The distribution of limnetic fish larvae in a flood control reservoir in Central Illinois. Trans. Am. Fish. Soc. 107:419-424. (WALLEYE; IMPOUNDMENTS; MOVEMENTS AND MIGRATIONS;).

2742. Stoudt, J. H. 1939. Creel census for Lake Winnibigoshish, 1939. Minn. Dept. Conserv., Invest. Rep. No. 3: 15 pp. (WALLEYE; CREEL CENSUS;).

2743. Stoudt, J. H. 1939. A study of the migration of the wall-eyed pike (Stizostedion vitreum) in waters of the Chippewa National Forests, Minnesota. Trans. Am. Fish. Soc. 68:163-169. (WALLEYE; MARKING; MOVEMENT AND MIGRATIONS; SPAWNING STUDIES;).

2744. Stoudt, J. H., and S. Eddy. 1939. Walleye pike tagging study, 1937-1938, Chippewa National Forest. Minn. Dept. Conserv., Invest. Rep. No. 20: 6 pp. (WALLEYE; MARKING; MOVEMENT AND MIGRATIONS; SPAWNING STUDIES;).

2745. Stoudt, J. H., and S. Eddy. 1939. Walleye pike tagging study, 1937-1938, Chippewa National Forest. Trans. 4th N. Am. Wildl. Conf. 4:305-310. (WALLEYE; MARKING; MOVEMENT AND MIGRATIONS; SPAWNING STUDIES;).

2746. Stoudt, J. H., and S. Eddy. 1939. Walleyed pike tagging report for Lake Winnibigoshish, 1939 data. Minn. Dept. Conserv., Invest. Rep. No. 21:9 pp. (WALLEYE; MARKING; SPAWNING STUDIES;).

2747. Stranahan, J. J. 1898. The microscope as practically applied to fish culture. Trans. Am. Fish. Soc. 27:88-93. (WALLEYE; PATHOLOGY; PROPAGATION;).

2748. Strand, R. F. 1973. Assessment of walleye spawning in the Mississippi River above Wolf Lake. Minn. Dept. Nat. Res., Fed. Aid Fish Wildl. Restor. Proj. F-26-R-5, Study 107.5 Completion Report: 7 pp. (WALLEYE; SPAWNING STUDIES;).

2749. Strand, R. F. 1980. The walleye (Stizostedion vitreum) sport fishery in three upper Mississippi reservoir Lakes: Cass, Andrusia, and Big Wolf, 1971-1975. Minn. Dept. Nat. Res., Invest. Rep. No. 368: 38 pp. (WALLEYE; CREEL CENSUS; MARKING; POPULATION STUDIES; PRODUCTIVITY; SPAWNING STUDIES;).

2750. Strathearn, M., and V. Ewing. 1985. Summer creel survey on Wolfe, Ruth and McQuaby Lakes 1984. Ont. Min. Nat. Res., Rep. 28 pp. (WALLEYE; AGE AND GROWTH; CREEL CENSUS;).

2751. Stringham, E. 1917. Fish laws of Mississippi River states: a digest of statutes relating to the protection of fish and miscellaneous aquatic animals of states bordering on the Mississippi River. U.S. Bur. Fish., Annu. Rep. (1916):1-16. (SAUGER; WALLEYE; COMMERCIAL FISHERIES;).

2752. Stringham, E. 1919. Fish laws of states bordering on Mississippi and Ohio Rivers: a digest of statutes relating to the protection of fishes and other cold-blooded aquatic animals. U.S. Bur. Fish., Annu. Rep. (1918):5-21. (SAUGER; WALLEYE; COMMERCIAL FISHERIES;).

2753. Stroud, R. H. 1948. Notes on growth of hybrids between the sauger and the walleye (Stizostedion canadense x Stizostedion vitreum) in Norris Reservoir, Tennessee. Copeia 4:297-298. (SAUGER; WALLEYE; AGE AND GROWTH; GENETICS; IMPOUNDMENTS;).

2754. Stroud, R. H. 1949. Growth of Norris Reservoir walleye (Stizostedion vitreum) during the first twelve years of impoundment. J. Wildl. Manage. 13:157-177. (SAUGER; WALLEYE; AGE AND GROWTH; CREEL CENSUS; IMPOUNDMENTS; SAMPLING METHODS;).

2755. Stroud, R. H. 1949. Rate of growth and condition of game and pan fish in Cherokee and Douglas Reservoirs, Tennessee, and Hiwassee Reservoir, North Carolina. J. Tenn. Acad. Sci. 24:60-74. (SAUGER; WALLEYE; AGE AND GROWTH; IMPOUNDMENTS;).

2756. Stroud, R. H. 1955. Fisheries report for some central, eastern, and western Massachusetts lakes, ponds, and reservoirs, 1951-1952. Mass. Div. Fish. Game, Bur. Wildl. Research Manage. 447 pp. (WALLEYE; ECOLOGY; INTRODUCTIONS;).

2757. Struthers, P. H. 1929. A biological survey of the Erie-Niagara system. X. Carp control studies in the Erie Canal. N.Y. Conserv. Dept., Suppl. 18th Annu. Rep. (1928):208-219. (WALLEYE; ECOLOGY; IMPOUNDMENTS;).

2758. Struthers, P. H. 1931. A biological survey of the St. Lawrence watershed. XI. Carp control studies in the Seneca, Canadaigua and Keuka Lake basins. N.Y. Conserv. Dept., Suppl. 20th Annu. Rep. (1930):217-229. (WALLEYE; ECOLOGY;).

2759. Stubbs, J. M. 1966. Elk River survey, fish population and creel census. Tenn. Game Fish Comm., Fed Aid Fish Wildl. Restor. Proj. F-17-R-10, Wk. Pl. 3, Job A-40 pp. (WALLEYE; CREEL CENSUS;).

2760. Summerfelt, R. C. 1967. Fishes of the Smoky Hill River, Kansas. Trans. Kans. Acad. Sci. 70:102-139. (WALLEYE; IMPOUND-

MENTS; MOVEMENT AND MIGRA-
TIONS; STOCKING;).

2761. Summers, G. L. 1979. Seasonal distribution
of adult walleye, *Stizostedion vitreum vitreum* (Mitchill) in Canton Reservoir, Oklahoma. M.S. Thesis, Univ. Okla., Norman,
Okla. 70 pp. (WALLEYE; BEHAVIOR;
MARKING; MOVEMENT AND MIGRA-
TIONS;).

2762. Summers, G. L. 1979. Seasonal distribution
of adult walleye as determined by ultrasonic
telemetry in Canton Reservoir, Oklahoma.
Proc. 33rd. Annu. Conf. Southeast Assoc.
Fish Wildl. Agencies 33:611-619. (WALL-
EYE; BEHAVIOR; MARKING; MOVE-
MENT AND MIGRATIONS;).

2763. Summers, P. B. 1954. Some observations on
the limnology and fish distribution in the Illinois River below Tenkiller Reservoir. Proc.
Okla. Acad. Sci. 35:15-20. (SAUGER;
ECOLOGY;).

2764. Sundin, L., and L. Walker. 1972. Esnagi Lake
creel census — 1971. Ont. Min. Nat. Res.,
Rep. 12 pp. (WALLEYE; CREEL CEN-
SUS;).

2765. Sundin, L., and L. Walker. 1972. Waba-
tongushi Lake creel census — 1971. Ont.
Min. Nat. Res., Rep. 13 pp. (WALLEYE;
CREEL CENSUS;).

2766. Surber, E. W. 1929. The utilization of sloughs
in the Upper Mississippi wildlife and fish
refuge as fish ponds. Trans. Am. Fish. Soc.
59:106-113. (WALLEYE; ECOLOGY;
HABITAT IMPROVEMENT;).

2767. Surber, T. 1929. Fish culture in Minnesota,
past, present, and future. Trans. Am. Fish.
Soc. 59:224-233. (WALLEYE; INTRODUC-
TIONS; PROPAGATION; STOCKING;).

2768. Surber, T. 1931. Fish cultural successes and
failures in Minnesota. Trans. Am. Fish. Soc.
61:240-246. (WALLEYE; AGE AND
GROWTH; ECOLOGY; INTRODUC-
TIONS; STOCKING;).

2769. Surface, H. A. 1899. Removal of lamprey
from the interior waters of New York. N.Y.
Comm. Fish., Game Forest. (1898):191-212.
(SAUGER; WALLEYE; COMMUNITY
DYNAMICS;).

2770. Suriano, D. M., and M. Beverely-Burton.
1981. *Urocleidus aculeatus* (Van Cleave and
Mueller, 1932) (Monogenea: Ancyrocephali-
nae) from *Stizostedion vitreum* (Mitchill)
(Pisces: Percidae) in Eastern North Amer-
ica: Anatomy and systematic position. Can.
J. Zool. 59:240-245. (WALLEYE; PATHOL-
OGY;).

2771. Svetovidov, A. N. 1963. The systematics, ori-
gin and history of distribution of the Eurasi-
atic and North American species of *Perca,
Lucioperca,* and *Stizostedion.* Proc. 16th
Int. Congr. Zool. 1:212 pp. (SAUGER;
WALLEYE; GEOGRAPHICAL DISTRI-
BUTION; TAXONOMY;).

2772. Svetovidov, A. N., and E. A. Dorofeeva.
1963. Systematics, origin, and history of
the distribution of the Eurasian and North
American perches and pike-perches (genera
Perca, Lucioperca and *Stizostedion*). Vo-
prosy Ikhtiologii 3:625-651. (SAUGER;
WALLEYE; MORPHOLOGY; TAXON-
OMY;).

2773. Swain, D. P. 1974. Fisheries resource impact
assessment of the upper Churchill River and
lower Hughes River, Manitoba. Appendix
B. An Analysis of commercial fish catches
from two Churchill River lakes in Manitoba
in relation to river discharge and air temperatures. Man. Dept. Mines, Res. Environ.
Manage. Research Branch: 81 pp. (WALL-
EYE; COMMERCIAL FISHERIES;
MORTALITY; PRODUCTIVITY;).

2774. Swanson, G. M., and F. J. Ward. 1985.
Growth of juvenile walleye, *Stizostedion vi-
treum vitreum* (Mitchill) in two man-made
ponds in Winnipeg, Canada. Int. Ver. Theor.
Angew. Limnol. Verh. 22:2502-2507.
(WALLEYE; AGE AND GROWTH; FOOD
STUDIES; PROPAGATION;).

2775. Swedberg, S. E. 1963. Inventory of waters of
the project area. Mont. Fish Game Dept.,
Fed. Aid Fish Wildl. Restor. Proj. F-5-R-12,
Job No. 1:3 pp. (SAUGER; IMPOUND-
MENTS; POPULATION STUDIES; SAM-
PLING METHODS;).

2776. Swedberg, S. E. 1964. Inventory of waters of
the project area. Mont. Fish Game Dept.,
Fed. Aid Fish Wildl. Restor. Proj. F-5-R-13,
Job No. 1:6 pp. (SAUGER; GEOGRAPHI-
CAL DISTRIBUTION;).

2777. Swedberg, S. E. 1980. South central Montana fisheries investigations — Bighorn Lake and Bighorn River post-impoundment study. Mont. Dept. Fish Game, Fed. Aid Fish Wildl. Restor. Proj. F-20-R-24, Job No. IV-a:12 pp. (WALLEYE; AGE AND GROWTH; CREEL CENSUS; IMPOUNDMENTS; POPULATION STUDIES; WATER LEVELS;).

2778. Swedberg, S. E., and M. Kraft. 1965. Evaluation of planting catchable sized rainbow trout into waters containing high population densities of less desirable species of fish. Mont. Fish Game Dept., Fed. Aid Fish Wildl. Restor. Proj. F-5-R-13, Job No. 4:8 pp. (SAUGER; CREEL CENSUS; IMPOUNDMENTS;).

2779. Swenson, W. A. 1972. Food competition between the walleye Stizostedion vitreum vitreum (Mitchill) and sauger, Stizostedion canadense (Smith) in Lake of the Woods, Minnesota. Ph.D. Dissertation, Univ. Minn., St. Paul, Minn. 157 pp. (WALLEYE; FOOD STUDIES;).

2780. Swenson, W. A. 1977. Food consumption of walleye (Stizostedion vitreum vitreum) and sauger (S. canadense) in relation to food availability and physical conditions in Lake of the Woods, Minnesota, Shagawa Lake, and western Lake Superior. J. Fish. Research Board Can. 34:1643-1654. (SAUGER; WALLEYE; BEHAVIOR; FOOD STUDIES; PHYSIOLOGY;).

2781. Swenson, W. A. 1978. Influence of turbidity on fish abundance in western Lake Superior. U.S. Environ. Prot. Agency, Ecol. Research Ser. EPA-600/3-78-067:84 pp. (WALLEYE; BEHAVIOR; ECOLOGY; FOOD STUDIES; POPULATION STUDIES;).

2782. Swenson, W. A., and L. L. Smith, Jr. 1973. Gastric digestion, food consumption, feeding periodicity and food conversion efficiency in walleye (Stizostedion vitreum vitreum). J. Fish. Research Board Can. 30:1327-1336. (WALLEYE; BEHAVIOR; FOOD STUDIES; PHYSIOLOGY;).

2783. Swenson, W. A., and L. L. Smith, Jr. 1976. Influence of food competition, predation, and cannibalism on walleye (Stizostedion vitreum vitreum) and sauger (S. canadense) populations in Lake of the Woods, Minnesota. J. Fish. Research Board Can. 33:1946-1954. (SAUGER; WALLEYE; COMMER-CIAL FISHERIES; COMMUNITY DYNAMICS; FOOD STUDIES;).

2784. Swingle, H. S. 1954. Fish populations in Alabama rivers and impoundments. Trans. Am. Fish. Soc. 83:47-57. (WALLEYE; HABITAT DEGRADATION; IMPOUNDMENTS; POPULATION STUDIES; PRODUCTIVITY; SAMPLING METHODS;).

2785. Sylvester, J. R., and J. D. Broughton. 1983. Distribution and relative abundance of fish in Pool 7 of the upper Mississippi River. N. Am. J. Fish. Manage. 3:67-71. (SAUGER; WALLEYE; ECOLOGY;).

2786. Sylvester, J. R., L. E. Holland, and T. K. Kammer. 1984. Observations on burrowing rates and comments on host specificity in the endangered mussel Lampsilis higginsi. J. Freshwater Ecol. 2:555-560. (WALLEYE; PATHOLOGY;).

2787. Symington, D. F. 1957. Fisheries resources of Saskatchewan. Sask Dept. Nat. Res., Conserv. Info. Serv., Conserv. Bull. 5:24 pp. (WALLEYE; COMMERCIAL FISHERIES;).

2788. Symington, D. F. 1959. The fish of Saskatchewan. Sask. Dept. Nat. Res., Conserv. Bull. 7: 25 pp. (SAUGER; WALLEYE; LIFE HISTORY;).

2789. Symons, G. E., and R. W. Simpson. 1939. Report on fish destruction in the Niagara River in 1937. Trans. Am. Fish. Soc. 68:246-255. (WALLEYE; HABITAT DEGRADATION; MORTALITY;).

2790. Sztramko, L. 1979. Summer creel census in the Canadian waters of the Western basin of Lake Erie 1978. Ont. Min. Nat. Res., Lake Erie Fish. Assess. Unit Rep. 1979-1: 49. (WALLEYE; AGE AND GROWTH; CREEL CENSUS;).

2791. Sztramko, L. 1979. Summer creel census in the Canadian waters of the Detroit River, 1978. Ont. Min. Nat Res., Lake Erie Fish. Assess. Unit Rep. 1979-2 49 pp. (WALLEYE; AGE AND GROWTH; CREEL CENSUS;).

2792. Sztramko, L. 1980. Summer creel census in the Canadian waters of the western basin of Lake Erie, 1979. Ont. Min. Nat. Res., Lake Erie Fish. Assess. Unit Rep. 1980-1:54 pp.

(WALLEYE; AGE AND GROWTH; CREEL CENSUS;).

2793. Sztramko, L. 1980. Summer creel census in the Canadian waters of the Detroit River, 1979. Ont. Min. Nat. Res., Lake Erie Fish. Assess. Unit Rep. 1980-2:49 pp. (WALLEYE; AGE AND GROWTH; CREEL CENSUS;).

2794. Sztramko, L., and J. R. Paine. 1982. Sport fishery data for the Canadian portion of Lake Erie and connecting waters 1948-1980. Ont. Min. Nat. Res., Lake Erie Fish. Assess. Unit Rep. 1982-3: 88 pp. (WALLEYE; AGE AND GROWTH; CREEL CENSUS;).

2795. Sztramko, L. K., and J. R. Paine. 1984. Sport fisheries in the Canadian portion of Lake Erie and connecting waters, 1948-1980. 1984 Ont. Fish. Tech. Rep. Serv. 13:43 pp. (WALLEYE; CREEL CENSUS;).

2796. Talbot, H. 1910. The invasion of the Potomac. Trans. Am. Fish. Soc. 39:168-173. (WALLEYE; INTRODUCTIONS;).

2797. Taliaferro, R. 1959. An evaluation of the walleye *Stizostedion vitreum vitreum*, in the Colorado fishery program. Colo. Game Fish. Dept., Spec. Purpose Rep. 61: 9 pp. (WALLEYE; COMMUNITY DYNAMICS; CREEL CENSUS; IMPOUNDMENTS; INTRODUCTIONS;).

2798. Talsma, A. 1976. Summarization of lake test netting data. S.D. Dept. Game Fish Parks, Fed. Aid Fish Wildl. Restor. Proj. F-015-R-11, Job No. 13:37 pp. (WALLEYE; AGE AND GROWTH; COMMUNITY DYNAMICS; POPULATION STUDIES; STOCKING;).

2799. Tarby, M. J. 1977. Energetics and growth of walleye *(Stizostedion vitreum vitreum)* in Onedia Lake, New York. Ph.D. Dissertation, Cornell Univ, Ithaca, N.Y. 120 pp. (WALLEYE; AGE AND GROWTH;).

2800. Tarby, M. J. 1981. Metabolic expenditure of walleye *(Stizostedion vitreum vitreum)* as determined by rate of oxygen consumption. Can. J. Zool. 59:882-889. (WALLEYE; PHYSIOLOGY;).

2801. Tarby, M. J. 1983. Relation of forage to growth, consumption, and energetics of walleye *(Stizostedion vitreum vitreum)* in Oneida Lake, New York. Ph.D. Dissertation, Cornell Univ., Ithaca, N.Y. 50 pp. (WALLEYE; AGE AND GROWTH; FOOD STUDIES; POPULATION STUDIES;).

2802. Tarleton, P. 1978. 1976 Remi Lake Kapuskasing District creel census report. Ont. Min. Nat. Res., Rep. 21 pp. (WALLEYE; CREEL CENSUS;).

2803. Tarleton, P. 1978. Opasatika Lake Complex Kapuskasing District creel survey report 1976. Ont. Min. Nat. Res., Rep. 47 pp. (WALLEYE; CREEL CENSUS;).

2804. Tarleton, P. 1979. Opasatika Lake Complex Kapuskasing District creel survey report, 1977. Ont. Min. Nat. Res., Rep. 32 pp. (WALLEYE; CREEL CENSUS;).

2805. Tarzwell, C. M. 1941. A second season of creel census on four Tennessee Valley Authority Reservoir. Trans. 6th N. Am. Wildl. Conf. 6:202-222. (SAUGER; COMMERCIAL FISHERIES; CREEL CENSUS; IMPOUNDMENTS;).

2806. Tarzwell, C. M. 1942. Fish populations in the backwaters of Wheeler Reservoir and suggestions for their management. Trans. Am. Fish. Soc. 71:201-214. (SAUGER; IMPOUNDMENTS; SAMPLING METHODS;).

2807. Tarzwell, C. M. 1945. The possibilities of a commercial fishery in the TVA impoundments and its value in solving the sport and rough fish problems. Trans. Am. Fish. Soc. 73:137-157. (SAUGER; COMMERCIAL FISHERIES; FISHING GEAR; IMPOUNDMENTS; POPULATION STUDIES;).

2808. Taylor, M. W. 1981. A generalized inland fishery simulator for management biologists. N. Am. J. Fish. Manage. 1:60-72. (WALLEYE; AGE AND GROWTH; COMMUNITY DYNAMICS; MORTALITY; PRODUCTIVITY;).

2809. Taylor, R. 1967. 1967 creel census report Upper Rideau, Lower Beverley and Rehorse Lakes. Ont. Min. Nat. Res. 61 pp. (WALLEYE; CREEL CENSUS;).

2810. Telford, H. S., and O. A. Stevens. 1942. Uses and management of ponds and lakes. N. D. Ag. Exp. Sta., N. D. State Game Fish Dept.,

Bull. 313:1-40. (WALLEYE; COMMUNITY DYNAMICS; ECOLOGY;).

2811. Temple, A. J., D. J. Price, and B. R. Murphy. 1985. An inexpensive method for sectioning otoliths of large fish. N. Am. J. Fish. Manage. 5:612. (WALLEYE; AGE AND GROWTH;).

2812. Templeman, W. 1965. Lymphocystis disease in American place of eastern Grand Bank. J. Fish Research Board Can. 22:1345-1356. (WALLEYE; PATHOLOGY;).

2813. Tester, A. L. 1930. Analysis of 16 stomach contents of *Stizostedion vitreum* ($15\frac{1}{4}$ — 18") from Lake Nipissing, Goose Is., 1929, 1930. Unpbl. Manuscript, Univ. Toronto, Great Lake Inst., Ont. pp. 1-6. (WALLEYE; FOOD STUDIES;).

2814. Thede, J. M. 1970. 1970 summer creel census in southeastern Georgian Bay, Lake Simcoe District. Ont. Min. Nat. Res., Rep. 11 pp. (WALLEYE; CREEL CENSUS;).

2815. Theis, G. L., and R. G. Howey. 1981. Dispenser for live food organisms. Prog. Fish-Cult. 43:161-162. (WALLEYE; PROPAGATION;).

2816. Thomas, D. B. J. 1966. Creel census report — Charleston Lake and Upper Rideau Lake, June 17 to Sept. 5, 1966. Ont. Min. Nat. Res., Rep. 28 pp. (WALLEYE; CREEL CENSUS;).

2817. Thomas, E. R. 1975. 1974 creel census White Lake. Ont. Min. Nat. Res., Rep. 24 pp. (WALLEYE; CREEL CENSUS;).

2818. Thomas, R. C. 1958. Alberta lake fisheries. Alta. Res. Conf., Queen's Printer, Edmonton, Alta. 18 pp. (WALLEYE; GEOGRAPHICAL DISTRIBUTION;).

2819. Thomas, R. E. 1960. Development of improved fish cultural methods. Neb. Game, Forest. Parks Comm. Fed. Aid Fish Wildl. Restor. Proj. F-4-R-6, Job 7:12 pp. (WALLEYE; PROPAGATION;).

2820. Thomas, R. E., and D. J. Jones. 1959. Development of improved fish culture methods. Neb. Game Forest. Parks Comm. Fed. Aid Fish Wildl. Restor. Proj. F-4-R-5, Wk. Pl. 4, Job 7:31 pp. (WALLEYE; IMPOUNDMENTS; MARKING; POPULATION STUDIES; PROPAGATION;).

2821. Thompson, D. H. 1933. The migration of Illinois fishes. Ill. Nat. Hist. Surv., Biol. Notes 1:25 pp. (WALLEYE; MARKING;).

2822. Thompson, E. S. 1898. A list of the fishes known to occur in Manitoba. Forest and Stream 51:214. (SAUGER; WALLEYE; GEOGRAPHICAL DISTRIBUTION;).

2823. Thoreson, N. A. 1956. Marias River fishery restoration. Mont. Fish Game Dept., Fed. Aid Fish Wildl. Restor. Proj. F-15-D-2, Job No. 1:11 pp. (SAUGER; HABITAT IMPROVEMENT; IMPOUNDMENTS;).

2824. Thorn, W. C. 1984. Effects of continuous fishing on the walleye and sauger population in Pool 4, Mississippi River. Minn. Dept. Nat. Res., Invest. Rep. No. 378:52 pp. (SAUGER; WALLEYE; CREEL CENSUS; IMPOUNDMENTS; MARKING; MORTALITY; POPULATION STUDIES; SPAWNING STUDIES; WATER LEVELS;).

2825. Thorpe, L. M. 1942. A fishery survey of important Connecticut lakes. Conn. Geol. Nat. Hist. Surv. 63:15-18, 122, 196, 198-201, 208-211, 216, 289-295 (Append. 1), 199 (Appen. 4), 300-302, 305-306, 329, 332, 335 (Append. 5). (WALLEYE; INTRODUCTIONS;).

2826. Threinen, C. W. 1951. Changes in the creel and fishing success as brought out in a five year creel census. Wis. Conserv. Dept., Invest. Rep. No. 801: 11 pp. (WALLEYE; AGE AND GROWTH; CREEL CENSUS; POPULATION STUDIES;).

2827. Threinen, C. W. 1952. History, harvest and management of the Lake Koshkonong fishery. Wis. Conserv. Dept., Invest. Rep. No. 668:33 pp. (WALLEYE; COMMERCIAL FISHERIES; ECOLOGY; HABITAT IMPROVEMENT; MORTALITY; POPULATION STUDIES;).

2828. Threinen, C. W. 1960. Results of walleye fingerling stocking in lakes with stunted panfish. Wis. Conserv. Dept., Summary Rep. 4 pp. (WALLEYE; COMMUNITY DYNAMICS; STOCKING;).

2829. Threinen, C. W., and W. T. Helm. 1952. Composition of the fish population and carrying capacity of Spaulding Pond, Rock County, as determined by rotenone treatment. Wis. Conserv. Dept., Invest. Rep. No. 656:19 pp. (WALLEYE; AGE AND GROWTH; COM-

MUNITY DYNAMICS; POPULATION STUDIES; PRODUCTIVITY;).

2830 Thuemler, T. F. 1969. The food habits of the walleye, *Stizostedion vitreum vitreum* (Mitchill) in Escanaba Lake, Vilas County, Wisconsin. M.S. Thesis, Univ. of Wis, Milwaukee. Wis. 34 pp. (WALLEYE; AGE AND GROWTH; FOOD STUDIES;).

2831. Thurston, C. E., M. E. Stansby, N. L. Karrick, D. T. Miyauchi, and W. C. Clegg. 1959. Composition of certain species of freshwater fish. II. Comparative data for 21 species of lake and river fish. Food Res. 24:493-502. (WALLEYE; GEOGRAPHICAL DISTRIBUTION;).

2832. Thurston, L. D. W. 1979. Results of the 1979 creel census conducted on the Lower Shawanaga River and waters around Shawanaga Island Georgian Bay. Ont. Min. Nat. Res., Rep. 13 pp. (WALLEYE; CREEL CENSUS;).

2833. Thurston, L. D. W. 1980. The winter walleye fishery on the Magnetawan River near Britt, Ontario. Ont. Min. Nat. Res., Rep. 11 pp. (WALLEYE; AGE AND GROWTH; CREEL CENSUS;).

2834. Thurston, L. D. W. 1981. Results of an intensive creel census conducted on Wahwashkesh Lake (McKenzie Twp.) during the summer of 1980. Ont. Min. Nat. Res., Rep. 20 pp. (WALLEYE; AGE AND GROWTH; CREEL CENSUS;).

2835. Thurston, L. D. W. 1981. Results of an intensive creel census conducted in the Bayfield area of Georgian Bay, Parry Sound District in 1980. Ont. Min. Nat. Res., Rep. 31 pp. (WALLEYE; AGE AND GROWTH; CREEL CENSUS;).

2836. Thurston, L. D. W. 1982. Results of an intensive creel census conducted on the Magnetawan River near Britt Ontario during the winter of 1981. Ont. Min. Nat. Res., Rep. 10 pp. (WALLEYE; AGE AND GROWTH; CREEL CENSUS;).

2837. Thurston, L. D. W. 1982. Results of the 1981 intensive creel census conducted on the Pointe Au Baril area of eastern Georgian Bay. Ont. Min. Nat. Res., Rep. 24 pp. (WALLEYE; AGE AND GROWTH; CREEL CENSUS;).

2838. Thurston, L. D. W. 1982. Results of an extensive creel census conducted on the eastern shore of Georgian Bay during 1980 and 1981. Ont. Min. Nat. Res., Rep. 17 pp. (WALLEYE; CREEL CENSUS;).

2839. Thurston, L. D. W. 1982. Results of the 1981 intensive creel census conducted in the Bayfield, Nares Inlet and Lower Naiscoot River areas of eastern Georgian Bay. Ont. Min. Nat. Res., Rep. 22 pp. (WALLEYE; AGE AND GROWTH; CREEL CENSUS;).

2840. Thurston, L. D. W. 1987. Results of the 1987 electrofishing project conducted on the Moon River and Iron City Bay Areas of Eastern Georgian Bay. Ont. Min. Nat. Res., Parry Sound Dis. Rep. 93 pp. (WALLEYE; SAMPLING METHODS; SPAWNING STUDIES; STOCKING; WATER LEVELS;).

2841. Tidan, R. J. 1981. Reproductive biology of *Lampsilis radiata silicoides, Pelecypoda unionidae.* Am. Midl. Nat. 106:243-248. (WALLEYE; PATHOLOGY;).

2842. Tiffany, L. H. 1921. The gizzard shad in relation to plants and game fishes. Trans. Am. Fish. Soc. 50:381-386. (WALLEYE; FOOD STUDIES;).

2843. Timmerman, A. J., and W. I. Dunlop. 1985. Evidence of yellow pickerel *(Stizostedion vitreum vitreum)* reproduction in the central basin of Lake Erie, 1984. Ont. Min. Nat. Res., Lake Erie Fish. Assessment Unit Rep. 1985-2:42 pp. (WALLEYE; ECOLOGY; MOVEMENTS AND MIGRATIONS; POPULATION STUDIES;).

2844. Titcomb, J. W. 1904. Report on the propagation and distribution of food-fishes. U.S. Comm. Fish Fish., Annu. Rep. (1902):22-102. (WALLEYE; PROPAGATION; STOCKING;).

2845. Titcomb, J. W. 1908. Fish-cultural practices in the United States Bureau of Fisheries. U.S. Bur. Fish., Bull. 28:699-757. (WALLEYE; PROPAGATION; SPAWNING STUDIES; STOCKING;).

2846. Titcomb, J. W. 1921. Some fish cultural notes. Trans. Am. Fish. Soc. 50:200-211. (WALLEYE; COMMUNITY DYNAMICS; PROPAGATION; SPAWNING STUDIES;).

2847. Todd, R. 1971. Winter creel census for White River District 1970-71. Ont. Min. Nat. Res., Rep. 42 pp. (WALLEYE; CREEL CENSUS;).

2848. Toner, G. C. 1933. Annotated list of fishes of Georgian Bay. Copeia 1933:133-140. (WALLEYE; GEOGRAPHICAL DISTRIBUTION;).

2849. Toner, G. C., and W. E. Edwards. 1938. Cold-blooded vertebrates of Grippen Lake, Leeds County, Ontario. Can. Field Nat. 52:40-43. (WALLEYE; GEOGRAPHICAL DISTRIBUTION;).

2850. Toner, G. C., and J. A. Stevenson. 1934. Notes on the fish fauna of the eastern Ontario shallow water lake. Can. Field Nat. 48:131-133. (WALLEYE; GEOGRAPHICAL DISTRIBUTION;).

2851. Toneys, M. L., and D. W. Coble. 1979. Size related, first winter mortality of freshwater fishes. Trans. Am. Fish. Soc. 108:415-419. (WALLEYE; ECOLOGY; MORTALITY;).

2852. Toole, J. E., and M. J. Ryan. 1975. Creel survey of Lake Cypress Springs. Tex. Parks Wildl. Dept., Fed. Aid Fish Wildl. Restor. Proj. F-31-R-1 Job VI Final Report. (WALLEYE; CREEL CENSUS;).

2853. Torp, B. L., T. A. Kucera, and B. W. Hawkinson. 1977. Annual report of the statewide creel census of 83 lakes and 35 trout streams in Minnesota, April, 1972 — February. 1973. Minn. Dept. Nat. Res., Invest. Rep. No. 339:102 pp. (WALLEYE; CREEL CENSUS;).

2854. Townes, M. A. 1976. Navigation and propagation. Ont. Fish Wildl. Rev. 15:7-8. (WALLEYE; HABITAT IMPROVEMENT; SPAWNING STUDIES;).

2855. Townsend, C. H. 1902. Statistics of the fisheries of the Great Lakes. U.S. Comm. Fish Fish., Annu. Rep. (1901):575-657. (SAUGER; WALLEYE; COMMERCIAL FISHERIES; FISHING GEAR;).

2856. Trautman, M. B. 1941. Fluctuations in lengths and numbers of certain species of fishes over a five-year period in Whitmore Lake, Michigan. Trans. Am. Fish. Soc. 70:193-208. (WALLEYE; GEOGRAPHICAL DISTRIBUTION;).

2857. Trautman, M. B. 1946. Artificial keys for the identification of the fishes of the State of Ohio. Franz Theodore Stone Lab. 52 pp. (SAUGER; WALLEYE; MORPHOLOGY; TAXONOMY;).

2858. Trautman, M. B. 1957. The fishes of Ohio. Ohio State Univ. Press 683 pp. (SAUGER; WALLEYE; LIFE HISTORY; MORPHOLOGY; TAXONOMY;).

2859. Trevredyn-Tait, S. 1985. Report of 1979 trap-netting Rice Lake. Ont. Min. Nat. Res., Kawartha Lakes Fish. Assess. Unit Rep. 1985-5:30 pp. (WALLEYE; COMMUNITY DYNAMICS; MARKING; POPULATION STUDIES;).

2860. Truitt, R. V. 1938. Sport fishing in Maryland. Chesapeake Biol. Lab. 26:16 pp. (WALLEYE; GEOGRAPHICAL DISTRIBUTION;).

2861. Truitt, R. V. 1952. Inventory. Md. Board Nat. Res., 9th Annu. Rep. pp. 8-12. (WALLEYE; IMPOUNDMENTS;).

2862. Truitt, R. V. 1953. Inventory. Md. Board Nat. Res., 10th Annu. Rep. pp. 20-23. (WALLEYE; IMPOUNDMENTS;).

2863. Truitt, R. V., and V. D. Vladykov. 1937. The importance of sport fishing in Maryland. Trans. Am. Fish. Soc. 66:403-405. (WALLEYE; GEOGRAPHICAL DISTRIBUTION;).

2864. Tubb, R. A., F. A. Copes, and C. Johnston. 1966. Fishes of the Sheyenne River of North Dakota. Proc. N.D. Acad. Sci. 19:120-128. (SAUGER; WALLEYE; GEOGRAPHICAL DISTRIBUTION;).

2865. Tucker, T. R. 1968. Aspects of the life history of the walleye *(Stizostedion vitreum)* in Hoover Reservoir, Ohio. M.S. Thesis, Ohio State Univ., Columbus, Ohio. 33 pp. (WALLEYE; AGE AND GROWTH; IMPOUNDMENTS; LIFE HISTORY; SAMPLING METHODS;).

2866. Tucker, T. R., and S. H. Taub. 1970. Age and growth of the walleye, *Stizostedion vitreum vitreum*, in Hoover Reservoir, Ohio. Ohio J. Sci. 70:314-318. (WALLEYE; AGE AND GROWTH; IMPOUNDMENTS;).

2867. Tunison, A., S. M. Mullin, and O. L. Meehean. 1949. Extended survey of fish culture in the

United States. Prog. Fish-Cult. 11:252-262. (WALLEYE; STOCKING;).

2868. Tunison, A. V., S. M. Mullin, and O. L. Meehean. 1949. Survey of fish culture in the United States. Prog. Fish-Cult. 11:31-69. (WALLEYE; STOCKING;).

2869. Tureson, F. 1978. A creel census of Lake Minnetonka, Hennepin County, Minnesota, from May 17 to October 19, 1975. Minn. Dept. Nat. Res., Fish Manage. Rep. No. 2:60 pp. (WALLEYE; CREEL CENSUS;).

2870. Tureson, F. 1978. A creel census and water surface use study of the Mississippi River from Coon Rapids Dam to the mouth of the Minnesota River May 8 to September 30, 1976. Minn. Dept. Nat. Res., Fish Manage. Rep. No. 3:39 pp. (SAUGER; WALLEYE; CREEL CENSUS;).

2871. Tureson, F. 1978. A creel census and water surface use study of five Metro Area lakes White Bear, Bald Eagle, Gervais, Keller and Vadnais, Ramsey, Washington and Anoka Counties. Minn. Dept. Nat. Res., Fish Manage. Rep. No. 11:55 pp. (WALLEYE; CREEL CENSUS;).

2872. Tureson, F., Jr., and C. A. Lessman. 1978. Attempts to induce ovulation of the walleye *(Stizostedion vitreum)* by the use of carp pituitary, steroids, and vertebrate gonadotropins. Minn. Dept. Nat. Res., Fish Manage. Rep. No. 8:22 pp. (WALLEYE; PROPAGATION; SPAWNING STUDIES;).

2873. U.S. Bureau of Fisheries. 1913. The distribution of fish and fish eggs during the fiscal year 1912. Bur. Fish. Doc., U.S. Government Printing Office, Washington. 770:108 pp. (WALLEYE; PROPAGATION; STOCKING;).

2874. U.S. Commission of Fish and Fisheries. 1903. Artificial propagation of the shad and pike perch. In the Fish Manual, Revised edition pp. 165-179. (SAUGER; WALLEYE; COMMERCIAL FISHERIES; COMMUNITY DYNAMICS; FOOD STUDIES; PROPAGATION; SPAWNING STUDIES;).

2875. U.S. Fish and Wildlife Service. 1976. Investigation of the walleye *(Stizostedion vitreum)* fishery in Franklin D. Roosevelt Lake. Wash., Dept. Game, U.S. Fish Wildl. Serv., Bur. Sport Fish. Wildl., May 15, 1974-May 14, 1975. 50 pp. (WALLEYE; AGE AND GROWTH; CREEL CENSUS; IMPOUNDMENTS;).

2876. Ulrikson, G. U., and P. W. Laarman. 1971. Serum protein analysis of walleyes. Mich. Dept. Nat. Res., Research and Develop. No. 240:10 pp. (WALLEYE; GENETICS;).

2877. UMRCC Technical Committee for Fisheries. 1945. Preliminary progress report. Upper Mississippi River Conserv. Surv. Comm., Tech. Comm. Fish., 1st Prog. Rep. 17pp. (SAUGER; WALLEYE; CREEL CENSUS;).

2878. Underhill, J. C. 1959. Fishes of the Vermillion River, South Dakota. Proc. S.D. Acad. Sci. 38:96-102. (SAUGER; WALLEYE; GEOGRAPHICAL DISTRIBUTION;).

2879. Unkenholz, D. G., P. H. Michaletz, and C. C. Stone. 1981. Fisheries studies related to the Gregory County pumped storage project, 1981. S.D. Dept. Game Fish and Parks, Prog. Rep. No. 81-8:52 pp. (SAUGER; WALLEYE; AGE AND GROWTH; COMMUNITY DYNAMICS; CREEL CENSUS; FOOD STUDIES; IMPOUNDMENTS; MARKING; MOVEMENTS AND MIGRATIONS; POPULATION STUDIES; SPAWNING STUDIES; WATER LEVELS;).

2880. Unkenholz, D. G., P. H. Michaletz, and C. C. Stone. 1983. Fisheries studies related to the Gregory County pumped storage project, 1982. S.D. Dept. Game Fish and Parks, Prog. Rep. No. 82-8:80 pp. (SAUGER; WALLEYE; AGE AND GROWTH; COMMUNITY DYNAMICS; CREEL CENSUS; FOOD STUDIES; IMPOUNDMENTS; MARKING; MOVEMENTS AND MIGRATIONS; POPULATION STUDIES; SPAWNING STUDIES; WATER LEVELS;).

2881. Unkenholz, D. G., P. H. Michaletz, and C. C. Stone. 1984. Fisheries studies related to the Gregory County pumped storage project, 1983. S.D. Dept. Game Fish and Parks, Prog. Rep. No. 84-5:129 pp. (SAUGER; WALLEYE; AGE AND GROWTH; COMMUNITY DYNAMICS; CREEL CENSUS; FOOD STUDIES; IMPOUNDMENTS; MARKING; MOVEMENTS AND MIGRATIONS; POPULATION STUDIES; SPAWNING STUDIES; WATER LEVELS;).

2882. Usher, A. J. 1987. Ontario Lake of the Woods fishery: economic and social analysis. Trans. Am. Fish. Soc. 116:352-366. (WALLEYE; SOCIO-ECONOMICS OF FISHERIES;).

2883. Uthe, J. F., E. Roberts, L. W. Clarke, and H. Tsuyuki. 1966. Comparative electrophero-grams of representatives of families Petromizontidae, Esocidae, Centrarchidae, and Percidae. J. Fish. Research Board Can. 23:1663-1671. (WALLEYE; TAXONOMY;).

2884. Uthe, J. F., and R. A. Ryder. 1970. Regional variation in muscle myogen polymorphism in walleye *(Stizostedion vitreum vitreum)* as related to morphology. J. Fish. Research Board Can. 27:923-927. (SAUGER; WALLEYE; MORPHOLOGY; TAXONOMY;).

2885. Vaillancourt, P. G. 1982. Study on the spawn-ing of yellow walleye, *Stizostedion vitreum vitreum* (Mitchill) in the Belle-Riviere in spring 1981 and some information on growth and maturity of capture specimens. Que. Min. du Loisir, de la Chasse at de la Peche. 40 pp. (WALLEYE; AGE AND GROWTH; SPAWNING STUDIES;).

2886. Valentine, J. J., and E. J. Peterson. 1974. Stocking walleye sac fry. Prog. Fish-Cult. 36:7. (WALLEYE; STOCKING;).

2887. Valiant, H., and T. Smith. 1979. Angler creel census in the Lake Winnipegosis, Waterhen, Lake Manitoba and Dauphin River areas in 1977 and 1978. Man. Dept. Nat. Res., Manu-script Rep. 79-68:88 pp. (SAUGER; WALLEYE; CREEL CENSUS; PRODUCTIVITY;).

2888. Van Cleave, H. J. 1923. Acanthocephala from the fishes of Oneida Lake, New York. Roosevelt Wildlife Annu. Bull. 2:73-84. (WALLEYE; PATHOLOGY;).

2889. Van Cleave, H. J., and J. F. Mueller. 1932. Parasites of Oneida Lake fishes. Part 1. De-scriptions of new genera and new species. N.Y. State Coll., Roosevelt WildLife Annu. Bull. 3:1-154. (WALLEYE; PATHOLOGY;).

2890. Van Cleave, H. J., and J. F. Mueller. 1934. Parasites of Oneida Lake fishes. Part III. A biological and ecological survey of the worm parasites. N.Y. State Coll. Forest., Roosevelt Wild Life Annu. Bull. 3:159-334. (WALLEYE; PATHOLOGY;).

2891. Vanexan, D. J. 1985. Volunteer creel census program in fly-in lakes in Hearst District, 1984. Ont. Min. Nat. Res., Rep. 27 pp. (WALLEYE; CREEL CENSUS;).

2892. Van Horn, W. M., and R. Balch. 1956. The re-action of walleyed pike eggs to reduced dis-solved oxygen concentrations. Purdue Univ. Eng. Ext. Dept., Ext. Serv. Bull. 91:319-341. (WALLEYE; HABITAT DEG-RADATION; MORTALITY; SPAWNING STUDIES;).

2893. Vanicek, C. D. 1964. Age and growth of sauger, *Stizostedion canadense* (Smith), in Lewis and Clark Lake. Iowa State J. Sci. 38:157-177. (SAUGER; AGE AND GROWTH; FOOD STUDIES; SAM-PLING METHODS;).

2894. Van Loon, J. C., and R. J. Beamish. 1977. Heavy-metal contamination by atmo-spheric fallout of several Flin Flon area lakes and the relation of fish populations. J. Fish. Research Board Can. 34:899-906. (WALLEYE; HABITAT DEGRADA-TION; TOXICANTS;).

2895. Van Meter, H. D., and M. B. Trautman. 1970. An annotated list of the fishes of Lake Erie and its tributary waters exclusive of the De-troit River. Ohio J. Sci. 70:65-78. (WALL-EYE; GEOGRAPHICAL DISTRIBU-TION;).

2896. Van Oosten, J. 1932. Experiments on the mesh of trapnets and legislation of commer-cial fisheries of Lake Erie. Trans. Am. Fish. Soc. 62:100-107. (SAUGER; WALLEYE; COMMERCIAL FISHERIES; FISHING GEAR;).

2897. Van Oosten, J. 1934. The value of question-naires in commercial fisheries regulations and surveys. Trans. Am. Fish. Soc. 64:107-117. (WALLEYE; COMMERCIAL FISH-ERIES; FISHING GEAR;).

2898. Van Oosten, J. 1935. Logically justified de-ductions concerning the Great Lakes fish-eries exploded by scientific research. Trans. Am. Fish. Soc. 65:71-75. (SAUGER; WALL-EYE; COMMERCIAL FISHERIES; FISHING GEAR; HABITAT DEGRADA-TION;).

2899. Van Oosten, J. 1937. Artificial propagation of commercial fish of the Great Lakes. Trans. 2nd N. Am. Wildl. Conf. pp. 605-612.

(SAUGER; WALLEYE; COMMERCIAL FISHERIES; MORTALITY; PROPAGATION; STOCKING;).

2900. Van Oosten, J. 1937. The Great Lakes fisheries: their proper management for sustained yields. Trans. Am. Fish. Soc. 66:131-138. (SAUGER; WALLEYE; COMMERCIAL FISHERIES;).

2901. Van Oosten, J. 1938. Mortality of fish on Lake Erie. Penn. Board Fish Comm., Combined Bienn. Rep. (1938):92-99. (WALLEYE; COMMERCIAL FISHERIES; MORTALITY;).

2902. Van Oosten, J. 1939. Migratory fish, a problem of interstate cooperation? Trans. 4th N. Am. Wildl. Conf. pp. 25-30. (SAUGER; WALLEYE; COMMERCIAL FISHERIES; MOVEMENT AND MIGRATIONS;).

2903. Van Oosten, J. 1940. Fishing industry of the Great Lakes. U.S. Fish Wildl. Serv., Mem. I-63:15. (SAUGER; WALLEYE; COMMERCIAL FISHERIES; FISHING GEAR;).

2904. Van Oosten, J. 1941. The age and growth of fresh-water fishes. Univ. Wis. Press, Madison Wis., Symp. Hydrobiol. pp. 196-205. (WALLEYE; AGE AND GROWTH; MORPHOLOGY; TAXONOMY;).

2905. Van Oosten, J. 1942. Relationship between the planting of fry and production of whitefish in Lake Erie. Trans. Am. Fish. Soc. 71:118-121. (WALLEYE; COMMERCIAL FISHERIES; STOCKING;).

2906. Van Oosten, J. 1948. Turbidity as a factor in the decline of Great Lakes fishes with special reference to Lake Erie. Trans. Am. Fish. Soc. 75:281-322. (SAUGER; WALLEYE; AGE AND GROWTH; ECOLOGY; HABITAT DEGRADATION; POPULATION STUDIES; PRODUCTIVITY;).

2907. Van Oosten, J. 1949. The present status of the United States commercial fisheries of the Great Lakes. Trans. 14th N. Am. Wildl. Conf. 14:319-330. (SAUGER; WALLEYE; COMMERCIAL FISHERIES;).

2908. Van Oosten, J., and H. J. Deason. 1957. History of Red Lakes fishery, 1917-38, with observations on population status. U.S. Fish Wildl. Serv., Spec. Sci. Rep. Fish. 229: 63 pp. (WALLEYE; AGE AND GROWTH; COM-

MERCIAL FISHERIES; ECOLOGY; MORTALITY; PHYSIOLOGY; POPULATION STUDIES; PROPAGATION; SPAWNING STUDIES;).

2909. Van Oosten, J., and H. J. Eschmeyer. 1956. Biology of young lake trout (Salvelinus namaycush) in Lake Michigan. U.S. Fish Wildl. Serv., Research Rep. 42:88 pp. (SAUGER; ECOLOGY;).

2910. Van Oosten, J., R. Hile, and F. W. Jobes. 1946. The whitefish fishery of Lakes Huron and Michigan with special reference to the deep-trap-net fishery. U.S. Fish Wildl. Serv., Fish. Bull. 50:297-394. (WALLEYE; COMMERCIAL FISHERIES; GEOGRAPHICAL DISTRIBUTION;).

2911. Van Vooren, A. R. 1978. Characteristics of walleye (Stizostedion vitreum) spawning stocks. Ohio Dept. Nat. Res., Fed. Aid Fish Wildl. Restor. Proj. F-35-R, Job No. 4:28 pp. (WALLEYE; COMMERCIAL FISHERIES; CREEL CENSUS; MARKING; MORTALITY; MOVEMENT AND MIGRATIONS; POPULATION STUDIES; SPAWNING STUDIES;).

2912. Van Vooren, A. R. 1983. Distribution and relative abundance of upper Mississippi River fishes. Upper Mississippi River Conserv. Comm., Fish Tech. Sec. 19 pp. (SAUGER; WALLEYE; ECOLOGY; GEOGRAPHICAL DISTRIBUTION;).

2913. Vasey, F. W. 1967. Age and growth of walleye and sauger in pool 11 of the Mississippi River. Iowa St. J. Sci. 41:447-466. (SAUGER; WALLEYE; AGE AND GROWTH; SPAWNING STUDIES;).

2914. Veith, G. D., D. W. Kuehl, E. N. Leonard, K. Welch, and G. Pratt. 1981. Polychlorinated biphenyls and other organic chemical residues in fish from major United States watersheds near the Great Lakes, 1978. Pestic. Monit. J. 15:1-8. (WALLEYE; TOXICANTS;).

2915. Vely, V. G. 1970. Identification of races, strains or sub-populations of walleye pike by the electrophoresis method. Ohio Dept. Nat. Res., Ohio AFS 3:68 pp. (WALLEYE; GENETICS; MOVEMENT AND MIGRATIONS;).

2916. Verduin, J. 1964. Changes in western Lake Erie during the period of 1948-1962. Verh.

Int. Verein. Limnol 15:639-644. (WALL-EYE; ECOLOGY; MORTALITY;).

2917. Vergeer, T. 1928. Canadian fish, a source of the broad tapeworm of man in the United States. J. Am. Med. Assn. 90:1687-1688. (SAUGER; WALLEYE; PATHOLOGY;).

2918. Vergeer, T. 1928. New sources of broad tapeworm infestations. Report of fourteen native cases. J. Am. Med. Assn. 91:369-397. (WALLEYE; PATHOLOGY;).

2919. Vergeer, T. 1928. An important source of broad tapeworm in America. Science 68:14-15. (WALLEYE; PATHOLOGY;).

2920. Vergeer, T. 1928. Dissemination of broad tapeworm by wild carnivora. Can. Med. Assn. J. 19:692-694. (WALLEYE; PATHOLOGY;).

2921. Vergeer, T. 1929. The broad tapeworm in America with suggestions for its control. J. Infect. Dis. 44:1-11. (SAUGER; WALLEYE; PATHOLOGY;).

2922. Vergeer, T. 1930. Causes underlying increased incidence of broad tapeworm in in North America. J. Am. Med. Assn. 95:1579-1581. (WALLEYE; PATHOLOGY;).

2923. VonRosen, H., and H. McLeod. 1985. White Lake fisheries assessment with a Pickerel Stocking Analysis. Ont. Min. Nat. Res., Rep. 30 pp. (WALLEYE; CREEL CENSUS; POPULATION STUDIES; WATER LEVELS;).

2924. Vukelich, M. F. 1980. Kabinakagami Lake creel census survey, 1979. Ont. Min. Nat. Res., Rep. 58 pp. (WALLEYE; AGE AND GROWTH; CREEL CENSUS;).

2925. Vukelich, M. F. 1983. A comparative assessment of the walleye (Stizostedion vitreum vitreum) and northern pike (Esox lucius) fisheries of Kabinakagami, Nagagamisis and Nagagami Lakes. Ont. Min. Nat. Res., Rep. 48 pp. (WALLEYE; AGE AND GROWTH; CREEL CENSUS;).

2926. Vukelich, M. F. 1984. An assessment of the walleye (Stizostedion vitreum vitreum) and northern pike (Esox lucius) sport fishery of Obakamiga and Granitehill Lakes, 1982. Ont. Min. Nat. Res., Rep. 29 pp. (WALLEYE; AGE AND GROWTH; CREEL CENSUS;).

2927. Vukelich, M. F. 1985. Nagagami Lake winter creel survey 1985. Ont. Min. Nat. Res., Rep. 14 pp. (WALLEYE; CREEL CENSUS;).

2928. Vukelich, M. F., and E. McGregor. 1984. Analysis of the volunteer creel census program on fly-in lakes in the Hearst District, 1980-1983. Ont. Min. Nat. Res., Rep. 96 pp. (WALLEYE; CREEL CENSUS;).

2929. Wagner, G. 1909. Notes of the fish fauna of Lake Pepin. Trans. Wis. Acad. Sci., Arts Letters 16:23-37. (SAUGER; WALLEYE; COMMERCIAL FISHERIES;).

2930. Wagner, W. C. 1972. Utilization of alewives by inshore piscivorous fish in Lake Michigan. Trans. Am. Fish. Soc. 101:55-63. (WALLEYE; ECOLOGY; FOOD STUDIES;).

2931. Wahl, D. H. 1982. Daily ratio, feeding periodicity and prey selection of sauger (Stizostedion canadense) in the Ohio River. M.S. Thesis. Virginia Polytechnic Institute and State University, Blacksburg, Va. 101 pp. (SAUGER; AGE AND GROWTH; COMMUNITY DYNAMICS; FOOD STUDIES;).

2932. Wahl, D. H., and L. A. Nielsen. 1985. Feeding ecology of the sauger (Stizostedion canadense) in a large river. Can. J. Fish. Aqaut. Sci. 42:120-128. (SAUGER; AGE AND GROWTH; COMMUNITY DYNAMICS; FOOD STUDIES;).

2933. Wahl, J. R., and A. Schalenkamp. 1983. Assessment of the Winnebago River sport fishery. Iowa Conserv.. Comm., Fish. Manage. Invest. 16 pp. (WALLEYE; AGE AND GROWTH; CREEL CENSUS; MARKING; MORTALITY; MOVEMENT AND MIGRATIONS; POPULATION STUDIES;).

2934. Wahtola, C. H., D. E. Miller, and J. B. Owen. 1972. The age and growth of walleye (Stizostedion vitreum) and sauger (Stizostedion canadense) in Lake Sakakawea, North Dakota. Proc. N.D. Acad. Sci. 25:72-83. (SAUGER; WALLEYE; AGE AND GROWTH; IMPOUNDMENTS;).

2935. Wainio, A. 1972. The sport fishery of Matchedash Sound. Ont. Min. Nat. Res., Rep. 159 pp. (WALLEYE; COMMUNITY DYNAMICS; CREEL CENSUS; ECOLOGY;

SOCIO-ECONOMICS OF FISHERIES;
TOXICANTS; WATER LEVELS;).

2936. Walburg, C. H. 1964. Fish population studies. Lewis and Clark Lake, Missouri River, 1956 to 1962. U.S. Fish Wildl. Serv., Spec. Sci. Rep. Fish No. 482:17 pp. (SAUGER; WALLEYE; AGE AND GROWTH; POPULATION STUDIES; SAMPLING METHODS; STOCKING;).

2937. Walburg, C. H. 1969. Fish sampling and estimation of relative abundance in Lewis and Clark Lake. U.S. Fish Wildl. Serv., Tech. Papers 18:15 pp. (SAUGER; FISHING GEAR; IMPOUNDMENTS; SAMPLING METHODS;).

2938. Walburg, C. H. 1971. Loss of young fish in reservoir discharge and year-class survival, Lewis and Clark Lake, Missouri River. Pages 441-448 in G.E. Hall, ed. Reservoir fisheries and limnology. Am. Fish. Soc. Sp. Publ. No. 8, Washington, D.C. (SAUGER; WALLEYE; IMPOUNDMENTS; MORTALITY; POPULATION STUDIES;).

2939. Walburg, C. H. 1972. Some factors associated with fluctuation in year-class strength of sauger, Lewis and Clark Lake, South Dakota. Trans. Am. Fish. Soc. 101:311-316. (SAUGER; AGE AND GROWTH; SPAWNING STUDIES; WATER LEVELS;).

2940. Walburg, C. H. 1976. Changes in the fish population of Lewis and Clark Lake, 1956-74, and their relation to water management and the environment. U.S. Fish Wildl., Research Rep. No. 79:34 pp. (SAUGER; WALLEYE; AGE AND GROWTH; ECOLOGY; IMPOUNDMENTS; POPULATION STUDIES; WATER LEVELS;).

2941. Walburg, C. H., G. L. Kaiser, and P. L. Hudson. 1971. Lewis and Clark Lake tailwater biota and some relations of the tailwater and reservoir fish populations . Pages 449-467 in G. E. Hall ed. Reservoir fisheries and limnology. Am. Fish. Soc. Sp. Publ. No. 8, Washington, D.C. (SAUGER; WALLEYE; AGE AND GROWTH; FOOD STUDIES; IMPOUNDMENTS; PRODUCTIVITY; SAMPLING METHODS;).

2942. Wales, D. L., and V. A. Liimatainen. 1987. Preliminary assessment of the current impact and potential risk of acidic deposition on walleye populations in Ontario. Ont.

Min. Nat. Res., Fish. Acidification Rep. Series. 87-11:51 pp. (WALLEYE; HABITAT DEGRADATION; TOXICANTS;).

2943. Walker, C. R., R. E. Lennon, and B. L. Berger. 1964. Preliminary observations on the toxicity of antimycin A to fish and other aquatic animals. Bur. Sport Fish. Wildl., Circ. 186:18 pp. (WALLEYE; TOXICANTS;).

2944. Walker, M. E., J. R. Brisbane, V. Macins, and J. A. Roos. 1982. An examination of the fishery in the eastern sector Lake of the Woods 1981. Ont. Min. Nat. Res., Lake of the Woods Fish. Assess. Unit Rep. 1982-02:125 pp. (SAUGER; WALLEYE; AGE AND GROWTH; COMMUNITY DYNAMICS; CREEL CENSUS; FOOD STUDIES; PATHOLOGY; POPULATION STUDIES; SPAWNING STUDIES;).

2945. Walker, R. 1947. Lymphocystis disease and neoplasia in fish. Anat. Rec. 99:559-560. (WALLEYE; PATHOLOGY;).

2946. Walker, R. 1958. Lymphocystis warts and skin tumors of walleyed pike. Rensselaer Rev. Grad. Stud. 14:1-5. (WALLEYE; PATHOLOGY;).

2947. Walker, R. 1962. Fine structure of lymphocystis virus of fish. Virology 18:503-505. (WALLEYE; PATHOLOGY;).

2948. Walker, R. 1963. The capsule of virus-induced lymphocystis cells of fish. Am. Zool. 3:490. (WALLEYE; PATHOLOGY;).

2949. Walker, R. 1965. Viral DNA and cytoplasmic RNA in lymphocystis cell of fish. N.Y. Acad. Sci., Annu. 126:386-395. (WALLEYE; PATHOLOGY;).

2950. Walker, R. 1969. Virus associated with epidermal hyperplasia in fish. Nat. Cancer Inst., Monogr. 31:195-207. (WALLEYE; PATHOLOGY;).

2951. Walker, R. 1985. Lymphocystis cells infected with retrovirus-like particles. Fish Health News 14: iii-v. (WALLEYE; PATHOLOGY;).

2952. Walker, R., and R. Weissenberg. 1965. Conformity of light and electron microscopic studies on virus particle distribution in lymphocystis cells of fish. N.Y. Acad. Sci.,

Annu. 126:375-385. (WALLEYE; PATHOL-OGY;).

2953. Walker, R., and K. Wolf. 1962. Virus array in lymphocystis cells of sunfish. Am. Zool. 2:556. (WALLEYE; PATHOLOGY;).

2954. Walker, R. E., and R. L. Applegate. 1976. Growth, food, and possible ecological effects of young of-the-year walleyes in a South Dakota prairie pothole. Prog. Fish-Cult. 38:217-220. (WALLEYE; AGE AND GROWTH; ECOLOGY; FOOD STUDIES; PRODUCTIVITY;).

2955. Waller, D. L., L. E. Holland, L. G. Mitchell, and T. W. Kammer. 1985. Artificial infestation of largemouth bass and walleye with glochidia of Lampsilis ventricosa (Pelecypoda: Uniconidae). Freshwater Invert. Biol. 4:152-153. (WALLEYE; PATHOLOGY;).

2956. Walroth, B. 1980. Analysis of the Onaman Lake creel census program 1977-1979, with particular reference to the 1979 field work. Ont. Min. Nat. Res., Rep. 27 pp. (WALLEYE; CREEL CENSUS;).

2957. Walroth, B. 1983. Onaman Lake creel census summary — 1983. Ont. Min. Nat. Res., Rep. 26 pp. (WALLEYE; AGE AND GROWTH; CREEL CENSUS;).

2958. Waltemyer, D. L. 1975. The effect of tannin on the motility of walleye (Stizostedion vitreum) spermatozoa. Trans. Am. Fish. Soc. 104:808-810. (WALLEYE; PROPAGATION;).

2959. Waltemyer, D. L. 1976. Tannin as an agent to eliminate adhesiveness of walleye eggs during artificial propagation. Trans. Am. Fish. Soc. 105:731-736. (WALLEYE; PROPAGATION;).

2960. Walter, G. S., and W. J. Hoagman. 1975. A method for estimating year class strength from abundance data with application to the fishery of Green Bay, Lake Michigan. Trans. Am. Fish. Soc. 104(2):245-263. (WALLEYE; AGE AND GROWTH; COMMERCIAL FISHERIES; COMMUNITY DYNAMICS; POPULATION STUDIES;).

2961. Walters, T. R. 1986. Dynamics and distribution of fishes occupying a South Dakota power plant cooling reservoir. M.S. Thesis, S.D. St. Univ., Brookings, S.D. 94 pp. (WALLEYE; AGE AND GROWTH; MOR-TALITY; POPULATION STUDIES; SPAWNING STUDIES;).

2962. Ward, F. J., and J. W. Clayton. 1975. Initial effects of fry introduction on year-class strength of West Blue Lake walleye, Stizostedion vitreum vitreum (Mitchell), using fry with distinctive malate dehydrogenase isozyme phenotypes as an identifying mark. Int. Ver. Theor. Angew. Limnol. Verh. 19:2394-2400. (WALLEYE; GENETICS; STOCKING;).

2963. Ward, F. J., and G. G. C. Robinson. 1974. A review of research on the limnology of West Blue Lake, Manitoba. J. Fish. Research Board Can. 31:977-1005. (WALLEYE; AGE AND GROWTH; COMMUNITY DYNAMICS; FOOD STUDIES; POPULATION STUDIES; PRODUCTIVITY;).

2964. Ward, H. B. 1912. The distribution and frequency of animal parasites and parasitic diseases in North American freshwater fish. Trans. Am. Fish. Soc. 41:207-244. (SAUGER; WALLEYE; PATHOLOGY;).

2965. Ward, H. B. 1929. Studies on the broad fish tapeworm in Minnesota. J. Am. Med. Assn. 92:389-390. (WALLEYE; PATHOLOGY;).

2966. Ward, H. B., and T. B. McGath. 1917. Notes on some nematodes from fresh-water fishes. J. Parisitol. 3:57-65. (WALLEYE; PA-THOLOGY;).

2967. Warnick, D. C. 1972. Walleye movements from Lake Kampeska based on anglers reports of tagged fish recoveries, 1966-72 South Dakota. S.D. Dept. Game, Fish Parks, Fed. Aid Fish Wildl. Restor. Proj. F-15-R-6, Job No. II-1:7 pp. (WALLEYE; MARKING; MOVEMENT AND MIGRATIONS; POPULATION STUDIES;).

2968. Washburn, F. L. 1886. Mortality of fish at Lake Mille Lac, Minnesota. Am. Nat. 20:896-897. (WALLEYE; MORTALITY; PATHOLOGY;).

2969. Waters, S. 1974. An evaluation of walleye fry and fingerling stocking and natural reproduction in Storm Lake, Iowa. Iowa Conserv.. Comm., 1974 Job Comp. Rep. Proj. 74-1-C-12:134-138. (WALLEYE; MARKING; MORTALITY; STOCKING;)

2970. Waters, S. 1975. An evaluation of walleye fry and fingerling stocking in Storm Lake,

Iowa. Iowa Conserv.. Comm., 1975 Job Comp. Rep. Proj. 75-I-C-115:33-40. (WALLEYE; MARKING; MORTALITY; STOCKING;).

2971. Watson, L. D., and B. W. Hawkinson. 1979. A recreational use survey of Pool 5 Upper Mississippi River, January 1 to December 31, 1978. Minn. Dept. Nat. Res., Invest. Rep. No. 362: 23 pp. (SAUGER; WALLEYE; CREEL CENSUS;).

2972. Watson, N. H. F., and G. H. Lawler. 1965. Natural infections of cyclopid copepods with procercoids of *Triaenophorus* sp.. J. Fish. Research Board Can. 22:1225-1343. (WALLEYE; PATHOLOGY;).

2973. Watson, S. W. 1953. Virus diseases of fish. Trans. Am. Fish. Soc. 83:331-341. (WALLEYE; PATHOLOGY;).

2974. Waybrant, R., and J. Shauver. 1979. Survey of larval fish in the Michigan waters of Lake Erie, 1975 and 1976. U.S. Environ. Protect. Agency, Ecol. Research Series 96 pp. (WALLEYE; MOVEMENT AND MIGRATIONS; POPULATION STUDIES;).

2975. Weaver, O. R. 1985. Evaluation of the walleye population of Lake Nottely. Geog. Dept. Nat. Res., Fed. Aid Fish Wildl. Restor. Proj. F-25:43 pp. (WALLEYE; COMMUNITY DYNAMICS; CREEL CENSUS; IMPOUNDMENTS; INTRODUCTIONS; POPULATION STUDIES; SPAWNING STUDIES; STOCKING;).

2976. Weber, D. T. 1960. Investigation of walleye reproduction and stocking success in northern South Dakota lakes, 1960. S.D. Dept. Game, Fish Parks, Fed. Aid Fish Wildl. Restor. Proj. F-1-R-10, Job No. 23:15 pp. (WALLEYE; AGE AND GROWTH; ECOLOGY; POPULATION STUDIES; SAMPLING METHODS; STOCKING;).

2977. Weber, D. T. 1960. Test netting and seining of northern lakes, 1959. Condition of fish. S.D. Dept. Game Fish and Parks, Fed. Aid Fish Wildl. Restor. Proj. F-1-R-9, Job No. 9: 34-49. (WALLEYE; AGE AND GROWTH;).

2978. Weber, D. T. 1962. Investigation of walleye reproduction and stocking success in northern South Dakota lakes 1961. S.D. Dept. Game, Fish Parks, Fed. Aid Fish Wildl. Restor. Proj. F-1-R-11, Job No. 19:26 pp. (WALLEYE; AGE AND GROWTH; POP-

ULATION STUDIES; SAMPLING METHODS; STOCKING;).

2979. Weber, D. T. 1963. Investigation of walleye reproduction and stocking success in eastern lakes 1962. S.D. Dept. Game, Fish Parks, Fed. Aid Fish Wildl. Restor. Proj. F-1-R-12, Job No. 19:16 pp. (WALLEYE; POPULATION STUDIES; SAMPLING METHODS; SPAWNING STUDIES; STOCKING;).

2980. Weber, D. T. 1965. Classification of lakes in South Dakota. S.D. Dept. Game, Fish Parks, Fed. Aid Fish Wildl. Restor. Proj. F-1-R-13, Job No. 20:21 pp. (WALLEYE; ECOLOGY;).

2981. Weber, D. T., and R. L. Imler. 1974. An evaluation of artificial spawning beds for walleye. Colo. Div. Wildl., Special Rep. No. 34:17 pp. (WALLEYE; AGE AND GROWTH; HABITAT IMPROVEMENT; IMPOUNDMENTS; POPULATION STUDIES; SPAWNING STUDIES;).

2982. Weber, D. T., T. G. Powell, and R. L. Imler. 1972. Warmwater fisheries investigations. Colo. Game, Fish Parks Div., Fed. Aid Fish Wildl. Restor. Proj. F-34-R-7, Job No. 3, 4. 5, 7 and 8:39 pp. (WALLEYE; CREEL CENSUS; HABITAT IMPROVEMENT; POPULATION STUDIES; SPAWNING STUDIES; STOCKING;).

2983. Weberg, C. A., and T. M. Lynch. 1955. 1954 creel census report. Colo. Dept. Game Fish. 14 pp. (WALLEYE; CREEL CENSUS; STOCKING;).

2984. Webster, B. O. 1931. A successful fishway. Trans. Am. Fish. Soc. 61:247-257. (WALLEYE; FISHWAYS;).

2985. Webster, D. A. 1942. The life histories of some Connecticut fishes. Conn. Geol. Nat. Hist. Surv., Bull., A Fishery Survey of Important Connecticut Lakes. 63: 122-127. (WALLEYE; INTRODUCTIONS; LIFE HISTORY; SPAWNING STUDIES;).

2986. Webster, D. A. 1962. Status of fish marking techniques in area covered by Northeast Division, American Fisheries Society, 1957-61. Northeast Fish. Wildl. Conf. 24 pp. (SAUGER; WALLEYE; MARKING;).

2987. Weed, A. C. 1927. Pike, pickerel and muskellunge. Field Mus. Nat. Hist., Zool. Leafl.

9:52. (SAUGER; WALLEYE; TAXONOMY;).

2988. Weilandt, P. 1984. Analysis of fisheries exploitation on the Woman River system during the summer of 1983. Ont. Min. Nat. Res., Red Lake District Rep. 61 pp. (WALLEYE; CREEL CENSUS; PRODUCTIVITY; REGULATIONS;).

2989. Weilandt, P. 1986. 1984 walleye tagging project on the Upper Chukuni River. Ont. Min. Nat. Res., Rep. 41 pp. (WALLEYE; MOVEMENTS AND MIGRATIONS; POPULATION STUDIES;).

2990. Weiler, W. C. 1969. 1969 Wildlife conservation officer creel census report and fish hatchery production report. Colo. Dept. Nat. Res., Fish Planning Serv. Rep. 25 pp. (WALLEYE; CREEL CENSUS; IMPOUNDMENTS; STOCKING;).

2991. Weinbauer, J. D., D. A. Thiel, V. W. Kaczynski, and C. S. Martin. 1980. Receiving stream fisheries studies relative to secondary treated pulp and paper mill effluents. Tappi 63:121-125. (WALLEYE; AGE AND GROWTH; COMMUNITY DYNAMICS; FOOD STUDIES; HABITAT DEGRADATION;).

2992. Weissenberg, R. 1939. Studies on virus diseases of fish. III. Morphological and experimental observations on the lymphocystis disease of pike perch, *Stizostedion vitreum.* Zool. 24:245-254. (WALLEYE; PATHOLOGY;).

2993. Weissenberg, R. 1945. Studies on virus disease in Centrarchidae. Zool. 30:169-184. (WALLEYE; PATHOLOGY;).

2994. Weissenberg, R. 1949. Studies on lymphocystis tumor cells of fish. I. The osmiophilic granules of the cytoplasmic inclusions and their interpretation as elementary bodies of the lymphocystis virus. Cancer Research 9:537-542. (WALLEYE; PATHOLOGY;).

2995. Weissenberg, R. 1951. Studies on lymphocystis tumor cells of fish. II. Granular structures of the inclusion substance as stages of the developmental cycle of the lymphocystis virus. Cancer Research 11:608-613. (WALLEYE; PATHOLOGY;).

2996. Weissenberg, R. 1965. Fifty years of research on the lymphocystis virus disease of fishes (1914-1964). Annu. N.Y. Acad. Sci. 126:362-374. (WALLEYE; PATHOLOGY;).

2997. Weithman, A. S. 1986. Economic benefits and costs associated with stocking fish. Pages 357-363 in R.H. Stroud, ed. Fish culture in fisheries management. Am. Fish. Soc., Bethesda, Maryland. (WALLEYE; SOCIO-ECONOMICS OF FISHERIES; STOCKING;).

2998. Welch, H. E. 1950. *Triaenophorus* investigation in the Thunder Bay District, Ontario. Fish. Research Board Can., Centr. Fish. Research Sta., Annu. Rep. 1950:22-23. (WALLEYE; PATHOLOGY;).

2999. Welham, S. 1983. Winter creel census on the Bay of Quinte, 1982. Ont. Min. Nat. Res., LOFAU Rep. 84-3:31 pp. (WALLEYE; CREEL CENSUS;).

3000. Welker, B. 1963. Desoto Bend fishery investigation, 1963. Iowa State Conserv. Comm., Quart. Biol. Rep. 16:67-73. (SAUGER; WALLEYE; ECOLOGY; HABITAT IMPROVEMENT; POPULATION STUDIES; STOCKING;).

3001. Welker, B. 1967. Fish population in five Missouri River ox-bow lakes. Proc. Iowa Acad. Sci. 72:230-237. (SAUGER; WALLEYE; AGE AND GROWTH; POPULATION STUDIES; STOCKING;).

3002. Welter, W. A. 1938. A list of the fishes of the Licking River drainage in eastern Kentucky. Copeia 1938:64-68. (WALLEYE; GEOGRAPHICAL DISTRIBUTION;).

3003. Wenke, T. L. 1968. Abundance of *Crepidostomum* and other intestinal helminths in fishes from Pool 19, Mississippi River. Iowa State J. Sci. 43:211-222. (SAUGER; WALLEYE; PATHOLOGY;).

3004. Wepruk, R. 1984. The Shebandowan Lake background data analysis for fisheries management directives. Ont. Min. Nat. Res., Interim. Rep. 64 pp. (WALLEYE; POPULATION STUDIES; WATER LEVELS;).

3005. Werner, W. H. R. 1952. Catch and year fishes Canadian waters of the Great Lakes. Five-year average (1921-1950), approximate figures for 1951. Ont. Dept. Lands Forests. 4 pp. (WALLEYE; COMMERCIAL FISHERIES;).

3006. Werner, W. H. R. 1961. Commercial fishing in Ontario. Annu. Rev. Fish. Council Can. 3 pp. (WALLEYE; COMMERCIAL FISHERIES; FISHING GEAR;).

3007. Werner, W. H. R., and M. J. Brubacher. 1960. Fisheries management in Georgian Bay. Ont. Dept. Lands Forests, Tech. Bull. 10:33 pp. (WALLEYE; COMMERCIAL FISHERIES;).

3008. Wesloh, M. L. 1959. A two-year creel census on Grace Lake in Beltrami County to evaluate the effect of perch removal on walleye fishing. Minn. Dept. Conserv., Invest Rep. No. 210:4 pp. (WALLEYE; COMMUNITY DYNAMICS; CREEL CENSUS;).

3009. Wesloh, M. L. 1959. A creel census of Long Lake, Becker County, with emphasis on the results of walleye fingerling stocking. Minn. Dept. Conserv., Invest. Rep. No. 208:3 pp. (WALLEYE; AGE AND GROWTH; CREEL CENSUS; STOCKING;).

3010. Wesloh, M. L. 1961. Sport fishery at Toad Lake, Becker County 1954-1956. Minn. Dept. Conserv., Invest. Rep. No. 235:9 pp. (WALLEYE; AGE AND GROWTH; CREEL CENSUS; STOCKING;).

3011. Wesloh, M. L., and D. E. Olson. 1962. The growth and harvest of stocked yearling northern pike, *Esox lucius* in a Minnesota walleye lake. Minn. Dept. Conserv., Invest. Rep. No. 242:9 pp. (WALLEYE; COMMUNITY DYNAMICS; CREEL CENSUS; ECOLOGY; STOCKING;).

3012. Westerman, F. A., P. I. Tack, and A. S. Hazzard. 1943. Michigan's program to encourage wider utilization of the less popular varieties of fish. Trans. 8th N. Am. Wildl. Conf. 8:251-259. (SAUGER; WALLEYE; COMMERCIAL FISHERIES;).

3013. Westerman, F. A., and Van Oosten. J. 1939. Report to the Michigan State Senate on the fisheries of Lake Michigan. Mich. Dept. Conserv. 82 pp. (WALLEYE; COMMERCIAL FISHERIES;).

3014. Wheeler, W. 1878. A partial list of the fishes of the Marais De Cygnes, at Ottawa. Trans. Kans. Acad. Sci. 6:33-34. (WALLEYE; GEOGRAPHICAL DISTRIBUTION;).

3015. Whitaker, H. 1890. Experiments in the impregnation of pike-perch eggs. Trans. Am. Fish Soc. 19:30-36. (WALLEYE; EMBRYOLOGY; PROPAGATION;).

3016. White, B. 1970. Winter creel census for White River District 1970. Ont. Min. Nat. Res., Rep. 17 pp. (WALLEYE; CREEL CENSUS;).

3017. White, C. E., Jr. 1959. Selectivity and effectiveness of certain types of commercial nets in the TVA lakes of Alabama. Trans. Am. Fish. Soc. 88:81-87. (SAUGER; COMMERCIAL FISHERIES;).

3018. White, C. E., Jr., and B. Jaco. 1961. Commercial and sport fishing on Guntersville Lake during the period of March 15-June 13, 1960. Proc. 15th Annu. Conf. Southeast Assoc. Game Fish Comm. 15:411-419. (SAUGER; COMMERCIAL FISHERIES; CREEL CENSUS;).

3019. White, T. F. 1977. Walleye spawning requirements in Thunderbird Reservoir. Okla. Wildl. Conserv., Fed. Aid Fish Wildl. Restor. Proj. F-34-R-3:48 pp. (WALLEYE; IMPOUNDMENTS; LIFE HISTORY; MORTALITY; SPAWNING STUDIES; STOCKING;).

3020. White, T. F. 1978. Evaluation of non-native fish introductions. Okla. Dept. Wildl. Conserv., Fed. Aid Fish Wildl. Restor. Proj. F-21-D-13, Job No. 1 & 2:26 pp. (WALLEYE; CREEL CENSUS; IMPOUNDMENTS; INTRODUCTIONS; MORTALITY; SPAWNING STUDIES;).

3021. Whitehead, V. M. 1978. Stream crossing design and construction implication to Manitoba fisheries. Man. Dept. Northern Affairs, Renew. Res. Transp. Serv. Tech. Rep. 78-10:171 pp. (WALLEYE; FISHWAYS; HABITAT IMPROVEMENT;).

3022. Whitehouse, F. 1919. Notes on some of the fishes of Alberta and adjacent waters. Can. Field Nat. 33:50-55. (SAUGER; WALLEYE; GEOGRAPHICAL DISTRIBUTION;).

3023. Whitney, A. N. 1953. Sampling fish populations in reservoirs. Mont. Fish Game Dept., Fed. Aid Fish Wildl. Restor. Proj. F-6-R-2, Job No. 1-B:4 pp. (WALLEYE; IMPOUNDMENTS;).

3024. Whitney, R. R. 1955. Walleye, *Stizostedion vitreum* (Mitchill), population of Clear Lake,

Iowa. Ph.D. Dissertation, Iowa St. Univ., Ames, Iowa 110 pp. (WALLEYE; POPULATION STUDIES;).

3025. Whitney, R. R. 1956. Walleye, *Stizostedion vitreum* population of Clear Lake, Iowa. Iowa State Coll. J. Sci. 30:454-455. (WALLEYE; POPULATION STUDIES;).

3026. Whitney, R. R. 1958. Numbers of mature walleyes in Clear Lake, Iowa, 1952-53, as estimated by tagging. Iowa State Coll. J. Sci. 33:55-79. (WALLEYE; AGE AND GROWTH; ECOLOGY; MARKING; MOVEMENT AND MIGRATIONS; POPULATION STUDIES; SPAWNING STUDIES;).

3027. Whitworth, W. R., P. L. Berrien, and W. T. Keller. 1968. Freshwater fishes of Connecticut. Conn. Bull. Nat. Hist. Surv. 101:134. (WALLEYE; INTRODUCTIONS;).

3028. Wickliff, E. L. 1934. Breeding habits of several fishes found in Ohio. Ohio Div. Conserv., Bur. Sci. Research, Bull. 66:4 pp. (SAUGER; WALLEYE; PROPAGATION; STOCKING;).

3029. Wickliff, E. L. 1936. Commercial fishing in Lake Erie. Ohio Div. Conserv., Bur. Sci. Research, Bull. 124:2 pp. (SAUGER; WALLEYE; COMMERCIAL FISHERIES; FISHING GEAR;).

3030. Wickliff, E. L. 1944. Suggestion for new fishing lakes. Ohio Div. Conserv. Nat. Res., Bull. 179:7 pp. (WALLEYE; IMPOUNDMENTS; STOCKING;).

3031. Wickliff, E. L. 1944. Notes on the American pike perches. Ohio Div. Conserv. Nat. Res., Bull. 191:6 pp. (SAUGER; WALLEYE; AGE AND GROWTH; COMMERCIAL FISHERIES; LIFE HISTORY; MARKING; MOVEMENT AND MIGRATIONS; STOCKING; TAXONOMY;).

3032. Wickliff, E. L., and M. B. Trautman. 1930. Suggestions for stocking certain species of fish in Ohio. Ohio Div. Conserv. Nat. Res., Bull. 23:4 pp. (WALLEYE; STOCKING;).

3033. Wickstrom, G. A. 1984. Intensive culture of largemouth bass and walleye fry in experimental systems. M.S. Thesis. S.D. State Univ., Brookings, S.D. 46 pp. (WALLEYE; MORTALITY; PROPAGATION;).

3034. Wiebe, A. H. 1928. Biological survey of the upper Mississippi River, with special reference to pollution. U.S. Bur. Fish., Bull. 43:137-167. (SAUGER; WALLEYE; COMMERCIAL FISHERIES; HABITAT DEGRADATION;).

3035. Wiener, J. G. 1983. Comparative analyses of fish populations in naturally acidic and circumneutral lakes in northern Wisconsin. U.S. Fish Wildl. Serv., FWS/OBS-80/40.16, Air Pollution and Acidic Rain Rep. No. 16:107 pp. (WALLEYE; HABITAT DEGRADATION;).

3036. Wiener, J. G., P. J. Rago, and J. M. Eilers. 1984. Species composition of fish communities in northern Wisconsin lakes: relation to pH. Pages 133-146 *in* G.R. Hendry, ed. Early biotic responses to advancing lake acidification. Acid precipitation series — Vol. 6: Butterworth Publishers, Woburn, MA. (WALLEYE; COMMUNITY DYNAMICS; ECOLOGY; HABITAT DEGRADATION;).

3037. Wiggins, T. A., T. R. Bender, Jr., R. A. Mudrak, Z. B. Bean, and S. E. Hood. 1981. Intensive culture of walleye fry *(Stizostedion vitreum)* using a commercially prepared dry diet and various live food feeding regimes. Penn. Fish Comm., 1981 Proj. Rep. 18 pp. (WALLEYE; FOOD STUDIES; PROPAGATION;).

3038. Wiggins, T. A., T. R. Bender, V. A. Murdak, and M. A. Takacs. 1983. Hybridization of yellow perch and walleye. Prog. Fish-Cult. 45:131-132. (WALLEYE; GENETICS; PROPAGATION;).

3039. Williams, H. J., and T. M. Lynch. 1953. 1953 creel census report. Colo. Game Fish Dept. 17 pp. (WALLEYE; CREEL CENSUS; STOCKING;).

3040. Williams, H. M. 1971. Walleye distribution and spawning success in reservoirs. S. C. Div. Game Boating, Fed. Aid Fish Wildl. Restor. Proj. F-15-R-2, Wk. Pl. C, Job 1: 78-90. (WALLEYE; IMPOUNDMENTS; POPULATION STUDIES; SPAWNING STUDIES;).

3041. Williams, M. Y. 1920. Notes on the fauna of the Moose River and the Mattagami and Abitibi tributaries. Can. Field Nat. 34:121-126. (WALLEYE; GEOGRAPHICAL DISTRIBUTION;).

3042. Williamson, J. L. 1965. Artificial stocking of walleye fry to augment native year class strength in Little John and Erickson Lakes, Vilas County, Wisconsin. Univ. Wis. Lab. Limnol., Progress Rep. 6-65:35 pp. (WALLEYE; POPULATION STUDIES; STOCKING;).

3043. Willis, D. W. 1982. Review of water level management on Kansas Reservoirs. Kans. Fish Game Comm. 30 pp. (WALLEYE; IMPOUNDMENTS; POPULATION STUDIES; WATER LEVELS;).

3044. Willis, D. W. 1984. A statewide summary of sampling data for white crappie, walleye, white bass, and largemouth bass collected in Kansas Reservoirs. Kans. Fish Game Comm., Fed. Aid Fish Wildl. Restor. Proj. FW-9-P3:45 pp. (WALLEYE; IMPOUNDMENTS; POPULATION STUDIES;).

3045. Willis, D. W. 1986. Use of gill-netting data to provide a recruitment index for walleye. Kans. Fish. Game Comm., Fish. I&D No. 86-10:6 pp. (WALLEYE; FISHING GEAR; IMPOUNDMENTS; POPULATION STUDIES; STOCKING;).

3046. Willis, D. W. 1986. Review of water level management on Kansas Reservoirs. Pages 110-114 in G.E. Hall and M.J. Van Den Avyles, eds. Reservoir fisheries management: strategies for the 80's. Reserv. Comm., S. Div. Am. Fish. Soc., Bethesda, Maryland. (WALLEYE; IMPOUNDMENTS; POPULATION STUDIES; WATER LEVELS;).

3047. Willis, D. W. 1987. Use of gill-net data to provide a recruitment index for walleyes. N. Am. J. Fish. Manage. 7:591-592. (WALLEYE; FISHING GEAR; POPULATION STUDIES;).

3048. Willis, D. W., and L. D. Jones. 1986. Fish standing crops in wooded and nonwooded coves of Kansas Reservoirs. N. Am. J. Fish. Manage. 6:105-108. (WALLEYE; COMMUNITY DYNAMICS; ECOLOGY; PRODUCTIVITY;).

3049. Willis, D. W., K. D. McCloskey, and D. W. Gabelhouse, Jr. 1985. Calculations of stock density indices based on adjustments for efficiencies of gill-net mesh size. N. Am. J. Fish. Manage. 5:126-137. (WALLEYE; POPULATION STUDIES; SAMPLING METHODS;).

3050. Willis, D. W., and J. L. Stephen. 1985. Relationships between storage ratio and population density, natural recruitment, and stocking success of walleye in Kansas reservoirs. Kans. Fish Game Comm., Fed. Aid Fish Wildl. Restor. Proj. FW-9-P4:27 pp. (WALLEYE; IMPOUNDMENTS; POPULATION STUDIES; STOCKING; WATER LEVELS;).

3051. Willis, D. W., and J. L. Stephen. 1987. Relationships between storage ratio and population density, natural recruitment, and stocking success of walleye in Kansas reservoirs. N. Am. J. Fish. Manage. 7:279-282. (WALLEYE; IMPOUNDMENTS; POPULATION STUDIES; STOCKING;).

3052. Willock, T. A. 1969. Distributional list of fishes in Missouri drainage of Canada. J. Fish. Research Board Can. 26:1439-1449. (SAUGER; WALLEYE; GEOGRAPHICAL DISTRIBUTION;).

3053. Wilson, C. B. 1916. Copepod parasites of fresh-water fishes and their economic relations to mussel glochidia. U.S. Bur. Fish., Bull. 34:333-374. (SAUGER; WALLEYE; PATHOLOGY;).

3054. Wilton, M. L. 1961. A preliminary report on the White Lake fishery. Ont. Min. Nat. Res., Rep. 15 pp. (WALLEYE; AGE AND GROWTH; CREEL CENSUS; POPULATION STUDIES;).

3055. Wingate, P. J., and D. H. Schupp. 1985. Large lake sampling guide. Minn. Dept. Nat. Res., Spec. Publ. No. 140:27 pp. (WALLEYE; POPULATION STUDIES; SAMPLING METHODS;).

3056. Wingo, W. M., and R. J. Muncy. 1985. Sampling walleye (Stizostedion vitreum) blood. Prog. Fish-Cult. 46:53-55. (WALLEYE; PHYSIOLOGY; SAMPLING METHODS;).

3057. Winterton, G. K. 1971. Georgian Bay yellow pickerel project progress report — 1970. Ont. Min. Nat. Res., Rep. 25 pp. (WALLEYE; AGE AND GROWTH; COMMERCIAL FISHERIES; CREEL CENSUS; MARKING; MORTALITY; PATHOLOGY; POPULATION STUDIES; SPAWNING STUDIES; TOXICANTS;).

3058. Winterton, G. K. 1972. Georgian Bay yellow pickerel project progress report — 1971.

Ont. Min. Nat. Res., Rep. 30 pp. (WALL-EYE; AGE AND GROWTH; COMMERCIAL FISHERIES; CREEL CENSUS; MARKING; MORTALITY; PATHOLOGY; POPULATION STUDIES; TOXICANTS;).

3059. Winterton, G. K. 1975. Structure and movement of a spawning stock of walleye, *Stizostedion vitreum vitreum* (Mitchill), in Georgian Bay. M.S. Thesis, Univ. Guelph, Guelph, Ontario. 95 pp. (WALLEYE; AGE AND GROWTH; MOVEMENTS AND MIGRATIONS; POPULATION STUDIES; SPAWNING STUDIES; STOCKING; WATER LEVELS;).

3060. Wisconsin Conservation Department. 1970. Population dynamics of the walleye *(Stizostedion vitreum)* and perch *(Perca* sp.) in lakes. Wis. Conserv. Dept., Fed. Aid Fish Wildl. Restor. Proj. F-83-R-6:20 pp. (WALL-EYE; LIFE HISTORY; MOVEMENT AND MIGRATIONS; POPULATION STUDIES; SAMPLING METHODS;).

3061. Wisconsin Conservation Department. 1971. Population dynamics of the walleye *(Stizostedion vitreum)* and perch *(Perca* sp.) in lakes. Wis. Conserv. Dept., Fed. Aid Fish Wildl. Restor. Proj. F-83-R-7:9 pp. (WALL-EYE; LIFE HISTORY; MOVEMENT AND MIGRATIONS; POPULATION STUDIES; SAMPLING METHODS;).

3062. Witkovosky, P., D. A. Burkhardt, and A. R. Nagy. 1979. Synaptic connections linking cones and horizontal cells in the retina of the pikeperch *(Stizostedion vitreum)*. J. Comp. Neurol. 186:541-560. (WALLEYE; MORPHOLOGY;).

3063. Witzel, L. 1981. Summer creel census in the Canadian waters of the western basin of Lake Erie, 1980. Ont. Min. Nat. Res., Lake Erie Fish. Assess. Unit Rep. 1981-1:52 pp. (WALLEYE; AGE AND GROWTH; CREEL CENSUS;).

3064. Witzel, L. 1981. Summer creel census in the Canadian waters of the Detroit River, 1980. Ont. Min. Nat. Res., Lake Erie Fish. Assess. Unit Rep. 1981-2:56 pp. (WALLEYE; AGE AND GROWTH; CREEL CENSUS;).

3065. Wolf, K. 1962. Experimental propagation of lymphocystis disease of fishes. Virology 18:249-256. (WALLEYE; PATHOLOGY;).

3066. Wolf, K. 1964. Characteristics of viruses found in fishes. Develop. Indus. Microbiol. 5:140-147. (WALLEYE; PATHOLOGY;).

3067. Wolfert, D. R. 1963. Age and growth of Lake Erie walleye. U.S. Bur. Sport Fish. Wildl. 34 pp. (WALLEYE; BEHAVIOR; MARKING; MOVEMENT AND MIGRATIONS;).

3068. Wolfert, D. R. 1963. The movements of walleye tagged as yearlings in Lake Erie. Trans. Am. Fish. Soc. 92:414-420. (WALLEYE; AGE AND GROWTH; MARKING; MOVEMENT AND MIGRATIONS;).

3069. Wolfert, D. R. 1964. Food of young-of-the-year walleye in Lake Erie. U.S. Fish Wildl. Serv., Fish. Bull. 65:489-494. (WALLEYE; COMMUNITY DYNAMICS; FOOD STUDIES; SAMPLING METHODS;).

3070. Wolfert, D. R. 1969. Maturity and fecundity of walleyes from the eastern and western basins of Lake Erie. J. Fish. Research Board Can. 26:1877-1888. (WALLEYE; AGE AND GROWTH; SPAWNING STUDIES;).

3071. Wolfert, D. R. 1977. Age and growth of the walleye in Lake Erie, 1963-1968. Trans. Am. Fish. Soc. 106:569-577. (WALLEYE; AGE AND GROWTH; SAMPLING METHODS;).

3072. Wolfert, D. R. 1979. The walleye *(Stizostedion vitreum)* in the New York waters of Lake Erie. U.S. Fish. Wildl. Serv., Great Lakes Fish. Lab., Ann Arbor, Mich. 15 pp. (WALLEYE; POPULATION STUDIES;).

3073. Wolfert, D. R. 1981. The commercial fishery for walleyes in the New York waters of Lake Erie, 1959-1978. N. Am. J. Fish. Manage. 1:112-126. (WALLEYE; COMMERCIAL FISHERIES; ECOLOGY; POPULATION STUDIES; PRODUCTIVITY;).

3074. Wolfert, D. R., V. C. Applegate, and L. N. Allison. 1967. Infection of walleye *(Stizostedion vitreum)* of western Lake Erie with *Bothricephalus cuspidatus*. Mich. Acad. Sci., Arts Letters 52:105-114. (SAUGER; WALLEYE; PATHOLOGY;).

3075. Wolfert, D. R., W. D. N. Busch, and C. T. Baker. 1975. Predation by fish on walleye eggs on a spawning reef in western Lake Erie, 1969-71. Ohio J. Sci. 75:118-125. (WALLEYE; COMMUNITY DYNAMICS;

EMBRYOLOGY; MORTALITY; SPAWN-
ING STUDIES;).

3076. Wolfert, D. R., and H. D. Van Meter. 1978.
Movements of walleyes tagged in eastern
Lake Erie. N.Y. Fish Game J. 25:16-22.
(WALLEYE; MARKING; MOVEMENT
AND MIGRATIONS;).

3077. Wollitz, R. E. 1968. Smallmouth bass stream
investigations. Va. Comm. Game Inland
Fish., Fed. Aid Fish Wildl. Restor. Proj. F-
14-R-6, Job No. 3:90 pp. (SAUGER; WALL-
EYE; AGE AND GROWTH; HABITAT
DEGRADATION; MORTALITY;).

3078. Woner, P. 1963. Lake Erie fish population gill
netting and shore seining survey. Ohio
Dept. Nat. Res., Fed. Aid Fish Wildl. Restor. Proj. F-35-R-1, Job No. 4:32 pp. (WALL-
EYE; SAMPLING METHODS;).

3079. Wood, D. 1984. 1982 fall electrofishing at
Lake Scugog. Ont. Min. Nat. Res., Kawar-
tha Lakes Fish. Assess. Unit Rep. 1984-3:42
pp. (WALLEYE; COMMUNITY DY-
NAMICS; FOOD STUDIES; POPULA-
TION STUDIES; SAMPLING METH-
ODS;).

3080. Wood, D. 1984. 1983 spring pickerel tagging
at Bobcaygeon, Pigeon Lake. Ont. Min.
Nat. Res., Kawartha Lakes Fish. Assess.
Unit Rep. 1984-4:31 pp. (WALLEYE; AGE
AND GROWTH; COMMUNITY DY-
NAMICS; MARKING; MORTALITY;
MOVEMENT AND MIGRATIONS; PA-
THOLOGY; SPAWNING STUDIES;).

3081. Wood, D. 1984. Report of 1983 trapnetting
Rice Lake. Ont. Min. Nat. Res., Kawartha
Lakes Fish. Assess. Unit Rep. 1984-5:43 pp.
(WALLEYE; AGE AND GROWTH; COM-
MUNITY DYNAMICS; POPULATION
STUDIES;).

3082. Wood, D. 1984. Report of 1983 trapnetting
Pigeon and Buckhorn Lakes. Ont. Min.
Res., Kawartha Lakes Fish. Assess. Unit
Rep. 1984-6:35 pp. (WALLEYE; AGE AND
GROWTH; COMMUNITY DYNAMICS;
POPULATION STUDIES;).

3083. Wood, D. 1985. Report of 1984 trapnetting
Balsam Lake. Ont. Min. Nat. Res., Kawar-
tha Lakes Fish. Assess. Unit Rep. 1985-6:44
pp. (WALLEYE; AGE AND GROWTH;
COMMUNITY DYNAMICS; POPULA-
TION STUDIES;).

3084. Wood, D. 1985. Report of 1984 trapnetting
Lake Scugog. Ont. Min. Nat. Res., Kawar-
tha Lakes Fish. Assess. Unit Rep. 1985-7:44
pp. (WALLEYE; AGE AND GROWTH;
COMMUNITY DYNAMICS; POPULA-
TION STUDIES;).

3085. Wood, D. 1985. Winter movements and
spawning locations of yellow pickerel (Stizostedion v. vitreum), Mitchill, in Pigeon,
Buckhorn and Chemung Lakes as determined by radio telemetry. Ont. Min. Nat.
Res., Kawartha Lakes Fish. Assess. Unit 60
pp. (WALLEYE; BEHAVIOR; MARK-
ING; MOVEMENT AND MIGRATIONS;
SPAWNING STUDIES;).

3086. Woodbury, L. A. 1942. A sudden mortality of
fishes accompanying a supersaturation of
oxygen in Lake Waubesa, Wisconsin. Trans.
Am. Fish. Soc. 71:112-117. (WALLEYE;
MORTALITY; PATHOLOGY; PHYSIOL-
OGY;).

3087. Wooding, F. H. 1959. The angler's book of Canadian Fishes. Collins, Don Mills, Ont. 303
pp. (SAUGER; WALLEYE; TAXON-
OMY;).

3088. Woodworth, H. C. 1975. Creel survey report
Remi Lake — 1975. Ont. Min. Nat. Res.,
Rep. 19 pp. (WALLEYE; CREEL CEN-
SUS;).

3089. Woolcott, W. S. 1953. Some percid fishes of
certain Tennessee counties. J. Tenn. Acad.
Sci. 28:245-246. (SAUGER; WALLEYE;
GEOGRAPHICAL DISTRIBUTION;).

3090. Worley, D. E., and R. V. Bangham. 1952.
Some parasites of fishes of the Upper Gati-
neau River Valley. Ohio J. Sci. 52:210-212.
(WALLEYE; PATHOLOGY;).

3091. Wort, W., and G. Brown. 1978. Fly-in fishery
creel census — 1978. Ont. Min. Nat. Res.,
Rep. 31 pp. (WALLEYE; CREEL CEN-
SUS;).

3092. Worth, S. G. 1895. Report on the propagation
and distribution of food-fishes. U.S. Comm.
Fish Fish., Rep (1893):78-135. (WALLEYE;
PROPAGATION; STOCKING;).

3093. Wrenn, W. B. 1974. Seasonal occurrence and
diversity of fish in a heated discharge channel, Tennessee River. TVA, Div. Forest.,
Fish. Wildl. Devel., Biothermal Research
Sec. 25 pp. (SAUGER; WALLEYE; COM-

MUNITY DYNAMICS; ECOLOGY; POP-ULATION STUDIES;).

3094. Wrenn, W. B. 1975. Temperature preference and movement of fish in relation to a long heated discharge channel. 2nd Thermal Ecology Symp. Proc., April 1975:18 pp. (WALLEYE; BEHAVIOR; ECOLOGY; MARKING;).

3095. Wrenn, W. B., B. J. Armitage, E. B. Rodgers, T. D. Forsythe, and K. L. Grannemann. 1979. Browns Ferry biothermal research series. II. Effects of temperature on bluegill and walleye, and periphyton, macroinvertebrate, and zooplankton communities in experimental ecosystems. U.S. Dept. Comm., Res. Develop. Rep. 81 pp. (WALLEYE; FISHWAYS; MORTALITY; PHYSIOLOGY;).

3096. Wrenn, W. B., and T. D. Forsythe. 1978. Effects of temperature on production and yield of juvenile walleyes in experimental ecosystems. Pages 66-73 in R.L. Kendall, ed. Selected coolwater fishes of North America. Am. Fish. Soc. Sp. Publ. No. 11, Washington, D.C. (WALLEYE; ECOLOGY; MORTALITY; PRODUCTIVITY;).

3097. Wrenn, W. B., and P. A. Hackney. 1979. Growth and survival of sauger (Stizostedion canadense) with surgically implanted dummy transmitters. Underwat. Telem. Newsl. 9:9-12. (SAUGER; AGE AND GROWTH; MARKING; MORTALITY;).

3098. Wright, A. H. 1918. Fish succession in some Lake Ontario tributaries. Sci. Monthly, December pp. 535-544. (WALLEYE; GEOGRAPHICAL DISTRIBUTION;).

3099. Wright, S., and M. Tidd. 1933. Summary of limnological investigations in western Lake Erie in 1929 and 1930. Trans. Am. Fish. Soc. 63:271-285. (WALLEYE; HABITAT DEGRADATION; SAMPLING METHODS;).

3100. Wyatt, E. J., and P. P. Economon. 1981. Parasites and selected anomalies of some fishes of the north central United States and Canada. Minn. Dept. Nat. Res., Spec. Publ. No. 131:197 pp. (SAUGER; WALLEYE; PATHOLOGY;).

3101. Wynne-Edwards, V. C. 1947. Northwest Canadian fisheries surveys in 1944-1945. III. The Mackenzie River. Fish. Research Board Can., Bull. 72:21-30. (WALLEYE; COM-MERCIAL FISHERIES; EMBRYOLOGY; PATHOLOGY;).

3102. Wynne-Edwards, V. C. 1952. Freshwater vertebrates of the arctic and subarctic. Fish. Research Board Can., Bull. 94:28 pp. (WALLEYE; GEOGRAPHICAL DISTRIBUTION;).

3103. Yamamoto, T., R. K. Kelly, and O. Nielsen. 1985. Epidermal hyperplasia of walleye (Stizostedion vitreum) associated with retrovirus-like type-C particles: prevalence histologic and electron microscopic observations. J. Fish Dis. 8:425-436. (WALLEYE; PATHOLOGY;).

3104. Yamamoto, T., R. K. Kelly, and O. Nielsen. 1985. Morphological differentiation of virus — associated skin tumors of walleye (Stizostedion vitreum vitreum). Fish Pathol. 20:361-372. (WALLEYE; PATHOLOGY;).

3105. Yamamoto, T., R. D. MacDonald, D. C. Gillespie, and R. K. Kelly. 1976. Viruses associated with lymphocystis disease and dermal sarcoma of walleye (Stizostedion vitreum vitreum). J. Fish. Research Board Can. 33:2408-2419. (WALLEYE; PATHOLOGY;).

3106. Yerger, R. W., and H. A. Beecher. 1975. First records of two percid fishes in Florida freshwaters. Quart. J. Fla. Acad. Sci. 38:142-143. (SAUGER; GEOGRAPHICAL DISTRIBUTION;).

3107. Young, J. K. 1971. Oba Lake creel census. Ont. Min. Nat. Res., Rep. 19 pp. (WALLEYE; CREEL CENSUS;).

3108. Young, J. K. 1973. Esnagi Lake creel census — 1972. Ont. Min. Nat. Res., Rep. 50 pp. (WALLEYE; AGE AND GROWTH; CREEL CENSUS;).

3109. Younk, J. A. 1987. Walleye stocking evaluation. Minn. Dept. Nat. Res., Fed. Aid Fish Wildl. Restor. Proj. F-26-R-18, Study No. 128:16 pp. (WALLEYE; MARKING; STOCKING;).

3110. Zarbock, W. M. 1977. Fish, fisheries, and water quality of the Great Lakes basin. Fisheries 2:2-4; 26-33. (SAUGER; WALLEYE; ECOLOGY;).

3111. Zimmerman, F. A. 1962. Some observation on the quality of angling in Lake Mindemoya,

Manitoulin Island. Ont. Dept. Lands Forest., Res. Manage. Rep. 64:35-42. (WALL-
EYE; CREEL CENSUS;).

3112. Zimmerman, F. A. 1965. Lake Mindemoya
creel census, 1961, 1962, 1963. Ont. Dept.
Land Forest., Res. Manage. Rep. 79:50-59.
(WALLEYE; CREEL CENSUS;).

3113. Zimmerman, J. F. 1967. Georgian Bay wall-
eye project progress report 1967 and six
year summary report of walleye trapping
and tagging on Georgian Bay, 1962-1967.
Ont. Dept. Lands For. 77 pp. (WALLEYE;
AGE AND GROWTH; COMMERCIAL
FISHERIES; CREEL CENSUS; MARK-
ING; MOVEMENT AND MIGRATIONS;
PATHOLOGY;).

3114. Zischke, J. A., and C. M. Vaughn. 1962. Hel-
minth parasites of young-of-the-year fishes
from the Fort Randall Reservoir. Proc. S.D.
Acad. Sci. 41:97-100. (SAUGER; ECOL-
OGY; IMPOUNDMENTS; PATHOL-
OGY;).

3115. Zuckerman, L. D., and R. J. Behnke. 1986. Introduced fishes in the San Luis Valley, Colorado. Pages 435-453 in R.H. Stroud, ed. Fish
culture in fisheries management. Am. Fish.
Soc., Bethesda, Maryland. (WALLEYE;
INTRODUCTIONS;).

3116. Zyanar, E. S., and M. A. Ali. 1975. An inter-
pretative study of the organization of visual
cells and tapetum lucidum of *Stizostedion*.
Can. J. Zool. 53:180-196. (WALLEYE; BE-
HAVIOR; MORPHOLOGY;).

KEYWORD INDEX

AGE AND GROWTH

SAUGER

14	58	137	139	154	177	214	229	235	274
275	276	283	284	286	314	352	357	375	379
385	386	389	394	395	396	433	434	435	480
611	612	616	617	632	775	788	791	804	810
812	818	819	889	890	896	904	905	906	909
969	972	985	988	992	1039	1092	1095	1139	1158
1159	1213	1216	1220	1222	1237	1284	1319	1356	1373
1375	1394	1413	1494	1498	1499	1601	1610	1634	1718
1722	1723	1724	1725	1726	1728	1729	1730	1732	1832
1886	1924	1983	1984	2037	2043	2044	2045	2047	2048
2049	2055	2089	2134	2165	2205	2225	2245	2246	2247
2288	2314	2329	2342	2351	2354	2355	2357	2365	2394
2497	2498	2524	2551	2563	2607	2608	2609	2610	2633
2640	2685	2691	2753	2754	2755	2879	2880	2881	2893
2906	2913	2931	2932	2934	2936	2939	2940	2941	2944
3001	3031	3077	3097						

WALLEYE

7	14	30	31	33	58	70	86	97	99
100	110	118	121	126	132	133	136	137	138
139	141	142	154	158	164	167	170	177	214
218	222	224	225	226	229	233	235	242	243
247	248	249	253	254	272	274	275	276	279
281	283	284	285	286	288	289	290	292	293
294	295	296	297	301	305	311	313	314	318
333	334	340	352	353	357	360	369	370	375
379	382	383	384	385	386	389	392	394	396
400	401	404	407	410	411	412	413	414	433
434	435	453	465	467	468	469	471	472	477
480	494	509	510	526	527	533	534	538	539
547	549	575	577	583	592	611	612	614	616
617	618	626	627	629	632	635	636	652	658
681	682	687	697	698	707	742	743	744	745
746	747	775	781	788	789	790	796	798	799
800	804	810	812	819	850	852	857	889	890
891	896	900	904	905	906	909	923	924	925
927	932	933	934	936	938	949	955	956	969
972	974	975	988	992	997	1005	1016	1025	1026
1029	1032	1045	1059	1062	1078	1082	1083	1091	1092
1093	1095	1097	1098	1103	1104	1106	1107	1108	1110
1114	1122	1126	1128	1139	1140	1160	1166	1174	1175
1178	1179	1180	1181	1182	1183	1184	1185	1186	1188
1189	1191	1192	1193	1195	1196	1197	1198	1199	1206
1213	1215	1220	1221	1222	1228	1237	1252	1253	1258
1261	1274	1282	1284	1315	1316	1319	1331	1334	1337
1350	1365	1372	1373	1375	1377	1378	1384	1385	1386
1387	1388	1389	1390	1391	1392	1393	1394	1410	1413
1415	1418	1431	1432	1433	1434	1436	1442	1443	1445
1446	1447	1451	1453	1457	1459	1461	1467	1480	1482
1486	1488	1489	1494	1498	1499	1510	1524	1534	1538
1545	1554	1557	1580	1581	1582	1586	1587	1601	1610
1620	1634	1636	1647	1650	1655	1660	1661	1666	1667
1668	1668	1671	1675	1676	1678	1680	1681	1684	1687
1688	1692	1698	1710	1712	1714	1716	1717	1718	1722
1723	1724	1725	1726	1727	1728	1729	1730	1739	1741
1746	1747	1759	1762	1770	1774	1799	1802	1807	1809
1816	1826	1832	1841	1842	1856	1863	1864	1865	1877

1886	1891	1892	1896	1897	1901	1914	1918	1927	1932
1933	1940	1942	1944	1949	1950	1973	1975	1981	1982
1983	1984	1985	1995	2012	2013	2019	2028	2037	2043
2044	2045	2049	2055	2057	2068	2073	2075	2076	2087
2089	2118	2119	2122	2125	2132	2133	2134	2140	2143
2144	2145	2147	2148	2152	2153	2156	2157	2160	2165
2176	2177	2184	2185	2187	2188	2193	2198	2201	2202
2203	2205	2207	2208	2209	2210	2212	2213	2220	2221
2222	2225	2237	2254	2261	2264	2268	2277	2279	2285
2286	2287	2288	2289	2297	2305	2306	2308	2314	2315
2316	2317	2319	2320	2326	2327	2328	2329	2337	2339
2340	2341	2342	2345	2346	2348	2351	2353	2354	2355
2357	2365	2366	2367	2388	2391	2394	2398	2410	2413
2414	2415	2416	2420	2421	2431	2440	2444	2467	2474
2475	2477	2478	2488	2489	2491	2495	2497	2498	2502
2507	2508	2509	2511	2512	2514	2515	2519	2520	2521
2522	2524	2526	2531	2535	2537	2538	2540	2543	2548
2550	2551	2552	2563	2565	2572	2584	2586	2587	2589
2591	2593	2595	2598	2607	2608	2609	2610	2616	2617
2628	2633	2637	2638	2639	2640	2652	2659	2661	2662
2666	2667	2668	2674	2675	2677	2678	2680	2681	2684
2685	2686	2687	2688	2691	2700	2701	2702	2710	2711
2720	2750	2753	2754	2755	2768	2774	2777	2790	2791
2792	2793	2794	2798	2799	2801	2808	2811	2826	2829
2830	2833	2834	2835	2836	2837	2839	2865	2866	2875
2879	2880	2881	2885	2904	2906	2908	2913	2924	2925
2926	2933	2934	2936	2940	2941	2944	2954	2957	2960
2961	2963	2976	2977	2978	2981	2991	3001	3009	3010
3026	3031	3054	3057	3058	3059	3063	3064	3068	3070
3071	3077	3080	3081	3082	3083	3084	3108	3113	

BEHAVIOUR

SAUGER

20	21	377	409	572	581	645	865	890	1212
2278	2362	2780							

WALLEYE

11	20	21	144	176	272	323	377	397	409
533	534	562	563	572	581	597	598	645	763
764	772	799	837	865	890	1005	1203	1212	1269
1279	1313	1442	1478	1479	1483	1497	1626	1696	1762
1783	1804	1824	1901	1922	1988	2068	2095	2106	2124
2128	2239	2278	2284	2362	2434	2435	2437	2462	2484
2485	2486	2544	2545	2622	2739	2761	2762	2780	2781
2782	3067	3085	3094	3116					

COMMERCIAL FISHERIES

SAUGER

4	17	58	59	67	68	72	75	79	80
123	154	162	177	234	284	286	332	352	368
374	375	379	389	393	425	426	431	433	434
439	442	476	505	516	524	531	551	601	602
616	617	619	669	670	671	672	720	724	752
819	834	863	867	869	870	970	972	1034	1049
1105	1219	1220	1222	1230	1231	1346	1394	1413	1465
1494	1499	1500	1507	1531	1537	1596	1598	1604	1605
1607	1635	1689	1702	1722	1723	1724	1725	1726	1728
1729	1730	1732	1764	1832	1845	1983	2056	2136	2159

2205	2299	2342	2357	2361	2362	2363	2389	2497	2498
2500	2501	2523	2524	2553	2562	2563	2640	2644	2648
2685	2699	2708	2713	2722	2751	2752	2783	2805	2807
2855	2874	2896	2898	2899	2900	2902	2903	2907	2929
3012	3017	3018	3029	3031	3034				

WALLEYE

3	4	5	6	17	45	49	58	59	64
67	68	72	75	79	80	82	84	85	108
118	123	127	132	133	135	154	162	177	227
234	241	254	255	263	267	284	285	286	289
290	332	337	338	352	353	368	370	374	375
379	381	389	390	393	425	426	431	433	434
439	442	445	446	450	453	459	476	477	483
484	485	487	488	490	505	516	523	524	525
530	531	533	551	577	594	596	601	602	604
616	617	619	620	638	652	653	670	671	672
675	697	720	724	752	780	782	819	834	863
867	868	869	870	891	917	932	965	970	972
990	1013	1034	1049	1065	1073	1091	1105	1127	1150
1160	1219	1220	1222	1227	1228	1230	1231	1232	1233
1236	1309	1312	1332	1346	1358	1369	1383	1394	1395
1411	1413	1433	1461	1465	1467	1494	1495	1496	1499
1500	1507	1531	1537	1538	1557	1573	1574	1596	1598
1604	1605	1607	1631	1635	1655	1687	1702	1707	1711
1722	1723	1724	1725	1726	1727	1728	1729	1730	1735
1737	1741	1746	1747	1764	1784	1826	1832	1842	1845
1871	1880	1912	1946	1983	2013	2027	2040	2056	2057
2132	2133	2136	2143	2144	2145	2147	2148	2149	2150
2152	2153	2155	2156	2159	2184	2185	2187	2205	2207
2210	2211	2215	2299	2309	2333	2334	2335	2339	2341
2342	2346	2347	2357	2360	2361	2362	2363	2372	2374
2389	2405	2413	2414	2415	2444	2447	2459	2460	2497
2498	2500	2501	2513	2523	2524	2540	2553	2562	2563
2625	2626	2640	2641	2642	2644	2648	2650	2652	2660
2661	2668	2681	2685	2697	2698	2699	2708	2713	2714
2751	2752	2773	2783	2787	2827	2855	2874	2896	2897
2898	2899	2900	2901	2902	2903	2905	2907	2908	2910
2911	2929	2960	3005	3006	3007	3012	3013	3029	3031
3034	3057	3058	3073	3101	3113				

COMMUNITY DYNAMICS

SAUGER

153	168	178	208	229	232	234	283	368	379
393	489	496	496	514	555	559	644	756	758
773	853	909	911	912	969	985	986	1069	1105
1216	1218	1222	1225	1373	1413	1494	1505	1624	1635
1718	1723	1724	1832	1852	1886	1911	1983	2024	2056
2205	2276	2282	2296	2324	2351	2362	2365	2562	2609
2690	2691	2699	2713	2769	2783	2874	2879	2880	2881
2931	2932	2944		3093					

WALLEYE

6	31	33	97	102	121	153	158	164	166
168	189	208	224	225	229	231	232	234	242
249	253	283	285	287	288	289	296	341	345
368	379	393	403	411	416	432	440	474	475
476	488	491	492	496	497	513	514	519	527
532	533	534	535	538	548	554	555	559	565
577	598	599	604	614	622	624	629	644	696

185

73?	756	758	773	783	820	823	850	853	855
855	891	909	911	912	926	927	930	931	932
934	935	936	959	969	973	974	986	991	1029
1032	1042	1043	1044	1045	1062	1069	1084	1090	1091
1105	1133	1140	1153	1154	1166	1203	1206	1218	1222
1225	1240	1242	1252	1253	1329	1330	1331	1341	1342
1352	1357	1367	1369	1373	1384	1385	1389	1390	1391
1393	1398	1403	1413	1418	1433	1434	1439	1442	1451
1454	1469	1485	1486	1487	1489	1492	1494	1505	1528
1529	1534	1576	1580	1586	1587	1623	1624	1625	1635
1541	1660	1661	1666	1667	1668	1672	1673	1674	1684
1696	1697	1708	1714	1718	1719	1721	1723	1724	1731
1749	1760	1795	1799	1807	1808	1832	1842	1856	1860
1861	1864	1867	1868	1869	1886	1888	1890	1911	1916
1921	1928	1929	1930	1931	1950	1977	1980	1981	1983
2000	2009	2016	2024	2056	2057	2068	2069	2074	2081
2085	2093	2094	2095	2115	2120	2129	2130	2131	2157
2169	2172	2176	2177	2186	2198	2200	2201	2202	2205
2228	2237	2242	2255	2260	2261	2267	2268	2269	2271
2276	2282	2284	2290	2296	2302	2307	2319	2324	2326
2327	2344	2346	2348	2351	2362	2365	2391	2414	2415
2416	2422	2428	2429	2438	2440	2443	2459	2460	2463
2468	2476	2488	2489	2490	2491	2492	2513	2515	2516
2517	2518	2535	2540	2543	2550	2562	2568	2577	2579
2603	2606	2609	2662	2671	2679	2684	2687	2690	2691
2699	2704	2705	2713	2714	2769	2783	2797	2798	2808
2810	2828	2829	2846	2859	2874	2879	2880	2881	2935
2944	2960	2963	2975	2991	3008	3011	3036	3048	3069
3075	3079	3080	3081	3082	3083	3084	3093		

CREEL CENSUS

SAUGER

14	15	35	137	177	185	275	276	283	286
302	316	349	394	396	435	436	438	439	441
443	476	612	671	758	805	809	810	813	815
816	819	871	890	896	904	905	906	907	909
964	966	987	1067	1087	1115	1288	1375	1394	1413
1465	1543	1725	1832	1881	1899	1900	1904	1970	1983
1984	2037	2043	2045	2055	2070	2088	2136	2205	2240
2329	2354	2355	2407	2523	2524	2532	2551	2553	2607
2609	2691	2715	2716	2717	2718	2733	2754	2778	2805
2824	2870	2877	2879	2880	2881	2887	2944	2971	3018

WALLEYE

1	2	14	15	35	63	64	65	70	87
93	97	100	109	111	112	113	114	115	119
125	126	128	129	130	136	137	138	140	165
167	177	182	183	184	185	219	220	221	222
228	242	243	247	248	262	275	276	278	279
280	283	286	289	292	296	298	302	310	311
312	313	318	337	338	342	349	351	354	355
356	358	361	262	364	373	394	396	410	411
417	418	435	436	438	439	441	443	444	447
448	449	450	451	452	453	468	476	479	485
493	495	517	518	520	533	537	547	549	566
567	568	577	578	580	591	592	612	618	624
627	629	631	647	648	649	654	655	660	665
666	668	671	700	701	702	703	704	705	706
707	713	714	715	734	736	737	739	757	758
766	768	769	770	771	779	782	794	798	801
802	803	805	809	810	813	815	816	819	851

852	857	871	872	873	877	878	890	892	893
895	896	897	898	899	900	901	903	904	905
906	907	909	932	934	950	955	957	959	961
962	964	966	976	977	978	981	987	1009	1010
1029	1030	1036	1037	1040	1041	1046	1047	1067	1078
1085	1086	1087	1088	1089	1091	1104	1106	1108	1109
1110	1120	1121	1122	1123	1124	1136	1137	1140	1141
1142	1144	1145	1146	1147	1162	1170	1174	1177	1179
1180	1182	1183	1184	1185	1186	1188	1189	1191	1192
1194	1196	1207	1229	1234	1239	1243	1244	1255	1267
1268	1273	1287	1288	1313	1331	1332	1333	1334	1335
1336	1337	1338	1339	1342	1347	1348	1350	1359	1360
1361	1365	1368	1375	1376	1377	1378	1380	1388	1389
1392	1393	1394	1399	1400	1401	1408	1409	1410	1413
1432	1433	1434	1435	1436	1437	1439	1443	1455	1458
1461	1463	1465	1467	1468	1485	1486	1488	1489	1502
1503	1510	1522	1524	1534	1539	1540	1541	1542	1543
1546	1553	1559	1560	1561	1568	1571	1580	1581	1582
1587	1588	1589	1591	1615	1616	1617	1618	1620	1636
1637	1653	1656	1657	1658	1659	1662	1663	1664	1665
1670	1671	1675	1695	1709	1710	1711	1712	1725	1734
1736	1737	1740	1741	1750	1761	1781	1785	1790	1791
1792	1793	1795	1798	1820	1825	1828	1829	1830	1832
1838	1839	1840	1842	1846	1848	1854	1859	1860	1861
1864	1865	1866	1881	1888	1889	1890	1891	1899	1900
1901	1902	1903	1904	1918	1932	1933	1937	1966	1970
1975	1978	1980	1983	1984	1985	1995	1997	2000	2005
2006	2007	2008	2020	2021	2022	2027	2029	2037	2042
2043	2045	2055	2070	2073	2088	2092	2119	2130	2133
2136	2138	2139	2140	2141	2142	2143	2144	2145	2146
2147	2148	2150	2151	2152	2153	2155	2156	2157	2160
2167	2169	2174	2176	2188	2193	2196	2201	2203	2204
2205	2206	2207	2208	2210	2211	2219	2220	2229	2240
2241	2253	2254	2258	2259	2260	2264	2269	2270	2274
2304	2308	2318	2319	2320	2329	2340	2354	2355	2366
2367	2376	2381	2395	2396	2397	2398	2404	2407	2413
2414	2415	2423	2424	2426	2430	2431	2449	2452	2454
2455	2460	2466	2473	2474	2477	2479	2480	2481	2493
2494	2496	2499	2506	2508	2512	2515	2517	2518	2523
2524	2532	2540	2546	2547	2548	2549	2550	2551	2552
2553	2570	2584	2587	2593	2594	2595	2597	2598	2599
2607	2609	2611	2614	2674	2675	2678	2691	2693	2694
2695	2715	2716	2717	2718	2720	2729	2733	2734	2742
2749	2750	2754	2759	2764	2765	2777	2790	2791	2792
2793	2794	2795	2797	2802	2803	2804	2809	2814	2816
2817	2824	2826	2832	2833	2834	2835	2836	2837	2838
2839	2847	2852	2853	2869	2870	2871	2875	2877	2879
2880	2881	2887	2891	2911	2923	2924	2925	2926	2927
2928	2933	2935	2944	2956	2957	2971	2975	2982	2983
2988	2990	2999	3008	3009	3010	3011	3016	3020	3039
3054	3057	3058	3063	3064	3088	3091	3107	3108	3111
3112	3113								

ECOLOGY

SAUGER

4	9	19	61	123	194	195	196	211	212
213	214	229	302	343	344	391	409	420	428
429	611	642	643	645	669	670	672	729	751
773	809	810	889	909	915	953	960	984	1000
1049	1055	1092	1125	1157	1158	1237	1257	1375	1494
1505	1519	1520	1532	1558	1569	1590	1599	1600	1602
1614	1624	1769	1773	1805	1852	1858	1962	2033	2034

2044	2047	2049	2050	2054	2055	2089	2104	2137	2216
2234	2240	2250	2288	2296	2362	2363	2377	2406	2408
2500	2527	2605	2607	2608	2640	2669	2672	2685	2763
2785	2906	2909	2912	2940	3000	3093	3110	3114	

WALLEYE

4	9	19	28	30	51	61	74	82	83
84	88	92	94	95	96	121	123	152	156
161	176	180	193	194	195	196	202	211	212
213	214	215	227	229	231	256	257	266	279
288	291	292	302	303	323	334	343	344	391
392	409	416	420	424	428	465	466	469	471
472	483	491	528	532	533	535	536	539	565
582	588	611	629	642	643	645	646	650	659
663	670	672	678	681	687	727	729	733	740
746	751	767	773	774	783	785	793	799	809
810	846	847	848	849	854	883	889	909	915
916	924	935	953	960	962	973	975	984	995
997	999	1000	1049	1055	1073	1083	1092	1097	1104
1106	1113	1116	1119	1125	1152	1153	1154	1157	1165
1166	1168	1235	1237	1242	1257	1262	1269	1278	1280
1281	1302	1306	1314	1316	1318	1325	1330	1331	1354
1375	1385	1398	1407	1417	1451	1454	1469	1475	1484
1493	1494	1497	1505	1514	1515	1516	1519	1520	1521
1524	1532	1538	1558	1565	1569	1577	1586	1599	1600
1602	1603	1606	1613	1614	1624	1646	1707	1719	1746
1747	1749	1762	1769	1770	1784	1804	1805	1807	1809
1812	1827	1837	1855	1858	1888	1906	1910	1913	1916
1948	1962	1974	1980	1990	1991	1998	2002	2004	2034
2044	2049	2050	2054	2055	2059	2075	2086	2089	2093
2095	2104	2105	2106	2116	2122	2124	2128	2133	2137
2164	2185	2194	2195	2197	2198	2199	2201	2202	2207
2209	2210	2216	2234	2239	2240	2241	2250	2254	2279
2281	2288	2289	2296	2326	2331	2332	2333	2334	2337
2343	2345	2346	2348	2349	2352	2353	2362	2363	2364
2377	2383	2391	2406	2408	2410	2428	2429	2438	2444
2461	2463	2468	2471	2484	2485	2491	2492	2495	2500
2507	2510	2513	2516	2535	2538	2540	2545	2564	2582
2591	2593	2603	2605	2607	2608	2616	2617	2621	2622
2632	2640	2653	2660	2662	2667	2669	2672	2679	2685
2705	2720	2723	2732	2738	2756	2757	2758	2766	2768
2781	2785	2810	2827	2843	2851	2906	2908	2912	2916
2930	2935	2940	2954	2976	2980	3000	3011	3026	3036
3048	3073	3093	3094	3096	3110				

EMBRYOLOGY

SAUGER

168	1080

WALLEYE

24	81	168	181	533	597	784	1080	1083	1149
1259	1518	1536	1767	1822	1833	1834	1835	1986	2121
2368	2534	2621	3015	3075	3101				

FISHING GEAR

SAUGER

17	75	208	282	286	375	376	377	379	388
389	393	394	396	791	890	969	1217	1220	1222
1284	1470	1537	1724	1725	1726	1728	1729	1732	1898
2052	2205	2377	2551	2563	2644	2648	2708	2807	2855
2896	2898	2903	2937	3029					

WALLEYE

17	75	127	158	164	186	208	255	263	282
285	286	321	370	372	375	376	377	379	388
389	393	394	396	397	410	423	509	510	533
576	659	782	890	921	969	979	989	1065	1083
1091	1111	1112	1161	1200	1217	1220	1222	1284	1370
1371	1386	1470	1495	1510	1537	1554	1567	1573	1584
1585	1655	1687	1724	1725	1726	1727	1728	1729	1821
1841	1869	1945	1994	2009	2010	2052	2082	2084	2132
2157	2205	2213	2267	2289	2364	2371	2377	2392	2393
2413	2414	2551	2563	2567	2588	2594	2644	2648	2668
2678	2705	2708	2855	2896	2897	2898	2903	3006	3029
3045	3047								

FISHWAYS

SAUGER

89	2562

WALLEYE

89	259	454	533	711	1134	1138	1853	2453	2555
2562	2728	2984	3021	3095					

FOOD STUDIES

SAUGER

4	154	159	194	196	379	435	514	545	559
609	611	644	669	791	835	890	909	910	911
912	914	918	972	985	986	1069	1213	1284	1319
1373	1375	1394	1505	1595	1605	1610	1634	1718	1832
1836	1852	1911	1924	1983	2043	2044	2045	2047	2165
2216	2245	2275	2276	2282	2288	2342	2351	2357	2362
2365	2402	2640	2685	2696	2780	2783	2874	2879	2880
2881	2893	2931	2932	2941	2944				

WALLEYE

1	4	33	83	102	121	151	154	155	159
160	179	194	196	222	224	227	233	244	245
246	247	248	249	250	252	271	289	322	333
340	341	348	363	370	379	403	411	435	440
453	467	474	475	490	503	514	515	533	542
545	547	556	559	562	563	564	570	575	577
597	598	599	604	609	611	614	623	626	629
641	644	681	682	687	728	763	793	799	823
835	857	858	890	909	910	911	912	914	918
920	924	926	927	931	934	936	938	955	972
980	986	1005	1016	1027	1032	1042	1043	1044	1045
1048	1059	1061	1069	1090	1093	1126	1201	1202	1204
1206	1209	1211	1213	1238	1252	1253	1256	1260	1275

1277	1284	1315	1316	1319	1328	1329	1331	1341	1352
1366	1367	1372	1373	1375	1385	1389	1390	1391	1393
1394	1410	1418	1440	1442	1443	1451	1475	1476	1477
1483	1492	1505	1506	1508	1515	1526	1527	1529	1533
1538	1545	1575	1576	1595	1605	1610	1622	1634	1646
1683	1685	1688	1696	1718	1719	1720	1721	1739	1757
1759	1762	1770	1789	1795	1800	1803	1806	1807	1808
1819	1826	1832	1837	1842	1856	1863	1877	1879	1887
1890	1892	1901	1911	1915	1916	1924	1928	1931	1932
1933	1949	1967	1968	1973	1974	1983	2016	2019	2028
2030	2031	2043	2044	2045	2068	2069	2074	2094	2108
2120	2124	2127	2158	2165	2172	2186	2190	2191	2195
2197	2198	2199	2201	2202	2203	2209	2210	2214	2216
2218	2242	2254	2272	2273	2275	2276	2282	2287	2288
2289	2294	2307	2308	2323	2326	2334	2337	2338	2339
2341	2342	2345	2346	2351	2357	2362	2365	2391	2399
2402	2410	2414	2415	2431	2444	2475	2478	2509	2511
2515	2522	2565	2568	2572	2578	2579	2593	2598	2618
2619	2620	2640	2654	2662	2666	2667	2680	2685	2696
2700	2701	2720	2774	2779	2780	2781	2782	2783	2801
2813	2830	2842	2874	2879	2880	2881	2930	2941	2944
2954	2963	2991	3037	3069	3079				

GENETICS

SAUGER

394	396	506	1173	1375	1702	2046	2053	2361	2362
2753									

WALLEYE

190	223	244	260	261	281	394	396	506	507
508	533	534	615	625	1173	1291	1293	1351	1375
1431	1578	1702	1801	1802	2025	2026	2046	2053	2122
2361	2362	2374	2401	2684	2753	2876	2915	2962	3038

GEOGRAPHICAL DISTRIBUTION

SAUGER

13	26	46	73	203	300	378	408	422	545
546	584	642	643	645	691	716	725	749	759
760	761	806	825	826	829	830	831	832	833
840	841	843	845	865	915	940	941	944	960
1038	1068	1092	1100	1117	1118	1157	1163	1205	1210
1226	1289	1290	1294	1297	1303	1355	1423	1430	1490
1513	1611	1642	1682	1704	1725	1831	1872	1873	1878
1963	2035	2036	2097	2162	2216	2223	2224	2235	2336
2358	2436	2465	2574	2580	2612	2615	2629	2631	2670
2685	2709	2771	2776	2822	2864	2878	2912	3022	3052
3089	3106								

WALLEYE

13	26	46	54	73	201	203	205	224	300
305	318	337	367	378	408	422	465	508	517
545	546	640	642	643	645	691	716	717	719
725	749	759	760	761	825	826	827	829	830
831	832	833	837	839	840	841	842	843	844
845	862	865	915	939	940	941	942	943	944
945	946	960	963	995	1038	1051	1068	1092	1100
1116	1117	1118	1119	1130	1135	1157	1163	1164	1168

1205	1210	1226	1235	1278	1294	1297	1303	1344	1396
1398	1422	1423	1442	1444	1448	1449	1456	1462	1490
1512	1513	1574	1608	1682	1690	1693	1694	1697	1704
1705	1725	1738	1752	1776	1777	1831	1872	1873	1874
1878	1901	1906	1907	1909	1947	1963	1964	2025	2035
2036	2096	2097	2106	2109	2162	2171	2178	2179	2180
2216	2224	2256	2257	2300	2301	2303	2310	2312	2313
2315	2326	2336	2337	2358	2378	2386	2436	2465	2483
2503	2504	2510	2540	2556	2569	2574	2580	2622	2629
2631	2670	2673	2685	2706	2707	2771	2818	2822	2831
2848	2849	2850	2856	2860	2863	2864	2878	2895	2910
2912	3002	3014	3022	3041	3052	3089	3098	3102	

HABITAT DEGRADATION

SAUGER

32	39	79	214	302	314	389	393	420	428
439	616	617	773	953	982	1020	1022	1023	1058
1087	1216	1519	1520	1558	1590	1634	1635	1725	1730
1744	1814	1844	2041	2056	2324	2357	2362	2363	2377
2394	2501	2505	2523	2524	2627	2683	2685	2736	2898
2906	3034	3077							

WALLEYE

32	39	79	84	85	117	134	161	163	169
187	205	214	215	268	302	314	347	370	389
393	419	420	428	439	454	498	501	528	533
548	554	580	582	616	617	657	723	753	773
854	874	916	917	948	953	974	993	1020	1021
1022	1023	1024	1058	1081	1087	1108	1110	1150	1152
1175	1241	1259	1262	1318	1327	1328	1330	1345	1395
1397	1414	1415	1456	1467	1474	1509	1516	1517	1518
1519	1520	1548	1558	1603	1631	1634	1635	1651	1652
1703	1725	1730	1744	1748	1751	1765	1772	1775	1783
1800	1814	1815	1823	1837	1844	1847	1855	1874	1948
2013	2041	2056	2133	2169	2189	2294	2305	2311	2324
2357	2362	2363	2373	2374	2377	2379	2394	2428	2459
2460	2482	2487	2501	2505	2513	2523	2524	2540	2571
2627	2651	2653	2655	2656	2657	2658	2659	2663	2666
2678	2679	2685	2784	2789	2892	2894	2898	2906	2942
2991	3034	3035	3036	3077	3099				

HABITAT IMPROVEMENT

SAUGER

89	232	954	1702	2823	3000

WALLEYE

1	12	89	120	232	533	646	659	663	709
933	954	1007	1088	1272	1393	1522	1549	1550	1556
1580	1702	1739	1742	1849	1855	1885	1992	2004	2064
2120	2204	2321	2390	2416	2427	2603	2692	2703	2720
2766	2827	2854	2981	2982	3000	3021			

IMPOUNDMENTS

SAUGER

```
  61   137   139   178   208   230   232   234   235   302
 343   408   425   429   436   496   531   642   643   644
 754   775   777   805   887   889   890   907   908   953
 954   985   987   988  1092  1102  1115  1167  1213  1223
1237  1356  1405  1406  1450  1610  1836  1886  1970  1971
2037  2038  2041  2043  2044  2045  2048  2050  2051  2054
2055  2183  2192  2235  2248  2249  2250  2314  2394  2527
2607  2608  2609  2610  2633  2634  2690  2691  2726  2733
2753  2754  2755  2775  2778  2805  2806  2807  2823  2824
2879  2880  2881  2934  2937  2938  2940  2941  3114
```

WALLEYE

```
   1    11    61    74    87    93   136   137   139   144
 167   207   208   222   228   231   232   234   235   272
 273   291   292   298   302   303   319   343   364   408
 425   430   436   496   520   531   533   538   539   575
 591   642   643   644   646   660   708   711   754   767
 775   776   785   792   793   794   805   847   849   850
 856   857   875   876   887   889   890   900   907   908
 953   954   955   956   958   959   987   988   997   998
 999  1029  1030  1042  1043  1044  1045  1078  1081  1082
1083  1084  1088  1092  1101  1122  1123  1124  1133  1140
1151  1171  1174  1201  1204  1206  1213  1223  1224  1237
1240  1254  1261  1264  1348  1353  1354  1365  1369  1371
1372  1419  1443  1450  1451  1454  1455  1510  1545  1546
1564  1571  1579  1580  1609  1610  1646  1679  1680  1681
1689  1708  1714  1739  1754  1783  1795  1807  1813  1816
1819  1856  1882  1885  1886  1887  1892  1931  1932  1933
1948  1956  1965  1970  1971  1975  1976  1977  1980  1985
2015  2017  2018  2019  2026  2037  2038  2039  2041  2043
2044  2045  2050  2051  2054  2055  2073  2105  2112  2169
2172  2176  2183  2188  2192  2196  2197  2198  2199  2201
2202  2241  2242  2248  2250  2260  2262  2263  2279  2307
2308  2314  2316  2317  2328  2349  2352  2353  2356  2384
2394  2397  2398  2410  2431  2475  2492  2526  2537  2538
2572  2607  2608  2609  2610  2633  2637  2638  2639  2680
2690  2691  2692  2703  2720  2725  2726  2727  2733  2734
2741  2753  2754  2755  2757  2760  2777  2784  2797  2820
2824  2861  2862  2865  2866  2875  2879  2880  2881  2934
2938  2940  2941  2975  2981  2990  3019  3020  3023  3030
3040  3043  3044  3045  3046  3050  3051
```

INTRODUCTIONS

SAUGER

```
 149   234   306   581   720   750   754   941   944  1050
1055  1883  1924  2351  2624
```

WALLEYE

```
   8    50    52    55    76    78   146   149   167   188
 192   193   217   234   249   264   265   277   288   306
 308   311   319   335   421   440   461   467   500   522
 533   536   556   575   581   582   589   720   750   754
 785   856   857   941   944   946   955   958   999  1035
1048  1050  1052  1053  1055  1056  1082  1085  1086  1103
1126  1151  1261  1296  1325  1353  1369  1372  1509  1510
1544  1545  1586  1612  1697  1714  1715  1766  1782  1807
```

1816	1883	1917	1975	1987	2065	2066	2087	2110	2168
2188	2193	2262	2263	2264	2265	2281	2332	2348	2349
2351	2352	2410	2531	2538	2559	2600	2601	2604	2623
2624	2637	2638	2641	2643	2647	2756	2767	2768	2796
2797	2825	2975	2985	3020	3027	3115			

LIFE HISTORY

SAUGER

206	346	426	718	750	914	918	960	985	1034
1131	1212	1245	1532	1570	1632	1858	2034	2137	2234
2362	2576	2624	2630	2722	2788	2858	3031		

WALLEYE

206	224	227	346	367	411	426	461	509	510
533	626	651	659	718	750	776	799	824	828
894	900	914	918	933	960	973	1034	1082	1083
1131	1176	1212	1245	1389	1532	1536	1555	1570	1593
1594	1632	1648	1688	1739	1746	1747	1762	1807	1826
1835	1856	1858	1865	1925	2012	2019	2034	2068	2075
2130	2137	2234	2262	2263	2264	2323	2340	2362	2409
2410	2428	2471	2483	2576	2597	2623	2624	2630	2788
2858	2865	2985	3019	3031	3060	3061			

MARKING

SAUGER

274	275	276	283	286	352	435	436	476	571
610	674	756	777	805	810	812	904	905	906
967	1105	1308	1310	1763	1773	1780	1969	1970	1971
2041	2048	2089	2136	2205	2239	2240	2351	2394	2432
2524	2527	2533	2607	2609	2610	2824	28792880	2881	2986
3031	3097								

WALLEYE

34	70	109	121	144	167	171	216	274	275
276	283	286	289	298	318	350	352	353	365
373	435	436	453	476	481	486	494	517	527
533	558	575	590	591	592	593	594	595	596
603	610	613	660	664	674	689	707	708	756
765	800	805	810	812	866	904	905	906	922
957	959	967	1006	1029	1057	1059	1091	1101	1104
1105	1106	1107	1122	1174	1238	1239	1240	1308	1310
1340	1362	1364	1365	1379	1392	1433	1436	1443	1460
1467	1482	1554	1587	1636	1669	1673	1674	1676	1677
1710	1712	1756	1759	1760	1763	1772	1802	1821	1824
1864	1865	1866	1918	1922	1939	1941	1950	1969	1970
1971	1972	1985	2012	2018	2023	2041	2089	2118	2119
2127	2128	2136	2157	2160	2182	2187	2193	2205	2207
2209	2210	2211	2239	2240	2254	2268	2271	2279	2284
2285	2305	2316	2317	2319	2340	2351	2394	2397	2419
2420	2421	2422	2425	2432	2433	2434	2440	2446	2451
2456	2459	2460	2477	2490	2492	2512	2519	2520	2521
2524	2526	2533	2542	2558	2561	2566	2607	2609	2610
2661	2678	2710	2711	2723	2728	2743	2744	2745	2746
2749	2761	2762	2820	2821	2824	2859	2879	2880	2881
2911	2933	2967	2969	2970	2986	3026	3031	3057	3058
3067	3068	3076	3080	3085	3094	3109	3113		

MORPHOLOGY

SAUGER

150	195	529	543	545	574	581	637	741	859
884	885	886	918	1018	1301	1304	1421	1425	1429
1570	1592	1640	1875	1883	1962	2034	2046	2161	2170
2288	2575	2630	2635	2636	2772	2857	2858	2884	

WALLEYE

76	150	191	195	209	210	325	413	526	529
533	543	545	560	574	581	597	637	726	741
784	836	859	886	918	1246	1301	1304	1351	1421
1425	1429	1453	1491	1521	1544	1570	1640	1758	1767
1783	1813	1833	1875	1883	1938	1962	2034	2046	2080
2090	2161	2170	2277	2288	2368	2400	2401	2575	2590
2630	2635	2636	2712	2737	2772	2857	2858	2884	2904
3062	3116								

MORTALITY

SAUGER

10	61	276	314	436	514	617	637	695	775
1031	1080	1092	1216	1222	1257	1373	1375	1599	1632
1718	1722	1723	1724	1726	1728	1729	1730	1886	2047
2051	2205	2365	2387	2432	2551	2669	2685	2824	2899
2938	3077	3097							

WALLEYE

10	33	51	57	61	83	100	101	109	134
161	167	180	193	225	226	242	247	248	249
253	254	276	288	301	314	318	320	363	398
402	436	440	453	469	471	472	474	482	494
514	527	533	536	540	542	547	549	579	617
621	627	637	663	689	695	696	707	712	755
775	850	858	891	902	913	925	927	930	934
935	975	997	1031	1057	1062	1080	1091	1092	1166
1201	1215	1222	1238	1239	1241	1248	1254	1257	1258
1259	1260	1262	1291	1309	1318	1331	1363	1365	1373
1375	1379	1382	1388	1389	1392	1393	1433	1436	1437
1442	1451	1467	1480	1482	1486	1488	1493	1501	1517
1518	1548	1554	1555	1581	1582	1586	1587	1599	1609
1623	1632	1641	1648	1679	1684	1685	1696	1703	1706
1714	1718	1722	1723	1724	1726	1727	1728	1729	1730
1748	1759	1760	1775	1822	1862	1863	1864	1866	1886
1932	1933	1935	1936	1950	1980	1981	1985	1995	2004
2013	2051	2059	2063	2068	2074	2086	2093	2118	2124
2132	2194	2205	2206	2213	2237	2254	2261	2268	2270
2271	2279	2289	2291	2364	2365	2384	2416	2428	2432
2440	2457	2460	2477	2490	2509	2511	2514	2515	2517
2519	2521	2534	2537	2550	2551	2552	2577	2581	2587
2589	2598	2616	2617	2621	2637	2651	2653	2655	2656
2658	2666	2668	2669	2681	2685	2773	2789	2808	2824
2827	2851	2892	2899	2901	2908	2911	2916	2933	2938
2961	2968	2969	2970	3019	3020	3033	3057	3058	3075
3077	3080	3086	3095	3096					

MOVEMENT AND MIGRATIONS

SAUGER

35	283	286	315	422	439	476	610	805	810
967	1167	1308	1310	2351	2394	2527	2551	2685	2879
2880	2881								

WALLEYE

35	158	167	176	216	225	257	272	283	286
311	315	422	439	476	610	652	707	805	810
851	967	973	1082	1101	1104	1106	1242	1269	1308
1310	1312	1331	1385	1392	1417	1554	1636	1710	1739
1756	1801	1824	1856	1863	1864	1866	2018	2019	2086
2127	2133	2160	2187	2289	2315	2316	2317	2340	2351
2394	2397	2410	2434	2446	2460	2475	2492	2512	2519
2550	2551	2572	2685	2701	2710	2741	2843	2879	2880
2881	2989	3059							

PATHOLOGY

SAUGER

4	29	159	173	174	175	269	387	435	476
553	633	634	1250	1251	1323	1627	1634	1691	1755
2067	2078	2079	2181	2342	2369	2917	2921	2944	2964
3003	3053	3074	3100	3114					

WALLEYE

4	16	27	29	34	98	159	172	173	174
175	197	236	237	268	269	289	326	339	359
370	387	411	435	476	533	534	552	553	586
587	597	622	633	634	661	688	707	727	730
731	732	796	821	822	879	880	881	882	883
1019	1093	1104	1106	1107	1228	1247	1249	1250	1251
1264	1266	1322	1323	1324	1387	1431	1467	1471	1472
1473	1530	1545	1562	1619	1621	1622	1627	1629	1634
1645	1669	1676	1691	1733	1754	1755	1768	1801	1802
1810	1811	1884	1905	1908	2014	2067	2077	2078	2079
2083	2113	2115	2166	2181	2217	2226	2238	2243	2244
2333	2334	2337	2339	2342	2350	2369	2380	2382	2385
2414	2415	2448	2457	2539	2557	2584	2606	2653	2731
2747	2770	2786	2812	2841	2888	2889	2890	2917	2918
2919	2920	2921	2922	2944	2945	2946	2947	2948	2949
2950	2951	2952	2953	2955	2964	2965	2966	2968	2972
2973	2992	2993	2994	2995	2996	2998	3003	3053	3057
3058	3065	3066	3074	3080	3086	3090	3100	3101	3103
3104	3105	3113							

PHYSIOLOGY

SAUGER

19	20	21	314	328	329	607	645	865	1080
1632	1924	1962	2252	2377	2780				

WALLEYE

19	20	21	24	25	106	176	225	260	261
314	327	328	329	330	533	608	630	645	667
692	727	753	865	993	996	1077	1080	1248	1258
1265	1280	1286	1320	1321	1329	1349	1441	1471	1547

1632	1654	1758	1775	1783	1823	1835	1847	1925	1951
1952	1962	1986	1988	2004	2106	2175	2252	2293	2348
2377	2486	2529	2579	2656	2659	2730	2780	2782	2800
2908	3056	3086	3095						

POPULATION STUDIES

SAUGER

123	137	139	208	229	232	234	235	275	276
283	284	286	332	357	429	439	476	496	505
511	610	617	632	729	756	775	788	791	805
819	853	861	890	907	908	909	937	953	954
968	969	971	972	982	983	984	985	988	1095
1223	1283	1284	1394	1413	1537	1558	1569	1599	1600
1610	1624	1723	1724	1725	1728	1729	1730	1732	1763
1773	1886	1904	1969	1970	1971	1983	1999	2001	2038
2039	2044	2045	2047	2048	2051	2052	2054	2055	2056
2134	2159	2192	2205	2248	2249	2324	2362	2365	2387
2394	2445	2524	2551	2553	2602	2607	2608	2609	2610
2613	2627	2685	2690	2691	2713	2726	2775	2807	2824
2879	2880	2881	2906	2936	2938	2940	2944	3000	3001
3093									

WALLEYE

8	30	31	33	37	38	87	93	116	118
121	123	136	137	138	139	156	157	158	164
166	167	189	207	208	228	229	231	232	233
234	235	242	243	244	253	254	255	257	270
275	276	279	283	284	285	286	288	289	290
291	296	303	304	318	321	332	357	363	369
370	381	398	402	403	412	415	416	439	453
468	475	476	477	486	487	496	503	505	511
512	520	532	533	547	549	558	577	579	590
610	617	627	629	632	651	653	660	675	687
689	707	729	738	756	775	781	788	792	794
800	805	819	850	852	853	857	861	864	876
890	891	907	908	909	921	923	925	927	928
930	932	933	936	937	953	954	955	956	957
959	962	968	969	971	972	973	974	975	983
984	988	995	1032	1041	1057	1062	1088	1093	1095
1098	1104	1107	1108	1110	1120	1132	1140	1160	1161
1168	1180	1181	1187	1190	1193	1195	1197	1198	1223
1224	1227	1239	1240	1263	1274	1276	1282	1284	1305
1307	1327	1329	1331	1342	1350	1360	1362	1364	1369
1371	1372	1378	1380	1383	1384	1385	1386	1388	1389
1390	1391	1393	1394	1404	1410	1413	1414	1418	1433
1438	1443	1452	1453	1454	1464	1469	1475	1482	1483
1484	1486	1487	1488	1489	1501	1510	1511	1521	1522
1523	1524	1534	1537	1554	1555	1558	1566	1567	1569
1578	1580	1581	1582	1585	1586	1587	1599	1600	1610
1615	1620	1623	1624	1633	1636	1646	1647	1660	1661
1666	1667	1668	1672	1673	1674	1676	1698	1703	1708
1710	1711	1712	1719	1721	1723	1724	1725	1727	1728
1729	1730	1736	1739	1741	1760	1763	1795	1798	1799
1801	1802	1807	1821	1842	1856	1863	1864	1865	1866
1867	1868	1869	1876	1877	1882	1885	1886	1891	1892
1901	1904	1920	1930	1931	1932	1933	1934	1935	1939
1941	1943	1945	1950	1969	1970	1971	1974	1976	1977
1980	1983	1985	1992	1995	1999	2001	2009	2011	2012
2037	2038	2039	2044	2045	2051	2052	2054	2055	2056
2057	2061	2076	2086	2087	2093	2118	2119	2128	2132
2133	2134	2135	2144	2149	2150	2155	2157	2159	2176

2177	2182	2184	2192	2193	2197	2199	2201	2202	2205
2207	2209	2210	2211	2212	2213	2227	2228	2232	2248
2254	2260	2261	2267	2268	2271	2279	2285	2289	2305
2307	2308	2309	2315	2319	2320	2324	2331	2339	2340
2344	2345	2359	2362	2364	2365	2366	2388	2391	2394
2395	2396	2405	2410	2414	2419	2420	2422	2426	2427
2430	2431	2440	2444	2445	2446	2448	2456	2459	2460
2468	2470	2472	2477	2478	2488	2489	2490	2491	2495
2508	2516	2518	2524	2526	2535	2540	2543	2548	2551
2552	2553	2554	2558	2560	2565	2584	2585	2587	2588
2591	2592	2593	2594	2595	2596	2597	2602	2607	2608
2609	2610	2611	2613	2616	2617	2627	2632	2638	2652
2660	2668	2678	2681	2684	2685	2690	2691	2704	2713
2720	2723	2725	2726	2727	2749	2777	2781	2784	2798
2801	2820	2824	2826	2827	2829	2843	2859	2879	2880
2881	2906	2908	2911	2923	2933	2936	2938	2940	2944
2960	2961	2963	2967	2974	2975	2976	2978	2979	2981
2982	2989	3000	3001	3004	3024	3025	3026	3040	3042
3043	3044	3045	3046	3047	3049	3050	3051	3054	3055
3057	3058	3059	3060	3061	3072	3073	3079	3082	3081
3083	3084	3093							

PRODUCTIVITY

SAUGER

137	213	389	394	396	399	476	480	673	695
758	987	1413	1805	2043	2205	2342	2389	2497	2498
2501	2523	2608	2610	2685	2887	2906	2941		

WALLEYE

6	33	36	60	137	198	199	213	225	243
247	248	249	288	290	334	389	394	396	399
406	412	449	450	465	469	471	472	476	480
483	493	530	533	534	535	547	548	554	579
605	618	622	636	652	673	683	695	758	850
925	930	935	987	1057	1059	1084	1097	1140	1165
1168	1253	1357	1378	1413	1480	1482	1483	1486	1535
1536	1538	1571	1580	1586	1631	1678	1684	1696	1701
1721	1770	1805	1821	1841	1862	1888	1895	1919	1921
1932	1933	1985	1990	1991	1993	1998	2002	2043	2114
2205	2213	2241	2261	2263	2264	2335	2341	2342	2346
2366	2389	2458	2464	2494	2497	2498	2501	2511	2514
2515	2523	2565	2584	2587	2595	2608	2610	2616	2617
2652	2662	2678	2685	2735	2749	2773	2784	2808	2829
2887	2906	2941	2954	2963	2988	3048	3073	3096	

PROPAGATION

SAUGER

4	90	194	695	750	918	1105	1427	1531	1601
1607	1632	1702	1989	2053	2724	2874	2899	3028	

WALLEYE

4	23	40	41	42	43	44	45	47	48
53	55	57	81	90	91143	169	170	179	190
194	197	200	226	227	245	246	250	251	252
258	267	320	324	333	336	348	363	455	457
458	461	462	463	467	469	470	471	472	473
499	500	502	521	533	541	542	561	562	563

600	621	624	676	677	679	680	684	685	686
692	693	694	695	710	722	750	762	796	888
901	918	994	1008	1012	1016	1028	1063	1079	1094
1105	1172	1201	1202	1227	1260	1271	1285	1311	1312
1315	1321	1326	1412	1416	1427	1487	1506	1522	1531
1551	1552	1583	1601	1607	1628	1630	1632	1683	1684
1685	1686	1702	1706	1707	1713	1743	1745	1753	1759
1787	1789	1794	1796	1797	1801	1802	1817	1870	1879
1894	1895	1917	1936	1951	1952	1965	1979	1989	1990
1991	1993	1996	1998	2003	2015	2030	2031	2032	2053
2058	2059	2060	2071	2072	2091	2101	2102	2103	2122
2123	2126	2163	2230	2231	2251	2266	2292	2293	2298
2320	2322	2375	2411	2417	2437	2439	2509	2529	2534
2572	2577	2646	2649	2650	2662	2686	2687	2688	2719
2724	2747	2767	2774	2815	2819	2820	2844	2845	2846
2872	2873	2874	2899	2908	2958	2959	3015	3028	3033
3037	3038	3092							

REGULATIONS

SAUGER

72	75	77	379	1105	1222	2136	2205

WALLEYE

72	75	77	87	93	114	243	304	311	379
493	533	573	618	902	933	934	1029	1030	1105
1140	1168	1222	1388	1438	1486	1489	1504	1522	1523
1620	1737	1985	2073	2087	2136	2143	2145	2147	2148
2150	2153	2155	2156	2205	2206	2356	2364	2376	2440
2514	2525	2584	2587	2598	2678	2988			

SAMPLING METHODS

SAUGER

137	139	208	376	427	437	611	673	777	807
811	818	887	953	970	1217	1230	1237	1722	1850
2104	2235	2245	2246	2250	2278	2450	2634	2754	2775
2806	2893	2936	2937	2941					

WALLEYE

1	8	30	34	99	118	131	137	138	139
156	186	208	291	303	372	376	410	427	437
533	594	611	659	673	687	699	707	742	747
792	797	807	811	836	837	838	887	922	928
953	970	979	989	997	998	999	1017	1148	1155
1156	1200	1217	1224	1230	1235	1237	1278	1371	1402
1404	1452	1453	1516	1521	1554	1555	1711	1722	1731
1762	1770	1771	1850	1851	1976	1994	2004	2062	2076
2082	2084	2104	2116	2250	2278	2285	2320	2337	2364
2372	2390	2392	2393	2427	2429	2450	2470	2471	2567
2594	2754	2784	2840	2865	2936	2941	2976	2978	2979
3049	3055	3056	3060	3061	3069	3071	3078	3079	3099

SOCIO-ECONOMICS OF FISHERIES

SAUGER

4	379	476	612	758	1725	2136	2501

WALLEYE

3	4	5	114	241	379	476	485	612	758
891	1060	1332	1433	1582	1725	1786	2027	2136	2481
2480	2501	2734	2882	2997					

SPAWNING STUDIES

SAUGER

4	22	154	168	194	195	196	208	229	232
283	496	504	545	551	581	606	617	669	754
775	817	904	905	906	909	918	953	954	983
984	985	988	992	1034	1055	1080	1092	1105	1159
1223	1257	1394	1427	1450	1499	1601	1632	1724	1725
1726	1728	1729	1730	1769	1971	1983	2037	2038	2047
2048	2049	2050	2051	2055	2089	2134	2159	2240	2280
2288	2351	2362	2365	2609	2633	2669	2685	2690	2691
2716	2724	2726	2824	2874	2879	2880	2881	2913	2939
2944									

WALLEYE

4	22	34	56	70	83	86	116	120	121
122	134	136	154	161	168	194	195	196	208
210	224	226	229	231	232	243	255	272	281
283	289	299	324	331	334	371	380	411	453
454	456	458	477	496	503	504	521	533	534
536	545	549	551	565	575	581	585	596	617
622	625	626	639	650	653	663	664	689	690
696	707	715	735	754	762	763	772	775	783
793	796	799	828	852	866	891	894	904	905
906	909	918	921	922	923	933	951	952	953
954	957	973	975	983	984	988	992	997	998
999	1004	1005	1007	1033	1034	1055	1080	1081	1082
1083	1091	1092	1104	1105	1106	1107	1129	1143	1174
1214	1223	1228	1257	1262	1276	1295	1317	1318	1331
1343	1363	1364	1372	1381	1382	1383	1387	1389	1388
1391	1394	1414	1415	1427	1442	1450	1451	1454	1466
1493	1499	1501	1510	1521	1524	1586	1587	1601	1632
1636	1649	1650	1655	1669	1688	1698	1724	1725	1726
1727	1728	1729	1730	1739	1741	1746	1753	1762	1765
1769	1771	1772	1783	1799	1801	1802	1807	1809	1822
1826	1834	1843	1849	1856	1876	1885	1922	1923	1948
1965	1971	1983	1995	2012	2013	2015	2017	2018	2019
2028	2037	2038	2039	2049	2050	2051	2055	2063	2064
2068	2087	2089	2098	2118	2127	2132	2133	2134	2135
2144	2159	2160	2164	2187	2195	2197	2201	2209	2240
2254	2261	2264	2266	2279	2280	2288	2289	2305	2316
2317	2319	2320	2325	2340	2351	2362	2365	2370	2384
2397	2413	2414	2415	2416	2428	2429	2430	2440	2441
2448	2459	2460	2467	2471	2490	2512	2513	2514	2526
2529	2530	2540	2545	2572	2583	2589	2590	2592	2596
2609	2633	2653	2657	2661	2667	2669	2678	2684	2685
2690	2691	2692	2701	2703	2710	2716	2720	2723	2724
2726	2728	2740	2743	2744	2745	2746	2748	2749	2824
2840	2845	2846	2854	2872	2874	2879	2880	2881	2885
2892	2908	2911	2913	2944	2961	2975	2979	2981	2982
2985	3019	3020	3026	3040	3057	3059	3070	3075	3080
3085									

STOCKING

SAUGER

344	389	476	550	581	695	1002	1105	1237	1374
1375	1531	1614	1632	1718	1989	2037	2248	2296	2351
2609	2690	2691	2899	2936	3000	3001	3028	3031	

WALLEYE

28	33	40	41	42	43	44	47	50	52
62	66	70	71	74	83	86	121	138	145
151	166	191	197	200	222	238	239	245	247
248	249	253	264	265	266	288	296	307	309
320	331	335	344	363	389	405	411	412	440
464	466	468	476	482	498	500	512	520	533
538	539	549	550	557	569	581	592	624	626
628	635	636	641	687	692	694	695	722	728
780	785	786	787	794	795	850	856	857	875
876	877	878	891	894	895	897	898	929	930
933	934	955	956	962	1001	1002	1015	1016	1017
1029	1030	1044	1052	1053	1057	1059	1061	1062	1064
1070	1071	1072	1074	1075	1076	1078	1082	1083	1084
1085	1094	1096	1103	1105	1108	1120	1121	1140	1161
1169	1201	1224	1227	1237	1240	1243	1261	1276	1281
1312	1331	1341	1348	1357	1369	1372	1374	1375	1379
1380	1386	1393	1412	1419	1452	1453	1467	1485	1488
1489	1501	1510	1516	1521	1531	1534	1546	1579	1580
1581	1582	1586	1587	1614	1618	1632	1677	1679	1684
1706	1708	1710	1718	1737	1746	1747	1760	1782	1788
1798	1801	1818	1826	1843	1849	1856	1857	1862	1863
1867	1868	1889	1892	1896	1897	1932	1933	1948	1950
1953	1954	1955	1956	1957	1958	1959	1960	1961	1980
1989	1995	1998	2000	2004	2012	2026	2037	2061	2069
2100	2101	2102	2103	2107	2110	2111	2112	2119	2130
2133	2154	2168	2176	2182	2199	2212	2233	2248	2260
2261	2263	2264	2284	2291	2296	2298	2302	2307	2308
2319	2320	2328	2330	2348	2351	2370	2395	2396	2403
2417	2419	2422	2431	2441	2443	2461	2475	2491	2507
2508	2511	2515	2528	2535	2537	2538	2541	2543	2558
2559	2564	2573	2577	2582	2583	2609	2611	2626	2637
2638	2639	2646	2649	2650	2660	2676	2690	2691	2721
2740	2760	2767	2768	2798	2828	2840	2844	2845	2867
2868	2873	2886	2899	2905	2936	2962	2969	2970	2975
2976	2978	2979	2982	2983	2990	2997	3000	3001	3009
3010	3011	3019	3028	3030	3031	3032	3039	3042	3045
3050	3051	3059	3092	3109					

TAXONOMY

SAUGER

10	69	147	150	194	195	196	204	206	460
504	543	544	545	551	574	581	637	662	718
721	741	748	751	826	859	884	885	886	918
919	1002	1014	1018	1034	1054	1131	1163	1212	1245
1292	1298	1299	1300	1301	1304	1421	1424	1425	1426
1427	1428	1429	1525	1570	1592	1597	1638	1639	1640
1875	1883	2046	2161	2170	2234	2283	2295	2536	2575
2624	2630	2689	2771	2772	2857	2858	2884	2987	3031
3087									

WALLEYE

10	54	69	124	147	148	150	194	196	195
204	206	210	224	277	317	421	460	504	533
543	544	545	551	560	574	581	637	662	718
721	741	748	751	774	778	826	828	859	886
918	919	996	1002	1014	1034	1054	1131	1163	1212
1245	1292	1298	1299	1301	1304	1420	1421	1424	1425
1426	1427	1428	1429	1442	1491	1544	1570	1572	1597
1638	1639	1640	1767	1813	1875	1883	1926	2046	2068
2090	2161	2170	2173	2234	2283	2295	2418	2536	2572
2575	2623	2624	2630	2645	2689	2712	2737	2771	2772
2857	2858	2883	2884	2904	2987	3031	3087		

TOXICANTS

SAUGER

39	478	546	1058	1519	1520	1643	1814	2236	2505

WALLEYE

18	39	60	104	105	161	166	240	268	273
478	533	546	657	860	947	1011	1058	1099	1208
1241	1259	1272	1397	1474	1481	1518	1519	1520	1563
1580	1644	1651	1652	1699	1700	1775	1778	1779	1814
1893	2099	2189	2311	2320	2379	2412	2428	2442	2469
2486	2487	2505	2571	2581	2582	2664	2665	2682	2894
2914	2935	2942	2943	3057	3058				

WATER LEVELS

SAUGER

61	230	232	234	235	393	904	905	906	1394
1450	2050	2055	2159	2609	2690	2691	2726	2824	2879
2880	2881	2939	2940						

WALLEYE

61	109	144	190	231	232	234	235	393	477
517	533	636	651	652	794	905	904	906	955
973	974	975	1369	1383	1394	1450	1454	1554	1739
1772	1841	1885	2050	2055	2073	2133	2159	2176	2199
2201	2319	2320	2591	2609	2690	2691	2726	2777	2824
2840	2879	2880	2881	2923	2935	2940	3004	3043	3046
3050	3059								

CPSIA information can be obtained at www.ICGtesting.com
Printed in the USA
LVOW021629011212

309647LV00006B/488/P